Mastering
Computing

Palgrave Master Series

Accounting
Accounting Skills
Advanced English Language
Advanced English Literature
Advanced Pure Mathematics
Arabic
Basic Management
Biology
British Politics
Business Communication
Business Environment
C Programming
C++ Programming
Chemistry
COBOL Programming
Communication
Computing
Counselling Skills
Counselling Theory
Customer Relations
Database Design
Delphi Programming
Desktop Publishing
Economic and Social History
Economics
Electrical Engineering
Electronic and Electrical Calculations
Electronics
Employee Development
English Grammar
English Language
Fashion Buying and Merchandising Management
Fashion Styling
French
Geography
German
Global Information Systems
Human Resource Management
Information Technology
Internet
Italian
Java
Management Skills
Marketing Management
Mathematics
Microsoft Office
Microsoft Windows, Novell Netware and UNIX
Modern British History
Modern European History
Modern United States History
Modern World History
Networks
Organisational Behaviour
Pascal and Delphi Programming
Philosophy
Physics
Practical Criticism
Psychology
Shakespeare
Social Welfare
Sociology
Spanish
Statistics
Strategic Management
Systems Analysis and Design
Team Leadership
Theology
Twentieth Century Russian History
Visual Basics
World Religions

www.palgravemasterseries.com

Palgrave Master Series
Series Standing Order ISBN 0–333–69343–4
(outside North America only)

You can receive future titles in this series as they are published by placing a standing order. Please contact your bookseller or, in case of difficulty, write to us at the address below with your name and address, the title of the series and the ISBN quoted above.

Customer Services Department, Macmillan Distribution Ltd
Houndmills, Basingstoke, Hampshire RG21 6XS, England

Mastering Computing

William Buchanan, Bsc (Hons), CE, Phd
Senior Lecturer
School of Computing
Napier University

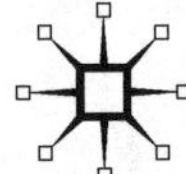

First published 2002 by
PALGRAVE MACMILLAN
Houndmills, Basingstoke, Hampshire RG21 6XS and
175 Fifth Avenue, New York, N.Y. 10010
Companies and representatives throughout the world

PALGRAVE MACMILLAN is the global academic imprint of the Palgrave Macmillan division of St. Martin's Press, LLC and of Palgrave Macmillan Ltd. Macmillan® is a registered trademark in the United States, United Kingdom and other countries. Palgrave is a registered trademark in the European Union and other countries.

ISBN 0–333–74806–9

This book is printed on paper suitable for recycling and made from fully managed and sustained forest sources.

A catalogue record for this book is available from the British Library.

10 9 8 7 6 5 4 3 2 1
11 10 09 08 07 06 05 04 03 02

Printed and bound in Great Britain by
Antony Rowe Ltd, Chippenham and Eastbourne

Contents

Preface

Computing has changed radically over the past few years and has readily adopted new technologies, especially, in recent years, in networking and the Internet. At one time it mainly involved computer architecture and computing programming. It now encapsulates many areas, from operating systems and processes to networking and the Internet. This book tries to cover some of these areas by investigating most of the key areas of computing.

1. **Computer Basics.** These chapters define some of the basic principles of computer systems, including the basic architecture, terminology and data representation.
2. **Operating Systems and Distributed Systems.** These chapters cover the principles of operating systems and how information and processing is distributed over networks.
3. **Data Communications and Compression.** These chapters introduce the techniques of transmitting data, and illustrate compression methods for data.
4. **Networking and the Internet.** These chapters introduce the theory and practice of computers that communicate over a network.
5. **Encryption and Security.** These chapters discuss some of the main principles used in securing the storage and transmission of data.
6. **Databases and Information.** These chapters discuss some of the main principles of using data to gather, process and store data, such as the use of agents to gather data, and databases to store it.
7. **Software Development.** This chapter covers the processes involved in developing software. This includes the principles of software programming, software design, and structured analysis and design.
8. **WWW, Electronic Mail and Multimedia.** These chapters cover the basic principles of WWW development, the usage of electronic mail, and multimedia.
9. **Ethernet, ATM, History of the Computer, and more.** To save space these chapters have been placed on the related WWW site.

The book has a good deal of material on the WWW site (`http://www.palgrave.com/studyskills/masterseries/buchanan`). This includes:

- **On-line tests.** Each chapter has a related on-line test, along with a complete on-line test taken from a database of all the material from the book.
- **Extra material.**
- **Fun quizzes.** This includes tests, such as networking hangman, and an Internet IQ test.
- **Registration and automated email updates.** Tutors and students can register from the WWW site, and will be kept up to date with activities relating to the book.
- **Sample lectures.** This includes an outline of the lectures for each of the chapters.
- **Chapter presentations.** This includes presentations for each of the units, in PPT, Flash, and PDF formats.
- **Source code.** All the related source code can be downloaded from the WWW site.
- **Teacher notes and sample schedules.** This shows examples of lesson plans and schedules.
- **Sample exam questions and FAQs.**

1 Introduction

1.1 Introduction

Never in the history of mankind has a technology advanced as fast as the computing industry. Bill Gates once quoted at a COMDEX that 'If GM kept up with technology like the computer industry has, we would be driving $25 cars that got 1000 miles to the gallon.' Unfortunately, the computing industry has been plagued with many problems, especially with continual updates in software and hardware, poor software reliability, and virtual monopolies on software and hardware systems. No other industry has ever led such a charmed life.

Computers are possibly the most useful and the most annoying pieces of technology of all time. If we bought a car and it failed at least a few times every day, we would take it back and demand another one. When that failed, we would demand our money back. Or, imagine a toaster that failed halfway through making a piece of toast, and we had to turn the power off, and restart it. We just wouldn't allow it.

These types of problems prompted GM in return to respond to Bill Gates' statement with:

'If GM had developed technology like Microsoft, we would all be driving cars with the following characteristics:

- For no reason whatsoever your car would crash twice a day.
- Every time they repainted the lines on the road, you would have to buy a new car.
- Occasionally your car would die on the freeway for no reason, and you would just accept this, restart and drive on.
- Occasionally, executing a maneuver such as a left turn would cause your car to shut down and refuse to start, in which case you would have to reinstall the engine.
- Only one person at a time could use the car, unless you bought "Car95" or "CarNT". But then you would have to buy more seats.
- Apple would make a car that was powered by the sun, reliable, five times as fast, and twice as easy to drive, but would only run on 5% of the roads.
- The oil, water temperature and alternator warning lights would be replaced by a single "general car default" warning light.
- New seats would force everyone to have the same size butt.
- The airbag system would say "Are you sure?" before deploying.
- Occasionally for no reason whatsoever, your car would lock you out and refuse to let you in until you simultaneously lifted the door handle, turn the key, and grabbed hold of the radio antenna.
- GM would require all car buyers to also purchase a deluxe set of Rand McNally road maps (now a GM subsidiary), even though they neither need them nor want them. Attempting to delete this option would immediately cause the car's performance to diminish by 50% or more. Moreover, GM would become a target for investigation by the Justice Department.
- Every time GM introduced a new model, car buyers would have to learn how to drive all over again because none of the controls would operate in the same manner as the old car.
- You'd press the "Start" button to shut off the engines.'

1.2 Aims of this book

The great thing about the computing industry is that it is moving so fast and in so many different directions. This book tries to encapsulate some of these strands, such as:

1. **Computer Basics**. This chapter and the next cover some of the basic principles of computer systems, including the basic architecture, terminology and data representation. Computers use binary digits to represent data, which, for humans, is not a very convenient method of representing numbers and characters. Thus, the second chapter discusses the techniques which can be used which allow humans to more easily interpret computer data. This includes the usage of hexadecimal, which is an easily interpreted method of representing binary digits, and ASCII, which represents characters.
2. **Operating Systems and Distributed Systems**. Chapters 3 to 6 cover the principles of operating systems and how information and processing is distributed over networks. Operating systems are important in that they allow users to easily interface to computer hardware, without actually knowing how the system works. For example, think about how difficult it would be to identify files on a disk drive using their actual physical location on the disk. To most people the logical layout of files within folders makes much more sense than the actual physical organization of the files on the disk.
3. **Data Communications and Compression**. Chapters 7 and 8 introduce the techniques of transmitting data, and illustrate compression methods for data. Either this compression reduces the amount of storage space, or the amount of time/bandwidth that data will take when transmitted over a communications channel. In the past data has typically been sent in a continuous manner (known as analogue communications), but modern communications focuses on transmitting binary digits, 0's and 1's (known as digital communications).
4. **Networking and the Internet**. Chapters 9 to 12 introduce the theory and practice of computers that communicating over a network. This network might be a local area network, where computers are physically connected to the same network, or might be wide area communications over the Internet. A key principle in understanding how computers communicate over a network is the OSI model, which abstracts the transmission of data, at different levels. For example, the OSI model allows someone to view the communications between two computers as a series of binary digits with a series of electrical or light pulses (physical layer). The model also allows the communication to be viewed as a collection of bits with information about the destination address location (data link layer), and so on. Chapter 10 presents the main types of networks, and The WWW site contains additional chapters which focus on two of the most important network types: Ethernet and ATM. Both have important concepts for the local transmission of data and for the global transmission of data. Networking technologies such as Ethernet and ATM only really provide a communications channel for the reliable transmission of data. A communications protocols is then required so that data can be properly addressed over a global communications channel, and the data can also to be split up into smaller data units, so that it can be transmitted over the channel. These are some of the main functions of a networking protocol, which, if it is standardized, allow two computers to communicate, no matter: their computer architecture, their type; their operating system; their network connection; and their physical location. The two most important networking protocols are IP and TCP. The IP part allows for a global

network addressing structure (using an IP address), and the TCP part allows data to be broken down into chunks, each with its own sequence number, and unique identification of the application that it is destined for. These protocols are covered in some detail in Chapters 11 and 12, and are key in understanding the organization and operation of the Internet.

5. **Encryption and Security.** Chapters 13 and 14 discuss some of the main principles used in securing the storage and transmission of data. Obviously no network can ever been totally secure, but most network administrators will try and protect data at different levels of abstraction, such as: physically securing transmission systems; filtering the content; and filtering based on the source and destination of the data. The only truly reliable method of securing data, though, is encryption. Chapter 13 discusses some of the main principles in encryption, and focuses on public-key encryption, which is now the most widely used encryption method. This method involves users generating two electronic keys, one of these private and the other is distributed to anyone who wants to send the user some encrypted data. Anyone sending the user some encrypted data uses the user's public key to encrypt the data; the only key that can then decrypt the data is then the user's private key. It is an ingenious method, which is used in many applications, such as in electronic commerce and in data security.
6. **Databases and Information.** Chapters 15 and 16 discuss some of the main principles of using data to gather, process and store present data, such as the use of agents to gather data, and databases to store it. Databases are key components of modern computing, thus a solid understanding of the way that they are designed and organized is essential for understanding any systems which are based around a database. Databases are now used in many disciplines, such as creating dynamic content for WWW sites, storage of banking details, storage of data samples from industrial plant, and so on.
7. **Software Development.** Chapter 17 covers the processes involved in developing software. This includes the principles of software programming, software design, and structured analysis and design. There is a great variety of software development principles, and programming languages, thus this chapter focuses on the choices that are made in practical development. The Internet and the WWW have obviously increased the requirement for intercommunication between computers, thus Chapter 12 gives a basic outline of a communications program over a network.
8. **WWW, Electronic Mail and Multimedia.** Chapters 18 to 20 cover the basic principles of WWW development, the usage of electronic mail, and multimedia.
9. **Multimedia, Ethernet, ATM, History of the Computer, and more.** To save space these chapters have been placed on the related WWW site.

1.3 Background

One of the major barriers to learning about computing is the use of jargon. Once this is mastered, the main principles involved are not too difficult. Table 1.1 outlines some of the most basic terms related to the units used in computing systems.

Planes and things

'We build systems like the Wright brothers built airplanes – build the whole thing, push it off the cliff, let it crash, and start over again.'

Software researcher on software development, 1968.

The binary digit is the most basic unit of a computer system. Computers use binary digits to represent program codes, numbers and characters. In a binary system there are only two digits: a 0 and a 1. In a normal decimal system there are 10 digits: 0 to 9, and in a hexadecimal system there are 16 digits (0 to 'F').

Electronic systems have a defined functionality. This could be to perform a simple operation, such as flashing a light bulb on and off, or could be an extremely complex one, such as controlling the operation of a nuclear power plant. Computer systems have been around for over a hundred years, and have evolved from mechanical devices, to electronic values (in the 1950s), onto discrete transistorized systems (in the 1960s), and then finally to integrated electronic devices (in the 1970s). Most of the major advances have already occurred, and the trend is now towards making the components parts of the computer smaller, and use less electrical power. This has been mainly achieved by integrating as much as possible of the electronics onto single devices (known as chips). The reliability and speed of computers systems has gradually improved over the years, mainly with stepwise changes in technology, and then with incremental changes of enhanced manufacturing and operation. The basic architecture of computer systems has not changed much over the years, and the concepts covered in Chapter 2 would be just as relevant 20 or 30 years ago. The main computer generations have been:

- **1st generation**. Valves (ENIAC). 1950s.
- **2nd generation**. Transistors (PDP-1). 1960s.
- **3rd generation**. Integrated circuits/time- sharing (IBM System/360). 1970s.
- **4th generation**. Large-scale integration (ZX81). 1980s.
- **5th generation**. Systems-on-a-chip (Pentium-based PCs). 1990s.
- **6th generation**. Mobile computing/embedded Internet/parallel processing. 2000 and beyond.

Modern computer systems have evolved from the development of digital electronics, which are electronic circuits that operate on binary digits. Initially digital systems had a fixed functionality, where they could not change their function without requiring a change of hardware. A great advancement came when, at the time, a relatively small company called Intel developed the 4004. This device was named a microprocessor, and was the first electronic device to change its functionality depending on the codes that were executed on it. It was rather limited as it could only process 4 bits at a time (a nibble), but it began the programmable hardware revolution. For the first time a general-purpose device could be used to execute many different functions. This type of hardware had many advantages over dedicated hardware, especially as it:

- Allows for easy updates, as a change of software updates the functionality.
- Allows easier development, as software can be more easily changed than hardware can.
- Allows software codes to be generated from a high-level programming language, which is easier to understand than electronic circuit diagrams. This high-level programming language is defined in a form which is similar to written English form.

An expensive error

One of the best-known software errors occurred on 22 July 1962 when the Mariner I rocket had to be blown-up, just after take-off, after it followed an erratic path. A single incorrect character in a FORTRAN statement for the motion equations caused it.

Table 1.1 Basic terminology

Unit	Representation	Description
b	Bit	A bit is a single binary digit of information, which can either be a zero (0) or a one (1). Computers can only understand binary information. Sometimes, to differentiate the unit from a byte (B), it is written as a bit without a space after the value (such as 8bit, as apposed to 8B, for 8 bytes).
bps	Bits per second	The number of bits transferred between one place and another, per second.
B	Byte	A byte is a group of 8 bits. Computers normally operate on multiples of 8 bits, such as 8 bits, 16 bits, 32 bits, 64 bits, and so on.
KB	Kilobyte	One thousand bytes. In binary, one thousand bytes is actually 1,024 bytes.
KB/s	Kilobyte/second	The number of KBs transferred per second.
MB	Megabyte	One million (1,048,576 or 1024 K) bytes.
MB/s	Megabyte/ second	The number of MBs transferred per second.
GB	Gigabyte	One billion (1,073,741,824 or 1024 M) bytes.

1.4 Data and information

What is the difference between data and information? Data is the raw form that is used to create information. For example, a weather forecaster may gather measurements of air pressure and temperature over a given time period and then create a trend graph to show how these varied over time. The air pressure and temperature measurements would be taken as data, while the trend graph would be the information. Then, based on these trends the forecaster might predict into the future. This generates new data. With this data the forecaster might produce a weather chart which converts the temperatures into colours, and the pressure data into isobars. This has converted data into information. Information thus involves some sort of processing of the data, such as converting temperature values into colours on a map, or points on a graph (as illustrated in Figure 1.1). There are many different types of processing, such as thresholding (is something hotter? is it darker? and so on), mathematical processing (such as calculating the average or standard deviation), filtering (such as sorting data into different ranges), or presentation processing (such as presenting numerical values in a graphical form). Obviously is it also possible to convert from one type of data to another, such as converting a temperature value from Centigrade to Fahrenheit.

Figure 1.2 illustrates the different methods of processing data. In this case a spreadsheet is used to process the data. These are:

- **Mathematical processing.** The processing determines the average value (in Microsoft Excel this is defined with `=AVERAGE(B2:B17)`) and the standard deviation (in Microsoft Excel this is defined with `=STDEV(B2:B17)`) of temperature over each of the days.

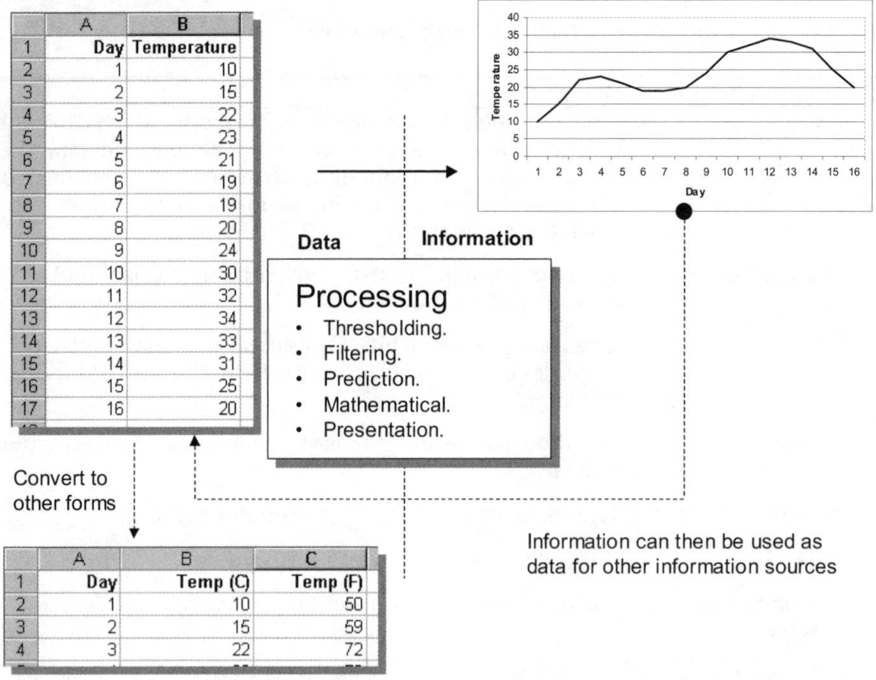

Figure 1.1 Data and information

- **Threshold processing**. The processing displays the value of 'Cool' if the temperature is 20°C, or below, else it will show the value of 'Warm' (in Microsoft Excel this is defined in the form of `=IF(B2>20,"Warm","Cool")`).
- **Filtering/ordering processing**. The processing displays the temperature values in a number of temperature frequency bins. In this case the bins are set between 0 –10, 11–15, 16–20, and so on (in Microsoft Excel this is defined in the form of `=FREQUENCY($B$2:$B$17,G25:K25)`).
- **Prediction processing**. The processing determines a forecasted formula for future days, using a basic average of the previous three days (in Microsoft Excel this is defined in the form of `=AVERAGE(B9:B11)`).
- **Presentation processing**. The processing displays the temperature values in the form of a bar chart. Most people prefer to view temperature trending in the form of a bar or a line graph, rather than as values.

The data that is collected is key to how well the information can be presented, and it can be operated on in many different ways to show different types of information. For example, in an election the voters complete a voting paper, and then submit it. This can be seen as the raw data. After this the raw data can be processed to present information in many ways (Figure 1.3), such as the:

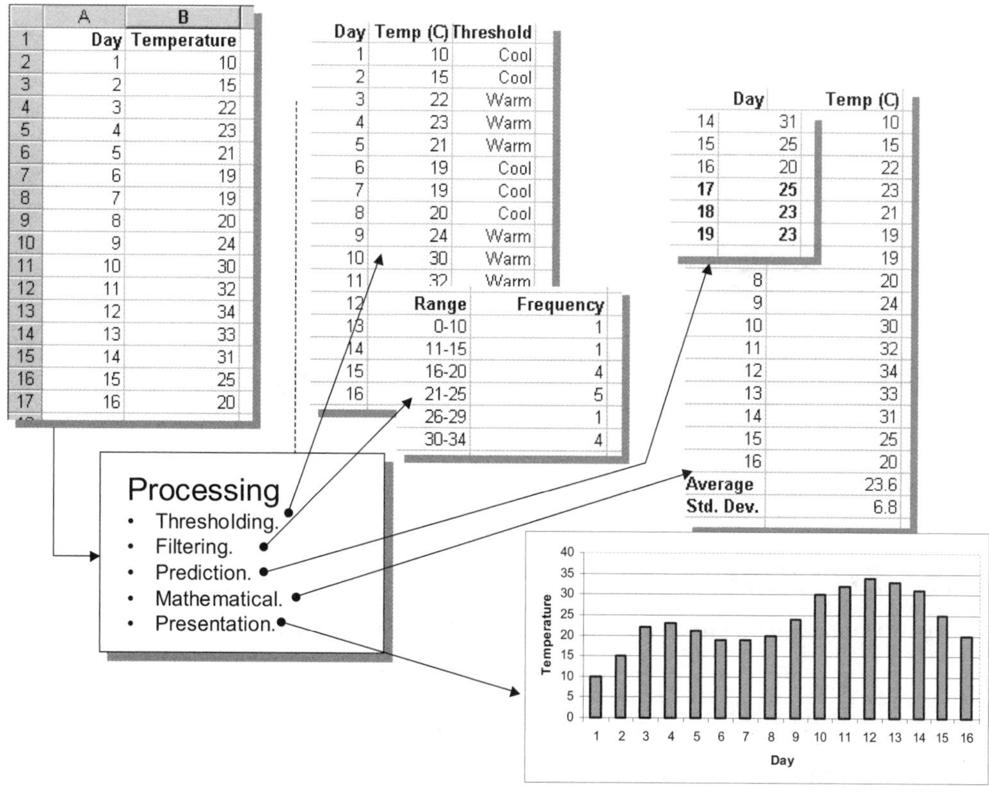

Figure 1.2 Data processing

- Split of the votes between the candidates, as the number of votes, and as a percentage of the total vote. It can be seen, from Figure 1.3, that the conversion to percentage figures helps the reader to interpret the relative weighting of the votes to each of the candidates. In this case nearly half of the votes were assigned to Smith (49.5%), around one-quarter of the votes were assigned to Arnold (26.9%), and around one-fifth of the votes went to Sinkly (20.8%).
- Split of correctly completed voting papers, against incorrectly completed ones. It can be seen, in Figure 1.3, that most of the voting papers were filled-in correctly, and only 2.7% were incorrectly completed. The correctly filled-in number relates to all the votes that were assigned to the candidates (Smith, Arnold and Sinkley), and give a total of 19,653 against the number of spoilt papers (555).
- Split of the votes for each of the geographical areas. From the information in Figure 1.3 it can be easily seen that more than half the votes were cast in the Greenwell area (53.5%), and very few votes, relatively, were cast in Downtown (2.1%).
- Split of the votes for their political bias, such as their tendency to be either a left-wing or a right-wing party. In Figure 1.3, the votes for Arnold and Sinkly have been added to give the total votes for the left-wing parties, and the votes for Smith have been taken for the ring-wing party. It can be seen that the split of the votes is virtually the same for left-wing against right-wing.

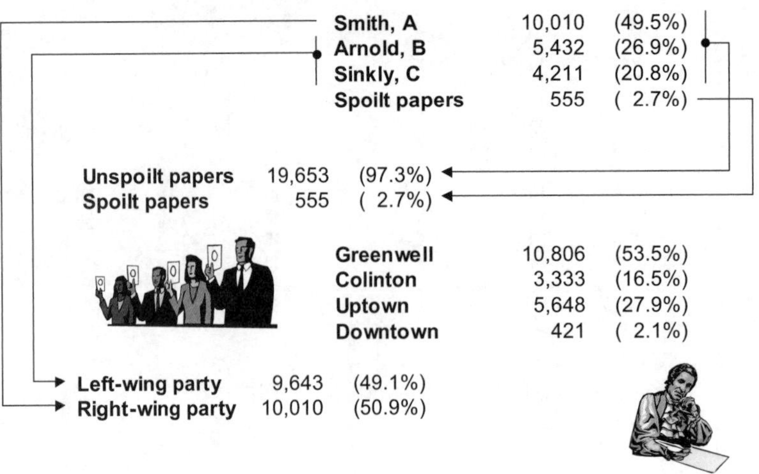

Figure 1.3 Voting in an election

1.5 Exercises

1.5.1 Define whether the following are either is likely to be data or information:

Type	Data	Information
Temperature samples	✓	
Television schedule		
Wind speed measurement		
Voltage sample		
Completed voting paper		
Election results		
User activity log		
Software package usage		
Telephone bill		

1.5.2 Match up, with a one-to-one relationship, the following information descriptions with possible data sources:

Information	**Data source**
Electricity bill	Odometer reading/fuel consumption
Isobar mappings	Speedometer
Temperature contours	Meter reading
Average speed results	Turnstile counter
Sports match attendance	Barometer
Average fuel consumption	Thermometer

Tutorial questions and exercises are available at:

`http://www.palgrave.com/studyskills/masterseries/buchanan`

2 Computer basics

2.1 History

> **Harvard architecture**
>
> Harvard architecture uses separate program and data spaces. It is also typically defined as architecture with uses separate program and data busses (and usually caches too). This architecture improves speed, though the address spaces are actually shared.
>
> The von Neumann architecture uses a stored program in the same writable memory that data is stored in.

During World War II, John Eckert at the University of Pennsylvania built the world's first large electronic computer. It contained over 19,000 electronic valves and was called ENIAC (Electronic Numerical Integrator and Computer). It was a poor acronym that just didn't quite roll-off the tongue, but technically it was so innovative that it ran for over 11 years before it was switched off. Not many modern day computers will run for more than a few years before they are considered unusable. In these days a computer has a typical usable age of just one or two years, before it is either cascaded onto someone who doesn't quite require the most modern computer, or, as is more typical in modern industry they are retired to the great computer graveyard in the sky, who are well looked after by some of the great, but departed innovators of the computer, such as:

- **Gary Kildall (1942–1994)**. Who, with CP/M was the innovator, and technical genius behind one of the first operating systems for microprocessor systems (and who developed many of the initial standards for the CD-ROM interface, and produced the first successful open-system architecture). If not for a blunder in arrangements with a meeting with IBM, CP/M may have become the standard operation system for the PC, rather than MS-DOS. Novell eventually bought his company, Digital Research, in 1991, and his products eventually disappeared under the weight and power of Microsoft Windows. He died in 1994 at the age of 52, after falling in a drunken state and hitting his head. Gary, unlike many others in the computer business, was always more interested in technical specifications, rather than financial statements and balance sheets.
- **John Eckert (1919–1995)** and **John von Neumann (1903–1957)**, of course, who would be totally amazed with modern computers, especially in the way that it is now possible to integrate millions of digital devices onto a single piece of silicon, which is smaller than a thumbprint. For them you could actually hold a digital device in your hand, and if it was working properly it would burn your hand. To them the invisible communications over an infrared link would seem more like magic than technology.
- **Herman Hollerith (1860–1929)**. Who, at the end of the 19th century, devised a machine that accepted punch cards with information on them. These cards allowed an electrical current to pass through a hole when there was a hole present (a 'true'), and did not conduct a current when a hole was not present (a 'false'). This was one of the first uses of binary information, which represents data in a collection of one of two states (such as true or false, or, 0 or 1). He would be amazed with current transfer rates for data storage. To him a few hundred bytes a second would seem fast, but would be totally amazed with the transfer rates that give many hundred of millions of bytes every second, all from invisible magnetic fields stored on a metal disk. Also imagine the number of punch cards that would be required to load many of our modern programs.

- **William Shockley (1910–1989).** Who, along with others at the Bell Labs, invented the electronic transistor, which allowed computers to migrate from reinforced concrete floors which occupied whole floors of a building, and need special electrical generators to power them, to ones which could be fitted onto a pin-head.
- **Grace Hopper (1906–1992).** Grace overcame one of the major problems in software development: how to write programs which could be easily understood and written by humans, and easily converted into a form which computers could understand. In the early1950s work had begun on assemblers which would use simple text representations of the binary operations that the computer understood (such as ADD A, B to add two numbers). The assembler would convert them into a binary form. This aided the programmer as they did not have to continually look up the binary equivalent of the command that they required. It also made programs easier to read. The great advance occurred around 1956 when Grace Hopper started to develop compilers for the UNIVAC computer. These graceful programs converted a language which was readable by humans into a form that a computer could understand. This work would lead to the development of the COBOL programming language (which has since survived to the present day, although it is still blamed for many of the Year 2000 problems).

By today's standards ENIAC was a lumbering dinosaur, and by the time it was dismantled it weighed over 30 tons and spread itself over 1,500 square feet. Amazingly, it also consumed over 25 kW of electrical power (equivalent to the power of over 400 60 W light bulbs), but could perform over 100,000 calculations per second (which, even by today's standards, is reasonable). Unfortunately, it was unreliable, and would work only for a few hours, on average, before an electronic valve needed to be replaced. Faultfinding, though, was much easier in those days, as a valve that was not working would not glow, and would be cold to touch.

While ENIAC was important in the history of the modern computer, its successor would provide a much greater legacy: the standard architecture that has been used in virtually every computer since built: the ENVAC (Electronic Discrete Variable Automatic Computer). Its real genius was due to John von Neumann, a scientific researcher who had already built up a strong reputation in the field of quantum mechanics. For computing, he used his superior logical skills to overcome the shortcomings of ENIAC: too little storage, too many valves, and too lengthy a time to program it. His new approach used the stored-program concept, which is used by virtually every computer made, ever since. With this the storage device of the computer (its memory) is used to hold both the program instructions and also the data used by the computer and the program. His computer, as illustrated in Figure 2.1, was designed around five major elements:

- **Central control.** Program instructions are read from the memory and then interpreted by the central control unit.
- **Central arithmetic unit.** This performs the arithmetic operations, such as add/subtract, multiply/divide, binary manipulation, and so on.
- **Memory.** This holds both the program instructions and program/system data.
- **Input device.** This is used to read data into the memory. Example input devices are keyboards, disk storage, punch card reader (which were used extensively before the large-scale introduction of disk storage devices). The input device loads both program instructions and data into memory.

- **Output device**. This is used to output data from memory to an output device, such as a printer or display device.

Typically, these days, the central control unit and the central arithmetical unit have been merged into a device known as a microprocessor. The environment in which to run programs, typically known as user programs, is defined by the operating system. The von Neumann architecture made it much easier to load programs as the operating system can load all its associated data in the same place as it loads the program. Previously to this architecture, a user would have to load the program into one area of memory, and all the associated data in another area. The computer would then read from the program area for its instructions, and then read and write to a data area.

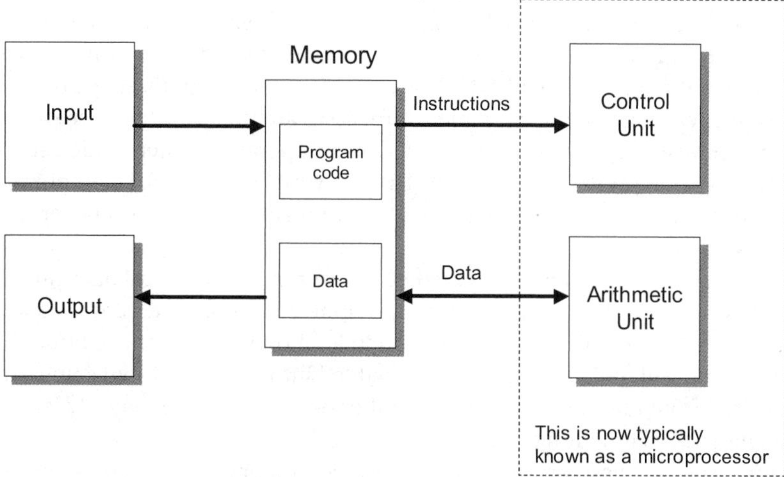

Figure 2.1 Stored-program architecture

2.2 System classification

Computer systems can be classified as either embedded systems or non-embedded systems. An embedded system typically has its operating system and programs integrated into the device. This allows for the system to be properly tested in most operating conditions, and they will thus be much more reliable. For example the controller in a washing machine is an embedded system, and will act correctly, within given specifications, and should hardly ever crash. An embedded system also normally has a limited range of hardware that can be added to the system. Again this makes the system more reliable, as many of the combinations of hardware can be tested for. It is thought that, in the near future, there could be as many as 10 times embedded systems sold than conventional computers, such as desktop PCs. The future is also likely to see the number of processing elements in devices increase, and automobiles of the future may contain hundreds of processing elements, each with their own specific function.

A non-embedded system is more general purpose and allows the operating systems and the user programs to be installed as required. They are thus less reliable as the system designer cannot test for all the possible combinations of hardware and software that could be installed or run on them.

Table 2.1 outlines some of the main classifications for computer systems. These vary in size from small embedded systems which perform simple operations, to large and complex systems which control industrial plants. The classifications include:

- **Small embedded systems**. These normally include small processing elements, which have minimal input and output, and have a simple program which runs on the processor. They typically also have their own local permanent memory, which can be written to so that they can be permanently programmed. These tend to be extremely reliable, and cope reasonably well with exceptional circumstances. Normally they do not require an operating system, and the code runs directly on the processing element.
- **Large embedded systems**. These typically have a powerful processor, which can have many inputs and outputs, and perform complex operations, that cannot be typically achieved within the required specification with a more general-purpose computer. These tend to be extremely reliable, and to cope well with exceptional circumstances. They are typically programmed once for their operation, and then not programmed again, until an upgrade is required. If they only run one program, they do not typically require an operating system, but if many processes are run at a time, there is normally a need for a robust operating system kernel (a basic operating system which supports the running of several programs at a time). There is very little need for a graphical user input for these system, as this typically adds too much of a processing overhead to the whole system.
- **Mobile devices**. These typical have medium-power processors, and have limited memory resources. They typically have a remote connection to another device, such as over an infrared link or a radio link (as with a mobile phone). As they have limited memory resources, many of their programs are embedded into the system, but some can also be downloaded from the Internet or from another device. They are typically fairly reliable, with an embedded operating system.
- **Desktop systems**. These are general-purpose computers, which can be installed with any type of operating system, and any user program which can be supported on the installed operating system. They typically do have the same reliability as embedded systems, as they can have a large range of hardware and software installed on them. A small software or hardware bug can cause the whole system to act unreliably.
- **Server systems**. These are systems which have a definite purpose of running server programs for client computers. Typical services as for WWW services, Internet access services, file transfer services, printer services, and electronic mail services. They are fairly robust, and have large amounts of memory to run many consecutive connections. Also, they are typically not used by a single user (as this would reduce the processing time available to client computers), and access to them is typically limited to the system manager, over a network. Many servers are contained within rack-mounted units, with power supplies which have backup systems which either allow the system to be properly shut-down when there is a power failure, or will sustain the power over a given time period. A server may also have several different storage sources, which allow for one or more to fail, without a loss of data. They are not as reliable as embedded systems, as they support a wide range of hardware and software, but these tend to be more robust than the types used in a desktop system. Server programs also tend to be much more reliable than general-purpose programs. Also a server typically runs a more robust operating system, which is more tolerant of incorrectly operating hardware/software, especially in faults in the network.

- **Supercomputers**. These are extremely fast computers, with an optimized architecture. Typically they also have multiple processors, with a fast communications channel between them. A supercomputer will typically have a base performance speed which is at least 10 times as great as a top-of-the-range desktop computer.

Winchester disks

Hard disks were at one time known as Winchester disks as they were initially available from IBM made from two spindles with 30 MB on each spindle. The 30-30 became known as Winchester disks after the 30-30 rifle.

Table 2.1 Computer classifications

Description	Processor power	Memory	Reliability	Input/ output connections	Programs	Typical application
Small embedded systems	L	L	H	L	Dedicated, but upgradable	Alarm system, car management system, mobile phones.
Large embedded systems	H	M	H	H	Dedicated, but upgradable	Radar processing, digital TV processing, network router.
Mobile devices	L-M	L-M	M-H	L	Integrated, with some installable programs	Hand-held computer, mobile phone with Internet access.
Desktop	M-H	M	L-M	L-M	General-purpose	Word processor, spreadsheet.
Workstation	M-H	M-H	M	L-M	Specialist programs, with other general-purpose software	Computer Aided Design, Multimedia.
Server	M-H	H	M-H	M	Server programs	WWW server, E-mail server.
Supercomputer	H	H	H	H	Specialized programs	High-power applications, such as genetic modelling, and scientific Simulations
Control system	H	H	H	H	Specialized programs	Industrial control.

L – Low; L-M – Low-to-Medium; M – Medium; M-H – Medium-to-High; H-High.

- **Control systems**. These support the interfacing of many devices, normally with some form of control program. As this control must be achieved within given time limits, there must be a robust and powerful operating system to support fast response speeds. For example it would be no good at all if the control program for a nuclear power plant crashed, just before the reactor temperature was increasing to dangerous levels. Also this type of system must also be able to prioritize signals, as the safety critical control should have a higher priority over optimization controls. The normal prioritization for an industrial plant will be (in this order):

    1. **Meet safety considerations**, such as making sure that the system does not overheat, explode, and so on. A system should not operate if it cannot meet its safety considerations. Any shutdown of the system must be carefully planned.
    2. **Meet regularity/legal obligations**, such as meeting omission levels, power considerations, operating times, and so on. A system can breach its regularity obligation, only if it does not meet its safety considerations.
    3. **Optimize system**. Once the system has met its safety considerations and its regularity obligations, it can then be optimized in order to maximize the profit/income of the product, or in the efficiency of its production. Optimization control/data has a lower priority that regularity obligation control/data, which in turn has a lower priority than safety critical control/data.

2.3 System definitions

A computer system consists of hardware, software and firmware, all of which interconnect. The basic definitions of each are:

- **Hardware**. These are the 'the bits that can be touched', that is, the components, the screws and nuts, the case, the electrical wires, and so on. Computer hardware can be split into different areas, such as: mechanical infrastructure (printed-circuit board, casing, screws, and so on); electrical power components (wires, electrical connectors, transformer, fuses, and so on); computer electronics infrastructure (microprocessor, memory, core components, and so on); and peripheral devices (keyboard, disk drives, video adaptor, and so on).
- **Software**. These are the programs that run on programmable hardware and change their operation depending on the inputs to the system. Inputs could be taken from a keyboard, interface hardware or from an external device. The program itself cannot exist without some form of programmable hardware such as a microprocessor or controller. Software programs typically require an operating system in which to run. This provides the program with all the necessary resources, so that it can run successfully, such as providing access to file systems, peripheral devices (such as disk drives, and printers), and access to specific hardware devices. The next chapter defines the types of operating systems that exist. An operating system, itself, is a piece of software which runs on the computer, and has a much closer level of control of the hardware, than user programs do.
- **Firmware**. These are hardware devices that are programmed using software. A good example of firmware is the serial port on a computer. With software this port can operate at one of many different operating transfer rates, or with differing communication

settings. Typically a firmware device must have some local memory in which to store the updated settings. This can be achieved with some permanent memory, such as an EEPROMs (Electrically Erasable Read Only Memories), or FLASH memory, where data can be stored in a permanent way, even when the power is taken away. An example is in a smart card which stores the bank details of a person. Other examples are storing the setup information for a PC (the BIOS settings), and using FLASH memory to store camera pictures. FLASH memory has many advantages over disk storage; especially that it does not require any mechanical movement of parts.

In most applications, dedicated hardware is faster than hardware that is running software, although systems running software programs tend to be easier to modify and require less development time.

Figure 2.2 shows an outline of operations that might occur in a computer system. There are many different data inputs that can occur in user programs, such as data being entered on a keyboard, or data from a network connection, or data movement on the mouse. The two main methods used to react to data input are:

- **Polling**. In this method the system scans all its input devices, at given time periods, and asks them if they have data that requires to be passed onto the system, to be processed. This is acceptable in systems which only have a few inputs, but it is very difficult to scan input devices which have a large number of data inputs. It is also inefficient as it wastes time in interrogating devices for input data when they have no data. Another major problem is that some devices may have a great deal of data, at a given time, and the system is not able to process it fast enough, as the system is too busy scanning other devices for data. Each input device typically has a temporary storage area for the data (known as a memory buffer). A typical problem in a polling system is buffer overruns. This is where the data cannot be extracted fast enough from the buffer, before it overflows, and part of the data is lost. Polling is typically only used when there is infrequent data arriving, or where the memory buffer is large enough, so that none of the data will be lost if the system cannot extract the data fast enough.
- **Event-driven**. The alternative to polling is event-driven, where programs respond to events as they occur in the system. This is more efficient for data input, and can also support other events, such as error and operating system events. It is also easier to write programs which are event-driven, as the program writer does not have to define exactly how the program scans for input data. The program basically just has to respond to specific events, such as when the user moves the cursor, or enters a key from the keyboard.

> **First bug**
>
> The first computer bug really was a bug. Grace Murray Hopper, who also invented COBOL, coined the term 'bug' when she traced an error in the Mark II to a moth trapped in a relay. She carefully removed the bug and taped it to her logbook.

Most general-purpose systems are now event-driven; as these are more efficient, but there can also be a number of programs which are polling-based, in the way that they get data input. Typically a system event causes the system to go into a certain state, such as: a data input state; a processing and analysis state; a data output state; or a defining data requirements state. For example if the user presses a key on the keyboard, then the system goes into the data input state. The character is then read from the keyboard, and processed and/or analysed in some way. Next the results of this can be outputted; typically to the monitor. After this there can be a requirement for more data to be input (the data requirements state). There are obviously many more states in a computer, but the data input, processing/analysis, data output and defining data requirements are typical system states.

Systems events can occur for many reasons, such as:

- Movement of a mouse.
- Pressing a key on the keyboard.
- Pressing a button on a window.
- Data arriving from a network.

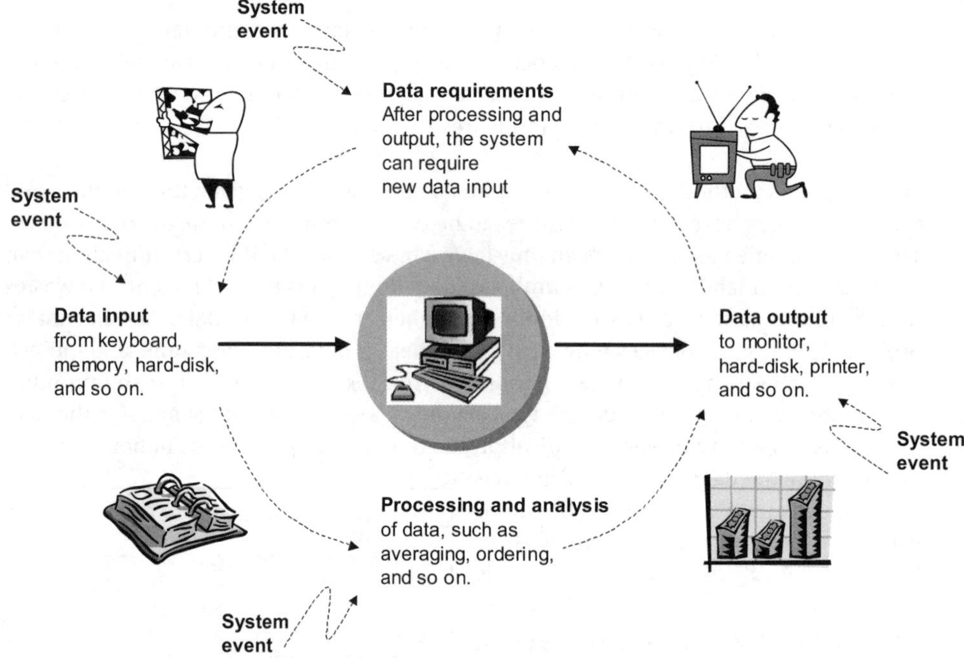

Figure 2.2 Block diagram of a simple computer system

2.4 Computer architecture

The stored-program concept was a great revolution in computer systems, and the basic architecture of a computer has varied very little since this time. Among the many changes that have happened is the integration of devices into single units, but the concept of stored-program and shared memory for program instructions and data stays the same. Some systems have been built using Harvard architecture, as this allows for data and program instructions to be kept separately, which is a much more logical approach. This overcomes the problem of data corrupting stored program instructions. It also actually requires a simpler approach to organizing data and program instructions in memory (as they are kept apart, so there are no problems in organizing the areas which are used by program instruction, and which are used by data). Unfortunately programmers would have to rewrite all their programs and operating system software for a different type of architecture. Also most system developers have been educated on systems which use von Neumann architecture, thus it now seems a more logical approach. Von Neumann architecture is much more efficient in memory than Harvard architecture, but this advantage is not so great in an era which has a large amount of memory. Von Neumann architecture was useful when memory was in short supply, but the case for it is not as strong, these days.

The main elements of a modern computer system are a CPU (central processing unit), memory, and input/output (I/O) interfacing circuitry. After von Neumann's new architecture the CPU and the arithmetic logic unit (ALU) were typically separate units. The invention of the microprocessor integrated the CPU and ALU into a single device.

A computer extracts data and instructions from memory, then processes the data, and places the results back into the memory. There must thus be some way to place a unique address tag for each element of data in memory. This tag is known as a memory address, and the address tag is passed to the memory though an address bus. A bus is a collection of common electrical connections grouped by a single name. The more connections in the address bus, the more address tags that can be used. Once the data is addressed, the data can be passed over the data bus. In order for the system to determine if the data is going to or from the processor, and whether there is valid data on the data bus, and other control definitions, a control bus is required. Thus the three main buses in a computer systems are: the address bus, the control bus and the data bus.

Figure 2.3 shows a basic system (based on von Neumann architecture). External devices such as a keyboard, display, disk drives can connect directly onto the data, address and control buses or through the I/O interface circuitry. It is normally preferable that they connect to the I/O interface as devices rather than connect straight onto the address and data buses as they could do some damage to the buses, especially by corrupting the data on these.

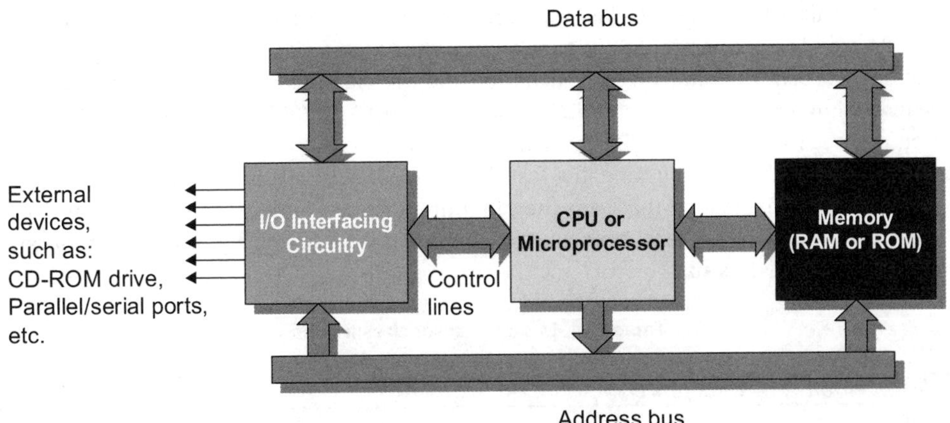

Figure 2.3 Block diagram of a simple computer system

Computers run programs which perform operations on stored data. This data can either be stored in electronic memory, or in a storage device, such as a hard disk or CD-ROM. Electronic memory normally provides a temporary storage of data, which can be accessed quickly (as compared to devices which use a mechanical method to access memory, such as hard disks, or CD-ROMs). Electronic memory consists of RAM (random access memory) and ROM (read only memory). ROM stores permanent binary information, whereas RAM is a non-permanent memory and loses its contents on a loss of power. Applications of RAM are to run programs and store temporary information. RAM is normally made up of either DRAM (Dynamic RAM) or SRAM (Static RAM). SRAM is typically much faster than DRAM, and is used when fast memory access is required. DRAM, though, is typically available in large amounts, and is cheaper for an equivalent memory size (typically a DRAM memory chip can store up to eight times the amount that a SRAM memory chip can). DRAM is typically used for the main memory of the system, and SRAM is used where fast memory is required, such as in memory for graphics devices. The other disadvantage of DRAM is that it looses its contents quickly and the system refreshes its contents many times every second. This operation causes DRAM to consume much more electrical power than SRAM.

"DOS addresses only 1 mega- byte of RAM because we cannot imagine any applications needing more."
Microsoft, 1980, on the development of DOS.

The microprocessor is the main controller of the computer. It only understands binary information and operates on a series of binary commands known as machine code. A system clock synchronizes every operation within the computer. Thus operations, such as reading and writing data to/from memory, occur on the tick of the clock. A system clock which runs at 1MHz (one million ticks per second) will have a single tick of the clock in one millionth of a second.

As the performance of electronic devices has improved, the microprocessor has been able to multiply the system clock, and use this as its operating rate. It will thus operate at a faster speed than the rest of the system. Unfortunately it must slow down to the rest of the system to communicate with devices outside itself. The main limitation on the speed of the system is now on the speed of the wires and interconnected circuit lines that connect the electronic devices together.

As the microprocessor is the heart of any of the operations that occur in the system, the number of bits that it can operate on at a time is an important measure of the system performance. This is knows as the classification of a microprocessor. The first microprocessor: the 4004 could only operate on 4 bits at a time, thus it was classified as a 4-bit processor. Next the Intel 8080 operated on 8 bits at a time and was classified as an 8-bit microprocessor The migration has since gone in multiples of two, from 16-bit (8086) to 32-bit (80386) and to 64-bit devices (Alpha). Table 2.2 shows some examples. Generally the more bits that a microprocessor can handle at a time, the fast the system will be. An important factor, though, is that the operating system that runs the program must also support this maximum size. If it does not, the improvement in speed may be lost, as the operating system cannot cope with the increased data size.

Table 2.2 Microprocessor classification

Classification	*Microprocessor*
4-bit	Intel 4004
8-bit	MOS Technologies 6502, Zilog Z80, Intel 8080, Motorola 6800
16-bit	TI TMS 9900, Intel 8086/8088, Motorola 68000, Intel 80286
32-bit	Zilog Z8000, Motorola 68020, Intel 80386/80486/Pentium
64-bit	DEC Alpha

The basic signals that we require in order to communicate between the microprocessor, memory and the I/O interface are:

- **Memory read or write.** This defines whether data is either being send from the microprocessor to the memory or I/O interface (with a memory write), or if data is being received by the microprocessor from the memory or I/O interface (with a memory read).
- **Memory or I/O interface select.** This defines whether the memory read or write is from the memory or the I/O interface.
- **Clock.** This synchronizes the events between the microprocessor and the memory or I/O interface.
- **Interrupt line.** This is used by external devices to get the attention of the processor (and thus cause an event).

The basic operation of the system is:

- Fetch binary instructions from memory.
- Decode these instructions into a series of simple actions.
- Carry out the actions in a sequence of steps.

To access a location in memory the following actions are conducted:

- The microprocessor puts the address of the location on the address bus.
- The contents at this address are then placed on the data bus.
- The microprocessor reads the data from the data bus.

To store data in memory the following actions are conducted:

- The microprocessor places the data on the data bus.
- The address of the location in memory is then put on the address bus.
- Data is read from the data bus into the memory address location.

2.5 Bits, bytes and words

Systems can be divided into two main classifications: digital systems and analogue systems. A digital system only understands 0's and 1's (binary information), whereas an analogue system can take on many values (this concept will be covered in more detail in Chapter 6).

2.5.1 Binary numbers

Imagine that you are an army scout whose job it is to sit on a hill and watch for an attacking army. You have been given two flags: a red flag and a green flag, which are inserted into a single flagpole. You could now represent two different conditions (or states). The green flag could represent that there were no armies approaching, and the red flag could represent that there was an army advancing on the city. Thus:

- Red flag – approaching army.
- Green flag – no approaching army.

Now, this does not give much information on the size of the army, at all, or if the approaching army is an aggressive one or a friendly one. Thus if we used two flags we could represent four different conditions (or states):

- Red flag, red flag – approaching large aggressive army. Get troops ready for battle.
- Red flag, green flag – approaching small aggressive army. Put troops on standby.
- Green flag, red flag – approaching friendly army. Set up greeting parade.
- Green flag, green flag – no approaching army.

It can be seen that we have to decide which of the flags is more significant than the other; as we need to differentiate between a Green, Red and a Red, Green condition. Thus we could signify that the flag on the left-hand side is more significant than the flag on the right-hand side, as this flag represents that there is an aggressive army approaching. This flag would be seen as the most-significant flag. Now let us represent the flags with either R (for red), and G (for green). Thus the states now become:

- RR – approaching large aggressive army. Get troops ready for battle.
- RG – approaching small aggressive army. Put troops on standby.
- GR – approaching friendly army. Set up greeting parade.
- GG – no approaching army.

The number of flags that we have thus determines the number of conditions that we can represent. If we only have one colour of flag, then we can only represent two states with one flag, four states with two flags, eight states with three flags (RRR, RRG, RGR, RGG, ... GGR and GGG), and so on. This type of representation with two conditions for each representation is known as binary. In computer systems the conditions for each representation is a '0' and a '1' (or sometimes as TRUE or FALSE). Thus, in binary, we could represent the red flag with a '1', and the green flag with a '0'. Our conditions (or states) are now: 00 (no approaching army); 01 (approaching friendly army); 10 (approaching small aggressive army); and 11 (approaching aggressive army).

A particular problem that we might have when we are signalling the information about the army is when our flags are changing. For example, say that we are currently in the condition of GG, and a large aggressive army started to approach. The scout would then have to change the flags from GG to RR. This will take two changes before he can reflect the new condition. How would he do it? If he changed the most-significant flag first, he would signal that there was an approaching friendly army, and the city would get a greeting parade ready, only then to be told that there was a large aggressive army approaching. This would obviously confuse everyone in the city. If he changed the least-significant flag, then the troops would be put on standby, only to be told that they would immediately be put on full alert. The problem we have is that we need some way to change the state of the flags, so that intermediate values are not taken as final values. Thus one way to do this would be to hide the changeover of the flags. This also occurs in a computer system where values of the binary digits change, and these should not be taken as valid values. This is overcome with clock signals and handshaking lines, which are used to define when the values on the computer's bus are actually valid, or not.

A computer operates on binary digits which use a base-2 numbering system. To determine the decimal equivalent of a binary number each column is represented by two raised to the power of 0, 1, 2, and so on. For example, the decimal equivalents of `1000 0001` and `0101 0011` are:

2^7	2^6	2^5	2^4	2^3	2^2	2^1	2^0	
128	*64*	*32*	*16*	*8*	*4*	*2*	*1*	*Decimal*
1	0	0	0	0	0	0	1	129
0	1	0	1	0	0	1	1	83

Thus `01010011` gives:
(0×128) + (1×64) + (0×32) + (1×16)+ (0×8) + (0×4) + (1×2) + (1×1) = 83

As seen the number of different representations of the binary digits is determined by the number of bits used to represent the value. With a single binary digit we can represent two values (2^1), with two binary digits we can represent four values (2^2), and so on. For example:

- 8 bits gives 0 to 2^8–1 (255) different representations.
- 16 bits gives 0 to 2^{16}–1 (65,535) different representations.
- 32 bits gives 0 to 2^{32}–1 (4,294,967,295) different representations.

Just as in the decimal system (with units, tens, hundreds, and so on), the most-significant bit (msb) is at the left-hand side of the binary number and the least-significant bit (lsb) on the right-hand side. To convert from decimal (base-10) to binary the decimal value is divided by two recursively and the remainder noted. The first remainder gives the lsb and the last gives the msb. For example:

2	54	
	27	r 0 <<< lsb
	13	r 1
	6	r 1
	3	r 0
	1	r 1
	0	r 1 <<< msb

Conversion to 2's complement

1. Convert to binary.
2. Invert all the bits
3. Add 1.

Thus 54 in decimal is `110110` in binary. Normally computer system use groups of 4 and 8 bits, thus it is important to memorize some of the key values for groups of 4 and 8, such as:

Binary	**Decimal**
0000	0
1111	15
1111 1111	255
1111 1111 1111	4095 (4k)
1111 1111 1111 1111	65,535 (64k)
1111 1111 1111 1111 1111 1111	16,777,215 (16M)
1111 1111 1111 1111 1111 1111 1111 1111	4,294,967,295 (4G)

Typical groupings of bits are:

- **Nibble**. A group of four bits. A nibble 16 (2^4) different combinations of ON/OFF, from 0000 to 1111.
- **Byte**. A group of eight bits. A byte gives 256 (2^8) different combinations of ON/OFF, from 0000 0000 to 1111 1111.
- **Word**. A group of 16 bits (2 bytes). A word gives 65,536 (2^{16}) different combinations of ON/OFF, from 00000000 00000000 to 11111111 11111111.
- **Long Word**. A group of 32 bits (4 bytes). A long word gives 4,294,967,296 (2^{32}) different combinations of ON/OFF.

2.5.2 Binary arithmetic

Computer systems must perform arithmetic operations on binary digits. In decimal we all know when we add a single digit (0 to 9) to another digit we get the rules of 0+0 equals 0, 0+1 equals 1, right up to 9+9 equals 18. When we perform these additions with other digits we align them up, and then carry any values into the next column. Thus 9+9 makes 8, with a one carried into the next column to be added with that column.

Binary addition is actually simpler as it only involves two values for each digit (but obviously we are now more accustomed to decimal addition). There are thus four possible combinations when adding two binary digits together (with a carry from the previous column):

$0+0 \;=0 \qquad 1+0 \;=1 \qquad 1+1 \;=10 \qquad 1+1+1=11$

We can then perform a binary addition as we do in decimal addition, by lining up the two values with the least significant bit at the right-hand side, and the most significant bit at the left-hand side. Any gaps in bits on the left-hand side are replaced with zero values (as we do with decimal addition, but we typically do not include preceding zeros). For example:

```
 0010001
 0001111
 -------
 0100000
 -------
  11111
```

2.5.3 Hexadecimal

Digital computers are digital systems, and operate on binary information (base-2), that is, 0's and 1's. Unfortunately, humans have difficulties in converting binary information into a decimal format. Some of the operations within the computer require that the user or programmer defines a binary value. Typically requirements are:

- **To specify a memory address**. Typically memory addresses in a computer are specified with their binary address, thus there must be a method to display this in a form which the user can easily convert to and from.
- **To display or set the value of a variable**. Sometimes the actual binary contents of a value needs to be interrogated or set, thus there must be a form in which the user can easily read and convert it into a binary form.
- **To specify network addresses**. A network address of a computer (such as 146.176.151.140) often needs to be converted into a form which the computer understands, thus there must be a conversion between decimal and binary, or vice versa.

These problems are solved by either converting between binary and decimal, or between binary and hexadecimal (base-16) or octal (base-8). Without the aid of a calculator, the conversion between binary and decimal is relatively difficult for large binary numbers, but hexadecimal and octal conversion make it easier, as they allow the binary digits to be split into groups of four (for hexadecimal) or three (for octal), and then converted. Hexadecimal is the conversion most often used to specify a memory address or in defining the contents of a memory address. Figure 2.4 shows an example of hexadecimal addresses.

Binary data is stored in memories which are either permanent or non-permanent. This data is arranged as bytes and each byte has a different memory address, as illustrated in Figure 2.5. The Read/Write defines whether data is read from (Read) the memory or written to (Write) the memory. In terms of size, the address bus defines the number of addressable locations, and the data bus size defines the maximum number of data bits that can be written to any addressable location. For example an 8-bit address bus can be used to access up to 256 bytes (256B), a 16-bit address bus can be used to access up to 65,636 bytes (64kB), a 24-bit address bus can be used to access up to 16,777,216 bytes (16MB), and a 32-bit address bus can be used to access up to 4,294,967,295 (4GB).

Top 20 computer people

1. Dan Bricklin (VisiCalc)
2. Bill Gates (Microsoft)
3. Steve Jobs (Apple)
4. Robert Noyce (Intel)
5. Dennis Ritchie (C Programming)
6. Marc Andreessen (Netscape Communications)
7. Bill Atkinson (Apple Mac GUI)
8. Tim Berners-Lee (CERN/WWW)
9. Doug Engelbart (Mouse/Windows/etc.)
10. Grace Murray Hopper (COBOL)
11. Philippe Kahn (Turbo Pascal)
12. Mitch Kapor (Lotus 123)
13. Donald Knuth (TEX)
14. Thomas Kurtz
15. Drew Major (NetWare)
16. Robert Metcalfe (Ethernet)
17. Bjarne Stroustrup (C++)
18. John Warnock (Adobe)
19. Niklaus Wirth (Pascal)
20. Steve Wozniak (Apple)

Byte, September 1995

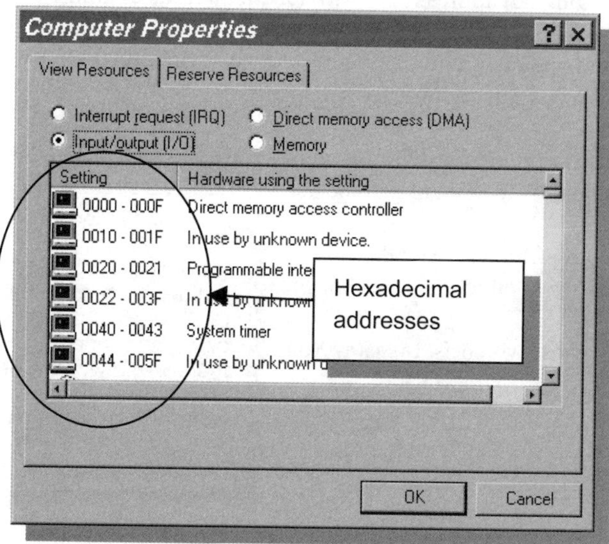

Figure 2.4 Hexadecimal memory addresses

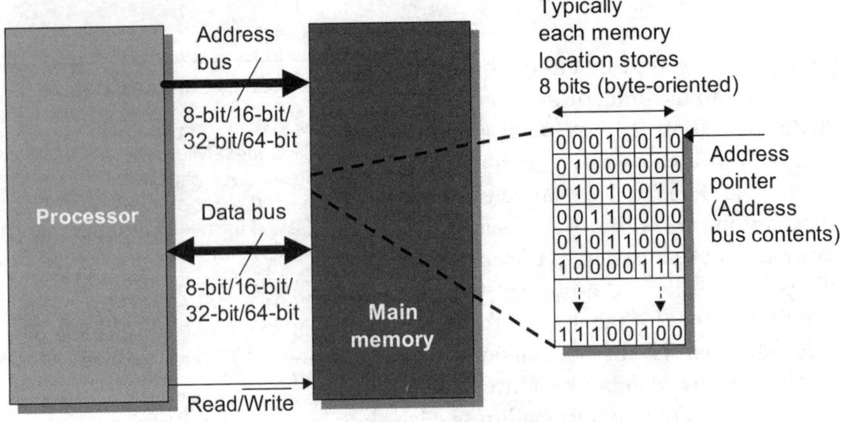

Figure 2.5 Memory storage (each address holds eight bits)

2.5.4 Address bus

The address bus is responsible for identifying the location into which the data is to be passed. Each location in memory typically contains a single byte (8 bits), but could also be arranged as words (16 bits), or long words (32 bits). Byte-oriented memory is the most flexible as it also enables access to any multiple of 8 bits. The size of the address bus thus indicates the maximum addressable number of bytes. Table 2.3 shows the size of addressable memory for a given address bus size. The number of addressable bytes is given by:

$$\text{Addressable locations} = 2^n \text{ B}$$

Addressable locations for a given address bus

where n is the number of bits in the address bus. For example (as defined in Table 2.3):

- A 1-bit address bus can address up to two locations (that is 0 and 1).
- A 2-bit address bus can address 2^2 or four locations (that is 00, 01, 10 and 11).
- A 20-bit address bus can address up to 2^{20} addresses (1 MB).
- A 32-bit address bus can address up to 2^{32} addresses (4 GB).

The units used for computers for defining memory are B (bytes), kB (kilobytes), MB (megabytes) and GB (gigabytes). These are defined as:

- Kilobyte: 2^{10} bytes, which is 1,024 B.
- Megabyte: 2^{20} bytes, which is 1,024 kB, or 1,048,576 B.
- Gigabyte: 2^{30} bytes, which is 1,024 MB, or 1,048,576 kB, or 1,073,741,824 B.

Don't mention computers!

For over a decade, Ken Olsen did not use the term computer to the DEC board of directors, as it was commonly thought, at the time, that there was a world-wide market for only up to 100 computers. Thus they were called Programmed Data Processing (PDP) units.

Table 2.3 Addressable memory (in bytes) related to address bus size

Address bus size	*Addressable memory (bytes)*	*Address bus size*	*Addressable memory (bytes)*
1	2	15	32 K
2	4	16	64 K
3	8	17	128 K
4	16	18	256 K
5	32	19	512 K
6	64	20	1 M†
7	128	21	2 M
8	256	22	4 M
9	512	23	8 M
10	1K*	24	16 M
11	2K	25	32 M
12	4K	26	64 M
13	8K	32	4G‡
14	16K	64	16GG

* 1K represents 1,024 bytes † 1M represents 1,048,576 (1024 K) bytes
‡ 1G represents 1,073,741,824 (1024 M) bytes

2.6 Data representation

The representation of data types is always a problem, as different computer systems use different ways to store and represent data. For example, the PC, which is based on Intel microprocessors, uses the little endian approach of representing a floating-point value. The little endian form starts with the least-significant byte in the lowest memory location, and the most-significant byte in the highest location. The big endian form, as used with Motorola-based systems, always starts with the high-order byte and ends with the lowest-order byte. For example with little endian, the value to store the 16-bit integer values of 4 (0000 0000 0000 0100b), 5,241 (0001 0100 0111 1001 b) and 26,152 (0110 0110 0010 1000b) would be:

Memory location	*Contents (hex)*	*Contents (binary)*	*Value*
00	04	0000 0100	4
01	00	0000 0000	
02	79	0111 1001	5,241
03	14	0001 0100	
04	28	0010 1000	26,152
05	66	0110 0110	

Whereas, in big endian, it would be stored as:

Memory location	*Contents (hex)*	*Contents (binary)*	*Value*
00	00	0000 0000	4
01	04	0000 0100	
02	14	0001 0100	5,241
03	79	0111 1001	
04	66	0110 0110	26,152
05	28	0010 1000	

Thus a program which has been written for a PC would incorrectly read data which has been written for a big endian program (typically for a UNIX workstation), and vice versa. Another particular problem is that different computer systems represent data (such as numeric values) in different formats. For example an integer can be represented with either 16 bits, 32 bits, 64 bits, or even, 128 bits. The more bits that are used, the larger the integer value that can be represented.

All these problems highlight the need for a conversion technique that knows how to read the value from memory, and convert it into a standard form that is independent of the operating system or the hardware of the computer. This is the function of eXternal Data Representation (XDR), which represents data in a standard format. In XDR the basic data types are:

- **Unsigned integer and signed integer.** An unsigned and signed integer uses a 32-bit value. The unsigned value uses the range from 0 to $2^{32}-1$ (4,294,967,295), whereas the signed integer uses 2's complement which gives a range of –2,147,483,648 (1111 1111 1111 ... 1111 1111) to +2,147,483,647 (0111 1111 1111 ... 1111).
- **Single-precision floating point.** A single-precision floating-point value uses a 32-bit IEEE format of a floating-point value. An example is given next. The range is from $\pm 3.4 \times 10^{-38}$ to $\pm 3.4 \times 10^{38}$.
- **Double-precision floating point.** A double-precision floating-point value uses a 64-bit IEEE format of a floating-point value. The range is from $\pm 1.7 \times 10^{-308}$ to $\pm 1.7 \times 10^{308}$.
- **String.** A string is represented with a number of bytes. The first four bytes define the number of ASCII characters defined. For example, if there were four characters in the string then the first four bytes would be: 0, 0, 0, 4, followed by the four characters in the string. Note that this differs from the way that the C programming language represents strings, as C uses the NULL ASCII character to define the end of a string.

Table 2.4 16-bit 2's complement notation

Decimal	*2's complement*
–32 768	10000000 00000000
–32 767	10000000 00000001
::::	::::
–2	11111111 11111110
–1	11111111 11111111
0	00000000 00000000
1	00000000 00000001
2	00000000 00000010
::::	::
32 766	01111111 11111110
32 767	01111111 11111111

2.6.1 Negative numbers

Signed integers use a notation called 2's complement to represent negative values. In this representation the binary digits have a '1' in the most-significant bit column if the number is negative, else it is a '0'. To convert a decimal value into 2's complement notation, the magnitude of the negative number is represented in binary form. Next, all the bits are inverted and a '1' is added. For example to determine the 16-bit 2's complement of the value –65, the following steps are taken:

+65	00000000 01000001
invert	11111111 10111110
add 1	11111111 10111111

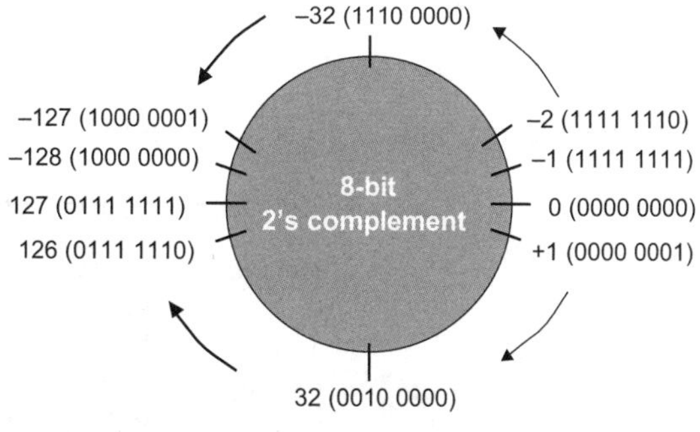

Thus, –65 is 11111111 1011111 in 16-bit 2's complement notation. Table 2.4 shows that with 16 bits the range of values that can be represented in 2's complement is from –32,768 to 32, 767 (that is, 65,536 values).

Two's complement is also useful in subtraction operations, where the value to be subtracted is converted in its negative form, and then added to the value it is to be subtracted from. For example to subtract 42 from 65, first 42 is converted into 2's complement (that is, –42) and added to the binary equivalent of 65. The result gives a carry-in to the sign bit and a carry-out (these are ignored).

65	`0100 0001`
–42	`1101 0110`
= 23	`(1) 0001 0111`

A 16-bit signed integer can vary from –32,768 (`1000 0000 0000 0000`) to 32,767 (`0111 1111 1111 1111`).

> 'There will be no software in this man's army!',
>
> General Dwight D. Eisenhower, 1947.

2.6.2 Hexadecimal and octal numbers

Often it is difficult to differentiate binary numbers from decimal numbers (as one hundred and one can be seen as 101 in binary, and vice-versa). A typical convention is to use a proceeding b for binary numbers, for example `0101 0111 1010b` and `1011 1110 1010b` are binary numbers. Hexadecimal and octal are often used to represent binary digits, as they are relatively easily to convert to and from binary. Table 2.5 shows the basic conversion between decimal, binary, octal and hexadecimal numbers. A typical convention is to append a hexadecimal value with an 'h' at the end (and octal number with an `o`). For example, `43F1h` is a hexadecimal value whereas `4310o` is octal.

To represent a binary digit as a hexadecimal value, the binary digits are split into groups of four bits (starting from the least-significant bit). A hexadecimal equivalent value then replaces each of the binary groups. For example, to represent `0111 0101 1100 0000b` the bits are split into sections of four to give:

Binary	`0111`	`0101`	`1100`	`0000`
Hex	`7`	`5`	`C`	`0`

Thus, `75C0h` represents the binary number `0111 0101 1100 0000b`. To convert from decimal to hexadecimal the decimal value is divided by 16 recursively and each remainder noted. The first remainder gives the least-significant digit and the final remainder the most-significant digit. For example, the following shows the hexadecimal equivalent of the decimal number `1103`:

```
16 | 1103
   |   68  rF <<< lsd (least-significant digit)
   |    4  r4
   |    0  r4 <<< msd (most-significant digit)
```

Thus, the decimal value `1103` is equivalent to `044Fh`.

Table 2.5 Decimal, binary, octal and hexadecimal conversions

Decimal	*Binary*	*Octal*	*Hex*
0	0000	0	0
1	0001	1	1
2	0010	2	2
3	0011	3	3
4	0100	4	4
5	0101	5	5
6	0110	6	6
7	0111	7	7
8	1000	10	8
9	1001	11	9
10	1010	12	A
11	1011	13	B
12	1100	14	C
13	1101	15	D
14	1110	16	E
15	1111	17	F

2.6.3 Floating-point representation

A single-precision floating-point value uses 32 bits, where the most-significant bit represents the sign bit (S), the next eight bits represents the exponent of the number in base 2, minus 127 (E). The final 23 bits represent the base-2 fractional part of the number's mantissa (F). The standard format is:

$$\text{Value} = -1^{S} \times 2^{(E-127)} \times 1.F$$

For example:

1.23 = 3F9D 70A4h
= 0 01111111 00111010111000010100100b
$= -1^{0} \times 2^{(127-127)} \times (1 + 2^{-3} + 2^{-4} + 2^{-5} + 2^{-9} + 2^{-10} + 2^{-11} + 2^{-16} + 2^{-18} + 2^{-21})$

-5.67 = COB5 70A4h
= 1 10000001 01101010111000010100100b
$= -1^{1} \times 2^{(129-127)} \times (1 + 2^{-2} + 2^{-3} + 2^{-5} + 2^{-7} + 2^{-9} + 2^{-10} + 2^{-11} + 2^{-15} + 2^{-17} + 2^{-20})$

100.442 = 42C8 E24Eh
= 0 10000101 10010001110001001001110b
$= -1^{0} \times 2^{(133-127)} \times (1 + 2^{-1} + 2^{-4} + 2^{-8} + 2^{-9} + 2^{-10} + 2^{-14} + 2^{-17} + 2^{-20} + 2^{-21} + 2^{-22})$

A single-precision floating-point value uses 64 bits, where the most-significant bit represents the sign bit (S), the next eight bits represents the exponent of the number in base 2, minus 1023 (E). The final 52 bits represent the base-2 fractional part of the number's mantissa (F).

2.6.4 ASCII

> **ANSI ASCII code**
>
> In 1963, ANSI defined the 7-bit ASCII standard code for characters. At the same time IBM had developed the 8-bit EBCDIC code which allowed for up to 256 characters, rather than 128 characters for ASCII. It is thought that the 7-bit code was used for the standard as it was reckoned that eight holes in punched paper tape would weaken the tape. Thus the world has had to use the 7-bit ASCII standard, which is still popular in the days of global communications, and large-scale disk storage.

As we have seen there are standard formats for integers and floating-point values. There are many standards for the representation of characters (known as character sets), but the most common one is known as ASCII. In its standard form it uses a 7-bit binary code to represent characters (letters, giving a range of 0 to 127). This is rather limited as it does not support symbols such as Greek lines, and so. To increase the number of symbols which can be represented, extended ASCII is used which has an 8-bit code.

Table 2.6 shows the standard ASCII character set (in binary, decimal, hexadecimal and also as a character). For example the 'a' character has the ASCII binary representation of 0110 0001b (61h), and the 'A' character has the binary representation of 0100 0001 (41h). One thing that can be noticed is that the upper and lower case versions of the letters ('a' to 'z') only differ by a single bit (the 6th bit, from the right-hand side).

2.7 Exercises

The following questions are multiple choice. Please select from a–d.

2.7.1 Which unit represents 1024 bytes:

(a) B (b) KB (c) MB (d) GB

2.7.2 Which unit represents bits per second:

(a) bps (b) bs (c) bits (d) bsec

2.7.3 Which unit represents a billion bytes:

(a) B (b) KB (c) MB (d) GB

2.7.4 Which of the following is 1GB:

(a) 1024KB (b) 100KB
(c) 1024MB (d) 1000MB

2.7.5 A processor can operate on four bytes at a time, which is its classification:

(a) 8-bit (b) 16-bit (c) 32-bit (d) 64-bit

2.7.6 How many bits are in a nibble:

(a) 4 (b) 8 (c) 16 (d) 32

Additional tutorial questions are available at:
`http://www.palgrave.com/studyskills/masterseries/buchanan`

Table 2.6 ASCII character set

Binary	*Decimal*	*Hex*	*Character*	*Binary*	*Decimal*	*Hex*	*Character*
00000000	0	00	NUL	00010000	16	10	DLE
00000001	1	01	SOH	00010001	17	11	DC1
00000010	2	02	STX	00010010	18	12	DC2
00000011	3	03	ETX	00010011	19	13	DC3
00000100	4	04	EOT	00010100	20	14	DC4
00000101	5	05	ENQ	00010101	21	15	NAK
00000110	6	06	ACK	00010110	22	16	SYN
00000111	7	07	BEL	00010111	23	17	ETB
00001000	8	08	BS	00011000	24	18	CAN
00001001	9	09	HT	00011001	25	19	EM
00001010	10	0A	LF	00011010	26	1A	SUB
00001011	11	0B	VT	00011011	27	1B	ESC
00001100	12	0C	FF	00011100	28	1C	FS
00001101	13	0D	CR	00011101	29	1D	GS
00001110	14	0E	SO	00011110	30	1E	RS
00001111	15	0F	SI	00011111	31	1F	US
00100000	32	20	SPACE	00110000	48	30	0
00100001	33	21	!	00110001	49	31	1
00100010	34	22	“	00110010	50	32	2
00100011	35	23	#	00110011	51	33	3
00100100	36	24	$	00110100	52	34	4
00100101	37	25	%	00110101	53	35	5
00100110	38	26	&	00110110	54	36	6
00100111	39	27	/	00110111	55	37	7
00101000	40	28	(	00111000	56	38	8
00101001	41	29	)	00111001	57	39	9
00101010	42	2A	*	00111010	58	3A	:
00101011	43	2B	+	00111011	59	3B	;
00101100	44	2C	,	00111100	60	3C	<
00101101	45	2D	-	00111101	61	3D	=
00101110	46	2E	.	00111110	62	3E	>
00101111	47	2F	/	00111111	63	3F	?
01000000	64	40	@	01010000	80	50	P
01000001	65	41	A	01010001	81	51	Q
01000010	66	42	B	01010010	82	52	R
01000011	67	43	C	01010011	83	53	S
01000100	68	44	D	01010100	84	54	T
01000101	69	45	E	01010101	85	55	U
01000110	70	46	F	01010110	86	56	V
01000111	71	47	G	01010111	87	57	W
01001000	72	48	H	01011000	88	58	X
01001001	73	49	I	01011001	89	59	Y
01001010	74	4A	J	01011010	90	5A	Z
01001011	75	4B	K	01011011	91	5B	[
01001100	76	4C	L	01011100	92	5C	\
01001101	77	4D	M	01011101	93	5D	]
01001110	78	4E	N	01011110	94	5E	`
01001111	79	4F	O	01011111	95	5F	_
01100000	96	60		01110000	112	70	p
01100001	97	61	a	01110001	113	71	q
01100010	98	62	b	01110010	114	72	r
01100011	99	63	c	01110011	115	73	s
01100100	100	64	d	01110100	116	74	t
01100101	101	65	e	01110101	117	75	u
01100110	102	66	f	01110110	118	76	v
01100111	103	67	g	01110111	119	77	w
01101000	104	68	h	01111000	120	78	x
01101001	105	69	i	01111001	121	79	y
01101010	106	6A	j	01111010	122	7A	z
01101011	107	6B	k	01111011	123	7B	{
01101100	108	6C	l	01111100	124	7C	:
01101101	109	6D	m	01111101	125	7D	}
01101110	110	6E	n	01111110	126	7E	~
01101111	111	6F	o	01111111	127	7F	DEL

3 Operating systems

3.1 Introduction

> 'I'm glad to be out of that bag', 'Hello, I am Macintosh. Never trust a computer you cannot lift.'
>
> Quotes from the Macintosh computer when it introduced itself.

A computer system is typically made up of hardware, an operating system and a user interface, as illustrated in Figure 3.1. The hardware includes the central processing unit (CPU), memory, and input/output devices, whereas an operating system allows an easy interface between the user and the hardware. Operating systems are key components of a computer system, and they provide a foundation for programs and the user to access the resources of a computer, in an easy-to-use way. They have evolved recently into systems which can sense the hardware of the system and set it up in the required way. At one time a computer program required to know how to access all the different types of hardware that it connected to. The user would then have to set it up in the settings of the program. These days the operating system hides much of the complexity of the hardware from user programs, and the user.

Also, in the past, computer systems required expert user operators who understood how to add and delete devices from the computer, how to start and stop the computer, and they knew how to control the computer with the required operating system commands. These days most modern operating systems start, and shutdown, automatically and scan the connected hardware. This allows the system to configure itself when booted.

Operating systems thus provide an easy-to-use interface to the hardware. Many older operating systems, such as DOS and UNIX, used text commands which were used to control the system. Most systems, these days, provide a graphical user interface (GUI) in which the user uses Windows, Icons, Menus and Pointers (WIMPs) to run programs and organize the system.

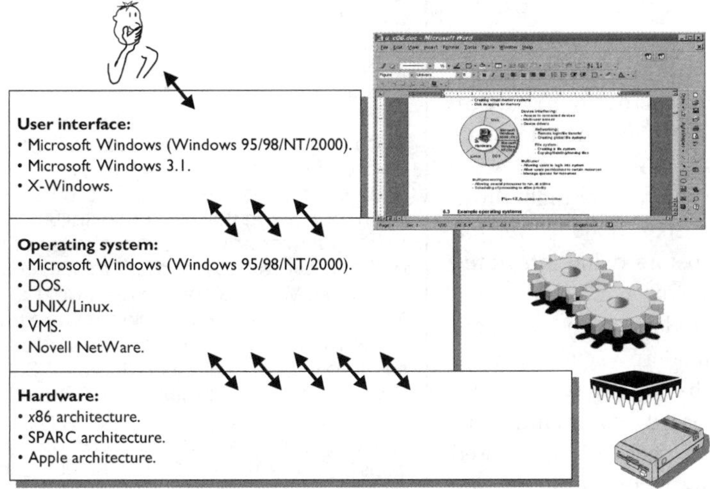

Figure 3.1 User interface, operating system and hardware

The two main functions of an operating system are to provide an interface between the user and the hardware of the computer, and to provide services to application programs. As computers are designed with a maximum size of address and data bus, an operating system is designed to operate on a maximum number of bits at a time. This typically defines the classification of the operating system, such as: 16-bit, 32-bit and 64-bit operating systems (although some super computers use 128-bit operating systems). Normally the more bits that an operating system can operate on, at a time, the faster it will run application programs. The limitation on the number of bits that the operating system can operate with, limits the software that can run on the operating system. For example 32-bit software (such as Microsoft Office 2000) will not run on a 16-bit operating system (such as DOS or Windows 3.x), but 16-bit software, such as old Windows and DOS programs, can typically run on a compatible 32-bit operating system.

The main operating systems which are currently available are:

- **DOS**. This was one of the first operating systems for the PC, and quickly become a standard, not because of its technical specifications, but because of its relative cheapness against the other PC operating systems. Initially there were several different flavours of DOS, from IBM (PC-DOS) and Microsoft (MS-DOS), but MS-DOS became the standard that most systems were measured by. It eventually lived through six major version changes, before being integrated into Microsoft Windows. It still lives on today in an emulated form in modern version of Windows. It had many weaknesses: its text-based command language; its lack of integrated networking; it could only run one program at a time (single tasking); it used 16-bit software (even

IBM and Microsoft

Unlike DEC, IBM could see the growing power of the personal computer market. So, their Corporate Management Committee gave permission to William Lowe to start Project Chess, which would have an extremely small team of just 12 engineers. Time was a critical factor, and to be able to deliver on time IBM could not conceivably write their own operating system. Thus IBM approached Bill Gates and Steve Ballmer, of Microsoft, and Gary Kildall at Digital Research. Bill Gates accepted the request from IBM to write the operating system for the IBM PC, but Gary Kildall rejected the offer for his CP/M-86 operating system.

After an initial prototype was produced, the Corporate Management Committee at IBM gave the go-ahead for full development. The code name was Acorn (which would indeed lead to greater things).

IBM had initially thought that the 8-bit 8080 processor would provide the heart of the system, but Bill Gates persuaded them to use the much higher-powered 16-bit 8086. Soon William Lowe assembled the engineers for Project Chess in Boca Raton, Florida.

Microsoft had previously had a good background in producing software compilers such as FORTRAN, BASIC (Radio Shack and Apple) and COBOL, and had just released their version of the UNIX operating system for the PC, called XENIX. As Microsoft's main strengths were in software compilers, Paul Allen of Microsoft contacted Tim Patterson at Seattle Computer Products to get the rights to sell their DOS (86-DOS) to an unnamed client (IBM). It was the deal of the century, and Microsoft only paid $100,000 for the rights. After this, Bill Gates, Paul Allen, and Steve Ballmer met with IBM to propose that Microsoft be put in charge of the entire software development for IBM PC. Microsoft and IBM then signed a contract for Microsoft to develop certain software products for IBM's microcomputer. IBM also asked Microsoft to produce BASIC, FORTRAN, COBOL and Pascal compilers for their PC. In 1981, IBM released DOS 1.0, and the rest is history. The following year, Microsoft released MS-DOS versions of FORTRAN, BASIC (GW-BASIC) and COBOL.

though the processor may be capable of running 32-bit software); it could only access up to 1MB of memory; and so on. It worked, though, and allowed the hardware to become powerful enough to support a proper multitasking operating system. For many businesses it gave them all the functionality that they required i.e. to run a single program on a stand-alone computer. Its only real advantage, though, was its compatibility with user programs, or, in most cases, the compatibility of user programs with it. If someone wanted to sell a program, it had to work with MS-DOS; otherwise it would be doomed to fail in the market. Thus any new operating system would have to provide exactly what MS-DOS did, and more. At the time, when DOS reined, PC hardware was not really up to running much more than a single program at a time, thus it was difficult to introduce a new operating system which properly competed with MS-DOS (IBM tried with several systems, and nearly succeeded with OS/2, but unfortunately it was too much of a compromised system). The coming wave of networking, the increased power of microprocessors (especially the 80486) and the power of graphical user interfaces would eventually kill off DOS. Luckily for Microsoft, they released their best version of Windows, at a time when PCs could properly support the new enhanced features of graphical user interfaces. Their new version of Windows (Windows 3.1) did not properly support networking, but with Novell NetWare, for the first time PCs could communicate over a network, and users could actually *see* their programs.

- **Microsoft Windows 3.x.** This was basically a graphical user interface (GUI), which used DOS as its operating system, and thus still had all the major problems of DOS (such as only being able to run 16-bit software, only being able to access a limited amount of memory, no networking, and so on). After two failed attempts at producing a graphical user interface for the PC (Windows Version 1.0 and Windows Version 2.0), Microsoft eventually succeeded with a winner with Microsoft Windows 3.1, which included many of the features that are standard in most modern GUIs, such as overlapping windows, menu systems, drag-and-drop, and so on. It has the advantage that it was still optional, as it built onto DOS, thus users could still use their DOS-based system, and then go into Windows when required. Some software companies who had extremely successful DOS-based versions, especially Lotus 123 and WordPerfect, failed to see the true potential of Windows, and did not create Windows versions fast enough for the market. Eventually these products were overtaken, especially with the Microsoft Office products, such as Microsoft Word for Windows, and Microsoft Excel for Windows, which incorporated the full power of the Windows interface.
- **Microsoft Windows.** In the mid-1980s, Microsoft spent a good deal of time working with IBM on OS/2. Unfortunately the partnership broke up, and Microsoft used their experience from this project and fed it into Microsoft NT Version 3.0. This was a radical redesign of an operating system for the PC. Its aim was to provided a robust environment for programs, and also properly supported networking. As Microsoft were releasing NT, in the mid-1990s, they were also releasing a new type of graphical user interface with Windows 95. The release of the two systems was a complete success and they were the start of complete operating systems which had an enhanced graphical user interface. Both properly supported networking, and could integrate with

> **Why is the PC clonable?**
>
> BIOS was a key element in making the PC clonable, as it contained all the hardware-specific information in a single place. Compaq successfully rewrote its version of BIOS, rather than copying it from the original IBM PC, which stopped any legal action from IBM.

virtually every type of network (especially with DECnet, Novell NetWare and IBM). They could also run more than one program at a time (multitasking). As they were designed to operate on 16 bits or 32 bits they could run 32-bit software. The next version of NT used the graphical user interface developed with Windows 95. Newer versions of Windows have included Windows 98, Windows ME and Windows 2000, and each has built on the robustness, networking infrastructure and GUI of its parents (Windows 95 and NT).

- **UNIX.** A powerful and robust operating system, which is typically used in high-powered workstations. It has a kernel, which interfaces to the hardware. This kernel has the advantage that it can be stripped away from the GUI and can be run on its own. This is a distinct advantage in embedded systems, which do not require user interfaces, or which might be slowed down by the extra code that is required to produce a GUI. It also has a main operating system, which runs commands, and will integrate with a GUI, typically X-Windows, to provide the interface between the user and the operating system. It typically supports either 32-bit or 64-bit software. Its greatest gift to the world have been its networking protocols, which it has nurtured over the years, and developed them so that they have become truly grown-up leaders in the world-wide Internet. Seldom has any parent been so successful in creating offspring that have truly united the world, and enhanced communication. The main contenders have been TCP/IP (for communications between computers over a network, no matter their architecture, type, operating system, or network connection), SMTP (for electronic mail), HTTP (for WWW access), TELNET (for remote login), FTP (for file transfer), RIP (for network routing) and many more.
- **Novell NetWare.** Around the time of DOS and Microsoft Windows 3.1, there was very little software which allowed computers to be connected to a network. Novell NetWare plugged this gap perfectly, with a networked operating system that provides access to networked resources, such as print queues, file services, and so on. It integrated seamlessly with DOS and Microsoft Windows, and could detect the commands which had to be run locally on the local operating system, and the ones which needed to be sent to the network server. It held a virtual monopoly on PC-based network operating systems, until Microsoft developed Windows NT.
- **VMS.** As with UNIX, a powerful and robust operating system. It is excellent at running batch processes, which are automatically started when the system is started. They then run quietly with little user input (typically described as batch processes).
- **Linux.** A version of UNIX for the PC, and one of the few PC-based operating systems to properly compete with Microsoft Windows.

Operating systems are basically split into two parts: the kernel component and the main operating system component, as illustrated in Figure 3.2. The operating system and kernel components can make access to user account databases, which contain the names of users who are allowed to log into the system, and their password. They also allow access to file systems and other resources, such as the scheduling of processes.

Operating systems are typically differentiated, as illustrated in Figure 3.3, by:

- **Single user** v. **Multi-user.** Single-user systems only allow a single user to login into the system at a time. They have no user account database, and have a low level of security, as users cannot protect their files from being viewed, copied or deleted. Typical single-user systems are DOS and Microsoft Windows. Multi-user operating systems have a user account database, which defines the rights that users have on certain resources. Multi-user systems are normally more secure than single user systems, as the access to resources can be limited. This security obviously protects against malicious damage, and also protects again non-malicious damage, where users cause damage to the system without knowing it. Most system administrators have seen users deleting files without actually meaning to. A multi-user system can guard against this, by protecting files against deletion.

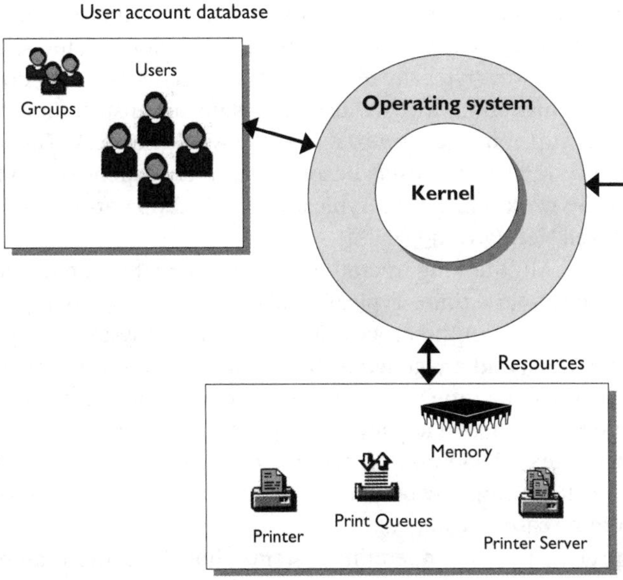

User account database
Groups
Users
Operating system
Kernel
Volumes
File system
Resources
Memory
Printer
Print Queues
Printer Server

Figure 3.2 Operating system components

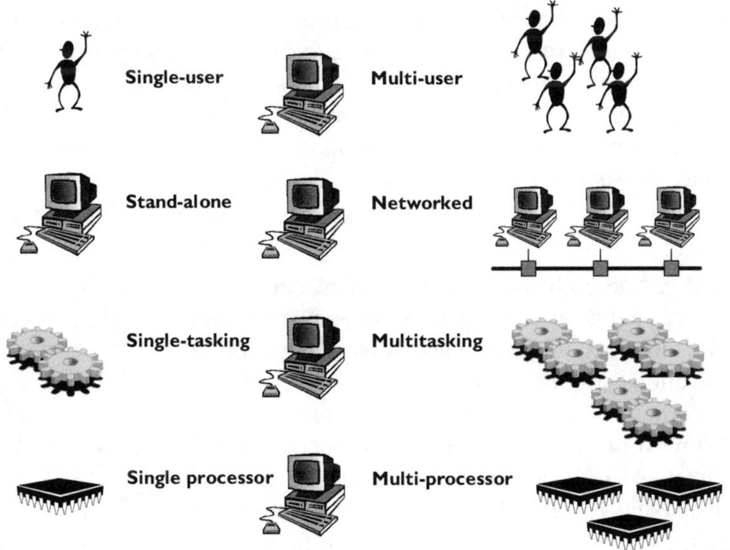

Figure 3.3 Operating system characteristics

- **Networked** v. **Stand-alone.** A stand-alone computer does not connect to a network, and thus cannot access any networked resources. This obviously creates a more secure environment as remote users cannot log into the computer. A networked operating system allows computers to interconnect and uses a standard communications protocol in order for them to communicate, no matter their computer type or their operating system. Typical networking protocols are TCP/IP (for UNIX networks and over the Internet) and IPX/SPX (for Novell NetWare networks). For example the TCP part allows large chunks of data to be split into segments which can be transmitted over the network. The IP part allows for computers to be addressable over interconnected networks. Networked systems are obviously less secure than stand-alone systems, and should thus be protected in some way (typically by creating user accounts). They do allow for improved system administration, as user accounts, software distribution and configuration, and system backup can be centralized over the whole network. The major problem with networked systems is that users become extremely dependent on the network, and cannot typically work without it. Typical networked operating systems are: Microsoft Windows, Novell NetWare and UNIX.
- **Multitasking** v. **Single-tasking.** Multitasking operating systems allow for one or more programs, or processes, to be run, at a time. Typically, this is achieved by giving each process a prioritized amount of time on the processor. Single-tasking systems only allow one program to run, at a time, and are generally faster than multitasking systems, as multitasking systems take up some time when switching between programs. Multitasking systems, though, are more efficient as they allow other tasks to run when a task is not performing any operations. Single-tasking systems are more robust, as multitasking programs often need to communicate with each other, which can cause synchronization problems (in some cases, deadlock).
- **Multiprocessor** v. **Single processor.** Some operating systems allow for more than one processor to be used on the system. This allows more than one task to be run, at a time, on different processors. Windows server operating systems supports multiprocessors (up to four processors). Single processor, multitasking involves running each of the processes for a given time slice on a single processor, whereas multiprocessor systems allow processes to be run at the same time, on different processors. A multiprocessor system can either use processors which are the same type and can thus run the same programs (known as homogeneous multiprocessing), or they can use processors of a different type (known as heterogeneous multiprocessing). A programming language such as Java allows programs to run over a network with different types of processor without requiring that the programs be converted to run on a different type of processor.
- **Embedded** v. **Non-embedded**. An embedded operating system is typically integrated into a device, and is used to perform a specific task, and support for specific applications. Embedded systems are especially written for certain applications and for a narrow range of additional hardware. These limitations allow the system to be tested for most of the conditions that can occur, and they can thus be made more robust than non-embedded systems. Generally, non-embedded systems are more general purpose and they are open to incorrectly operating software and incorrectly configured hardware. They are thus more prone to computer

By the middle of the 1990s, Intel and Microsoft were so profitable that they accounted for nearly half of the entire profits in the worldwide PC industry (which was worth over $100 billion, each year).

crashes and incorrectly configured software. As more equipment now supports embedded computers systems, there are much more embedded operating systems in equipment than there are non-embedded. For example an automobile may have more then 10 embedded systems which each communicate with each other. Typical embedded systems include car engine management systems, mobile phones and Internet routers (which direct data packets around the Internet). Typically embedded systems are more robust, and their programs are permanently stored so that they, and their operating system, are started-up automatically when the system is started. Examples of an embedded operating system include LINUX (kernel), Windows CE and Palm OS. In an embedded system the operating system and programs are typically stored in a permanent electronic memory (know as FLASH memory), which retains its contents when the power is taken away. An embedded system can also vary widely in its computing power, from a small system, which could control a central heating system in a home, to large and complex embedded systems which process radar signals.

- **Distributed processing** v. **Localized processing**. Most processing is achieved locally within the computer system (localized processing), but some processing can be distributed to other computers. A good example of this is with a distributed file system where remote computers provide access to file systems which are not local to the local computer, thus any access to these is actually achieved on the remote computer rather than the local computer. In some case specialized processing is required, which could not be provided locally. This is especially relevent in high-powered applications, such as biological research, or mathematical modelling. For this a computer could initiate programs on another computer system which had enhanced facilities, such as large amounts of physical memory, enhanced processing power, or parallel processing.

Figure 3.4 lists some of the basic functions that a non-embedded operating system should implement. These functions are:

- **File system.** All operating systems create and maintain a file system, where users can create, copy, delete and move files around a structured file system. Most systems organize the files in directories (or folders). In a multi-user system these folders can have associated user ownership, and associated access rights. All files have an owner, who can define the rights of the file, some of which are defined in the box given on the right-hand side of this text.
- **Device interfacing.** Operating systems should try and hide the complexity of interfacing to devices from user programs and the user. Typically, at start-up, an operating system will try and configure devices connected, by scanning all its connected interface buses (rather than getting the user to set them up). Increasingly it is also possible to add equipment to a system while the system is still powered on (hot plugging). A device driver contains much of the methods which define how a device is operated, and the operating system should

File attributes

- **Read** (r). User can or cannot read, or view, the file.
- **Write** (w). User can or cannot write to the file.
- **Execute** (x). User can or cannot execute the file.
- **Hidden** (h). User can or cannot view the file in a listing of the directory which contains the file.
- **Delete** (d). User can or cannot delete the file.
- **Permissions** (p). User can or cannot change the permissions of the file.
- **Ownership** (O). User can take ownership of a file.

integrate this into its own environment. The user programs do not, thus, have to know how to interface to specific devices, as the operating system will deal with the detail of its control. User programs thus issue commands to the operating system, which then convert these commands into the actual control signals required to interface to the equipment. The operating system can also set up queues on devices, typically for printers, so that multiple accesses can occur when a device is busy.

- **Multi-user.** This allows one or more users to log into the system. For this, the operating system must contain a user account database, which contains user names, default home directories, user passwords, user rights, and so on. If possible the operating system should support login over a network, where users can log into any computer within the logical extent of a network (typically known as a domain), and still have the same environment as they had when they last logged into the system.
- **Multitasking.** This allows for one or more tasks to run on a system, at a time. Typically this is achieved by giving each task a certain amount of time on the processor (known as a quanta time slice), and the state of the task at the end of the quanta is stored to memory, and recalled when it is next run. As far as the user is concerned the programs are all being run at the same time (and not given time slices).
- **Multiprocessing.** This allows two or more processors to be used, at a time. When running with more than one processor the operating system must decide if it can run the processes on the different processors, or it has to determine if the processes require to be run sequentially (that is, one at a time). It must also manage the common memory and common resources (such as the data and address buses) between the processors.
- **Multi-threaded applications.** Processes are often split into smaller tasks, named threads. These threads allow for smoother process operation. Threads of a program use a common area for their data. They allow smaller processes to run, as larger processes will typically get stuck waiting for resources to be freed, or data to be inputted. A thread-based approach allows other threads to continue their operation, while others wait for some form of input, or access to a certain resource.

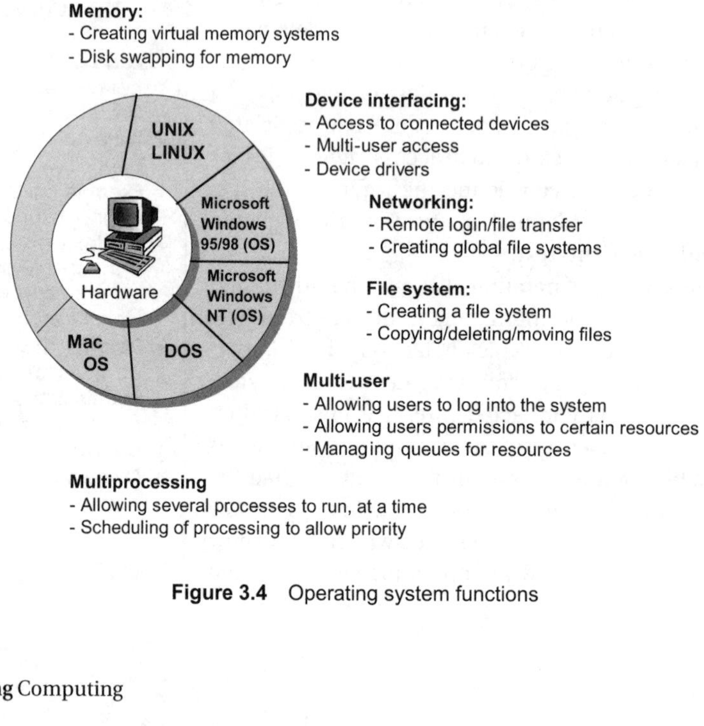

Figure 3.4 Operating system functions

- **Multiple access to devices.** Some devices allow many programs to access it, without causing any problems, while others require that only one program at a time can have access. Memory and disk access allow multiple access for programs, whereas modems and printers typically only allow one program to access them at a time. Thus the operating system must put locks on devices, so that other programs cannot access them while another program is accessing it. Note that the multiple access to a device is really a virtual thing, in that two or more programs should not be able to access the same resource, before another program has finished with it. Thus locks are also applied to multi-access devices if they are accessing the same area of memory or the same file.
- **Driver loading.** A device driver is a special piece of software which knows how to communicate with a specific device. For example a mouse driver will know how to receive data from a mouse and then convert it into a form which can be used by a program. An operating system is thus responsible for loading device drivers, and making sure that they act reliably. The operating system must thus be able to handle any error message from the device, and take the required actions (such as isolating it from the rest of the system). Typically when the computer starts-up the operating system scans all the connected hardware and loads the required device drivers. This is a more dynamic approach than was implemented in the past, where device drivers were loaded once, and then loaded every time the computer was started, no matter if the device was present, or not. Device drivers cause many of the problems in modern systems, as there is no guarantee that the loaded device drivers are reliable in their operation, and that they will not have a detrimental effect on the rest of the system. One bad device driver can cause a whole system to act unreliably. There is an increasing focus on providing operating systems which have protected areas for device drivers, so that users cannot replace existing ones, without a high level of privilege. At one time it was possible to delete every device driver on the system, with a single command.
- **Managing memory.** This involves allocating memory to processes, and often involves creating a virtual memory for programs. Virtual memories were an invention of the VMS operating system, where programs could be given an almost infinite amount of memory, even though there was a limited physical memory. For example, in Microsoft Windows, programs are given access to several gigabytes of memory, even though there may only be a few hundred megabytes of physical memory, which is shared with other programs, and the operating system. This virtually memory is typically created by using other memory storage devices, such as the hard disk for the additional memory space. Two techniques are: paging (organizing programs so that the program data is loaded into pages of memory) and swapping (which involves swapping the contents of memory to disk storage).

First Microprocessor

Around the late 1960s, the electronics industry was producing cheap pocket calculators, which led to the development of affordable computers, when the Japanese company Busicom commissioned Intel to produce a set of between eight and 12 ICs for a calculator. Then instead of designing a complete set of ICs, Ted Hoff, at Intel, designed an integrated circuit chip that could receive instructions, and perform simple integrated functions on data. The design became the 4004 microprocessor. Intel then produced a set of ICs, which could be programmed to perform different tasks. These were the first ever microprocessors and soon Intel (short for *Int*egrated *El*ectronics) produced a general-purpose 4-bit microprocessor, named the 4004.

- **Networking**. Typically an operating system must make provision to create a network either to connect to an external network (such as the Internet), or in a local network (or domain). This normally involves loading the required networking protocol, such as TCP/IP for communications with the Internet. An operating system can arrange for several networking protocols to be used, such as TCP/IP for the Internet and IPX/SPX for communicating with a Novell NetWare server, or NetBEUI when communicating in a Microsoft networking domain.

The concept of the operating system interfacing with devices drivers is illustrated in Figure 3.5. When the operating system starts-up it will typically scan all its interface busses for devices. Any device which can identify itself causes the operating system to load the required device driver. Newer operating systems are plug-and-play where the operating system will automatically detect a new device, and try and configure it so that it does not conflict with any other device. This allows users to add new equipment to their computer without having to worry about its configuration. New interface busses, such as USB, allow for hot plug-and-play where devices can be added and deleted to/from a system while the power is on. USB has the advantage that each USB device tells the operating system about its type (such as it being a soundcard, a printer or a video monitor), and the operating system can automatically search for the best driver for it.

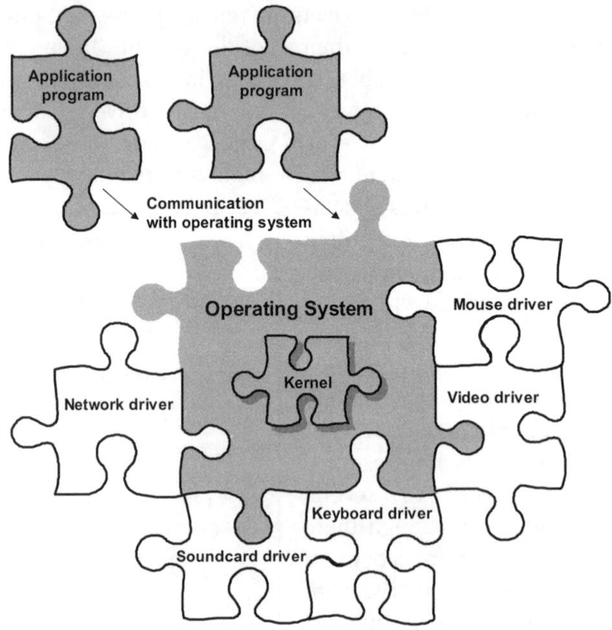

Figure 3.5 Operating system components

3.2 Multitasking and threading

These days, networking and operating systems are almost intertwined, and most operating systems now directly support networking as part of their functionality. Without networks, operating systems could not provide the required user functionality, such as access to networked resources (printers, file systems, and so on), connection to the Internet or an Intranet, transferring of files, and so on. Typical network operating systems are Novell NetWare, Windows NT/2000/XP and UNIX.

The computer in the film *Space Odyssey* was named **HAL** which is one letter removed from **IBM**.

The boundaries where processes run have now expanded from only running on local computers, to being distributed over networks. In the most extreme case it is possible to run processes over a large geographical area. This leads to the concept of distributed processing. Normally, each process must communicate with another, and there thus must be some mechanism for synchronization between them. Local computers use techniques such as hardware and software interrupts to generate events, and then signals or messages to pass the information between the processes.

Figure 3.6 shows an example of data passed between processes. These processes could be running locally on a computer, or could be run over a network on different computers. For example, initially a process on a computer sends an interrupt to the computer to identify that it is ready to transmit data. When the interrupt is received on the local computer, or a remote computer, it informs the destination process that a process wants to communicate with it. A message or a signal is then sent between the two processes to identify the type of data to be passed (if any). The data can then be passed between the processes.

Multitasking involves running several tasks at the same time. It normally involves running a process for a given amount of time, before releasing it and allowing another process a given amount of time. The two main forms of multitasking are illustrated in Figure 3.7 and Figure 3.8; and are:

- **Pre-emptive multitasking.** This type of multitasking involves the operating system controlling how long a process stays on the processor. This allows for smooth multitasking and is used in 32-bit Microsoft Windows programs and in the UNIX operating system.
- **Co-operative multitasking.** This type of multitasking relies on a process giving up the processor. It is used with Windows 3.x programs and suffers from processor hogging, where a process can stay on a processor and the operating system cannot kick it off.

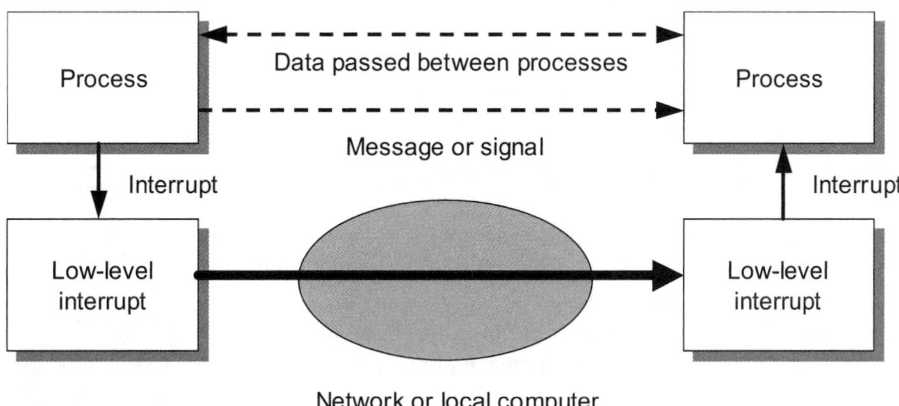

Figure 3.6 Information passed between processes

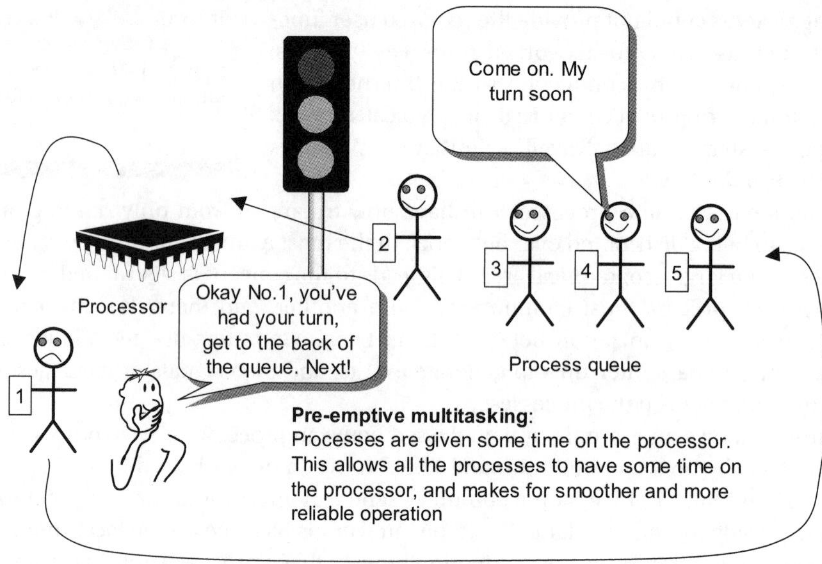

Figure 3.7 Pre-emptive multitasking

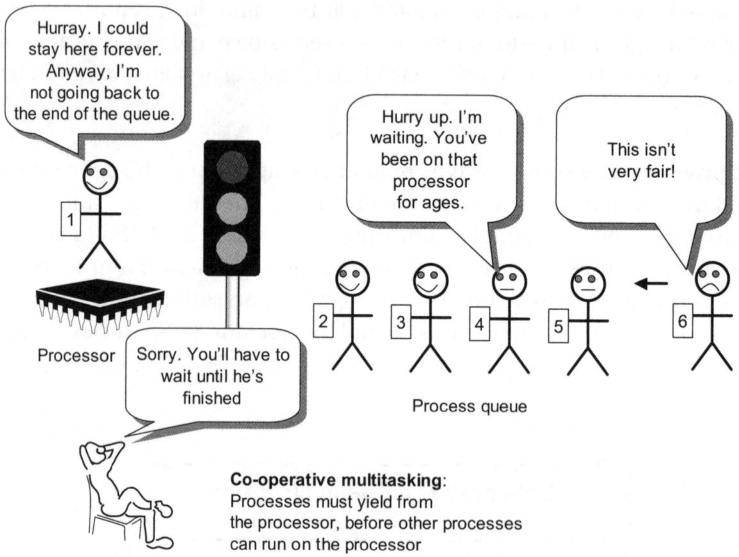

Figure 3.8 Co-operative multitasking

The logical extension to multitasking programs is to split a program into a number of parts (threads) and run each of these on a multitasking system (multi-threading). Multi-threading can be likened to splitting sequential tasks, into a number of interrelated tasks. For example, let's say that you have to cook a meal with the following recipe:

1. Put potatoes on to boil.
2. Put pie in the microwave, on HIGH for 10 minutes.
3. Wait for potatoes to become soft.
4. Take potatoes out of pan, and place on the plates.
5. Wait for pie to complete.
6. Take pie out of microwave and place on the plates.
7. Put carrots in pan, and boil.
8. Wait for carrots to become soft.
9. Take carrots out of pan, and place on the plates.

Ethernet (n): something used to catch the etherbunny

The problem with this recipe is that someone could be waiting for step 4 to complete, while they could be checking the pie to see if it has completed. An improved method would use independent subtasks, which were interrelated. In this case the pie and the potatoes are not interrelated, but the potatoes and the carrots are (assuming that we only have one pan). Figure 3.9 shows a possible schedule using subtasks (or threads of the main task), where we now have six main threads. Each of the threads can run independently, but some cannot run until they have received something from another thread. For example it is not possible for the 'Put potatoes on plate' thread to start until it has received the potatoes from the 'Boil potatoes' thread.

A threads-based approach allows us to create specialized tasks, which have a small definitive goal. It is much easier to test a small program which has a definitive task, than to test a large and complex piece of software. It is also easier to upgrade a thread, without affecting the overall operation of the complete program.

A program that is running more than one thread at a time is known as a multi-threaded program. These have many advantages over non-multi-threaded programs, including:

- They make better use of the processor, where different threads can be run when one or more threads are waiting for data. For example, a thread could be waiting for keyboard input, while another thread could be reading data from the disk.
- They are easier to test, as each thread can be tested independently of other threads.
- They can use standard threads, which are optimized for given hardware.

They also have disadvantages, including:

- The program has to be planned properly so that threads know on which other threads they depend.
- A thread may wait indefinitely for another thread which has crashed or terminated.

The main difference between multiple processes and multiple threads is that each process has independent variables and data, while multiple threads share data from the main program, as illustrated in Figure 3.10.

In April 1970, Wayne Pickette proposed to Intel that they use the computer-on-a-chip for the Busicom project. Then, in December, Gilbert Hyatt filed a patent application entitled 'Single Chip Integrated Circuit Computer Architecture', the first basic patent on the microprocessor.

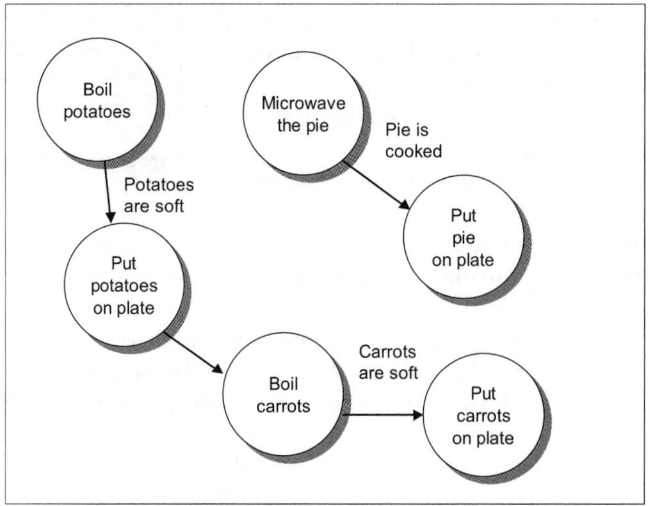

Figure 3.9 Threads in a task

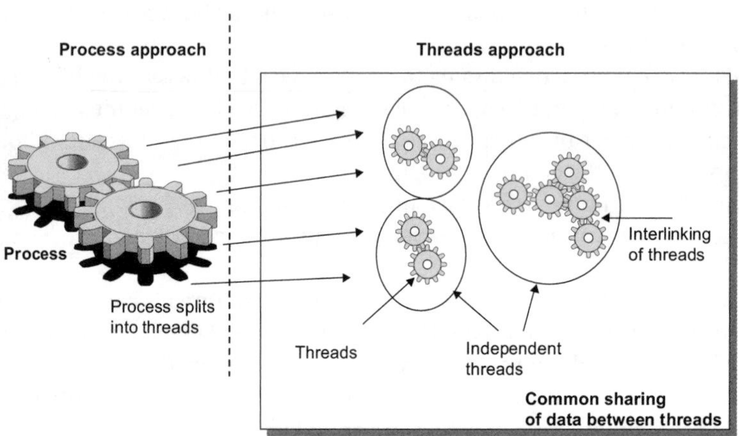

Figure 3.10 Process splitting into threads

3.3 Exercises

The following questions are multiple choice. Please select from a–d.

3.3.1 Which type of operating system allows processes to yield themselves from the processor:

(a) Pre-emptive multitasking (b) Co-operative multitasking
(c) Thread-based multitasking (d) Interrupt multitasking

Additional tutorial questions and material are available at:
`http://www.palgrave.com/studyskills/masterseries/buchanan`

4 Processes and scheduling

4.1 Introduction

A process is a self-contained program which has all the required elements for it to be run on a processor. It is unlikely that it will be able to run on its own, and it is likely to require the help of other processes to provide it with data, or to take data from it, and must thus have some form of communication device to signal its intentions to other processes (and vice-versa). The requirement for many processes to run, at a time, results in the need for a scheduler, which must try and be as fair as possible to all the processes, but which has the main aim of keeping the system running as smoothly as possible, without any system crashes.

The perfect environment for a process is run on the processor, without any disturbance from any other process. Unfortunately this would be inefficient in the usage of the system for many reasons, such as:

- **Inefficient use of the processor.** The process being run could be waiting for some input from a device, or waiting to send to an output device. This is inefficient as other processes could be run while the current process is waiting.
- **Not allowing other processes to run, at the same time.** On a general-purpose computer, the user should be able to run other processes at the same time, such as running multiple Internet sessions, and word processor programs.
- **Not running any support programs.** The system should be able to run other processes which provide support to the user's processes. Typical to these might be a process which responded to the user printing a document. This process would then take the output from a process and then store it. It would then communicate with the printer, and allow the user program to get on with other tasks, without having to communicate with the printer.
- **Not allowing the sharing of resources.** If each process were allowed dedicated access to the processor, it would not allow for sharing of resources, as resources would remain fixed to the processes.

Most modern operating systems now run multiple processes, and systems try to simulate the isolated environment with a virtual machine environment, which simulates the stand-alone, single-tasking environment, where other processes cannot affect the current process.

Processes, themselves, can either run locally within a computer system, or can be run over a network, such as in a distributed system. When several processes run at the same time, there must be some mechanism for them to intercommunicate and pass information. Another requirement is when processes share the same resource. This tends to be reasonably easy when the resource can be shareable, but problems can occur when the resource must be dedicated to one process at a time. This type of situation can lead to deadlock where resources, which are dedicated to processes, do not yield to other processes which are waiting on them.

The first multitasking systems were based on batch processing, which would run user programs with a high priority, but could also run background processes which required virtually no interaction with users (batch programs). Thus batch files would typically use most of the processing time when the system was not being used by other user programs. A batch program normally involves reading data from one or more file(s), and processing it, into one or more output files. This suited many situations, especially where programs could be run overnight, without any interaction with any users. Batch processing was especially important in the days before personal computers, when the cost of processing was high, and many users competed to access to the system. In mathematical modelling it was typical that processes would have to run for hours, days, or even weeks, on processes that would take minutes by today's standards. But, of course, the range of applications which need to be processed have also moved on, and many large-scale processing problems can take many days or weeks to complete. Thus batch processing is still an important issue, and many batch processes are happily working in systems, and using its resources, only when the system can spare the time. One extension of this is towards using spare processing power over a network (and possibly over the Internet), as this allows the spare computing power of many computers to be used, at a time. This will be covered in more detail in the next chapter, as we look at distributed processing methods.

4.2 Scheduling

Multitasking operating systems can run many programs at the same time, but these must be organized in some way. This is the task of the process scheduler, which must allow each process some time on the processor. A badly designed scheduler simply allows each of the processes the same period of time. Whereas a well-designed scheduler allows for priority levels, and can make decisions on which processes should be run, at a given time. Typically system processes are more important than user programs, and need to be run at regular intervals, and will thus be given a higher priority over user programs.

The scheduler operates on a queue of processes, each of which can either be:

- **Running.** This is where the process is actually currently running on the processor.
- **Waiting.** This is where the process is waiting on another process to run and provide it with some data, or if a process is waiting to access a resource. The waiting process can sometimes turn into a zombie process, where a process terminates for some reason, but whose parent process has not yet waited for it to terminate. A zombie process is not a big problem, as it has no resources allocated to it. Normally the only way to get rid of zombie processes is to reboot the system.
- **Ready.** This is where the process is ready to be run on the processor, and is not waiting for any other processes or has terminated.
- **Terminated.** This is where a process has finished its run, and all resources that have been allocated to it must be taken away from it.

These concepts are illustrated in Figure 4.1. The scheduler must thus make a decision on when to change state, such as:

- Running to waiting.
- Waiting to ready.
- Running to ready.
- Running to terminated.

A preemptive scheduler uses a timer to allow each process some time on the processor and coordinates access to shared data. Along with this, it requires a kernel designed to protect the integrity of its own data structures. Kernels must be robust in the way that they are designed, as any problems in the kernel will affect the whole system.

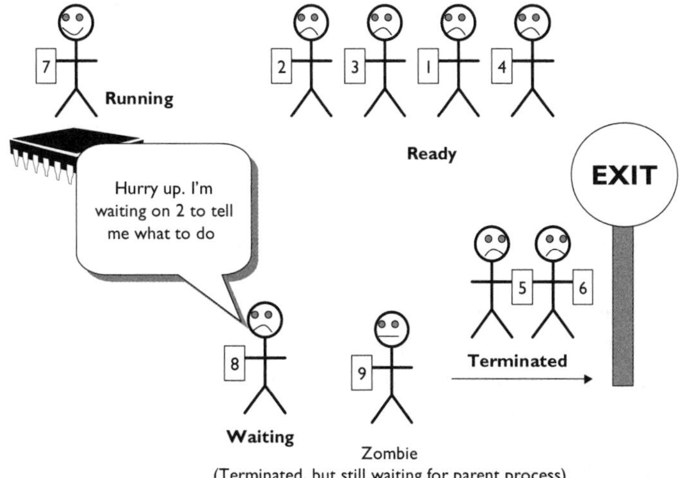

Figure 4.1 Running, ready, waiting and terminated

4.2.1 Scheduling queues

There are three main system queues: Job Queue – incoming jobs; Ready Queue and Device Queues (blocked processes). Normally the type of scheduler chosen depends on the type of system that is required, such as:

- **Long-term (Job) scheduler.** This type of scheduler is used in batch systems.
- **Short-term scheduler.** This type of scheduler typically uses a FIFO (First In, First Out) queue, or a priority queue.
- **Medium-term scheduler.** This type of scheduler swaps processes in and out to improve the job mix. Normally it schedules on the following:
  - **Time since swapped in or out**. Swapping involves moving the running process to some temporary storage space (such as the local disk). A process which has been swapped out for a longer time than another one, is more likely to be chosen by the scheduler, over the one which has waited the least time. As much as possible users should not get the feeling that their processes are not being serviced, at all.
  - **Processor time used.** In order to be fair, a scheduler might pick a process that has had a lesser time on the processor; over one that has had more time. The time that a process has spent on the processor is no guarantee that it has used its time efficiently.
  - **Size.** Typically a small process will most likely take the least amount of resources, and processing time (but this is no guarantee), thus the scheduler may pick the process which has the smallest size. An improved method is for the scheduler to make an estimate about the amount of resources that the process will require to complete, and then chose the next process on the basis of this. An efficient schedule is to try and complete processes which can be completed in the shortest time. This type of scheduling is know as shortest-first, and many busy people reckon that this is the best way to organize their work, where they tackle tasks that can be com-

pleted quickly, before the larger tasks. Unfortunately this may cause problems as the larger tasks may never get completed, as too much time is taken by completing the smaller tasks.

- **Priority**. This is possibly one of the best methods that can be used to determine which process should be run next. But who or what decides the priority of a process? It is well known that users will always believe that their process is more important than anyone else's. Thus there must be some independent method of determining the priority of a process. One of the best methods is to boost the priority of a process if it has not been on the processor for a while, and reduce the priority of a process if it has been given some time on the processor.

Processes often require different processing requirements, such as:

- **Processor I/O burst cycle**. This normally involves a large number of short bursts, along with a number of longer processor bursts.
- **Processor bound**. This involves long processor bursts.
- **I/O bound**. This involves short processor bursts.

4.2.2 Scheduling algorithms

Every scheduler must be fair in the way that it assigns tasks, much of which should be automatic, and should not require user input. Figure 4.2 outlines some of the main objectives, which are:

Objectives	*Description*	*Scheduler must try to:*
Fairness	Each process has a fair share of the processor	Maximize
Efficiency	Efficient use of the processor	Maximize
Throughput	Number of processes completed	Maximize
Turnaround	Time taken for processes to complete	Maximize
Waiting time	Time taken in the queue	Minimize
Predictability	Allowing a dependable response	Maximize
Response time	Time to react to actions	Minimize

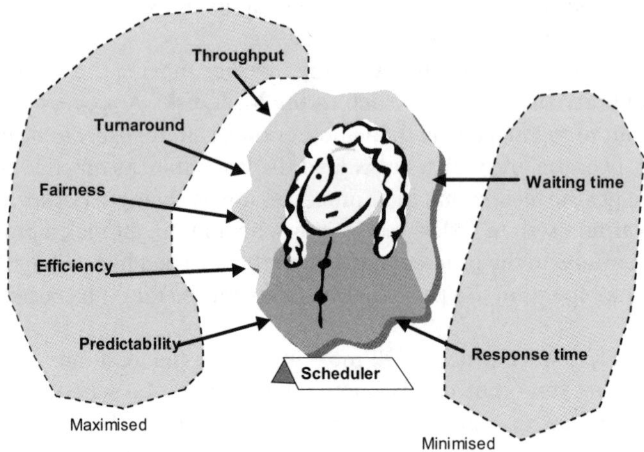

Figure 4.2 Decisions for a scheduler

The two main classifications for scheduling are:

- **Policy**. Sets priority on individual processes.
- **Mechanism**. Implements a scheduling policy.

There are various methods that the scheduler can use to implement a scheduling algorithm:

- **First-Come, First-Served** (FCFS). This type of scheduling is used with non-preemptive operating systems, where the time that a process waits in the queue is totally dependent on the processes which are in front of it, as illustrated in Figure 4.3. The response of the system is thus not dependable.
- **Round Robin** (RR). This is a first-come, first-served schedule with preemption, where each process is given a finite time slice on the processor. The queue is circular, thus when a process has been run, the queue pointer is moved to the next process, as illustrated in Figure 4.4. This is a relatively smooth schedule and gives all processes a share of the processor. As children we would typically be assigned to things in a round-robin way, especially when there were too many demands on a certain resource, and we didn't get enough time on it. A good example is when children want to get access to a bouncy castle, and there's a limit on the number that can be on the castle at any one time. An example schedule might be to allow a child onto the castle for a minute, and then they must come off, and go back to the end of the queue. The next child in the queue can then take their place on the castle, and so on.

STRANGE, BUT TRUE

A customer phoned a customer support line, and complained that their computer would not work. All the wires were plugged in the right place, and it had been plugged-in. After many other questions the operator asked the user, 'What happens when you press the power switch', 'What's a power switch?', came the reply.

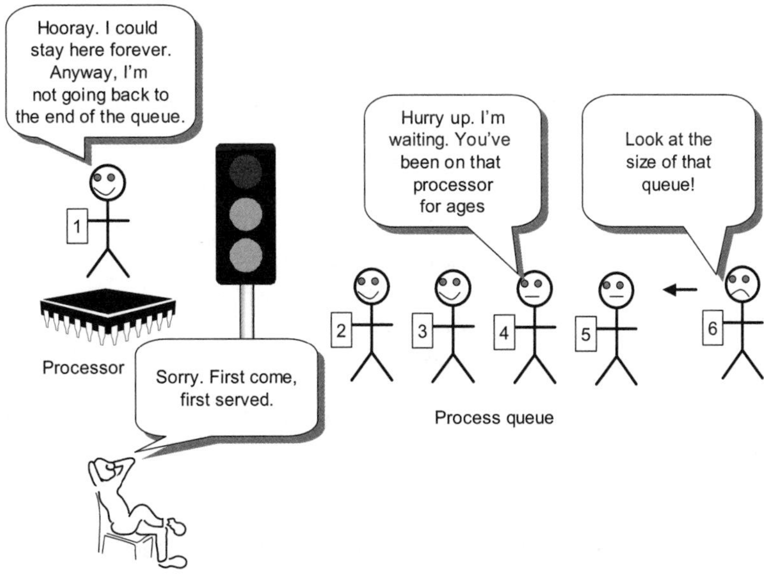

Figure 4.3 First come, first served

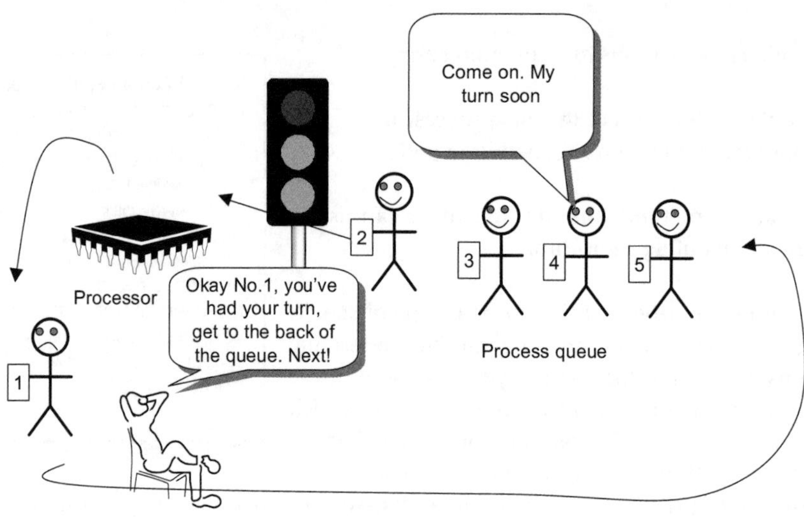

Figure 4.4 Round robin

- **Shortest-Job-First** (SJF). This is one of the most efficient algorithms, and involves estimating the amount of time that a process will run for, and taking the process which will take the shortest time to complete. A problem for the scheduler is thus to determine the amount of time that the process will take to complete its task. This is not an easy task. For example, let's say that we've got four tasks to complete. Task one will take 1 hour, task two takes 2 hours, task three will take 3 hours, and finally task four will take 8 hours to complete. We could schedule the task to each get half-an-hour of processing time. Once we have finished this time, we make a decision on what task to do next. Thus within four hours we would have the following:

ROUND ROBIN

Time slot (in half-hour blocks)	Task (remaining time to completion)
1	Task 1 (0:30)
2	Task 2 (1:30)
3	Task 3 (2:30)
4	Task 4 (7:30)
5	Task 1 (**complete**)
6	Task 2 (1:00)
7	Task 3 (2:00)
8	Task 4 (7:00)

It can be seen that we have only completed one task, but if we were to take the shortest-job first, then:

SHORTEST-JOB-FIRST

Time slot (in half-hour blocks)	Task (remaining time to completion)
1	Task 1 (0:30)
2	Task 1 (**complete**)
3	Task 2 (1:30)
4	Task 2 (1:00)

5	Task 2 (0:30)
6	Task 2 (**complete**)
7	Task 3 (2:30)
8	Task 3 (2:00)

We can see that we've now completed two tasks, and we're at the same point as the previous example with Task 3. From a user's point of view this will be perceived as possibly the most satisfying as more tasks have actually been completed in a shorter time. From a computer system point of view the user will perceive that the processes are running faster, as they are being completed at a perceived faster rate (although Task 4 is being starved on processing time, in order to achieve this). The only problem is that some of the processes will not make any progress until they are allowed access to the processor. The time remaining in each of the cases will be the same as the first scheme will require a further 10 hours to complete (Task 2 requires 1 hour, Task 3 requires 2 hours and Task 4 requires 7 hours), and the shortest-job-first scheme requires a further 10 hours (Task 3 requires 2 hours and Task 4 requires 8 hours). Thus the shortest-job-first is only perceived to be running tasks faster. Shortest-job-first is very efficient on processor time with batch systems, as batch processes are less susceptible to process starvation.

- **Priority Scheduling**. This type of scheduling assigns each process a priority. It is typically used in general-purpose operating systems (such as Microsoft Windows and UNIX) and can be used with either preemptive or non-preemptive operating systems. The main problem is to assign a priority to each process, where priorities can either be internal or external. Internal priorities relate to measurable system resources, such as time limits, memory requirements, file input/output, and so on. A problem is that some processes might never get the required priority and may never get time on the processor (which leads to process starvation). To overcome this, low-priority waiting processes can have their priority increased, over time (known as ageing).
- **Multilevel Queue Scheduling.** This scheme supports several different queues, and sets priorities for them. For example, a system could run two different queues: foreground (interactive) and background (batch), as illustrated in Figure 4.5. The foreground task could be given a much higher priority over the background task, such as 80%–20%.

Each of the queues can be assigned different priorities. Microsoft Windows runs a preemptive scheme where certain system processes are given a higher priority than other non-system processes. An example priority might be (in order of priority):

1. **System processes**. Top priority. These must have a top priority as the system could act unreliably if they were not executed within a given time.
2. **Interactive processes**. These are processes which require some user input, such as from the keyboard or mouse. It is important that users feel that these processes are running with a high priority, otherwise they may try to delete them, and try to rerun the process.
3. **Interactive editing processes**. These processes tend to run without user input for long periods, but occasionally require some guidance on how they run.
4. **Batch processes**. Lowest priority. These tend to be less important processes which do not require any user input.

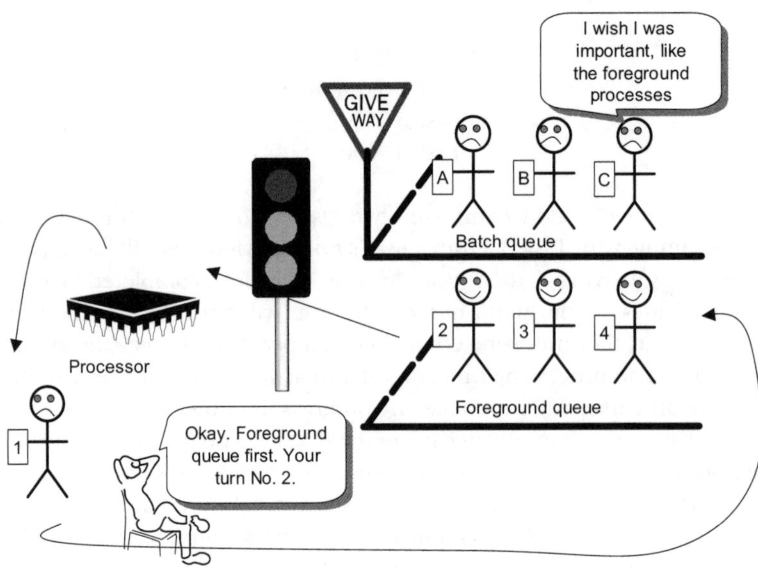

Figure 4.5 Multilevel queue scheduling

- **Multilevel Feedback Queue Scheduling.** This scheme is the most complex, and allows processes to move between a number of different priority queues. Each queue has an associated scheduling algorithm. To support this there must be a way to promote and relegate processes for their current queues.

4.2.3 Multiprocessor scheduling

The two main classifications of multiprocessor scheduling are:

- **Heterogeneous.** This is where there are a number of different types of processors, each with their own instruction set. This is typically the case in distributed computing, where a process is run over a number of computers on a network. For it to work there must be a high-level protocol that allows communication between the computers. Java is an excellent programming language for this, as it can produce machine-independent code.
- **Homogeneous.** This is where all the processors can run the same code. In the scheduler there is either a common queue for all processors (and they take processes from the queue once they have completed a process) or there is a separate queue for each process (this involves a scheduler deciding on what processes should be given to each of the processors). The processing can either be asymmetric multiprocessor where a single processor looks after scheduling, I/O processing and other system activities, or symmetric multiprocessing, where each processor is self-scheduling or has a master-slave structure.

> **REAL STUDENT ANSWER**
>
> Gravity was invented by Isaac Walton. It is chiefly noticeable in the autumn when the apples are falling off the trees.

The problem with multiprocessor systems is segmenting a problem up so that it can be run on the individual processors. For example, if a program was to compute the result of:

$z = (a+3) \times (a-4)$; where $a=10$;

Then this can be broken down to the following:

$a=10$;
$x= a + 3$;
$y = a - 4$;
$z = x \times y$;

Then both processors could be passed the value of *a*, and one processor could run the operation *a*+3, and the other *a*–4, in parallel. Next one of the processors would tell the other processor its result, and the processor that receives the value could then multiply the two results together. This has resulted in **three** consecutive operations, as apposed to **four** consecutive operations in the non-parallel method (1. Pass value of 10; 2. Compute (*a*+3); 3. Compute (*a*–4); 4. Multiply the results of Step 2. and Step 3.).

Another example is for matrix multiplication. For example if a parallel system was to compute the result of the multiplication of two 3×3 matrices. The result would be:

$$Arr = \begin{bmatrix} a & b & c \\ d & e & f \\ g & h & i \end{bmatrix} \begin{bmatrix} j & k & l \\ m & n & o \\ p & q & r \end{bmatrix} = \begin{bmatrix} aj+bm+cp & ak+bn+cq & al+bo+cr \\ dj+em+fp & dk+en+fq & dl+eo+fr \\ gj+hm+ip & gk+hn+iq & gl+ho+ir \end{bmatrix}$$

For example:

$$Arr = \begin{bmatrix} 1 & 2 & 3 \\ 4 & 5 & 6 \\ 7 & 8 & 9 \end{bmatrix} \begin{bmatrix} 1 & 2 & 1 \\ 2 & 5 & 3 \\ 1 & 2 & 3 \end{bmatrix} = \begin{bmatrix} 8 & 18 & 16 \\ 20 & 45 & 37 \\ 32 & 72 & 58 \end{bmatrix}$$

This would normally take nine mathematical operations, with a mixture of addition and multiplication. To run it in parallel, we need to partition the problem so that the processors can run the problem in parallel. Thus for example if we have a system with three processors, we could do the following:

- **Processor 1**. Pass the values of **first** column of the second matrix {*j,m,p*}, and all the values of the first matrix {*a,b,c;d,e,f;g,h,i*}.
- **Processor 2.** Pass the values of **second** column of the second matrix {*k,n,q*}, and all the values of the first matrix {*a,b,c;d,e,f;g,h,i*}.
- **Processor 3.** Pass the values of **third** column of the second matrix {*l,o,r*}, and all the values of the first matrix {*a,b,c;d,e,f;g,h,i*}.

Next each of the processors can calculate using the column from the second matrix and the values from the first matrix, in parallel:

- **Processor 1**. Calculate element 1 as *aj+bm+cp*; element 2 as *dj+em+fp*; element 3 as *gj+hm+ip*. Operations = 12 (nine multiply and three summations).
- **Processor 2**. Calculate element 4 as *ak+bn+cq*; element 5 as *dk+en+fq*; element 6 as *gk+hn+iq*. Operations = 12 (nine multiply and three summations).

- **Processor 3**. Calculate element 7 as *al+bo+cr*; element 8 as *dl+eo+fr*; element 9 as *gl+ho+ir*. Operations = 12 (nine multiply and one summation).

The results from each of the processors can then be collated in the complete matrix. Thus on a single processor it would have taken **nine** mathematical calculations (**36** mathematical operations: 27 multiply and nine summations). This has been reduced to **three** parallel processing calculations (**12** mathematical operations). The only overhead is that we must communicate a single column of the second array, and the values of the first array. This does not typically have a great overhead when there are just a few processors, but with many processes it can have a relatively large overhead.

If we had nine processors, then we could partition the problem as follows:

- Processor 1: Compute *aj+bm+cp*. Operations = 4 (three multiple and one summation).
- Processor 2: Compute *dj+em+fp*. Operations = 4 (three multiple and one summation).
- Processor 3: Compute *gj+hm+ip*. Operations = 4 (three multiple and one summation).
- Processor 4: Compute *ak+bn+cq*. Operations = 4 (three multiple and one summation).
- Processor 5: Compute *dk+en+fq*. Operations = 4 (three multiple and one summation).
- Processor 6: Compute *gk+hn+iq*. Operations = 4 (three multiple and one summation).
- Processor 7: Compute *al+bo+cr*. Operations = 4 (three multiple and one summation).
- Processor 8: Compute *dl+eo+fr*. Operations = 4 (three multiple and one summation).
- Processor 9: Compute *gl+ho+ir*. Operations = 4 (three multiple and one summation).

Which will only take **one** mathematical calculation (**four** mathematical operations). Unfortunately this mathematical calculation takes three multiplications and a summation. Thus if we optimize the system with 27 processors, we could partition the problem as:

- Processor 1: Compute *aj*. Processor 2: Compute *bm*. Processor 3: Compute *cp*.
- Processor 4: Compute *dj*. Processor 5: Compute *em*. Processor 6: Compute *fp*.
- Processor 7: Compute *gj*. Processor 8: Compute *hm*. Processor 9: Compute *ip*.
- Processor 10: Compute *ak*. Processor 11: Compute *bn*. Processor 12: Compute *cq*.
- Processor 13: Compute *dk*. Processor 14: Compute *en*. Processor 15: Compute *fq*.
- Processor 16: Compute *gk*. Processor 17: Compute *hn*. Processor 18: Compute *iq*.
- Processor 19: Compute *al*. Processor 20: Compute *bo*. Processor 21: Compute *cr*.
- Processor 22: Compute *dl*. Processor 23: Compute *eo*. Processor 24: Compute *fr*.
- Processor 25: Compute *gl*. Processor 26: Compute *ho*. Processor 27: Compute *ir*.

Next:

- **Processor 1:** Gets results from Processor 1, Processor 2 and Processor 3, and then summates the result to get element 1.
- **Processor 4:** Gets results from Processor 4, Processor 5 and Processor 6, and then summates the result to get element 2.
- **Processor 7:** Gets results from Processor 7, Processor 8 and Processor 9, and then summates the result to get element 3.
- **Processor 10:** Gets results from Processor 10, Processor 11 and Processor 3, and then summates the result to get element 4.
- **Processor 13:** Gets results from Processor 13, Processor 14 and Processor 15, and then summates the result to get element 5.

- **Processor 16:** Gets results from Processor 16, Processor 17 and Processor 18, and then summates the result to get element 6.
- **Processor 19:** Gets results from Processor 19, Processor 20 and Processor 21, and then summates the result to get element 7.
- **Processor 25:** Gets results from Processor 25, Processor 26 and Processor 27, and then summates the result to get element 8.

Thus with 27 processors we now get down to **two** mathematical operations. We cannot get it down to one mathematical operation as the summation process must **wait** for the multiply operation to complete. Thus, in summary:

Processors	**Mathematical operations**
1	36
3	12
9	4
27	2

Thus it can be seen, in this case, that the best saving in mathematical operations possibly occurs between 1 and 3 processors. An increasing number of processors does not really help to reduce the number of mathematical operations by a great deal. There is also, for an increased number of processor, an increase in the time that it takes to communicate the parameters to each of the processors, and then the intercommunications of their results. Thus in some cases it is possible for the processing time to actually increase with an increasing number of processors.

Timing

To simulate the time taken, we can estimate each of the timings, such as:

- Time to transmit one value over the network is 5 time units.
- Time for a two-value multiplication is 8 time units.
- Time for a three-value summation is 2 time units.

Let's assume that the model uses a server which receives values from client processors. Also assume that the processors already know the values from both matrices.

For a one-processor system, there will be:

- 27 multiply operations (216 time units).
- 9 summations (18 time units).
- 9 transmissions of the result (45 time units).

which gives 279 time units.

For a three-processor system, there will be:

- 9 multiply operations (72 time units).
- 3 summations (6 time units).
- 9 transmissions of the result (45 time units).

Time taken for 3-by-3 problem

Processors	Time taken	Computation
1	279	100%
3	123	44%
9	71	25%
27	145	52%

which gives 123 time units. Thus the communications of the parameters is starting to have a large effect on the total time.

For a nine-processor system, there will be:

- 3 multiply operations (24 time units).
- 1 summation (2 time units).
- 9 transmissions of the result (45 time units).

which gives 71 time units. Thus we have increased the number of processors by a factor of three but we've only reduced the processing time by about 25% on the total time for three-processors.

Finally for 27 processors, there will be:

- 1 multiply operation (8 time units).
- 1 summation (2 time units).
- 27 transmissions of the result (135 time units). This is because two out of three of the processors must report their result to another processor in order to inform them of the result. Thus for example Processor 1 would calculate *aj*; Processor 2 would calculate *bm* and Processor 3 would calculate *cp*. Next Processor 2 and Processor 3 would send their results to Processor 1, who would then perform the summation. After which it would send the result to the server. The transmission of the intermediate results gives 18 transmissions, and the transmission of the final results gives nine transmissions. Thus the total number of transmissions is 27.

which gives 145 time units. This is actually an increase in time over the nine-processor system.

A great investment

$10,000 invested in shares of Cisco Systems when they were initially floated on the stock market in 1990 was worth $6.5million at the end of the millennium.

4.2.4 Problem segmentation and processing time

A major problem with parallel processing, in some cases, is that the communication overhead increases as the number of processors increase. The computation time is likely to reduce as the number of processing elements increases, but the communication time will increase. An example is shown in Figure 4.6, which shows a system which determines the average value for a number of adjacent pixels. In this case we could segment the problem into four physical domains and assign a 2×2 processor array to the problem. The problem that we have is that at the end of the calculations, the processors must communicate the values of the pixels at their boundary to their adjacent neighbour. For a 2×2 processor array there will be two interfaces. If we increase the array to a 3×3 processor array then there will be four interfaces, and with a 4×4 processor array there will be six interfaces. In general, an $n \times n$ array will have $2(n-1)$ interfaces. The total computation time is thus the addition of the processing time plus the communication time.

In this case the computation time for the problem will reduce as the number of processors increase, but the communication time between the physical domains will increase, as the number of interfaces increase. Figure 4.7 shows a typical characteristic for total computation time. It can be seen that there is likely to be an optimal number of processors which minimizes the total computation time.

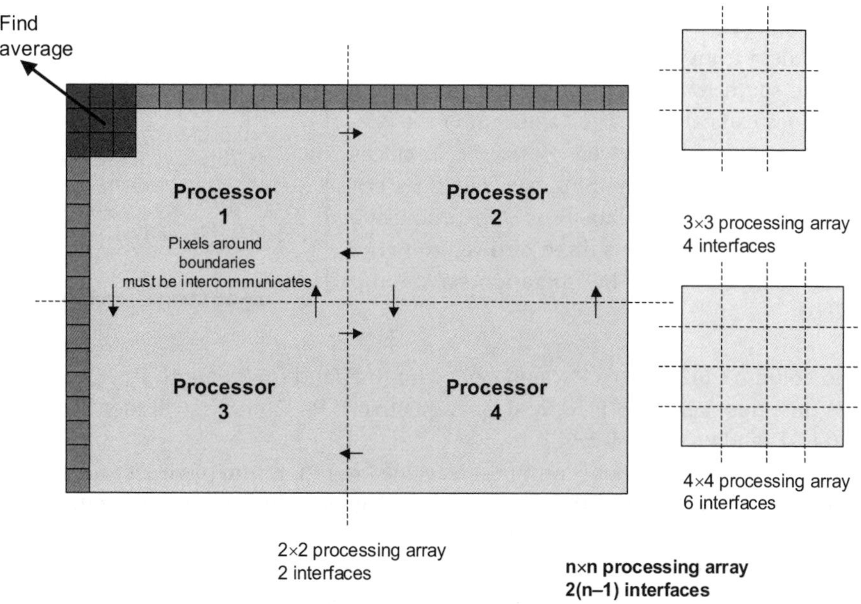

Figure 4.6 Segmentation of a problem for parallel processing

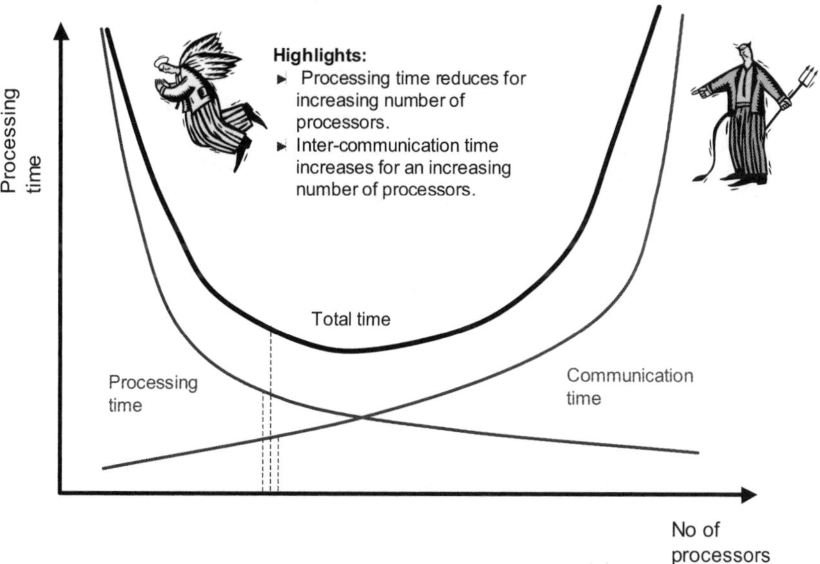

Figure 4.7 Computation time

4.2.5 Processor arrays

Typically in parallel processing the problem involves processors communicating with their adjacent neighbour (as illustrated in Figure 4.6). In the matrix multiplication, we assumed that we were using a single bus to connect on the processors. An improved method could use an array structure, as illustrated in Figure 4.8. With this the column of the matrix is passed to the array elements from the north to south, and the results are computed from east to west. Each of the processors knows one of the matrices and then waits for the column data to be passed to them from the north. They then pass then data to the south to the next processor in the line. After this they can calculate their value, after the partial result has been received from the east, as illustrated in Figure 4.9. The Sink basically does not do anything but receive data from the processing element, and the Zero passes three zero values to the next processing element. The operation for the top row will be:

> **Supersonic**
>
> In their first year (1981), Compaq Computers generated $110 million, two years on it was $503.9 million, and two years after that it was $1 billion. The following year it was $2 billion. From zero to $2 billion, in six years (a world record at the time).

1. Send column Col1 data to P_1, send Col2 data to P_2 and Col3 data to P_3. P_1, P_2 and P_3 will then pass this data onto P_4, P_5 and P_6, respectively. P_4, P_5 and P_6 will then pass this data onto P_7, P_8 and P_9, respectively.
2. P_3 receives a zero value, and computes its value (*al+bo+cr*) and passes it to P_2;
3. P_2 receives a partial vector from P_3, adds its computed value (*ak+bn+cq*). It then adds it to the partial vector, and passes this to P_1.
4. P_1 receives a partial vector for P_2 and adds its computed value (*aj+bm+cp*) and adds it to the partial vector, which will now be the completed row of the calculation, and passes this onto the Result {*aj+bm+cp*; *ak+bn+cq*; *al+bo+cr*}.

There will be a similar parallel action for P_4, P_5 and P_6, and also P_7, P_8 and P_9.

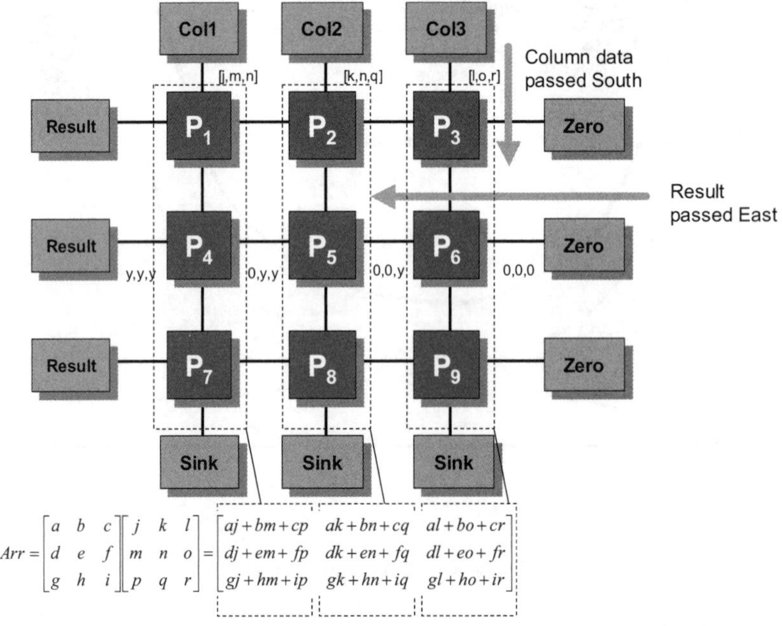

Figure 4.8 Processor array

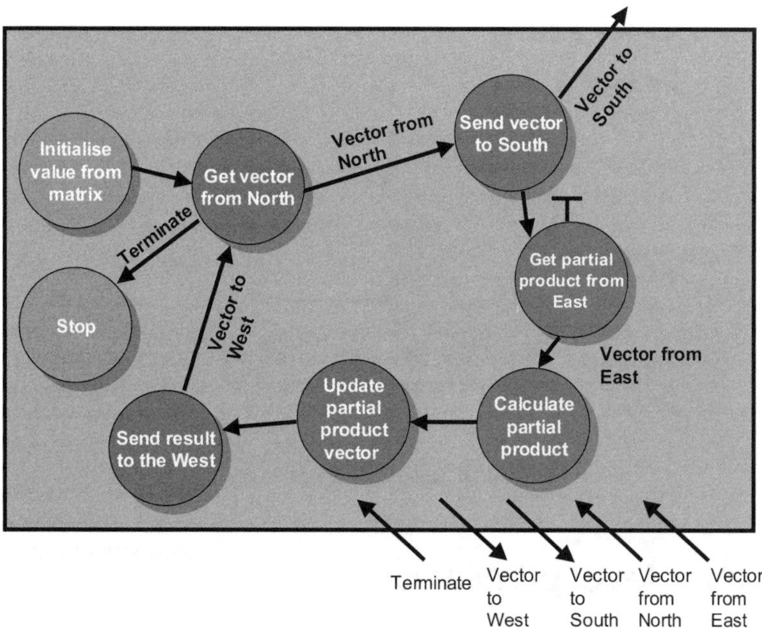

Figure 4.9 Modelling of the processes run on each of the processors

4.2.6 Real-time scheduling

Real-time systems normally have key processes which should be serviced before other processors. The two main classifications are:

- **Hard real time.** This is where a critical process is completed within a critical time, and cannot be stored in second memory.
- **Soft real time.** This is where critical processes receive a higher priority than less critical processes. Soft real time can lead to process starvation, and also an unfair allocation of system resources. This type of real-time system is typically implemented in systems which require high-speed data transfer, especially in multimedia (such as MPEG movies) and high-speed, processor intensive graphics (such as 3D graphics).

4.3 Interrupts

An interrupt allows a program or an external device to interrupt the execution of a program. The generation of an interrupt can occur by hardware (hardware interrupt) or software (software interrupt). When an interrupt occurs an interrupt service routine (ISR) is called. For a hardware interrupt the ISR then communicates with the device and processes any data. When it has finished the program execution returns to the original program. A software interrupt causes the program to interrupt its execution and goes to an interrupt service routine. Typical software interrupts include reading a key from the keyboard, outputting text to the screen and reading the current date and time. The operating system must respond to interrupts from external devices, as illustrated in Figure 4.10.

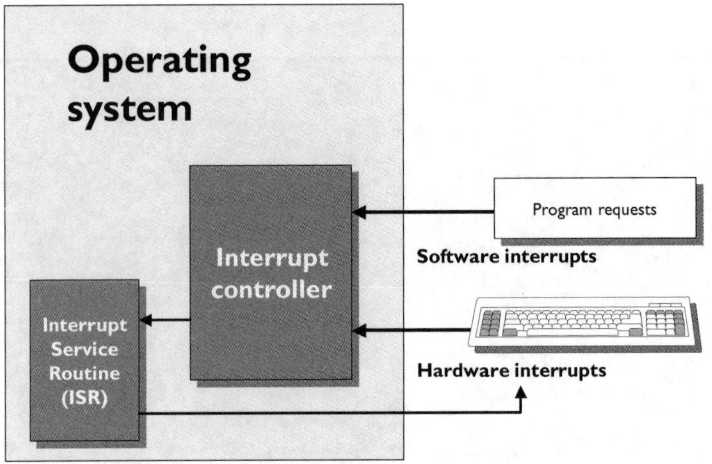

Figure 4.10 Interrupt service routine

4.4 Higher-level primitives

> **REAL STUDENT ANSWER**
> The sun never set on the British Empire because the British Empire is in the East and the sun sets in the West.

Processes often need to identify that they are waiting for another process to give them data or are busy, waiting for some I/O transfer. They must thus support higher-level primitives to identify these. On shared memory systems the following are used:

- **Semaphores.** This involves setting flags, which allow or bar other processes from getting access to certain resources. An analogy of a semaphore is where two railway trains are using a single-track railway line. When one train enters the single-track line, it sets a semaphore which disallows the other train from entering the track. Once the train on the single track has left the single track, it resets the semaphore flag, which allows the other train to enter the single track.
- **Signals.** Signals are similar to interrupts, but are implemented in software, rather than hardware. This is a primitive interrupt handler and involves a signal handler which controls process signals.

On non-shared memory systems the following are used:

- **Message passing.** Messages are sent between processes, such as SEND and RECEIVE.
- **Pipes.** Pipes allow data to flow from one process to another, in the required way.
- **Remote procedure calls** (RPC).

4.5 Signals, pipes and task switching (UNIX)

UNIX does not implement a sharing system. In a sharing system, like Microsoft Windows and MAC OS, the operating system only changes to a different process when the current process identifies that it is ready to swap tasks. UNIX implements its scheduling using signals and pipes.

4.5.1 Signals

UNIX uses signals in a similar way to interrupts, but they are implemented at a higher level. Events rather than hardware devices generate these interrupts. Typically, software interrupt service routines are called on certain signals. The signal handler sets the status of a process, but a process may also put itself in a sleep mode, waiting for a signal. One problem with this is that signals may get lost if they are sent before the process goes into a waiting mode. One solution is to set a flag in the process whenever it receives a signal. The process can then test this flag before it goes into the wait state, if it is set; the wait operation does not block the process.

4.5.2 Pipes

Pipes allow data to flow from one process to another, in the required way. Typically they are implemented with a fixed size storage area (a buffer) in which one process can write to it, while the other reads from it (when the data is available). UNIX implements pipes with a file-like approach, and uses the same system calls to write data to a pipe and read data from a pipe; as those for reading and writing files. Each process which creates a pipe receives two identifiers: one for the reading and one for the writing. Typically, the creating process forks-off two child processes, one of which looks after one end of the pipe, and the other looks after the other end of the pipe. The two child processes can then communicate.

UNIX uses the '`|`' character to implement the pipe command in the command prompt. For example the '`ps -ef`' command shows all the running processes with an identification of the owner of the process. The output of this command can be piped into the `grep` command to search for any occurrence of the word 'bill', with the following:

```
chimera:~ > ps -ef | grep bill
    bill  2319  2296  1 23:29:42 pts/2    0:00 grep bill
    bill  2296  2294  1 23:28:00 pts/2    0:01 -tcsh
```

Figure 4.11 shows an example of a pipe, and also illustrates that pipes can also be implemented on two remote computers. This is normally defined as a connection, and the ends of the pipes, over a connection, are known as sockets.

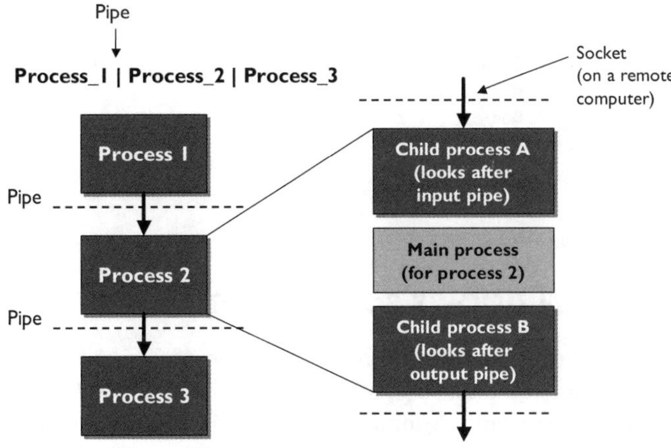

Figure 4.11 Pipes

4.5.3 Task switching

The dispatcher receives orders from the scheduler as to the processes that are to be run. It is part of the kernel and has privileges on process information. One of its main tasks is to extract information from the previous state of the process, such as process registers, stack pointers, and so on. It then switches the processor from kernel mode to user mode (basically enabling the hardware memory protection), and the process begins to run.

> **REAL STUDENT ANSWER**
>
> The nineteenth century was a time of a great many thoughts and inventions. People stopped reproducing by hand and started reproducing by machine.

4.6 Messages

The best method of interprocess communication is messages, as these allow information on the actual process to be passed between processes. Messages can be of a fixed length, but are most generally of any length, and typically are unstructured. This is the method that Microsoft Windows uses to pass data between processes.

In a message system, each process communicates with a port (or message port), which is a data structure in which messages are sent to. Most systems have a single port, but others can have several message ports. In most cases, the system implements two system calls: SEND and RECEIVE, as illustrated in Figure 4.12.

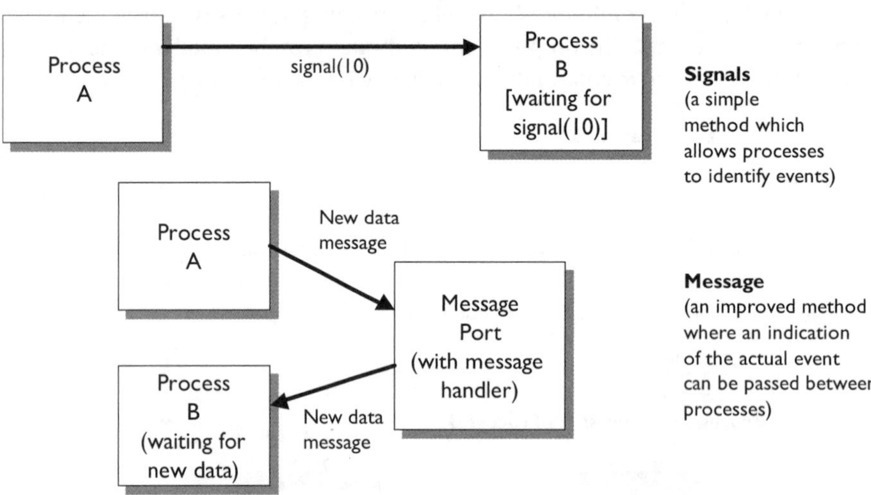

Figure 4.12 Message passing

4.7 Microsoft Windows scheduling

Scheduling involves determining which thread should be run on the processor at a given time. This element is named a time slice, and its actual value depends on the system configuration. Each thread currently running has a base priority, which is set by the programmer who created the program. It defines how the thread is executed in relation to other system threads, and the thread with the highest priority gets use of the processor.

Microsoft Windows has 32 priority levels. The lowest priority is 0 and the highest is 31. A scheduler can change a thread's base priority by increasing or decreasing it by two levels, thus changing the thread's priority.

The scheduler is made up of two main parts:

- **Primary scheduler.** This scheduler determines the priority numbers of the threads which are currently running. It then compares their priority and assigns resources to them, depending on their priority. Threads with the highest priority are executed for the current time slice. When two or more threads have the same priority then the threads are put on a stack. One thread is run and then put to the bottom of the stack, then the next is run and it is put to the bottom, and so on. This continues until all threads with the same priority have been run for a given time slice.
- **Secondary scheduler.** The primary scheduler runs threads with the highest priority, whereas the secondary scheduler is responsible for increasing the priority of non-executing threads (which are all other threads apart from the currently executed thread). It is thus important for giving low priority threads a chance to run on the operating system. Threads which are given a higher or lower priority are:

    - A thread which is waiting for user input has its priority increased.
    - A thread that has completed a voluntary wait also has its priority increased.
    - Threads with a computation-bound thread get their priorities reduced. This prevents the blocking of I/O operations.

Apart from these, all threads get a periodic increase. This prevents lower-priority threads hogging shared resources that are required by higher-priority threads.

4.8 UNIX process control

REAL STUDENT ANSWER

Handel was half German half Italian and half English. He was very large.

UNIX is a multitasking, multi-user operating system, where many tasks can be running at any given time. Typically there are several processes which are started when the computer is rebooted; these are named daemon processes and they run even when there is no user logged into the system, as illustrated in Figure 4.13. Only the system administrator can kill these processes.

UNIX uses special characters (called metacharacters) to define how a process runs, these are:

- **Redirect output.** The '>' operator (greater-than sign) redirects the output from the standard output (normally the user's screen) to another output, such as to a file.
- **Redirect input.** The '<' operator (less-than sign) redirects the input from the standard input (normally the keyboard) to another input, such as from a file.
- **Background task.** The '&' operator (ampersand sign) sends a process into the background. The process will execute quietly while the user conducts another task, and only the output to the console will be seen.
- **Pipe.** The '|' character (vertical bar) is used to pipe data from one process into another.

Some of these operators will be used in the following UNIX sessions.

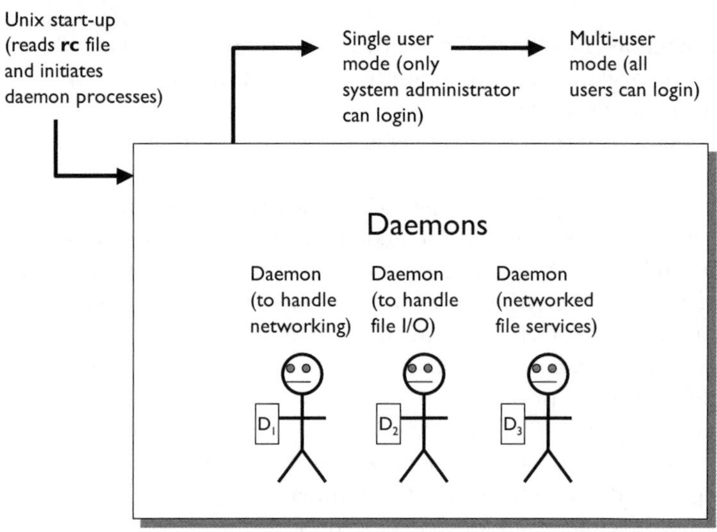

Figure 4.13 Daemon processes

4.8.1 ps (process status)

The ps command prints information about the current process status. The basic ps list gives a list of the current jobs of the user. An example is given in Sample session 4.1.

> **REAL STUDENT ANSWER**
>
> Johann Bach wrote a great many musical compositions and had a large number of children. In between he practiced on an old spinster which he kept up in his attic.

Sample session 4.1

```
% ps
  PID  TTY  TIME  CMD
   43   01  0:15  csh
   51   01  0:03  ls -R /
  100   01  0:01  ps
```

The information provided gives:

- **PID.** The unique process identification number.
- **TTY.** Every connected computer is identified with a unique name. The TTY name identifies the place at which the process was started.
- **TIME.** Identifies the amount of CPU time that has been used. Typically the format is HH:MM (for min:sec).
- **CMD.** Identifies the actual command line that was used to run the process.

> **STRANGE, BUT TRUE**
>
> A support line operator asked a customer to put the floppy disk back in the drive and close the door. After a short delay and the padding of footsteps, the customer came back to the phone and told the operator that the floppy was back in the drive and the door was now closed.

A process can be stopped using the kill command.

A long listing is achieved using the -l option and for a complete listing of all processes on the system the -a option is used, as shown in Sample session 4.2.

Sample session 4.2

```
% ps -al
F S UID PID PPID CPU PRI NICE ADDR SZ WCHAN TTY TIME CMD
1 S 101 43   1    3  30   20   3211 12 33400 01  0:15 csh
1 S 104 44   2    2  27   20   4430 12 51400 04  0:08 sh
1 S 104 76  32    3  30   20   3223 12 33400 04  0:03 vi tmp
1 S 104 89   1    3  30   20  10324 02 44103 04  0:01 ls
1 R 101 99  55   43  52   20   4432 12 33423 01  0:01 ps
```

The main additional columns are:

- **UID.** This identifies the process owner (User ID), which is generated from the value for the user in the `/etc/passwd` file.
- **PRI.** This is used to define the priority of the process, where the higher the number the lower the priority it has.
- **F.** This identifies the flags that are associated with the process (0 – swapped, 1 – in core, 2 – system process, and so on).
- **STIME.** Start time for the process (the date is printed instead, if the process has been running for more than 24 hours).
- **ADDR.** Memory address of the process.
- **NI.** Nice value, which is used to determine process priority.
- **S.** This identifies the state of the process. An S identifies that the process is sleeping (the system is doing something else); W specifies that the system is waiting for another process to stop and R specifies that the process is currently running. In summary:
    - **R.** Process is running.
    - **T.** Process has stopped.
    - **D.** Process is in disk wait.
    - **S.** Process is sleeping (that is, less than 20 secs).
    - **I.** Process is idle (that is, longer than 20 secs).

The 586

After the Intel 80486, most people expected to see the 80586, but it never happened. The reason for this was that Intel had tried to make the 386 one of their trademarks. Unfortunately, the US courts believed that the 386 number was so prevalent that it was almost a generic name (which led to the introduction of the term Intel386 for an Intel 386 processor). Instead of 586, they used the Pentium, so that they could trademark the name. This allowed Intel to invest their own money into developing the Pentium brand.

4.8.2 kill (send a signal to a process, or terminate a process)

The `kill` command sends a terminate signal to a process. The general format is:

`kill` *–sig processid*

The *processid* is the number given to the process by the computer, which can be found by using the `ps` command. The *sig* value defines the amount of strength that is given to the kill process. A value of `9` is the strongest value, others are: 1 (hang up); 2 (interrupt); 3 (quit); 4 (alarm); 5 (terminate) and 6 (abort). The owner of a process can kill their own processes, but only the system administrator can kill any process.

REAL STUDENT ANSWER

Louis Pasteur discovered a cure for rabbis.

Sample session 4.3 gives an example session.

Sample session 4.3

```
% ps
   PID  TTY  TIME  CMD
   112  01   1:15  csh
   145  01   0:05  lpr temp.c
   146  01   0:01  ps
% kill -9 145
% ps
   PID  TTY  TIME  CMD
   112  01   1:15  csh
   146  01   0:01  ps
% find / -name "*.c" -print > listing &
% ps
   PID  TTY  TIME  CMD
   112  01   1:15  csh
   177  01   0:03  find -nam
   179  01   0:01  ps
% kill -9 177
```

4.8.3 nice (run a command at a low priority)

The `nice` command runs a command at a low priority. The standard format is as follows:

`nice` *–number command* [*arguments*]

The lowest priority is –20 and the default is –10. Sample session 4.4 gives a sample session.

Sample session 4.4

```
% nice -15 ls -al
% nice -20 find / -name "*.c" -print > Clistings &
```

4.8.4 at (execute commands at later date)

The `at` command, when used in conjunction with another command, executes a command at some later time. The standard format is:

`at` *time* [*date*] [*week*]

where *time* is given using from 1 to 4 digits, followed by either 'a', 'p', 'n' or 'm' for am, pm, noon or midnight, respectively. If no letters are given then a 24-hour clock is assumed. A 1- or 2-digit time is assumed to be given in hours, whereas a 3- or 4-digit time is assumed to be hours and minutes. A colon may also be included to separate the hours from the minutes.

The *Date* can be specified by the month followed by the day-of-the-month number, such as Mar 31. A *Week* can be given instead of the day and month. Sample session 4.5 shows a session where a program is compiled at quarter past eight at night.

Most Granted Patents

1 IBM (2,886)
2 NEC Corporation (2,020)
3 Canon (1,890)
4 Samsung. (1,441)
5 Lucent (1,411)
6 Sony (1,385)
7 Micron Technology (1,304)
8 Toshiba (1,232)
9 Motorola Inc. (1,196)
10 Fujitsu Limited (1,147)

United States Patent and Trademark Office, 2000

Sample session 4.5

```
% at 20:15
   cc - test test.c
  ^D
   520776201.a at Tue May 26 20:15:00 1997
```

and to send `fred` a message at 14:00:

Sample session 4.6

```
% at 14:00
   echo "Time for a tea-break" | mail fred
   ^D
   520777201.a at Mon Jun 4 14:00:00 1989
```

To remove all files with the .o extensions from the current directory on September 9th at 1 noon.

Sample session 4.7

```
% at 1n sep 9
   rm *.o
   ^D
   520778201.a at Sat Sep 9 13:00:00 1989
```

To list all jobs that are waiting to be executed at some later time use the `-l` option.

Sample session 4.8

```
% at -l
  520776201.a  Mon Jun 4 20:15:00 1989
  520778201.a  Sat Sep 9 13:00:00 1989
  520777201.a  Mon Jun 4 14:00:00 1989
```

To remove jobs from the schedule the `-r` option can be used, giving the job number.

Sample session 4.9

```
  % at -r 520777201.a
```

> **REAL STUDENT ANSWER**
>
> Milton wrote *Paradise Lost*. Then his wife died and he wrote *Paradise Regained*.

4.9 Finite-state machines

Finite-state machines (FSM) are at the heart of most computer systems. They define the system as a finite number of states, each of which is linked by a series of events. Often complex systems can be easily modelled in this way. Figure 4.14 shows an example of a FSM for a traffic light controller. The system is started in State 1 (Red light ON, and Don't Walk ON, which is a safe starting state). After this, the system then goes from State 2 to State 3 and to State 4 (with a finite time delay between each state). When leaving State 4, the system goes back to either State 1 if the pedestrian button has not been pressed, or State 5, if it has been pressed. If the system goes into State 5, the traffic light goes to RED and the Don't Walk is still ON. Next, in State 6, the pedestrian light goes to Walk, and so on. Unfortunately, there is no state for a safe start-up (traffic lights OFF) and a shutdown state. Figure 4.15 overcomes this, with a safe shutdown from State 1. Only in State 1 can the system be shutdown (as it is unsafe to shut it down in any other state).

STRANGE, BUT TRUE

Some computer companies are considering changing the message: 'Press any key to continue' as some users phone up their support lines to ask where the 'Any' key is.

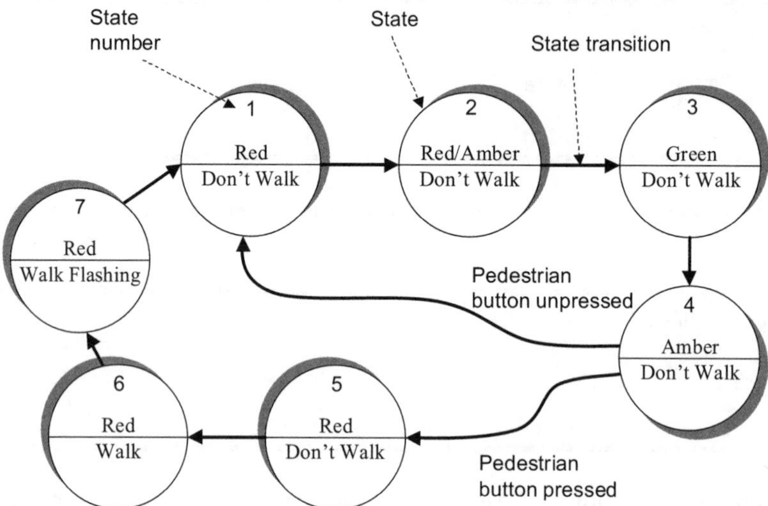

Figure 4.14 State transition for a traffic light controller

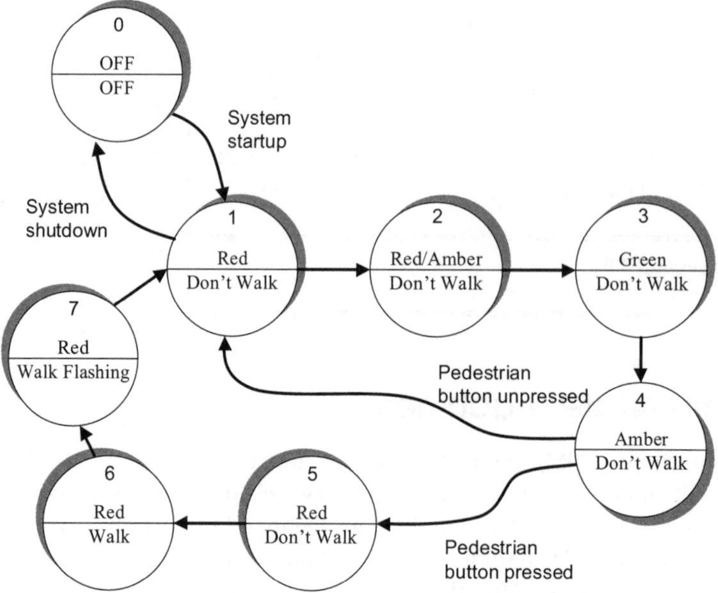

Figure 4.15 State transition for a traffic light controller with start-up/shutdown state

4.10 Exercises

The following questions are multiple choice. Please select from a–d.

4.10.1 Which of the following is not a process state:

(a) Running (b) Waiting
(c) Synchronizing (d) Ready

4.10.2 Which is the UNIX metacharacter for running a process in the background:

(a) | (b) &
(c) < (d) >

4.10.3 Which type of scheduler is used for batch systems:

(a) Long-term scheduler (b) Short-term scheduler
(c) Medium-term scheduler (d) Swapping scheduler

4.10.4 Which of the following best describes a zombie process:

(a) A terminated process, but still waiting for parent process
(b) A virus process
(c) A process that cannot be killed
(d) A process that is hogging the processor

4.10.5 Which of the following is not a major objective of a scheduler:

(a) Fairness (b) Throughput
(c) Predictability (d) Allowing user intervention

4.10.6 Which scheduling algorithm has a circular process queue:

(a) Shortest-job-first (b) Round-robin
(c) Multilevel queue (d) First-come, first-served

4.10.7 Which of the following is used in a non-pre-emptive operating system:

(a) Shortest-job-first (b) Round-robin
(c) Multilevel queue (d) First-come, first-served

4.10.8 Which is the UNIX metacharacter for redirecting the input to a program:

(a) | (b) &
(c) < (d) >

4.10.9 Which of the following is the fairest to all the running processes:

(a) Shortest-job-first (b) Round-robin
(c) Multilevel queue (d) First-come, first-served

4.10.10 Which of the following is the best for allowing key system processes to run smoothly:

(a) Shortest-job-first (b) Round-robin
(c) Multilevel queue (d) First-come, first-served

Additional tutorial questions are available at:

`http://www.palgrave.com/studyskills/masterseries/buchanan`

5 Distributed elements

5.1 Introduction

The following chapters cover the theory of distributing data and processing over a network, thus we need to understand the main principles involved in data distribution. The main principle is the concept of peer-to-peer systems, and client-server systems. A server is a system which provides a particular service (such as remote login, or file services) to a client. The server must wait on connections from clients. A peer-to-peer network works on co-operation, where peer computers share resources. Small networks (typically with fewer than 10 computers) normally work best with a peer-to-peer network, and larger networks work best with a client-server architecture. It must be noted that client-server and peer-to-peer architectures can easily co-exist together, and many networks operate this way. A good example is that a computer will use a client-server architecture when contacting a WWW server, but it might use a peer-to-peer architecture when it is sharing a printer with its neighbour.

The Internet supports many server applications, including remote login (telnet), remote file transfer (ftp), electronic mail transfer (smtp), domain name services (dns), and so on.

A traditional method of presenting distributed elements is to define: the concept of analogue and digital data; the concept of a communications model; and the coverage of the communications channel. Thus some of this chapter discusses these topics. These will be more important in the chapters on Data Communications and Networks, but they have been covered here in order to present distributed elements as a single entity.

Data is available in either an analogue form or in a digital form, as illustrated in Figure 5.1. Computer-generated data can be easily stored in a digital format, but if a computer is to be able to interpret analogue signals, such as speech and video, they must first be sampled at regular intervals and then

DEAR JARGON-BUSTER

Question: *I've just had a lecture on the WWW and the Internet, and my head is spinning. I counted 20 acronyms that I have got a clue about. Can you help? They included HTML, HTTP, VB Script, ASP, PHP, CGI, PERL, CSS, RSA, DHCP, TCP/IP, IP, and many more.*

Oh dear. Computing is a difficult enough learning the principles, without have to try and understand some of the term. If you're ever struggling with a term, just put your hand up and ask what it means.

Well here goes. I assume that you don't just want to know what the acronym stands for, so I'll try and give you a quick overview of the terms. Well, **HTML** is the standard computer language that is read by a WWW browser, and contains special tags which identify the format of the WWW page, such as text contained with <B> and </B> will be shown as **bold**. HTML is fine for basic formatting, but it is not so good at getting user interaction, thus **VBScript** (Visual Basic) is a simplified form of Visual Basic (which is the most popular programming language in the world) and is used to provide some basic functions, such as time() to display the current time. VB script integrates into HTML, and can hide itself from WWW browsers by embedding it in-between the <SCRIPT LANGUAGE="VBSCRIPT"> and the </SCRIPT> tags.

```
<SCRIPT LANGUAGE="VBSCRIPT">
   sub myheader_onClick
     myheader.Style.Color = "BLACK"
   end sub
</SCRIPT>
```

to be continued ...

converted into a digital form. This process is known as digitization and has the following advantages:

- **Less susceptible to noise**. Digital data is less affected by noise, as illustrated in Figure 5.2. Noise is any unwanted signal and has many causes, such as static pick-up, poor electrical connections, electronic noise in components, cross-talk, and so on. It makes the reception/storage of a data more difficult and can produce unwanted distortion on the received/stored data.
- **Less error prone**. Extra information can be added to digital data so that errors can either be detected or corrected.
- **Digital data tends not to degrade over time**.
- **Easier processing**. Processing of digital data is relatively easy, either in real time (on-line processing) or non real time (off-line processing).
- **Easier to store.** A single type of storage media can be used to store many different types of information (such as video, speech, audio and computer data being stored on tape, hard disk or CD-ROM). This is more difficult in an analogue media. For example in an analogue environment, images are stored on photographic paper, video and audio are stored on magnetic tape, temperatures are stored as numerical values, and so on.
- **More dependable and predictable**. A digital system has a more dependable response, whereas an analogue system's accuracy depends on its operating parameters and its design characteristics such as its component tolerance, its operating temperature, power supply variations, and so on. Analogue systems thus produce a variable response and no two analogue systems are identical. This obviously gives analogue systems more of a personality, and they must be carefully setup in order to produce a dependable performance. Many methods, though, have been used in analogue systems to ensure that they have a more dependable performance. One of the most widely used is to provide feedback from the output and then compare this with the required output, and make some correction on the output. Unfortunately these corrections take time, and can lead to under or over compensation, which cause the system either to be too slow to respond to changes, or respond too quickly.

DEAR JARGON-BUSTER (cont...)

Okay. I've explained **HTML** and **VBScript** (*look two pages back*), so I'll continue. **ASP** is similar to VBScript, but rather than the browser processing the script, the WWW server actually does it before it sends the page to the WWW browser. ASP is a Microsoft technology and will typically only run on a Microsoft server (such as with an Microsoft IIS server).

ASP pages are named with an asp file extension (such as default.asp). An example is:

<B>Current time is <%=Time()%> </B>

which will display the current time. When this is sent to the WWW browser it will have the Time() function expanded into HTML code, such as:

<B>Current time is 10:35pm</B>

for which the WWW browser will display as:

Current time is 10:35pm

ASP is a Microsoft technology for server-side includes in HTML pages, whereas **PHP** is a UNIX equivalent, and typically runs on an Apache WWW server.

to be continued ...

- **Easier to upgrade**. Digital systems are more adaptable and can be reprogrammed with software. Analogue systems normally require a change of hardware for any functional changes (although programmable analogue devices are now available). This makes upgrades and bug fixes easier, as all that is required is a change of software.

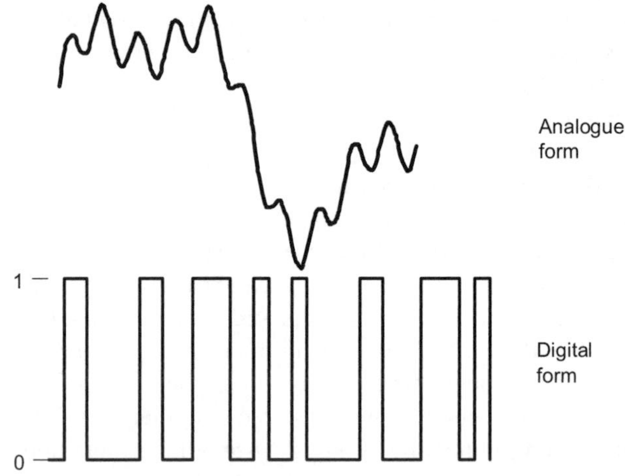

Figure 5.1 Analogue and digital format

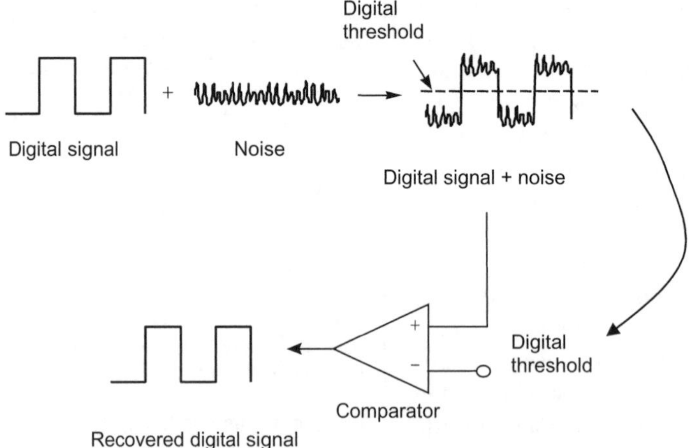

Figure 5.2 Recovery of a digital signal with noise added to it

As an analogue signal must be sampled at regular intervals, digital representations of analogue waveforms require large amounts of storage space. For example, 70 minutes of hi-fi quality music requires over 600 MB of data storage. Fortunately we now live in a time where large amounts of digital storage are available, in a reliable form, for a modest amount of money.

The data once stored tends to be reliable and will not degrade over time. Typically, digital data is stored either as magnetic fields on a magnetic disk or as pits on an optical disk. A great advantage of digital technology is that once the analogue data has been converted to digital, it is relatively easy to store it with other purely digital data. This is known as media integration. Once stored in digital form it is relatively easy to process the data before it is converted back into analogue form. Analogue signals are relatively easy to store, such as video and audio signals as magnetic fields on tape or a still picture on photographic paper. These media, though, tend to add noise (such as tape hiss) during storage and recovery. It is also difficult preserve the data over time, and to recover the original analogue data, once it has degraded in some way (especially if it is affected in a random way). Most methods of reducing this degradation (which is due to noise) involve some form of filtering or smoothing of the data.

The accuracy of a digital system depends on the number of bits used for each sample, whereas an analogue system's accuracy depends on the specification of the components used in the system. Analogue systems also produce a differing response for different systems whereas a digital system has a more dependable response.

5.2 Conversion to digital

Figure 5.3 outlines the conversion process for digital data (the upper diagram) and for analogue data (the lower diagram). The lower diagram shows how an analogue signal (such as speech or video) is first sampled at regular intervals of time. These samples are then converted into a digital form with an ADC (analogue-to-digital converter). The digital samples then are compressed and/or stored in a defined digital format (such as WAV, JPG, and so on). This digital form is then converted back into an analogue form with a DAC (digital-to-analogue converter). When data is already in a digital form (such as text or animation) it is converted into a given data format (such as BMP, GIF, JPG, and so on). It can be further compressed before it is stored, transmitted or processed.

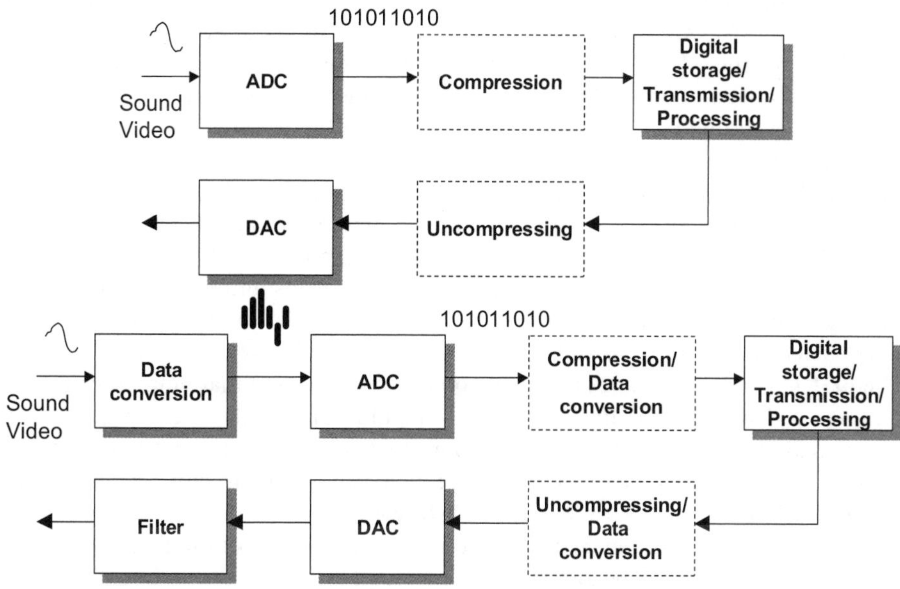

Figure 5.3 Information conversion into a digital form

5.3 Communications model

Figure 5.4 shows a communications model in its simplest form. An information source transmits data to a destination through a transmission media. This transmission can either be with a direct communication (using a physical or wireless connection) or through an indirect communication (via a number of physical or wireless connections).

The information, itself, can either be directly sent through an electrical cable, or it can be carried on an electromagnetic wave. Electromagnetics waves act as a carrier of the data, in the same way that the postal service, or telephone providers, support channels for post and telephone information to be sent and received in a reliable way. The type of electromagnetic carrier depends on the communication media which the data is to be sent through. Each carrier has a specific frequency (which is indirectly proportional to its wavelength), which is used to tune into the wave at the receiver. The frequency typically defines how well the carrier propagates through a media channel. Typical electromagnetic carrier types are:

- **Radio waves.** The lower the frequency of a radio wave the more able it is to bend around objects. Defence applications use low frequency communications as they can use this to transmit over large distances, and up and over solid objects (such as hills and mountains). The trade-off is that the lower the frequency of the radio wave, the less the information that can be carried. LW (MF) and AM (HF) signals can propagate large distances, but FM (VHF) signals require repeaters because they cannot bend round and over solid objects such as trees and hills.
- **Microwaves.** Microwaves have the advantage over optical waves (light, infrared and ultraviolet) in that they propagate reasonably well through water and thus can be transmitted through clouds, rain, and so on. One of the first applications of microwaves was in radar, as the microwave pulses could propagate through clouds, and bounce off a metal target (normally an airplane, a missile, or a ship), and return to the transmitter. If the microwaves were of a high enough frequency they can even propagate through the ionosphere and out into outer space. This is the property that is used in satellite communications where the transmitter bounces microwave energy off a satellite, which is then picked up at a receiving station. Their main disadvantage is that they will not bend round large objects, as their wavelength is too small.
- **Infrared.** Infrared is used in optical communications, and allows for a much greater amount of data to be sent, than radio and microwaves. Infrared is extensively used for line-of-site communications (and fibre optic communication), especially in remote control applications. The amount of data that can be transmitted is normally limited by the electronics at the transmitter and the receiver, but it is possible to get many billions of bits to be transmitted, in each second.
- **Light.** Light is the only part of the electromagnetic spectrum that humans can 'see' (although we can feel the affect of infrared radiation on the air around us). It is a very small part of the spectrum and ranges from 300 to 900 nm (a nanometre is one billionth of a metre). Colours contained are red, orange, yellow, green, blue, indigo and violet (ROY.G.BIV or **R**ichard **O**f **Y**ork **G**ave **B**attle **I**n **V**ain).
- **Ultraviolet.** As with infrared, ultraviolet is used in optical communications (typically with fibre optic communications). In high enough exposures, it can cause skin cancer. Fortunately for humans, the ozone layer blocks out much of the ultraviolet radiation from the sun. Note that you should not look directly into a fibre optic cable which is currently operating, as invisible radiation (especially infrared radiation) may damage your eye.

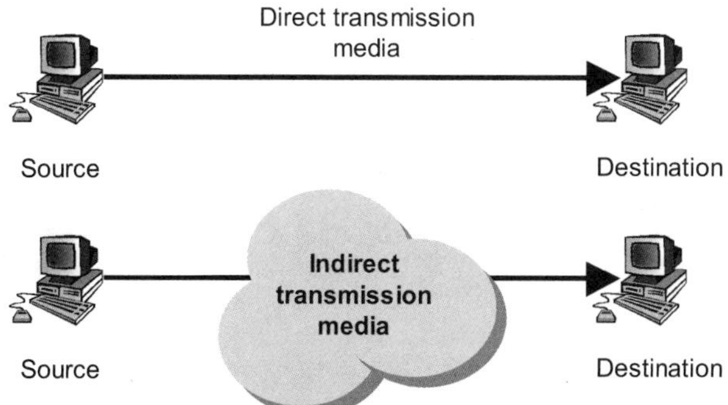

Figure 5.4 Simple communications model

5.4 Cables

The cable type used to transmit the data over the communications channel depends on several parameters, including:

- The **reliability** of the cable, and the maximum **length** between nodes.
- The possibility of electrical **hazards**, and the **power** loss in the cables.
- Tolerance to **harsh** conditions, and **expense** and general **availability** of the cable.
- Ease of **connection** and **maintenance**, and the ease of **running** cables, and so on.
- The signal **bandwidth.** The amount of information that can be sent directly relates to the bandwidth of the system, and typically the main limitation on the bandwidth is the channel between the transmitter and the receiver. With this, the lowest bandwidth of all the connected elements defines the overall bandwidth of the system (unless there are alternative paths for the data).

The main types of cables used for the digital communications channels are illustrated in Figure 5.5, and include:

- **Coaxial.** Coaxial cable has a grounded metal sheath around the signal conductor. This limits the amount of interference between cables and thus allows higher data rates. Typically, they are used at bit rates of 100 Mbps for maximum lengths of 1 km.
- **Fibre optic.** The highest specification of the three cables is fibre optic, and allows extremely high bit rates over long distances. Fibre optic cables do not interfere with nearby cables and give greater security. They also provide more protection from electrical damage by external equipment and greater resistance to harsh environments, as well as being safer in hazardous environments.
- **Unshielded twisted-pair (UTP) copper.** Twisted-pair and coaxial cables transmit electric signals, whereas fibre-optic cables transmit light pulses. Unshielded twisted-pair cables are not shielded and thus interfere with nearby cables. Public telephone lines generally use twisted-pair cables. In LANs they are generally used up to bit rates of 100 Mbps and with maximum lengths of 100 m. UTP cables are typically used to connect a computer to a network. There are various standards for twisted-pair cables, such as Cat-5 cables, which can transmit up to 100 Mbps (100,000,000 bits per second), and Cat-3, which support the transmission of up to 16 Mbps (16,000,000 bits per second).

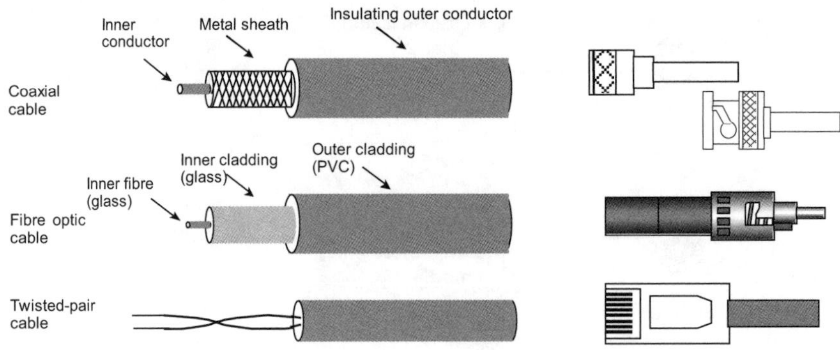

Figure 5.5 Types of network cable and their connectors

5.4.1 Cable characteristics

The main characteristics of cables are:

- **Attenuation.** Attenuation defines the reduction in the signal strength at a given frequency for a defined distance. It is normally specified in decibels (dB) per 100 m. As a basic measure a value of 3dB/100 m gives a reduction of half the signal power every 100 m.
- **Crosstalk.** Crosstalk is an important parameter as it defines the amount of signal that crosses from one signal path to another. This causes distortion on the transmitted signal. Shielded twisted-pair cables have less crosstalk than unshielded twisted-pair cables.
- **Characteristic impedance.** The characteristic impedance (as measured in Ω – ohms) of a cable and its connectors are important, as all parts of the transmission system need to be matched to the same impedance. This impedance is normally classified as the characteristic impedance of the cable. Any differences in the matching results in a reduction of signal power and can produce signal reflections (or ghosting). For example, twisted-pair cables have a characteristic impedance of approximately 100 Ω, and coaxial cable used in networking has a characteristic impedance of 50 Ω (or 75 Ω for TV systems).

DEAR JARGON-BUSTER (cont...)

So what about RSA, DHCP, TCP/IP and IP addresses? Well **RSA** is the encryption technique which allows a user to generate to encryption keys: one public and one private one. The public one is advertised to anyone who wants to send the user an encrypted message. Once the message has been encrypted with the public key, only the private key can then decrypt it. The great advantage of public-key encryption is that you can use the same public key for all your messages.

Every computer (or node) on the Internet requires a unique address, which is known as an IP address. An example **IP** address is 144.44.55.66. This address identifies the location of the computer. Devices called routers are used to pass information about the location of destination IP addresses. An IP address can either be permanently assigned to a computer, or it can be allocated to it dynamically, when a computer requires an IP address, with a **DHCP** server which contains a table of IP addresses. This table could be generated from a pool of addresses, or could be based on the physical address of the network adaptor. This gives enhanced security.

to be continued ...

5.5 Peer-to-peer and client-server

An important concept in Computing is the differentiation between a peer-to-peer connection and a client-server connection. With a client-server connection, servers provide services to client, and must wait for clients to connect to these services. Typical services might be to allow the printing of documents to a networked printer, or provide access to a networked file system. A peer-to-peer architecture allows for two systems to actively seek connections, without involving a server. An example of a client-server network in human terms might be a travel agent, who will wait for customers (clients) to get in contact with them in order to book the best holiday for them. A peer-to-peer network would be equivalent to someone phoning a friend (who isn't a travel agent) and asking them of the best holiday that they could get. The friend might then go and book the holiday over the Internet. This is a peer-to-peer network, as the friend does not actively seek questions on holiday arrangements, or in booking holidays.

A peer-to-peer connection allows users on a local network to access a local computer. Typically, this might be access to:

Local printers. Printers, local to a computer, can be accessed by other users if the printer is shareable. This can be password protected, or not. Shareable printers on a Microsoft network have a small hand under the icon.

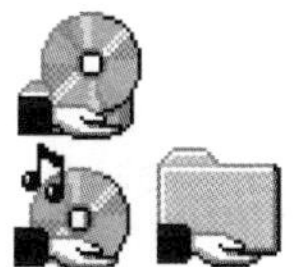

Local disk drives and folders. The disk drives, such as the hard disk or CD-ROM drives can be accessed if they are shareable. Normally the drives must be shareable. On a Microsoft network a drive can be made shareable by selecting the drive and selecting the right-hand mouse button, then selecting the Sharing option. User names and passwords can be set-up locally or can be accessed from a network server. Typically, only the local computer grants access to certain folders, while others are not shared.

These shared resources can also be mounted as objects on the remote computer. Thus, the user of the remote computer can simply access resources on the other computers as if they were mounted locally. This option is often the best when there is a small local network, as it requires the minimum amount of set-up and does not need any complicated server set-ups. Figure 5.6 shows an example of a peer-to-peer network where a computer allows access to its local resources. In this case, its local disk drive and printer are shareable.
Normally a peer-to-peer network works best for a small office environment. Care must be taken, though, when setting up the attributes of the shared resources. Figure 5.7 shows an example of the sharing setting for a disk drive. It can be seen that the main attributes are:

- **Read-only.** This should be used when the remote user only requires to copy or execute files. The remote user cannot modify any of the files.
- **Full.** This option should only be used when the remote user has full access to the files and can copy, erase or modify the files.
- **Depends on Password.** In this mode, the remote user must provide a password to get either read-only access or full access.

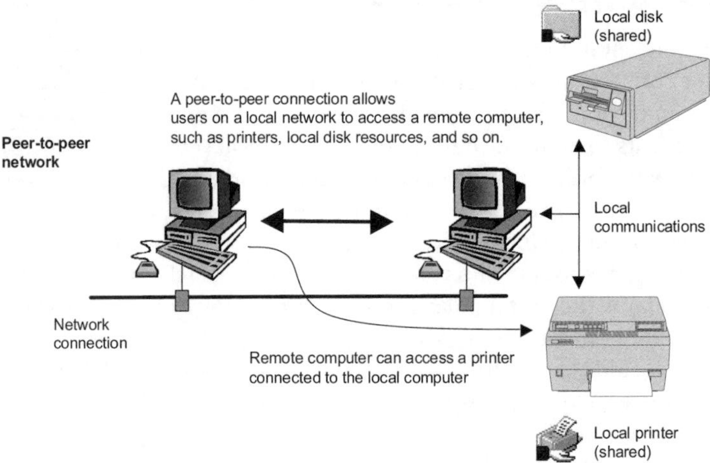

Figure 5.6 Peer-to-peer network

If the peer-to-peer network has a local server, such as Novell NetWare or Windows NT/2000 then access can be provided for certain users and/or groups, if they provide the correct password.

A client-server network has a central server which proves services to clients, as illustrated in Figure 5.8. These clients can either be local to the network segment, or from a remote network. The server typically provides one or more of the following services:

- Store usernames, group names and passwords.
- Run print queues for networked printers.
- Allocate IP addresses for Internet accesses.
- Provide system back-up facilities, such as CD-ROM disk drives and DAT tape drives.
- Provide centralized file services, such as networked hard disks or networked CD-ROM drives.
- Centralize computer settings and/or configuration.
- Provide access to other centralized peripherals, such as networked faxes and dial-in network connections.
- Provide WWW and TCP/IP services, such as remote login and file transfer.

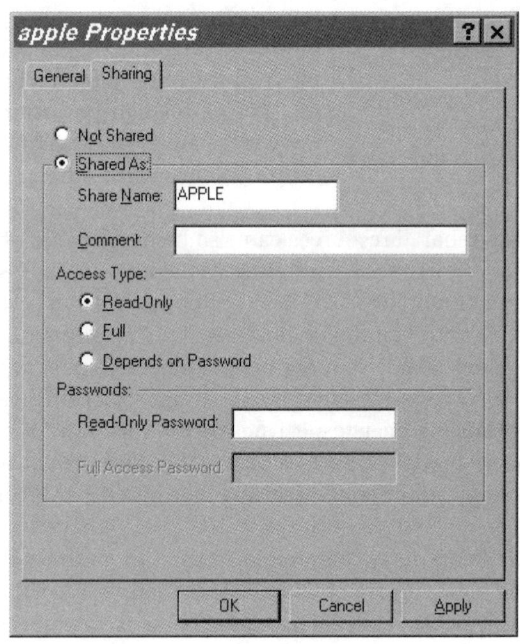

Figure 5.7 File access rights

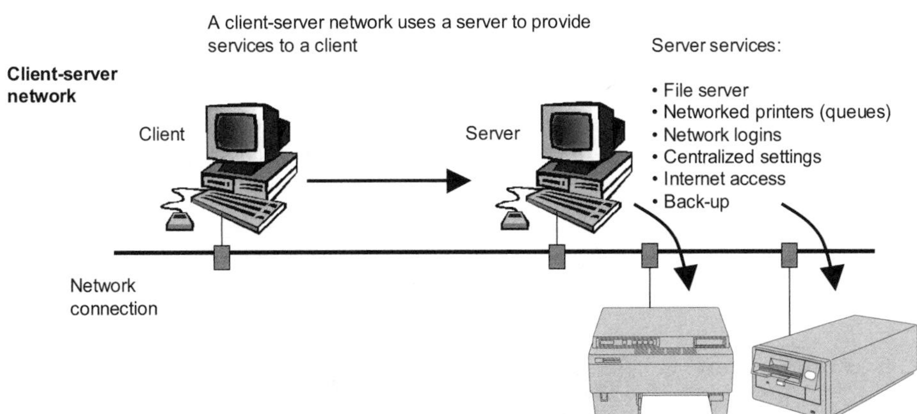

Figure 5.8 Client/server network

A network operating system server typically provides file and print services, as well as storing a list of user names and passwords. Typical network operating systems are Windows NT/2000, Novell NetWare and UNIX.

Internet and WWW services are typically run from an Internet server. Typical services include:

- **HTTP** (Hyper Text Transfer Protocol), for WWW (World-Wide Web) services. On the WWW, WWW servers and WWW clients pass information between each other using HTTP. A simple HTTP command is GET, which a WWW client (the WWW browser) sends to the server in order to get a file.
- **FTP** (File Transfer Protocol), which is a standard protocol and used to transfer files from one computer system to another. In order for the transfer to occur the server must run an FTP server program.
- **TELNET**, which is used for remote login services.
- **SMTP** (Simple Mail Transport Protocol), which is used for electronic mail transfer.
- **TIME**, which is used for a time service.
- **SNMP** (Simple Network Management Protocol), which is used to analyse network components.

DEAR JARGON-BUSTER (cont...)

TCP/IP. What can you say about TCP/IP? It's one of the most successful inventions of all time. It has allowed computers, and any electronic devices to connect to each other over the Internet. The IP part allows for addressing on a word-wide basis, while the TCP part allows for the data to be split into segments, each which are uniquely identified so that the receive can build them back into the transmitted data. You can think of TCP a bit like a writer sending his manuscript to the publisher. On each chapter that he sends he marks it with the chapter number, and the page numbers. Then he puts each chapter in a parcel and addresses it (which is equivalent to the function of the IP protocol). The postal service will then route the parcel to find the destination (these are equivalent to routers on the Internet). When the publisher receives the parcels they will be opened up and the chapters will each be reordered in the correct order (just as TCP does). When received the publisher will phone up the writer to say that they have received the parcel. This provides an acknowledgement to the writer that his manuscript has been received correctly (the postal service could not guarantee that the manuscript had been read, all they could say was that the parcels had been delivered to the right address). This acknowledgement is also part of the TCP protocol, and allows for data to be acknowledged.

Figure 5.9 shows an example network which has two local network servers. One provides file and print services, while the other supports Internet services. The local computer accesses each of these for the required service. It can also access a remote Internet server through a router. This router automatically determines that the node is accessing a remote node and routes the traffic out of the local network.

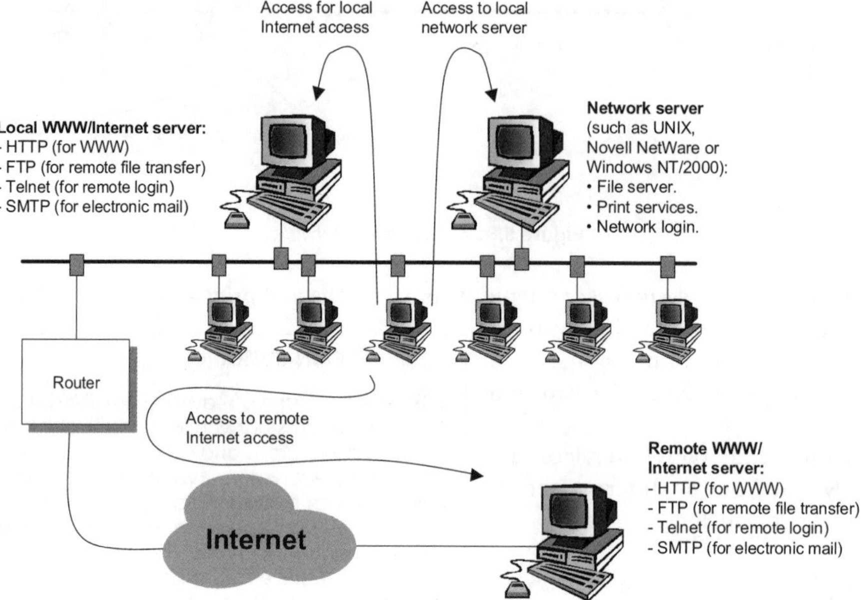

Figure 5.9 Local and remote servers

5.6 Exercises

The following questions are multiple choice. Please select from a–d.

5.6.1 Which type of communication transmission is typically used for remote transmission for short distances:
(a) Infrared (b) Microwaves
(c) Light (d) Ultraviolet

5.6.2 Which type of communication transmission is typically used for transmission over long distances:
(a) Infrared (b) Microwaves
(c) Light (d) Ultraviolet

Additional material and tutorial questions are available at:
`http://www.palgrave.com/studyskills/masterseries/buchanan`

6 Distributed processing and file systems

6.1 Introduction

> **CLASSIC SOFTWARE**
>
> **1. VisiCalc** (Original authors: Dan Bricklin, Bob Frankston). VisiCalc is the classic case of a software package that helped sell a computer. It was released in 1979, and helped the Apple II to become quickly adopted. VisiCalc was the first ever spreadsheet, and preceded Lotus 1-2-3 by three years.

Chapter 4 covered running processing on a local machine, and how these could run in a multitasking environment. With the advent of networking and the Internet it is now possible to distribute processing over a network. An extreme example involves The National Foundation for Cancer Research (NFCR) Centre for Drug Discovery in the Department of Chemistry at the University of Oxford, England. They are working on a project which uses the CPU time of users on the Internet, when a registered computer uses their screen saver (http://www.ud.com). The program that runs on the computer is one which searches for new drugs in the treatment of cancer. By July 2001 this program had achieved 213,568,434 hours of CPU time using over 760,000 devices. This has achieved one of the world's largest computers. Most people understand the concept of not using up available local memory, or disk resources, or even network capacity, but one of the largest underutilized resources is CPU time. Many computers, especially in the office, lie idle for many hours in the day. These computers could easily be performing other tasks, such as providing solutions to state-of-the-art research projects.

A good example of a centralized system against a distributed system is in the banking industry. Figure 6.1 shows how a bank might want to organize its business. In this case it devolves decision making, account management and logistics to regional offices, which then devolves these to local offices. This allows for a distribution of the activities, and, for example, a holiday in one regional area will not affect the rest of the business. If the bank had a centralized model, all the customers, staff and logistics would be centralized in a single place. This would obviously be inefficient and would cause a great deal of strain on the central site. It would also not be possible to set-up an efficient system so that every customer would be able to withdraw cash from the central site. A more efficient model is to use ATMs distributed to local offices. Most governments around the world operate with this distributed model, where the central government creates the rules and policies, which are then distributed on a regional basis with regional councils. These are then passed onto local councils, which implement the policies. A centralized government would create all the policies, then decide how these would be implemented, and then would be in total control of its implementation.

Distributed processing has many advantages over localized processing, especially in:

- **Using specialized resources**, which would not normally be accessible from a local computer, such as enhanced processing or increased amount of memory storage.
- **Using parallel processing**, where a problem is split into a number of parallel tasks, which are distributed over the network.

- **Reducing the loading on the local computer**, as tasks can be processed on remote computers.

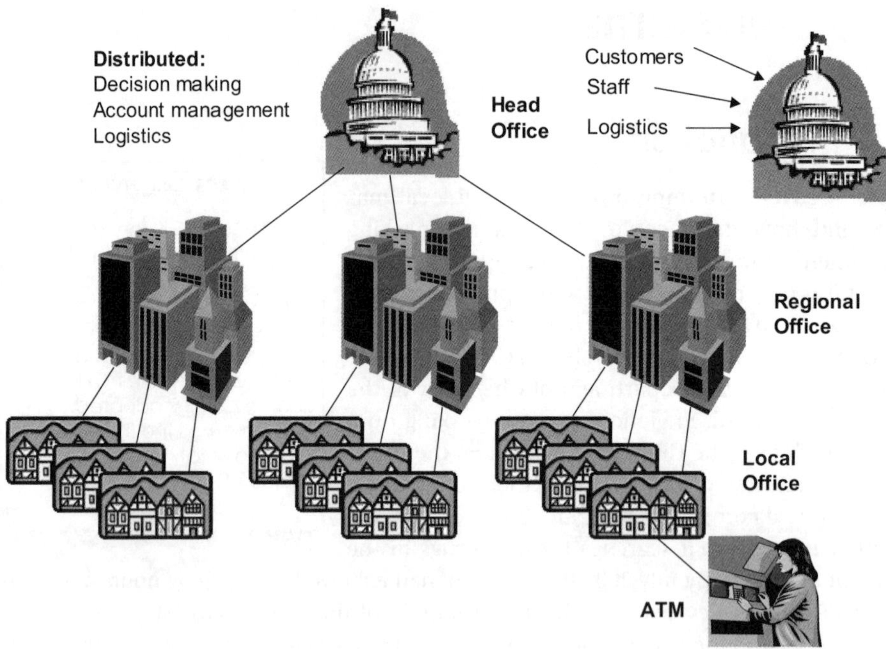

Figure 6.1 Distributed v. centralized

One of the most common mechanisms for running remote processes over a network is RPC (Remote Procedure Call). With this an RPC server waits for a request from a client. When it receives one it runs a specified process and returns the results to the client, as illustrated in Figure 6.2.

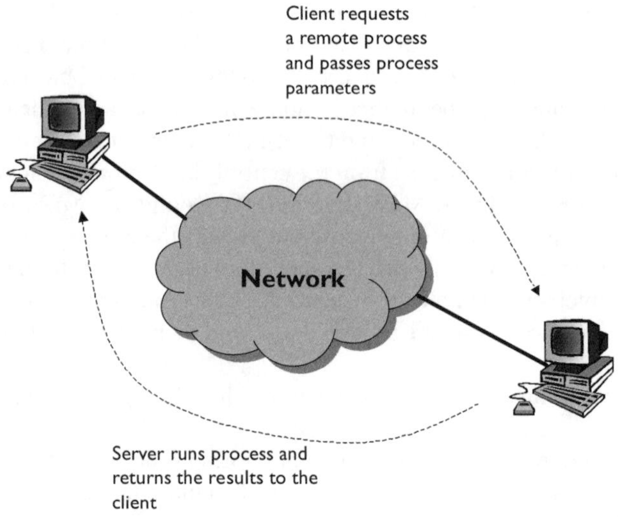

Figure 6.2 Distributed processing

Some processes can be distributed over a network, while others need to be run locally. The main criterion for determining if a process can be distributed is the communications overhead. If the communications channel is relatively slow compared with the speed of processing the task, the distribution of the processing can be inefficient. One great advantage of distributing processes is when processing moves from a server to a client. This allows the server to perform high-level operations, while the client does most of the processing. An example of distributing a process is when a user runs a word processor from a server. The files that are executed reside on the server, but the actual running of the program occurs on the client.

CLASSIC SOFTWARE

2. WordStar (Original author: Seymour Rubinstein). For a time in the 1980s, WordStar was the standard word processing package. It was released in 1979, and quickly became the standard word processor. Often other word processors imitated WordStar's keystrokes, such as Cntrl-Q-F to find a piece of text.

3. dBase II (Original author: Wayne Ratliff). Initially written for CP/M, dBase II was a massive success in its DOS version. It was bought by Aston-Tate, but has since lost its large market share, especially due to the bug-ridden dBase IV (1988) and their slowness to develop a Windows version (1994).

6.2 Interprocess communication

Interprocess communication (IPC) is a set of interfaces that allow programmers to communicate between processes, and allow programs to run concurrently. Figure 6.3 illustrates some of the methods, these include:

- **Pipes.** Pipes allow data to flow from one process to another, and have a common process origin. Data only flows in the one direction, typically from the output of one process to the input of another. The data from the output is buffered until the input process receives it. In UNIX the single vertical bar character (|) is used to represent a pipe, and operates in a similar way to a pipe system call in a program. Two-way communication can be constructed with two pipes, one for each direction.
- **Named pipe.** A named pipe uses a pipe which has a specific name for the pipe. Unlike unnamed pipes, a named pipe can be used in processes that do not have a shared common process origin. Typically a named pipe is known as a FIFO (first in, first out), as the data written to a pipe is read in the order that it was written to.
- **Message queuing.** Message queues allow processes to pass messages between themselves, using either a single message queue or several message queues. The system kernel manages each message queue, and puts messages on the queue which identify the message (message type). Messages can vary in length and be assigned different types or usages. The queues can be created by one process and used by multiple processes that read and/or write messages to the queue. Application programs (or their processes) create message queues and can send and receive messages using an application program interface (API).
- **Semaphores.** These will be discussed later in this chapter, and are used to synchronize events between processes. Semaphores are integer values which are greater than or equal to zero. A zero value puts a process to sleep, while a non-zero value causes a sleeping process to awaken (when certain operations are performed). A signal is sent to a semaphore when an event occurs which then increments the semaphore.

- **Shared memory.** Shared memory allows processes to interchange data through a defined area of memory. For example, one process could write to an area of memory and another could read from it. To do this the writing process must check to see if the reading process is actually reading from the memory, at the same time, and vice versa. If this is occurring the other process must wait for the other process to complete. This is implemented using semaphores, where only one process is allowed to access the memory at a time.
- **Sockets.** These are typically used to communicate over a network, between a client and a server (although peer-to-peer connections are also possible). Sockets are end points of a connection, and allow for a standard connection that is independent of the type of computer and its operating system.

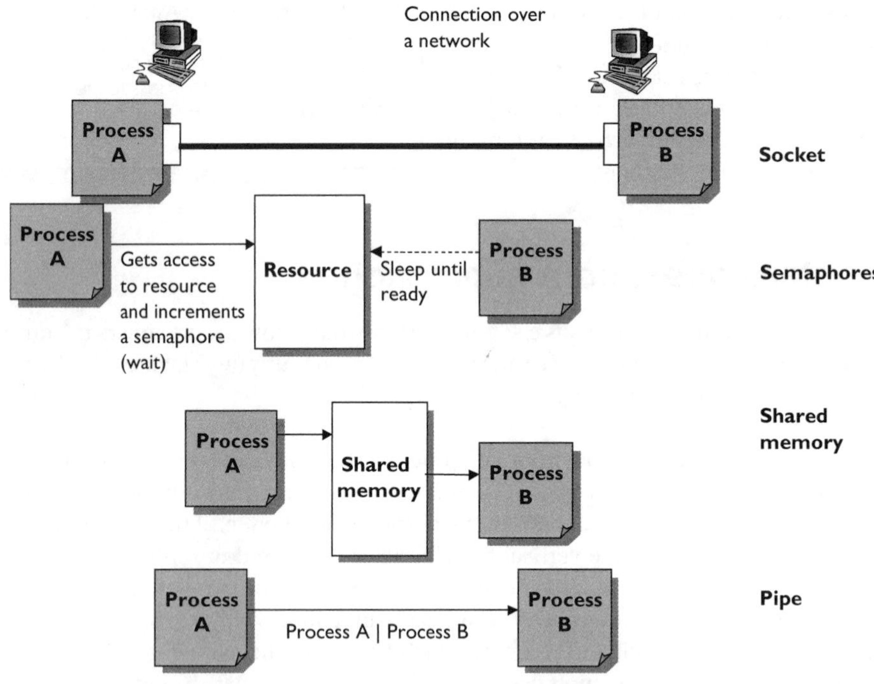

Figure 6.3 IPC methods

6.3 Flags and semaphores

Flags are simple variables which take on a binary state (0 or a 1), and are used to identify that an event has occurred, or to pass binary information. Semaphores are positive integer values which can take on any range of values, but can also be binary values (for mutual exclusion applications). An example of using a semaphore is when a process uses a resource, and sets a semaphore flag to indicate that it is currently accessing the resource. Any device, which then accesses the resource while the semaphore flag was set, will

> **CLASSIC SOFTWARE**
>
> **4. Lotus 1-2-3** (Developer: Lotus). Lotus 1-2-3 became the best- selling application of all time. It considerably enhanced the VisiCalc program, and was written specifically for the IBM PC.

know that the resource is still being used, and must thus wait until the flag is unset. Semaphores were initially developed by Dijkstra and are implemented in IPC. Two common uses of semaphores are:

- **Memory**. This allows processes to share a common area of memory.
- **File access**. This allows processes to share access to files.

> **CLASSIC SOFTWARE**
>
> **5. AutoCAD** (Developer: Autodesk). Initially written for CP/M, and ported to DOS and Windows. It allowed designers to access powerful mechanical design software, which was previously only available on mini and mainframe computers (1994).

A semaphore could simply be a memory location in which processes go to and test the value. If the semaphore is set to a given value, a process may have to sleep until the value is changed to a value which allows orderly access to the resource. Semaphores can also be used to define *critical code regions*. These are parts of a process which must wait for code in another process to complete. A practical example of this is when we imagine two trains (two processes) approaching a region of single-track rail. For safety considerations there must only be one train on the single-track line, at a time. The trains must then have some way of signalling to the other train that they are now on the track. A signal (the semaphore) could be set up so that it is set either to a red or a green light at the entrance of the track. When a train enters the track the signal will change to red, and stop any other trains from entering the track. When it has left the track the signal will be set to green, and the other train can enter the track. In software terms, the trains could be processes which require exclusive access to a resource. When one of the processes gets access to it, all other processes must wait for the resource to be released.

Most operating systems run more than one process at a time (using time multiplexing). This can cause many problems, especially in synchronizing activities and allowing multiple processes access to shared resources. Semaphores can overcome these problems, as they are operating system variables that each process can check and change, if required. They are basically a counter value which can be zero or positive, but never negative. There are only two operations on the semaphore:

- **UP** (signal). Increments the semaphore value, and, if necessary, wakes up a process which is waiting on the semaphore. This is achieved in a single operation, to avoid conflicts.
- **DOWN** (wait). Decrements the semaphore value. If the counter is zero there is no decrement. Processes are blocked until the counter is greater than zero.

> **CLASSIC SOFTWARE**
>
> **6. The Norton Utilities** (Original author: Peter Norton). Early computers were difficult to use, and were often unreliable. DOS was always a very basic operating system which lacked a great deal of system tools. Norton Utilities allowed users to gain access to the hardware and firmware of the computer. A typical utility was one which recovered data from a corrupted hard disk (which often happened, as hard disks had to be parked before they were moved).

Figure 6.4 shows an example of two processes running with mutually exclusive code. Each piece of protected code is surrounded with a `wait()` at the start and a `signal()` at the end. The wait() operation decrements the semaphore value (which has an initial value of 1), and the signal() operation increments the semaphore value. Process A is the first process to execute the mutually exclusive code, and decrements the semaphore so that it is zero. When Process B tries the wait, it tests the semaphore, and since it is zero, the process will go into sleep mode. It will not waken until Process A has executed the signal() operation. When Process B is awoken it executes the wait() which sets the semaphore to 1, thus Process A cannot execute the mutually exclusive code. When finished, Process B will set the semaphore back to a 1 with the signal().

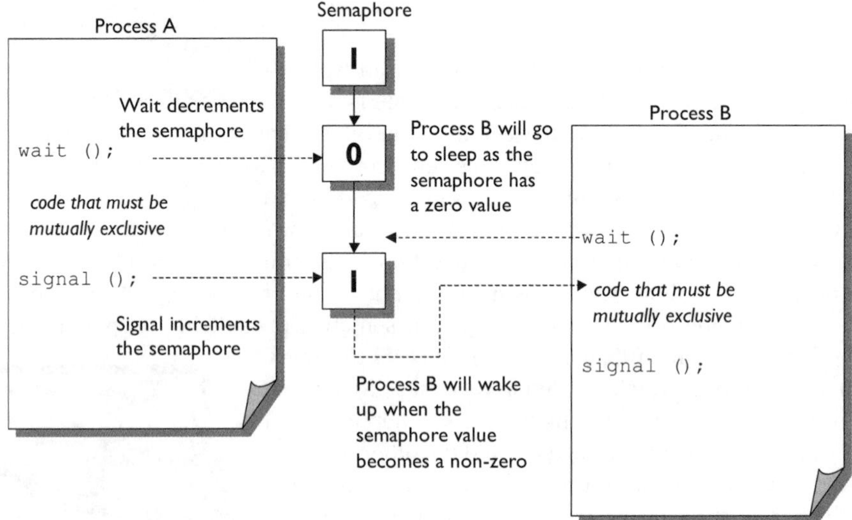

Figure 6.4 Example usage of semaphore in mutually exclusive code

6.3.1 Semaphore values

A signal is like a software interrupt, and can be viewed as a flag, as it does not give any indication on the number of events that have occurred, it is only possible to know that it has occurred. Whereas, a semaphore can be regarded as a generalized signal, which has an integer counter to record the number of signals that have occurred. Processes can put themselves to sleep while waiting for a signal.

Semaphores are operated on by signal and wait operations. A wait operation decrements the value of a semaphore and a signal operation increments it. The initial value of a semaphore identifies the number of waits which may be performed on the semaphore. Thus:

$$V = I - W + S$$

where I is the initial value of the semaphore.
W is the number of completed wait operations performed on the semaphore.
S is the number of signal operations performed on it.
V is the current value of the semaphore (which must be greater than or equal to zero).

As $V \geq 0$, then $I - W + S \geq 0$, which gives:

$$I + S \geq W$$

or

$$W \leq I + S$$

Thus, the number of wait operations must be less than or equal to the initial value of the semaphore, plus the number of signal operations. A binary semaphore will have an initial value of 1 ($I = 1$), thus:

$$W \leq S + 1$$

> So why did Dijkstra use 'P' (for DOWN) and 'V' (for UP) for the operations? Well, one theory is that the lifts on the 13th floor of the Livvy tower are engraved with a 'P' instead of an arrow.

In mutual exclusion, waits always occur before signals, as waits happen at the start of a critical piece of code, with a signal at the end of it. The above equations state that no more than one wait may run to completion before a signal has been performed. Thus, no more than one process may enter the critical section at a time, as required.

6.3.2 P and V operations

A simple process can either be in RUNNING, SLEEPING or WAKEUP mode. A process is put to sleep if it is waiting for a resource which is currently being used by another process. When the resource is released, and no other processes need to access the resource, a sleeping process can be sent a WAKEUP, where it will reactivate itself. Semaphores with a value of zero can identify that there are no processes waiting on a resource, and the process can gain access to it. A positive value can then identify that there are a number of wakeups pending.

Two operations, P and V, are generalizations of SLEEP and WAKEUP and can be used to operate on the semaphore as follows:

- P operation (the DOWN operation). This checks the semaphore, and if the value of the semaphore is greater than zero, it decrements its value. A zero value puts the process to sleep without completing the P operation.
- V operation (the UP operation). This increments a referenced semaphore, and identifies that there are one or more processes that require some processing time (as they have been put to sleep with an earlier P operation). A sleeping process is chosen at random, and is allowed to complete a P operation.

> **CLASSIC SOFTWARE**
>
> **7. MS-DOS 2.0** (Developer: Microsoft). DOS was the solid foundation that the PC was built on. It was never a startling operating system, and just did enough to get by. Its true strength was its basic compatibility with all previous versions (this makes it extremely unusual in the computer industry). Programs were almost guaranteed to run on earlier versions of DOS.

There must be no interrupts when checking a semaphore, changing a semaphore and waking up a process, and it must be done in a single indivisible operation (an atomic action). This overcomes timing hazards (see Section 6.3.3) as no other process can get access to the semaphore until the process has completed or is blocked.

6.3.3 Producer-consumer problem

The producer–consumer problem involves two processes sharing a common, fixed-size buffer. The producer puts information into the buffer, and the consumer process reads and removes information from the buffer. This is an exclusion problem as the consumer could be reading the buffer when the producer tries to write to the buffer. The solution to this is to put the producer to sleep when the consumer is reading and removing the data from the buffer, and then is awoken when complete. When the consumer wants to read and remove the data, and the producer is writing to the buffer, it must go to sleep, and then is awoken when the producer is finished.

Program 6.1 shows an example program. There can be a number of items in the buffer, which is identified with a variable called `buffer_count`, and the maximum number of items that can be stored in the buffer is `MAX_BUFF`. In the program, the producer keeps filling the buffer with data. When, if ever, the buffer is full it will go to sleep (`if (buffer_count== MAX_BUFF) sleep();`). It will then wait on the consumer to wake it up when it has read at least one item from the buffer (`if (buffer_count==MAX_BUFF-1) wakeup (producer_buffer);`). The consumer goes to sleep when there are no items in the buffer (`if (buffer_count==0) sleep();`), and will be woken-up when the producer has put at least one item in the buffer (`if (buffer_count==1) wakeup(consumer);`).

Unfortunately there is a timing problem in the code. This can happen with an empty buffer and when the operating system scheduler has just run the consumer but stops it before it can check the empty buffer. The scheduler then runs the producer which then adds an item to the buffer, and thinks that the consumer should be sleeping (as the buffer was empty). This signal will be lost on the consumer, as it is not sleeping. When the scheduler runs the consumer again, it will have an incorrect count value of zero, as it has already checked the count, and will thus go to sleep. The producer will thus not wake the consumer up, as the producer will fill the buffer up, and then go to sleep. Both consumer and producer will be sleeping, awaiting the other to wake them up. One solution to this is to have a bit which defines that there is a wake up waiting, which is set by a process which is still awake. If the process then tries to go to sleep, it cannot as the wake up-waiting bit is set. The process would thus stay awake, and reset the wake up-waiting bit.

CLASSIC SOFTWARE

8. Flight Simulator (Developer: Microsoft). By today's standards, Microsoft's Flight Simulator was hardly startling, but in the 1980s its graphics were state of the art. It led to a great market for supplying different terrains and cities to fly over. For many it was their first sight of New York from the sky.

Program 6.1

```
#define MAX_BUFF 100            /* maximum items in buffer          */
int buffer_count=0;             /* current number of items in buffer   */

int main(void)
{
   /* producer_buffer();   on the producer    */
   /* consumer_buffer();   on the consumer    */
}
void producer_buffer(void)
{
 while (TRUE){                       /* Infinite loop */
  put_item();                        /* Put item*/
```

```
  if (buffer_count==MAX_BUFF) sleep(); /* Sleep, if buffer full */
  enter_item();                        /* Add item to buffer*/
  buffer_count = buffer_count + 1;     /* Increment number of items in the
                                          buffer */
  if (buffer_count==1) wakeup(consumer); /*was buffer empty?*/
 }
}
void consumer_buffer(void)
{
 while (TRUE) {                        /* Infinite loop */
  if (buffer_count==0) sleep();        /* Sleep, if buffer empty */
  get_item();                          /* Get item */
  buffer_count = buffer_count - 1;     /* Decrement number of items in the
                                          buffer*/
  if (buffer_count==MAX_BUFF-1) wakeup(producer_buffer);
                                       /* if buffer not full
                                          anymore, wake up producer*/
  consume_item();                      /*remove item*/
 }
}
```

6.3.4 Deadlock

Deadlock is a serious problem when running processes in both a local and a distributed system. It occurs when a process is waiting for an event that will never occur. This typically occurs when:

- **Resource locking.** This is where a process is waiting for a resource which will never become available. Some resources are preemptive, where processes can release their access on them, and give other processes a chance to access them. Others, though, are non-preemptive, and processes are given full rights to them. No other processes can then get access to them until the currently assigned process is finished with them. An example of this is with the transmission and reception of data on a communication system. It would not be a good idea for a process to send some data that required data to be received, in return, to yield to another process which also wanted to send and receive data. The non-preemptive resources would thus be locked so that no other processes could access them. This can cause a problem when the resource which is accessing the resource never gets the event which will release the lock, or if the process crashes. Many examples of resource locking relate to the physical access for users. A good example is when a user is writing to a CD drive (with a writeable CD). It would not make any sense if the current session was interrupted, and another user was allowed to use it, as the CD would have to be changed for the new user, and then changed back again for the other user. This would continue, as the time on the resource would share. Obviously the reading of data from a CD-ROM drive could be shared, if the users were both using the CD-ROM disk.

CLASSIC SOFTWARE

9. Novell NetWare (Developer: Novell). NetWare became the first company to properly bring together PCs to make a local area network. For this it used its own, propriety protocol: IPX/SPX, and is the only networking operating system which can compete against the strength of UNIX (which uses the TCP/IP protocol) and Windows 95/98/NT/2000. It held an almost monopoly on networks in the commercial market, but has suffered recently due to the might of Microsoft Windows, as Windows can support many different protocols.

- **Starvation.** This is where other processes are run, and the deadlocked process is not given enough time to catch the required event. This can occur when processes have a low priority compared with other ones, as higher priority tasks tend to have a better chance to access the required resources.

6.3.5 Deadlock

We've all seen deadlock occurring in real life, especial with automobiles. Figure 6.5 illustrates a typical case of deadlock. In this case two cars are blocking the junction (at A and D), and do not allow any of the other cars behind them to move. Unfortunately both automobiles cannot move as there are automobiles blocking their entry into the junction. The only way to clear the deadlock, apart from the two cars who are turning into the junctions to give up and go straight ahead, is for one of the automobiles which is blocking one of the junctions to reverse. Unfortunately, in this case, they cannot, as there are automobiles behind them. This is a deadly embrace. In resource terms, both of the car lanes of the main road has one of the junctions, and requires the other, but none of the car lanes can give their lane up.

In process terms, resource deadlock occurs when Process 1 holds Resource A, and Process 2 holds Resource B, but Process 1 wants to gain access to Resource B, and vice-versa. Each process then waits for the other to yield their exclusive access to their resource. This is a deadly embrace. A typical problem can occur when data buffers can become full. For example a print spooler can be setup so that it must receive the full contents of a print file, before it will actually send it to the printer. If print buffer is receiving print data from several sources, it can fill up the buffer before any of the print jobs have completed. The only way round this problem would be to increase the data buffer size, which can be difficult.

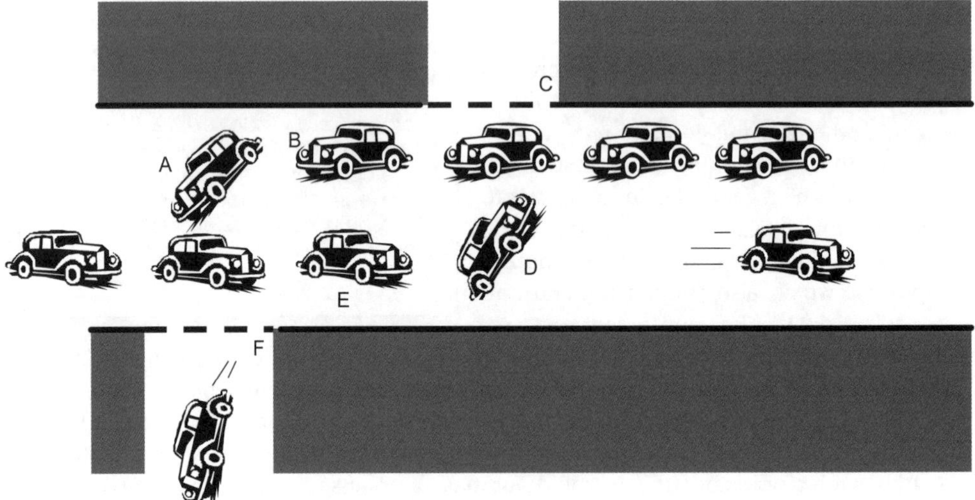

Figure 6.5 Deadlock on a road junction

The four conditions that must hold for deadlock to occur are:

- **Mutual exclusion condition.** This is where processes get exclusive control of required resources, and will not yield the resource to any other process.
- **Wait for condition.** This is where processes keep exclusive control of acquired resources while waiting for additional resources.
- **No preemption condition.** This is where resources cannot be removed from the processes which have gained them, until they have completed their access on them.
- **Circular wait condition.** This is a circular chain of processes on which each process holds one or more resources that are requested by the next process in the chain.

In our example of deadlock in Figure 6.5 we can see that this passes all of these conditions. A car blocking the junction defines mutual exclusion, and since the cars cannot move away from the junction (in the deadlock case) there will be a condition for wait and preemption. As both automobile lanes are waiting for each other, we have a circular wait. Note that deadlock may occur very infrequently, but when it does occur it normally requires some form of user input, to try and recover the situation. In the case of the automobile deadlock, we would need someone to make directions as to the best plan to overcome the deadlock (possibly, a traffic policeman).

6.3.6 Deadlock avoidance

If possible, processes should run without the problem of deadlock, as systems normally require a reboot to clear the problem. One of the best-known avoidance algorithms is the Banker algorithm, which tries to avoid deadlock by estimating the amount of a given resource that processes are likely to require, in order to run to completion. It is typically applied to define the amount of resources of the same type, but can be extended to resource pools with differing resource types. In our automobile deadlock, we could have applied the same principle, in that an automobile is not allowed to turn to go into the junction, unless both junctions can be cleared. Thus if one automobile could not get into the junction, then the other automobile who wants to turn into the other junction would not be allowed to enter the junction, and would have to proceed without turning into the junction. For example let's say that A is allowed to wait at the junction, while there is an automobile waiting at junction F. It will be allowed to do this, as deadlock will be avoided if there is no automobile turning at D. If this continues, but an automobile now requested to turn into C, and its path is blocked, then it will not be allowed to do this as it can cause deadlock.

> **CLASSIC SOFTWARE**
>
> **10. UNIX System V** (Distributor: AT&T). System V was the first real attempt at unifying UNIX into a single standardized operating system, and succeeded in merging Microsoft XENIX, SunOS, and UNIX 4.3 BSD. Unfortunately, after this there was still a drift by hardware manufacturers to move away from the standard (and define their standards). Although it has been difficult to standardize UNIX, its true strength is its communications protocols, such as TCP/IP, which are now world-wide standards for communicating over the Internet. The biggest challenge to UNIX has been from Windows NT/2000, which has tried to create a hardware independent operating system. UNIX has, in the main, survived because of its simplicity and its reliability.

In the Banker algorithm, the operating system has a number of resources of a given type (N), which are allocated a number of users (M). The operating system is told by each process the maximum number of resources that it requires (n), which must be less than N. The operating system gives access to one of the resources of a process, one at a time. Thus processes can be guaranteed access to one of the resources within a given time. A safe condition is when one of the processes can complete with the amount of resources that are left unallocated. For example, if the operating system allocated memory to processes, and the operating system has a total of 100 MB (N = 100), with four processes currently running (M = 4). Each process tells the operating system about the maximum amount of memory that it will require (n). Processes must then ask the operating system for an allocation of the resources. The algorithm then checks to see if there is enough allocation left, after the new allocation has been granted, and that at least one of the processes with allocated resources can complete, even if it asks for its maximum allocation. The best way to illustrate this is with an example:

> **CLASSIC SOFTWARE**
>
> **11. Mac OS and System 7** (Developer: Apple). Microsoft has relied on gradual improvement to its software, especially in its operating systems, while Apple got it right first time with its Mac OS system. Many reckon that it was 10 years ahead of all other systems. With the PC there were many difficulties, such as keeping compatibility with the original DOS, difficulties with the Intel 8086/88 memory model, support for a great number of peripherals, and the slowness of its internal buses (including the graphics adaptor). These all made software development of the PC difficult. Apple did not have compatibility to deal when it designed the Macintosh as it had a blank piece of paper to work with. It spent as much money on the operating system as it did on developing the hardware for the Macintosh.

Process A requires a maximum of 50 MB.
Process B requires a maximum of 40 MB.
Process C requires a maximum of 60 MB.
Process D requires a maximum of 40 MB.

The current state would be safe:

Process	*Current allocation*	*Maximum allocation required*
A	40	50
B	20	40
C	20	60
D	10	40
Resource unallocated	10	

This is safe as Process A can still complete, as there is still 10 MB to be allocated. This will be enough to complete this process, but no other processes would be given any more resources as all of the unallocated memory must be reserved for Process A. Process B possibly requires another 20 MB, Process C also possibly requires another 40 MB, and Process D possibly requires another 30 MB.

An unsafe condition would be:

Process	*Current allocation*	*Maximum allocation required*
A	15	50
B	30	40
C	40	60
D	10	40
Resource unallocated	5	

This is unsafe as there is only 5 MB of memory left, and this is not enough for any of the processes to complete. Thus we can have deadlock (unless a process is willing to give up its memory allocation). The operating system would reject any allocation which took it into the unsafe region. In summary the algorithm assumes:

- Each resource has exclusive access to resources that have been granted to it.
- Allocation is only granted if there is enough allocation left for at least one process to complete, and release its allocated resources.
- Processes which have a rejection on a requested resource must wait until some resources have been released, and that the allocated resource must stay in the safe region.

The main problems with the Banker algorithm are:

- Requires processes to define their maximum resource requirement.
- Requires the system to define the maximum amount of a resource.
- Requires a maximum amount of processes.
- Requires that processes return their resources in a finite time.
- Processes must wait for allocations to become available. A slow process may stop many other processes from running as it hogs the allocation.

6.3.7 Deadlock detection and recovery

The main technique that is used to detect a deadlocked situation is the existence of a circular wait. This detection process has a time overhead on the operation system, but the operating system can try and release deadlocked resources, rather than the user rebooting the system. A typical technique is to use resource allocation graphs, which indicate resource allocations and requests. An arrow from a process to a resource maps the request currently under consideration, and an arrow from a resource to a process indicates the resource has been allocated to that process. Squares represent processes, large circles represent classes of identical devices, and small circles drawn inside large circles indicate the number of identical devices of each class. This graph can be used to determine the processes that can complete their execution and the processes that will remain deadlocked. The graph will reduce for a process when all the requests have been granted, and will release the resources. If a graph cannot be reduced for a set of processes, deadlock occurs.

To undeadlock a system, one of the four deadlock conditions must be broken. This normally involves determining the deadlocked processes (which is often a difficult task). Once identified it is often necessary to kill one or more of the deadlocked processes, and release

> **CLASSIC SOFTWARE**
>
> **12. Netscape (Navigator/Communicator)/ Internet Explorer** (Developer: Netscape Communications Corporation (Navigator/Communicator)/Microsoft (Internet Explorer)). Web browsers interpret special hypertext pages which consist of the hypertext markup language (HTML) and JavaScript. They then display it in the given format. Netscape Navigator is one of the most widely used WWW browsers and is available for PCs (running Microsoft Windows), Unix workstations and Macintosh computers. It has since become the standard WWW browser and has many add-ons and enhancements, which have been added through continual development by Netscape, and other software developers (the source code is now freely available to anyone who wants it).

the resources which are allocated to it. The released resources will hopefully be released to the currently deadlocked processes, which can then complete successfully.

Memory allocation can cause a good deal of contention problems, especially if the system has a limited amount of memory that can be allocated. Most systems now operate a virtual memory system, where the storage memory of the system is used as additional memory over the physical memory. Unfortunately many systems use up their spare capacity, and the virtual memory system become limited. Thus processes which are currently running may not be able to complete, as there is a limit on the amount of allocatable memory. Thus some prediction on the maximum requirements of a process is useful in predicting how easy it will be to complete a process.

CLASSIC SOFTWARE

13. SideKick 1.0 (Developer: Borland International). Borland developed SideKick to provide a pop-up notepad, calendar, and calculator whenever the user wanted them. It used a TSR (Terminate and stay resident), and a hotkey, so that the user could quickly move from its current application to SideKick. In days of single-tasking DOS, around 1984, this was revolutionary, but in these days of multitasking Windows, it does not seem so.

6.4 RPC

Remote processing has many advantages over local processing, especially as it removes the loading on the local computer. In an attempt to standardize the protocol used to communicate and initiate remote processes, Sun Microsystems Inc. developed Remote Procedure Control (RPC), which has since been standardized in the RFC1050 document. It defines:

- **Servers**. This is software which implements the network services.
- **Services**. This is a collection of one or more remote programs.
- **Programs**. These implement one or more remote procedures.
- **Procedures**. These define the procedures, the parameters and the results of the RPC operation.
- **Clients**. This is the software that initiates remote procedure calls to services.
- **Versions**. This allows servers to implement different versions of the RPC software, in order to support previous versions.

Remote Procedure Call (RPC) provides the ability for clients to transparently execute procedures on remote systems of the network. RPC fits into the session layer of the OSI model (this model will be covered in more detail in a later chapter), as illustrated in Figure 6.6. This has the advantage of being able to communicate with most transport and network layer protocols, such as TCP/IP, UDP/IP or SPX/IPX. Typically, though, it uses TCP/IP as the transport/network layer, as this allows for reliable communications. TCP/IP itself allows for a virtual connection between two hosts and the data is checked for errors, whereas UDP/IP does not setup a connection, and does not provide any guarantee that the data has been received correctly by the session layer of the OSI model.

In a local procedure call model, a calling program inserts parameters into a predefined location, and then transfers control to the procedure, which reads the parameters from the predefined location. Eventually the calling procedure will regain control, and reads from a predefined location for the results of the called procedure. An RPC is similar to this, with a calling process on the client, and a server process on the server. The operation of the client and server is illustrated in Figure 6.7, and is as follows:

- The caller process sends a call message, with all the procedure's parameters, to the server process and waits for a reply message.
- On the arrival of a call message the server process extracts the procedure's parameters, and wakes up a dormant process, which is then run with the required parameters.
- After the process has completed, the server sends a reply message with the procedure's results. Once the reply message is received, the results of the procedure are extracted, and caller's execution is resumed.
- The server process then waits, dormant, for the next call message.

6.4.1 Transports, semantics and authentication

RPC does not provide any form of reliability, as it assumes that the protocol used to transmit and receive it is reliable, which is the reason that TCP/IP is typically used, as it provides for reliable transmissions. There may be several requests from a client to a server at a time, thus each client request has a transaction ID, which is used by the client to keep track of requests. Transaction IDs do not have to be unique and can be used with different requests (obviously the previous request would have to be completed, before the same ID is used again). The server has no choice on the ID, and must only use it to identify its response to the client.

An important part of RPC is authentication, as a server would be open to abuse if any client was allowed to remotely run processes on it. This is a typical attack on a system, and, if too many processes are run on a computer, it will eventually grind to a halt, and typically requires to be rebooted. RPC supports various different types of authentication protocols.

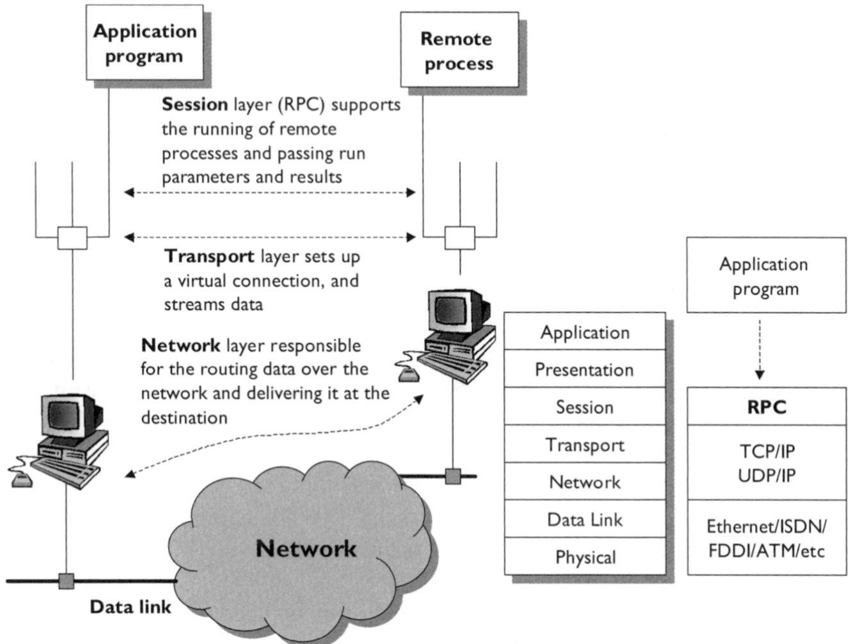

Figure 6.6 OSI model with RPC

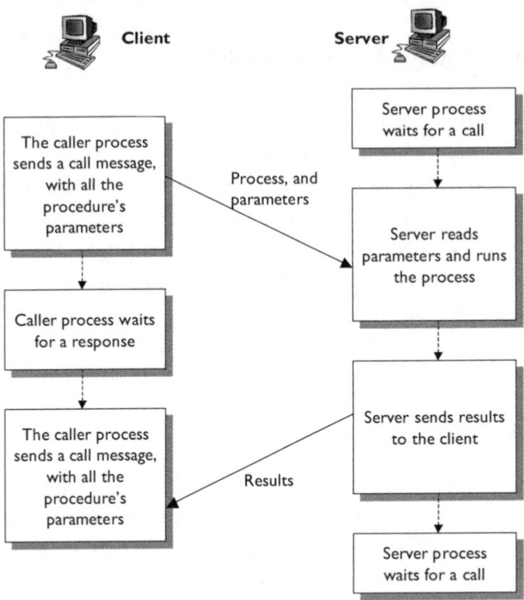

Figure 6.7 Operation of RPC

6.4.2 RPC protocol

The RPC protocol provides:

- A unique specification of the called procedure.
- A mechanism for matching response parameters with request messages.
- Authentication of both callers and servers. The call message has two authentication fields (the credentials and verifier), and the reply message has one authentication field (the response verifier).
- Protocol errors/messages (such as incorrect versions, errors in procedure parameters, indication on why a process failed and reasons for incorrect authentication).

RPC has three unsigned fields which uniquely identify the called procedure:

- **Remote program number.** These are numbers which are defined by a central authority (like Sun Microsystems).
- **Remote program version number.** This defines the version number, and allows for migration of the protocol, where older versions are still supported. Different versions can possibly support different message calls. The server must be able to cope with this.
- **Remote procedure number.** This identifies the called procedure, and is defined in the specification of the specific program's protocol. For example, file service may define that an 8 defines a read operation and a 10 defines a write operation.

The reply message can give some indication of the cause of an error, including:

- Version number not supported. The returned message contains the upper and lower version of the version number that is supported.

- Remote program is not available on the remote system.
- Requested procedure number does not exist.
- Parameters passed are incorrect.

The RPC message has the following format:

- Message type. This is either CALL (0) or REPLY (1).
- Message status. There are two different message status fields, depending on whether it is a CALL or a REPLY. These are:

  - o CALL. Followed by a field which gives the status of: SUCCESS (executed successfully – 0), PROG_UNAVAIL (remote does not support the requested program – 1), PROG_MISMATCH (cannot support version – 2), PROC_UNAVAIL (procedure unavailable – 3).
  - o REPLY. Followed by MSG_ACCEPTED (0) and MSG_DENIED (1). If the message was denied the field following defines the reason, such as: RPC_MISMATCH (Version mismatch – 0) or AUTH_ERROR (cannot authenticate the caller – 1).

Call messages then have:

- Rpcvers. RPC version number (unsigned integer).
- Prog, vers and proc. Specifies the remote program, its version number and the procedure within the remote program (all unsigned integers).
- Cred. authentication credentials.
- Verf. authentication verifier.
- Procedure specific parameters.

6.4.3 RPC authentication

Authentication is important as it should authenticate both the caller and the server, as this bars invalid callers from getting access to the server, and vice versa. The call message has two authentication fields (the credentials and verifier), and the reply message has one authentication field (the response verifier). This can either be:

- **No authentication** (AUTH_NULL). No authentication is made when callers do not know who they are or when the server does not care who the caller is. This type of method would be used on a system that did not have external connections to networks, and assumes that all the callers are valid.
- **Unix authentication** (AUTH_UNIX). Unix authentication uses the Unix authentication system, which generates a data structure with a stamp (an arbitrary ID which the caller machine may generate), machine name (such as 'Apollo'), UID (caller's effective user ID), GID (the caller's effective group ID) and GIDS (an array of groups which contain the caller as a member).
- **Short authentication** (AUTH_SHORT).

CLASSIC SOFTWARE

14. Excel for the Macintosh (Developer: Microsoft). Microsoft stole the thunder from VisiCalc and Lotus 1-2-3 when it produced a graphical version of a spreadsheet. Microsoft saw the potential of a graphical spreadsheet and quickly ported it to the PC. In the end, Lotus was too slow to convert Lotus 1-2-3 to Windows (going initially for an OS/2 version), and lost a considerable market share that would never be recovered.

- **DES authentication** (AUTH_DES). Unix authentication suffers from two problems: the naming is too Unix oriented and there is no verifier (so credentials can easily be faked). DES overcomes this by addressing the caller using its network name (such as 'unix.111@mycomputer.net') instead of by an operating system specific integer. These network names are unique on the Internet. For example unix.111@mycomputer.net identifies user ID number 111 on the mycomputer.net system.

Apart from providing a unique network name, DES authentication also provides authentication of the client, and vice versa. It does this by the client generating a 128-bit DES key which is passed to the server in the first RPC call. In any communications, the client then reads the current time, and encrypts it with the key. The server will then be able to decrypt the encrypted timestamp, as it knows the encryption key. If the decrypted timestamp is close to the current time, then the server knows that the client must be valid. Thus it is important that both the client and server keep the correct time (perhaps by consulting an Internet Time Server at regular intervals). After the initial timestamp has been validated, the server then authenticates following timestamps so that they have a later time than the previous timestamp and that the timestamp has not expired. This timestamp window is defined in the first RPC call, and thus defines the lifetime of the conversation.

The server authenticates itself to the client by sending back the encrypted timestamp it received from the client, minus one second. If the client gets anything different than this, it will reject it.

6.4.4 RPC programming

Distributed programming is an art that should produce robust, and reliable problems, as many programs provide a foundation for many other programs. The level of control depends on how well the programmer wants to control the operation of the remote process control. For this RPC defines three main layers:

CLASSIC SOFTWARE

15. PageMaker (Developer: Aldus). A classic package which has been used in millions of publications. Its approach was simple; it made the computer invisible, and made the users feel as if they were using traditional page design methods.

- **Highest layer.** At this level the calls are totally transparent to the operating system, the computer type and the network. With this the programmer simply calls the required library routine, and does not have to worry about any of the underlying computer type, operating system or networking. For example, the `rnusers` routine returns the number of users on a remote computer (as given in Program 6.2).
- **Middle layer.** At this level the programmer does not have to worry about the network connection (such as the TCP sockets), the UNIX system, or other low-level implementation mechanisms. It just makes a remote procedure call to routines on other computers, and is the most common implementation as it gives increased amount of control over the RPC call. These calls are made with: `registerrpc` (which obtains a unique system-wide procedure identification number); `callrpc` (which executes a remote procedure call); and `svc_run`. The middle layer, in some more complex applications, does not allow for timeout specifications, choice of transport, UNIX process control, or error flexibility in case of errors. If these are required, the lower layer is used.
- **Lowest layer.** At this level there is full control over the RPC call, and this can be used to create robust and efficient connections.

At the highest layer the programmer simply uses a call to the RCP library. In UNIX this library is typically named `librpcsvc.a`, and the program is compiled with:

```
cc progname.c -l lrpcsvc
```

Program 6.2

```
#include <stdio.h>
int main(int argc, char *argv[])
{
    int users;
    if (argc != 2) {
        fprintf(stderr, "Use: rnusers hostname\n");
        return(1);
    }
    if ((users = rnusers(argv[1])) < 0) {
        fprintf(stderr, "Error: rnusers\n");
        exit(-1);
    }
    printf("There are %d users on %s\n", users, argv[1]);
    return(0);
}
```

Example RPC server library routines are:

- `rnusers`. Returns number of users on remote machine.
- `rusers`. Returns information about users on remote machine.
- `havedisk`. Determines if remote machine has a disk.
- `rstats`. Gets performance data from remote kernel.
- `rwall`. Writes to specified remote machines.
- `yppasswd`. Updates user password in Yellow Pages.

CLASSIC SOFTWARE

16. Adobe Type (Developer: Adobe). An important change in desktop publishing was the use of enhanced fonts, such as the Type 1 PostScript fonts available from Adobe. Adobe has also produced one of the standard methods to transfer files around computer systems, without losing any layout information. This form is named PDF (Portable Document Format), and is now well integrated with the WWW.

At the next level, the middle layer, the programmer has more control over the RPC call using `callrpc` and `registerrpc`. Program 6.3 determines the number of remote users, and uses the `callrpc` routine which has the following parameters:

`argv(1)`	Remote server name
`RUSERSPROG`	Program
`RUSERSVERSION`	Version
`RUSERSPROCVAL`	Procedure number. Together with the program and version numbers, this defines the procedure to be called.
`xdr_void`	Defines the data type for the next argument (which is the parameter to be sent to the remote procedure). As there are no arguments to be sent the data type is void. Other XDR types for basic data types are: `xdr_bool`, `xdr_char`, `xdr_u_char`, `xdr_enum`, `xdr_int`, `xdr_u_int`,

xdr_long, xdr_u_long, xdr_short, xdr_u_short and xdr_wrapstring.

`0`	An argument to be encoded and passed to the remote procedure.
`xdr_u_long`	Defines the return type for next variable to be a long integer (users).
`&users`	Pointer to the users variable, in which the number of users is returned to.

If the routine is successful the returned value will be zero, otherwise it will contain a status value, which is defined in `clnt.h`.

Program 6.3

```
#include <stdio.h>
#include <rpc.h>
#define RUSERSPROG          10002 /* Program number    */
#define RUSERSVERSION       2     /* Version number    */
#define RUSERPROCVAL        1     /* Procedure number  */
int main(int argc, char *argv[]) {
unsigned long  users;
int            rtn;
    if (argc != 2) {
         fprintf(stderr, "Use: nusers hostname\n"); exit(-1);
    }
    if (rtn = callrpc(argv[1], RUSERSPROG, RUSERSVERSION, RUSERSPROCVAL,
                      xdr_void, 0, xdr_u_long, &users) != 0) {
           clnt_perrno(stat); return(1);
    }
    printf("There are %d users on %s\n", users, argv[1]);
    return(0);
}
```

Typically a server registers all its RPC calls, and then goes into an infinite wait loop. Program 6.4 shows an example of a program on a server which registers the `nuser` RPC call. The program assumes that the `nuser` routine exists in the RPC library. The `svc_run` routine responds to remote calls and initiates the remote procedure.

Program 6.4

```
#include <stdio.h>
#include <rpc.h>
#define RUSERSPROG          10002 /* Program number    */
#define RUSERSVERSION       2     /* Version number    */
#define RUSERPROCVAL        1     /* Procedure number  */

char   *nuser();
int    main(void)
{
    registerrpc(RUSERSPROG, RUSERSVERS, RUSERSPROC_NUM, nuser,
                                        xdr_void, xdr_u_long);

    svc_run();

    fprintf(stderr, "Error: server terminated\n");
    return(1);
}
```

In UNIX the `/etc/rpc` file contains a listing of the RPC services (notice that 100002 corresponds to `rusers`). The first column defines the RPC process name, the second the procedure number, and the third defines an alias for the process (the fourth column has been added to give extra information). An example is:

`portmapper`	`100000`	`portmap sunrpc`	*Port mapper*
`rstatd`	`100001`	`rstat rstat_svc rup perfmeter`	*Remote stats*
`rusersd`	**`100002`**	**`rusers`**	*Number of users*
`nfs`	`100003`	`nfsprog`	*Network File System (NFS)*
`ypserv`	`100004`	`ypprog`	*Network Information Service (NIS)*
`mountd`	`100005`	`mount showmount`	*Mount daemon*
`ypbind`	`100007`		*NLS binder*
`walld`	`100008`	`rwall shutdown`	*Shutdown message*
`yppasswdd`	`100009`	`yppasswd`	*yppasswd server*
`etherstatd`	`100010`	`etherstat`	*Ether stats*
`rquotad`	`100011`	`rquotaprog quota rquota`	*Disk quotas*
`sprayd`	`100012`	`spray`	*Spray packets*
`selection_svc`	`100015`	`selnsvc`	*Selection service*
`database_svc`	`100016`		*Remote database access*
`rexd`	`100017`	`rex`	*Remote execution*
`sched`	`100019`		*Scheduling service*
`llockmgr`	`100020`		*Local lock manager*
`nlockmgr`	`100021`		*Network lock manager*

6.5 Multiprocessor systems

Computer systems have generally evolved around a single centralized processor with an associated area of memory. This main processor performs most of the operations within the computer and also controls reads and writes to and from memory. This type of arrangement is useful in that there is little chance of a conflict when addressing any peripheral as only the single processor can access it. With the evolution of microelectronics it is now possible to build computers with many processors. This has the advantage over a distributed system over a network, as the communications can be faster, as the distances involved are smaller.

It is typical on modern computers to have several processors, apart from the central processor. For example many computers now have dedicated processors to control the graphical display, processors to control the input/output functions of the computer, processors to control the hard-disk drive, and so on.

CLASSIC SOFTWARE

17. Windows 3.x (Developer: Microsoft). The first two versions of Microsoft Windows were pretty poor. They had a poor interface, and still had all of the constraints of DOS (which are, of course, great). Microsoft Windows 3.0 changed all that with an enhanced usage of icons and windows, greater integration, increased memory usage. It was still 16-bit, but started to make full use of the processor, and gave a hint of the forthcoming multitasking (two processes at a time, using time sharing). Other enhancements were OLE, True Type fonts, and drag-and-drop commands. Windows for Workgroups was Microsoft's first attempt at trying to network PCs together, but it was too complicated to setup, and not very powerful.

Computer systems, especially servers, are also now being designed with several processors that can run application programs, at a time. Each of these processors can access its own localized memory and/or a shared memory. This type of multiprocessor system, though, leads to several problems, including device conflicts and processor synchronization. Figure 6.8 illustrates the two types of systems.

A memory conflict occurs when a process tries to read from or write to an area of memory at the same time as another is trying to access it. Normally, multiprocessor systems have mechanisms that lock areas of memory when a processor is accessing it. This is known as bus mastering, and there must be some arbitration mechanism between the processors to synchronize the access to the system buses.

Parallel systems require processor synchronization because one or more processors may require data from other processors. This synchronization can either be hard-wired into the system using data and addressing buses, or by a master controlling processor that handles the communication among slave processors (processor farms). They may also be controlled by the operating system software.

The two main classifications of parallel systems are:

- **Small-scale parallelized systems**. This normally involves just a few processors, and is typically used on server systems. As many programs on general-purpose servers cannot run totally in parallel there will not be a direct scaling between the number of processors and the processing power of the system. Small-scale parallelization is normally used to overcome the limitations in maximum processing power of current systems. For example a system may require a processing power of 1 billion operations, but current systems may only give 50% of this power. Thus a four-processor array may give the required processing power.
- **Large-scale parallelized systems**. This normally involves a massive number of processors running in parallel in specialized applications, and typically has a specialized architecture which runs specialist software. Only certain applications scale well with large-scale parallelization. These tend to be the ones which do not require a great deal of processor intercommunication (as relative to processing time per processor). Searching and permutation programs are good examples of large-scale parallalization, such as decryption programs and biological gene searching.

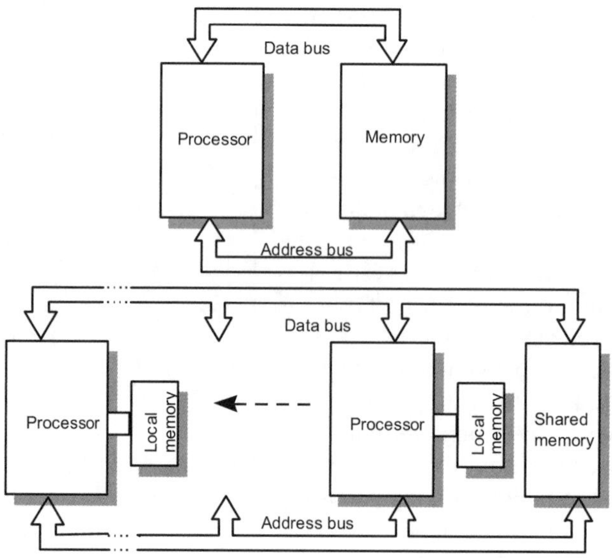

Figure 6.8 Single and multiprocessor systems

6.5.1 Parallel techniques

There are two main methods used when dividing computational tasks to individual processors. These are either to divide the task into stages in a pipeline or to divide them into parallel streams, as illustrated in Figure 6.9. A mixed method uses a mixture of pipelines and parallel streams.

The pipeline method is preferable when there is a large number of computations on a small amount of data. Distributing data between streams can be awkward, since calculations often involve two or more consecutive items of data. Parallel streams are preferable for simple operations on large amounts of data, such as mathematical processing operations.

A major problem with pipelines is that it is difficult to ensure that all the processors have an equal loading. If one processor has a heavier workload than its neighbours then this processor holds up the neighbours while they are waiting for data from the burdened processor.

It is always important to recognize the inherent parallelism in the problem and whether to allocate fast processors to critical parts and slower ones for the rest, or to equalize the workload, called load balancing.

6.5.2 Processor farms

Processor farming is a technique for distributing work with automatic load balancing. It uses a master processor to distribute tasks to a network of slaves. The slave processors only get tasks when they are idle.

It is important in a parallel system that processor tasks are large enough because each task has its overheads. These include the handling overhead of the master controller and also the interprocessor communication. If the tasks are too small then these overheads take a significant amount of time and cause bottlenecks in the system. The major problem in distributing tasks to an increasing number of processors is that as the actual processing time reduces, the amount of time spent passing the results between the processors increases.

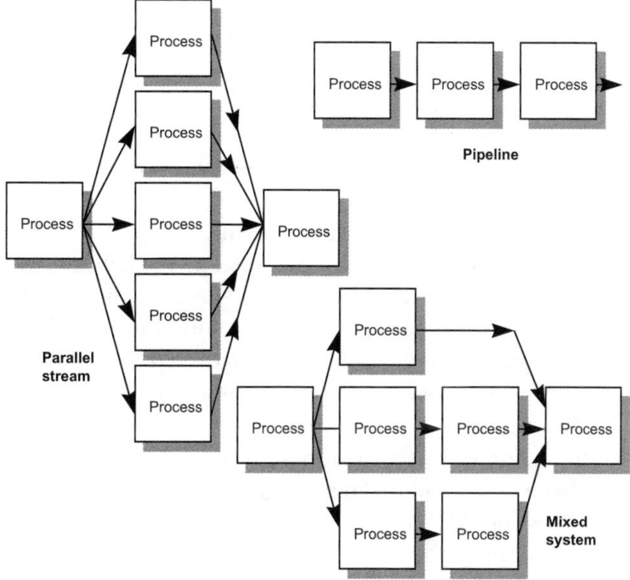

Figure 6.9 Pipeline, parallel stream and mixed systems

6.6 Distributed file systems

Files systems typically use a directory structure which is based on folders which contain files and/or subfolders. They store three main types of files:

> **CLASSIC SOFTWARE**
>
> **18. Microsoft Office.** The revenues from DOS allowed Microsoft to continue developing its application packages, such as Word, Excel, Access and PowerPoint, when many of its first attempts were inferior to its competitors, and typically were bug ridden. A classic example of this was Word 3.0, which had over 700 bugs, some of which caused the system to destroy data, or caused the computer to crash. Microsoft eventually had to give customers free upgrades, at a cost of over $1 million. Classic versions were Word for Windows 2.0, Word 6.0 and Excel 5.0.

- **Information**. This will typically be user files, such as word processor files, spreadsheets, and e-mail messages.
- **Program files**. These will typically be application programs, such as a WWW browser program, word processor program, spreadsheet program, and so on.
- **Configuration data**. These will be important data which define the configuration of the user's computer. Typical storage will be hardware configuration data for the computer, the setup of user's desktop, and so on.

In the past, most information was stored locally on a computer, or centrally on a mainframe computer, but there is now a trend to distribute information around networks. This has many advantages over traditional localized information (Figure 6.10):

- **File system mirrors the corporate structure.** File systems can be distributed over a corporate network, which might span cities, countries or even continents. The setup of a complete network file system over a corporation can allow the network to mirror the logical setup of the organization, rather than its physical and geographical organization. For example the Sales Department might be distributed around the world, but the network in which they connect to is identical to the way that the Sales Department is organized.
- **Easier to protect the access rights on file systems**. In a distributed file system it is typical to have a strong security policy on the file system, and each file will have an owner who can define the privileges on this file. File systems on user computers tend to have limited user security.
- **Increased access to single sources of information**. Many users can have access to a single source of information. Having multiple versions of a file can cause a great deal of problems, especially if it is not known as to which one is the most up to date.
- **Automated updates**. Several copies of the same information can be stored, and when any one of them is updated they are synchronized to keep each of them up-to-date. Users can thus have access to a local copy of data, rather than accessing a remote copy of it. This is called mirroring files.
- **Improved backup facilities.** A user's computer can be switched-off, but their files can still be backedup from the distributed file system.
- **Increased reliability**. The distributed file system can have a backbone which is constructed from reliable and robust hardware, which are virtually 100% reliable, even when there is a power failure, or when there is a hardware fault.

- **Larger file systems.** In some types of distributed file systems it is possible to build-up large file systems from a network of connected disk drives.
- **Easier to administer.** Administrators can easily view the complete file system.
- **Interlinking of databases.** Small databases can be linked together to create large databases, which can be configured for a given application. The future may also bring the concept of data mining, where agent programs will search for information with a given profile by interrogating databases on the Internet.
- **Limiting file access.** Organizations can setup an organization file structure, in which users can have a limited view of the complete file system.

The structure of file systems has, in the past, been based on the physical connection of file systems to the network. An enhanced method of organizing file systems is to setup a structure which mirrors the organizational structure of the organization. This makes it easier for users to view the file system, as it is more logical in its structure. This is important because for most users the organizational structure makes more sense to them than the structure of files on a computer system. Figure 6.11 shows two file structures. The one on the left-hand side is possibly easier for an experienced user to use, and the one on the right-hand side is more intuitive to someone who understands the organizational structure of the organization. File systems, such as Novell NDS and Microsoft Active Directory try to setup file systems which have a global file structure which try to mirror the structure of the organization. In these systems, resources, other than files such as printers, and file servers can be mapped onto the file system.

Most file systems have a hierarchical file structure, which has directories that contain subdirectories files and devices. The file system, itself, is a tree on a single server (normally a single disk or a physical partition) which has a specified root. Some systems use a mount system that mounts file systems onto a single tree, while others use a forest of file systems, where the file systems appear individually. If possible, the mounting of a drive system should be transparent to the user, and should be done automatically so that the user treats the mounted drive just as a local resource. A major problem, though, is the security of the remotely connected drive, thus each mounted drive must have strict rules on the access rights for the local user.

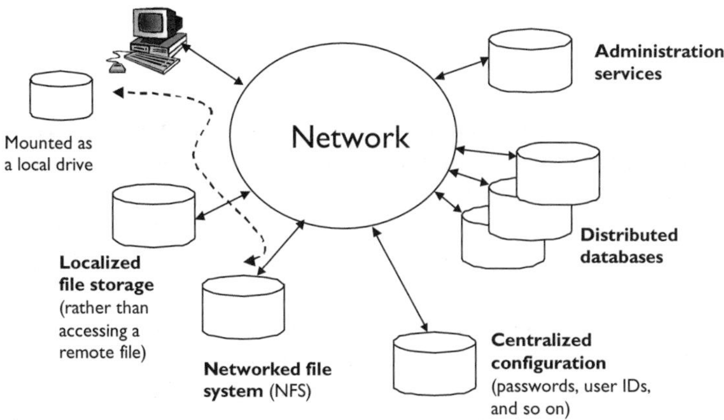

Figure 6.10 Distributed file system

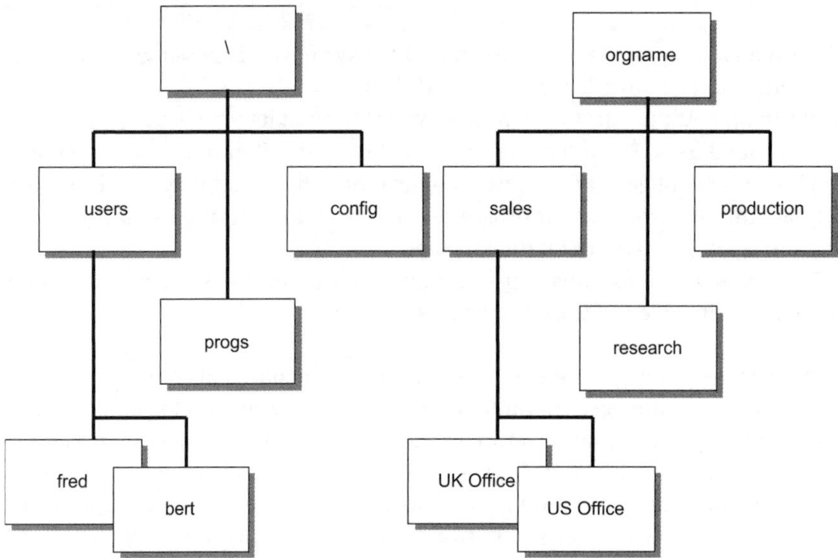

Figure 6.11 Traditional file structure v. corporate structure

Drives can either be mounted locally to a computer as a single tree (as UNIX) or as a forest of drives (as used with Microsoft Windows). In Figure 6.12, one of the computers has created a single tree that uses its local drives to create the /etc and /user directories, and then mounts two networked drives to give /progs and /sys. The global file system will then be mounted onto the common tree, with four subdirectories below the top-level directory (/). The advantages of this type of system are:

- The structure of the file system, and the drives that are mounted are transparent to the user. As far as the user is concerned the complete file system is viewable.
- Every user can view the complete file system, if required.
- The file system is consistent around the network, and can be setup on a per computer basis.

With the forest of disks, a disk drive is mounted locally as if it is a local drive. In the example in Figure 6.12, the remote drives have been mounted as E: and F:. Its main advantage over the global file system is that:

- It is easier to determine if the remote drive is mounted, as it will appear as a mounted resource. With a single tree it is often difficult to determine if a drive is loaded onto the global file system as the basic structure still exists.
- Less complex than a global file, and easier to mount drives, but can become complex to setup if there are many remote drives to be mounted.

Its main disadvantage is it is more difficult to setup than the single tree system as the local mount drive must be specified, along with the path. In the global file system, files are mounted on the system in a consistent way, such as with E:\FREDS_DRIVE. If the local system does not mount the remote drive onto the required disk partition, there may be problems in the configuration of the system.

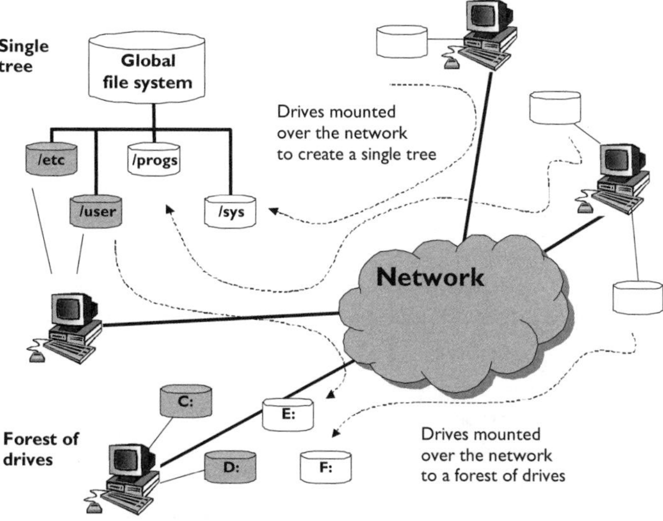

Figure 6.12 Distributed file system

6.6.1 NFS

The Network File System (NFS) is defined in RFC1094 and allows computers to share the same files over a network. It was originally developed by Sun Microsystems, and has the great advantage that it is independent of the host operating system and can provide data sharing among different types of systems (heterogeneous systems). This is achieved using Remote Procedure Call (RPC), on top of XDR, which provides a standard method of representing data types. RPC is defined in RFC1057, and XDR is RFC1014.

NFS uses a client-server architecture where a computer can act as an NFS client, an NFS server or both. An NFS client makes requests to access data and files on servers; the server then makes that specific resource available to the client. NFS servers are passive and stateless. They wait for requests from clients and do not maintain any information on the client. One advantage of servers being stateless is that it is possible to reboot servers without adverse consequences to the client. Servers do not preserve the current status of any of their clients, which means that a client can simply retry a request from a server, if it fails to get a response (in the event of a failure of the network or the server). If the server was stateful, the client would have to know that a server had crashed or that the network connection had broken, so that it knew which state is should be in, when the connection was returned, or when the server came back on-line.

The server grants remote access privileges to a restricted set of clients, which allows clients to mount remote directory trees onto their local file system. The components of NFS are as follows (Figure 6.13 shows how the protocols fit into the OSI model):

- **NFS** remote file access may be accompanied by network information service (NIS).
- External data representation (**XDR**), which is a universal data representation, used by all nodes, and provides a common data representation if applications are to run transparently on a heterogeneous network or if data is to be shared among heterogeneous systems. Each node translates machine-dependent data formats to XDR format when

sending and translating data. It is XDR that enables heterogeneous nodes and operating systems to communicate with each other over the network.

- Remote Procedure Call (**RPC**) allows clients to transparently execute procedures on remote systems of the network. NFS services run on top of the RPC, which corresponds to the session layer of the OSI model.
- Network lock manager (`rpc.lockd`) allows users to coordinate and control access to information on the network. It supports file locking and synchronizes access to shared files.

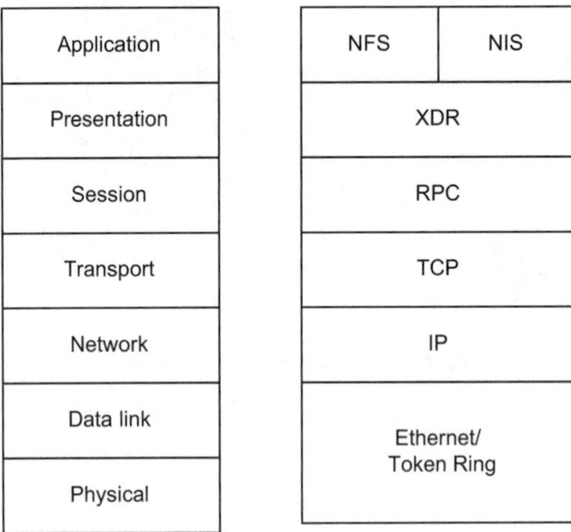

Figure 6.13 NFS services protocol stack

6.6.2 NFS protocol

NFS assumes a hierarchical file structure. It can be used to mount file systems which map into a single tree (as the UNIX file system), or it can be used to add a file system as one of a forest of drives (as Microsoft Windows). NFS looks up one component of a pathname, at a time, as different file systems use different separators to identify a pathname (for example, UNIX uses '/' and Microsoft Windows uses '\', while others use periods).

The main NFS protocol is defined as a set of procedures with arguments and results defined using the RPC language. Each of the procedures is synchronous, and the client can assume that a response from a request completes the operation. The procedures used are:

No.	*Procedure*	*Name*
0	void NULL(void)	No operation
1	attrstat GETATTR(fhandle)	Get file attributes
2	attrstat SETATTR(sattrargs)	Set file attributes
6	readres READ(readargs)	Read from file
8	attrstat WRITE(writeargs)	Write to file
9	diropres CREATE(createargs)	Create file
10	stat REMOVE(diropargs)	Remove file
11	stat RENAME(renameargs)	Rename file
12	stat LINK(linkargs)	Create link to file
13	stat SYMLINK(symlinkargs)	Create symbolic link
14	diropres MKDIR(createargs)	Create directory
15	stat RMDIR(diropargs)	Remove directory
16	readdirres READDIR(readdirargs)	Read from directory

Figure 6.14 shows a client sending RPC procedures to the server, which responds back with the required data, parameters or with a status flag. Typical status flags are: NFS_OK (success), NFSERR_PERM (not owner), NFSERR_NOENT (no such file or directory), NFSERR_IO (some sort of hard error occurred), NFSERR_NXIO (no such device or address), NFSERR_ACCES (permission denied), NFSERR_EXIST (the file specified already exists), NFSERR_NODEV (no such device) and NFSERR_NOTDIR (not a directory).

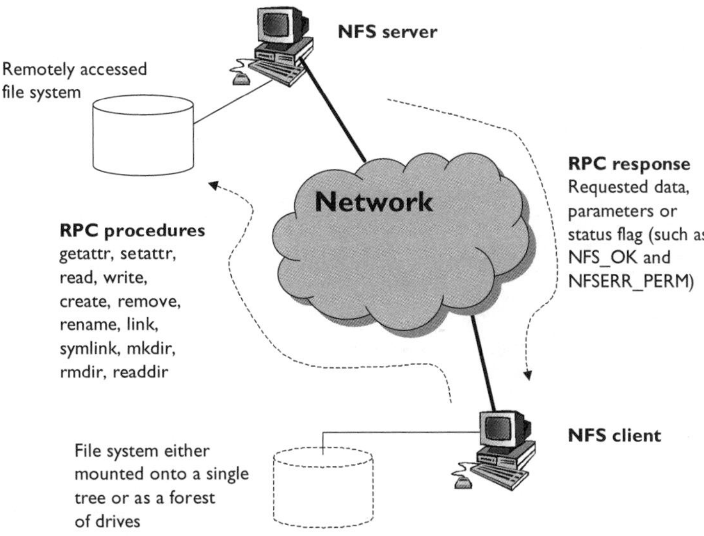

Figure 6.14 RPC procedures and responses

Network Information Service (NIS)

As networks grow in size it becomes more difficult for the system administrator to maintain the security of the network. An important factor is the maintenance of a passwords file, where new users are added with the group, and any other information (such as their default home directory). In most networks a user should be able to log into any computer within a domain. Thus a global password and configuration files are required. This can be achieved with NIS, which is an optional network control program which maintains the network configuration files over a network. NIS allows the system manager to centralize the key configuration files on a single master server. If anyone wants to log into the network the master server is consulted (or one of its slave servers). Figure 6.15 illustrates some of the files that the server maintains; these include password (which contains the passwords for all the users within the domain), and groups (the group that the user is associated with). It is thus easy for the system administrator to add and delete users from the NIS server, and these changes will be reflected over the domain. A user cannot log into any of the clients, without the client checking with the server to see if they have a valid login and password.

Previously NIS was named *Yellow Pages* (**YP**), but has changed its name as this is a registered trademark of the British Telecommunications company. NIS normally administers the network configuration files such as `/etc/group` (which defines the user groups), `/etc/hosts` (which defines the IP address and symbolic names of nodes on a network), `/etc/passwd` (which contains information, such as user names, encrypted passwords, home directories, and so on). An excerpt from a `passwd` file is:

```
root:FDEc6.32:1:0:Super user:/user:/bin/csh
fred:jt.06hLdiSDaA:2:4:Fred Blogs:/user/fred:/bin/csh
fred2:jtY067SdiSFaA:3:4:Fred Smith:/user/fred2:/bin/csh
```

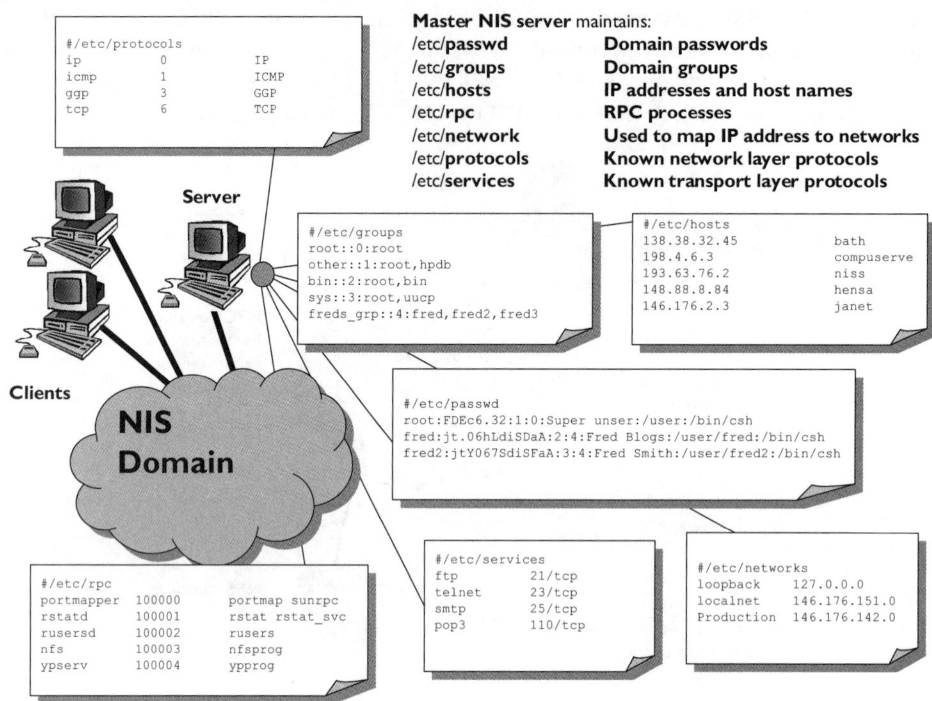

Figure 6.15 NIS domain

This passwd file has three defined users; these are root, fred and fred2. The encrypted password is given in the second field (between the first and second column), and the third field is a unique number that defines the user (in this case fred is 2 and fred2 is 3). The fourth field in this case defines the group number (which ties up with the /etc/groups file). An example of a groups file is given next. It can be seen from this file that group 4 is defined as freds_grp, and contains three users: fred, fred2 and fred3. The fifth field is simply a comment field and in this case it contains the user's names. In the next field each user's home directory is defined and the final field contains the initial UNIX shell (in this case it is the C-shell).

```
root::0:root
other::1:root,hpdb
bin::2:root,bin
sys::3:root,uucp
freds_grp::4:fred,fred2,fred3
```

A sample listing of a directory shows that a file owned by fred has the group name freds_grp.

```
> ls -l
-r-sr-xr-x   1 fred     freds_grp  24576    Apr 22  2000 file1
```

```
-r-xr-xr-x  13 fred     freds_grp  40       Apr 22  2000 file2
dr-xr-xr-x   2 fred     freds_grp  1024     Aug  5 14:01 myfile
-r-xr-sr-x   1 fred     freds_grp  24576    Apr 22  2000 text2.ps
-r-xr-xr-x   2 fred     freds_grp  16384    Apr 22  2000 temp1.txt
```

An excerpt from the `/etc/hosts` file is shown next.

```
138.38.32.45      bath
198.4.6.3         compuserve
193.63.76.2       niss
148.88.8.84       hensa
146.176.2.3       janet
146.176.151.51    sun
```

The `/etc/protocols` file contains information with known protocols used on the Internet.

```
# The form for each entry is:
# <official protocol name> <protocol number> <aliases>
# Internet (IP) protocols

ip       0  IP       # internet protocol, pseudo protocol number
icmp     1  ICMP     # internet control message protocol
ggp      3  GGP      # gateway-gateway protocol
tcp      6  TCP      # transmission control protocol
egp      8  EGP      # exterior gateway protocol
pup      12 PUP      # PARC universal packet protocol
udp      17 UDP      # user datagram protocol
hmp      20 HMP      # host monitoring protocol
xns-idp  22 XNS-IDP  # Xerox NS IDP
rdp      27 RDP      # "reliable datagram" protocol
```

The `/etc/netgroup` file defines network-wide groups used for permission checking when doing remote mounts, remote logins, and remote shells. Here is a sample file:

```
# The format for each entry is: groupname  member1  member2 ...
#  (hostname, username, domainname)
engineering hardware software (host3, mikey, hp)
hardware (hardwhost1, chm, hp)   (hardwhost2, dae, hp)
software (softwhost1, jad, hp)   (softwhost2, dds, hp)
```

NIS master server and slave server

With NIS, a single node on a network acts as the NIS master server, with a number of NIS slave servers, which receive their NIS information from the master server. The slaves are important in that they hold copies of the most up-to-date version of the NIS database, so if the master were to crash, or become uncontactable, the slaves could still provide password, group, and other NIS information to the clients in the domain. The slaves also relieve the workload on the master, as it may become busy responding to many NIS requests. When a client first starts up it sends out a broadcast to all NIS servers (master or slaves) on the network and waits for the first one to respond. The client then binds to the first that responds and addresses all NIS requests to that server. If this server becomes inoperative then an NIS client will automatically rebind to the first NIS server which responds to another broadcast. Figure 6.16 illustrates this.

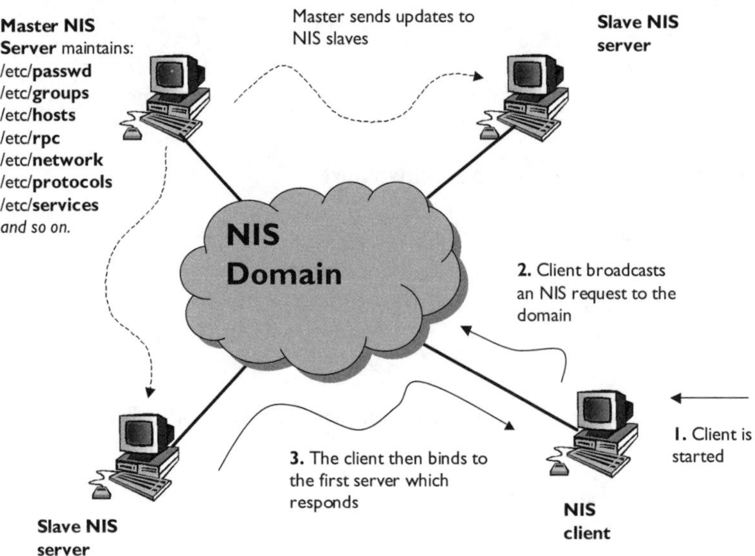
Master NIS
Server maintains:
/etc/passwd
/etc/groups
/etc/hosts
/etc/rpc
/etc/network
/etc/protocols
/etc/services
and so on.
Master sends updates to
NIS slaves
Slave NIS
server
NIS
Domain
2. Client broadcasts
an NIS request to the
domain
1. Client is
started
3. The client then binds to
the first server which
responds
NIS
client
Slave NIS
server

Figure 6.16 NIS domain

NIS domain

An NIS domain is a logical grouping of the set of maps contained on NIS servers. The rules for NIS domains are:

- All nodes in an NIS domain have the same domain name.
- Only one master server exists on an NIS domain.
- Each NIS domain can have zero or more slave servers.

An NIS domain is a subdirectory of `/usr/etc/yp` on each NIS server, where the name of the subdirectory is the name of the NIS domain. All directories that appear under `/usr/etc/yp` are assumed to be domains that are served by an NIS server. Thus to remove a domain being served, the user deletes the domain's subdirectory name from `/etc/etc/yp` on all of its servers.

The start-up file on most UNIX systems is the `/etc/rc` file. This automatically calls the `/etc/netnfsrc` file which contains the default NIS domain name, and uses the program `domainname`.

NFS remote file access

To initially mount a remote directory (or file system) onto a local computer the superuser must do the following:

- On the server, export the directory to the client.
- On the client, mount (or import) the directory.

For example suppose the remote directory `/user` is to be mounted onto the host `miranda` as the directory `/win`. To achieve this operation the following are setup:

1. The superuser logs on to the remote server and edits the file `/etc/exports` adding the

/user directory.

2. The superuser then runs the program exportfs to make the /user directory available to the client.

```
% exportfs -a
```

3. The superuser then logs into the client and creates a mount point /win (empty directory).

```
% mkdir /mnt
```

4. The remote directory can then be mounted with:

```
% mount miranda:/user /win
```

NFS maintains the file /etc/mnttab which contains a record of the mounted file systems. The general format is:

special_file_name dir type opts freq passno mount_time cnode_id

where *mount_time* contains the time the file system was mounted using mount. Sample contents of /etc/mnttab could be:

```
/dev/dsk/c201d6s0    /                  hfs   defaults 0 1 850144122 1
/dev/dsk/c201d5s0    /win               hfs   defaults 1 2 850144127 1
castor:/win          /net/castor_win    nfs   rw,suid  0 0 850144231 0
miranda:/win         /net/miranda_win   nfs   rw,suid  0 0 850144291 0
spica:/usr/opt       /opt               nfs   rw,suid  0 0 850305936 0
triton:/win          /net/triton_win    nfs   rw,suid  0 0 850305936 0
```

In this case there are two local drivers (/dev/dsk/c201d6s0 is mounted as the root directory and /dev/dsk/c201d5s0 is mounted locally as /win). There are also four remote directories which are mounted from remote servers (castor, miranda, spica and triton). The directory mounted from castor is the /win directory and it is mounted locally as /net/castor_win.hfs defines a UNIX format disk and nfs defines that the disk is mounted over NFS.

A disk can be unmounted from a system using the umount command, e.g.

```
% umount miranda:/win
```

Network configuration files

The main files used to setup networking are as follows:

/etc/checklist	is a list of directories or files that are automatically mounted at boot time.
/etc/exports	contains a list of directories or files that clients may import.
/etc/inetd.conf	contains information about servers started by inetd (the Internet daemon). Listing 6.5 shows an example of the inetd.conf file. It can be seen that it includes the service name, socket type (stream or datagram), the protocol (TCP or UDP), flags, the owner, the server

path, and any other arguments. Lines which begin with the '#' character are ignored by `inetd`. It can be seen that many of the Internet-related programs, such as FTP and TELNET are started here, as well as the login program (LOGIN).

`/etc/netgroup` contains a mapping of network group names to a set of node, user, and NIS domain names.

`/etc/netnfsrc` is automatically started at run time and initiates the required daemons and servers, and defines the node as a client or server.

`/etc/rpc` maps the RPC program names to the RPC program numbers and vice versa.

`/usr/adm/inetd.sec` checks the Internet address of the host requesting a service against the list of hosts allowed to use the service.

Listing 6.5 (inetd.conf)

```
# <service_name> <sock_type> <proto> <flags> <user> <server_path> <args>
# Echo, discard and daytime are used primarily for testing.
echo     stream   tcp   nowait   root   internal
echo     dgram    udp   wait     root   internal
discard  stream   tcp   nowait   root   internal
discard  dgram    udp   wait     root   internal
daytime  stream   tcp   nowait   root   internal
daytime  dgram    udp   wait     root   internal
time     dgram    udp   wait     root   internal
# These are standard services.
ftp      stream   tcp   nowait   root   /usr/sbin/tcpd /usr/sbin/wu.ftpd
telnet   stream   tcp   nowait   root   /usr/sbin/tcpd /usr/sbin/in.telnetd
#
# Shell, login, exec and talk are BSD protocols.
shell    stream   tcp   nowait   root   /usr/sbin/tcpd /usr/sbin/in.rshd
login    stream   tcp   nowait   root   /usr/sbin/tcpd /usr/sbin/in.rlogind
talk     dgram    udp   wait     root   /usr/sbin/tcpd /usr/sbin/in.ntalkd
ntalk    dgram    udp   wait     root   /usr/sbin/tcpd /usr/sbin/in.ntalkd
#
# Pop mail servers
pop3     stream   tcp   nowait   root   /usr/sbin/tcpd /usr/sbin/in.pop3d
#
bootps   dgram    udp   wait     root   /usr/sbin/tcpd /usr/sbin/in.bootpd
#
finger   stream   tcp   nowait   daemon    /usr/sbin/tcpd /usr/sbin/in.fingerd
systat   stream   tcp   nowait   guest     /usr/sbin/tcpd /usr/bin/ps -auwwx
netstat  stream   tcp   nowait   guest     /usr/sbin/tcpd /bin/netstat -f inet
```

Daemons

Networking programs normally initiate networking daemons which are background processes and are always running. Their main function is to wait for a request to perform a task. Typical daemons are:

`biod` which is asynchronous block I/O daemons for NFS clients.

`inetd` which is an Internet daemon that listens to service ports. It listens for service requests and calls the appropriate server. The server it calls depends on the contents of the `/etc/inetd.conf` file.

`nfsd` which is the NFS server daemon. It is used by the client for reading and writing to a remote directory and it sends a request to the remote server `nfsd` process.

`pcnfsd` which is a PC user authentication daemon.

`portmap` which is an RPC program to port number conversion daemon. When a client makes an RPC call to a given program number, it first contacts `portmap` on the server node to determine the port number where RPC requests should be sent.

Here is an extract from the processes that run a networked UNIX workstation:

```
 UID   PID  PPID  C     STIME TTY        TIME COMMAND
root   100     1  0  Dec  9  ?          0:00 /etc/portmap
root   138     1  0  Dec  9  ?          0:00 /etc/inetd
root   104     1  0  Dec  9  ?          9:20 /usr/etc/ypserv
root   106     1  0  Dec  9  ?          0:00 /etc/ypbind
root   122   120  0  Dec  9  ?          0:00 /etc/nfsd 4
root   116     1  0  Dec  9  ?          0:00 /usr/etc/rpc.yppasswdd
root   123   120  0  Dec  9  ?          0:00 /etc/nfsd 4
root   128     1  0  Dec  9  ?          0:02 /etc/biod 4
root   131     1  0  Dec  9  ?          0:00 /etc/pcnfsd
root   133     1  0  Dec  9  ?          0:00 /usr/etc/rpc.statd
root   135     1  0  Dec  9  ?          0:00 /usr/etc/rpc.lockd
root  4649     1  0 14:33:15 ?          0:00 /usr/etc/rpc.mountd
```

6.7 Exercises

The following questions are multiple choice. Please select from a–d.

6.7.1 In which application is a binary semaphore used:
(a) Sockets (b) Mutual exclusion
(c) Message handling (d) Producer-client

6.7.2 In which application is a non-binary semaphore value typically used:
(a) Sockets (b) Mutual exclusion
(c) Message handling (d) Producer-client

6.7.3 Which of the following is not a communication device used in IPC:
(a) Sockets (b) Message handling
(c) Synchronization (d) Semaphores

6.7.4 What does a signal operation do to a semaphore:
(a) Increment it (b) Decrement it
(c) Read it (d) Negate it

6.7.5 What does a wait operation do to a semaphore:
(a) Increment it (b) Decrement it
(c) Read it (d) Negate it

Additional material and tutorial questions are available at:
`http://www.palgrave.com/studyskills/masterseries/buchanan`

7 Data communications

7.1 Introduction

Communication has always been important to mankind, and lack of communication in the past has resulted in terrible wars and tragedies. It could be said that the reason that we have had world peace for so long is more to do with global communications, than it has to do with diplomacy. The great growth of communications has revolved around three main technologies: the telephone, television and radio. All three initially involved the transmission of analogue signals over wires or with radio waves. On an analogue telephone system, the voltage level from the telephone varies with the voice signal. Unwanted signals from external sources easily corrupt these signals. In a digital communication system, a series of digital codes represents the analogue signal, which are then transmitted as 1's and 0's. These digit forms are less likely to be affected by noise and thus have become the predominant form of communications.

Digital communication also offers a greater number of services, greater traffic and allows for high-speed communications between digital equipment. The usage of digital communications includes cable television, computer networks, facsimile, mobile digital radio, digital FM radio and so on.

7.2 History

Communications, whether from smoke signals or pictures or the written word, is as old as mankind. Before electrical communications, man has used fire, smoke and light to transmit messages over long distances. For example, Claude Chappe developed the semaphore system in 1792, which has since been used to transmit messages with flags and light.

The history of communication can be traced to four main stages:

- The foundation of electrical engineering and radio wave transmission which owes a lot to the founding fathers of electrical engineering who were Coulomb, Ampère, Ohm, Gauss, Faraday, Henry and Maxwell, who laid down the basic principles of electrical engineering.
- The electronics revolution, which brought increased reliability, improved operations, improved sensitization and increased miniaturization.
- The desktop computer revolution, which has accelerated the usage of digital communication and has finally integrated all forms of electronic communications: text, speech, images and video.
- The usage of modern communications techniques, such as satellite communications, local area networks and digital networks.

7.2.1 History of electrical engineering

The Greek philosopher Thales appears to have been the first to document the observations of electrical force. For this he noted that rubbing a piece of amber with fur caused it to attract feathers. It is interesting that the Greek name for amber was *elektron* and the name has since been used in electrical engineering.

An important concept in electrical systems is that electrical energy is undoubtedly tied to magnetic energy. Thus when there is an electric force, there is an associated magnetic force. The growth in understanding of electrics and magnetics began during the 1600s when the court physician of Queen Elizabeth I, William Gilbert, investigated magnets and found that the Earth had a magnetic field. From this he found that a freely suspended magnet tends to align itself with the magnetic field lines of the Earth. From then on, travellers around the world could easily plot their course because they knew which way was North.

Much of the early research in magnetics and electrics was conducted in the Old World, mainly in England, France and Germany. However, in 1752, Benjamin Franklin put the USA on the scientific map when he flew a kite in an electrical storm and discovered the flow of electrical current. This experiment is not recommended and resulted in the untimely deaths of several scientists.

In 1785, the French scientist Charles Coulomb showed that the force of attraction and repulsion of electrical charges varied inversely with the square of the distance between them. He also went on to show that two similar charges repel each other, while two dissimilar charges attract.

Two scientists who would be commemorated by electrical units made most of their major findings in the 1820s. The French scientist André Ampère studied electrical current in wires and the forces between them, and then, in 1827, the German scientist Georg Ohm studied the resistance to electrical flow. From this, he determined that resistance in a conductor was equal to the voltage across the material divided by the current through it. Soon after this, English scientist Michael Faraday produced an electric generator when he found that the motion of a wire through an electric field generated electricity. From this, he mathematically expressed the link between magnetism and electricity.

Morse code:

A	•—	W	•——
B	—••	X	—••—
C	—•—•	Y	—•——
D	—••	Z	——••
E	•	1	•————
F	••—•	2	••———
G	——•	3	•••——
H	••••	4	•••—
I	••	5	•••••
J	•———	6	—••••
K	—•—	7	——•••
L	•—••	8	———••
M	——	9	————•
N	—•	10	—————
O	———	.	•—•—•—
P	•——•	,	——••——
Q	——•—	?	••——••
R	•—•	:	———•••
S	•••	;	—•—•—•
T	—	-	—•••—
U	••—	/	—••—•
V	•••—		

The root of modern communication can be traced back to the work of Henry, Maxwell, Hertz, Bell, Marconi and Watt. American Joseph Henry produced the first electromagnet when he wrapped a coil of insulated electrical wire around a metal inner. Henry, unfortunately, like many other great scientists, did not patent his discovery. If he had he would have enjoyed his retirement years as a very wealthy man, rather than on his poor pension. The first application of the electromagnet was in telegraphy, which was the beginning of the communications industry. Henry sent coded electrical pulses over telegraph wires to an electromagnet at the other end. It was a great success, but it was left to the artist Samuel Morse (the American Leonardo, according to one of his biographers) to take much of the credit. Morse, of course, developed Morse Code, which is a code of dots and dashes. He used Henry's system and installed it in a telegraph system from Washington to Baltimore. The first transmitted message was 'What hath God wrought'. It received excellent publicity and after eight years there were over 23,000 miles (37,000 km) of telegraph wires in the USA. Several of the first companies to develop telegraph systems went on to become very large corporations, such as the Mississippi Valley Printing Telegraph Company which later became the Western Union. One of the first non-commercial uses of telegraph was in the Crimean War and the American Civil War, where a communications line from New York to San Francisco was an important mechanism for transmitting information to and from troops.

Other important developers of telegraph systems around the world were P.L. Shilling in Russia, Gauss and Weber in Germany, and Cooke and Wheatstone in Britain. In 1839 Cooke and Wheatstone opened a telegraph system alongside the main railway route running west from London.

Famous Edinburghers

Alexander Graham Bell (1847–1922) and James Clerk Maxwell (1831–79) were both born in Edinburgh, Scotland. Other famous Edinburghers include:

- Adam Smith, 1723–90. Economist.
- Sir Arthur Conan Doyle, 1859–1930. Writer.
- David Hume, 1711–76. Philosopher.
- Elsie Inglis, 1864–1917. Medical pioneer.
- Sir Harry Lauder, 1870–1950. Entertainer.
- James Boswell, 1740–95. Writer.
- John Knox, 1505–72. Theologian.
- Muriel Spark, 1918–. Writer.
- Robert Adam, 1728–92. Architect.
- Robert Louis Stevenson, 1850–94. Writer.
- Sean Connery, 1930– Actor.
- Sir Walter Scott, 1771–1832. Writer.

One of the all-time greats was James Clerk Maxwell, who was born in Edinburgh in 1831. His importance to science puts him on par with Isaac Newton, Albert Einstein, James Watt and Michael Faraday. Maxwell's most famous formulation was a set of four equations that define the basic laws of electricity and magnetism (Maxwell's equations). Before Maxwell's work, many scientists had observed the relationship between electricity and magnetism. However, it was Maxwell, who finally derived the mathematical link between these forces. His four short equations described exactly the behaviour and interaction of electric and magnetic fields. From this work, he also proved that all electromagnetic waves, in a vacuum, travel at 300,000 km per second (or 186,000 miles per second). This, Maxwell recognized, was equal to the speed of light and from this, he deduced that light was also an electromagnetic wave. He then reasoned that the electromagnetic wave spectrum must contain many invisible waves, each with its own wavelength and characteristic. Other practical scientists, such as Hertz and Marconi soon discovered these 'unseen' waves. The electromagnetic spectrum was soon filled with infrared waves, ultraviolet, gamma ray, X-rays and radio waves (and some even proposed waves which did not even exist).

While Maxwell would provide a foundation for the transmission of electrical signals, another Scot, Alexander Graham Bell, would provide a mechanism for the transmission and reception of sound: the telephone. From his time in Scotland he always had a great interest in the study of speech and elocution. In the USA, he fully developed his interest and opened the Boston School for the Deaf. His other interest was in multiple telegraphy and he worked on a device which he called a harmonic telegraph, which he used to aid the teaching of speech to deaf people. In 1876, out of this research he produced the first telephone with an electromagnet for the mouthpiece and the receiver. Alexander Graham Bell actually made the telephone call to his assistant with the words 'Mr Watson, come here, I want you.' Unlike many other great inventions it got good press coverage. 'It talks' was one of the headlines (it has not stopped since). Even the great Maxwell was amazed that anything so simple could reproduce the human voice and, in 1877, Queen Victoria acquired a telephone. Edison then enhanced it by using carbon powder in the diaphragm, to create a basic microphone. This produced an increased amount of electrical current. To fully commercialize his invention, Bell along with several others formed the Bell Telephone Company which fully developed the telephone so that, by 1915, long-distance telephone calls were possible. Bell's patent number 174 465 is the most lucrative ever issued. At the time, a reporter wrote, about the telephone, 'It is an interesting toy ... but it can never be of any practical value.'

Around 1851, the brothers Jacob and John Watkins Brett laid a cable across the English Channel between Dover and Cape Griz Nez. It was the first use of electrical communications between England and France (unfortunately a French fisherman mistook it for a sea monster and trawled it up). The British maintained a monopoly on submarine cables and laid cables across the Thames, Scotland to Ireland, England to Holland, as well as cables under the Black Sea, the Mississippi River and the Gulf of St Lawrence. Submarine cables have since been placed under most of the major seas and oceans around the world.

Around 1888, German Heinrich Hertz detected radio waves (as predicted by Maxwell) when he found that a spark produced an electrical current in a wire on the other side of the room. Then, Guglielmo Marconi, in 1896, succeeded in transmitting radio waves over a distance of two miles. From this humble start, he soon managed to transmit a radio wave across the Atlantic Ocean.

Scot Robert Watson-Watt made RADAR (radio detection and ranging) practicable in 1935, by transmitting microwave electromagnetic pulses which were reflected by metal objects (normally planes or ships) and were detected by a receiver. Today it is used in many applications from detect missiles and planes, to detecting rain clouds and the speed of motor cars. Microwave signals have been important in the development of satellite communications.

7.2.2 History of modern communications

The main developments of modern communications have been:

- **Automated telephone switching.** After the telephone's initial development, call switching was achieved by using operators. This tended to limit the range of the calls, and was particularly unreliable (and not very secure, as operators would often listen to the telephone conversation). However, in 1889, Almon Strowger, a Kansas City undertaker, patented an automatic switching system. In one of the least catchy advertising slogans, it was advertised as a 'girl-less, cuss-less, out-of-orderless, wait-less telephone system.' His motivation for the invention was to prevent his calls being diverted to a business competitor by his local operator. It used a pawl-and-ratchet system to move a wiper over a set of electrical contacts. This led to the development of the Strowger exchange, which was used extensively until the 1970s. Another important improvement came with the crossbar, which allowed many inputs to connect to many outputs, simply by addressing the required connection. The first inventor is claimed to be J.N Reynolds of Bell Systems, but it is normally given to G.A. Betulander.

Shakespeare's networking sayings:

- To contend or to not contend. That is the Ethernet question.
- Whether it is nobler to Ethernet than to ATM.
- A path, a path, my kingdom for a virtual path.
- Oh poor, Token Ring. I knew him so well.

– W. Buchanan

- **Radio transmission.** One of the few benefits of war (whether it be a real war or a cold war) is the rapid development of science and technology. Radio transmission benefited from this over World War I. A byproduct of this work was frequency modulation (FM) and amplitude modulation (AM). In these, signals to be carried on (modulated) high frequency carrier waves which travelled through the air better than unmodulated waves. Another by-product of the war effort was frequency division multiplexing (FDM) which allowed many signals to be transmitted over the same channel, but with a different carrier frequency.
- **Trans-continental cables.** After World War II, the first telephone cable across the Atlantic was laid from Oban, in Scotland to Clarenville in Newfoundland. Previously, in 1902, the first Pacific Ocean cable was laid. A cable, laid in 1963, stretches from Australia to Canada. These trans-continental cables are now important trunk routes for the global Internet. Their capacity has increased over the years, especially with the introduction of fibre-optic cables.
- **Satellites.** The first artificial satellite was Sputnik 1, which was launched by the USSR in 1957. This was closely followed in the following year by the US satellite, Explorer 1. The great revolution when the ATT-owned Telstar satellite started communicating over large distances using microwave signals. It used microwave signals which could propagate through rain and clouds and bounce off the satellite. The amount of information that can be transmitted varies with the bandwidth of the system, and is normally limited by the transmission system. A satellite system can carry as much as 10 times the amount of information that a radio wave can carry. This allows several TV channels to be transmitted simultaneously and/or thousands of telephone calls. Satellite TV stations are popular in transmitting TV stations over large areas.
- **Digital transmission and coding.** Most information transmitted is now transmitted in the form of digital pulses. A standard code for this transmission, called pulse code modulation (PCM), was invented by A.H. Reeves in the 1930s, but was not used until the 1960s. A major problem in the past with computer systems was that they used different codes to transmit text. To overcome this Baudot developed a 5-unit standard code for telegraph systems. Unfortunately, it had a limited alphabet of upper-case letters and had only a few punctuation symbols. In 1966, ANSI defined a new standard code called ASCII. This has since become the standard coding system for text-based communications. It has only recently been upgraded with Unicode (which uses 16 bits). In its standard form it uses 7 bits and can thus only represent up to 128 characters. It has since been modified to support an 8-bit code (called Extended ASCII).
- **Fibre-optic transmissions.** Satellite communications increased the amount of data that could be transmitted over a channel, but in 1965 Charles Kao laid down the future of high-capacity communication with the proof that data could be carried using optical fibres. Optical fibres now provide the backbone to many networks, including the Internet. Satellites supported the transmission of many hundreds of bits per second, but fibre optics could support billions of bits per second over a single fibre. They are reliable, and have excellent capacity for future upgrading with a new transfer rate.

7.3 Background

The communications industry has moved from transmitting a single character every second, to transmission of many billions of characters every second. The great breakthrough was to communicate faster than someone could type. One of the most basic communications rate is actually based on the speed of a typist. For this a good typist will type at around 75 words per minute. If we assume that there are five characters on average in every word (with an extra character for a space). Thus the typist will type, on average, 450 characters per minute. This will give 7.5 characters every second. Thus, as each character is represented, in ASCII, with 8 bits. The maximum transfer rate will be:

Transfer rate = 7.5 (characters per second) x 8 (bits per character) = **60 bps**

This was the basic bit rate that a communications link would have to support if it were to receive the speed of a fast typist. When a faster rate was required, the basic rate was doubled to 120 bps (although the standard rate was typically set at 110 bps). The speed then jumped to 300 bps, and multiples of this followed with 1200 bps, 2400 bps, 9600 bps, 19,200 bps (19 bkps), 38,400 bps (37 kbps), 57,600 bps (56 kbps), 115,200 bps (112 kbps), and so on. Most serial communications ports for computers and modems support many of these rates.

From the starting rate of 60 bps, the rates have increased over the years, as more people have used communications links, and backbone data traffic can have a capacity of tens of billions of bits per second (a 166,666,667 fold increase). For example, this chapter contains over 84,000 characters. With a 60 bps transfer rate it would take over **3 hours** to transmit it, while at 10 billion bits per second it would be transmitted in less than **100 millionth of a second** (assuming a transfer rate of 10,000,000,000 bps for 672,000 bits). The basic bit rate of transmission will increase over the years as the demand for data communications increases, and the number of applications for it increases.

The growth in data communications is creating one of the largest and most important industries in the world. It is a technology that brings benefits to virtually all individuals. Without it many organizations could not work efficiently. They are also creating industries that never existed before, such as digital TV, electronic commerce, electronic delivery of video and music, and, best of them all, electronic mail. The trend for transmitting data is to transmit digital information, thus if the original information is in the form of an analogue signal, it must first be converted into a digital form. This can then be transmitted over a digital network. At one time computer type data was sent over a network which was matched to transmitting this type of data, such as Ethernet and Token Ring, and speech was sent over a telephone-type network. The future will see the total integration of both real time (such as speech) and non-real time (such as computer-type data) into a single integrated digital network (IDN), as illustrated in Figure 7.1. The true integrator is ATM, which is covered in one of the WWW-based chapters. Networking technologies such as Ethernet are likely to remain a standard network connection onto a network, as they have become de facto standards.

The communications channel normally provides the main limitation on the amount of data that can be transmitted. This normally relates to its bandwidth, which can either be dedicated to the transmission of data from one source to a destination, or can be shared between more than one source, to more than one destination. Communications systems vary a great deal in the way they setup a connection, such as:

- **Bandwidth contention, bandwidth sharing or reserved bandwidth.** Some communication systems reserve bandwidth for a connection (such as ISDN and ATM), while others allow systems to contend for it (such as Ethernet). Normally the most efficient scheme is to allow systems to share the bandwidth. In this, some nodes can have more of the available bandwidth, if they require, while others can have a lesser share.
- **Virtual path, dedicated line or datagram.** Some communication systems allow for a virtual path to be setup between the two connected systems, while others support a dedicated line between the two systems. A dedicated line provides a guaranteed bandwidth for the length of the conversation, while a virtual path should support a certain amount of bandwidth, as a connection has been setup to support the data being transmitted. In a datagram-based system, there is no setup for the route and all of the transmitted datagrams (data packets) take an independent path from the source to the destination.
- **Global addressing, local addressing or no addressing.** An addressing structure provides for individual data packets to have an associated destination address. Each of the devices involved in the routing of the data read this address and send the data packet off on the optimal path. This type of addressed system normally uses datagrams. A typical global addressing structure is IP addressing, which is the standard addressing scheme for the Internet. In a non-addressed system the data is not tagged with the destination address, and only contains enough information to get it from one device to another. This is the technique that is typically used in setting up a virtual path. No addressing is used when circuit connection is setup, as all the data takes the same route.

Most communication channels are sequential in their nature, where the data from one connection goes straight into another channel. Each of the channels has their own bandwidth limitation, thus the bandwidth of a complete system is limited to the bandwidth of the element of the system which has the least bandwidth (unless there are parallel paths around this element). This is similar to hi-fi systems where the performance of the system is limited by the worst element in the system, as illustrated in Figure 7.5.

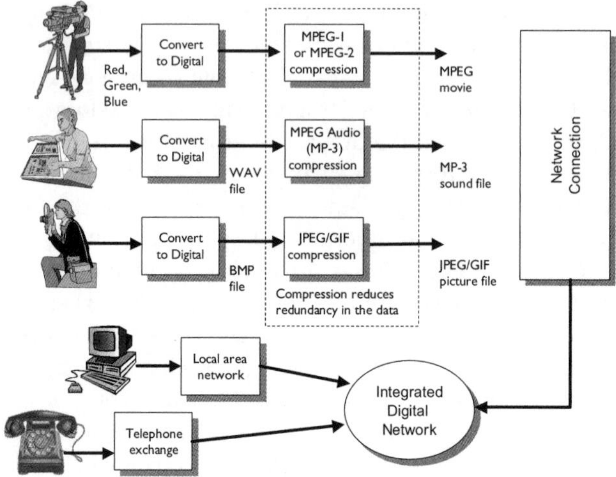

Figure 7.1 Conversion of information into an integrated digital network

7.4 Electrical signals

Any time-varying quantity can either be represented as a time-varying signal, or in terms of frequencies. For example when we describe sound we typically refer to it in terms of frequencies, such as an A is described as 440 Hz. Table 7.1 illustrates some of the frequencies for notes for given octaves. It can be seen that A, in the middle C octave 4, has a frequency of 440Hz. One octave down from this it is half the frequency (220Hz), and in the octave above this it is double this (880Hz).

Table 7.1 Note frequencies (Hz) for different octaves

	Octave 1	Octave 2	Octave 3	Octave 4	Octave 5	Octave 6	Octave 7
C	32.70	65.41	130.81	261.63	523.25	1046.50	2093.00
C#,Db	34.65	69.30	138.59	277.18	554.36	1100.73	2217.46
D	36.71	73.42	146.83	293.66	587.33	1174.66	2349.32
D#,Eb	38.89	77.78	155.56	311.13	622.25	1244.51	2489.02
E	41.20	82.41	164.81	329.63	659.26	1318.51	2367.02
F	43.65	87.31	174.61	349.23	698.46	1396.91	2637.02
F#,Gb	46.25	92.45	185.00	369.99	739.99	1474.98	2959.96
G	49.00	98.00	196.00	392.00	783.99	1567.98	3135.96
G#,Ab	51.91	103.83	207.65	415.30	830.61	1661.22	3322.44
A	**55.00**	**110.00**	**220.00**	**440.00**	**880.00**	**1760.00**	**3520.00**
A#,Bb	58.27	116.54	233.08	466.16	932.33	1664.66	3729.31
B	61.74	123.47	246.94	493.88	987.77	1975.53	3951.07

Any electrical signal can be analysed either in the time domain or in the frequency domain. A time-varying signal contains a range of frequencies. If the signal is repetitive (that is, it repeats after a given time) then the frequencies contained in it will also be discrete.

The standard form of a single frequency signal is:

$$V(t) = V\sin(2\pi ft + \theta)$$

where $v(t)$ is the time-varying voltage (V), V is the peak voltage (V), f the signal frequency (Hz) and θ its phase (°).

A signal in the time domain is a time-varying voltage, whereas in the frequency domain it is voltage amplitude against frequency. Figure 7.2 shows how a single frequency is represented in the time domain and the frequency domain. It shows that for a signal with a period T the frequency of the signal is $1/T$ Hz. The signal frequency is represented in the frequency domain as a single vertical arrow at that frequency, where the amplitude of the arrow represents the amplitude of the signal.

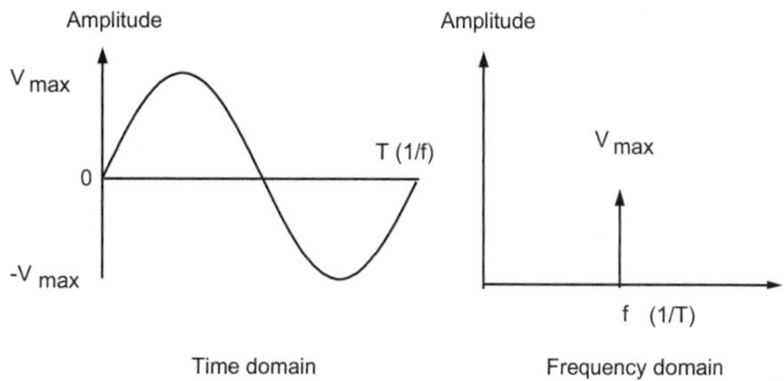

Figure 7.2 Representation of signal in frequency and time domains

7.5 Bandwidth

In general, in a communication system, bandwidth is defined as the range of frequencies contained in a signal. As an approximation it is the difference between the highest and the lowest signal frequency, as illustrated in Figure 7.3. For example, if a signal has an upper frequency of 100 MHz and a lower of 75 MHz then the signal bandwidth is 25 MHz. Normally, the larger the bandwidth the greater the information that can be sent. Unfortunately, normally, the larger the bandwidth the more noise that is added to the signal. The bandwidth of a signal is typically limited to reduce the amount of noise and to increase the number of signals transmitted. Table 7.2 shows typical bandwidths for different signals.

The two most significant limitations on a communication system performance are noise and bandwidth. In a data communications system the bandwidth is normally defined in terms of the maximum bit rate. As will be shown this can be approximated to twice the maximum frequency of transmission through the system.

Table 7.2 Typical signal bandwidths

Application	*Bandwidth*
Telephone speech	4 kHz
Hi-fi audio	20 kHz
FM radio	200 kHz
TV signals	6 MHz
Satellite comms	500 MHz

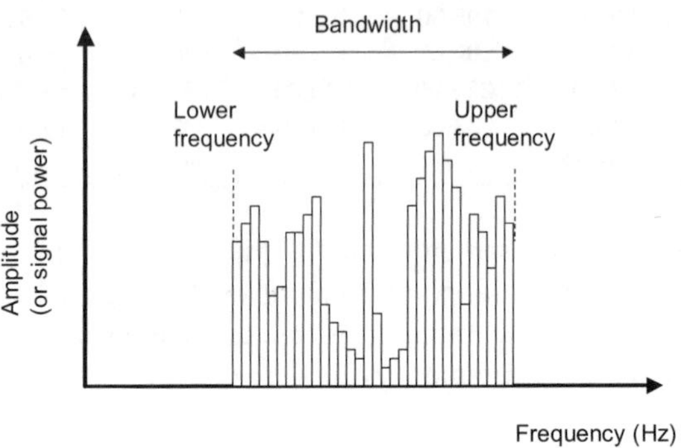

Figure 7.3 Signal bandwidth

> **Intel inside**
>
> Few companies have ever managed to get their logo on other manufacturers' products. The Intel Inside logo was one of these successes. Others include:
>
> - Dolby noise reduction.
> - Teflon non-stick material.
> - Nutrasweet.

7.6 Bandwidth requirements

The greater the rate of change of an electronic signal the higher the frequencies that will be contained in its frequency content. Figure 7.4 shows two repetitive signals. The upper signal has a DC component (zero frequency) and four frequencies, f_1 to f_4. The lower signal has a greater rate of change than the upper signal and it thus contains a higher frequency content, from f_1 to f_6.

Typically, in a cascaded system, the overall bandwidth of the system is defined by the lowest bandwidth of the cascaded elements. Digital pulses have a very high rate of change around their edges. Thus, digital signals normally require a larger bandwidth than analogue signals. In a digital system made up of cascaded elements, each with its own bandwidth, the overall bandwidth will be given by the lowest bandwidth element (as defined in bps), as illustrated in Figure 7.5. This changes if there are parallel channels, as the bandwidth capacity of a parallel route is equal to the sum of the two parallel routes. For example if data could take two channels, each with a bandwidth of 1 Mbps. Then the total bandwidth would be 2 Mbps, as 1 Mbps could flow over each channel (assuming that the data can be split between the two streams). Typically also bandwidth is not dedicated to a single connection, and must thus be divided by several connections. For example if the maximum bandwidth of a channel is 10 Mbps, and that this is split between 10 users. If each of the users were equally using the channel then the bandwidth available to each user will be 1 Mbps. This type of equal sharing may not be the best solution, thus in some cases users may be allocated a given share of the allocation.

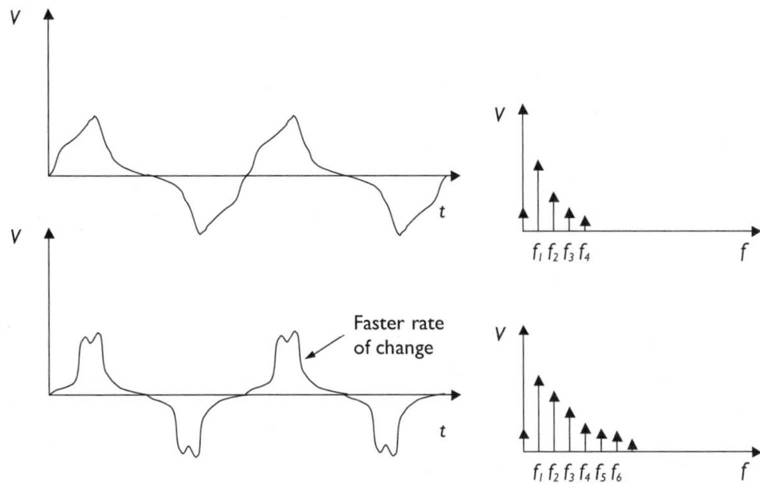

Figure 7.4 Frequency content of two repetitive signals

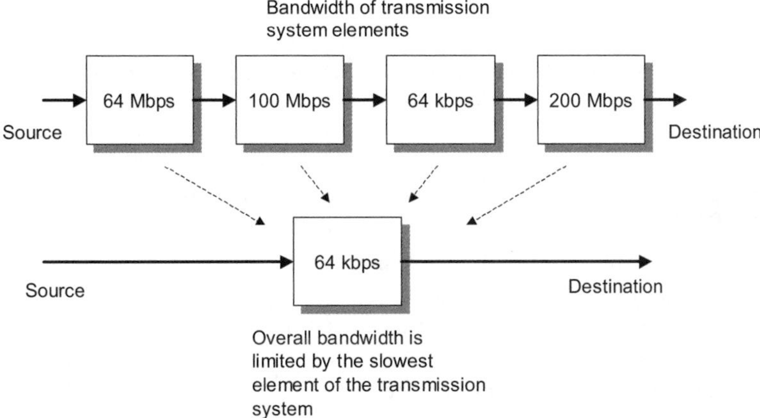

Figure 7.5 Overall bandwidth related to the system bandwidth elements

7.7 Noise and signal distortion

Noise is any unwanted signal added to information transmission. The main sources of noise on a communication system are:

- **Thermal noise.** Thermal noise occurs from the random movement of electrons in a conductor and is independent of frequency. The noise power can be predicted from the formula:

  $$N = k\,T\,B$$

  where N is the noise power in watts, k is Boltzman's constant (1.38×10^{-23} J/K), T is the temperature (in K) and B the bandwidth of channel (Hz). Thermal noise is predictable and is spread across the bandwidth of the system. It is unavoidable but can be reduced by reducing the temperature of the components causing the thermal noise. Many receivers which detect very small signals require to be cooled to a very low temperature in order to reduce thermal noise. A typical example is in astronomy where the temperature of the receiving sensor is reduced to almost absolute zero. Thermal noise is a fundamental limiting factor of any communications system.
- **Cross-talk.** Electrical signals propagate with an electric and a magnetic field. If two conductors are laid beside each other then the magnetic field from one couples into the other. This is known as crosstalk, where one signal interferes with another. Analogue systems tend to be affected more by crosstalk than digital ones, but noise in a digital system can could severe errors, if the noise is large enough to change a 0 to a 1, or a 1 to a 0.
- **Impulse noise.** Impulse noise is any unpredictable electromagnetic disturbance, such as from lightning or from energy radiated from an electric motor. It is normally characterized by a relatively high energy, short duration pulse. It is of little importance to an analogue transmission system as it can usually be filtered out at the receiver. However, impulse noise in a digital system can cause the corruption of a significant number of bits.

A signal can be distorted in many ways, especially due to the electrical characteristics of the transmitter and receiver and also the characteristics of the transmission media. An electrical cable contains inductance, capacitance and resistance. The inductance and capacitance have the effect of distorting the shape of the signal whereas resistance causes the amplitude of the signal to reduce (and also to lose power).

7.8 Capacity

The information-carrying capacity of a communications system is directly proportional to the bandwidth of the signals it carries. The greater the bandwidth, the greater the information-carrying capacity. An important parameter for determining the capacity of a channel is the *signal-to-noise ratio* (SNR). This is normally defined in decibels as the following:

For example, if the signal power is 100 mW, and the noise power is 20 nW, then:

$$\frac{S}{N}(\text{dB}) = 10\log_{10}\frac{100\times10^{-3}}{20\times10^{-9}}\,\text{dB}$$

$$\frac{S}{N}(\text{dB}) = 10\times\log_{10}\left[5\times10^{6}\right]\text{dB}$$

$$\frac{S}{N}(\text{dB}) = 6.7\,\text{dB}$$

$$\frac{S}{N}(dB) = 10\log_{10}\frac{Signal\ Power}{Noise\ Power}$$

In a digital system, Nyquist predicted that the maximum capacity, in bits/sec, of a channel subject to noise is given by:

$$Capacity = B.\log_2\left[1+\frac{S}{N}\right] \quad \text{bits/sec}$$

where B is the bandwidth of the system and S/N is the signal-to-noise ratio. For example if the signal-to-noise ratio is 10,000 and the bandwidth is 100 kHz, then the maximum capacity is:

$$\begin{aligned} Capacity &= 10^5.\log_2\left(1+10^4\right) \text{ bits/sec} \\ &\approx 10^5.\frac{\log_{10}\left(10^4\right)}{\log_{10}(2)} \text{ bits/sec} \\ &= 13.3\times10^5 \text{ bits/sec} \end{aligned}$$

$$\log_x(y) = \frac{\log_{10}(y)}{\log_{10}(x)}$$

Attenuation is the loss of signal power and is normally frequency dependent. A low-pass channel is one which attenuates, or reduces, the high frequency components of the signal more than the low frequency parts. A band-pass channel attenuates both high and low frequencies more than a band in the middle.

The bandwidth of a system is usually defined as the range of frequencies passed which are not attenuated by more than half their original power level. The end points in Figure 7.6 are marked at 3 dB (the –3 dB point) above the minimum signal attenuation.

Bandwidth is one of the most fundamental factors as it limits the amount of information which can be carried in a channel at a given time. It can be shown that the maximum possible symbol bit rate of a digital system on a noiseless, band-limited channel is twice the channel bandwidth, or:

Maximum symbol rate (symbols/sec) $= 2 \times$ Bandwidth of channel

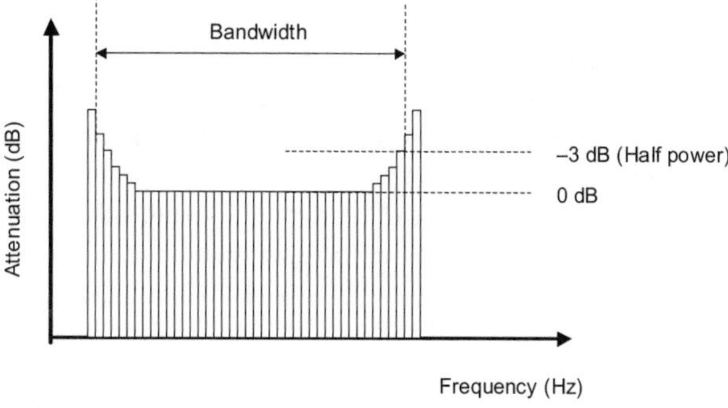

Figure 7.6 Bandwidth of a channel

If a signal is transmitted over a channel which only passes a narrow range of frequencies than is contained in the signal then the signal will be distorted. This is illustrated in Figure 7.7, where the maximum frequency content occurs when the 10101... bit sequence occurs. The minimum frequency content of this bit pattern will be *B* Hz. The symbol bit rate will thus be twice the highest frequency of the channel. The reason that the rate is referred to as a symbol rate, and not a bit rate, is that the symbol rate can differ from the bit rate. This is because more than one bit can be sent for each symbol. This typically happens with modems, where more than one bit is sent for every symbol. For example, several amplitudes of symbols can be sent, such as four amplitudes can be used to represent two bits. The symbol rate for speech limited channels will be 8,000 symbols per second (as the maximum frequency is 4 kHz). As four bits can be sent for every symbol, the bit rate will be 32 kbps.

If the frequency characteristics of the channel are known then the receiver can be given appropriate compensatory characteristics. For example, a receiving amplifier could boost higher frequency signals more than the lower frequencies. This is commonly done with telephone lines, where it is known as channel equalization.

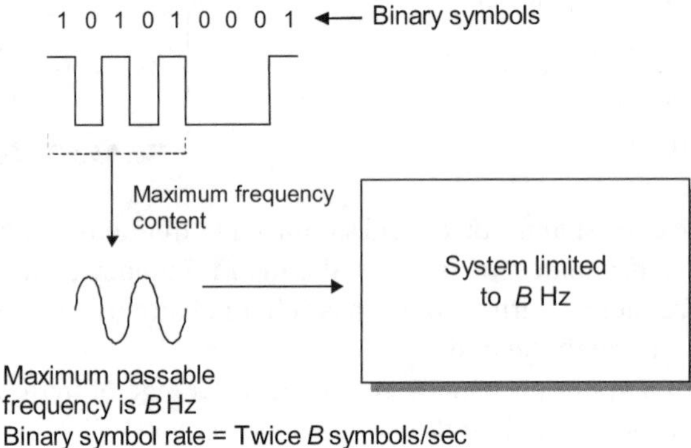

Figure 7.7 Maximum binary symbol rate is twice the frequency of the bandwidth

7.9 Modulation

Do witches run spell checkers?

A computer's attention span is as long as its power cord.

Modulation allows the transmission of a signal through a transmission medium by carrying it on a carrier wave (which can propagate through a given media). It also adds extra information that allows the receiver to pick-up the signal (allowing the modulated signal to be 'tuned-into'). For example, audio signals do not propagate well through air for any great distances. If they are added onto radio waves, the waves can propagate for vast distances. With long waves they can actually even transverse the planet. The other advantage of using a radio wave to carry the audio signal is that each audio signal can be transmitted using a different radio frequency. This then allows for many audio signals to be transmitted at the same time. This is known as frequency division multiplexing (FTM). Anyone who tunes to the correct carrier frequency can receive the signal, thus there can be one transmitter of the signal and many receivers. This is similar to the transmission of radio signals, where each radio station has its own carrier frequency, and receivers are tuned into these. This is also known as broadband communications, where a wide band is used to transmit the signals.

There are three main methods used to modulate: amplitude, frequency and phase modulation. With amplitude modulation (AM) the information signal varies the amplitude of a carrier wave. In frequency modulation (FM) it varies the frequency of the wave and with phase modulation (PM) it varies the phase.

7.9.1 Amplitude modulation (AM)

AM is the simplest form of modulation where the information signal modulates a higher frequency carrier. The modulation index, m, is the ratio of the signal amplitude to the carrier amplitude, and is always less than or equal to 1. It is given by:

$$m = \frac{V_{signal}}{V_{carrier}}$$

Figure 7.8 shows three differing modulation indices. In Figure 7.8 (a) the information signal has a relatively small amplitude compared with the carrier signal, giving a relatively small modulation index. In Figure 7.8 (b) the signal amplitude is approximately half of the carrier amplitude, and in Figure 7.8 (c) the signal amplitude is almost equal to the carrier's amplitude (giving a modulation index of near unity).

AM is generally susceptible to noise and fading as it is dependent on the amplitude of the modulated wave. Binary information can be transmitted by assigning discrete amplitudes to bit patterns.

7.9.2 Frequency modulation (FM)

Frequency modulation involves the modulation of the frequency of a carrier. FM is preferable to AM as it is less affected by noise because the information is contained in the change of frequency and not the amplitude. Thus, the only noise that affects the signal is limited to a small band of frequencies contained in the carrier. The information in an AM waveform is contained in its amplitude which can be easily affected by noise.

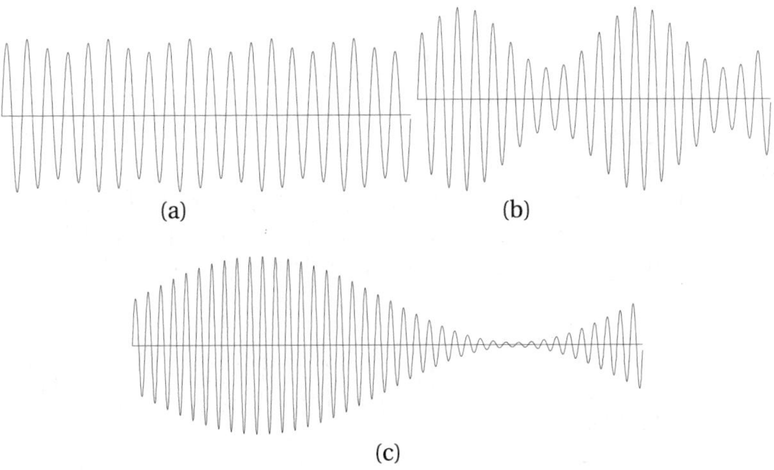

Figure 7.8 AM waveform

Figure 7.9 shows a modulator/demodulator FM system. A typical device used in FM is a Phased-Locked Loop (PLL) which converts the received frequency-modulated signal into a signal voltage. It locks onto frequencies within a certain range (named the capture range) and follows the modulated signal within a given frequency band (named the lock range). Typically binary information can be sent by using two frequencies, the upper frequency representing a zero, and the lower frequency representing a one. Modems can transmit binary information by using different frequencies to represent bit patterns.

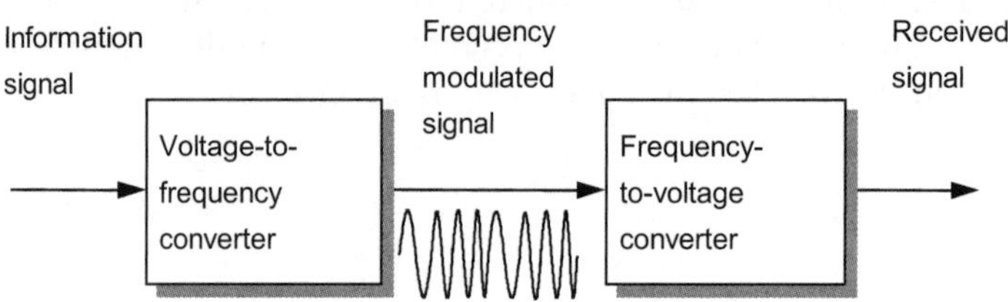

Figure 7.9 Frequency modulation

7.9.3 Phase modulation (PM)

Phase modulation involves modulating the phase of the carrier. PM is less affected by noise than AM because the information is contained in the change of phase and, like FM, not in its amplitude. As with FM, binary information can be transmitted by assigning discrete phases to bit sequences. For example, a zero phase could represent a zero, and a 180° phase shift could represent a one.

7.10 Digital modulation

Digital modulation changes the characteristic of a carrier according to binary information. With a sine wave carrier the amplitude, frequency or phase can be varied. Figure 7.10 illustrates the three basic types: amplitude-shift keying (ASK), frequency-shift keying (FSK) and phase-shift keying (PSK).

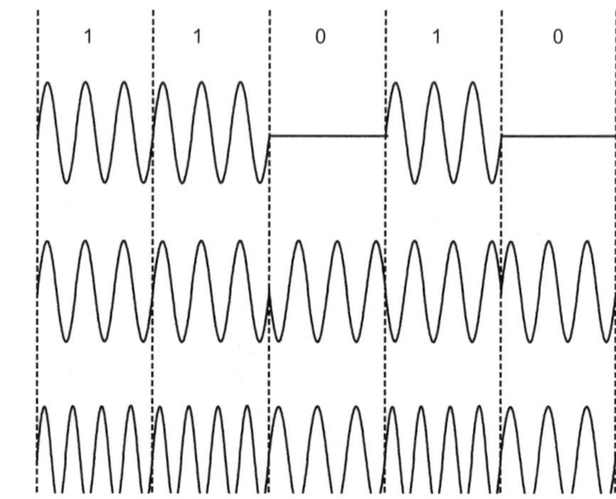

Figure 7.10 Waveforms for ASK, PSK and FSK

7.10.1 Frequency-shift keying (FSK)

FSK, in the most basic case, represents a 1 (a mark) by one frequency and a 0 (a space) by another. These frequencies lie within the bandwidth of the transmission channel. On a V.21, 300 bps, full-duplex modem the originator modem uses the frequency 980 Hz to represent a mark and 1180 Hz a space. The answering modem transmits with 1650 Hz for a mark and 1850 Hz for a space. These four frequencies allow the caller originator and the answering modem to communicate at the same time; that is, full-duplex communication.

FSK modems are inefficient in their use of bandwidth, with the result that the maximum data rate over normal telephone lines is 1800 bps. Typically, for rates over 1200 bps, other modulation schemes are used.

7.10.2 Phase-shift keying (PSK)

In coherent PSK a carrier gets no phase shift for a 0 and a 180° phase shift for a 1, such as:

$$0 \Rightarrow 0^\circ \qquad\qquad 1 \Rightarrow 180^\circ$$

Its main advantage over FSK is that as it uses a single frequency it uses much less bandwidth. It is thus less affected by noise, and has an advantage over ASK because its information is not contained in the amplitude of the carrier, thus again it is less affected by noise

7.10.3 *M*-ary modulation

With *M*-ary modulation a change in amplitude, phase or frequency represents one of *M* possible signals. It is possible to have *M*-ary FSK, *M*-ary PSK and *M*-ary ASK modulation schemes. This is where the baud rate differs from the bit rate. The bit rate is the true measure of the rate of the line, whereas the baud rate only indicates the signalling element rate, which might be a half or a quarter of the bit rate.

For four-phase differential phase-shift keying (DPSK) the bits are grouped into two and each group is assigned a certain phase shift. For two bits there are four combinations: a 00 is coded as 0°, 01 coded as 90°, and so on:

$$\begin{array}{llll} 00 \Rightarrow & 0^\circ & 01 \Rightarrow & 90^\circ \\ 11 \Rightarrow & 180^\circ & 10 \Rightarrow & 270^\circ \end{array}$$

It is also possible to change a mixture of amplitude, phase or frequency. *M*-ary amplitude-phase keying (APK) varies both the amplitude and phase of a carrier to represent *M* possible bit patterns.

M-ary quadrature amplitude modulation (QAM) changes the amplitude and phase of the carrier. 16-QAM uses four amplitudes and four phase shifts, allowing it to code four bits at a time. In this case, the baud rate will be a quarter of the bit rate.

Typical technologies for modems are:

FSK	– used up to 1200 bps
Four-phase DPSK	– used at 2400 bps
Eight-phase DPSK	– used at 4800 bps
16-QAM	– used at 9600 bps

Most modern modems operate with V.90 (56 kbps), V.22bis (2400 bps), V.32 (9600 bps), V.32bis (14 400 bps); some standards are outlined in Table 7.3. The V.32 and V.32bis modems can be enhanced with echo cancellation. They also typically have built-in compression using either the V.42bis standard or MNP level 5.

Table 7.3 Example modems

Type	*Bit rate (bps)*	*Modulation*
V.21	300	FSK
V.22	1,200	PSK
V.22bis	2,400	ASK/PSK
V.27ter	4,800	PSK
V.29	9,600	PSK
V.32	9,600	ASK/PSK
V.32bis	14,400	ASK/PSK
V.34	28,800	ASK/PSK

7.10.4 V.42bis and MNP compression

There are two main standards used in modems for compression. The V.42bis standard is defined by the ITU and the MNP (Microcom Networking Protocol) has been developed by a company named Microcom. Most modems will try to compress using V.42bis but if this fails they try MNP level 5. V.42bis uses the Lempel-Ziv algorithm, which builds dictionaries of code words for recurring characters in the data stream. These code words normally take up fewer bits than the uncoded bits. V.42bis is associated with the V.42 standard which covers error correction.

7.10.5 V.22bis modems

V.22bis modems allow transmission at up to 2400 bps. It uses four amplitudes and four phases. Figure 7.11 shows the 16 combinations of phase and amplitude for a V.22b is modem. It can be seen that there are 12 different phase shifts and four different amplitudes. Each transmission is known as a symbol, thus each transmitted symbol contains 4 bits. The transmission rate for a symbol is 600 symbols per second (or 600 baud), thus the bit rate will be 2,400 bps.

Trellis coding tries to ensure that consecutive symbols differ as much as possible.

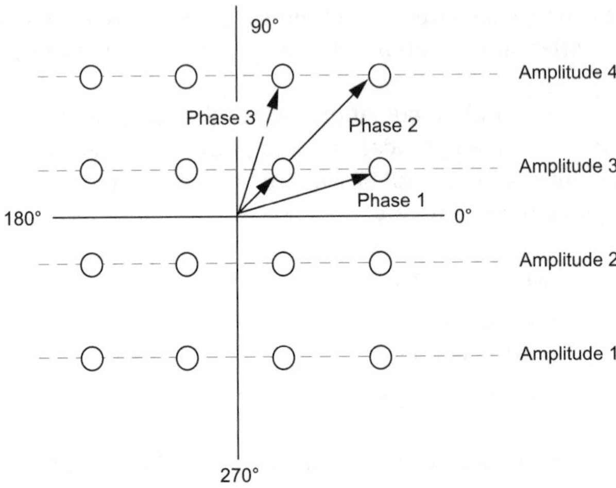

Figure 7.11 Phase and amplitude coding for V.32

7.10.6 V.32 modems

V.32 modems include echo cancellation which allows signals to be transmitted in both directions at the same time. Previous modems used different frequencies to transmit on different channels. Echo cancellation uses DSP (digital signal processing) to subtract the sending signal from the received signal.

V.32 modems use trellis encoding to enhance error detection and correction. They encode 32 signalling combinations of amplitude and phase. Each of the symbols contains four data bits and a single trellis bit (for error detection). The basic symbol rate is 2,400 bps; thus the actual data rate will be 9,600 bps. A V.32bis modem uses seven bits per symbol; thus the data rate will be 14,400 bps (2,400 × 6).

Intel processors that shook the world

4004: Nov 1971, 108 kHz, 4-bit data bus, 2,300 transistors, 640 B of addressable memory.

8008: Apr 1972, 200 kHz, 8-bit data bus, 3,500 transistors, 16 kB of addressable memory.

8080: Apr 1974, 2 MHz, 8-bit data bus, 6,000 transistors, 64 kB of addressable memory.

8086: June 1978, 5/8/10 MHz, 16-bit data bus, 29,000 transistors, 1 MB of addressable memory.

8088: June 1979, 5/8 MHz, 8-bit data bus, 29,000 transistors, 1 MB of addressable memory.

80386: Oct 1985, 16/20/25/33 MHz, 32-bit data bus, 275,000 transistors, 4 GB of addressable memory.

80486: Apr 1989, 25/33/50 MHz, 32-bit data bus, 1.2 million transistors, 4 GB of addressable memory.

Pentium: Mar 1993, 60/66 MHz, 64-bit data bus, 3.1 million transistors, 4 GB of addressable memory.

Pentium II/III: Mar 1997, 200 MHz and on, 64-bit data bus, 7.5 million transistors, 64 GB of addressable memory.

7.11 Multiplexing

Multiplexing is a method of sending information from many sources over a single transmission media. For example, satellite communications and optical fibres allow many information channels to be transmitted simultaneously. There are two main methods of achieving this, either by separation in time with time-division multiplexing (TDM) or separation in frequency with frequency-division multiplexing (FDM).

7.11.1 Frequency-division multiplexing (FDM)

With FDM each channel uses a different frequency band. An example of this is FM radio and satellite communications. With FM radio, many channels share the same transmission media but are separated into different carrier frequencies. Satellite communication normally involves an earth station transmitting on one frequency (the up-link frequency) and the satellite relays this signal at a lower frequency (the down-link frequency).

Figure 7.12 shows an FDM radio system where each radio station is assigned a range of frequencies for their transmission. The receiver then tunes into the required carrier frequency.

7.11.2 Time-division multiplexing (TDM)

With TDM different sources have a time slot in which their information is transmitted. The most common type of modulation in TDM systems is pulsed code modulation (PCM). With PCM, analogue signals are sampled and converted into digital codes. These are then transmitted as binary digits.

In a PCM-TDM system, several voice-band channels are sampled and converted into PCM codes. Each channel gets a time slot and each time slot is built up into a frame. The complete frame has extra data added to it to allow synchronization. Figure 7.13 shows a PCM-TDM system with three sources.

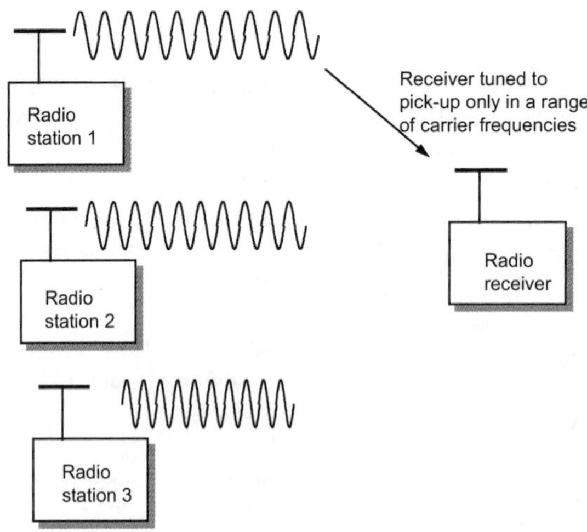

Figure 7.12 FDM radio system

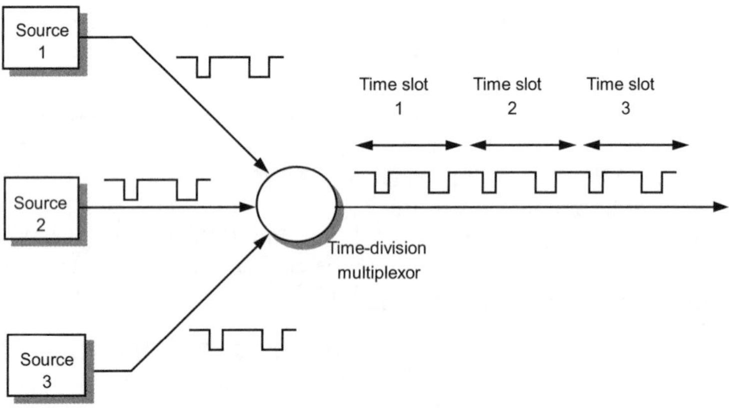

Figure 7.13 TDM system

7.12 Frequency carrier

Often a digital signal cannot be transmitted over channel without it being carried on a carrier frequency. The frequency carrier of a signal is important and is chosen for several reasons, such as the:

- signal bandwidth.
- signal frequency spectrum.
- transmission channel characteristics.

Figure 7.14 shows the frequency spectrum of electromagnetic (EM) waves. The microwave spectrum is sometimes split into millimetre wave and microwaves and the radio spectrum splits into seven main bands from ELF (used for very long distance communications) to VHF (used for FM radio).

Normally, radio and lower frequency microwaves are specified as frequencies. Whereas, EM waves from high frequency (millimetre wavelength) microwaves upwards are specified as a wavelength.

The wavelength of a signal is the ratio of its speed of propagation (u) to its frequency (f). It is thus given by:

> In a coaxial cable the dielectric constant is approximately 9.
>
> Thus, the speed of propagation will be one-third the speed of light, that is:
>
> **100,000,000 m/s**
>
> In 1 ns (1×10^{-9}s), it will travel:
>
> Distance $= 1\times10^{8}\times10^{-9}$
> $= 0.1$ m = **10 cm**

$$\lambda = \frac{u}{f}$$

In free space an electromagnetic wave propagates at the speed of light (300,000,000 m s^{-1} or 186,000 miles s^{-1}). For example, if the carrier frequency of an FM radio station is 97.3 MHz then its transmitted wavelength is 3.08 m. If an AM radio station transmits at 909 kHz then the carrier wavelength is 330 m. Typically, the length of radio antenna is designed to be half the wavelength of the received wavelength. This is the reason why FM aerials are normally between 1 and 2 m in length whereas in AM and LW aerials a long coil of wire is wrapped round a magnetic core. Note that a 50 Hz mains frequency propagates through space with a wavelength of 6,000,000m.

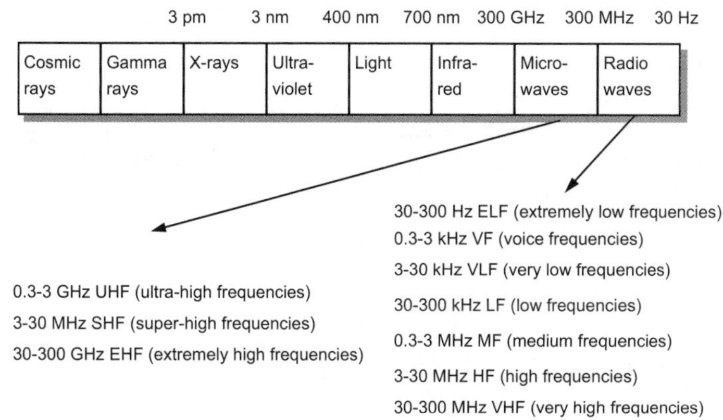

Figure 7.14 EM frequency spectrum

If an EM wave propagates through a dense material then its speed slows. In terms of the dielectric constant, ε_r of a material (which is related to density) then the speed of propagation is:

$$u = \frac{c}{\sqrt{\varepsilon_r}}$$

Each classification of EM waves has its own characteristics. The main classifications of EM waves used for communication are:

- **Radio waves.** The lower the frequency of a radio wave the more able it is to bend around objects. Defence applications use low frequency communications, as they can be transmitted over large distances, and over and round solid objects. The trade-off is that the lower the frequency the less the information that can be carried. LW (MF) and AM (HF) signals can propagate over large distances, but FM (VHF) requires repeaters because they cannot bend round and over solid objects such as trees and hills. Long wave radio (LW) transmitters operate from approximately 100 to 300 kHz, medium wave (AM) from 0.5 to 2 MHz and VHF radio (FM) from 87 to 108 MHz.
- **Microwaves.** Microwaves have the advantage over optical waves (light, infrared and ultraviolet) in that they can propagate well through water and thus can be transmitted through clouds, rain, and so on. If they are of a high enough frequency they can propagate through the ionosphere and out into outer space. This property is used in satellite communications where the transmitter bounces microwave energy off a satellite, which is then picked up at a receiving station. Radar and mobile radio applications also use these properties. Their main disadvantage is that they will not bend round large objects, as their wavelength is too small. Included in this classification is UHF (used to transmit TV signals), SHF (satellite communications) and EHF waves (used in line-of-sight communications).
- **Infrared.** Infrared is used in optical communications. When it is used as a carrier frequency the transmitted signal can have a very large bandwidth because the carrier frequency is high. It is extensively used in fibre optic communications and for line-of-site communications, especially in remote control applications. Infrared radiation is basically the propagation of heat, and heat received from the sun propagates as infrared radiation.
- **Light.** Light is the only part of the spectrum that humans can 'see'. It is a

Radio waves:

- **Low frequency**: Propagate over long distances. Waves can bend around objects. Low bandwidth.
- **Medium frequency**: Long wave (LW) – long wave radio. High frequency (HF) – AM radio.
- **High frequency**: Normally used in line-of-sight communications. Very high frequency (VHF) – FM radio.

Microwaves:
Ultra-high frequency – UHF (TV).
Extra high frequency – EHF (Mobile radio).
Millimetre waves (Military communications). Propagates well through clouds. Medium bandwidth, such as one TV channel.

Infrared/Ultraviolet:
Does not propagate well through free space. Normally used in light-of-sight communications. Very high bandwidth. For example, a 900 nm wave has a frequency of 3.33×10^{14} Hz, which allows for a bandwidth of 3.33×10^{13} Hz. It could thus provide for millions of TV channels, all at the same time.

very small part of the spectrum and ranges from 300 to 900 nm. Colours contained are red, orange, yellow, green, blue, indigo and violet.

- **Ultraviolet.** As with infrared it is used in optical communications. In high enough exposures it can cause skin cancer. Luckily the ozone layer around the Earth blocks much of the ultraviolet radiation from the sun.

7.13 Routing of data

Data communications involves the transmission of data from a transmitter to a receiver, over some physical distances. This could involve short distances, such as within a computer system, or a building, or could involve large distances, such as countrywide or even worldwide (or in the most extreme case, planet-wide). In order for data to be delivered to a recipient, a path must exist for it. Normally this path is setup by either mechanical switching, electronic switching (where the mechanical switch is replaced by an electronic switch) or virtual switching (where no physical or electronic connection exists between the sender and the receiver, but data is routed over virtual paths). The different types of switching include:

- **Circuit switching.** This type of switching uses a dedicated line to make the connection between the source and destination, just as a telephone line makes a connection between the caller and the recipient. As the connection is dedicated to the connection, the bit rate can vary as required, and possibly underutilized, but there tends to very little delay in transmitting the data.
- **Packet switching.** This type of switching involves splitting data into data packets. Each packet contains the data and a packet header which has the information that is used to route the packet through the network. Typical information contained in the packet header are source and destination addresses. These addresses may only have local significance (such as the address of the next switching device) or could have global significance (such as the Internet address of the source and destination devices). If the addresses have local significance it is likely that they will change as the data packet is passed from place to place, whereas global addresses will stay fixed. With packet switching each switching device on the path reads the data packet and sends it onto the next in the path. The transport can either be:

    - **Datagram**. This is where the data packets travel from the source to the destination, and can take any path through the interconnected network. This technique has an advantage, over setting up a fixed path, that data packets can take alternative paths. This is important when there is heavy traffic on parts of the network, or when links become unavailable. It also does not require a call setup.
    - **Virtual circuit**. This is where all the data packets are routed along the same path. It differs from circuit switching in that there is no dedicated path for the data. Virtual circuits must be setup before any data can be transmitted, and normally the route taken by the data can be chosen so that it gives the required link quality. This quality typically relates to propagation delay (latency), error rate and bandwidth limitations. Data packets in a virtual circuit also normally have some information in the header which identifies the virtual circuit, and this is likely only to have significance to the actual circuit setup.

- **Multirate circuit switching.** Traditionally TDM (time division multiplexing) is used to transmit data over a PSN (public switched network). This uses a circuit switching technology with a fixed data rate, and has fixed channels for the data. Multirate rates allow transmitters to transmit to different destinations over a single physical connection. For example, in ISDN a node can transmit to two different destinations with a single connection (each of 64 kbps). The bit rate, though, is fixed at 64 kbps, and it is difficult to achieve a variable bit rate (VBR).
- **Frame relay.** This method is similar to packet switching, but the data packets (typically known as data frames in frame relays) have a variable length and are not fixed in length. This allows for variable bit rates. As the data packets are of variable length there must be some way of defining the start and end of the data packet. For this the special bit sequence of 01111110 is typically used at the start and the end of the frame. A special technique, known as bit stuffing, is then used to stop the start and end sequence from occurring at any other place, apart from at the start and the end of the data frame.
- **Cell relay.** This method uses fixed packets (cells), and is a progression of the frame relay and multirate circuit switching. Cell relay allows for the definition of virtual channels with data rates dynamically defined. Using a small cell size allows almost constant data rate even though it uses packets.

Local connections are typically either made with a direct connection, or over a local area network (LAN). For a connection over a large area the connection is typically made over a wide area network (WAN) which connects one node to another over relatively large distances via an arbitrary connection of switching nodes. Typically the WAN can use the public data network (PDN) or through dedicated company connections. Figure 7.15 illustrates the two main types of connection over the public telephone network: circuit switching and packet switching.

> **Pentium bug**
>
> The Pentium bug was found in October 1994 by Thomas Nicely, a mathematician from Lynchburgh College, Virginia. He found that one divided by 824,633,702,441 gave the wrong answer. This bug eventually cost Intel over half a billion dollars, as they offered to replace bug-ridden Pentiums with correctly operating ones.

With circuit switching, a physical, or a reserved multiplexed, connection exists between two nodes. This type of connection is typical in a public-switched telephone network (PSTN), as telephone connections have been made, in the past, with this method. As with a telephone call, the connection must be made before transferring any data. Until recently this connection took a relatively long time to setup (typically over 10 seconds), but with the increase in digital switching it has reduced to less than a second. The usage of digital switching has also allowed the transmission of digital data, over PSTNs, at rates of 64 kbps and greater. This type of network is known as a circuit-switched digital network (CSDN). Its main disadvantage is that a permanent connection is setup between the nodes, which is wasteful in time and can be costly. Another disadvantage is that the transmitting and receiving nodes must be operating at the same speed. A CSDN, also, does not perform any error detection or flow control.

Packet switching involves segmenting data into packets that propagate within a digital network. They either follow a predetermined route or are routed individually to the receiving node via packet-switched exchanges (PSE) or routers. These examine the destination addresses and based on an internal routing directory pass it to the next PSE on the route. As with circuit switching, data can propagate over a fixed route. This differs from circuit switching in that the path is not an actual physical circuit (or a reserved multiplexed channel). As it is not a physical circuit it is normally defined as a virtual circuit. This virtual circuit is less wasteful on channel resources as other data can be sent when there are gaps in the data flow. Table 7.4 gives a comparison of the two types.

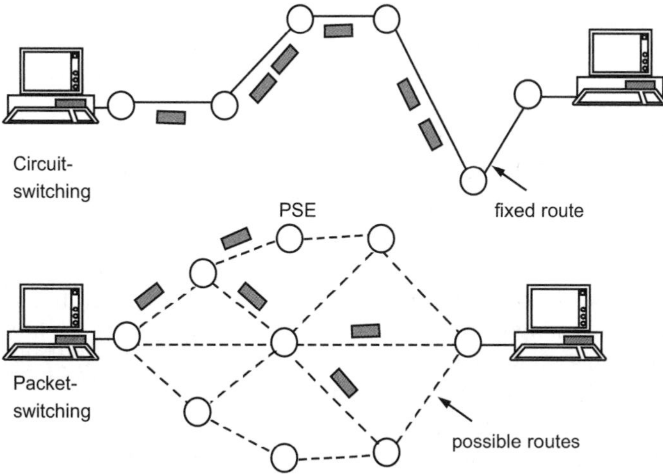

Figure 7.15 Circuit and packet switching

Table 7.4 Comparison of switching techniques

	Circuit-switching	*Packet-switching*
Investment in equipment	Minimal as it uses existing connections	Expensive for initial investment
Error and flow control	None, this must be supplied by the end users.	Yes, using the FCS in the data link layer
Simultaneous transmissions and connections	No	Yes, nodes can communicate with many nodes at the same time and over many different routes
Allows for data to be sent without first setting up a connection	No	Yes, using datagrams
Response time	Once the link is setup it provides a good reliable connection with little propagation delay	Response time depends on the size of the data packets and the traffic within the network

7.14 Exercises

7.14.1 What is the most fundamental limitation on the maximum amount of data that can be transmitted over a channel:

(a) The application program (b) The type of data being transmitted
(c) Noise on the channel (d) The delay in transmission

Additional material and tutorial questions are available at:
`http://www.palgrave.com/studyskills/masterseries/buchanan`

8 Compression

8.1 Introduction

Very few things in life are 100% efficient. Just think how wonderful it would be if a car engine could convert the fuel straight into engine power, and not even get hot. This would, of course, use much less fuel, and the reliability of the engine also would improve. With computer data the key to efficiency typically relates to the amount of bandwidth that it uses, the size of the data, and the delay in the transmission. The optimum efficiency would be to make every single bit of data count for some information. This would be very difficult, but where resources are low, data must be optimized in the amount of the resources that it uses.

The key factors in reducing the amount of data storage are:

DEAR COMPRESSION AGENT

Question: *You say that high-quality audio uses 16 bits for each sample, but my CD player says that it uses **1- bit** conversion. Is this right?*

Yes. It does. It uses one bit at a time, as this is thought to give a smoother response. A major problem with CD recordings is that they sometimes lack warmth, and are a little sharp (as they are too perfect). One-bit tracking tries to follow the movement of the audio signal. So your CD still uses 16-bit coding.

- **Getting rid of redundant data**. This involves determining the parts of the data that are not required. For example, a database could hold data on one hundred people. Each person could have their time and date of birth stored in the database, but if the system simply displayed the person's age, then there is no need for the time of their birth to be stored, in this case, as their age does not depend on the time of birth. Thus, the time of birth could be deleted from the database, as, in this example, it is not required.
- **Identifying irrelevant data**. This involves identifying the parts of the data which are perceived to be irrelevant. A good example of this is music, where a loud instrument, such as a trombone, will often drown-out the sound of a quiet instrument, such as a triangle. Thus the sound of the triangle can be reduced when there are loud sections of trombone, and brought back to normal in quieter sections. This is a technique that is often used in modern digital music compression. In the days of analogue tape recording a perceivable hiss would be heard when there were quiet sections of music, but it couldn't be perceived when there were loud sections (even though it was still there).
- **Converting the data into a different format**. This will typically involve changing the way that the data is processed and stored. A good example is to change a graphics image from a bitmap, where the colour of each pixel is stored, to a metafile, where shapes and sizes are stored. This type of conversion is also used in music files, where the time-varying musical signal is converted into sound frequencies, and then processed. This conversion makes compression much simpler.
- **Reducing the quality of the data**. Often the user does not require the specified quality of the data. For example if an image is stored with 1200 pixels by 1200 pixels, and the user can only view a 800 pixel by 600 pixel size, then the high resolution is not required. There can thus be a saving of 400% of the data size, if the image was reduced to 600 by 600 pixels. If this image was downloaded over the Internet in its raw format, the larger format would take four times longer to download than the small version (360,000 pixels

as apposed to 1,440,000 pixels). Also, the number of colours used can also be much greater than can actually be viewed on a graphics display. For example a 24-bit colour image uses 16,777,216 colours, which may be too many colours for some displays. A reduction to 65,536 colours would reduce the number of bits used to store the colour down to 16 bits. This would bring a 50% saving in data size (if it was stored in its raw format).

A key factor in improving the efficiency of the data is to determine the information that is required, and the parts of it that could be lost. Often computer data, in its raw form, is typically stored in an inefficient way, where the data contains a great deal of redundant information.

Computer-type data on the Internet is typically already stored in a fairly efficient manner (especially if it is a large file, as, in the past, disk storage was a precious resource). Computer networks and the Internet have also grown up transmitting computer-type data. These files are relatively easy to transmit as they are already in a digital format, and, in most cases, do not have a large requirement in the amount of data transmitted from each user. The next great wave of usage of networks is from the transmission of video, audio and speech. Each of these types of data, in their raw form, contains a great amount of data, and will generally swamp the rest of the network. Thus, a key to their acceptance will be compression, which tries to reduce the size of the stored/transmitted data, while still retaining the required information.

Information must be converted into a digital format before it can be stored on a computer or transmitted over a network. This is achieved by:

DEAR COMPRESSION AGENT

Question: *Someone told me that I couldn't use the GIF file format for my program. Are they correct?*

Well it's a difficult one. In 1987 CompuServe released the GIF (Graphics Interchange Format) format as a free and open specification in 1987. It quickly became a standard way to present graphics on the WWW. Unfortunately many developers started to write software supporting GIF without even acknowledging the existence of CompuServe. Along with this GIF used a compression technique called LZW (Lempel-Ziv-Welch), which Unisys holds a patent on.

The GIF format became so successful that by at the end of December 1994, CompuServe Inc. and Unisys Corporation announced that developers would have to pay a license fee in order to continue to use technology patented by Unisys. This, though, only applied to certain categories of software supporting the GIF format. These first statements caused immediate reactions and some confusion. With all these legal discussions, it is likely that GIF will be replaced, in the future, by other formats which do not have any patent or licensing problem, especially the PNG format. The great strength of GIF over JPEG is that it supports transparent colours (which will show through the colour of the background), where JPEG does not. PNG also supports this.

After a great deal of anger (including an article in *Time*), and with statements like:

'The announcement by CompuServe and Unisys that users of the GIF image format must register by January 10 and pay a royalty or face lawsuits for their past usage, is the online communications community's equivalent of the sneak attack at Pearl Harbor.'

In the end it has been ruled the GIF file format cannot be patented, but the usage of the LZW algorithm is patented (by Unisys). So as long as you do not breach the patent for this, you are not breaching any patents. If you are you must pay a royalty for its usage.

- **Images.** Images are converted into digital data by converting each of the pixels in the image into a digital value which represents the colour of the pixel. The more colours that are used, the greater the amount of data that is required to store the image.
- **Motion video.** Motion video is basically a series of stored images, which are updated at

a constant rate (often known as the scanning rate). For TV signals this rate is 50 times per second for UK-type TV quality (PAL) and 60 times per second for US-type TV quality (NSTC). Often the overall scan rate is reduced to half of this with interlaced updates, where every second scanned line is sent in every screen update.

- **Audio.** An audio file is converted by sampling the audio waveform at a constant rate (8000 times per second for telephone quality speech, and 44,100 times per second for hi-fi audio).

The basic conversion of this data into a digital form creates extremely large amounts of digital data. For example:

Content	*Description*	*Storage requirement*
Bitmapped image	1024 × 800, 65,536 colours	1.5 MB
Motion video	20 frames per second, 1024 × 800, 65,536 colours, 10 seconds	300 MB
Audio	60 minutes, hi-fi, stereo	600 MB

Cameras contain a red, a green, and a blue sensor. The output from this is typically known as RGB, where the intensities of each of the primary colours are stored. This type of image is known as a bitmap, where the colour of each pixel is stored in RGB format. Typically these values are packed into a single value. For example if 8 bits is used for each of the primary colours then the number of bits used to store each of the colours will be 24 bits. This type of format is typically known as True colour. With 8 bits for each of the primary colours there will be 256 different intensities hues, and the total number of colours will be 16.7 million colours (256×256×256). A typical format is to show the colour as a hexadecimal value, with the three primary colours (in RGB format). For example:

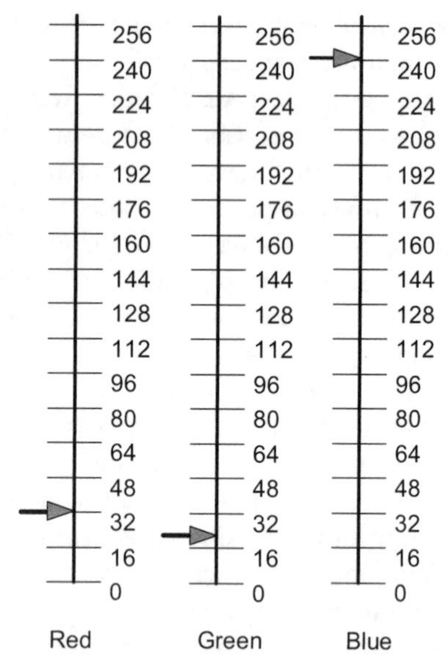

#2016F1

defines 20h (32, in decimal) for the red intensity, 16h (22, in decimal) or the green intensity, and F1 (241, in decimal) for the blue intensity. Thus the colour has a strong blue element, and a lesser red and green intensity. The graphic on the right-hand side illustrates the different intensities.

The raw form of image, video and audio contains massive amounts of redundant information, as there tends to be very little changes between one data sample and the next (Figure 8.1). One method used to compress the data is to store the changes between one data sample and the next. For example, in motion video, there are very few changes between one frame and the next (maybe just a few pixels). Thus, all that is required is to store the initial image, and then store the changes between the stored frame and the next, and so on. Occasionally it is important to store the complete frame, as the user may want to scan through the video, and start at any given point.

Motion video image compression relies on two facts:

- Images have a great deal of redundancy (repeated images, repetitive, superfluous, duplicated, exceeding what is necessary, and so on).
- The human eye and brain have limitations on what they can perceive.

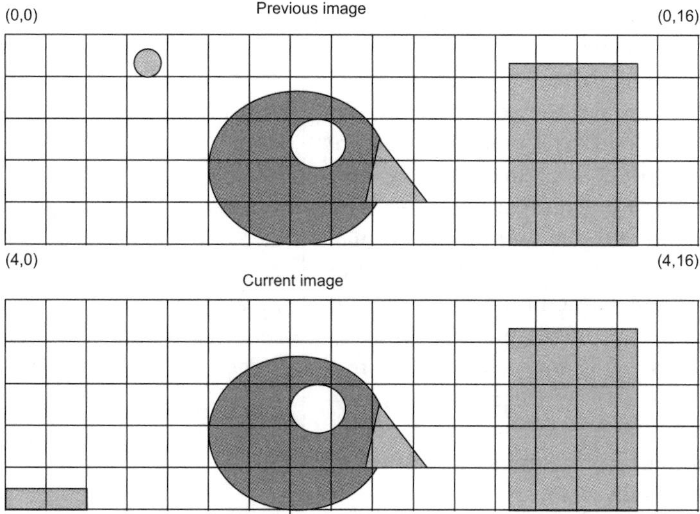

Figure 8.1 Information conversion into a digital form

The main forms of compression for images, video and audio are:

- **JPEG/GIF**. The JPEG (Joint Photographic Expert Group) compression technique is well matched to what the human eye and the brain perceive. For example, the brain is more susceptible to changes in luminance (brightness) and not so susceptible to colour changes. Thus to save storage space, more information on luminance can be stored, as apposed to information on colour changes. JPEG can compress a photograph which is over 1 MB to less than 20 KB. Another typical image compression standard is GIF. GIF and JPEG operate in different ways, and GIF is aimed at compressing images, while JPEG is focused on photographs. A major limitation with GIF is that it can only display up to 256 colours at a time (but these colours can be virtually any colour).
- **MPEG.** MPEG (Motion Picture Experts Group) uses many techniques to reduce the size of the motion video data. It uses the techniques that JPEG uses, to compress each of the images in the motion

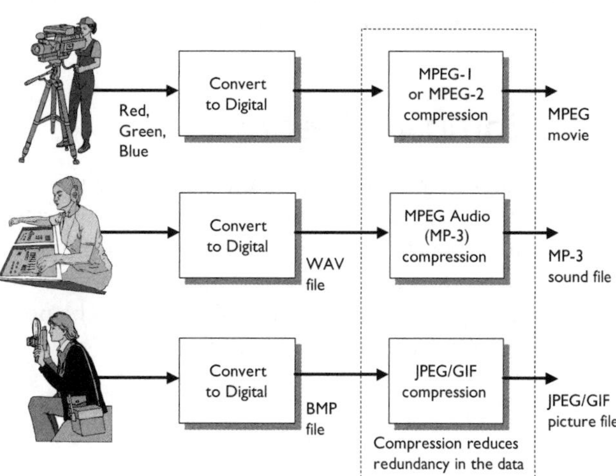

video. It also compresses between frames by only storing the information that is changing between frames. Typical compression rates are 130:1. Another typical video compression standard is AVI.

- **MPEG (MP-3).** The digital storage of audio allows for the data to be compressed. Typically, on an audio CD, a stereo, hi-fi quality song uses about 10 MB for every minute of music (600 MB for 1 hour). The storage requirements are thus extremely large, as a few hours of music would fill many currently available hard disk drives. MP-3 audio uses a compression technique that understands the parts of the music that the human brain perceives, and retains this information, while discarding parts that it does not perceive. For example, the ear will generally only listen to loud instruments, and ignore instruments which are playing quietly. MP-3 is so successful that it can compress hi-fi quality audio into one-tenth of its normal, uncompressed, size. A standard, 60 min music CD can be compressed to around 60 MB. With the increasing size of electronic memory, it is now possible to store a whole music CD in electronic memory, rather than storing it on a CD or a hard disk. Another typical audio compression standard is Dolby AC-3.

Monster or the Great Unifier?

With the growth in the Internet and global communications, we have created a global village, but have we also created an unregulated monster that is out of control? Well I think that Albert Einstein sums it best:

'Concern for man himself and his fate must always be the chief interest of all technical endeavors ... in order that the creations of our minds shall be a blessing and not a curse to mankind. Never forget that in the midst of your diagrams and equations.'

8.2 Conversion to digital

Figure 8.2 outlines the conversion process for digital data (the upper diagram) and for analogue data (the lower diagram). When data is already in a digital form (such as text or animation) it is converted into a given data format (such as BMP, GIF, JPG, and so on). It can be further compressed before it is either stored, transmitted or processed. The lower diagram shows how an analogue signal (such as speech or video) is first sampled at regular time intervals. These samples are then converted into a digital form with an ADC (analogue-to-digital converter). They can then be compressed and/or stored in a defined digital format (such as WAV, JPG, and so on). This digital form is then converted back into an analogue form with a DAC (digital-to-analogue converter).

8.3 Sampling theory

As an analogue signal may be continually changing, a sample of it must be taken at given time intervals. The rate of sampling depends on its rate of change. For example, the temperature of the sea will not vary much over a short time but a video image of a sports match will. To encode a signal digitally it is normally sampled at fixed time intervals. Sufficient information is then extracted to allow the signal to be processed or reconstructed. Figure 8.3 shows a signal sampled every T_s seconds.

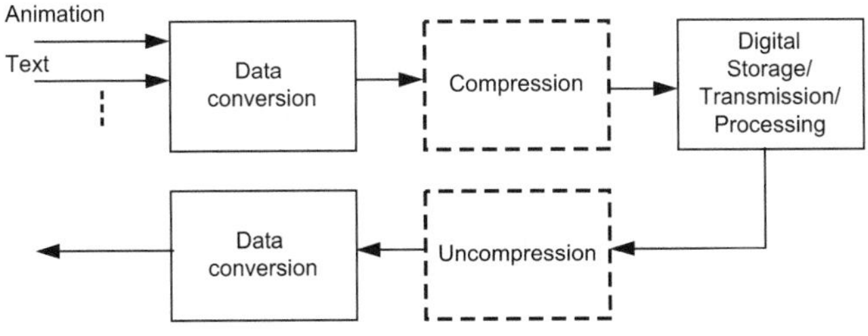

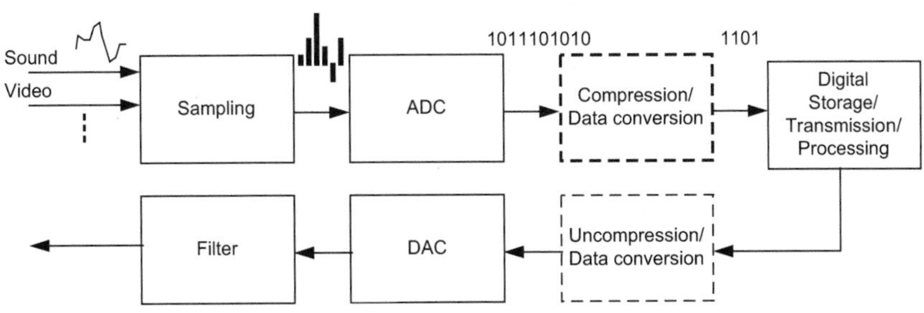

Figure 8.2 Information conversion into a digital form

The faster that the signal is sampled, the larger the amount of data that will be used. Thus it is important that the sampling rate is kept to a minimum, in order to reduce the amount of data required. Luckily Nyquist came up with a criterion which defines that if a signal is to be reconstructed as the original signal it must be sampled at a rate which is **twice** the highest frequency of the signal.

For telephone speech channels, the maximum signal frequency is limited to 4 kHz and must thus be sampled at least 8000 times per second (8 kHz). This gives one sample every 125 µs. Hi-fi quality audio has a maximum signal frequency of 20 kHz and must be sampled at least 40,000 times per second (many professional hi-fi sampling systems sample at 44.1 kHz). Video signals have a maximum frequency of around 6 MHz, thus a video signal must be sampled at 12 MHz (or once every 83.3 ns).

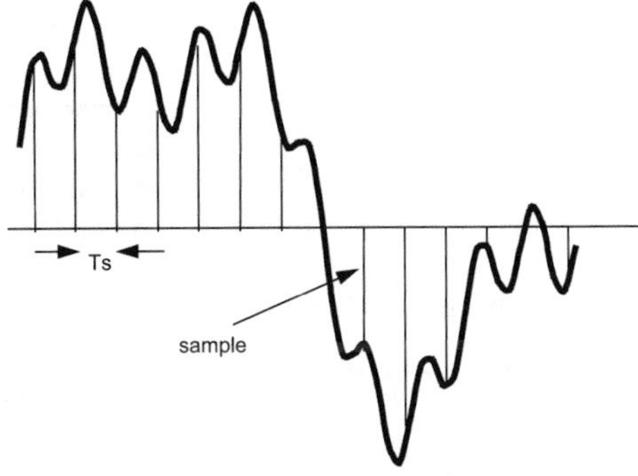

Figure 8.3 The sampling process

8.4 Quantization

Quantization involves converting an analogue level into a discrete quantized level. Figure 8.4 shows the conversion of an example waveform into a 4-bit digital code. In this case there are 16 discrete levels which are represented with the binary values 0000 to 1111. Value 1111 represents the maximum voltage level and value 0000 the minimum. It can be seen, in this case, that the digital codes for the four samples are 1011, 1011, 1001, 0111.

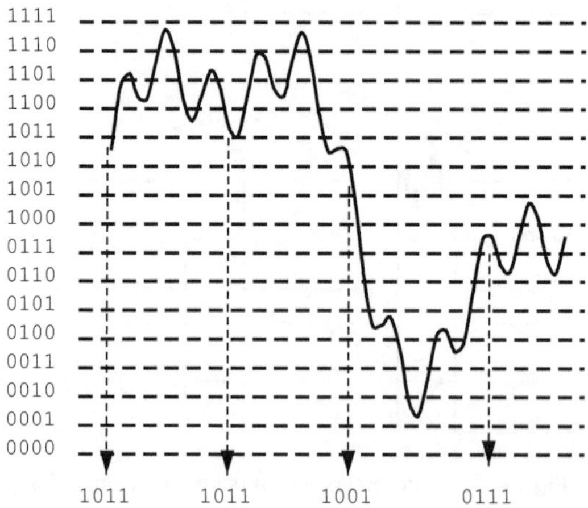

Figure 8.4 Converting an analogue waveform into a 4-bit digital form

The quantization process approximates the level of the analogue level to the nearest quantized level. This approximation leads to an error known as quantization error. The greater the number of levels the smaller the quantization error. Table 8.1 gives the number of levels for a given number of bits.

The maximum error between the original level and the quantized level occurs when the original level falls exactly halfway between two quantized levels. The maximum error will be half of the smallest increment or

$$\text{Max error} = \pm\frac{1}{2}.\frac{\text{Full Scale}}{2^N}$$

If the range of a signal is between +5V and -5V, then a 12-bit convertor would give a maximum error of:

$$\text{Max error} = \pm\frac{1}{2}\frac{10}{2^{12}}$$
$$= 0.00122 \text{ V}$$

Table 8.1 states the quantization error (as a percentage) of a given number of bits. For example the maximum error with 8 bits is 0.2%, while for 16 bits it is only 0.000 76%.

Table 8.1 Number of quantization levels as a function of bits

Bits (N)	Quantization levels	Accuracy (%)	Bits (N)	Quantization levels	Accuracy (%)
1	2	25	8	256	0.2
2	4	12.5	12	4 096	0.012
3	8	6.25	14	16 384	0.003
4	16	3.125	16	65 536	0.000 76

8.5 Compression methods

Most transmission channels have a restricted bandwidth, either because of the limitations of the channel or because the bandwidth is shared between many users. Many forms of data have redundancy, thus if the redundant information was extracted the transmitted data would make better use of the bandwidth. This extraction of the information is normally achieved with compression.

When compressing data it is important to take into account three important characteristics: whether it is possible to lose elements of the data; the type of data that is being compressed; and how it is interpreted by the user. These three factors are normally interrelated. For example the type of data normally defines whether it is possible to lose elements of the data. For computer data, normally if a single bit is lost, then all of the data is corrupted, and cannot be recovered. In an image, it is normally possible to loose data, but it could still contain the required information. For example, when we look at a photograph of someone, do we really care that every single pixel displays the correct colour. In most cases the eye is much more sensitive to changes in brightness, and less sensitive to changes in colour. Thus in compressing an image, we could actually reduce the amount of data in an image, by actually losing some of the original data. Compression which loses some of the elements of the data is defined as lossy compression, while lossless compression defines compression which does not lose any of the original data. Video and sound images are normally compressed with a lossy compression whereas computer-type data has a lossless compression. The basic definitions are:

> **DEAR COMPRESSION AGENT**
>
> **Question:** I can't understand it. I've just bought a brand new, state-of-the-art 56 kbps modem, and all I ever get is a maximum transfer speed of 4.19 KB/s. Where am I going wrong, do I need a new ISP?
>
> No. Your ISP is providing an excellent service, as 56 kbps is split between sending and receiving. As users who access the Internet from modems typically need to receive more data than they send, the bandwidth for receiving is greater than the bandwidth for sending. You can thus receive at a faster rate than you can send. The maximum receiving rate is 33 kbps, which relates to a maximum transfer rate of 4.125 KB/s (there are 8 bits in a byte). If you need a higher-rate you should try ISDN which gives a total transfer rate of 128 kbps (16 KB/s). Otherwise consider ADSL (Asymmetric Digital Subscriber Line), which gives up to 9 Mbps receiving and 1.1 Mbps sending, over standard telephone lines.

- **Lossless compression.** Where the data, once uncompressed, will be identical to the original uncompressed data. This will obviously be the case with computer-type data, such as data files, computer programs, and so on, as any loss of data may cause the file to be corrupted.
- **Lossy compression.** Where the data, once uncompressed, cannot be fully recovered. It normally involves analysing the data and determining which data has little effect on the perceived information. For example, there is little difference, to the eye, between an image with 16.7 million colours (24-bit colour information) and an image stored with 1024 colours (10-bit colour information), but the storage will be reduced to 41.67% (many computer systems cannot even display 24-colour information in certain resolutions). Compression of an image might also be achieved by reducing the resolution of the image. Again, the human eye might compensate for the loss of resolution (and the eye might never require the high resolution, if the image is viewed from a distance).

Apart from lossy and lossless compression, an important parameter is the encoding of the data. This is normally classified into two main areas:

- **Entropy coding.** This does not take into account any of the characteristics of the data and treats all the bits in the same way. As it does not know which parts of the data can be lost, it produces lossless coding. As an example, imagine that you had a system which received results from sports matches, around the world. With this there would be no way of knowing the scores that would be expected, and the maximum size of the name that is stored for the result. For example a UK soccer match might have a result of **Mulchester 3 Madchester 2**, and the results of an American football match might be **Smellmore Wanderers 60 Drinksome Wanderers 23**. Thus, all the information would have to be stored as characters, where each character is stored in an ASCII format (such as with 8 bits for each character), with some way to delimit the end of the score. We could compress this, though, even not knowing the content of the result. For example there are repeated sequences in the scores: *chester* and *Wanderers*. These we could store each of these once, and then just make reference to it in some way. This technique of finding repeated sequences is a typical one in compression, and is used in ZIP compression (which is a general-purpose compression technique).

  Typically entropy coding uses:

  - Statistical encoding – where the coding analyses the statistical pattern of the data. For example if a source of text contains many more 'e' characters than 'z' characters then the character 'e' could be coded with very few bits and the character 'z' with many bits.
  - Suppressing repetitive sequences – many sources of information contain large amounts of repetitive data. For example this page contains large amounts of 'white space'. If the image of this page were to be stored, a special character sequence could represent long runs of 'white space'.

- **Source encoding.** This normally takes into account characteristics of the information. For example images normally contain many repetitive sequences, such as common pixel colours in neighbouring pixels. This can be encoded as a special coding sequence. In video pictures, also, there are very few changes between one frame and the next. Thus typically the data encoded only stores the changes from one frame to the next. In our example of sports matches we could identify the type of sport, and then

> **DEAR COMPRESSION AGENT**
> **Question:** *Everyone seems to be talking about MP-3, but what's so good about it?*
>
> MP-3 audio is set to revolutionize the way that music is distributed and licensed. A typical audio track is sampled at 44,100 times per second, for two channels at 16 bits per sample. Thus the data rate is 1.411 Mbps (176,400 B/s), giving a total of 52,920,000B (50.47 MB) for a five-minute song. As the storage of a CD is around 650 MB, it is possible to get 64 minutes from the CD.
>
> Obviously it would take too long, with present bandwidths to download a five-minute audio file from the Internet in its raw form (over 3 hours with a 56 kbps modem). If the audio file was compressed with MP-3, it can be reduced to one-tenth of its original size, without losing much of its original content.
>
> So, it is now possible, with MP-3, to get over 10 hours of hi-fi quality music on a CD. But the big change is likely to occur with songs being sampled, and downloaded over the Internet. Users would then pay for the license to play the music, and not for purchasing the CD.

compress the data based on this. For example in a UK soccer match we could have a table of all the names of the sports clubs that we were storing the results for. Thus, for example, we may have 256 professional clubs, which would require 8 bits to store a reference value for each of these (number 0 to 256). So that 0 could be Mudchester, 1 could be Malchester, 2 could be Readyever United, and so on. We can also compress the scores, as we know that the goals scored for a team is very unlikely to be more than 31, thus we could use 5 bits to encode the score (0 to 31). Thus each score could be sent as an 8-bit reference for the home team, followed by a 5-bit value for their score, followed by an 8-bit reference for the away team, and finally by a 5-bit value for their score. Thus we only need 26 bits to store each of the scores, which is a large saving. In fact we could compress the data even more, as we know that the most probable goals scored will be 0, 1 or 2. Thus we could store zero goals as 00 (in binary), one goal as 01 (binary), two goals as 10 (in binary), three goals as 110 (in binary), four goals as 1110 (in binary), and so on. Thus, as most scores will only have between zero and two goals scored for each team, the average number of bit will be just over 2 bits. For example if the scores were: 0, 1, 0, 2, 3, 2, 2, 1 and 1 (which would be stored as 00, 01, 00, 10, 110, 10, 10, 01 and 01), this would require 19 bits, which is an average of 2.11 bits. This is a reduction from 5 bits for each score.

8.6 Entropy encoding

Normally, general data compression does not take into account the type of data which is being compressed and is lossless. As it is lossless it can be applied to computer data files, documents, images, and so on. The two main techniques are statistical coding and repetitive sequence suppression. This section discusses two of the most widely used methods for general data compression: Huffman coding and Lempel-Ziv coding.

8.6.1 Huffman coding

Huffman coding uses a variable length code for each of the elements within the data. This normally involves analysing the data to determine the probability of its elements. The most probable elements are coded with a few bits and the least probable coded with a greater number of bits. This could be done on a character-by-character basis, in a text file, or could be achieved on a byte-by-byte basis for other files.

The following example relates to characters. First, the textual data is scanned to determine the number of occurrences of a given letter. For example:

Letter:	'b'	'c'	'e'	'i'	'o'	'p'
No. of occurrences:	12	3	57	51	33	20

Next the characters are arranged in order of their number of occurrences, such as:

'e'	'i'	'o'	'p'	'b'	'c'
57	51	33	20	12	3

After this the two least probable characters are assigned either a 0 or a 1. Figure 8.5 shows that the least probable ('c') has been assigned a 0 and the next least probable ('b') has been assigned a 1. The addition of the number of occurrences for these is then taken into the next column and the occurrence values are again arranged in descending order (that is, 57, 51, 33, 20 and 15). As with the first column, the least probable occurrence is assigned a 0 and the next least probable occurrence is assigned a 1. This continues until the last column. When complete, the Huffman-coded values are read from left to right and the bits are listed from right to left.

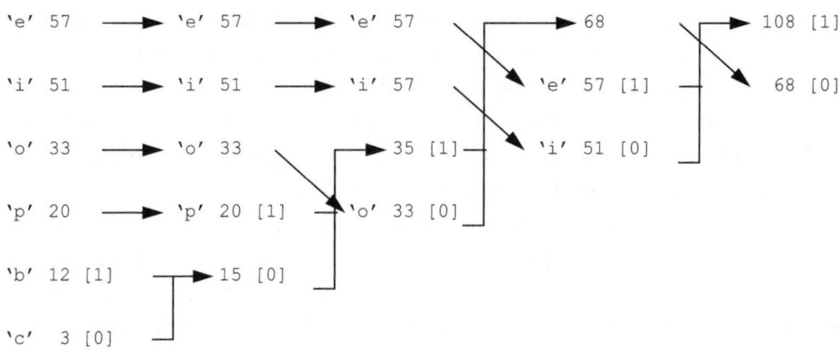

Figure 8.5 Huffman coding example

> **Alpha channels**. Control the amount of transparency in an image.
> **Gamma correction**. Control of image brightness on different computers.

The final coding will be:

'e'	11	'i'	10
'o'	00	'p'	011
'b'	0101	'c'	0100

The great advantage of Huffman coding is that, although each character is coded with a different number of bits, the receiver will automatically determine the character whatever their order. For example if a 1 is followed by a 1 then the received character is an 'e'. If it is then followed by two 0s then it is an 'o'. Here is an example:

11 00 011 0100 10 011 0100

will be decoded as:

'e' 'o' 'p' 'c' 'i' 'p' 'c'

When transmitting or storing Huffman-coded data, the coding table needs to be stored with the data (if the table is generated dynamically). It is generally a good compression technique but it does not take into account higher order associations between characters. For example, the character 'q' is normally followed by the character 'u' (apart from words such as Iraq). An efficient coding scheme for text would be to encode a single character 'q' with a longer bit sequence than a 'qu' sequence.

In a previous example we used soccer matches as an example of how data could be compressed. In a small sample of UK soccer matches the following resulted:

0 goals – 21 times; 1 goal –34 times; 2 goals- 15 times; 3 goals– 14 times;
4 goals – 5 times; 5 goals – 2 times; 6 goals – 1 time.

We could then order them as follows:

1 goal – 34 times; 0 goals – 21 times; 2 goals - 15 times; 3 goals – 14 times;
4 goals – 5 times; 5 goals – 2 times; 6 goals – 1 time.

This is obviously a small sample, and there are thus no codes for 7 goals or more. With a larger sample, there would be an associated number of occurrences. Figure 8.6 shows the resulting Huffman coding for these results. Thus, for example, a binary value of 01 will represent zero goals scored, and so on. This code could be combined with a table of values that represent each of the soccer teams. So, if we have 256 different teams (from 0 to 255), and use 00000000b to represent Mulchester, and 00000001b to represent Madchester, then the result:

Mulchester 2 Madchester 0

would be coded as:

00000000 **00** 00000001 **01**

where the bold digits represent the score. If the next match between the two teams resulted in a score of 4–1 then the code would be:

00000000 **1001** 00000001 **11**

Notice that the number of bits used to code the score can vary in size, but as we use a Huffman code we can automatically detect the number of bits that it has.

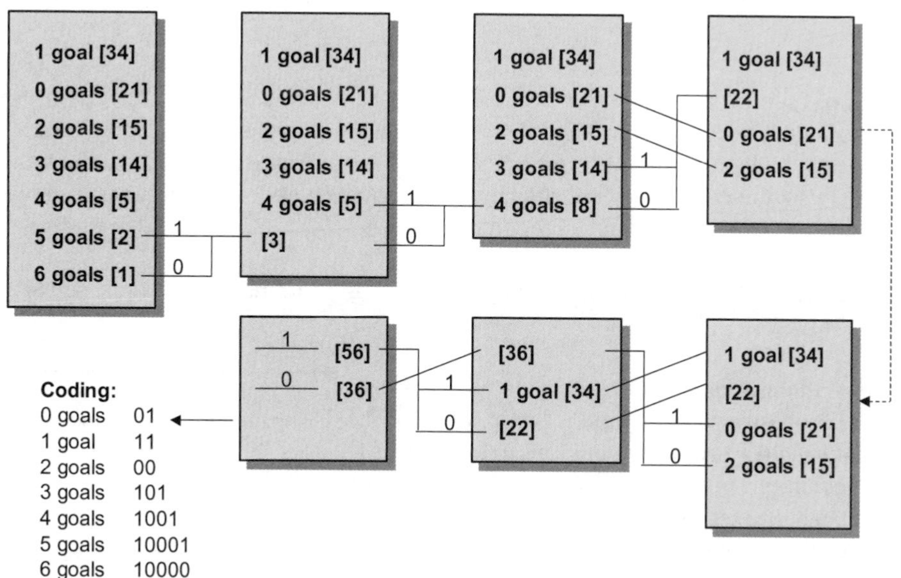

Figure 8.6 Huffman coding example

8.6.2 Adaptive Huffman coding

Adaptive Huffman coding was first conceived by Faller and Gallager and then further refined by Knuth (so it is often called the FGK algorithm). It uses defined word schemes which determine the mapping from source messages to code words. These mappings are based upon a running estimate of the source message probabilities. The code is adaptive and changes so as to remain optimal for the current estimates. In this way, the adaptive Huffman codes respond to locality and the encoder thus learns the characteristics of the source data. It is thus important that the decoder learns the encoding along with the encoder. This will be achieved by continually updating the Huffman tree so as to stay in synchronization with the encoder.

A second advantage of adaptive Huffman coding is that it only requires a single pass over the data. In many cases the adaptive Huffman method actually gives a better performance, in terms of number of bits transmitted, than static Huffman coding.

8.6.3 Lempel-Ziv coding

Around 1977, Abraham Lempel and Jacob Ziv developed the Lempel–Ziv class of adaptive dictionary data compression techniques (also known as LZ-77 coding), which are now some of the most popular compression techniques. The LZ coding scheme is especially suited to data which has a high degree of repetition, and makes back references to these repeated parts. Typically a flag is normally used to identify coded and unencoded parts, where the flag creates back references to the repeated sequence. An example piece of text could be:

'The **recei**ver **re**quires a **recei**pt for **it**. This **is** automatically s**en**t wh**en it is recei**ved.'

This text has several repeated sequences, such as ' is ', 'it', 'en', 're' and ' receiv'. For example the repetitive sequence 'recei' (as shown by the underlined highlight), and the encoded sequence could be modified with the flag sequence #*m*#*n* where *m* represents the number of characters to trace back to find the character sequence and *n* the number of replaced characters. Thus the encoded message could become:

'The receiver**#9#3**quires a**#20#5**pt for it. This is automatically sent wh**#6#2** it **#30#2#47#5**ved.'

Normally a long sequence of text has many repeated words and phases, such as 'and', 'there', and so on. Note that in some cases this could lead to longer files if short sequences were replaced with codes that were longer than the actual sequence itself.

> 'But what ... is it good for?' Engineer at the Advanced Computing Systems Division of IBM, 1968, commenting on the microchip.

Using the previous example of sport results:

Mulchester 3 Madchester 2
Smellmore Wanderers 60 Drinksome Wanderers 23

we could compress this with:

Mulchester 3 Mad#13#7 2
Smellmore Wanderers 60 Drinksome#23#1123

8.6.4 Lempel-Ziv-Welsh coding

The Lempel–Ziv–Welsh (LZW) algorithm (also known LZ-78) builds a dictionary of frequently used groups of characters (or 8-bit binary values). Before the file is decoded, the compression dictionary must be sent (if transmitting data) or stored (if data is being stored). This method is good at compressing text files because text files contain ASCII characters (which are stored as 8-bit binary values) but not so good for graphics files, which may have repeating patterns of binary digits that might not be multiples of 8 bits.

A simple example is to use a six-character alphabet and a 16-entry dictionary, thus the resulting code word will have 4 bits. If the transmitted message is:

```
ababacdcdaaaaaaef
```

Then the transmitter and receiver would initially add the following to its dictionary:

0000	'a'	0001	'b'
0010	'c'	0011	'd'
0100	'e'	0101	'f'
0110–1111	empty		

First the 'a' character is sent with 0000, next the 'b' character is sent and the transmitter checks to see that the 'ab' sequence has been stored in the dictionary. As it has not, it adds 'ab' to the dictionary, to give:

0000	'a'	0001	'b'
0010	'c'	0011	'd'
0100	'e'	0101	'f'
0110	'ab'	0111–1111	empty

The receiver will also add this to its table (thus the transmitter and receiver will always have the same tables). Next the transmitter reads the 'a' character and checks to see if the 'ba' sequence is in the code table. As it is not, it transmits the 'a' character as 0000, adds the 'ba' sequence to the dictionary, which will now contain:

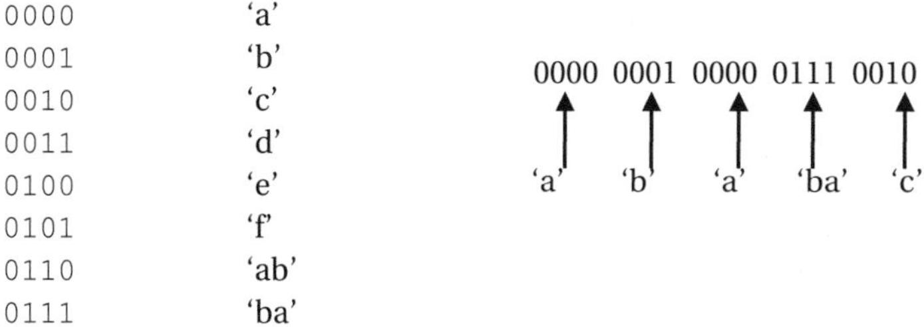

1000–1111 empty

Next the transmitter reads the 'b' character and checks to see if the 'ba' sequence is in the table. As it is, it will transmit the code table address which identifies it, i.e. 0111. When this is received, the receiver detects that it is in its dictionary and it knows that the addressed sequence is 'ba'.

Next the transmitter reads a 'c' and checks for the character in its dictionary. As it is included, it transmits its address, i.e. 0010. When this is received, the receiver checks its dictionary and locates the character 'c'. This then continues with the transmitter and receiver maintaining identical copies of their dictionaries. A great deal of compression occurs when sending a sequence of one character, such as a long sequence of 'a'.

Typically, in a practical implementation of LZW, the dictionary size for LZW starts at 4 K (4096). The dictionary then stores bytes from 0 to 255 and the addresses 256 to 4095 are used for strings (which can contain two or more characters). As there are 4096 entries then it is a 12-bit coding scheme (0 to 4096 gives 0 to $2^{12}-1$ different addresses).

> **DEAR COMPRESSION AGENT**
> **Question:** *When there is JPEG, why do we still use GIF files for graphics in WWW page?*
>
> Well, the only two standard graphics files for WWW pages are JPEG and GIF. JPEG gives excellent compression, especially for photographs. It also gives 16.7 million colours, and has been designed to compress objects which have a good deal of change within the graphic. GIF files are limited in that they can only display 256 colours at a time (from a range of 16.7 million colours). But GIF is very good a compressing graphics which do not have a great amount of change, especially small graphics, such as little images. The other great advantage is that GIF files support transparency, where parts of the images can be made transparent, so that the background colour will be shown wherever there is transparency.

8.6.5 Statistical encoding

Statistical encoding is an entropy technique which identifies certain sequences within the data. These 'patterns' are then coded so that they have fewer bits. Frequently used patterns are coded with fewer bits than less common patterns. For example, text files normally contain many more '*e*' characters than '*z*' characters. Thus the '*e*' character could be encoded with a few bits and the '*z*' with many bits. Statistical encoding is also known as arithmetic compression.

A typical statistical coding scheme is Huffman encoding. Initially the encoder scans through the file and generates a table of occurrences of each character. The codes are assigned to minimize the number of encoded bits, then stored in a codebook which must be transmitted with the data.

Table 8.2 shows a typical coding scheme for the characters '*a*' to '*z*'. It uses the same number of bits for each character. Morse code is an example of statistical encoding. It uses

> **DEAR COMPRESSION AGENT**
> **Question:** *So it GIF the future?*
>
> No. It's unlikely. GIF, and the compression method that it uses (LZW) are proprietary. Unisys hold the patent on LZW, and many software and equipment makers pay a small royalty to use it; CompuServe developed GIF and widely promoted it. It has allowed free use in the past but may not do this in the future.
>
> The future is likely to be the PNG (Portable Network Graphics), which is supported by most new WWW browsers. PNG is a good format as it has strong compression for images, as there is no loss of graphic image data when an image is uncompressed. PNG also supports variable transparency of (alpha channels) and control of image brightness on different computers (gamma correction). It can be used for both small images and complex ones, such as photographs.

dots (a zero) and dashes (a one) to code characters, where a short space in time delimits each character. It uses short codes for the most probable letters and longer codes for less probable letters. In the form of zeros and ones it is stated in Table 8.3.

Thus:

```
this an
```

would be encoded as:

```
Message:      t      h      i      s             a      n
Simple code:  10011  00111  01000  10010  11010  00000  01101
Morse code:   1      0000   00     000       0011   01     10
```

This has reduced the number of bits used to represent the message from 35 (7×5) to 18.

Table 8.2 Simple coding scheme

a	00000	b	00001	c	00010	d	00011	e	00100
f	00101	g	00110	h	00111	i	01000	j	01001
k	01010	l	01011	m	01100	n	01101	o	01110
p	01111	q	10000	r	10001	s	10010	t	10011
u	10100	v	10101	w	10110	x	10111	y	11000
z	11001	SP	11010						

Table 8.3 Morse coding scheme

a	01	b	1000	c	1010	d	100	e	0
f	0010	g	110	h	0000	i	00	j	0111
k	101	l	0100	m	11	n	10	o	111
p	0110	q	1101	r	010	s	000	t	1
u	001	v	0001	w	011	x	1001	y	1011
z	1100	SP	0011						

8.6.6 Repetitive sequence suppression

Repetitive sequence suppression involves representing long runs of a certain bit sequence with a special character. A special bit sequence is then used to represent that character, followed by the number of times it appears in sequence. For example typically 0's (zero) and ' ' (spaces) occur repetitively in text files. For example the data:

> 'I think there is a world market for maybe five computers.'
> Thomas Watson, chairman of IBM, 1943

```
8.3200000000000
```

could be coded as:

```
8.32F11
```

where F represents the flag. In this case the number of stored characters has been reduced from 16 to 7.

Graphics images typically have long sequences of the same pixel colour, thus a technique called run-length encoding (RLE), has been developed to compress long sequences of the same value. RLE uses a special flag to encoded repeated character sequences. For example:

```
Fred       has     when.........
```

could be coded as:

```
FredF7 hasF7 whenF9.
```

where F represents the flag. In this case the number of stored characters has been reduced from 32 to 20. The 'F7 ' character code represents seven ' ' (spaces) and 'F9.' represents nine '.' characters.

8.7 Source compression

Source compression takes into account the type of information that is being compressed, and is typically used with image, video and audio information. All these data sources have a great deal of redundant data in their raw form, either in that they have little relevance on the perceived media form, or contain no information at all. The main compression techniques for these are JPEG, MPEG and MP-3.

An example of the redundancy is contained in audio samples, where high-quality audio compression involves sampling the audio signal 44,000 times per second. The audio signal does not change much between samples, and will definitely not change outside a given range, thus it is possible to code the difference between samples, rather than coding for the complete range of the samples. For example the following might be integer values for the samples:

321, 322, 324, 324, 320, 317, 310, 311

This could be coded as difference values as:

320, +1, +2, 0, –4, –3, –7, +1

where the first value is stored, and then only the change is then coded. The advantage with this technique is that the maximum value of change can be defined, and this is likely to reduce the number of bits required to code the samples. For example, in this case, the sample difference ranges between –7 and +7, thus we only require 4 bits for each difference sample (7 could be represented by 0111, 6 by 0110, 5 by 0101, ... 0 by 0000, –1 by 1111, –2 by 1110, ... –6 by 1001 and –7 by 1000). This would only take 4 bits per sample (after the initial sample), as apposed to at least 8 bits for the non-difference system.

8.7.1 Image compression

Data communication increasingly involves the transmission of still and moving images. Most of these images are compressed using standard compression format. Some of these forms are outlined in Table 8.4. The main parameters in a graphics file are:

Table 8.4 Typical standard compressed graphics formats

File	*Compression type*	*Max. resolution or colours*	
TIFF	Huffman RLE and/or LZW	48-bit colour	TIFF (tagged image file format) is typically used to transfer graphics from one computer system to another. It allows high resolutions and colours of up to 48 bits (16 bits for red, green and blue).
GIF	LZW	65,563 × 65,536 (24-bit colour, but only 256 displayable colours)	Standardized graphics file format which can be read by most graphics packages. It has similar graphics characteristics to PCX files and allows multiple images in a single file and interlaced graphics.
JPG	JPEG compression (DCT, quantization and Huffman)	Depends on the compression	Excellent compression technique which produces lossy compression. It normally results in much greater compression than the methods outlined above.

- **The picture resolution.** This is defined by the number of pixels in the *x*- and *y*-directions.
- **The number of colours per pixel.** If N bits are used for the pixel colour then the total number of displayable colours will be 2^N. For example an 8-bit colour field defines 256 colours, a 24-bit colour field gives 2^{24} or 16.7 M colours.
- **Palette size.** Some systems reduce the number of bits used to display a colour by reducing the number of displayable colours for a given palette size. Typically each colour in the palette is defined in a relatively large number of bits (such as 24-bit or 32-bit colour), but there is only a limited number of colours which can be displayed. For example the GIF format uses 24-bit colour, within an 8-bit palette.

Comparison of the different methods

This section uses example bitmapped images and shows how much the different techniques manage to compress them. The left-hand side of Figure 8.7 shows an image and Table 8.4 shows the resultant file size when it is saved in different formats. It can be seen that the BMP file format has the largest storage. The two main forms of BMP files are RGB (red, green, blue) encoded and RLE encoded. RGB coding saves the bitmap in an uncompressed form, whereas the RLE coding will reduce the total storage by compressing repetitive sequences. The GIF format manages to compress the file to around 40% of its original size and the TIF file achieves similar compression (mainly because both techniques use LZH compression). It can be seen that by far the best compression is achieved with JPEG which in both forms has compressed the file to under 10% of its original size.

The reason that the compression ratios for GIF, TIF and BMP RLE are relatively high is that the image on the left-hand side of Figure 8.7 contains a lot of changing data. Most images will compress to less than 10% because they have large areas which do not change much. The right-hand side of Figure 8.7 shows a simple graphic of 500 × 500, 24-bit, which has large areas with identical colours. Table 8.5 shows that, in this case, the compression ratio is low. The RLE encoded BMP file is only 1% of the original as the graphic contains long runs of the same colour. The GIF file has compressed to less than 1%. Note that the PCX, GIF and BMP RLE files have saved the image with only 256 colours. The JPG formats have the advantage that they have saved the image with the full 16.7 M colours and give compression rates of around 2%.

Figure 8.7 Sample graphics image

Table 8.5 Compression on a graphics file

Type	*Size(B)*	*Compression (%)*	
BMP	308 278	100.0	BMP, RBG encoded (640 × 480, 256 colours)
BMP	301 584	97.8	BMP, RLE encoded
GIF	124 304	40.3	GIF, Version 89a, non-interlaced
GIF	127 849	41.5	GIF, Version 89a, interlaced
TIF	136 276	44.2	TIF, LZW compressed
TIF	81 106	26.3	TIF, CCITT Group 3, MONOCHROME
JPG	28 271	9.2	JPEG – JFIF Complaint (Standard coding)
JPG	26 511	8.6	JPEG – JFIF Complaint (Progressive coding)

Table 8.6 Compression on a graphics file with highly redundant data

Type	*Size (B)*	*Compression (%)*	
BMP	750 054	100.0	BMP, RBG encoded (500 × 500, 16.7 M colours)
BMP	7 832	1.0	BMP, RLE encoded (256 colours)
PCX	31 983	4.3	PCX, Version 5 (256 colours)
GIF	4 585	0.6	GIF, Version 89a, non-interlaced (256 colours)
TIF	26 072	3.5	TIF, LZW compressed (16.7 M colours)
JPG	15 800	2.1	JPEG (Standard coding, 16.7 M colours)
JPG	12 600	1.7	JPEG (Progressive coding, 16.7 M colours)

JPEG compression

The GIF format is an excellent format for compressing images which have a limited range of colours. This is fine for simple images, but it does not suit the compression of photographs, thus the JPEG standard was developed by the Joint Photographic Expert Group (JPEG), which is a subcommittee of the ISO/IEC. It was based on research into compression ratios on images and their resulting image quality. The standards produced can be summarized as follows:

It is a compression technique for grey-scale or colour images and uses a combination of discrete cosine transform, quantization, run-length and Huffman coding.

JPEG is an excellent compression technique which produces lossy compression (although in one mode it is lossless). As seen from the previous section it has excellent compression ratios when applied to a colour image. The main steps are:

- Data blocks — Generation of data blocks
- Source encoding — Discrete cosine transform and quantization
- Entropy encoding — Run-length encoding and Huffman encoding

Unfortunately, compared with GIF, TIFF and PCX, the compression process is relatively slow. It is also lossy in that some information is lost in the compression process. This information is perceived to have little effect on the decoded image.

GIF files typically use 24-bit colour information (8 bits for red, 8 bits for green and 8 bits for blue) and convert it into an 8-bit colour palette (thus reducing the number of bits stored to approximately one-third of the original). It then uses LZW compression to further reduce the storage. JPEG operates differently in that it stores changes in colour. As the eye is very sensitive to brightness changes it is particularly sensitive to changes in brightness. If these changes are similar to the original then the eye will perceive the recovered image as similar to the original.

> Best file compression around:
>
> DEL *.* {DOS}
>
> or rm –r *.* {UNIX}
>
> gives 100% compression

Colour conversion and subsampling

In the first part of the JPEG compression, each colour component (red, green and blue) is separated in luminance (brightness) and chrominance (colour information). JPEG allows more losses on the chrominance and less on the luminance. This is because the human eye is less sensitive to colour changes than to brightness changes. In an RGB image, all three channels carry some brightness information but the green component has a stronger effect on brightness than the blue component.

A typical scheme for converting RGB into luminance and colour is known as CCIR 601, which converts the components into Y (can be equated to brightness), C_b (blueness) and C_r (redness). The Y component can be used as a black and white version of the image. The components are computed from the RGB components:

> **DEAR COMPRESSION AGENT**
>
> **Question:** *Why, with video and images, do you convert from RGB into something else?*
>
> Video cameras have sensors for Red, Green and Blue (the primary colours for video information). In TV, before colour TV, these colours were converted into luminance (Y). When colour TV arrived they had to hide the extra colour information and then send it as U and V (Redness and Blueness). Thus for TV, RGB is converted into YUV. With images, the human eye is very sensitive to changes in brightness in any object, and not so sensitive to colour changes. Thus colour changes can be compressed more than the luminance. This is why RGB is converted in YC_bC_r. For example, 4:2:2 uses twice as many samples for luminance than redness and blueness, and 4:1:1 uses four times as many samples.

$$Y = 0.299R + 0.587G + 0.114B$$
$$C_b = 0.1687R - 0.3313G + 0.5B$$
$$C_r = 0.5R - 0.4187G + 0.0813B$$

For the brightness it can be seen that green has the most effect and blue has the least. For the redness, the red colour (of course) has the most effect and green the least, and for the blueness, the blue colour has the most effect and green the least. Note that the YC_bC_r components are often known as YUV.

A subsampling process is then conducted which samples the C_b and C_r components at a lower rate than the Y component. A typical sampling rate is four samples of the Y component to a single sample on the C_b and C_r component. This sampling rate is normally set with the compression parameters. The lower the sampling, the smaller the compressed data and the shorter the compression time. All the required information on how to decode the JPEG data is contained in the JPEG header.

DCT coding

The DCT (discrete cosine transform) converts intensity data into frequency data, which can be used to tell how fast the intensities vary. In JPEG coding the image is segmented into 8×8 pixel rectangles, as illustrated in Figure 8.8. If the image contains several components (such as Y, C_b, C_r or R, G, B), then each of the components in the pixel blocks is operated on separately. If an image is subsampled, there will be more blocks of some components than of others. For example, for 2×2 sampling there will be four blocks of Y data for each block of C_b or C_r data.

The data points in the 8×8 pixel array start at the upper right at $(0, 0)$ and finish at the lower right at $(7, 7)$. At the point (x, y) the data value is $f(x, y)$. The DCT produces a new 8×8 block $(u \times v)$ of transformed data using the formula:

$$F(u,v) = \frac{1}{4} C(u) C(v) \left[\sum_{x=0}^{7} \sum_{y=0}^{7} f(x,y) \cos \frac{(2x+1)u\pi}{16} \cos \frac{(2y+1)v\pi}{16} \right]$$

$$\text{where} \quad C(z) = \frac{1}{\sqrt{2}} \quad \text{if } z = 0$$

$$\text{or} \quad = 1 \quad \text{if } z \neq 0$$

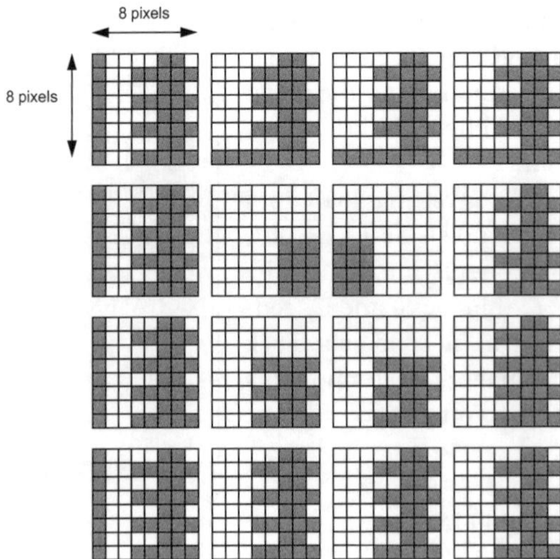

Figure 8.8 Segment of an image in 8x8 pixel blocks

This results in an array of space frequency $F(u, v)$ which gives the rate of change at a given point. These are normally 12-bit values which give a range of 0 to 4095. Each component specifies the degree to which the image changes over the sampled block. For example:

- $F(0,0)$ gives the average value of the 8×8 array.
- $F(1,0)$ gives the degree to which the values change slowly (low frequency).
- $F(7,7)$ gives the degree to which the values change most quickly in both directions (high frequency).

The coefficients are equivalent to representing changes of frequency within the data block. The value in the upper left block (0, 0) is the DC or average value. The values to the right of a row have increasing horizontal frequency and the values to the bottom of a column have increasing vertical frequency. Many of the bands end up having zero or almost zero terms, which is useful when we compress long runs of zero values.

8.7.2 Motion video compression

Motion video contains massive amounts of redundant information. This is because each image has redundant information and also because there are very few changes from one image to the next.

Motion video image compression relies on two facts:

- Images have a great deal of redundancy (repeated images, repetitive, superfluous, duplicated, exceeding what is necessary, and so on).
- The human eye and brain have limitations on what they can perceive.

DEAR COMPRESSION AGENT

Question: *Why when I watch digital TV, or a DVD movie, does the screen sometimes display large rectangular blocks, or objects which seem to move incorrectly across the screen?*

MPEG splits images up into blocks. As part of the compression process, MPEG splits each frame into a series of blocks. These blocks are then transformed. To increase compression, MPEG sends the complete picture every so often, and then just sends updates in the differences between the frames. Thus if your reception is not very good then you may fail to get the complete update of the picture, and only receive parts of the update. Also MPEG tries to track moving objects, it will then group the moving object, and transmit how the object moves. Sometimes this has not been encoded very well, and the object seems to move incorrectly across the screen. Normally this is because there are not enough updates to the complete frame.

Question: *Why does MPEG have to send/store the complete picture every few frames? Would it not be possible to send/store one complete frame, and then just send/store the changes from frame to frame?*

This would work fine, and would give excellent compression, but the user would not be able to move quickly through the MPEG film, as the decoder would have to read the initial frame, and then all the updates to determine how the frames changed. Also if there were corrupt data, it would propagate through the whole film. Thus there is a compromise between the number of intermediate frames and the number of main frames.

As with JPEG, the Motion Picture Experts Group (MPEG) was setup to develop an international open standard for the compression of high-quality audio and video information. At the time, CD-ROM single-speed technology allowed a maximum bit rate of 1.2 Mbps and this was the rate that the standard was built around. These days, $\times 12$ and $\times 20$ CD-ROM bit rates are common, which allow for smoother and faster animations.

MPEG's main aim was to provide good quality video and audio using hardware processors (and in some cases, on workstations with sufficient computing power, to perform the tasks using software). Figure 8.9 shows the main processing steps of encoding:

- **Image conversion** – normally involves converting images from RGB into YUV (or YC_rC_b) terms with optional colour subsampling.
- **Conversion into slices and macro-blocks** – a key part of MPEG's compression is the detection of movement within a frame. To detect motion a frame is subdivided into slices then each slice is divided into a number of macroblocks. Only the luminance component is then used for the motion calculations. In the subblock, luminance (*Y*) values use a 16×16 pixel macroblock, whereas the two chrominance components have 8×8 pixel macroblocks.
- **Motion estimation** – MPEG uses a motion estimation algorithm to search for multiple blocks of pixels within a given search area and tries to track objects which move across the image.
- **DCT conversion** – as with JPEG, MPEG uses the DCT method. This transform is used because it exploits the physiology of the human eye. It converts a block of pixels from the spatial domain into the frequency domain. This allows the higher-frequency terms to be reduced, as the human eye is less sensitive to fast changes of colour, or luminance.
- **Encoding** – the final stages involve organizing the data into a pattern which will tend to produce long runs of zero value. These are then compressed with run-length encoding and then finally with fixed Huffman code to produce a variable-length code.

Colour space conversion

The first stage of MPEG encoding is to convert a video image into the correct colour space format. In most cases, the incoming data is in 24-bit RGB colour format and is converted in 4:2:2 YC_rC_b (or YUV) form. Some information will obviously be lost in the conversion of the colour components, as there will only be half the number of samples for the redness and the blueness as there is for the luminance, but it results in some compression.

Slices and macroblocks

MPEG compression tries to detect movement within a frame. This is done by subdividing a frame into slices and then subdividing each slice into a number of macroblocks. For example, a PAL format which has:

352×288 pixel frame (101 376 pixels)

can, when divided into 16×16 blocks, give a whole number of 396 macroblocks. Dividing 288 by 16 gives a whole number of 18 slices, and dividing 352 gives 22. Thus the image is split into 22 macroblocks in the *x*-direction and 18 in the *y*-direction, as illustrated in Figure 8.10.

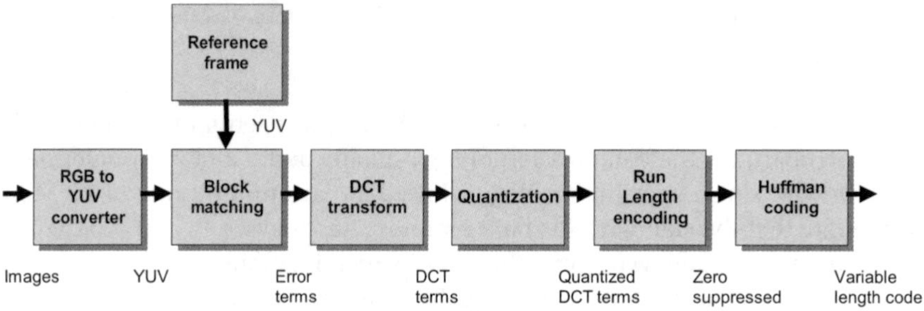

Figure 8.9 MPEG encoding with block matching

Luminance (Y) values use a 16×16 pixel macroblock, whereas the two chrominance components have 8×8 pixel macroblocks. Note that only the luminance component is used for the motion calculations.

Motion estimation

MPEG uses a motion estimation algorithm to search for multiple blocks of pixels within a given search area and tries to track objects which move across the image. Each luminance (Y) 16×16 macroblock is compared with other macroblocks within either a previous or future frame to find a close match. When a close match is found, a vector is used to describe where the block is to be located, as well as any difference information from the compared block. As there tend to be very few changes from one frame to the next, it is far more efficient than using the original data.

Figure 8.1 shows two consecutive images of 2D luminance made up into 16×5 megablocks. Each of these blocks has 16×16 pixels. It can be seen that, in this example, there are very few differences between the two images. If the previous image is transmitted in its entirety then the current image can be transmitted with reference to the previous image. For example, the megablocks for $(0,0)$, $(0,1)$ and $(0,2)$ in the current block are the same as in the previous blocks. Thus they can be coded simply with a reference to the previous image. The $(0,3)$ megablock is different to the previous image, but the $(0,3)$ block is identical to the $(0,2)$ block of the previous image, thus a reference to this block is made. This can continue, as most of the blocks in the image are identical to the previous image. The only other differences in the current image are at $(4,0)$ and $(4,1)$; these blocks can be stored in their entirety or specified with their differences to a previous similar block.

DEAR COMPRESSION AGENT

Question: *Why don't we just use the ZIP format for everything? It seems to be a good compression technique.*

Well, the ZIP format uses entropy compression, which does not take into account the type of data being compressed. With audio and video compression there are lots of little tricks that can be done to enhance the compression, such as:

- The human eye is more sensitive to changes to luminance than it is to changes in colour. Thus we can reduce the amount of information on changes of colour.
- The human ear tends to perceive only the music that is playing in the foreground, thus any background sounds can be suppressed.
- In video compression, there tends to be very few changes from frame to frame, thus it is better to just store the difference between two frames. This can also go for audio, where the audio samples will only vary within a certain range, thus only the difference between the samples needs to be stored.
- In audio and video, repetitive sequences can be located, and then reference can be made to them from previous instances, giving information on how they have changed.
- Audio and video information tends to be stored in a time-based format, but if is it converted into the frequency or the spatial domain, it can considerably enhance compression, as these components tend to vary less over time. Have a look at a graphical equalizer on a hi-fi and you'll see that the frequency component in audio tends not to vary too much.

A major objective of the MPEG encoder is to spend a much greater time compressing the video information into its most efficient form. Each macroblock is compared mathematically with other blocks in a previous frame, or even in a future frame. The offset information to another block can be over a macroblock boundary or even over a pixel boundary. This comparison then repeats until a match is found or the specified search area within the frame has been exhausted. If no match is available, the search process can be repeated using a different frame or the macroblock can be stored as a complete set of data. As previously stated, if a match is found, the vector information specifying where the matching macroblock is located is used along with any difference information.

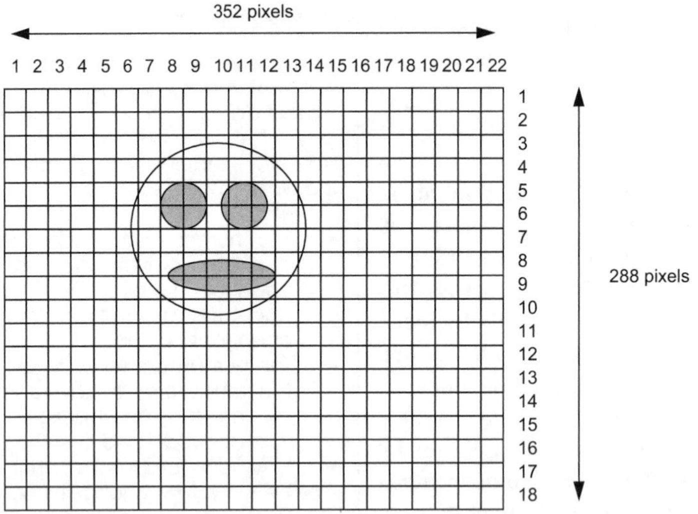

Figure 8.10 Segmentation of an image into subblocks

As the technique involves very many searches over a wide search area and there are many frames to be encoded, the encoder must normally be a high-powered workstation. This has several implications:

- **Asymmetrical compression**. MPEG uses an asymmetrical compression process, where a relatively large amount of computing power is required for the encoder and much less for the decoder. The encoding process is normally achieved in non-real time whereas the decoder reads the data in real time (as the user requires to view the video, without having large pauses, while the decoder processes the compressed data). As processing power and memory capacity increase, more computers will be able to compress video information in real time. Even mobile devices will have the processing power and memory to be able to process MPEG in real time.
- **Compression quality**. Encoders influence the quality of the decoded image dramatically. If the encoder takes shortcuts, such as limited search areas and macroblock matching, it can result in poor picture quality, irrespective of the quality of the decoder.
- **Memory requirements**. The decoder normally requires a large amount of electronic memory to store past and future frames, which may be needed for motion estimation.

With the motion estimation completed, the raw data describing the frame is now converted by DCT algorithm to be ready for Huffman coding.

I, P and B-frames

As video frames tend not to change much between frames, MPEG video compression uses either full frames (which contain all the frame data), or partial frames (which refer back to other frames). The three frames types are defined as:

> **The Disappearing Internet**
>
> 'Many people talk about the disappearing computer. Well, it has already disappeared. Computer chips may seem relatively large, but the actual silicon that they use covers a very small area. It's really just the casing and the pins that take up the space. If there were no interfaces to anything then the computer would be the size of this bookmark. Look at computer monitors, disk drives, and so on. All of these could blend themselves into our lives. Hard disks could be replaced by small pieces of silicon (Flash RAMs) and a computer monitor by a thin display. The most important thing though, will not be the processor, or the amount of memory, or whether it can play DVD movies, it will be its connection to the Internet. If you have access to the Internet, you are part of the world's biggest mainframe. Part of the largest distributed system ever created (or should I say to evolve, as the Internet was never really created, or was it?). A living, breathing, digital world. The future is towards computers which will become a part of the fabric of our lives. So, what's going to disappear? The Internet, as it will become part of the fabrics of our lives. For too long our communications have been controlled by governments, large corporations and monopolistic telephone companies, but not any more.

- **Intra frame (I-frame).** An intra frame, or I-frame, is a complete image and does not require any extra information to be added to it to make it complete. As it is a complete frame, it cannot contain any motion estimation processing. It is typically used as a starting point for other referenced frames, and is usually the first frame to be sent.
- **Predictive frame (P-frame).** The predictive frame, or P-frame, uses the preceding I-frame as its reference and has motion estimation processing. Each macroblock in this frame is supplied as referenced to an I-frame as either a vector and difference, or if no match was found, as a completely encoded macroblock (called an intracoded macroblock). The decoder must thus retain all I-frame information to allow the P-frame to be decoded.
- **Bidirectional frame (B-frame).** The bidirectional frame, or B-frame, is similar to the P-frame except that it references frames to the nearest preceding or future I- or P-frame. When compressing the data, the motion estimation works on the future frame first, followed by the past frame. If this does not give a good match, an average of the two frames is used. If all else fails, the macroblock can be intracoded. As B-frames reference preceding and future frames, it requires that many I- and P-frames are retained in memory, which will require a relatively large amount of memory, as apposed to using I-frames, and P-frames, only.

Other enhancements include:

- **Any order of frames**. MPEG also allows frames to be ordered in any sequence. Unfortunately a large amount of reordering requires many frame buffers that must be stored until all dependencies are cleared.
- **Random access**. MPEG allows random access to a video sequence, thus the file must contain regular I-frames. Regular I-frames also allow enhanced modes such as fast forward, which means that an I-frame is required every 0.4 seconds, or 12 frames between each I-frame (at 30 fps).

At 30 fps, a typical sequence starts with an I-frame, followed by two B-frames, a P-frame, followed by two B-frames, and so on. This is known as a group of picture (GOP):

I⇒B⇒B⇒P⇒B⇒B⇒ I⇒B⇒B⇒P⇒B⇒B⇒ I⇒B⇒B⇒P⇒...

When decoding, the decoder must store the I-frame, and the next two B-frames until the B-frame arrives. The next two B-frames have to be stored locally until the P-frame arrives. The P-frame can be decoded using the stored I-frame and the two B-frames can be decoded using the I- and P-frames. One solution of this is to reorder the frames so that the I- and P-frames are sent together followed by the two intermediate B-frames. Another more radical solution is not to send B-frames at all, simply to use I- and P-frames.

On computers with limited memory and limited processing power, the B-frames are difficult to process as they:

- Increase the encoding computational load and memory storage. The inclusion of the previous and future I- and P-frames as well as the arithmetic average greatly increases the processing needed. The increased frame buffers to store frames allow the encode and decode processes to proceed. This argument is again less valid with the advent of large and high-density memories.
- They do not provide a direct reference in the same way that an I- or P-frame does.

The advantage of B-frames is that they lead to an improved signal-to-noise ratio because of the averaging out of macroblocks between I- and P-frames. This averaging effectively reduces high-frequency random noise. It is particularly useful in lower bit rate applications, but is of less benefit with higher rates, which normally have improved signal-to-noise ratios.

DEAR COMPRESSION AGENT

Question: *All music seems to be becoming digital, but what's the great advantage when you* ***lose*** *something in the conversion?*

Yes. Something is lost in the conversion (the quantization error), but this stays constant, whereas the analogue value is likely to change. The benefits of converting to digital audio outweigh the drawbacks, such as:

- The quality of the digital audio system only depends on the conversion process, whereas the quality of an analogue audio system depends on the component parts of the system.
- Digital components tend to be easier and cheaper to produce than high-specification analogue components.
- Copying digital information is relatively easy and does not lead to a degradation of the signal.
- Digital storage tends to use less physical space than equivalent analogue forms.
- It is easier to transmit digital data.
- Information can be added to digital data so that errors can be corrected.
- Improved signal-to-noise ratios and dynamic ranges are possible with a digital audio system.

Practical MPEG compression

Most MPEG encoders typically have a range of parameters which can be changed to give the required quality. The following outline some of the main parameters.

Frame rate and data rate

The frame rate and data rate are two parameters which greatly affect the quality of the encoded bitstream. The frame rate is normally set by the frame rate of the input format, such as 23.976, 24, 25, 29.97, 30, 50, 59.94, and 60 frames/sec. Many encoders do not support all of these rates for the output so there are two modes which can be used to reduce or increase the frame rate, these are:

- Keep original number of frames. In this mode the frames are encoded frames as they are ordered in the input file, but the MPEG decoder plays these files at the wrong speed, such as slowing them down with a lower frame rate or faster to give a faster frame rate.
- Keep original duration. In this mode the encoder either duplicates (to increase rate) or skips some of the input frames (to reduce the rate) to provide the correct playback frame rate.

Most encoding systems allow the user to specify the data rate of the encoded bitstream, and the encoder then tries to keep to this limit when it is encoding the input bitstream. For example, a single-speed CD-ROM requires a maximum data rate of 150 KB/sec. This rate is relatively low and there may be some degradation of quality to produce this. Reasonable quality requires at least 300 KB/sec.

DCT conversion

As with JPEG, MPEG uses the DCT, and transforms macroblocks of luminance (16 × 16) and chrominance (8 × 8) into the frequency domain. This allows the higher-frequency terms to be reduced as the human eye is less sensitive to high-frequency changes.

Frames are broken up into slices 16 pixels high, and each slice is broken up into a vector of macroblocks having 16 × 16 pixels. Each macroblock contains luminance and chrominance components for each of four 8 × 8 pixel blocks. Colour decimation can be applied to a macroblock, which yields four 8 × 8 blocks for luminance and two 8 × 8 blocks (C_b and C_r) of chrominance, using one or two chrominance values for each of the four luminance values. This is called the 4:1:1 or 4:2:2 format, respectively.

For each macroblock, a spatial offset difference between a macroblock in the predicted frame and the reference frame(s) is given if one exists (a motion vector), along with a luminance value and/or chrominance difference value (an error term) if needed. Macroblocks with no differences can be skipped except in intra frames. Blocks with differences are internally compressed, using a combination of a discrete cosine transform (DCT) algorithm on pixel blocks (or error blocks) and variable quantization on the resulting frequency coefficient (rounding off values to one of a limited set of values).

The DCT algorithm accepts signed, 9-bit pixel values and produces signed 12-bit coefficients. The DCT is applied to one block at a time, and works much as it does for JPEG, converting each 8 × 8 block into an 8 × 8 matrix of frequency coefficients. The variable quantization process divides each coefficient by a corresponding factor in a matching 8 × 8 matrix and rounds to an integer.

Quantization

As with JPEG the converted data is divided, or quantized, to remove higher-frequency components and to make more of the values zero. This results in numerous zero coefficients, particularly for high-frequency terms at the high end of the matrix. Accordingly, amplitudes are recorded in run-length form following a diagonal scan pattern from low frequency to high frequency.

Encoding

After the DCT and quantization state, the resultant data is then compressed using Huffman coding with a set of fixed tables. The Huffman code not only specifies the number of zeros, but also the value that ended the run of zeros. This is extremely efficient in compressing the zigzag DCT encoding method.

8.7.3 Audio compression

Initially when audio was converted to digital information (using PCM), no-one actually knew how many bits would be required to code each of the sample. The greater the number of bits used, the more accurate the decoded value will be. For every sample, an error results, which will result in noise. This noise is known as quantization noise, and it can become noticeable when it becomes relatively large, as compared with the signal. Thus, as no-one knew how this noise would be perceived, it was decided that the best test would be to let users listen to the digitized audio for differing sample sizes, and decide the one which gave the required quality. For telephone quality speech it was found that 8 bits are required, and for hi-fi quality it was found that at least 14 bits are required. Any increase in the number of bits used will improve the quality, and reduce any noise in the digitized bit stream. Unfortunately this increases the amount of bits used to encode the audio.

Audio signals normally use PCM (pulse coded modulation) codes which can be compressed to reduce the number of bits used to code the samples. For high-quality monochannel audio, the signal bandwidth is normally limited to 20 kHz, thus it is sampled at 44.1 kHz. If each sample is coded with 16 bits then the basic bit rate will be:

$$\text{Digitized audio signal rate} = 44.1 \times 16 \text{ kbps} = 705.6 \text{ kbps}$$

For stereo signals the bit rate would be 1.4112 Mbps. Many digital audio systems add extra bits from error control and framing, which increases the bit rate, but results in a more robust signal.

Digital audio normally involves the processes of:

- Filtering the input signal.
- Sampling the signal at twice the highest frequency.
- Converting it into a digital form with an ADC (analogue-to-digital converter).
- Converting the parallel data into a serial form.
- Storing or transmitting the serial information.
- When reading (or receiving) the data the clock information is filtered out using a PLL (phase-locked loop).
- The recovered clock is then used with a SIPO (serial-in parallel-out) converter to convert the data back into a parallel form.
- Converting the digital data back into an analogue voltage.
- Filtering the analogue voltage.

These steps are illustrated in Figure 8.11. The clock recovery part is important; and there is no need to save or transmit separate clock information because it can be embedded into the data. It also has the advantage that a fixed clock becomes jittery when it is affected by noise, thus if the clock information is transmitted separately over relatively long distances it will be jittery.

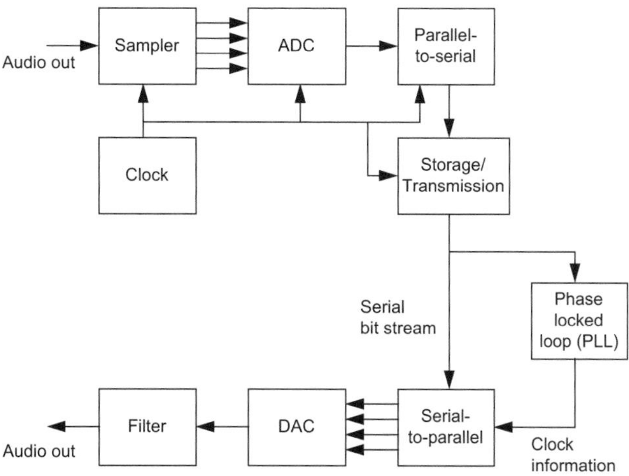

Figure 8.11 A digital audio system

CD-quality stereo audio requires a bit rate of 1.411200 Mbps (2×16 bits $\times 44.1$ kHz). A single-speed CD-ROM can only transfer at a rate of 1.5 Mbps, and this rate must include both audio and video. Thus there is a great need for compression of both the video and audio data. The need to compress high-quality audio is also an increasing need as consumers expect higher-quality sound from TV systems and the increasing usage of digital audio radio.

A number of standards have been put forward for digital audio coding for TV/video systems. One of the first was MUSICAM, which is now part of the MPEG-1 coding system. The FCC Advisory Committee considered several audio systems for advanced television systems, but there was generally no agreement on the best technology. As it is often difficult to determine the performance of an audio system purely by its technical performance, it was finally decided to conduct a side-by-side test. The winner was Dolby AC-3, and in second place was MPEG coding. Many cable, cinemas and satellite TV systems now use either MPEG or Dolby AC-3 coding.

Psycho-acoustic model

MPEG and Dolby AC-3 use the psycho-acoustic model to reduce the data rate, which exploits the characteristics of the human ear. This is similar to the method used in MPEG video compression which uses the fact that the human eye has a lack of sensitivity to the higher-frequency video components (that is, sharp changes of colour or contrast). The psycho-acoustic model allows certain frequency components to be reduced in size without affecting the perceived audio quality as heard by the listener.

A well-known audio effect is the masking effect, where noise is only heard by a person when there are no other sounds to mask it. A typical example is in high-frequency hiss from a compact cassette when there are quiet passages of music. When there are normal periods of music the louder music masks out the quieter hiss and it is not heard. In reality, the brain is masking out the part of the sound it wants to hear, even though the noise component is still there. When there is no music to mask the sound, the noise is heard.

Noise, itself, tends to occur across a wide range of frequencies, but the masking effect also occurs with sounds. A loud sound at a certain frequency masks out a quieter sound at a similar frequency. As a result the sound heard by the listener appears only to contain the loud sounds, which masks out the quieter one. The psycho-acoustic model tries to reduce the levels to those that would be perceived by the brain.

Figure 8.12 illustrates this psycho-acoustic process. In this case a masking level has been applied and all the amplitudes below this level have been reduced in size. Since these frequencies have been reduced in amplitude, and any noise associated with them is also significantly reduced. This basically has the effect of limiting the bandwidth of the signal to the key frequency ranges.

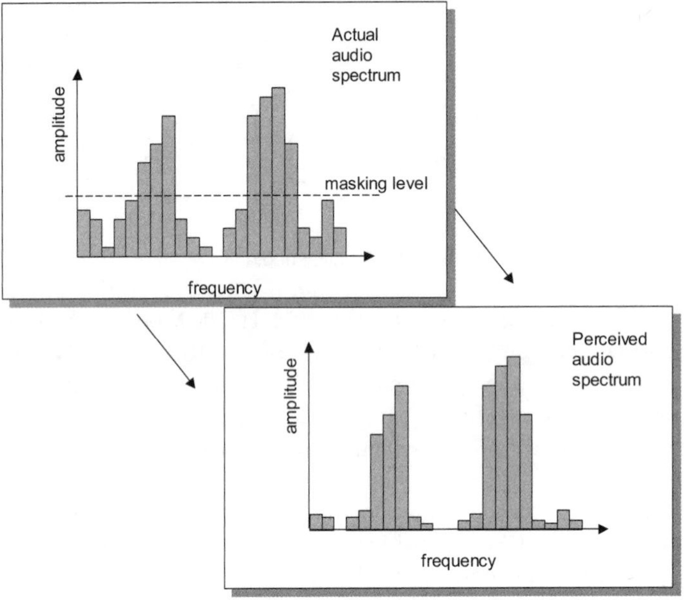

Figure 8.12 Difference between actual and perceived audio spectrum

The psycho-acoustic model also takes into account non-linearities in the sensitivity of the ear. The ear's peak sensitivity is between 2 and 4 kHz (the range of the human voice) and it is least sensitive around the extremes of the frequency range (that it, high and low frequencies). Any noise in the less sensitive frequency ranges is more easily masked, but it is important to minimize any noise in the peak range because it has a greater impact.

Masking can also be applied in the time domain, where it can be applied just before and after a strong sound (such as a change of between 30 and 40 dB). Typically, premasking occurs for about 2–5 ms before the sound is perceived by the listener and the postmasking effect lasts for about 100 ms after the end of the source.

For audio, MPEG basically has three different levels:

- MPEG-Audio Level I – This uses the psycho-acoustic model to mask and reduce the sample size. It is basically a simplified version of MUSICAM and has a quality which is nearly equivalent to CD-quality audio. Its main advantage is that it allows the construction of simple encoders and decoders with medium performance and which will operate fairly well at 192 or 256 kbps.
- MPEG-Audio Level II – This is identical to the MUSICAM standard. It is also nearly equivalent to CD-quality audio and is optimized for a bit rate of 96 or 128 kbps per monophonic channel.

- MPEG-Audio Level III (MP-3) – This is a combination of the MUSICAM scheme and ASPEC, a sound compression scheme designed in Erlangen, Germany. Its main advantage is that it can produce reasonable quality audio at rates of 64 kbps per audio channel. At that speed, the quality is very close to CD quality and produces a sound quality which is better than MPEG Level-II operating at 64 kbps.

The three levels are basically supersets of each other with Level III decoders being capable of decoding both Level I and Level II data. Level I is the simplest, while Level III gives the highest compression but is the most computational in coding.

The forward and backward compatible MPEG-2 system, following recommendations from SMPTE, EBU and others, has increased the audio capacity to five channels. Figure 8.13 shows an example of a 5-channel system; the key elements are:

- A centre channel.
- Left and right surround channels.
- Left and right channels (as hi-fi stereo).

MPEG-2 also includes a low-frequency effects channel (called LFE, essentially a sub-woofer). This has a much lower bandwidth than the other channels. This type of system is often called a 5.1-channel system (5 main channels and LFE channel).

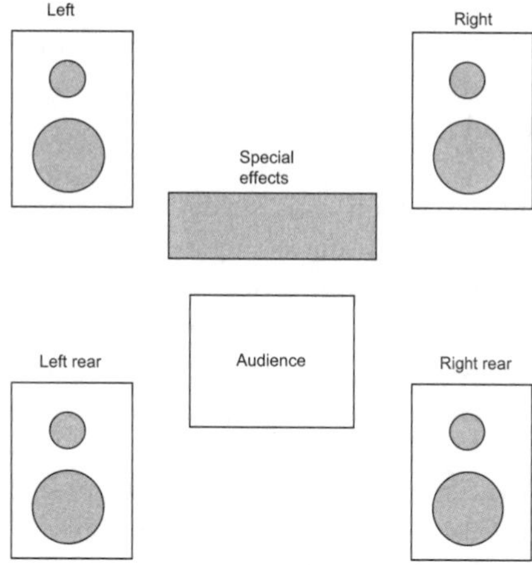

Figure 8.13 A 5.1 channel audio surround sound system

8.8 Exercises

8.8.1 How much memory would an uncompressed 640×480 image with 256 colours take in memory:

(a) 300 KB (b) 2400 KB (c) 76800 KB (d) 1 MB

Additional material and tutorial questions are available at:

`http://www.palgrave.com/studyskills/masterseries/buchanan`

9 Introduction to networks

9.1 Introduction

Networking involves the interconnection of workstations, terminals and other networked devices. In most cases a network allows computers of different types to intercommunicate using a network protocol. The protocol that the computers use is thus more important to communication, than their actual make. Thus, in order for them to intercommunicate, computers on a network must have a common protocol.

Many of the first computers were standalone devices, and thus worked independently from other computers. This caused many problems, including:

- The difficulty to intercommunicate between computers.
- The difficulty in managing the configuration of the computers.
- The requirement for duplication of resources, as each computer required its own resource, such as a dedicated printer, a dedicated modem, and so on.

These problems were solved with local area networks (LANs), which connect computers and other devices within a single building. One of the great advantages of LANs was that they allowed the sharing of files and printers. They are also efficient in transferring files within an organization, but it was still difficult to transmit data over a large geographical area. This led to the development of WANs (wide area networks), and MANs (metropolitan area networks).

The order of size for networks are:

- **Local area networks** (LANs), which connect over a relatively small geographical area, typically connecting computers within a single office or building. In most cases they connect to a common electronic connection – commonly known as a network backbone. LANs can connect to other networks either directly or through a WAN or MAN.
- **Metropolitan area networks** (MANs), which normally connect networks around a town or city. They are smaller than a WAN, but larger than a LAN. An example of a MAN is the EaStMAN (Edinburgh and Stirling MAN) network that connects universities and colleges in Edinburgh and Stirling, UK, as illustrated in Figure 9.1.
- **Wide area networks** (WANs), which connect networks over a large geographical area, such as between different buildings, towns or even countries.

The four main methods of connecting a network (or an independently connected computer) to another network are:

- Through a **modem** connection. A modem converts digital data into an analogue form that can be transmitted over a standard telephone line.
- Through an **ISDN** connection. An ISDN (integrated services digital network) connection uses the public telephone service and differs from a modem connection in that it sends data in a digital form.
- Through a **gateway**. A gateway connects one type of network to another type.
- Through a **bridge** or **router**. Bridges and routers normally connect one type of network to one of the same type. Normally, these days, gateways are routers.

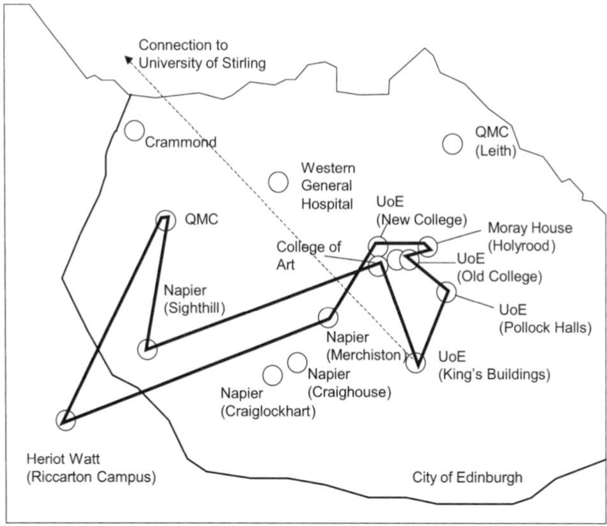

Figure 9.1 Layout of the EaStMAN network

The 1980s saw a growth in networks, but in many cases they became difficult to configure as new networking technologies used different types of hardware and software implementations, which caused incompatibilities with other types of networking equipment. Soon a number of specifications started to appear, each of which had difficulty in communicating with other types. To overcome this, in 1984, the International Organization for Standardization (ISO) developed a new model called the OSI Reference Model, which was based on research into network technologies such as:

- **SNA** (Systems Network Architecture). Developed by IBM in the 1970s. It is large and complex, and is similar in its approach to the developed OSI reference model, especially, as it also has seven layers.
- **DECNET.** Developed by DEC, and has been recently developed into DECnet/OSI which supports both OSI protocols and proprietary DEC protocols.
- **TCP/IP** (Transmission Control Protocol/Internet Protocol). Developed by US Department of Defense in the 1970s. Its main function was to allow the intercommunication of computers over a global network (the Internet). It is now used by all of the computers which connect to the Internet.

The developed model has since allowed:

- Compatibility – allows manufacturers to create networks which are compatible with each other.
- Interoperability – allows the transfer of data between different types of computers, no matter their architecture, their operating system, or their network connection type.

Along with the developed model, a number of standards have been defined, which are basically a set of rules or procedures that are either widely used or officially specified.

9.2 Advantages and disadvantages of networks

Networks allow the orderly flow of information between connected nodes. Their main advantages are that:

- It is easier to set up new users and equipment.
- It allows the sharing of resources (see Figure 9.2).
- It is easier to administer users.
- It is easier to administer software licenses.
- It allows electronic mail to be sent between users.
- It allows simple electronic access to remote computers and sites.
- It allows the connection of different types of computers which can communicate with each other.

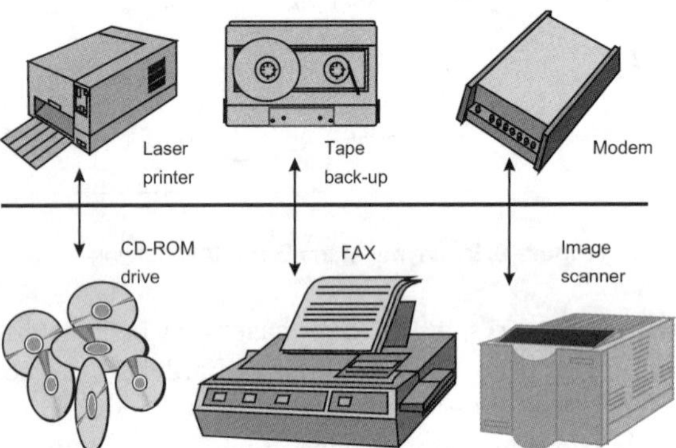

Figure 9.2 Local network with a range of facilities

9.2.1 Sharing information

A major advantage of LANs is their ability to share information over a network. Normally, it is easier to store application programs at a single location and make them available to users rather than having copies individually installed on each computer (unless the application program requires special configurations or there are special licensing agreements). This saves on expensive disk space and increases the availability of common data and configurations. The disadvantage of this is that it increases the traffic on a network.

Most networks have a network manager, or network group, who manage the users and peripherals on a network. On a well-maintained network the network manager will:

- Control the users on the network, that is, who can and cannot login.
- Control which of the users are allowed to use which facilities.
- Control which of the users are allowed to run which application programs.
- Control the usage of software packages by limiting users to license agreements.
- Standardize the set up of application programs to a single source.
- Back-up important files on a regular basis onto a mass back-up system.
- Set up simple-to-use procedures to access programs, such as icons, menus, and so on.
- Possibly control PC (personal computer) viruses by running automatic scanning programs.
- Update application programs by modifying them at a single source.

9.2.2 Sharing disk resources (network file servers)

Many computer systems require access to a great deal of information and to run many application programs such as word processors, spreadsheets, compilers, presentation packages, computer-aided design (CAD) packages, and so on. Most local hard disks could not store all the required data and application programs, thus a network allows users to access files and application programs on remote disks.

Some distributed, multitasking operating systems such as UNIX and VMS allow all the hard disks on a network to be electronically linked as a single file system. Most PCs normally are networked to file servers, which provide networked file systems. A network file server thus allows users to access a central file system (for PCs) or a distributed file system (for UNIX/VMS). This is illustrated in Figure 9.3.

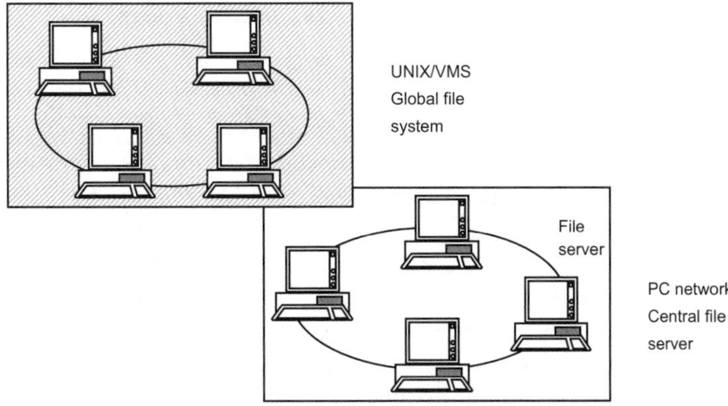

Figure 9.3 Sharing disk space with UNIX/VMS and PC network

9.2.3 Sharing resources

Computers not connected to a network may require extra peripherals such as printers, fax machines, modems, plotters, and so on. This may be resource inefficient, as other users cannot get access to them unless they are physically disconnected and connected to their own computer. Normally, it is more efficient to share resources over a network.

Access to networked peripherals is also likely to be simpler as the system manager can standardize configurations. Peripherals that are relatively difficult to set up such as plotters, fax machines and modems can be set up once and their configuration stored. The network manager can also bar certain users from using certain peripherals.

There is normally a trade-off between the usage of a peripheral and the number required. For example a single laser printer in a busy office may not be able to cope with the demand. A good network copes with this by segmentation, so that printers are assigned to different areas or users. The network may also allow for re-direction of printer data if a printer was to fail, or become busy.

9.2.4 Electronic mail

Electronic mail (e-mail) is one use of the Internet, which, according to most businesses, improves productivity. Traditional methods of sending mail within an office environment are inefficient, as it normally requires an individual requesting a secretary to type the letter. This must then be proofread and sent through the internal mail system, which is relatively slow and can be open to security breaches.

A faster, and more secure method of sending information is to use electronic mail, where messages are sent almost in an instant. For example, a memo with 100 words can be sent within a fraction of a second. It is also simple to send to specific groups, various individuals, company-wide, and so on. Other types of data can also be sent with the mail message such as images, sound, and so on. It may also be possible to determine if a user has read the mail. The main advantages can be summarized as:

- It is normally much cheaper than using the telephone (although, as time equates to money for most companies, this relates any savings or costs to a user's typing speed).
- Many different types of data can be transmitted, such as images, documents, speech, and so on.
- It is much faster than the postal service.
- Users can filter incoming e-mail easier than incoming telephone calls.
- It normally cuts out the need for work to be typed, edited and printed by a secretary.
- It reduces the burden on the mailroom.
- It is normally more secure than traditional methods.
- It is relatively easy to send to groups of people (traditionally, either a circulation list was required or a copy to everyone in the group was required).
- It is usually possible to determine whether the recipient has actually read the message (the electronic mail system sends back an acknowledgement).

First microprocessor

In the late 1960s, the electronics industry was producing cheap pocket calculators, which led to the development of affordable computers when the Japanese company Busicom commissioned Intel to produce a set of between eight and 12 ICs for a calculator. Then, instead of designing a complete set of ICs, Ted Hoff at Intel designed an integrated circuit chip that could receive instructions and perform simple integrated functions on data. The design became the 4004 microprocessor. Intel produced a set of ICs that could be programmed to perform different tasks. These were the first ever microprocessors and soon Intel produced a general-purpose 4-bit microprocessor, named the 4004.

The main disadvantages are:

- It stops people using the telephone.
- It cannot be used as a legal document.
- Electronic mail messages can be sent impulsively and may be later regretted (sending by traditional methods normally allows for a rethink). In extreme cases messages can be sent to the wrong person (typically when replying to an e-mail message, where a message is sent to the entire mailing list [Reply to All] rather than the originator).
- It may be difficult to send to some remote sites. Some organizations have either no electronic mail or merely an intranet. Large companies are particularly wary of Internet connections and limit the amount of external traffic.
- Not everyone reads his or her electronic mail on a regular basis (although this is changing as more organizations adopt e-mail as the standard communications medium).

9.2.5 Peer-to-peer communication

A major problem with computers is to make them communicate with a different computer type or with another that possibly uses a different operating system. A local network allows different types of computers running different operating systems to share information over the network. This is named peer-to-peer exchange and is illustrated in Figure 9.4.

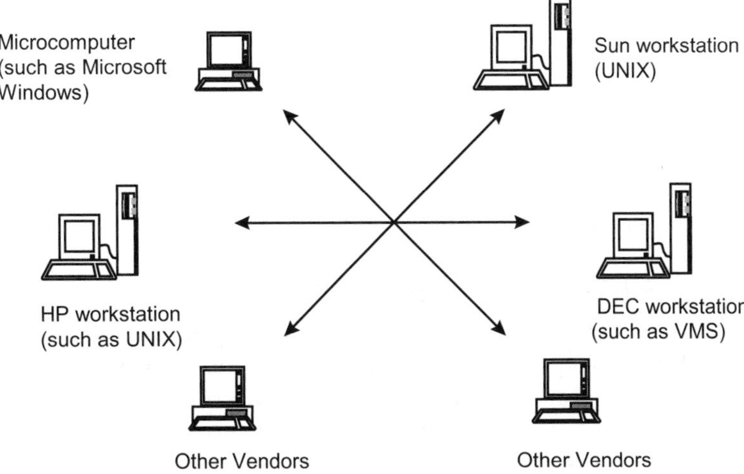

Figure 9.4 Peer-to-peer exchange over a network

9.2.6 Remote login

A major advantage of networks is that they allow users to remotely log into other computers. The computer being logged into must be running a multitasking operating system, such as UNIX. Figure 9.5 shows an example of three devices (a workstation, an X-windows terminal and a PC) logging into a powerful workstation. This method allows many less powerful computers to be linked to a few powerful machines.

9.2.7 Protecting information

Most computers have information which must not be read or modified by certain users. It is difficult to protect information on a stand-alone computer, as typically all that is required is to wait until the user is not using the computer. On a network each user can be granted certain rights and privileges to stored information, which can be protected by a password.

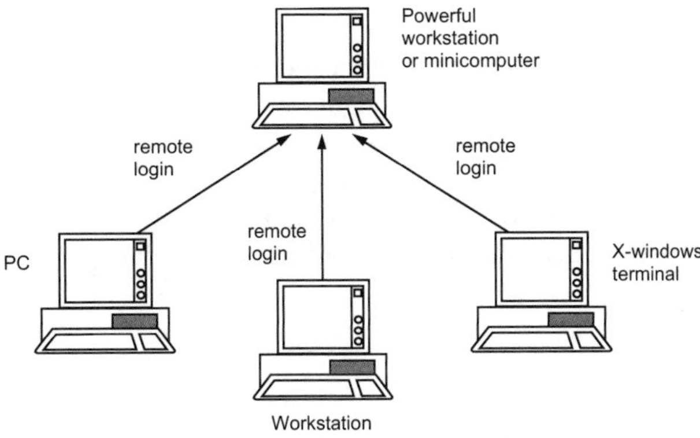

Figure 9.5 Remote login into other nodes

9.2.8 Centralized storage and backup of information

A particular problem with stand-alone computers is that when they crash the user can lose a lot of information, especially if they have not taken regular backups. As file sizes have increased it has also become more difficult for users to perform these backups as it normally involves spanning several floppy disks. Thus a better solution is to have a networked central storage and backup device. The network manager can then schedule backups at regular intervals (typically each day). If a network crash occurs on the central storage the manager can recover the previous backup, thus only losing a small amount of newly created data.

9.2.9 Disadvantages and potential pitfalls of networks

The main disadvantage of networks is that users become dependent upon them. For example, if a network file server develops a fault then many users may not be able to run application programs and get access to shared data. To overcome this a back-up server can be switched into action when the main server fails. A fault on a network may also stop users from being able to access peripherals such as printers and plotters. To minimize this, a network is normally segmented so that a failure in one part of it does not affect other parts.

Another major problem with networks is that their efficiency is very dependent on the skill of the system manager. A badly managed network may operate less efficiently than non-networked computers. Also, a badly run network may allow external users into it with little protection against them causing damage. Damage could also be caused by novices causing problems, such as deleting important files.

The main disadvantages are summarized:

- If a network file server develops a fault then users may not be able to run application programs.
- A fault on the network can cause users to lose data (especially if they have not saved the files they have recently been working with).
- If the network stops operating then it may not be possible to access various resources.
- Users' work-throughput becomes dependent upon the network and the skill of the system manager.
- It is difficult to make the system secure from hackers, novices or industrial espionage (again this depends on the skill of the system manager).
- Decisions on resource planning tend to become centralized, for example, what word processor is used, what printers are bought, and so on.
- Networks that have grown with little thought can be inefficient in the long term.
- As traffic increases on a network the performance degrades unless it is designed properly.
- Resources may be located too far away from some users.
- The larger the network becomes the more difficult it is to manage.

9.3 OSI model

The OSI reference model makes networks more manageable and then eases the problem of moving information between computers by dividing the problem into seven smaller and more manageable tasks. A layer of the model solves each of the seven problem areas, these are: the physical layer, the data link layer, the network layer, the transport layer, the session layer, the presentation layer, and the application layer.

A major problem in the electronics industry is the interconnection of equipment and software compatibility. Other problems can occur in the connection of electronic equipment in one part of the world to another, in another part. For these reasons, the International Standards Organization (ISO) developed a model known as the OSI (open systems interconnection) model. Its main objects were to:

- Allow manufacturers of different systems to interconnect their equipment through standard interfaces.
- Allow software and hardware to integrate well and be portable on differing systems.
- Create a model which all the countries of the world would use.

OSI mnemonics

All
People
Seem
To
Need
Data
Processing

Please
Do
Not
Throw
Sausage
Pizza
Away

Figure 9.6 shows the OSI model. Data passes from the top layer of the sender to the bottom and then up from the bottom layer to the top to the recipient. Each layer on the sender, though, communicates directly to the recipient's corresponding layer, which creates a virtual data flow between layers.

The top layer (the application layer) initially gets data from an application and appends it with data that the recipient's application layer reads. This appended data passes to the next layer (the presentation layer). Again, it appends it with its own data, and so on, down to the physical layer. The physical layer is then responsible for transmitting the data to the recipient. The data sent can be termed as a data frame, whereas data sent by the network and the transport layers are typically referred to as a data packet and a data segment, respectively.

The basic function of each of the layers are:

1. **Physical.** TRANSMISSION OF BINARY DATA. Defines the electrical characteristics of the communications channel and the transmitted signals, such as voltage levels, connector types, cabling, and so on.
2. **Data link.** MEDIA ACCESS. Ensures that the transmitted bits are received in a reliable way, such as adding extra bits to define the start and end of the data frame, adding extra error detection/correction bits and ensuring that multiple nodes do not try to access a common communication channel at the same time.
3. **Network.** ADDRESSING AND DETERMINING THE BEST PATH. Routes data packets through a network. If data packets need to go out of a network then the transport layer routes them through interconnected networks. Its task may involve, for example, splitting data for transmission and re-assembling it upon reception. The IP part of TCP/IP is involved with the network layer (or IPX in Novell NetWare).

OSI model gives:

- Increased evolution.
- Modular engineering.
- Interoperable technology.
- Reduced complexity.
- Simplified teaching and learning.
- Standardized interfaces.

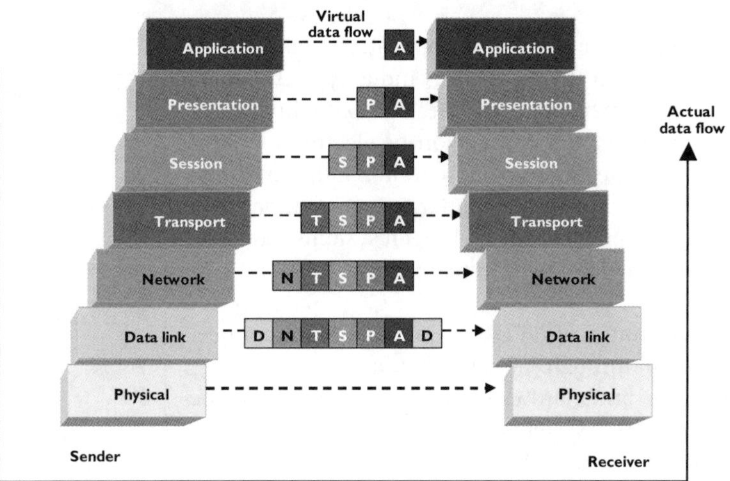

Figure 9.6 Seven-layer OSI model

4. **Transport.** END-TO-END CONNECTION RELIABILITY. Network transparent data transfer and transmission protocol, which supports the transmission of multiple streams from a single computer. The TCP part of TCP/IP is involved with the transport layer (or SPX in Novell NetWare).
5. **Session.** INTERHOST COMMUNICATION. Provides an open communications path with the other system. It involves the setting up, maintaining and closing down of a session. The communication channel and the internetworking of the data should be transparent to the session layer. A typical session protocol is telnet, which allows for remote login over a network.
6. **Presentation.** DATA REPRESENTATION and INTERPRETING. Uses a set of translations that allows the data to be interpreted properly. For example it may have to translate between two systems if they use different presentation standards, such as different character sets or differing character codes. The presentation layer can also add data encryption for security purposes.

OSI model layers:

- **A**pplication. Provides application programs, such as file transfer, print access and electronic mail.
- **P**resentation. Transforms the data into a form which the session layer and the application layer expect. It can perform encryption, translating character sets (such as converting binary values into text for transmitting a binary program over a text-based system), data compression and network redirections.
- **S**ession. Setting up, maintaining and closing down of a session. It should not depend on any specific transport or network layer, and should be able to communicate as if the session was created on a stand-alone computer (that is, the network is transparent to the session layer).
- **T**ransport. Provides for reliable end-to-end error and flow control. The network layer does not validate that the data packet has been successfully received, thus it is up to the transport layer to provide for error and flow control.
- **N**etwork. Defines the protocols that are responsible for delivering the data to the required destination.
- **D**ata link. Provides for the access to the network media and thus builds on the physical layer. It takes data packets from the upper level and frames it so that it can be transmitted from one node to another.
- **P**hysical. Provides for the actual transmission of the binary digits.

7. **Application.** NETWORK SERVICES TO APPLICATION PROGRAMS. Provides network services to application programs, such as file transfer and electronic mail.

> **Choosing the right cable:**
> - Bandwidth (such as bit rate). Fibre-optic cable has the greatest bandwidth, followed by coaxial, and then by twisted-pair.
> - Location (such as flammable environment, security).
> - Expense. Fibre-optic cable is the most expensive, and twisted-pair the least.
> - Long-term use (upgradeability over the years).

Figure 9.7 shows how typical networking systems fit into the OSI model. The data link and physical layers are covered by networking technologies such as Ethernet, Token Ring and FDDI. The networking layer is covered by IP (internet protocol) and transport by TCP (transport control protocol).
The layers can be grouped as follows:

- **Media layers.** This covers the physical and data link layers, as they control the physical delivery of messages over the network.
- **Host layers.** This covers the application, presentation, session and transport layers, as they provide for accurate delivery of data between computers on the network.

In general the OSI model has:

- **Increased evolution.** Systems are allowed to quickly change, as they still integrate well with existing systems. This speeds evolution.
- **Allows modular engineering.** This allows for systems to be designed in a modular way so that each of the components, whether they be hardware or software, can interface well with each other.
- **Guarantees interoperable technology.** This allows the transfer of data between computers of different types, either in their software, operating system, network hardware or computer hardware.

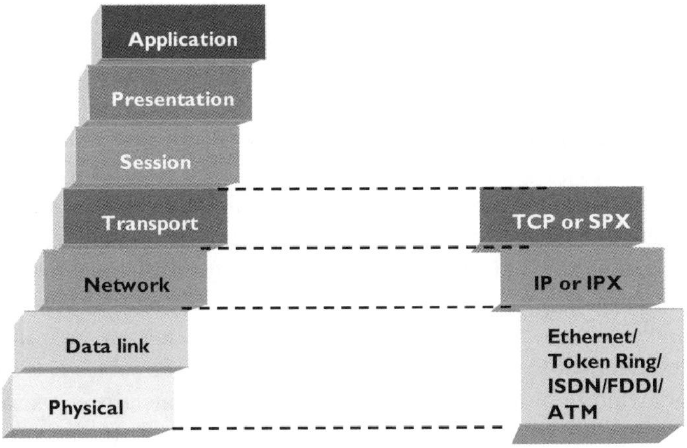

Figure 9.7 Typical technologies used in network communications

- **Reduced complexity.** The task of transmitting data from one application to another over a network is reduced in complexity as it is reduced to seven smaller tasks.
- **Simplifies teaching and learning.** The OSI model has been used as a standard method for teaching networking, and, as it is built up of layers, allows for easier learning of networking. Students can easily visualize the network in a given layer of abstraction.
- **Standardizes interfaces.** This allows for designers to design their products so that they can be easily plugged into one or more of the layers of the model. The actual implementation of the layer can be invisible to other layers.

9.4 Foundations of the OSI model

The OSI reference model is purely an abstract model, and provides a conceptual framework which defines the network functions at each layer. It thus defines how data from the source (the network device that is sending data) is transmitted to the destination (the network device that is receiving data). This data is transmitted in the form of data packets. At the source the data is passed through all of the layers of the OSI model, with each layer adding its own information. The process of adding the extra information is known as encapsulation. The data packet is thus wrapped in a particular protocol header. For example, Ethernet networks require an Ethernet protocol header before transmitting onto the Ethernet network.

Figure 9.8 shows how the data link, network and transport layers are responsible for transporting data between applications (which basically covers the session, presentation and application layers). The data link layer delivers data between devices on a network segment, and the network layer is responsible for passing it between network segments and delivers the data at the destination (using routers). The transport layer concentrates (multiplexes) the data into a single data stream for transmission, and demultiplexes it at the destination.

9.4.1 Physical layer – cables, voltages and connectors

Computers store information using digital digits (or bits), which have a level of a '0' or a '1'. The foundation level of the OSI model is the physical layer, and provides for the actual transmission of the binary digits. In most cases this is converted to an electrical voltage and sent over a copper cable, or converted in pulses of light and transmitted over a fibre-optic cable. The physical layer is thus responsible for the electrical, mechanical, procedural, and functional specifications for activating, maintaining, and deactivating the physical link between end systems (the end-user device on a network) and covers:

- **Cable.** Typically these are coaxial cable, twisted-pair cable or fibre-optic cable. Fibre-optic cable gives the best specification, and can be run for longer lengths than the other two types. Twisted-pair cable has the advantage over the other two in that it is relatively inexpensive to install, but does not have as good a specification as the others. The main decision for choosing a cable type relates to how much data can be transmitted over it (the required bandwidth), its location (for example copper cables can cause electrical sparks, so they tend not to be used in flammable situations), its expense and its long-term usage. Typically cabling should have a lifetime of over 10 years (which is much longer than most of the computers that connect to the network), thus they must have the potential to support future growth.

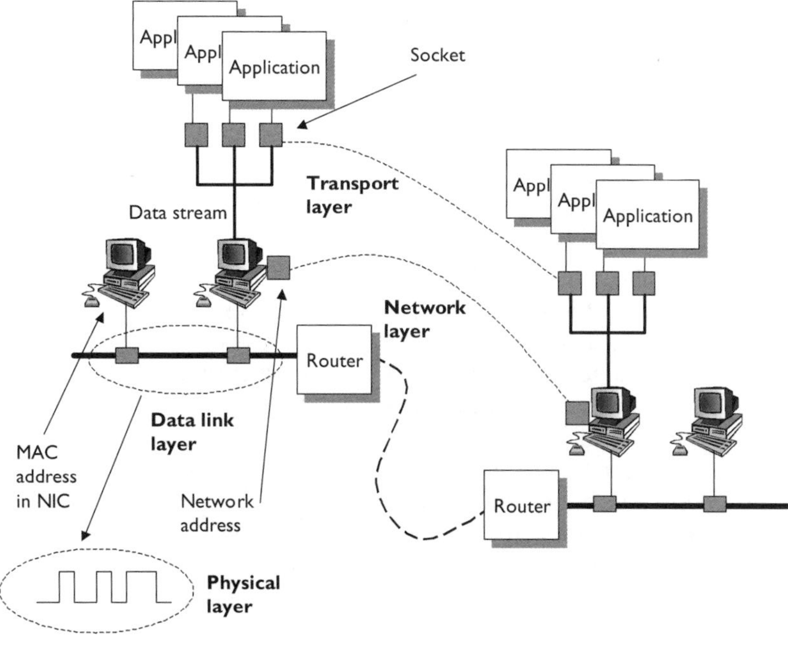

Figure 9.8 Networking showing lower-level layers

- **Electrical voltages, electrical currents, and intensities of light pulses.** Defines the levels of the voltages or light levels for transmission of the binary digits over the cable. Electrical impulses representing data are known as signals.
- **Connectors.** Defines the physical specifications of the connector, and the connections that are made.
- **Encoding.** Defines how the bits are represented by electrical or light signals. This normally involves matching the transmission of binary digits to the required transmission specification. Important considerations are to embed the clock signal into the transmitted signals (which is important to properly recover the received data), or to try and reduce the average transmitted value to zero (as the average value does not contain any embedded information). A typical encoding scheme is Manchester encoding which encodes the 0 and 1 as either a positive edge or a negative edge.

9.4.2 Data link layer – MAC addresses and NICs

Computers connect to the physical media using an NIC (network interface card). The data link layer provides for the access to the network media and thus builds on the physical layer. It takes data packets from the upper levels and frames them so that they can be transmitted from one node to another. The data link layer provides for:

- **Error control.** This provides for the addition of binary digits that can be used to identify if there has been an error in the transmission of one of more bits. If possible, there should be some mechanism for the destination to tell the source that it has received bits in error, and to request a retransmission.

- **Flow control.** This is where there is an orderly flow of transmitted data between the source and the destination, so that the source does not swamp the destination with data. Typically the destination sends back messages that indicate whether the destination can receive data, or not.
- **Line discipline.** This provides for the orderly access to the network media. If there was no orderly access, many nodes could try and get access to the network, at the same time, thus swamping the network. Typically only one node is allowed access to the network at a time. Techniques which allow an orderly access are collision detection (which detects when other nodes are trying to transmit at the same time) and token passing (which involves nodes passing an electronic token from one node to the next, nodes can only transmit when they capture the token).
- **Network topology.** Physical arrangement of network nodes and media within an enterprise networking structure.
- **Ordered delivery of frames.** This provides for sequencing of the data frames in the correct order, and allows the recipient to determine if there are any gaps in the sequence of the received data frames.
- **Physical addressing.** Each node on a network has a unique physical address (or hardware address), this is normally known as a MAC (Media Access Control) address. This address must be used if a node is to receive the transmitted data frame. The only other data frame that a node can receive is when the destination address is a broadcast (which is also received by all the nodes on the network). On Ethernet networks, the MAC address has six bytes, which is allocated by the IEEE.

OSI LAYERS

Physical (TRANSMISSION OF BINARY DATA):

- Cable.
- Electrical voltages, electrical currents and intensities of light pulses.
- Connectors.
- Encoding.

Data link (MEDIA ACCESS):

- Error control.
- Flow control.
- Line discipline.
- Network topology.
- Orderly delivery of frames.
- Physical addressing.

Network (ADDRESSING AND BEST PATH):

- Network addresses.
- Routing.

Transport (END-TO-END CONNECTION RELIABILITY):

- Connection type (connection-less/ connection-oriented).
- Name service.

Session (INTERHOST COMMUNICATION):

- Setting up, maintaining and closing down of a session.

Physical addresses and network addresses

The MAC address identifies the physical address of the NIC, and differs from the network address (which is also known as a protocol address) which is used by the network layer. An Ethernet address takes the form of a hexadecimal number, such as:

`0000.0E64.5432` or `00-00-0E-64-54-32`

and the network address, for IP, takes the form of a dot address, such as:

146.176.151.130

All computers that connect onto the Internet must have a unique IP address.

IPX addresses (for Novell NetWare) use an eight-digit hexadecimal address for the network address and the node portion is the 12-digit MAC address. From example:

F5332B10:00000E645432

Network address | Node address

> **Network addresses:**
>
> 146.176.151.130 (IP)
> F5332B10:00000E645432 (IPX)
>
> **MAC address:**
>
> 00-00-0E-64-54-32

AppleTalk uses alphabet characters, such as:

NewPrinter

The physical address is physically setup in the NIC when it is manufactured and cannot be changed. It gives no information on the physical location of the NIC. The network address, on the other hand, is a software address, and gives some information on where a computer is logically located. The only way that a MAC address can be changed is to change the NIC card, whereas the network address is changed when the computer is moved from one network to another.

In Ethernet networks the following occurs:

- A data frame is transmitted onto the network with the destination MAC address.
- All the devices on the network read the destination MAC address to see if it matches their address.
- If it does not match the physical address, the device ignores the rest of the data frame, otherwise, the NIC card copies the data frame into its buffer, which is then read when the device is ready.

> **NETWORK LAYER**
>
> **Network address** (such as IP and IPX):
>
> - NETWORK PART (146.176).
> - HOST PART (151.130).
>
> Network address changes when a computer is moved from one network to another.
>
> **Routing protocol** (such as RIP, BGP and OSPF):
>
> - Allows the communication between routers so that they can determine the optimal route to a destination.
> - **RIP** is the most popular, and uses the number of hops that it takes to get to a destination (a hop is one router). It is limited to 16 hops.
> - **OSPF** uses other metrics to determine the best route (known as route costs). It also allows for additional hierarchy, authentication of routing messages (using a password) and route load balancing.
> - **BGP** (Border Gateway Protocol) is less complex than OSPF, but uses an Internet-like structure which assumes that the Internet is connected with a number of AANs (autonomously attached networks). These create boundaries around an organization, Internet service provider, and so on.

9.4.3 Network layer - protocols for reliable delivery

The network layer defines the protocols that are responsible for data delivery at the required destination, and requires:

- **Network addresses.** This identifies the actual logical location of the node (the network address), and the actual node (the node address). The form of the network address depends on the actual protocol. IP uses a dot address, such as 146.176.151.130 that identifies the network and the host. IPX address (for Novell NetWare) uses an eight-digit hexadecimal address to identify the network address and the node portion with a 12-digit MAC address, such as F5332B10: 00000E645432. Network addresses are setup in software and are loaded into the computer when it starts (assuming that it has some storage device to store its network address). This differs from the MAC address which is setup in the hardware. Like MAC addresses, no two computers on a network can have the same network address.
- **Routing.** This is passing of the data packets from one network segment to another, and involves routers. A router reads the network address and decides on which of its connections it should pass the data packet on to. Routing information is not static and must change as the conditions on the network change. Thus each route must maintain a routing table which is used to determine the route that the data packet takes. These routing tables are updated by each of the routers talking to each other using a routing protocol. Two typical routing protocols are Routing Information Protocol (RIP) and Open Shortest Path First (OSPF). RIP uses the least number of hops (which relates to the number of routers between the destination and the current router), whereas OSPF uses other metrics to determine the best route (such as latency and bandwidth capacity).

9.4.4 Transport layer – validates transmission and structures messages

The transport layer provides for reliable end-to-end error and flow control. This is required as the network layer does not validate that any data packets have been successfully received, thus it is up to the transport layer to provide for error and flow control. It involves:

- **Connection type.** This defines the method of handshaking of data between the source and the destination, and can be connection-oriented or connectionless. In a connectionless connection there are no acknowledgements and responses when the data is transmitted from the source to the destination. In a connection-oriented system, a virtual connection is set up, and data is acknowledged by the destination, by sending acknowledgement data from the destination to the source. The source will thus know if the data has been received correctly. In order to detect if data segments

TRANSPORT LAYER

Connection type:

- **Connection-oriented** (or virtual circuit). The source and the destination set up a unique connection (typically known as a socket) and the destination acknowledges the successful receipt of data segments. Connection-oriented is thus reliable for system crashes on both the source and destination and data segment loss/error.
- **Connection-less** (or datagram). There is no virtual connection between the source and the destination, thus there is no guarantee that the data segments have been received correctly (or whether the destination is even there).

Name resolution:

Resolves logical names to network addresses. For example:

- **DNS**. Operates on the Internet and is used when a user uses a domain name (such as www.fred.co). DNS is thus used to return the IP address of the destination (such as 11.22.33.44). No data on the Internet can be transmitted unless the IP address is known.

have been lost or are in error, each data segment has a sequence number. The destination sends back the acknowledgement with the data packet segment that it expects to receive from the source (thus acknowledging all previously transmitted data segment to the acknowledged data segment number). Figure 9.9 shows an example flow of information. Initially, for a connection-oriented connection, the transport layer creates a connection by negotiation, where both the source and destination pass the details of their connection, such as details of their socket (which is a unique number that defines the connection) and the data segment number that they will start to send on.

- **Name resolution.** This allows for the resolution of logical names to logical network addresses. It is often easier to access networked devices using a logical name, rather than their logical address, as these are easier to remember. A typical implementation on TCP/IP networks is the Domain Name Service (DNS) which resolves domain names to IP addresses. For example, a domain name of www.fredandco.com could be resolved to the network address of 11.22.33.44.

> **Internetworking:**
>
> - Increases the number of nodes that can connect to a network.
> - Extends the physical distance of a network.
> - Localizes the traffic with network segments.
> - Merges existing networks.
> - Isolates network faults.

9.4.5 Session layer

The session layer involves the setting up, maintaining and closing down of a session. This builds on the transport layer which provides the foundation for the connection over the network. The session provides a higher-level connection, such as a login procedure, or a remote connection. It is important that the session layer does not depend on any specific transport or network layer, and should be able to communicate as if the session was created on a stand-alone computer (that is, the network is transparent to the session layer). A typical session protocol is telnet, which allows for the remote login over a network.

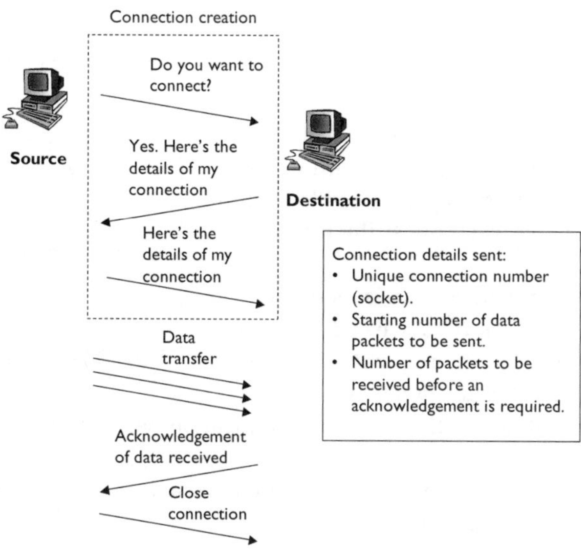

Figure 9.9 Basic transport layer connection-oriented protocol

9.4.6 Presentation layer

The presentation layer transforms the data into a form which the session layer and the application layer expect. It can perform encryption, translate character sets (such as converting binary values into text for transmitting a binary program over a text-based system), data compression and network redirections. An example protocol for the presentation layer is XDR.

9.4.7 Application layer

The application layer provides application programs, such as file transfer, print access and electronic mail.

9.5 Internetworking

Networks can be constructed using a common connection for all the nodes that connect to the network. Unfortunately, the more devices that connect, the slower the network becomes. Thus there is a need for devices that split networks into segments, each of which contain locally attached nodes. Internetworking devices have many advantages, such as:

- They increase the number of nodes that can connect to the network than would be normally possible. Limitations on the number of nodes that connect to a network relate to the cable lengths and traffic constraints.
- They extend the physical distance of the network (the range of the network).
- They localize traffic within a network. Typically computers, which are geographically located close to each other, need to communicate with each other. Thus local communications should not have an effect on communications outside a given network segment.
- Merge existing networks. This allows connected networks to intercommunicate.
- Isolate network faults. This allows faults on one network to be contained within a given network, so that they do not affect other connected networks.

Typical internetworking devices are:

- **Repeater.** These operate at Layer 1 of the OSI model, and extend the physical length of a connection that would normally be possible with the cable type. They basically boost the electrical or light signals.
- **Bridges.** These pass data frames between networks using the MAC address (Layer 2 address).
- **Hubs.** These allow the interconnection of nodes and create a physically attached network.
- **Switches.** These allow simultaneous communication between two or more nodes, at a time.
- **Routers.** These pass data packets between connected networks, and operate on network addresses (Layer 3 address).

Internetworking devices:

- **PHYSICAL LAYER**: Repeaters and hubs.
- **DATA LINK LAYER**: Bridges and switches. Uses MAC address.
- **NETWORK LAYER**: Routers. Uses network address.

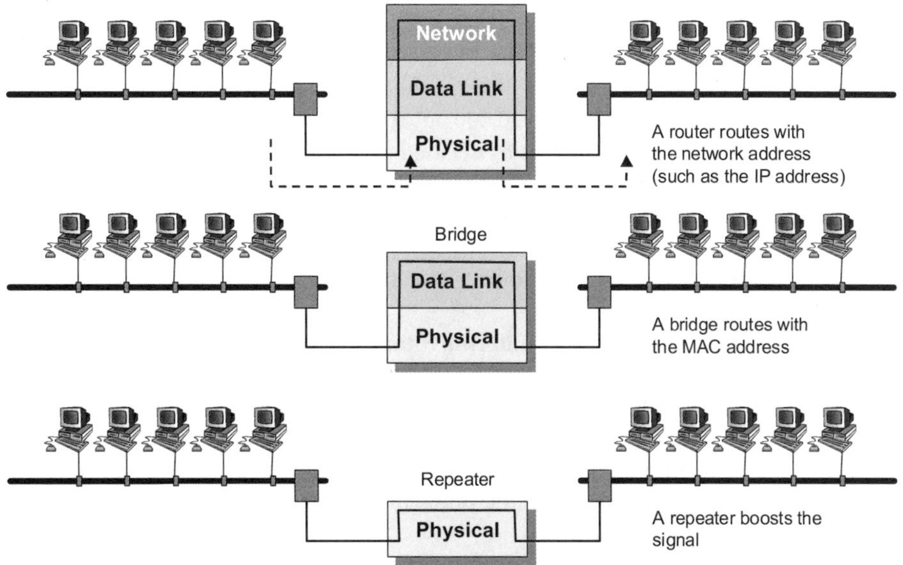

Figure 9.10 Repeaters, bridges and routers

Networks connect to other networks through repeaters, bridges or routers. A repeater corresponds to the physical layer of the OSI model and routes data from one network segment to another. Bridges, on the other hand, route data using the data link layer (with the MAC address), whereas routers route data using the network layer (that is, using a network address, such as an IP address). Normally, at the data link layer, the transmitted data is known as a data frame, while at the network layer it is referred to as a data packet. Figure 9.10 illustrates the three interconnection types.

9.5.1 Repeaters

All network connections suffer from a reduction in signal strength (attenuation) and digital pulse distortion. Thus, for a given cable specification and bit rate, each connection will have a maximum cable length that can be used to transmit the data reliably. Repeaters can be used to increase the maximum interconnection length, and may do the following:

- Reshape signal pulses.
- Pass all signals between attached segments.
- Boost signal power.
- Possibly translate between two different media types (such as between fibre-optic and twisted-pair cable).

Transmit to more than one network. These are multiport repeaters and send data frames from any received segment to all the others. Multiport repeaters do not filter the traffic, as they blindly send received data frames to all the physically connected network segments.

9.5.2 Bridges

Bridges filter input and output traffic so that only data frames distended for another network segment are actually routed into that segment and only data frames destined for the outside are allowed out of the network segment.

The performance of a bridge is governed by two main factors:

- **The filtering rate.** A bridge reads the MAC address of the Ethernet/Token ring/FDDI node and then decides if it should forward the frames into the network. Filter rates for bridges range from around 5000 to 70,000 pps (packets per second).
- **The forward rate.** Once the bridge has decided to route the frame into the internetwork, the bridge must forward the frame onto the destination network. Forwarding rates range from 500 to 140,000 pps and a typical forwarding rate is 90,000 pps.

An example Ethernet bridge has the following specifications:

Bit rate: 10 Mbps **Filtering rate:** 17,500 pps
Forwarding rate: 11,000 pps
Connectors: Two DB15 AUI (female), one DB9 male console port, two BNC (for 10BASE2) or two RJ-45 (for 10BASE-T).
Algorithm: Spanning tree protocol. This automatically learns the addresses of all devices on both interconnected networks and builds a separate table for each network.

Spanning tree architecture (STA) bridges

The IEEE 802.1 standard has defined the spanning tree algorithm, and is normally implemented as software on STA-compliant bridges. On power-up they automatically learn the addresses of all the nodes on both interconnected networks and build up a separate table for each network.

They can also support two connections between two LANs so that when the primary path becomes disabled, the spanning tree algorithm re-enables the previously disabled redundant link, as illustrated in Figure 9.11.

Source route bridging

With source route bridging, a source device, not the bridge, is used to send special explorer packets. These are then used to determine the best path to the destination. Explorer packets are sent out from the source routing bridges until they reach their destination workstation.

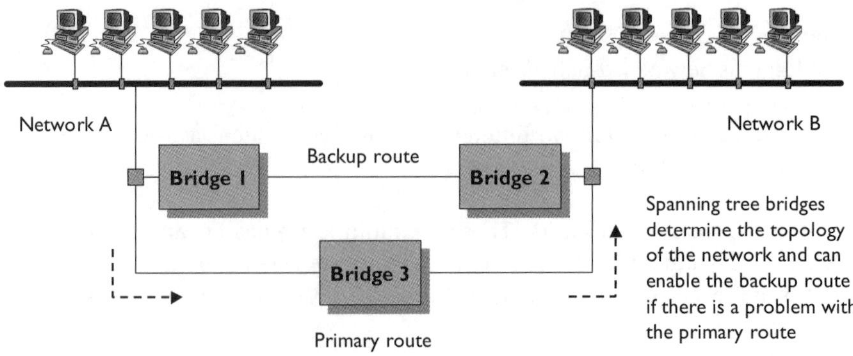

Figure 9.11 Spanning tree bridges

Each source routing bridge along the route enters its address in the routing information field (RIF) of the explorer packet. The destination node then sends back the completed RIF field to the source node. When the source device has determined the best path to the destination, it sends the data message along with the path instructions to the local bridge, which then forwards the data message according to the received path instructions.

9.5.3 Routers

Routers examine the network address field and determine the best route for a data packet. They have the great advantage in that they normally support several different types of network layer protocols.

Routers need to communicate with other routers so that they can exchange routing information. Most network operating systems have associated routing protocols which support the transfer of routing information. Typical routing protocols for Internet communications are:

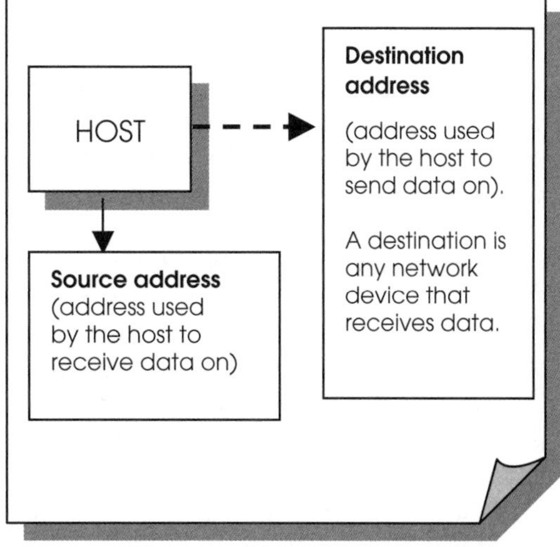

- BGP (border gateway protocol).
- EGP (exterior gateway protocol).
- OSPF (open shortest path first).
- RIP (routing information protocol).

Most routers support RIP and EGP. In the past, RIP was the most popular router protocol standard, and its widespread use is due, in no small part, to the fact that it was distributed along with the Berkeley Software Distribution (BSD) of UNIX (from which most commercial versions of UNIX are derived). It suffers from several disadvantages and has been largely replaced by OSFP and EGB. These newer protocols have the advantage over RIP in that they can handle large internetworks, as well as reducing routing table update traffic.

RIP uses a distance-vector algorithm, which measures the number of network jumps (known as hops), up to a maximum of 16, to the destination router (a value of 16 identifies that the destination is not reachable). This has the disadvantage that the smallest number of hops may not be the best route from a source to a destination. The OSPF and EGB protocol uses a link state algorithm that can decide between multiple paths to the destination router. These are based, not only on hops, but also on other parameters such as delay (latency), capacity, reliability and throughput.

Bridges:

- Forward broadcasts.
- Forward traffic to unknown addresses.
- Do not modify data frame.
- Build tables of MAC addresses.
- Use the same network address for all of its ports.

Routers:

- Do not forward broadcasts.
- Do not forward traffic to unknown addresses.
- Modify data packet header.
- Build tables of network addresses.
- Use a different network address for each of its ports.

With distance-vector routing, each router maintains routing tables by communicating with neighbouring routers. The number of hops in its own table are then computed as it knows the number of hops to local routers. Unfortunately, their routing tables can take some time to be updated when changes occur, because it takes time for all the routers to communicate with each other (known as slow convergence).

9.6 Broadcasts

A puzzling question that most people ask is how the host knows what the network address of the computer it is communicating with is, and how it knows the MAC address of the host that it communicates with. In order to determine these a host must send out a broadcast to all of the hosts on its network segment. There are two main types of broadcasts:

- **Requests for a destination MAC address.** If a host does not know what the destination MAC address is, it sends out a broadcast request to all the hosts on the network segment. The host which has a matching network address responds back with its MAC address in the source MAC address field. The MAC and network addresses are then stored in the memory of the host, so that they can be used in future communications. This process is known as ARP (Address Resolution Protocol), and is illustrated in Figure 9.12.
- **Requests for a network address.** If a host does not know the network address for a given MAC address, it sends out a request with the MAC address. A server on the network normally then responds back with the network address for the given MAC address. This process is known as RARP (Reverse Address Resolution Protocol), as it is only really used when a node needs to know what its own network address is (as it has no local storage to store it).

Most networking technologies have a special MAC address for a broadcast. Ethernet uses the address:

FF-FF-FF-FF-FF-FF

for a broadcast. There are also network broadcast addresses using the network address (known as multicast), where all the nodes on the network listen to the communication (such as transmitting a video conference to many nodes on a network, at the same time), but they are used for different purposes than broadcast MAC addresses, which are used to get network information.

Bridges always forward broadcast addresses, but routers do not. Another advantage of routers over bridges is that a router will not forward to an unknown address, whereas a bridge will. The blocking of broadcasts is a great advantage in routers as it stops the broadcasts being sent to hosts on other networks, thus limiting the traffic on other networks.

9.7 Bits, frames, packets and segments

As has been seen, each of the OSI layers communicates directly with the equivalent layer on the receiving host. The data that is transmitted in each of the lower layers is referred to in a different way. Data that passes from layer to layer is called protocol data units (PDUs).

These PDUs are referred to in different ways in each of the layers. At the physical level they are referred to as bits, at the data link layer they are referred to as frames, at the network layer they are referred to as packets, and at the transport layer they are referred to as segments. This is illustrated in Figure 9.13.

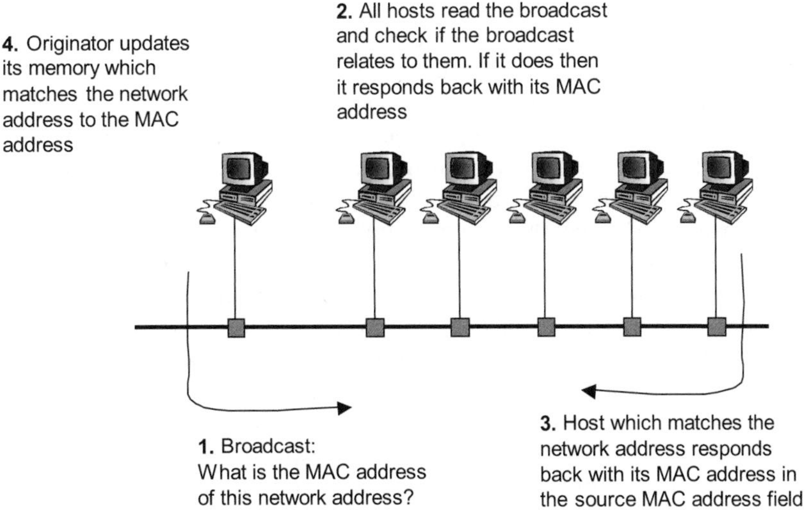

4. Originator updates its memory which matches the network address to the MAC address
2. All hosts read the broadcast and check if the broadcast relates to them. If it does then it responds back with its MAC address
1. Broadcast: What is the MAC address of this network address?
3. Host which matches the network address responds back with its MAC address in the source MAC address field

Figure 9.12 Broadcasts for MAC address

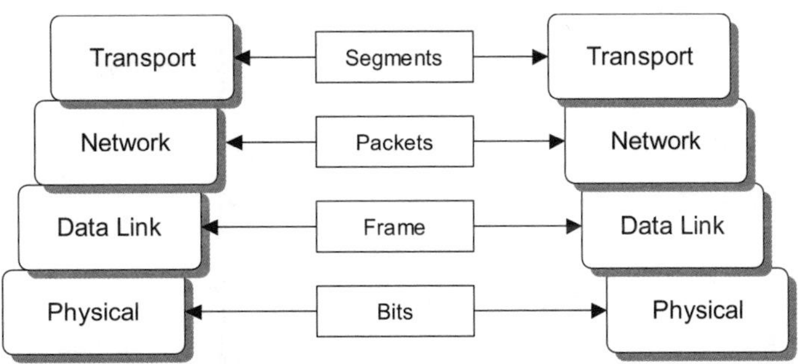

Transport
Segments
Transport
Network
Packets
Network
Data Link
Frame
Data Link
Physical
Bits
Physical

Figure 9.13 Bits, frames, packets and segments

9.8 Exercises

The following questions are multiple choice. Please select from a–d.

9.8.1 What must be common to computers if they are to communicate over a network:

(a) Use the same operating system (b) Use the same protocol
(c) Manufactured by the same company (d) Use similar hardware

Additional material and tutorial questions are available at:
`http://www.palgrave.com/studyskills/masterseries/buchanan`

10 Networking types

10.1 Introduction

Most computers in organizations connect to a network using a LAN (local area network). These networks normally consist of a backbone, which is the common link to all the other networks within the organization. This backbone allows users on different network segments to communicate and allows data into and out of the local network. Figure 10.1 shows a local area network which contains various segments: LAN A, LAN B, LAN C, LAN D, LAN E and LAN F. These are connected to the local network via the BACKBONE 1. Thus, if LAN A communicates with LAN E then the data must travel out of LAN A, onto BACKBONE1, then into LAN D and through onto LAN E.

Networks are partitioned from other networks either using a bridge, a gateway or a router. A bridge links a network of one type to an identical type, such as Ethernet to Ethernet, or Token Ring to Token Ring. A gateway connects two dissimilar types of networks and routers operate in a similar way to gateways and can either connect similar or dissimilar networks. The essential operation of a gateway, bridge or router is that they only allow data traffic through that is intended for another network, which is outside the connected network. This filters traffic and stops traffic, not intended for the network, from clogging-up the backbone. Most modern bridges, gateways and routers are intelligent and can automatically determine the topology of the network. They do this by intercommunicating with each other.

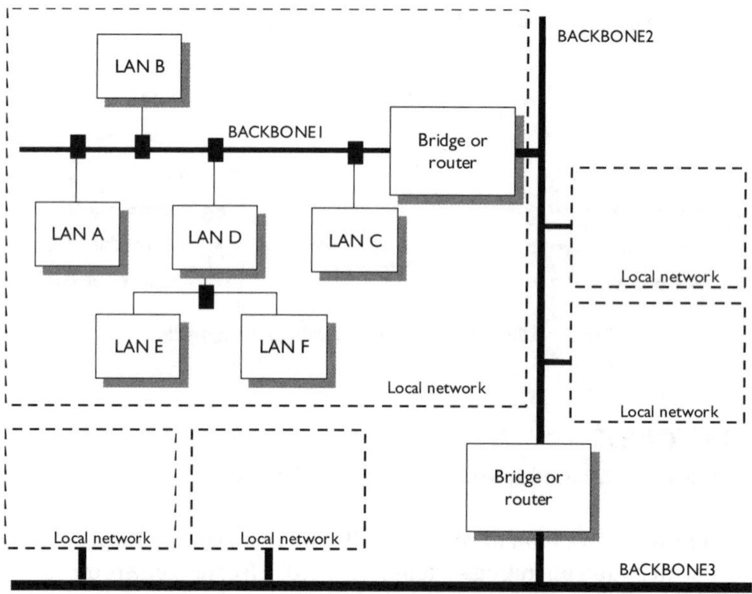

Figure 10.1 Interconnection of local networks

10.2 Network topologies

There are three basic topologies for LANs, which are shown in Figure 10.2. These are:

- A **star** network. This type of network uses a central server to route data between clients.
- A **ring** network. This type of network uses a ring in which data is passed from node to node, either in a clockwise or an anti-clockwise direction. Normally a token is passed from node to node, and a node can only transmit when it gets the token.
- A **bus** network. In this type of network all the nodes on a network segment connect to the same physical cable. They must thus contend to get access to the network.

> **Enterprise network**
> An enterprise network is a network which binds together data, communication, computing and file services in a single organization. They typically require the services of a WAN to provide interconnection between sites, and a LAN to provide interconnection between computers and file servers.

There are other topologies which are either a combination of two or more of the basic topologies or are derivatives of the main types. A typical topology is a **tree** topology, that is essentially a combined star and a bus network, as illustrated in Figure 10.3. A concentrator (or hub) is used to connect the nodes to the network.

10.2.1 Star network

In a star topology, a central server (or switching hub) switches data around the network (Figure 10.4). Data traffic between nodes and the server will thus be relatively low. Its main advantages are:

- Since the data rate is relatively low between central server and the node, a low-specification twisted-pair cable can be used to connect the nodes to the server.
- A fault on one of the nodes will not affect the rest of the network. Typically, mainframe computers use a central server with terminals connected to it.

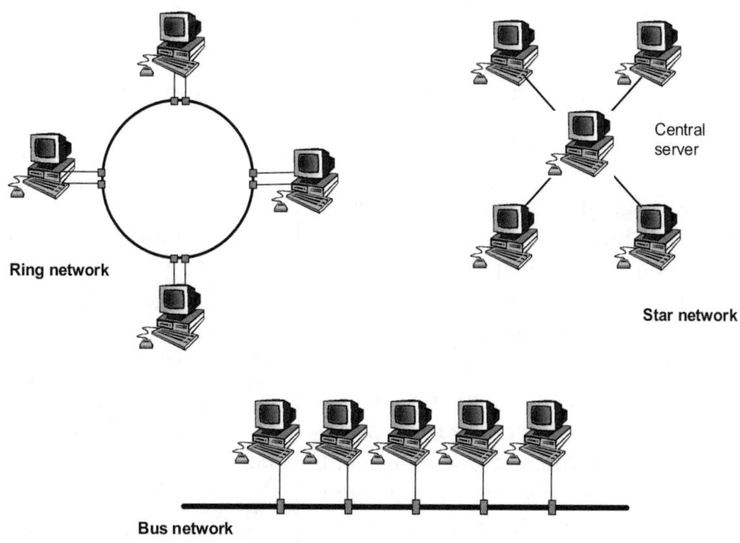

Figure 10.2 Network topologies

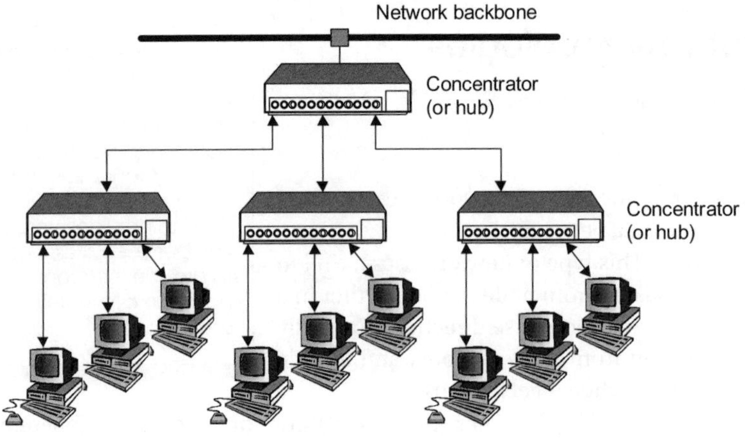

Network backbone
Concentrator
(or hub)
Concentrator
(or hub)

Figure 10.3 Tree topology

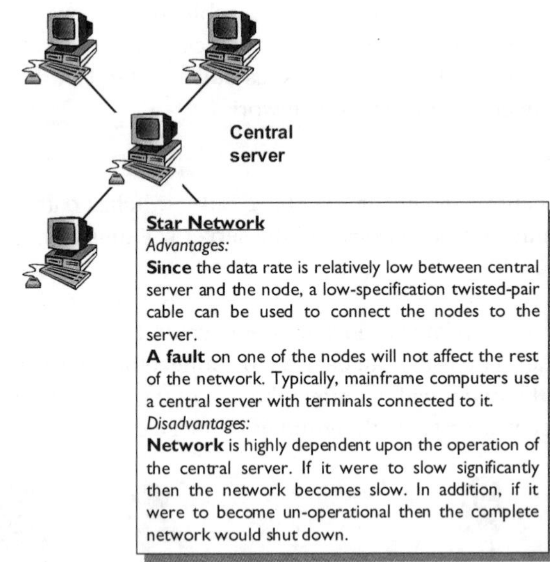

Central
server
Star Network
Advantages:
Since the data rate is relatively low between central server and the node, a low-specification twisted-pair cable can be used to connect the nodes to the server.
A fault on one of the nodes will not affect the rest of the network. Typically, mainframe computers use a central server with terminals connected to it.
Disadvantages:
Network is highly dependent upon the operation of the central server. If it were to slow significantly then the network becomes slow. In addition, if it were to become un-operational then the complete network would shut down.

Figure 10.4 Star topology

The main disadvantage of this type of topology is that the network is highly dependent upon the operation of the central server. If it were to slow significantly then the network becomes slow. In addition, if it were to become un-operational then the complete network would be shut down.

An Ethernet hub acts as multiport repeaters (a concentrator). They can be either active or passive. An active hub connects to the network media, and also regenerates the signal, whereas a passive hub simply connects devices onto the networking media.

Logical and physical star

Ethernet networks use a bus-type network, but when it connects to a hub the network can be seen as a physical star topology as the hub can be seen as a central point. If it were to fail, then the whole network may fail. Inside the hub the Ethernet connection still uses a bus network.

This is also the case for a ring network which uses MAU (Multistation Access Units) which is like a hub but creates a virtual ring. The MAU can be seen as a physical star, although the actual network is a ring topology.

10.2.2 Ring network

In a ring network, computers link together to form a ring. To allow an orderly access to the ring, a single electronic token passes from one computer to the next around the ring, as illustrated in Figure 10.5. A computer can only transmit data when it captures the token. In a manner similar to the star network, each link between nodes is a point-to-point link and allows the usage of almost any type of transmission medium. Typically twisted-pair cables allow a bit rate of up to 16 Mbps, but coaxial and fibre-optic cables are normally used for extra reliability and higher data rates.

A typical ring network is IBM Token Ring. The main advantage of token ring networks is that all nodes on the network have an equal chance of transmitting data. Unfortunately, it suffers from several problems; the most severe is that if one of the nodes goes down then the whole network may go down (as it is not able to pass the token onto the next node).

10.2.3 Bus network

A bus network uses a multi-drop transmission medium, as shown in Figure 10.6, where all nodes on the network share a common bus and thus share communications. This allows only one device to communicate at a time. A distributed medium access protocol determines which station is to transmit. As with the ring network, data frames contain source and destination addresses, where each station monitors the bus and copies frames addressed to itself.

Twisted-pair cables give data rates up to 100 Mbps, whereas, coaxial and fibre-optic cables give higher bit rates and longer transmission distances. A bus network is a good compromise over the other two topologies as it allows relatively high data rates. Also, if a node goes down, it does not normally affect the rest of the network. The main disadvantage of this topology is that it requires a network protocol to detect when two nodes are transmitting at the same time. It also does not cope well with heavy traffic rates. A typical bus network is Ethernet 2.0.

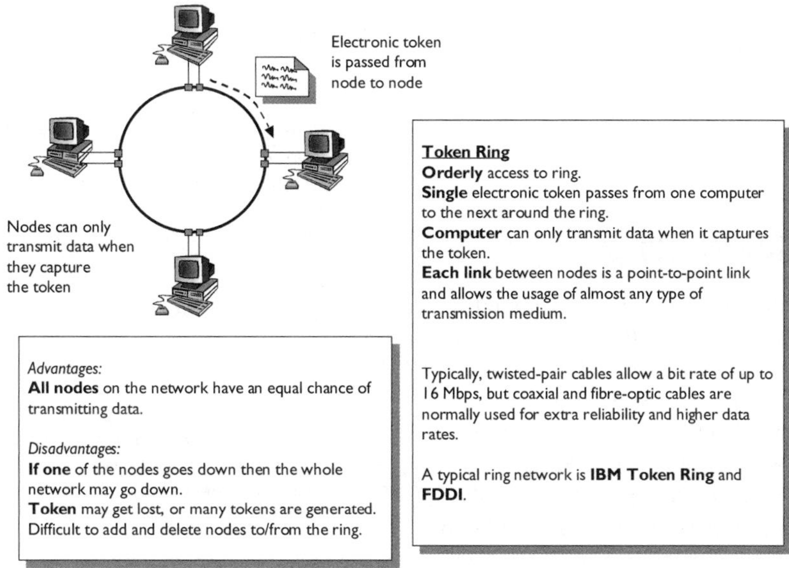

Figure 10.5 Token passing ring network

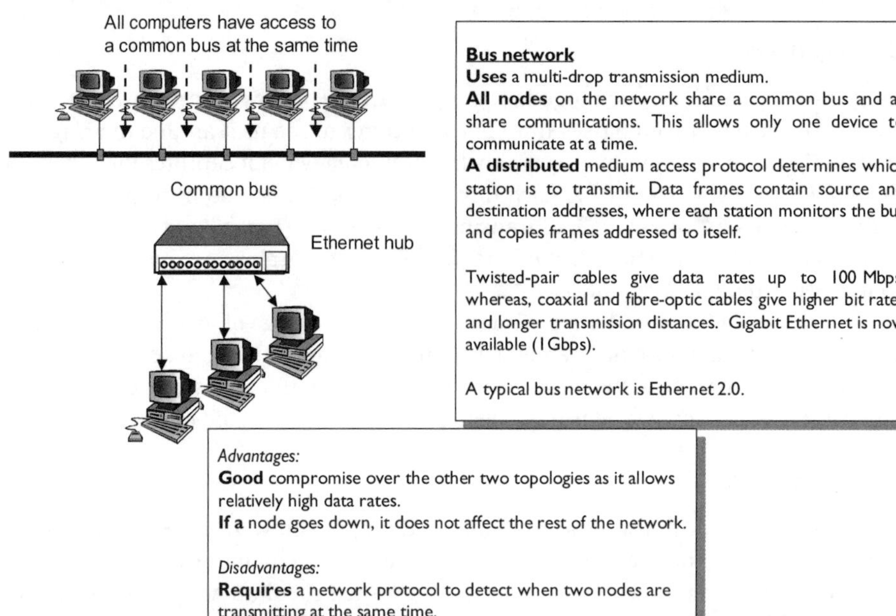
All computers have access to
a common bus at the same time
Common bus
Ethernet hub
Bus network
Uses a multi-drop transmission medium.
All nodes on the network share a common bus and all share communications. This allows only one device to communicate at a time.
A distributed medium access protocol determines which station is to transmit. Data frames contain source and destination addresses, where each station monitors the bus and copies frames addressed to itself.
Twisted-pair cables give data rates up to 100 Mbps, whereas, coaxial and fibre-optic cables give higher bit rates and longer transmission distances. Gigabit Ethernet is now available (1 Gbps).
A typical bus network is Ethernet 2.0.
Advantages:
Good compromise over the other two topologies as it allows relatively high data rates.
If a node goes down, it does not affect the rest of the network.
Disadvantages:
Requires a network protocol to detect when two nodes are transmitting at the same time.
Does not cope well with heavy traffic rates.

Figure 10.6 Bus topology

Bus networks require a termination at either end of the bus, as the signal needs to be absorbed at the end of the bus (else it would bounce off the end of the open-circuited bus). This prevents signals from bouncing back and being received again by workstations attached to the bus. Ring and star networks do not require termination as they are automatically terminated. With a star network the connected nodes automatically terminate the end of the connection.

Collision:
This is the result of two nodes transmitting at the same time. The frames from each node are damaged when they meet each other on the physical media.
Collision domain:
On an Ethernet network, when two or more nodes try and transmit at the same time the data frame is damaged, and the nodes must backoff from the network. The network area within which data packets originate and collide is called a collision domain.
Backoff:
The retransmission delay enforced when a collision occurs.
Broadcasts:
Data frames that are sent to all the nodes within a network segment. They are identified by a broadcast address.
Network architecture:
A combination of existing standards (rules or procedures that the network complies with) and protocols (set of rules and conventions that govern how networked nodes intercommunicate).

10.3 Token Ring

Token Ring networks were developed by several manufacturers, the most prevalent being the IBM Token Ring. Unlike Ethernet, they cope well with high network traffic loadings, and were at one time extremely popular but Ethernet has since overtaken their popularity. Token Ring networks have, in the past, suffered from network management problems and poor network fault tolerance.

10.3.1 Operation

A Token Ring network circulates an electronic token (named a control token) around a closed electronic loop. Each node on the network reads the token and repeats it to the next node. The control token circulates around the ring even when there is no data being transmitted.

Nodes on a Token Ring network wishing to transmit must await a token. When they get it, they fill a frame with data and add the source and destination addresses then send it to the next node. The data frame then circulates around the ring until it reaches the destination node. It then reads the data into its local memory area (or buffer) and marks an acknowledgement on the data frame. This then circulates back to the source (or originating) node. When it receives the frame, it tests it to determine whether it contains an acknowledgement. If it does then the source node knows that the data frame was received correctly, else the node is not responding. If the source node has finished transmitting data then it transmits a new token, which can be used by other nodes on the ring.

Figure 10.7(a)–(d) shows a typical interchange between node B and node A. Initially, in (a), the control token circulates between all the nodes. This token does not contain any data and is only a few bytes long. When node B finally receives the token it then transmits a data frame, as illustrated in (b). This data frame is passed to node C, then to node D and finally onto A. Node A then reads the data in the data frame and returns an acknowledgement to node B, as illustrated in (c). After node B receives the acknowledgement, it passes a control token onto node C and this then circulates until a node wishes to transmit a data frame. No nodes are allowed to transmit data unless they have received a valid control token. A distributed control protocol determines the sequence in which nodes transmit. This gives each node equal access to the ring, as each node is only allowed to send one data frame (although some Token Ring systems, such as FDDI, allow for a time limit on transmitting data, before the token is released). It must then give up the token to the next node, and wait for the token to return before it can transmit another data frame.

> **DEAR NET-ED**
>
> **Question:** *What do I need to create a basic network?*
>
> All you really need is two computers, two Ethernet NICs, a hub, and some patch cables. The patch cables connect the computers to the hub, and the hub creates the network. The computers can then simply make a peer-to-peer connection with each.
>
> UNIX/Linux will allow you to access one computer from another, using TELNET, FTP, NDS, and so on, but you would have to assign each computer a unique IP address. As long as you do not connect onto the Internet, you can choose any IP address.
>
> Microsoft Windows uses its own protocol (NetBEUI) to make a peer-to-peer connection (with file/printer sharing).

10.3.2 Token Ring maintenance

A Token Ring system requires considerable maintenance; it must perform the following functions:

- Ring initialization – when the network is started, or after the ring has been broken, it must be reinitialized. A co-operative decentralized algorithm sorts out which node starts a new token, which goes next, and so on.
- Deletion from the ring – a node can disconnect itself from the ring by joining together its predecessor and its successor. Again, the network may have to be shut down and re-initialized.
- Adding to the ring – if a new node is to be physically connected to the ring then the network must be shut down and reinitialized.

- Fault management – typical Token Ring errors occur when two nodes think it is their turn to transmit or when the ring is broken as no node thinks that it is their turn.

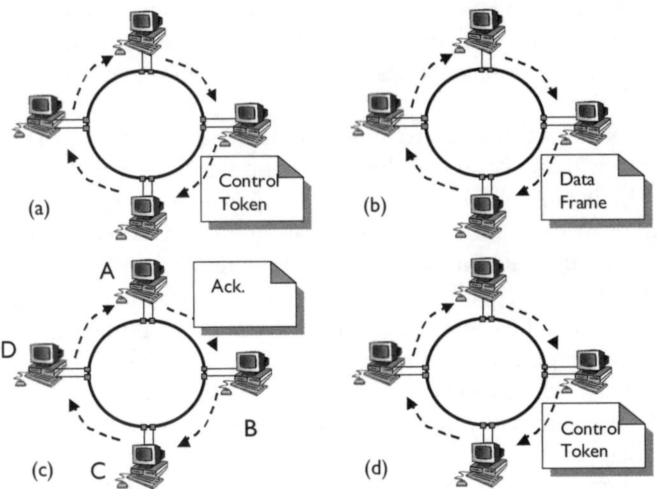

Figure 10.7 Example data exchange

10.3.3 Token Ring multistation access units (MAUs)

The problems of adding and deleting nodes to or from a ring network are significantly reduced with a multistation access unit (MAU). Normally, a MAU allows nodes to be switched in and out of a network using a changeover switch or by automatic electronic switching (known as auto-loopback). This has the advantage of not shutting down the network when nodes are added and deleted or when they develop faults.

10.4 Ethernet

Most of the computers in business now connect through a LAN and the most commonly used LAN is Ethernet. DEC, Intel and the Xerox Corporation initially developed Ethernet and the IEEE 802 committee has since defined standards for it, the most common of which are Ethernet 2.0 and IEEE 802.3.

In itself Ethernet cannot make a network and needs some other protocol such as TCP/IP to allow nodes to communicate. Unfortunately, Ethernet in its standard form does not cope well with heavy traffic, but this is offset by the following:

- Ethernet networks are easy to plan and cheap to install.
- Ethernet network components, such as network cards and connectors, are cheap and well supported.
- It is a well-proven technology, which is fairly robust and reliable.
- It is simple to add and delete computers on the network.
- It is supported by most software and hardware systems.

A major problem with Ethernet is that, because computers must contend to get access to the network, there is no guarantee that they will get access within a given time. This contention also causes problems when two computers try to communicate at the same time, they must both back off and no data can be transmitted. In its standard form Ethernet allows a bit rate of 10 Mbps, but new standards for fast Ethernet systems minimize the problems of contention and also increase the bit rate to 100 Mbps (and even 1Gbps). Ethernet uses coaxial, fibre-optic or twisted-pair cable.

Ethernet uses a shared-media, bus-type network topology where all nodes share a common bus. These nodes must then contend for access to the network as only one node can communicate at a time. Data is then transmitted in frames which contain the MAC (media access control) source and destination addresses of the sending and receiving node, respectively. The local shared media is known as a segment. Each node on the network monitors the segment and copies any frames addressed to it.

Ethernet uses carrier sense, multiple access with collision detection (CSMA/CD). On a CSMA/CD network, nodes monitor the bus (or Ether) to determine if it is busy. A node wishing to transmit data waits for an idle condition then transmits its message. Unfortunately, collisions can occur when two nodes transmit at the same time, thus nodes must monitor the cable when they transmit. When a collision occurs, both nodes stop transmitting frames and transmit a jamming signal. This informs all nodes on the network that a collision has occurred. Each of the nodes involved in the collision then waits a random period of time before attempting a re-transmission. As each node waits for a random delay time then there can be a prioritization of the nodes on the network, as illustrated in Figure 10.8.

Each node on the network must be able to detect collisions and be capable of transmitting and receiving simultaneously. These nodes either connect onto a common Ethernet connection or can connect to an Ethernet hub, as illustrated in Figure 10.8. Nodes thus con-

DEAR NET-ED

Question: *Everywhere I read, it says that Ethernet has so many problems, and isn't really a very good networking technique. So why is it so popular?*

Local area networks have evolved over the years. At one time the big contest was between Token Ring, and Ethernet. Which was best? Well Token Ring was always better at coping with network traffic than Ethernet, especially when the network traffic was heavy. But, remember these were the days before hubs. Thus most network connections were made from computer to computer with coaxial cable. The big problem with Token Ring was when there was a bad connection or when a computer was disconnected from the network, as this brought the whole network down. Ethernet (10BASE) proved much easier to add and delete computers to and from the network. Thus it triumphed over Token Ring. Soon Ethernet NICs cost much less than Token Ring cards, and were available from many sources (typically, these days, Token Ring cards will cost up to over five times as much as Ethernet ones).

Ethernet has coped well with the evolving networks, and the new hubs made it even easier to connect computers to a network. It faced a big problem, though, when the number of users of a network increased by a large factor. Its answer to this was 100BASE, which ramped up the bit rate by a factor of ten. This worked well, but it suffered when handling traffic over wide areas. Ethernet had a final trump card: 1000BASE, which gives a bit rate of 1 Gbps.

Thus, whatever we throw at Ethernet, it fights back by either ramping up the bit rate (from 10 Mbps to 100 Mbps to 1 Gbps) or it allows multiple simultaneous network connections (through Ethernet switches). So, don't dismiss the King, he's going to be around for a while yet.

tend for the network and are not guaranteed access to it. Collisions generally slow the network.

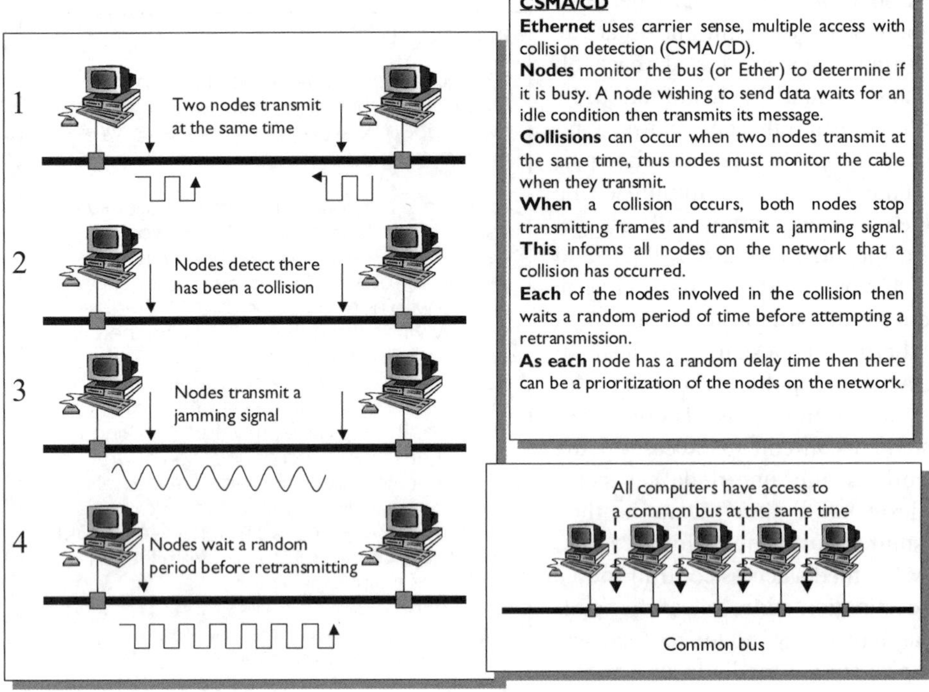

Figure 10.8 CSMA/CD

10.4.1 Hubs, bridges and routers

Repeaters operate at layer 1 of the OSI model, and are used to increase the number of nodes that can connect to a network segment, and the distance that it can cover. They do this by amplifying, retiming and reshaping the digital signals. A hub is a repeater with multiple ports, and can be thought of as being the centre point of a star topology network. It is often known as a multiport repeater (or as a concentrator in Ethernet). Hubs generally:

> **DEAR NET-ED**
>
> **Question:** *How do you connect a fibre-optic cable to a connector?*
>
> It takes a little bit of skill, but basically it is just glued onto the end.
>
> **Question:** *And, how do you get an RJ-45 connector onto twisted-pair cable?*
>
> You strip about 0.5 inch of the outer jacket and fan out the wires in the correct order. Next you push them fully into the RJ-45 connector, and finally use the special crimping tool to clamp the cable, and make the required contacts. No soldering is involved.

- Amplify signals.
- Propagate the signal through the network.
- Do not filter traffic. This is a major disadvantage with hubs and repeaters as data arriving at any of the ports is automatically transmitted to all the other ports connected to the hub.
- Do not determine the path.

- Centralize the connection to the network. This is normally a major problem when using a star connected network, but hubs are normally reliable and can be easily interchanged if they do not operate properly.

Hubs do not filter traffic, so that collisions affect all the connected nodes within the collision domain. The more collisions there are the slower the network segment becomes. There are two main ways to overcome this:

- **Bridges.** These examine the destination MAC address (or station address) of the transmitted data frame, and will not retransmit data frames which are not destined for another network segment. They maintain a table with connected MAC addresses, and do not forward any data frames if the MAC address is on the network segment that originated it, else it forwards to all connected segments.
- **Router.** These examine the network (typically the IP or IPX address) of the transmitted data packet, and will only transmit it out of a network segment if it is destined for a node on another network.

Bridges and routers bound a network segment, whereas a repeater extends it, as illustrated in Figure 10.9. As they are outside the network segment, bridges and routers thus do not forward collisions. Broadcast data frames are sent out by a node if it does not know the MAC address of the destination. Bridges forward these broadcasts to all the connected network segments, and every device on the connected network segments must listen to these data frames. Broadcast storms result when too many broadcasts are sent out over the network, which can cause network time-outs, where the network slows down. Routers do not forward broadcasts and thus cope better with broadcast storms.

Routers

Routers are the key components of the Internet. They communicate with each other and try and determine the best way to get to a remote network. As every computer which connects to the Internet must have an IP address, they use these addresses to route data around the Internet. Without routers we would not have an Internet. Routers are generally the best devices to isolate traffic from one network and another, as they will only forward data packets if the destination is not on the current network.

Advantages of routers:

- Intelligently route data to find the best path using the network address. A bridge will route if the MAC address is not on the originating segment, whereas a router will intelligently decide whether to forward, or not.
- They do not forward broadcasts, thus they reduce the effect of broadcast storms.

Disadvantages of routers:

- Slower than bridges, as they must process the data packet at a higher level. The data frame is then forwarded in a modified form.
- They are network protocol dependent, whereas bridges will forward any high-level protocol as it is operating on the level 2 (as long as it connects two networks of the same types, such as Ethernet-to-Ethernet). Routers interpret the network level data using the required protocol, such as IP or IPX.

Hail the Router. Along with TCP/IP, the true uniter of the People of the World.

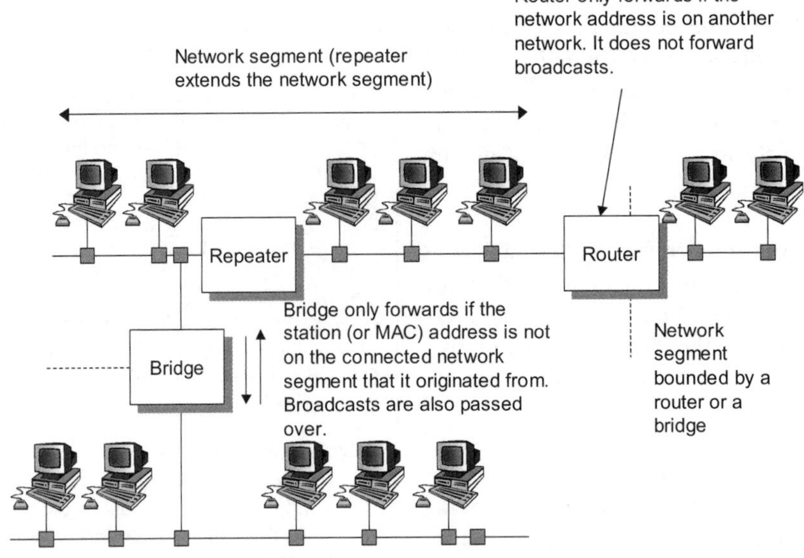
Router only forwards if the network address is on another network. It does not forward broadcasts.
Network segment (repeater extends the network segment)
Repeater
Router
Bridge
Bridge only forwards if the station (or MAC) address is not on the connected network segment that it originated from. Broadcasts are also passed over.
Network segment bounded by a router or a bridge

Figure 10.9 Repeaters, bridges and routers

10.5 LAN components

LANs are high-speed, low-error data networks that span a relatively small geographic area. They connect workstations, peripherals, terminals, and other devices in a single building or other geographically limited area. The required hardware is:

> **Advantages of bridges:**
>
> - Segment networks.
> - Reduce collision domains.
> - Filter network traffic.
> - Bridges work best in connecting network segments which do not require a great amount of inter-network traffic.
> - They forward any high-level protocol (TCP/IP, SPX/IPX, and so on).
>
> **Disadvantages of bridges:**
>
> - If the internetwork traffic is large, the bridge can become a bottleneck for traffic.
> - Bridges forward broadcast data frames to all connected networks.

- **Workstations.** These are the devices that users use to gain access to the network. Typically they are PCs, and they run the application programs, thus important decisions in purchasing a computer are: whether they run the required application software packages; whether they run the required network operating system; and whether they can run as a stand-alone computer (when the network fails).
- **Networking media.** This is the media that connects the parts of the network. There are four main types of media: unshielded twisted-pair cable, shielded twisted-pair cable, coaxial cable, and fibre-optic cable. Network media is fundamentally important, as the rest of the network will not work without it. It is often said that a network is as reliable as its cabling, and that the networking media is the most important part of the whole network. It is the most limiting factor in the network, and sets the maximum

limit for network traffic. In most cases it has a life of more than ten years, and thus must be chosen to support expansion over that time.

- **NIC cards.** This is the device that connects the workstation or file server to the network, and is where the physical or MAC address is located. Every workstation and file server has a NIC card, which typically plugs into one of the expansion slots on the motherboard. Its three main functions are:

    - To form data frames and send them out onto the networking media.
    - To receive data frames coming from the networking media and transform them into information that the workstation can understand.
    - To provide an orderly access to the shared networking media.

- **Hub or wiring centre.** In networks with a file server it is not possible to connect every workstation to it, each with a separate NIC card within the server. Thus most LANs use a hub, which is a network device that serves as the center of a star-topology network, each of the connections being independent. On Ethernet networks, hubs are multiport repeaters and are used to provide for multiple connections.

Additionally a network may have one or more file servers, which are used to store important network information, and are a central storage facility for the network. Typically they contain networked application programs and have several general features:

- **Highly optimized**. As many users have access to them they must operate quickly and are thus generally built to a high specification with an optimized architecture. Normally they contain a large amount of memory and storage facilities.
- **Located in a convenient place** for the workstations that connect to it. This is important as most of the workstations which connect to the network require the file server to provide application software, and other networking facilities, such as being a print server, login validation, and so on. Thus the file server must be located in an optimum place so that each workstation can have fast access to it.

Coaxial cable is typically available in two main flavours:

- **Thicknet.** Thick and rigid cable which is difficult to bend and often difficult to install. It typically has a distinctive yellow outer cover.
- **Thinnet.** Thinner cable which is easier to work with (0.18 inch).

Advantages of coaxial cable

- Outer copper braid or metallic foil provides a shield to reduce the amount of interference.
- They can be run unboosted for longer distances than either shielded or unshielded twisted-pair cable.
- Less expensive than fibre-optic.
- Well-known technology. Coaxial cable has been used extensively in the past, especially in radio, TV and microwave applications.

Disadvantages of coaxial cable

- The cable is relatively thick, and the thicker the cable the more difficult it is to work with.
- More expensive than twisted-pair cable.
- In thinnet, the outer copper or metallic braid of the cable comprises half the electrical circuit. Thus special care must be taken to ensure that it is properly grounded, at both ends of the cable. If it is not properly grounded, it can result in electrical noise that interferes with transmittal of the signal on the networking media.

- **Reliable connection.** The file server is typically the most important computer on the network, and if it were to fail to communicate with the rest of the network it may cause a significant loss of service. Thus the file server is typically connected using reliable cabling with a robust network connection.

10.5.1 Cables

Cabling is one of the most important elements in a network, and is typically the limiting factor on the speed of the network. The four main types of networking media are:

- Shielded twisted-pair cable (STP).
- Unshielded twisted-pair cable (UTP).
- Coaxial cable.
- Fibre-optic cable.

The type of network media determines how fast the data travels along the media, and also the maximum data rate that can be carried. Twisted-pair and coaxial cable use copper wires to carry electrical signals, while fibre-optic cable carries light pulses. Fibre-optic cables generally support the fast data transfer rate.

All signals are affected by degradation when they are applied onto networking media. These are either internal or external, such as:

- **Internal.** In copper cables electrical parameters such as resistance (opposition to the flow of electrons), capacitance (the opposition to changes in voltage) and inductance (the opposition to changes in current) can cause signals to degrade. Resistance causes a loss of power (or signal attenuation), whereas capacitance and inductance cause the signals to lose their shape.
- **External.** These are external sources of electrical impulses that cause the electrical signals to change their shape. They are caused either by electromagnetic interference (EMI) or radio frequency interference (RFI), and are typically generated from lighting, electrical motors, and radio systems. In copper cables, each wire of the cable acts as an antenna, and absorbs electrical signals from other wires in the cable (know as crosstalk) and from EMI and RFI sources outside the cable. These sources are known as noise and can distort the electrical signals so that it is difficult to determine the original data.

Advantages of UTP:

- The cable is thin and easy to work with. This makes it easy to install.
- Less expensive than other types of networking media.
- When used with an RJ connector (RJ-45 or RJ-11), it provides a reliable connection.
- Data rates can be as fast as coaxial cables (as UTP cables now have an excellent specification).

Disadvantages of UTP:

- More prone to electrical noise and interference than other types of networking media (as there is no shield between the pairs).
- Can carry electrical surges.

Methods used to reduce signal attenuation, and coupled noise are:

- **Cancellation.** Electrical conductors produce a small circular magnetic field around themselves when an electrical current flows in them. If two wires are placed beside each other, and there is an opposite current flowing, then the magnetic fields will tend to cancel. This magnetic field can be reduced to almost zero by twisting the two opposite wires together. This technique is called twisted-pairs. The same goes for external magnetic fields coupling into the twisted-pairs, again they will cancel each other out. Thus twisted-pairs (or self-shielding) are useful for reducing external coupling of electromagnetic noise and crosstalk. The direction of these magnetic lines of force is determined by the direction in which current flows along the wire. If two wires are part of the same electrical circuit, electrons flow from the negative voltage source to the destination along one wire and from the destination to the positive voltage source along the other wire.

- **Shielding.** This combats EMI and RFI by wrapping a metal braid or foil around each wire pair or group of wire pairs, which acts as a barrier from external noise. This increases the size and cost of the cable, and is typically only used when there are large sources of external radiation, such as when placed near electrical motors. However, as with increasing the size of the conductors, using braid or foil covering increases the diameter of the cable, and it will increase the cost as well. Therefore, cancellation is the more commonly used technique to protect the wire from undesirable interference.
- **Match cables.** The characteristic impedance of a cable is important, and cables and connectors must always be chosen so that they have the same characteristic impedance. If they are not matched there can be a significant power loss or pulse reflections from the junction between the cable and the connection. For twisted-pair cables, this characteristic impedance is typically 100 Ω, and for coaxial cable it is 50 Ω (for networking) and 75 Ω (for TV applications).
- **Improve the cable.** Increasing the thickness of the conductors reduces the electrical resistance, and increasing the thickness of the insulating material reduces the amount of crosstalk. These changes tend to be expensive and increase the size of the cable.

Advantages of fibre optics:

- Excellent reliability, and are extensively used as network backbones.
- Immune from crosstalk, EMI and RFI.
- Can be run for longer distances than copper cables.
- They do not create grounding problems, thus they can be used to connect between two sites with a different ground potential.
- Very thin flat cable that can be easily run within confined spaces.
- Can be used in hazardous conditions, as it does not create electrical sparks.
- Immune from lightning strikes.

Disadvantages of fibre optics:

- More expensive and more difficult to install than any other networking media.
- Requires a trained installer to create a good cable connection.
- Too expensive in most situations to provide fibre connections to every workstation.

An important consideration when selecting a cable, especially in hazardous areas, is its jacket. Typically it is made from plastic, Teflon, or composite material. Problem areas are:

- **Carrying fire.** This is where the cable can carry fire from one part of a building to another. Typically it is where cables are installed between walls, in an elevator shaft or pass through an air-handling unit.
- **Producing toxic smoke when lit.** When burnt, plastic cable jackets can create toxic smoke.

To protect against these problems, network cables must always comply with fire codes, building codes, and safety standards. These are more important than other factors, such as cable size, speed, cost, and difficulty of installation.

10.5.2 Unshielded twisted-pair cable

The most popular type of cabling is unshielded twisted-pair, which comprises four-wire pair. Unshielded twisted-pair cable does not have a shield around each of the pairs, it thus relies on:

- **Cancellation effect.** The twists of each pair produces a cancellation effect which limits degradation caused by EMI and RFI.
- **Variation of twists.** With this the number of twists in the wire pairs varies from one to the other, which reduces the amount of crosstalk between the pairs. There are strict limits on the maximum number twists or braids per foot of cable.
- **Accurate characteristic impedance.** For this the characteristic impedance is around 100 Ω in order to produce a good match between the cable and any connection.

10.5.3 Shielded twisted-pair cable

STP cable is similar to UTP but has shielding on each of the pairs, thus reducing the effect of crosstalk, EMI and RFI. Unlike coaxial cable, the shielding does not act as part of the circuit, but it must be properly grounded at each end to enhance the shielding effect (as a non-ground shield will act like an antenna and pick up electrical noise). Its only disadvantage is that it is more expensive than UTP, although it can suffer from the same problems of coaxial cable if either end of the shield is not grounded.

> **DEAR NET-ED**
>
> **Question:** *I live in Edinburgh, and my friend lives in London. How long does it take for a digital pulse to travel from Edinburgh to London?*
>
> Well, there are a lot of assumptions to be made. First we'll assume that there are no intermediate devices in the cable that connects Edinburgh and London, and we'll assume that it is fibre-optic cable, which propagates light pulses at one-third the speed of light (10^8 m/s). Thus for a distance of 500 miles (804.65km) the time will be:
>
> $$T = \frac{Distance}{Speed} = \frac{804.65\times10^3}{1\times10^8} = 0.0080465$$
> $$= 8.05\,\text{ms}$$

10.5.4 Fibre-optic cables

One of the greatest revolutions in data communications is the usage of light waves to transmit digital pulses through fibre-optic cables. A light carrying system has an almost unlimited information capacity, and theoretically, it has more than 200,000 times the capacity of a satellite TV system.

Optoelectronics is the branch of electronics which deals with light, and uses electronic devices that use light which operate within the optical part of the electromagnetic frequency spectrum, as shown in Figure 10.10. There are three main bands in the optical frequency spectrum, these are:

- Infrared – the band of light wavelengths that are too long to been seen by the human eye.
- Visible – the band of light wavelengths that the human eye responds to.
- Ultraviolet – band of light wavelengths that are too short for the human eye to see.

10.5.4.1 Wavelength and colour

Wavelength is defined as the physical distance between two successive points of the same electrical phase. Figure 10.11 (a) shows a wave and its wavelength. The wavelength is dependent upon the frequency of the wave f, and the velocity of light, c (3×10^{8} m/s) and is given by:

$$\lambda = \frac{c}{f}$$

The optical spectrum ranges from wavelengths of 0.005 mm to 4000 mm. In frequency terms these are extremely large values from 6×10^{16} Hz to 7.5×10^{10} Hz. It is thus much simpler to talk in terms of wavelengths rather than frequencies.

The human eye sees violet at one end of the colour spectrum and red on the other. In-between, the eye sees blue, indigo, green, yellow and orange. Two beams of light that have the same wavelength are seen as the same colour and the same colours usually have the same wavelength. Figure 10.11 (b) shows the colour spectrum.

DEAR NET-ED

Question: *Everyone keeps telling me how good network switches are. So what's so good about them?*

Network switches, unlike network hubs, allow more than one port to talk to another port, at a time. Thus the bandwidth can be a multiple of the base bandwidth. For example a four-port switch could have a total network maximum throughput of 400 Mbps (for a base transfer rate of 100 Mbps). The other example of network switches is that it is possible to configure them to set up virtual LANs (vLAN), which enhances security and also allows networks to be defined by software rather than physical location.

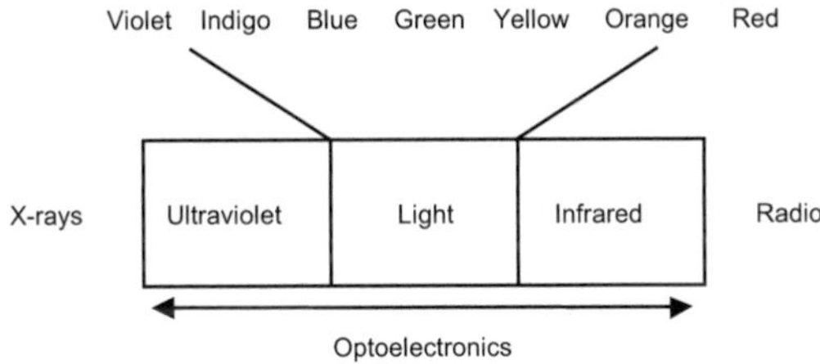

Figure 10.10 EM optoelectronics spectrum

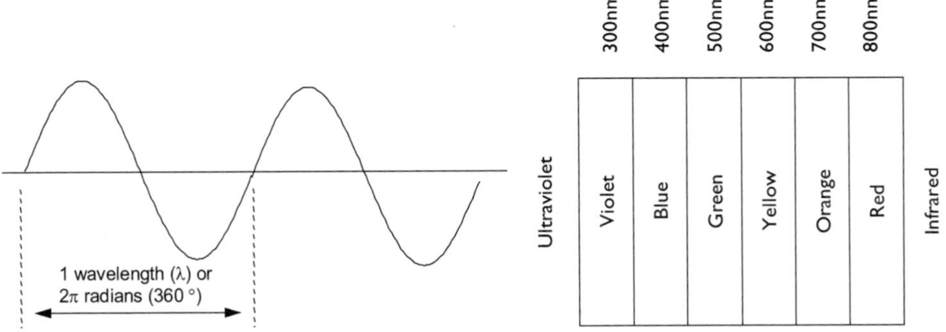

Figure 10.11 Wavelength of wave and colour spectrum

10.5.4.2 Velocity of propagation and refractive index

In free space electromagnetic waves travel at approximately 300,000,000m/sec (186,000 miles/sec). However, their velocity is lower when they travel through denser materials. When travelling from one material to another which is less dense the light ray is refracted (or bent) away from the normal, as illustrated in Figure 10.12.

The amount of bending or refraction at the interface between two materials of different densities depends on the refractive index of the two materials. This index is the ratio of the velocity of propagation of a light ray in free space to the velocity of propagation of a light ray in the material, as given by:

$$n = \frac{c}{v}$$

where c is speed of light in free space and v is the speed of light in a given medium. Typical refractive indexes are given in Table 10.1.

> **DEAR NET-ED**
>
> **Question:** *Why do they put cables in the ocean? Can't they just use satellites?*
>
> Satellites can transmit at hundred of megabits per second. The data which travels between continents is increasing all the time, and can be many tens of gigabits per second. Thus satellite systems would require hundreds of channels to be able to cope with the capacity. A fibre optic system has an almost infinite bandwidth, which is typically limited by the electronics that it uses, and having to boost the laser signal at regular intervals. Thus satellite communications provide a good short-term solution, but nothing can really beat fibre optic transmission. A big problem with fibre optic cables under the sea is that the seabed is forever moving, which eventually breaks the cable. Thus cables have to be re-run at regular intervals.

10.5.4.3 Optical fibres

Optical fibres are transparent, dielectric cylinders surrounded by a second transparent dielectric cylinder. Light is transported by a series of reflections from wall to wall from the interface between a core (inner cylinder) and its cladding (outer cylinder). A cross-section of a fibre is given in Figure 10.13.

Reflections occur because the core has a higher reflective index than the cladding (it thus has a higher density). Abrupt differences in the refractive index cause the light wave to bounce from the core/cladding interface back through the core to its opposite wall. Thus the light is transported from a light source to a light detector at the other end of the fibre.

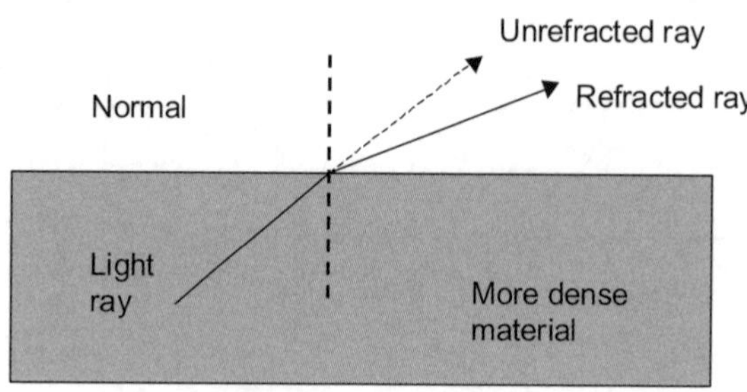

Figure 10.12 Refracted ray

Table 10.1 Refractive index of sample materials

Medium	*Refractive index*
Air	1.0003
Water	1.33
Glass fibre	1.5–1.9
Diamond	2.0–2.42
Gallium arsenide	3.6
Silicon	3.4

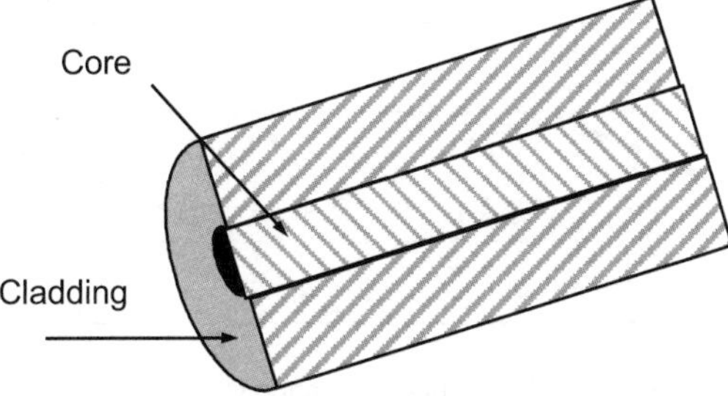

Figure 10.13 Cross-section of an optical fibre

Optical fibres transmit light by total internal reflection (TIR), where light rays passing between the boundaries of two optically transparent media of different densities experience refraction, as shown in Figure 10.14. This changed direction can be determined according to Snell's law:

$$n_1 \sin\theta_1 = n_2 \sin\theta_2$$

Thus
$$\theta_2 = \sin^{-1}\left[\frac{n_1}{n_2}\sin\theta_1\right]$$

The angle at which the ray travels along the interface between the two materials is called the critical angle (θ_c). If the incident ray is greater than this angle, the ray will be totally reflected from the outer cladding. It then propagates along the fibre being reflected by the cladding on the way, as shown in Figure 10.15. The angle at which the reflection occurs is called the acceptance angle, and if the initial ray is entered at an angle of at least the acceptance angle, then the ray will bounce along the inner core.

DEAR NET-ED

Question: *What? The light pulses bounce along the cable?*

Yes. They do. The light pulses do not travel straight through the fibre, they bounce along it. Just imagine that you're underwater. When you look at the water, at a certain angle, you can actually see a mirror image of the sky.

Question: *If we're transmitting voice or audio along the fibre-optic cable, are we transmitting the analogue version of the signal, or a digital one?*

Normally we transmit the digital version, which means that we send digital pulses of light over the fibre. It is possible to transmit different intensities of light to represent the amplitude of the signal, but this is susceptible to reduction in amplitude of the light rays.

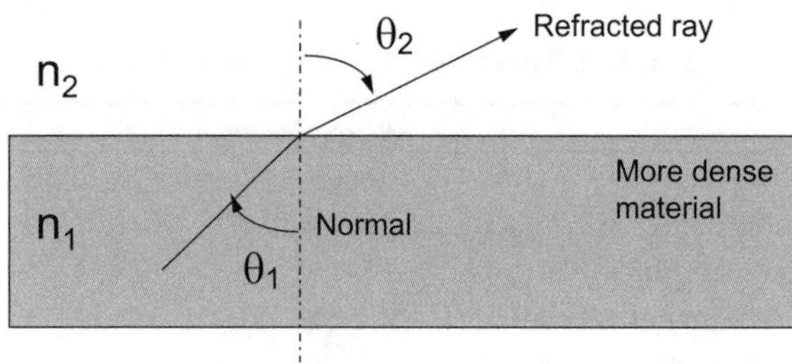

Figure 10.14 Refraction

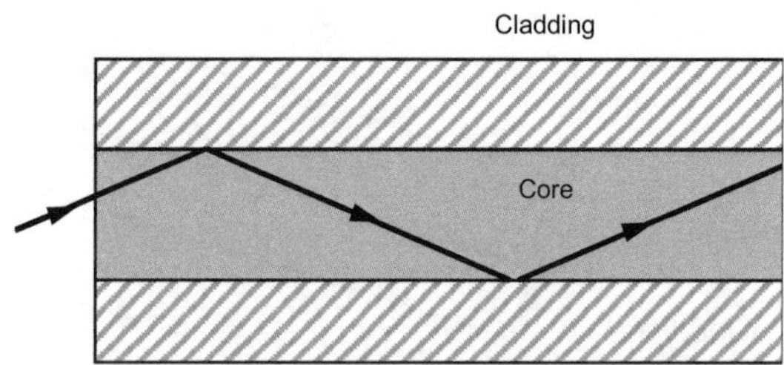

Figure 10.15 Light propagating in an optical fibre

Fibre-optic losses result in a lower transmitted light power, which reduces the system bandwidth, information transmission rate, efficiency and overall system capacity. The main losses are:

- **Absorption losses.** Impurities in the glass fibre cause the transmitted wave to be absorbed and converted into heat.
- **Material scattering.** Extremely small irregularities in the structure of the cable cause light to be diffracted. This causes the light to disperse or spread out in many directions. A greater loss occurs at visible wavelengths than at infrared.
- **Chromatic distortion.** Caused by each wavelength of light travelling at differing speeds. They thus arrive at the receiver at different times causing a distorted pulse shape. Monochromatic light reduces this type of distortion.
- **Radiation losses.** Caused by small bends and kinks in the fibre that scatters the wave.
- **Modal dispersion.** Caused by light taking different paths through the fibre. This will each have a different propagation time to travel along the fibre. These different paths are described as modes. Figure 10.16 shows two rays taking different paths. Ray 2 will take a longer time to get to the receiver than ray 1.
- **Coupling losses.** Caused by light being lost at mismatches at terminations between fibre/fibre, light source/fibre, and so on.

Optical fibre cables are either glass-based or plastic-based, and typically carry infrared signals (it is thus important to never look directly into a fibre optic cable which is transmitting infrared signals, as it can damage your eyes). Table 10.2 shows the characteristics of two typical fibre-optic cables, one using glass, and the other plastic. It can be seen that the inside core and the cladding diameters are relatively small, i.e. fractions of a millimetre. Normally the cladding is covered in a coating which is then covered in a jacket. These give the cable mechanical strength and also make it easier to work with. In the case of the

50/125 μm glass cable in Table 10.2 the outer diameter of the cable is 3.2 mm but the inner core diameter is just 50 μm. Normally glass fibre cables have better electrical characteristic over plastic equivalents, but are more prone to breakage and damage. It can be seen that the glass cable has improved bandwidth and lower attenuation over the plastic equivalent.

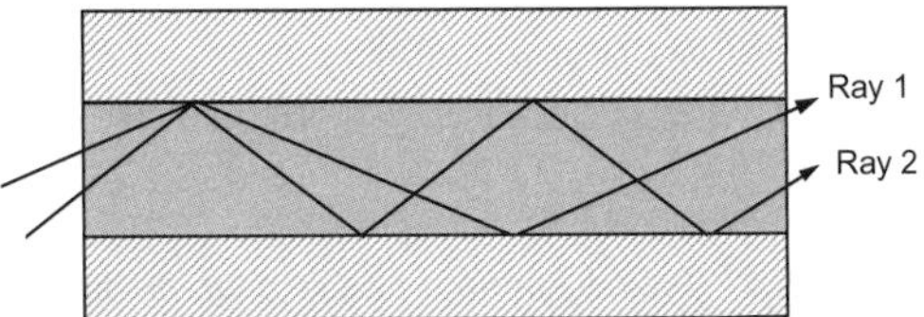

Figure 10.16 Light propagating in different modes

> **DEAR NET-ED**
>
> **Question:** *I've been told that I should not use copper cables to connect networks between two buildings. Why?*
>
> Networks use digital signals. These digital signals are referenced to a local ground level (which eventually connects to the earth connection). The ground level can vary between different buildings (and can be large enough to give someone an electrical shock). Thus the ground connection between the two buildings must be broken. If possible for safety, and for reliable digital transmission, you should use a fibre-optic connection.
>
> Also, copper cables can carry electrical surges (such as from lightning strikes), and airborne electrical noise. Electrical surges can cause great damage, and noise can cause the network performance to degrade (as it can cause bit errors).
>
> If possible use fibre-optic cables for any long run of networking media. They tend to produce fewer problems, and allow for easy upgrades (as they have a much greater bandwidth than copper-based cables).

There are many advantages in using fibre optics, including:

- Fibre systems have a greater capacity due to the inherently larger bandwidths available with optical frequencies. Metallic cables contain capacitance and inductance along their conductors, which cause them to act like low-pass filters. This limits bandwidth and also the speed of propagation of the electrical pulse.
- Fibre systems are immune from cross-talk between cables caused by magnetic induction. Glass fibres are non-conductors of electricity and therefore do not have a magnetic field associated with them. In metallic cables, the primary cause of cross-talk is magnetic induction between conductors located near each other.
- Fibre cables do not suffer from static interference caused by lightning, electric motors, fluorescent lights, and other electrical noise sources. This immunity is because fibres are non-conductors of electricity.
- Fibre systems have greater electrical isolation thus allowing equipment greater protection from damage due to external sources. For example if a part of a network was hit by a lightning pulse then it may damage one of the optical receivers but a high voltage pulse cannot travel along the optical cable and damage sensitive equipment on other parts of the network. They also prevent electrical noise travelling from one part of a network to another, as illustrated in Figure 10.17.
- Fibre cables do not radiate energy and therefore cannot cause interference with other communications systems. This characteristic makes fibre systems ideal for military applications, where the effect of nuclear weapons (EMP-electromagnetic pulse interference) has a devastating effect on conventional communications systems.

- Fibre cables are more resistant to environmental extremes. They operate over a larger temperature variation than copper cables and are affected less by corrosive liquids and gases.
- Fibre cables are safer to install and maintain, as glass and plastic have no electrical currents or voltages associated with them. Optical fibres can be used around volatile liquids and gases without worrying about the risk of explosions or fires. They are also smaller and more lightweight than copper cables.
- Fibre cables are more secure than copper cables and are virtually impossible to tap into without users knowing about it.

Table 10.2 Typical fibre-optic cable characteristics

	50/125 μm glass	*200 μm PCS*
Construction	Glass	Plastic coated silica (PCS)
Core diameter	50 μm	200 μm
Cladding diameter	125 μm	389 μm
Coating diameter	250 μm	600 μm
Jacket material	Polyethylene	PVC
Overall diameter	3.2 mm	4.8 mm
Connector	9 mm SMA	9 mm SMA
Bandwidth	400 MHz/km	25 MHz/km
Minimum bend radius	30 mm	50 mm
Temperature range	–15 °C to +60 °C	–10 °C to +50 °C
Attenuation @820 nm	3 dB/km	7 dB/km

High voltages or electrical noise cannot propagate back to the transmitter

Data flow

Figure 10.17 Fibre-optic isolation

10.6 Exercises

The following question is multiple choice. Please select from a–d.

10.6.1 The cable type which offers the highest bit rate is:

(a) Fibre-optic cable (b) Twisted-pair cable
(c) Coaxial cable (d) Untwisted-pair cable

Additional material and tutorial questions are available at:

`http://www.palgrave.com/studyskills/masterseries/buchanan`

11 Internet Protocol

11.1 Introduction

> **InterNIC** (International Network Information Center) is the organization that serves the Internet community and supplies user assistance, documentation, training, and other services.

Networking technologies such as Ethernet, Token Ring and FDDI provide a data link layer function, that is, they allow a reliable connection between one node and another on the same network. They do not provide internetworking where data can be transferred from one network to another or from one network segment to another. For data to be transmitted across a network requires an addressing structure which is read by a gateway or a router. The interconnection of networks is known as internetworking (or an internet). Each part of an internet is a subnetwork (or subnet), and Transmission Control Protocol (TCP) and Internet Protocol (IP) are a pair of protocols that allow one subnet to communicate with another.

A protocol is a set of rules that allows the orderly exchange of information. The IP part corresponds to the network layer of the OSI model and the TCP part to the transport layer. Their operation is transparent to the physical and data link layers and can thus be used on Ethernet, FDDI or Token Ring networks. This is illustrated in Figure 11.1. The address of the data link layer corresponds to the physical address of the node, such as the MAC address (in Ethernet and Token Ring) or the telephone number (for a modem connection). The IP address is assigned to each node on the internet, and is used to identify the location of the network and any subnets.

TCP/IP was originally developed by the US Defense Advanced Research Projects Agency (DARPA), and its objective was to connect a number of universities and other research establishments to DARPA. The resultant internet is now known as the Internet. It has since outgrown this application and many commercial organizations now connect to the Internet. The Internet uses TCP/IP to transfer data, where each node on the Internet is assigned a unique network address, called an IP address. Note that any organization can have its own internets, but if it is to connect to the Internet then the addresses must conform to the Internet addressing format. Common applications that use TCP/IP communications are remote login and file transfer. Typical programs used in file transfer and login over TCP communication are `ftp` for file transfer program and `telnet` which allows remote log into another computer. The `ping` program determines if a node is responding to TCP/IP communications.

The ISO has adopted TCP/IP as the basis for the standards relating to the network and transport layers of the OSI model, and is known as ISO-IP. Most currently available systems conform to the IP addressing standard.

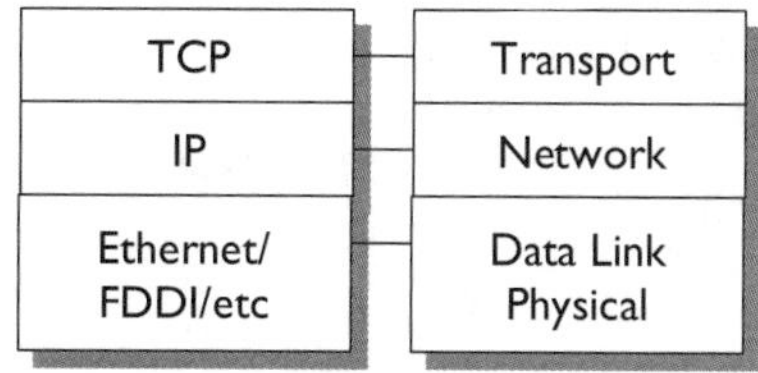

Figure 11.1 TCP/IP and the OSI model

11.2 Data encapsulation

The OSI model provides a clear model in understanding how data is transferred from one system to another. Each layer of the OSI model depends on the layers above and/or below it to provide a certain function. To achieve this data is encapsulated when passing from one layer to the next. Encapsulation happens when a lower layer gets a PDU (Protocol Data Unit) from an upper layer and uses this as a data field. It then adds to its own headers and trailers so that it can perform the required function. For example, as illustrated in Figure 11.2, if a user was sending an e-mail to another user the host computer would go through the following:

- **Step 1.** The application program makes contact with a network application program for electronic mail transfer [Application].
- **Step 2.** The computer converts the data into a form that can be transmitted over the network [Presentation].
- **Step 3.** The computer sets up a connection with the remote system and asks if it is willing to make a connection with it. Once accepted it will ask the remote system as to whether the user for whom the e-mail message is destined for actually exists on that system [Session].
- **Step 4.** The transport layer negotiates with the remote system about how it wants to receive the data, it then splits the data into a number of segments, each of which are numbered. Any problems with lost segments will be dealt with at this step [Transport]. DATA SEGMENT.
- **Step 5.** The network address of the destination and source are added to all the data segments [Network]. DATA PACKET.
- **Step 6.** The data packet is then framed in a format so that it can be transmitted over the local connection [Data link]. DATA FRAME.
- **Step 7.** The data frame is then taken and converted into a binary form and transmitted over a physical connection. BITS.

Media layers

These layers control the physical delivery of messages of the network. They include:

- **Network** (addressing and best path).
- **Data link** (access to media)
- **Physical layers** (bit transmission).

Network: ROUTERS
Data link: BRIDGES/SWITCHES
Physical: HUBS/REPEATERS

Host layers

These layers provide accurate delivery of data between interconnected nodes. They are:

- **Application** (provides network services to user applications, such as file transfer to an application program).
- **Presentation** (provides data representation and encoding, and ensures that the data is in a form that can be used by the application or able to be transmitted over the network).
- **Session** (establishes, maintains, and manages sessions between applications),
- **Transport** (segments at the send and reassembles the data into a data stream).

Bits→Frames→Packets→
Segments→Data (Bottom-Up)
Data→Segments→Packets→
Frames→Bits (Top-Down)

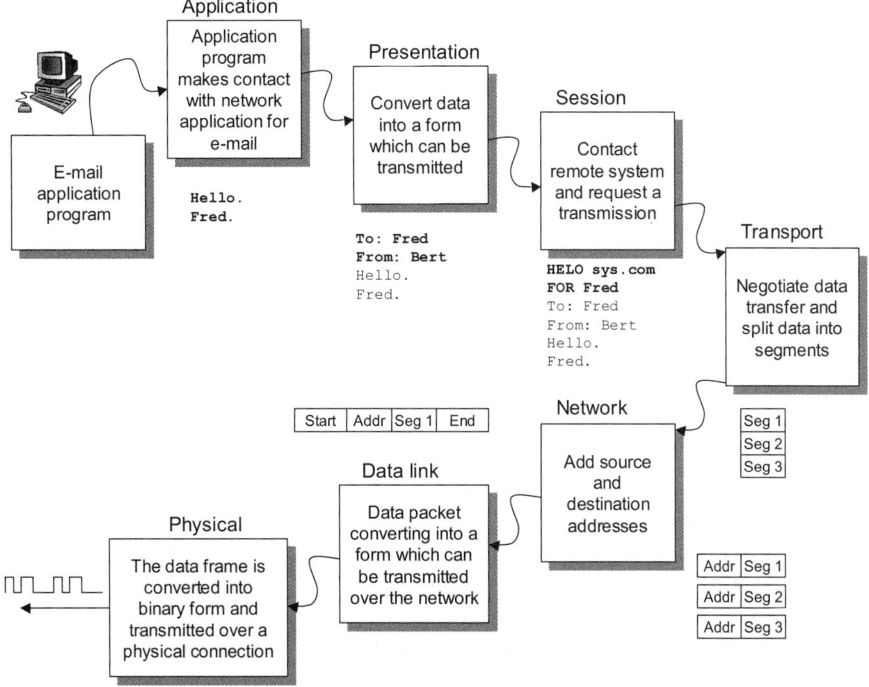

Figure 11.2 Data encapsulation

11.3 TCP/IP gateways and hosts

TCP/IP hosts are nodes which communicate over interconnected networks using TCP/IP communications. A TCP/IP gateway node connects one type of network to another. It contains hardware to provide the physical link between the different networks and the hardware and software to convert frames from one network to the other. Typically, it converts a Token Ring MAC layer to an equivalent Ethernet MAC layer, and vice versa.

A router connects a network of a similar type to another of the same kind through a point-to-point link. The main operational difference between a gateway, a router, and a bridge is that for a Token Ring and Ethernet network, the bridge uses the 48-bit MAC address to route frames, whereas the gateway and router use the IP network address. As an analogy to the public telephone system, the MAC address would be equivalent to a randomly assigned telephone number, whereas the IP address would contain the information on where the telephone is logically located, such as which country, area code, and so on.

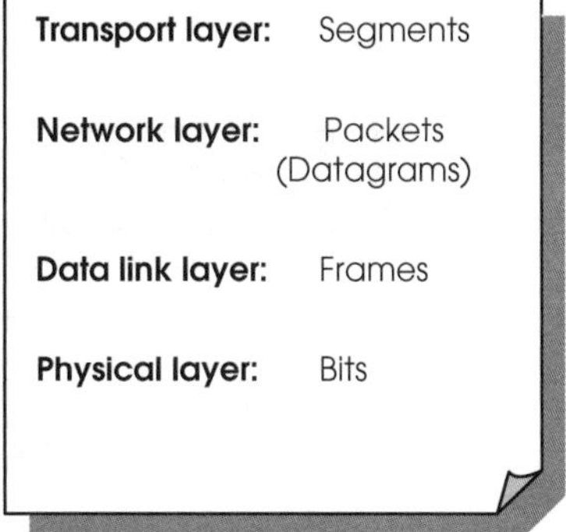

Transport layer: Segments
Network layer: Packets (Datagrams)
Data link layer: Frames
Physical layer: Bits

Figure 11.3 shows how a gateway (or router) routes information. It reads the data frame from the computer on network A, and reads the IP address contained in the frame and makes a decision whether it is routed out of network A to network B. If it does then it relays the frame to network B.

11.4 Functions of the IP protocol

The main functions of the IP protocol are to:

- Route IP data packets – which are called internet datagrams – around an internet. The IP protocol program running on each node knows the location of the gateway on the network. The gateway must then be able to locate the interconnected network. Data then passes from node to gateway through the internet.
- Fragment the data into smaller units, if it is greater than a given amount (64 kB). Most data packets will be much smaller than 64kB. For example the maximum size of a data packet that can be contained in an Ethernet frame is 1500 bytes.
- Report errors. When a datagram is being routed or is being reassembled an error can occur. If this happens then the node that detects the error reports back to the source node. Datagrams are deleted from the network if they travel through the network for more than a set time. Again, an error message is returned to the source node to inform it that the Internet routing could not find a route for the datagram or that the destination node, or network, does not exist.

> **APPLICATION LAYER**
>
> Computer applications make use of network applications.
>
> Computer applications:
>
> - Spreadsheets.
> - Word processor.
> - Database.
> - WWW browser.
>
> Network applications (application layer of OSI model):
>
> - Electronic mail.
> - File transfer.
> - Remote access.
> - WWW access.

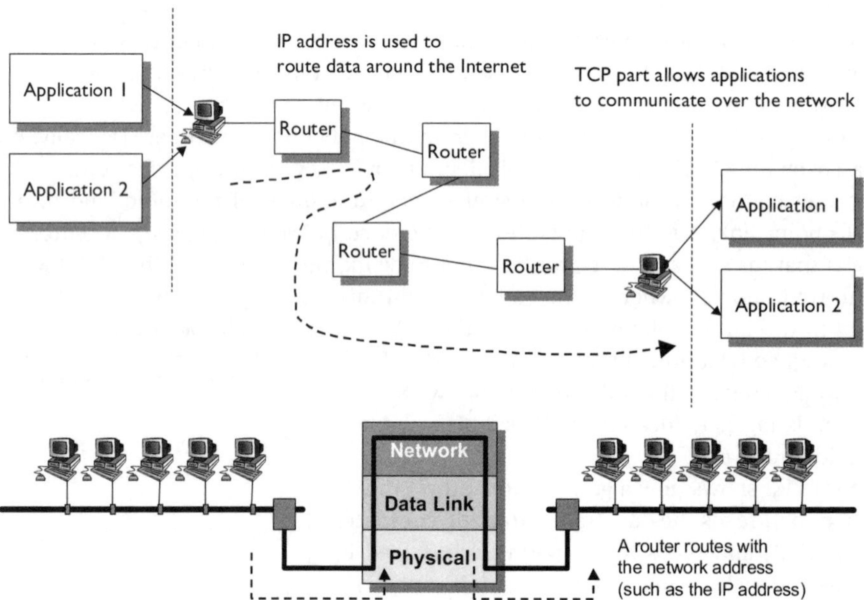

Figure 11.3 Internet gateway layers

11.5 Internet datagram

The IP protocol is an implementation of the network layer of the OSI model. It adds a data header onto the information passed from the transport layer, the resultant data packet is known as an internet datagram. The header contains information such as the destination and source IP addresses, the version number of the IP protocol and so on. Figure 11.4 shows its format.

The datagram can contain up to 65,536 bytes (64 KB) of data. If the data to be transmitted is less than, or equal to 64 KB, then it is sent as one datagram. If it is more than this then the sender splits the data into fragments and sends multiple datagrams. When transmitted from the source each datagram is routed separately through the internet and the received fragments are finally reassembled at the destination.

The fields in the IP datagram are:

- **Version.** The TCP/IP `version number` helps gateways and nodes interpret the data unit correctly. Differing versions may have a different format. Most current implementations will have a version number of four (IPv4).
- **Type of service.** The `type of service` bit field is an 8-bit bit pattern in the form `PPPDTRXX`, where `PPP` defines the priority of the datagram (from 0 to 7). The precedence levels are:

  111 (Network control)
  110 (Internetwork control)
  001 (Priority)

  `D` sets a low delay service (0 – normal delay, 1 – low delay).
  `T` sets high throughput (0 – normal throughput, 1 – high throughput).
  `R` sets high reliability (0 – normal reliability, 1 – high reliability).

- **Header length** (4 bits). The `header length` defines the size of the data unit in multiples of four bytes (32 bits). The minimum length is five bytes and the maximum is 65,536 bytes. Padding bytes fill any unused spaces.
- **Identification** (16 bits). A value which is assigned by the sender to aid the assembly of the frames of a datagram.

PRESENTATION LAYER

The presentation layer allows for code formatting and encoding. This ensures that the data is in a form that can be transmitted and received at the destination. A typical function is to translate from one system to another. Encryption is also another important function. Typical conversions and formats used at the presentation layer are:

- Text. ASCII, EBCDIC, Encryption, Binary-to-text, Character conversion.
- Graphics. JPEG, TIFF, GIF.
- Audio. MP-3, WAV, MIDI.
- Video. MPEG, QuickTime (AVI).

Typical encryption standards are:

- **RSA.** Rivest, Shamir and Aldeman (the creators of the RSA method). An encryption method where a user generates two keys: a public one and a private one. The public key is freely available to anyone who wants to send the user some encrypted data. It is used to encrypt the data destined for the user, and only the private key can decrypt the data.
- **PGP.** Pretty Good Privacy. Based on the RSA method, but highly optimized and fast.
- **DES.** Data Encryption Standard. A private-key standard where both the sender and the receiver use the same private key to encrypt and decrypt the data.
- **IDEA.** International Data Encryption Standard. Private-key method

- **D and M bits.** A gateway may route a datagram and split it into smaller fragments. The `D` bit informs the gateway that it should not fragment the data and thus it signifies that a receiving node should receive the data as a single unit or not at all. The `M` bit is the 'more fragments' bit and is used when data is split into fragments. The `fragment offset` contains the fragment number. The bit settings are:

  D – Don't fragment. 0 – may fragment, 1 – don't fragment.
  M – Last fragment. 0 – last fragment, 1 – more fragments.

- **Fragment offset** (13 bits). Indicates which datagram this fragment belongs to. The fragment offset is measured in units of 8 bytes (64 bits). The first fragment has an offset of zero.
- **Time-to-live** (8 bits). A datagram could propagate through the internet indefinitely. To prevent this, the 8-bit `time-to-live` value is set to the maximum transit time in seconds and is set initially by the source IP. Each gateway then decrements this value by a defined amount. When it becomes zero the datagram is discarded. It can also be used to define the maximum amount of time that a destination IP node should wait for the next datagram fragment.
- **Protocol** (8 bits). Different IP protocols can be used on the datagram. The 8-bit `protocol` field defines the type to be used. Typical values are: 1 – ICMP and 6 – TCP.
- **Header checksum** (16 bits). The `header checksum` contains a 16-bit pattern for error detection. Since values within the header change from gateway to gateway (such as the time-to-live field), it must be recomputed every time the IP header is processed. The algorithm is:

  The 16-bit 1's complement of the 1's complement sum of all the 16-bit words in the header. When calculating the checksum the header checksum field is assumed to be set to a zero.

- **Source and destination IP addresses** (32 bits). The `source` and `destination IP addresses` are stored in the 32-bit source and destination IP address fields.

SESSION LAYER

The session layer establishes, manages and terminates sessions between applications. Typical session protocols are:

- **FTP.** File transfer protocol. Used to transfer files.
- **HTTP.** Hypertext transmission Protocol. Used to transfer files between a WWW server and a client.
- **NFS.** Network File Service. Used to link file systems.
- **RPC.** Remote procedure call. Used to run remote applications.
- **SMTP.** Simple mail transport protocol. Used to transmit e-mail.
- **SNMP.** Simple network management protocol. Used to investigate network devices.
- **SQL.** Structured query language. Used to transfer database information over a network.
- **TELNET.** Used to remotely log into a remote computer.
- **DNS.** Domain name services. Used to convert logical names into network addresses.
- **bootp.** Boot protocol. Used to assign network address (typically IP addresses), based on station addresses (typically, MAC addresses).
- **DHCP.** Dynamic host control protocol. Used to assign network addresses.
- **WINS.** Used to assign network addresses.
- **NNTP.** Network news transfer protocol.
- **NTP.** Network time protocol.
- **FINGER.** Used to determine information on a user.

- **Options**. The `options` field contains information such as debugging, error control and routing information.

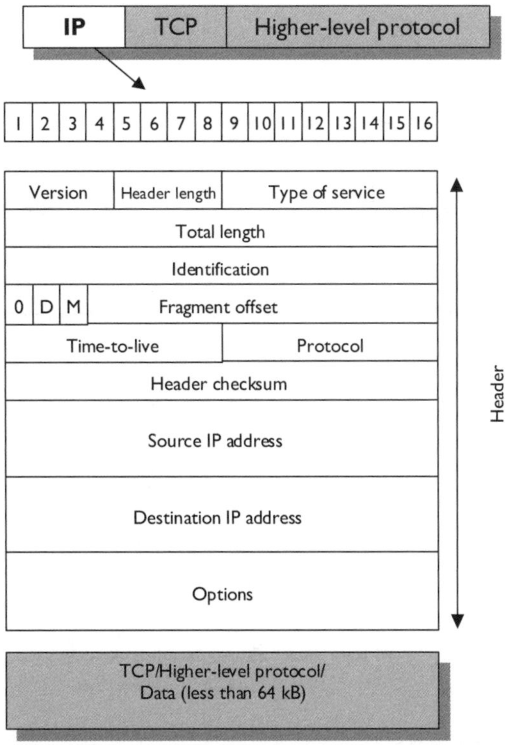

Figure 11.4 Internet datagram format and contents

11.6 TCP/IP internets

Figure 11.5 illustrates a sample TCP/IP implementation. A gateway MERCURY provides a link between a Token Ring network (NETWORK A) and the Ethernet network (ETHER C). Another gateway PLUTO connects NETWORK B to ETHER C. The TCP/IP protocol allows a host on NETWORK A to communicate with VAX01.

> **Transport layer.** Segments and reassembles data into a data stream. It is also responsible for connection synchronization, flow control and error recovery.
>
> **Network layer.** Determines the best route for data to take from one place to another. Routers operate at this layer.

11.6.1 Selecting internet addresses

Each node using TCP/IP communications requires an IP address which is then matched to its Token Ring or Ethernet MAC address. The MAC address allows nodes on the same segment to communicate with each other. In order for nodes on a different network to communicate, each must be configured with an IP address.

Nodes on a TCP/IP network are either hosts or gateways. Any node that runs application software or are terminals are hosts. Any node that routes TCP/IP packets between networks is called a TCP/IP gateway node. This node must have the necessary network controller boards to physically interface to other networks it connects with.

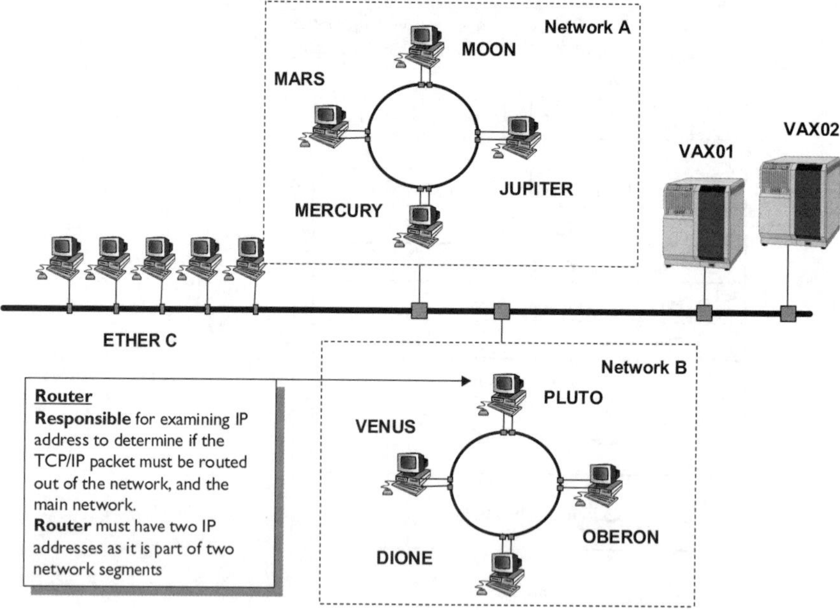

Figure 11.5 Example internet

11.6.2 Format of the IP address

A typical IP address consists of two fields: the left field (or the network number) identifies the network, and the right number (or the host number) identifies the particular host within that network. Figure 11.6 illustrates this. The IP address is 32 bits long and can address over four billion physical addresses (2^{32} or 4,294,967,296 hosts). There are three main address formats and these are shown in Figure 11.7.

Each of these types is applicable to certain types of networks. Class A allows up to 128 (2^7) different networks and up to 16,777,216 (2^{24}) hosts on each network. Class B allows up to 16,384 (2^{14}) networks and up to 65,536 (2^{16}) hosts on each network. Class C allows up to 2,097,152 (2^{21}) networks each with up to 256 (2^8) hosts.

The class A address is thus useful where there are a small number of networks with a large number of hosts connected to them. Class C is useful where there are many networks with a relatively small number of hosts connected to each network. Class B addressing gives a good compromise of networks and connected hosts.

When selecting internet addresses for the network, the address can be specified simply with decimal numbers within a specific range. The standard DARPA IP addressing format is of the form:

```
W.X.Y.Z
```

where `W`, `X`, `Y` and `Z` represent 1 byte of the IP address. As decimal numbers they range from 0 to 255. The 4 bytes together represent both the network and host address.

Table 11.1 Ranges of addresses for type A, B and C internet address

Type	*Network portion*	*Host portion*
A	1 – 126	0.0.1 – 255.255.254
B	128.1 – 191.254	0.1 – 255.254
C	192.0.1 – 223.255.254	1 – 254

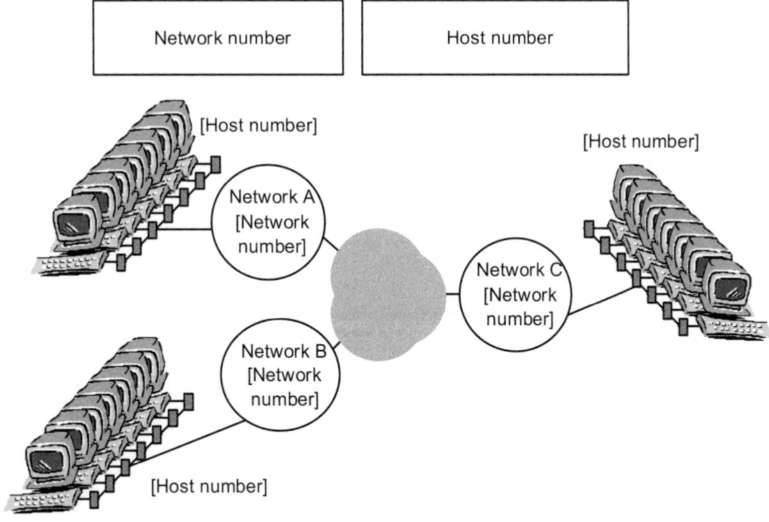

Figure 11.6 IP addressing over networks

The valid range of the different IP addresses given in Table 11.1 defines the valid IP addresses. Thus for a class A type address there can be 127 networks and 16,711,680 (256×256×255) hosts. Class B can have 16,320 (64×255) networks and class C can have 2,088,960 (32×256×255) networks and 255 hosts. Addresses above `223.255.254` are reserved, as are addresses with groups of zeros.

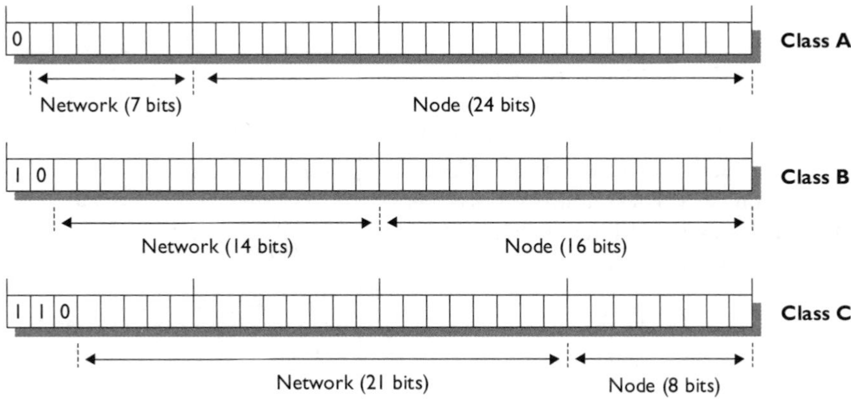

Figure 11.7 Type A, B and C IP address classes

11.6.3 Range of IP addresses

The IP address splits into two main parts: the network part (which is assigned by InterNIC), and the host part (which is assigned by the local system administrator). The type of address that is allocated depends on the size of the organization and the number of hosts that it has on its network. Figure 11.8 shows how the binary notation can be represented in dotted notation, of which there are three commercial address classifications, these are:

- **Class A.** Large organizations with many nodes. MIT has a Class A address (18.0.0.0).
- **Class B.** Medium sized organizations with an average number of hosts. For example, Napier University has a Class B address (146.176.0.0).
- **Class C.** Small organizations or setups, with only a few hosts on each network.

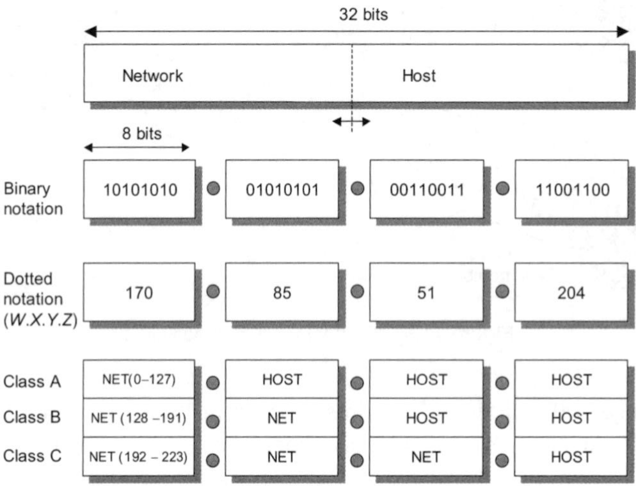

Figure 11.8 IP address format

The other two address classifications are used for multicast and research purposes. These are:

- **Class D.** Multicast. Single packets copied by the network and sent to a specific subset of network addresses. These addresses are specified in the destination address field.
- **Class E.** Research purposes.

Not all the IP addresses in the host part can be used to assign to a host. The two exceptions are:

- **All 0's in the host part** are reserved for the entire network. For example:

  32.0.0.0 (Class A network address).
  146.176.0.0 (Class B network address).

> The ping command allows a user to determine if a host is responding to TCP/IP communications. It also gives an indication of a host's IP address.
>
> ping www.mit.edu
> Ping statistics for **18.181.0.31**:
> Packets: Sent = 4, Received = 4, Lost = 0 (0% loss).
>
> ping www.napier.ac.uk
> Ping statistics for **146.176.1.8**:
> Packets: Sent = 4, Received = 4, Lost = 0 (0% loss).
>
> ping www.ja.net
> Ping statistics for **194.82.140.71**:
> Packets: Sent = 4, Received = 4, Lost = 0 (0% loss).

199.20.30.0 (Class C network address).

- **All 1's in the host part** are reserved for the broadcast address, which is used to send a data packet to all the hosts on the network. For example:

  32.255.255.255 (Class A broadcast address for the network 32.0.0.0).
  146.176.255.255 (Class B broadcast address for the network 146.176.0.0).
  199.20.30.255 (Class C broadcast address for the network 199.20.30.0).

The other broadcast address is 255.255.255.255. Routers will not transmit broadcast addresses from one network segment to another.

11.6.4 Creating IP addresses with subnet numbers

Besides selecting IP addresses of internets and host numbers, it is also possible to designate an intermediate number called a subnet number. Subnets extend the network field of the IP address beyond the limit defined by the type A, B, C scheme. They thus allow for a hierarchy of internets within a network. For example, it is possible to have one network number for a network attached to the internet, and various subnet numbers for each subnet within the network. This is illustrated in Figure 11.9. For an address `W.X.Y.Z` and type for a type A address, typically `W` specifies the network and `X` the subnet. For type B the `Y` field typically specifies the subnet, as illustrated in Figure 11.10.

To connect to a global network a number is normally assigned by a central authority. For the Internet network it is assigned by the Network Information Center (NIC). Typically, on the Internet an organization is assigned a type B network address. The first two fields of the address specify the organization network, the third specifies the subnet within the organization and the final value specifies the host.

TRANSPORT LAYER

The transport layer provides the required reliability in the delivery of data, and end-to-end services. It supports:

- **Segmentation and reassembly.** This involves splitting data from one or more applications into segments, which are then transmitted onto a single data stream. The receiver must reassemble these segments back into the original data block.
- **Flow control.** This allows the destination to control the amount of data but informing the source that it cannot receive any more data at the present.
- **Acknowledgement and retransmission.** Acknowledgements are sent by the receiver after it has successfully received the transmitted data segments. This allows the transmitter to determine if the data has been received correctly, if not, it can retransmit the data.

Typical transport protocols are:

- **TCP.** The standard protocol that is used on the Internet.
- **UDP.** Similar to TCP, but does not have acknowledgement or flow control. It is thus unreliable, as the sender cannot guarantee that the data segments were received correctly.
- **SPX.** The transport protocol that is used with Novell NetWare.

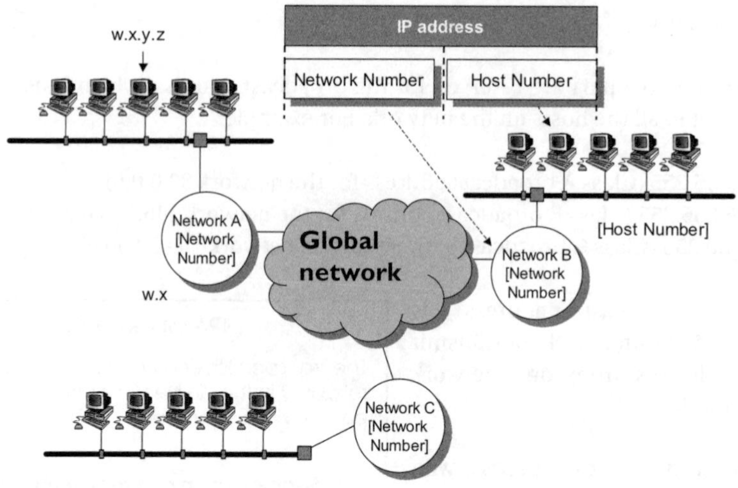

Figure 11.9 IP addresses with subnets

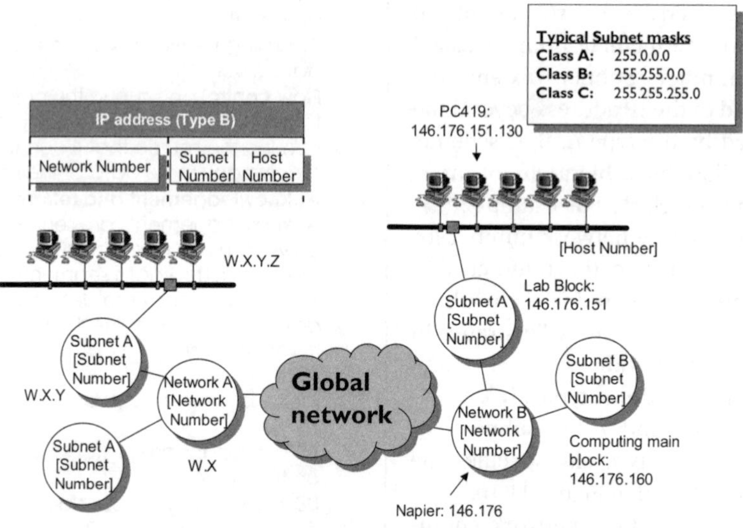

Figure 11.10 Internet addresses with subnets

11.6.5 Specifying subnet masks

If a subnet is used then a bit mask, or subnet mask, must be specified to show which part of the address is the network part and which is the host. The subnet mask is a 32-bit number that has 1's for bit positions specifying the network and subnet parts and 0's for the host part. A text file called `hosts` is normally used to set up the subnet mask. Table 11.2 shows example subnet masks. To set up the default mask the following line is added to the `hosts` file.

```
Hosts file
255.255.255.0defaultmask
```

Table 11.2 Default subnet mask for type A, B and C IP addresses

Address type	*Default mask*
Class A	255.0.0.0
Class B	255.255.0.0
Class C and Class B with a subnet	255.255.255.0

The subnet can use any number of bits from the host portion of the address. Table 11.3 outlines the subnet masks for Class B addresses, and Table 11.4 outlines the subnet masks for Class C addresses. The number of bits borrowed from the host address defines the maximum number of subnetworks. For example four bits borrowed from the host field will allow 14 different subnetworks (2^4-2, as 0000 is reserved for the whole network and 1111 is reserved for the broadcast address). The subnets will thus be defined by 0001, 0010, 0011 ... 1101 and 1110. The maximum number of hosts will be the number of bits left in the host part, after the bits have been borrowed for the subnet, to the power of two, less two. The reason that the value is reduced by two is that the 0.0 address is reserved for the network, and the all 1's address is reserved for a broadcast address to that subnet.

Table 11.3 Subnet masks for a Class B address

Binary subnet address	*Dotted notation*	*Maximum number of subnets*	*Maximum number of hosts on each subnet*
11111111.11111111.11000000.00000000	255.255.192.0	2	16382
11111111.11111111.11100000.00000000	255.255.224.0	6	8190
11111111.11111111.11110000.00000000	255.255.240.0	14	4094
11111111.11111111.11111000.00000000	255.255.248.0	30	2046
11111111.11111111.11111100.00000000	255.255.252.0	62	1022
11111111.11111111.11111110.00000000	255.255.254.0	126	510
11111111.11111111.11111111.00000000	255.255.255.0	254	254
11111111.11111111.11111111.10000000	255.255.255.128	510	126
11111111.11111111.11111111.11000000	255.255.255.192	1022	62
11111111.11111111.11111111.11100000	255.255.255.224	2046	30
11111111.11111111.11111111.11110000	255.255.255.240	4094	14
11111111.11111111.11111111.11111000	255.255.255.248	8190	6
11111111.11111111.11111111.11111100	255.255.255.252	16382	2

Table 11.4 Subnet masks for a Class C address

Binary subnet address	*Dotted notation*	*Max. subnets*	*Max. hosts on each subnet*
11111111.11111111. 11111111.11000000	255.255.255.192	2	62
11111111.11111111. 11111111.11100000	255.255.255.224	6	30
11111111.11111111. 11111111.11110000	255.255.255.240	14	14
11111111.11111111. 11111111.11111000	255.255.255.248	30	6
11111111.11111111. 11111111.11111100	255.255.255.252	62	2

For example for a subnet with a subnet mask of 255.255.248.0, which has been given a Class B address of 144.32.Y.Z. Then the first usable subnet address will be (the brackets signify the binary address, and the bold text identifies the subnet address):

144.32.[**00001** 000].[0000 0000]
which is 144.32.8.0 (this starts from **00001** as 00000 is reserved for the whole network)

The addresses that can be allocated to the computers will then be:

First address: 144.32.8.1.
Second address: 144.32.8.2.
...
Last address: 144.32.15.254 (143.32.[00001 111].[1111 1110]).

The second subnet of the network will be:

144.32.[**00010** 000].[0000 0000]
which is 144.32.16.0 (this will be the network address of the subnet)

The addresses that can be allocated to the computers will then be:

First address: 144.32.16.1. (144.32.16.0 cannot be used as it is the address for all the subnets)
Second address: 144.32.16.2.
...
Last address: 144.32.23.254 (143.32.[00010 111].[1111 1110]).
The last subnet of the network will be:

144.32.[**11110** 000].[0000 0000]
which is 144.32.240.0 (this will be the network address of the subnet)

The addresses that can be allocated to the computers will then be:

First address: 144.32.240.1.
Second address: 144.32.240.2.
...
Last address: 144.32.247.254 (143.32.[11110 111].[1111 1110]).

11.7 Internet naming structure

The Internet naming structure uses labels separated by periods; an example is `dcs.napier.ac.uk`. It uses a hierarchical structure where organizations are grouped into primary domain names, such as `com` (for commercial organizations), `edu` (for educational organizations), `gov` (for government organizations), `mil` (for military organizations), `net` (Internet network support centers) or `org` (other organizations). The primary domain name may also define the country in which the host is located, such as `uk` (United Kingdom), `fr` (France), and so on. All hosts on the Internet must be registered to one of these primary domain names.

The labels after the primary field describe the subnets within the network. For example in the address eece.napier.ac.uk, the ac label relates to an academic institution within the uk, napier to the name of the institution and eece the subnet within that organization. An example structure is illustrated in Figure 11.11.

11.8 Domain name system

IP addresses are difficult to remember, thus Domain Name Services (DNS) are used to allow users to use symbolic names rather than IP addresses. DNS computers on the Internet determine the IP address of the named destination resource or application program. This dynamic mapping has the advantage that users and application programs can move around the Internet and are not fixed to an IP address. An analogy relates to the public telephone service. A telephone directory contains a list of subscribers and their associated telephone number. If someone looks for a telephone number, first the user name is looked up and their associated telephone number found. The telephone directory listing thus maps a user name (symbolic name) to an actual telephone number (the actual address). When a user enters a domain name (such as www.fred.co.uk) into the WWW browser, the local DNS server must try and resolve the domain name to an IP address, which can then be used to send the data to it. If it cannot resolve the IP address then the DNS server interrogates other servers to see if they know the required IP address, as illustrated in Figure 11.12. If it cannot be resolved then the WWW browser displays an error message.

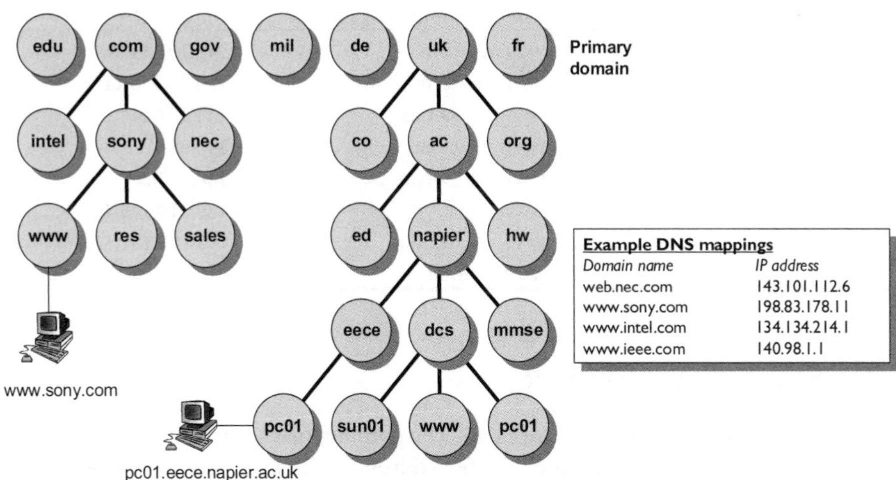

Figure 11.11 Example of domain naming

Table 11.5 lists some Internet domain assignments for WWW servers. Note that domain assignments are not fixed and can change their corresponding IP addresses, if required. The binding between the symbolic name and its address can thus change at any time.

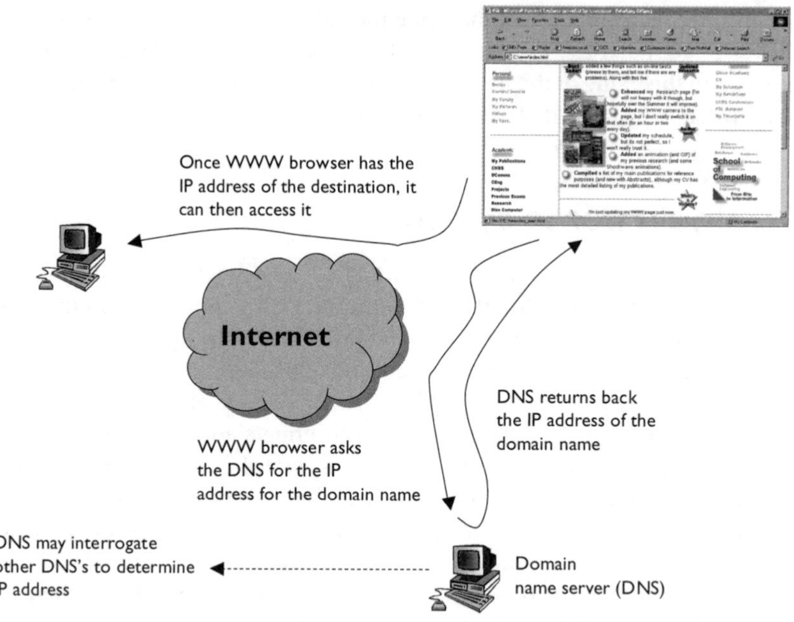

Figure 11.12 Domain name server

Table 11.5 Internet domain assignments for web servers

Web server	*Internet domain name*	*Internet IP address*
NEC	web.nec.com	143.101.112.6
Sony	www.sony.com	198.83.178.11
Intel	www.intel.com	134.134.214.1
IEEE	www.ieee.com	140.98.1.1
University of Bath	www.bath.ac.uk	136.38.32.1
University of Edinburgh	www.ed.ac.uk	129.218.128.43
IEE	www.iee.org.uk	193.130.181.10
University of Manchester	www.man.ac.uk	130.88.203.16

11.9 Example network

A university network is shown in Figure 11.13. The connection to the outside global Internet is via the Janet gateway node and its IP address is `146.176.1.3`. Three subnets, `146.176.160`, `146.176.129` and `146.176.151`, connect the gateway to departmental bridges. The Computer Studies router address is `146.176.160.1` and the Electrical Department router has an address `146.176.151.254`.

The Electrical Department router links, through other routers, to the subnets `146.176.144`, `146.176.145`, `146.176.147`, `146.176.150` and `146.176.151`. The main bridge into the department connects to two Ethernet networks of PCs (subnets `146.176.150` and `146.176.151`) and to another router (`Router 1`). `Router 1` connects to the subnet `146.176.144`. Subnet `146.176.144` connects to workstations and X-terminals. It also connects to the gateway `Moon` that links the Token Ring subnet `146.176.145` with the Ethernet subnet `146.176.144`. The gateway `Oberon`, on the

146.176.145 subnet, connects to an Ethernet link 146.176.146. This then connects to the gateway Dione that is also connected to the Token Ring subnet 146.176.147.

The topology of the Electrical Department network is shown in Figure 11.14. Each node on the network is assigned an IP address. The *hosts* file for the set up in Figure 11.14 is shown next. For example the IP address of Mimas is 146.176.145.21 and for miranda it is 146.176.144.14. Notice that the gateway nodes, Oberon, Moon and Dione, all have two IP addresses.

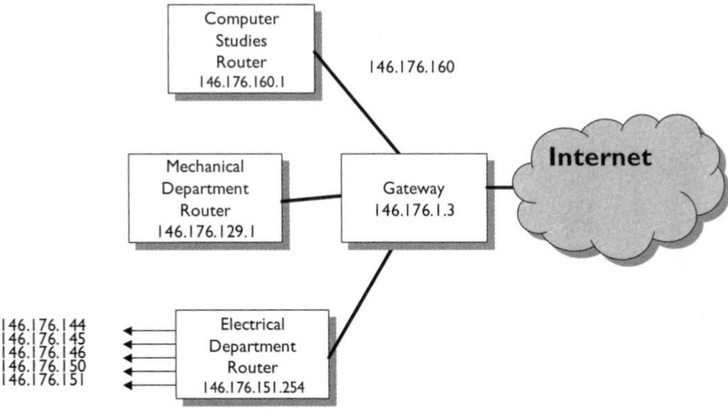

Figure 11.13 A university network

Contents of host file

```
146.176.1.3          janet
146.176.144.10       hp
146.176.145.21       mimas
146.176.144.11       mwave
146.176.144.13       vax
146.176.144.14       miranda
146.176.144.20       triton
146.176.146.23       oberon
146.176.145.23       oberon
146.176.145.24       moon
146.176.144.24       moon
146.176.147.25       uranus
146.176.146.30       dione
146.176.147.30       dione
146.176.147.31       saturn
146.176.147.32       mercury
146.176.147.33       earth
146.176.147.34       deimos
146.176.147.35       ariel
146.176.147.36       neptune
146.176.147.42       pluto
 :: ::
146.176.144.58       spica
146.176.151.254      cubridge
146.176.151.99       bridge_1
146.176.151.98       pc2
146.176.151.97       pc3
           :::::
146.176.151.70       pc30
146.176.151.99       ees99
146.176.150.61       eepc01
255.255.255.0        defaultmask
```

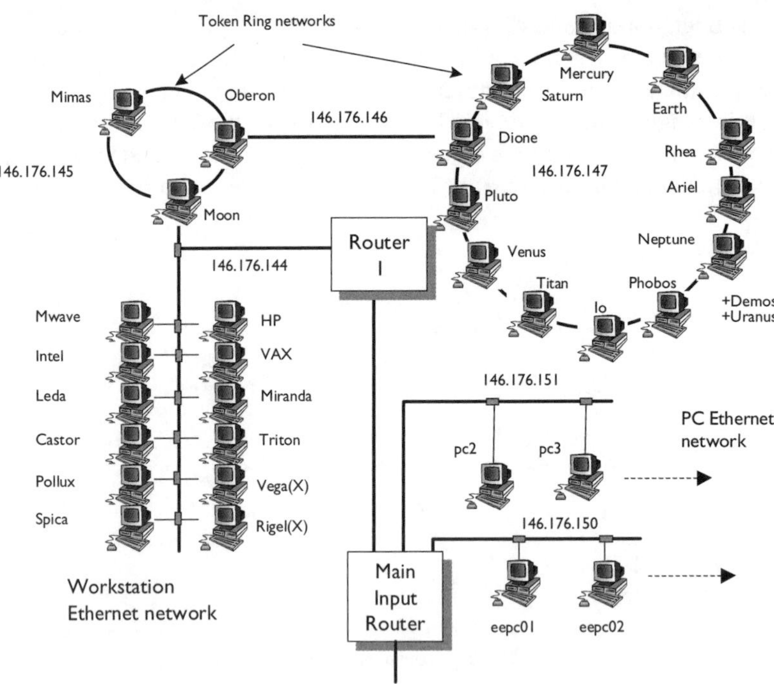

Figure 11.14 Network topology for the Department network

11.10 IP addresses for routers

Routers require an IP address for each of their ports, but they cannot use the zero host address as this is used to identify the whole network. For example, if there were five nodes on the 177.132.1 network (NETA), and six nodes on the 177.131.2 network (NETB), which are interconnected by a router (AB). Then the IP address could be assigned as:

Node NETA_1 177.131.1.2 Node NETA_2 177.131.1.3
Node NETA_3 177.131.1.4 Node NETA_4 177.131.1.5
Node NETA_5 177.131.1.6

Node NETB_1 177.131.2.2 Node NETB_2 177.131.2.3
Node NETB_3 177.131.2.4 Node NETB_4 177.131.2.5
Node NETB_5 177.131.2.6 Node NETA_6 177.131.2.7

Router AB_E0177.131.1.1 Router AB_E1 177.131.2.1

The router, in this case, has two ports. These have been defined with the IP address 177.131.1.1 (which connects to the 177.131.1 network), and 177.131.2.1 (which connects to the 177.131.2 network).

11.11 IP multicasting

Many applications of modern communications require the transmission of IP datagrams to multiple hosts. Typical applications are video conferencing, remote teaching, and so on. This is supported by IP multicasting, where a host group is identified by a single IP address. The main parameters of IP multicasting are:

- The group membership is dynamic.
- Hosts may join and leave the group at any time.
- There is also no limit to the location or number of members in a host group.
- A host may be a member of more than one group at a time.
- A host group may be permanent or transient. Permanent groups are well known and are administratively assigned a permanent IP address. The group is then dynamically associated with this IP address. IP multicast addresses that are not reserved to permanent groups are available for dynamic assignment to transient groups.
- Multicast routers forward IP multicast datagrams into the Internet.

ICMP messages

- Destination unreachable.
- Time-to-live exceeded.
- Parameter problem.
- Source quench.
- Redirect.
- Echo.
- Echo reply.
- Timestamp.
- Timestamp reply.
- Information request.
- Information reply.
- Address request.
- Address reply.

ICMP is used to send error and control messages.

11.11.1 Group addresses

A special group of addresses are assigned to multicasting. These are known as Class D addresses, and they begin with 1110 as their starting 4 bits (Class E addresses with the upper bits of 1111 are reserved for future uses). The Class D addresses thus range from:

224.0.0.0
(11100000 00000000 00000000 00000000)
239.255.255.255
(11101111 11111111 11111111 11111111)

The address 224.0.0.0 is reserved. 224.0.0.1 is also assigned to the permanent group of all IP hosts (including gateways), and is used to address all multicast hosts on the directly connected network.

DEAR NET-ED
Question: *If IP has been such a success, why do we need a new address scheme?*

IP has been a victim of its own success. No one could have imagined how popular it would be. As it has a 32-bit address it can only support up to 4 billion addresses. Unfortunately not all these addresses can be used, as network addresses are allocated to organizations for their maximum requirement. Also, if an organization uses subnets, then it is unlikely that every subnet has its maximum capacity of hosts.

There are possibly enough IP addresses for all the computers in the world, but the next big wave is going to come from granting IP addresses to virtually every electronic device, such as mobile phones, faxes, printers, traffic lights, telephones, and so on. The stage after this is to grant every object in the world an IP address. This could include cars, trains, people, and even our pets.

11.12 IPv6

The IP header (IP Ver4) is added to higher-level data (as defined in RFC791). This header contains a 32-bit IP address of the destination node.

Unfortunately, the standard 32-bit IP address is not large enough to support the growth in nodes connecting to the Internet. Thus a new standard, IP Version 6 (IP Ver6, aka, IP, The Next Generation, or IPng), has been developed to support a 128-bit address, as well as additional enhancements, such as authentication and data encryption.
The main techniques being investigated are:

- **TUBA** (TCP and UDP with bigger addresses).
- **CATNIP** (common architecture for the Internet). The main idea was to define a common packet format which was compatible with IP, CLNP (Connectionless Network Protocol) and IPX. CLNP was proposed by the OSI as a new protocol to replace IP, but it has never really been adopted (mainly because it was too inefficient).
- **SIPP** (Simple Internet protocol plus). This scheme increases the number of address bits from 32 to 64, and gets rid of unused fields in the IP header.

It is likely that none of these will provide the complete standard and the resulting standard will be a mixture of the three. The RFC1883 specification outlines the main changes as:

- **Expanded addressing capabilities.** The size of the IP address will be increased to 128 bits, rather than 32 bits. This will allow for more levels of addressing hierarchy, an increased number of addressable nodes and a simpler auto-configuration of addresses. With multicast routing, the scalability is improved by adding a scope field to the multicast addresses. As well as this, an anycast address has been added so that packets can be sent to any one of a group of nodes.
- **Improved IP header format.** This tidies the IPv4 header fields by dropping the least used options, or making them optional.
- **Improved support for extensions and options.** These allow for different encodings of the IP header options, and thus allow for variable lengths and increased flexibility for new options.
- **Flow labelling capability.** A new ca-

DEAR NET-ED

Question: *Can devices have more than one IP address?*

Yes. Many devices have more than one IP address. In fact each port that connects to a network must have an IP address. A good example of this is with routers, as they connect to two or more networks. Each of the ports of the router must have an IP address which relates to the network to which it connects to. For example if a router connects to three networks of:

146.176.151.0
146.176.152.0
146.176.140.0

then one IP address from each of the networks must be assigned to the router. Thus it could be assigned the following addresses for its ports:

146.176.151.1
146.176.152.1
146.176.140.1

Question: *Can these addresses be used again for one of the hosts on the connected networks?*

No way. No two ports on the Internet can have the same address.

Question: *Okay, sorry I asked. So what addresses cannot be used for the ports, or the hosts?*

All zeros in the host field, as this identifies the network, and all ones in the host field as this identifies the broadcast address. Thus in the example above, 146.176.151.0 and 146.176.151.255 could not be used (these addresses use a Class B address with a subnet in the third field).

pability is added to enable the labelling of packet belonging to particular traffic *flows* for which the sender requests special handling, such as non-default quality of service or *real-time* service.

- **Authentication and privacy capabilities**. Extensions to support authentication, data integrity, and (optional) data confidentiality are specified for IPv6.

11.12.1 Autoconfiguration and multiple IP addresses

IPv4 requires a significant amount of human intervention to set up the address of each of the nodes. IPv6 improves this by supplying autoconfiguration renumbering facilities, which allows hosts to renumber without significant human intervention.

IPv4 has a stateful address structure, which either requires the user to manually set up the IP address of the computer or to use DHCP servers to provide IP addresses for a given MAC address. If a node moves from one subnet to another, the user must reconfigure the IP address, or request a new IP address from the DHCP. IPv6 supports a stateless autoconfiguration, where a host constructs its own IPv6. This occurs by adding its MAC address to a subnet prefix. The host automatically learns which subnet it is on by communicating from the router which is connected to the network that the host is connected to.

IPv6 supports multiple IP addresses for each host. These addresses can be either *valid*, *deprecated* or *invalid*. A valid address would be used for new and existing communications. A deprecated address could be used only for the existing communications (as they perhaps migrated to the new address). An invalid address would not be used for any communications. When renumbering, a host would deprecate the existing IP address, and set the new IP address as valid. All new communications would use the new IP address, but connections to the previous address would still operate. This allows a node to gradually migrate from one IP address to another.

DEAR NET-ED

Question: *Sometimes when I connect to the Internet everything seems fine, but I cannot access WWW sites, and it seems to load pages from a WWW cache?*

This is a common problem, and it is likely that you are connected to the Internet, but the Domain Name Server is not reachable. This means that you cannot resolve domain names into IP addresses. The way to check this is to use the IP address in the URL. For example:

http://www.mypage.com/index.html

could be accessed with:

http://199.199.140.10/index.html

If you can get access with this, you should investigate your DNS. Remember you can normally specify several DNSs, thus find out the address of a remote DNS, just in case your local one goes off-line.

11.12.2 IPv6 header format

Figure 11.15 shows the basic format of the IPv6 header. The main fields are:

- Version number (4 bits) – contains the version number, such as 6 for IP Ver6. It is used to differentiate between IPv4 and IPv6.
- Priority (4 bits) – indicates the priority of the datagram, and gives 16 levels of priority (0 to 15). The first eight values (0 to 7) are used where the source is providing congestion control (which is traffic that backs-off when congestion occurs), these are:
    - 0 defines no priority.

- 1 defines background traffic (such as netnews).
- 2 defines unattended transfer (such as e-mail), 3 (reserved).
- 4 defines attended bulk transfer (FTP, NFS), 5 (reserved).
- 6 defines interactive traffic (such as telnet, X-windows).
- 7 defines control traffic (such as routing protocols, SNMP).

The other values are used for traffic that will not backoff in response to congestion (such as real-time traffic). The lowest priority for this is 8 (traffic which is the most willing to be discarded) and the highest is 15 (traffic which is the least willing to be discarded).

- Flow label (24 bits) – still experimental, but will be used to identify different data flow characteristics. It is assigned by the source and can be used to label data packets which require special handling by IPv6 routers, such as defined QoS (Quality of Service) or real-time services.
- Payload length (16 bits) – defines the total size of the IP datagram (and includes the IP header attached data).
- Next header – this field indicates which header follows the IP header (it uses the same IPv4). For example: 0 defines IP information; 1 defines ICMP information; 6 defines TCP information and 80 defines ISO-IP.
- Hop limit – defines the maximum number of hops that the datagram takes as it traverses the network. Each router decrements the hop limit by 1; when it reaches 0 it is deleted. This has been renamed from IPv4, where it was called time-to-live, as it better describes the parameter.
- IP addresses (128 bits) – defines IP address. There will be three main groups of IP addresses: unicast, multicast and anycast. A unicast address identifies a particular host, a multicast address enables the hosts within a particular group to receive the same packet, and the anycast address will be addressed to a number of interfaces on a single multicast address.

There are various assigned values for the IP version label. These are:

Value	*Keyword*	*Description*
0		Reserved
4	IP	Internet Protocol (RFC791)
5	ST	ST Datagram Mode (RFC1190)
6	SIP	Simple Internet Protocol
7	TP/IX	TP/IX: The Next Internet
8	PIP	The P Internet Protocol
9	TUBA	TUBA
10–14		Unassigned
15		Reserved

IPv6 has a simple header, which can be extended if required. These are:

- Routing header.
- Authentication header.
- Destinations options header.
- Fragment header.
- Encrypted security payload.

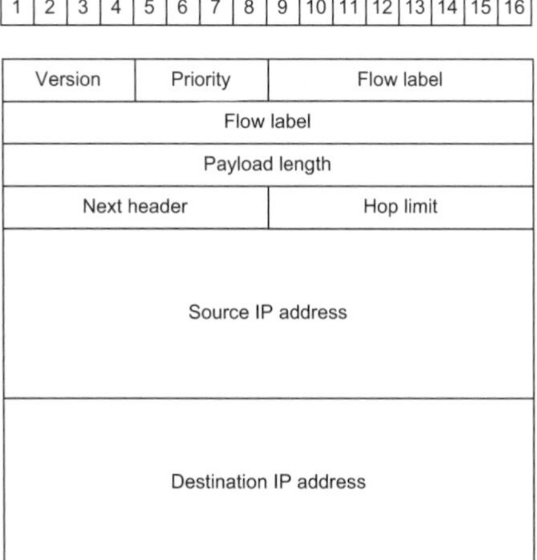

Figure 11.15 IP Ver6 header format

11.13 Allocating IP addresses

IP addresses can either be allocated statically or dynamically. A static address is permanently assigned to a node, whereas a dynamically allocated address is assigned to a host when it requires connecting to the Internet. Dynamically assigned addresses have the following advantages over static addresses:

- **Limiting access to the Internet.** IP addresses can be mapped to MAC addresses. A node which requires an IP address will ask the IP granting server for an IP address. The server then checks the host's MAC address to determine if it is allowed to access the Internet. If it is not, the server does not return an IP address. The system administrator can thus set up a table which only includes the hosts which are required to connect to the Internet.
- **Authenticating nodes.** A typical hacking method is to steal an IP address and use it for the time of a connection. This can be overcome by making all of the nodes on the network ask the IP granting server for their IP address. It is thus not possible to steal an address, as the IP granting server will check the MAC address of the host.
- **Allocating from a pool of IP addresses.** An organization may be granted a limited range of IP addresses which is not enough to allocate to all the nodes in the organization. The IP granting server can thus be set up to allocate IP addresses to nodes as they require them. When all the IP addresses have been allocated, no more IP addresses can be given out. When a node is finished with its IP address, the IP address that was granted to it can be put back in the pool when it is finished with it.
- **Centralized configuration of IP addresses.** The system manager can easily setup IP addresses to nodes from the central IP granting server.
- **Barring computers from connecting to a network.** Some networks are set up so that they must get a valid IP address before they can connect to the network (typically in UNIX-type networks). The IP granting server will check the MAC address of the requester, if it is not allowed the server will not grant it an IP address.

The two main protocols which are used to dynamically allocate IP addresses are DHCP (Dynamic Host Configuration Program) and bootp (Bootstrap Protocol). DHCP is typically used by Microsoft Windows to get IP addresses, while bootp is sometimes used in UNIX environments. The main disadvantage of dynamically assigned IP addresses is that the network is centralized on the single DHCP server. If this were to crash, no IP addresses can be assigned.

11.14 Domain name server and DHCP

Each institution on the Internet has a host that runs a process called the domain name server (DNS). The DNS maintains a database called the directory information base (DIB) which contains directory information for that institution. When a new host is added, the system manager adds its name and its IP address. It can then access the Internet.

Dynamic Host Configuration Protocol (DHCP) allows for the transmission of configuration information over a TCP/IP network. Microsoft implemented DHCP on its Microsoft Windows operating system and many other vendors are incorporating it into their systems. It is based on the Bootstrap Protocol (bootp) and adds additional services, such as:

- Automatic allocation of reusable IP network addresses.
- Additional TCP/IP configuration options.

It has two components:

DEAR NET-ED

Question: *Apart from increasing the number of IP addresses, why change the format, the Internet works, doesn't it, so why change it?*

Ah. Your perception of the Internet is based on what's available now. Few technologies have expanded so fast, and without virtually any inputs from the governments of the world. Look at the world-wide telephone system infrastructure, if it was based on the system that we had 30 years ago there's no way we could communicate as efficiently as we do. The Internet must do the same, if it is to keep pace with the increase in users, devices and the amount of information that can be transferred. At present, you possibly imagine that the Internet is an infrastructure of computers that have big boxes and sit on your desk, and are congregated around servers, and ISPs. In 10 or 20 years this perception will change, and computers will almost become invisible, as will the Internet. To cope with this change we need a different infrastructure. To do this we need to identify its weaknesses:

- The Internet and its addressing structure was never really designed to be a global infrastructure and is constraining the access to resources and information.
- Information and databases tend to be static, and fixed to location.
- Difficult to group individual objects into larger objects.
- Difficult to add resources to the Internet (requires an ISP and a valid IP address).
- Search engines are not very good at gathering relevant information. On the WWW, typically users get pages of irrelevant information, which just happens to have the keyword which they are searching for.
- Resources are gathered around local servers.
- Resources are tied to locations with an IP address.
- IP addresses are not logically organized. The IP address given does not give any information about the geographical location of the destination. This then requires complex routing protocols in which routers pass on information about how to get to remote networks.

- A protocol for delivering host-specific configuration parameters from a DHCP server to a host.
- A mechanism for allocation of network addresses to hosts.

DHCP uses a client-server architecture, where the designated DHCP server hosts (servers) allocate network addresses and deliver configuration parameters to dynamically configured hosts (clients).

The three techniques that DHCP uses to assign IP addresses are:

- **Automatic allocation**. DHCP assigns a permanent IP address to a client.
- **Dynamic allocation**. DHCP assigns an IP address to a client for a limited period of time or when the client releases the address. It allows for automatic reuse of IP addresses that are no longer used by clients. It is typically used when there is a limited pool of IP addresses (which is less than the number of hosts) so that a host can only connect when it can get one of the IP addresses from the pool.
- **Manual allocation**. DHCP is used to convey an IP address which has been assigned by the network administrator. This allows DHCP to be used to eliminate assigning an IP address to a host through its operating system.

Networks can use several of these techniques.

DHCP messages are based on bootp messages, which allows DHCP to listen to a bootp relay agent and to allow integration of bootp clients and DHCP servers. A bootp relay agent is an Internet host or router that passes DHCP messages between DHCP clients and DHCP servers. DHCP uses the same relay agent behaviour as the bootp protocol specification. bootp relay agents are useful because they eliminate the need for having a DHCP server on each physical network segment.

Some of the objectives of DHCP are:

- DHCP should be a mechanism rather than a policy. DHCP must allow local system administrators control over configuration parameters where desired.
- No requirements for manual configuration of clients.
- DHCP does not require a server on each subnet and should communicate with routers and bootp relay agents and clients.
- Ensure that the same IP address cannot be used by more than one DHCP client at a time.
- Restore DHCP client configuration when the client is rebooted.
- Provide automatic configuration for new clients.
- Support fixed or permanent allocation of configuration parameters.

DEAR NET-ED

Question: *When I connect to an ISP, what is my IP address, and my domain name? Can I have the same IP address each time, and the same domain name?*

When you connect to your ISP you will be granted an IP address from a pool of assigned IP addresses. There is no guarantee that this will be the same each time you connect. Your domain name will also change, as it is bound to the IP address. It is possible to be allocated a static IP address, but you would have to pay some money to your ISP for the privilege. The advantage of this is that remote computers could connect to you when you connected via your ISP.

You can determine your current IP address if you use the command WINIPCFG (or IPCONFIG). This is particularly useful if you are playing games over the Internet.

11.15 WINS

The Windows Internet Naming Service (WINS) is an excellent companion to DHCP. WINS provides a name registration and resolution on TCP/IP. It extends the function of DNS which will only map static IP addresses to TCP/IP host names. WINS is designed to resolve NetBIOS names on TCP/IP to dynamic network addresses assigned by DHCP. As it resolves NetBIOS names it is obviously aimed at Microsoft Windows-based (and DOS) networks.

For more material on WINS please visit our website at:
`http://www.palgrave.com/studyskills/masterseries/buchanan`

11.16 ICMP

Messages, such as control data, information data and error recovery data, are carried between Internet hosts using the Internet Control Message Protocol (ICMP). These messages are sent with a standard IP header. Typical messages are:

- Destination unreachable (message type 3) – which is sent by a host on the network to say that a host is unreachable. The message can also include the reason the host cannot be reached.
- Echo request/echo reply (message type 8 or 0) – which is used to check the connectivity between two hosts. The `ping` command uses this message, where it sends an ICMP 'echo request' message to the target host and waits for the destination host to reply with an 'echo reply' message.
- Redirection (message type 5) – which is sent by a router to a host that is requesting its routing services. This helps to find the shortest path to a desired host.
- Source quelch (message type 4) – which is used when a host cannot receive anymore IP packets at the present (or reduce the flow).

An ICMP message is sent within an IP header, with the Version field, Source and

DEAR NET-ED

Question: *If I move my computer from one network to another, does the IP and MAC address stay the same, and what do I need to change?*

The MAC address will not change as the network card stays with the computer. If the computer is moved to a different subnet or onto a completely different network, the IP address must change, or the data will be routed back to the wrong network. Data would leave the relocated computer, and would arrive at the destination, but any data coming back would be routed to the previously attached network (and thus get lost). Another thing that is likely to change is the gateway. Nodes cannot communicate with the hosts outside their network if they do not know the IP address of the gateway (normally a router), thus if the network changes then the gateway is likely to be different.

The user may also have to set a new Domain Name Server (although a host can have several DNS entries). The first one listed in the DNS entries should be the one that is the most reliable and, possibly, the fastest.

Other changes may be to change the subnet mask (on a Class B network, with a subnet this is typically 255.255.255.0).

Question: *So why do you only have to specify the IP address of the gateway?*

Because the host uses an ARP request to determine the MAC address of the gateway.

Destination IP Addresses, and so on. The Type of Service field is set to a 0 and the Protocol field is set to a 1 (which identifies ICMP). After the IP header, follows the ICMP message, which starts with three fields, as shown in Figure 11.17. The message type has eight bits and identifies the type of message; as Table 11.6. The code fields are also eight bits long and a checksum field is 16 bits long. The checksum is the 1's complement of the 1's complement sum of all 16-bit words in the header (the checksum field is assumed to be zero in the addition).

The information after this field depends on the type of message, such as:

- For echo request and reply, the message header is followed by an 8-bit identifier, then an 8-bit sequence number followed by the original IP header.
- For destination unreachable, source quelch and time, the message header is followed by 32 bits which are unused and then the original IP header.
- For timestamp request, the message header is followed by a 16-bit identifier, then by a 16-bit sequence number, followed by a 32-bit originating timestamp.

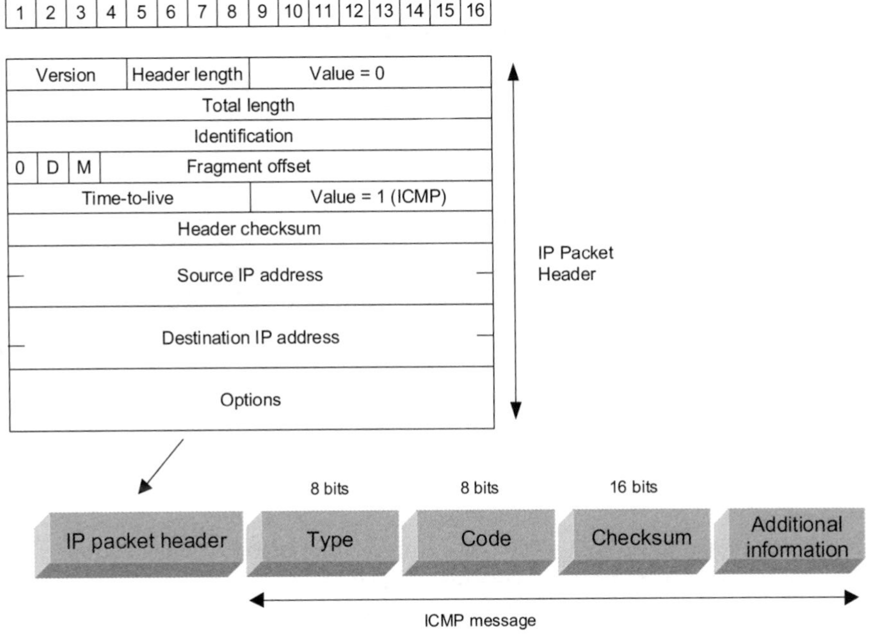

Figure 11.16 ICMP message format

Where:

- Pointer (8-bit). Identifies the byte location of the parameter error in the original IP header. For example, a value of 9 would identify the Protocol field, and 12 would identify the Source IP address field.
- Identifier (16-bit). Helps the matching of requests and replies (possibly set to zero). It can be used to identify a unique connection.
- Sequence Number (16-bit). Helps in matching request and replies (possibly set to zero).
- Timestamps (32-bit) – This is the time in milliseconds since midnight UT (Universal

Time). If this is not possible then it is anytime, as long as the high-order bit of the timestamp is set to a 1 to indicate that it is non-standard time.

- Gateway address (32-bit). The address of the gateway to which network traffic specified in the original datagram should be sent to.
- Internet Header + 64 bits of Data Datagram. This is the original IP header and the first 64 byte of the data part. It is used by the host to match the match to the required high-level application (such as TCP port values).

For more material on ICMP please visit our website at

`http://www.palgrave.com/studyskills/masterseries/buchanan`

11.17 Additional

Table 11.6 outlines the values that are used in the protocol field of the IP header.

Table 11.6 Assigned Internet protocol numbers

Value	*Protocol*	*Value*	*Protocol*
0	Reserved	18	Multiplexing
1	ICMP	19	DCN
2	IGMP (Internet group management)	20	TAC monitoring
3	Gateway-to-gateway	21–62	
4	CMCC gateway monitoring message	63	Any local network
5	ST	64	SATNET and backroom EXPAK
6	TCP	65	MIT subnet support
8	EGP (exterior gateway protocol)	69	SATNET monitoring

11.18 Exercises

11.18.1 Which OSI layer does the IP layer correspond to:
(a) Data link (b) Network (c) Transport (d) Session

11.18.2 When transmitting data, what is the correct order of data encapsulation:
(a) Bits→Frames→Packets→Segments→Data
(b) Frames→Bits→Packets→Data→Segments
(c) Bits→Frames→Segments→Packets→Data
(d) Bits→Frames→Packets→Data→Segments

11.18.3 What is another name for a network-level data packet:
(a) Data frame (b) Data unit (c) Datagram (d) Data segment

11.18.4 Which OSI layer does the TCP layer correspond to:
(a) Data link (b) Network (c) Transport (d) Session

Additional tutorial questions and material are available at:

`http://www.palgrave.com/studyskills/masterseries/buchanan`

12 TCP/UDP

12.1 Introduction

> **RFCs**
>
> RFC (Request For Comment) documents are published by the IAB (Internet Advisor Board) and are a quick way to quickly define new standards, in which anyone can comment on. They are continually updated, but various documents define the main standards used on the Internet, these are:
>
> | | |
> |---|---|
> | RFC768 | UDP |
> | RFC791 | IP |
> | RFC792 | ICMP |
> | RFC793 | TCP |
> | RFC821 | SMTP |
> | RFC822 | Format of email messages |
> | RFC854 | Telnet |
> | RFC959 | FTP |
> | RFC1034 | Domain names |
> | RFC1058 | RIP |
> | RFC1157 | SNMP |
> | RFC1521 | MIME Pt. 1 |
> | RFC1522 | MIME Pt. 2 |
> | RFC1939 | POP Version 3 |

The transport layer is important as it segments the data from the upper layers, and passes these onto the network layer, which adds the network address to the segments (these are then called packets). The network layer allows for delivery of these segments at the receiver. Once delivered the transport layer then takes over and reassembles the data segments back into a form that can be delivered to the layer above. These services are often known as end-to-end services, as the transport layer provides a logical connection between two end points on a network.

The network layer cannot be considered reliable, as the transmitter has no idea that the data packets have been received correctly. It is thus up to the transport layer to provide this, using:

- **Synchronization and acknowledgement.** Initially, when the transmitter makes contact with the receiver it makes a unique connection. The transmitter thus knows that the receiver is on-line, and willing to receive data.
- **Acknowledgements and retransmissions.** This allows the receiver to send back acknowledgements which tell the transmitter that the data segments have been received correctly. If no acknowledgements have been received, the transmitter can either resend the data, or can assume that the receiver has crashed and that the connection is to be terminated.
- **Flow control.** This allows the receiver to tell the transmitter that it cannot receive any more data at present. This typically happens when the receiver has filled-up its receiving buffer.
- **Windowing.** This is where the transmitter and the receiver agree on a window size when the connection is initially made. The window then defines the number of data segments that can be sent before the transmitter must wait for an acknowledgement from the receiver.
- **Multiple connections onto a single data stream.** The transport layer takes data from one or more applications; it then marks them with a unique connection number and segment number. At the receiver these can be demultiplexed to the correct application program.
- **Reordering of data segments.** All the data segments that are transmitted are marked with a sequence number. Thus if any are delivered in the incorrect order, or if any of them are missing, the receiver can easily reorder them or discard segments if one or more are missing.

The most important transport protocol is TCP, which is typically uses IP as an addressing scheme. TCP and IP (TCP/IP) are the standard protocols that are used on the Internet and also on UNIX networks (where TCP/IP grew up, but have since dwarfed their parent). TCP works well because it is simple, but reliable, and it is an open system where no single vendor has control over its specification and its development.

An important concept of TCP/IP communications is the usage of ports and sockets. A port identifies a process type (such as FTP, TELNET, and so on) and the socket identifies a unique connection number. In this way, TCP/IP can support multiple simultaneous connections of applications over a network, as illustrated in Figure 12.1.

The IP header is added to higher-level data, and contains the 32-bit IP address of the destination node. Unfortunately, the standard 32-bit IP address is not large enough to support the growth in nodes connecting to the Internet. Thus a new standard, IP Version 6, has been developed to support 128-bit addresses, as well as additional enhancements.

TCP/IP protocol stack

- Protocols to support file transfer, e-mail, remote login, and other applications.
- Reliable and unreliable transports (TCP/UDP).
- Connectionless datagram delivered at the network layer.
- Connection-oriented with TCP, connection-less with UDP.

The transport layer really provides a foundation for the application program to create a data stream were from one application program to another, just as if they two programs running on the same computer, thus the data transfer operation should be transparent to the application program. It is thus important that the network protocol and the network type are invisible to the layers about the transport layer, as illustrated in Figure 12.2. This is important as application programmers can write programs which will run on any type of network protocol (such as SPX/IPX or TCP/IP) or any network type (such as, over ISDN, ATM or Ethernet). The protocol stack is the software that is used to provide the transport and network layers.

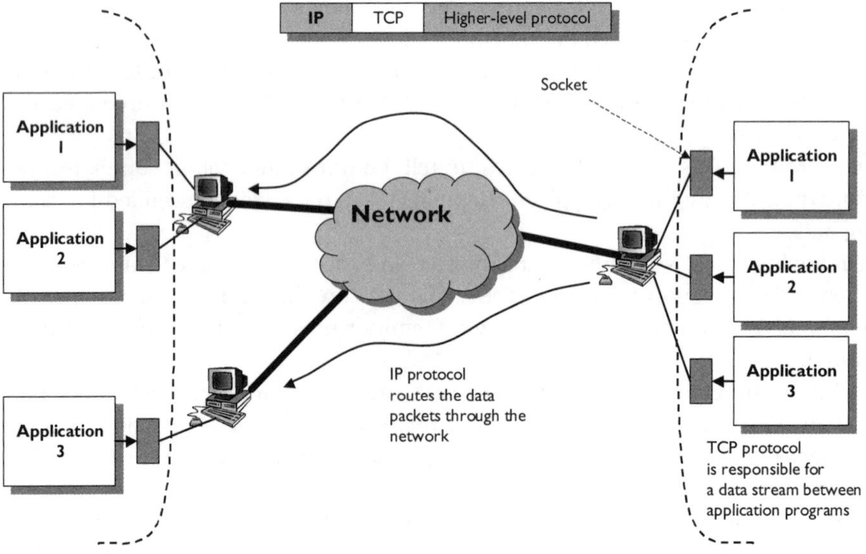

Figure 12.1 Roles of TCP and IP

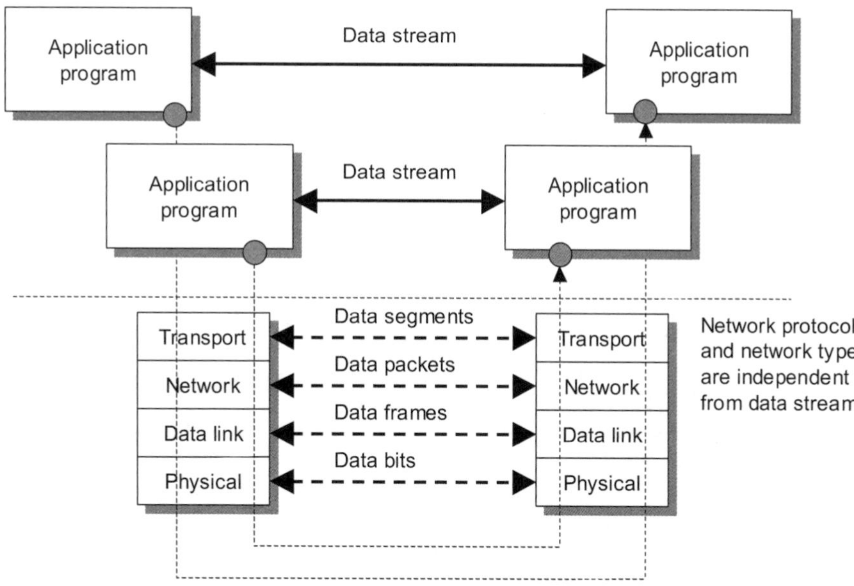

Figure 12.2 Data streams

12.2 Functions of the transport layer

The great trick of the transport level is to allow multiple applications to communicate over a network, at the same time. This is achieved by identifying each connection with a unique value (a socket number) and adding sequence numbers on each of the segments. Segments can also be sent to many different destinations (using the network layer to identify the destination).

> **Spoof networking exam question**
>
> Show how it is possible to avoid a network collision in Ethernet with users waving flags when they are about to send data. How is priority of transmission built into this system, and how is it difficult for a user to predict when they are about to receive data?
>
> Also, how might different coloured flags be used? Finally, if different coloured t-shirts are used instead, what effect does this have on the latency of the data packet, that coloured flags would not?

12.2.1 Establishing connections

An important concept in the transport layer is to make a reliable connection with a destination node. This requires that the transport layer on one host makes contact with the transport layer on the destination host, and create a connection-oriented session with the peer system. Before data can be transmitted the sender and the receiver negotiate the connection and agree the parameters for the data to be sent, such as how many data segments that can be sent before an acknowledgement, the unique connection number, and so on. This process is called synchronization. Once the connection has been agreed, the data can pass between the transmitter and receiver on a data stream.

Figure 12.3 shows an example of the negotiation between a transmitter and a receiver. Initially the transmitter requests synchronization, after which the transmitter and the receiver negotiate the connection parameters. If acceptable the receiver sends a synchronization signal, after which the transmitter acknowledges this with an acknowledgement. The connection is now made, and a data stream can flow between the two systems.

> **DARPA**
>
> The Defense Advanced Research Projects Agency, which is a US government agency that has funded research relating to the Internet. Now known as ARPA.
>
> **TCP/IP**
>
> Two of the protocols developed by the US DoD in the 1970s to support the interconnection of networks.

12.2.2 Flow control

Data that is received is typically buffered in memory, as the processor cannot deal with it immediately. If there is too much data arriving to be processed, the data buffer can often overflow, and all newly arriving data will be discarded (as there is no place to store it). Another problem can occur when several hosts are transmitting to a single host. There is thus a need for a mechanism which can tell hosts to stop sending data segments, and to wait until the data has been properly processed.

The transport layer copes with these problems by issuing a Not Ready indicator, which tells a transmitter not to send any more data, until the host sends a Ready indicator. After this the transmitter can send data. This process is illustrated in Figure 12.4.

12.2.3 Acknowledgement and windowing

The transport layer uses a technique called positive acknowledgement which only acknowledges correctly received data segments. The transmitter thus assumes that, after a certain period of time, if no acknowledgement has been received then the data has not been received correctly, and will thus retransmit the unacknowledged data segments. These will be sent with the same segment numbers as the original data segments so that the receiver does not end up with identical data segments. Thus two or more received data segments with the same sequence number will be deleted so that only a single copy is left.

Windowing provides for a method where the transmitter is forced to wait for an acknowledgement for the data segments that it has sent. The number of data segments that it is allowed to be sent before an acknowledgement, is set up when the connection is made. If the transmitter does not receive an acknowledgement within a given time limit, it will assume that the data did not arrive at the destination, and will then retransmit the data segments which were sent after the last acknowledged data segment.

> **Spoof networking exam question**
>
> 1. Explain the technology that allows gigabit per second speeds down a standard piece of doorbell cable. How is it possible to transmit data, and also front door bell signals, along the same cable? Also carefully explain how the doorbell signals could be decoded by any host on the Internet, and then how these could be used to open the door (Note: do not use the example of a person actually getting up to go to the door).
> 2. Describe the purpose of each of the following smilies:
>
>   (9--+)
>   (#@-0)

If the window were set to unity, every data segment would have to be acknowledged. This, of course, would be inefficient and slow, as the transmitter would have to wait for every segment to be acknowledged. Thus the window allows for a number of segments to be transmitted before the requiring acknowledgements.

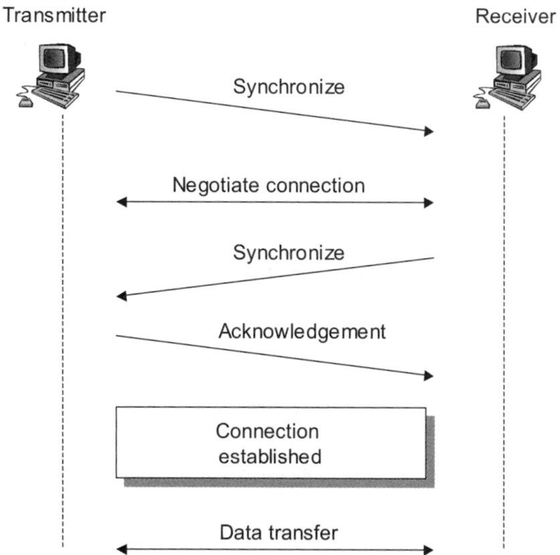

Figure 12.3 Synchronization and acknowledgement

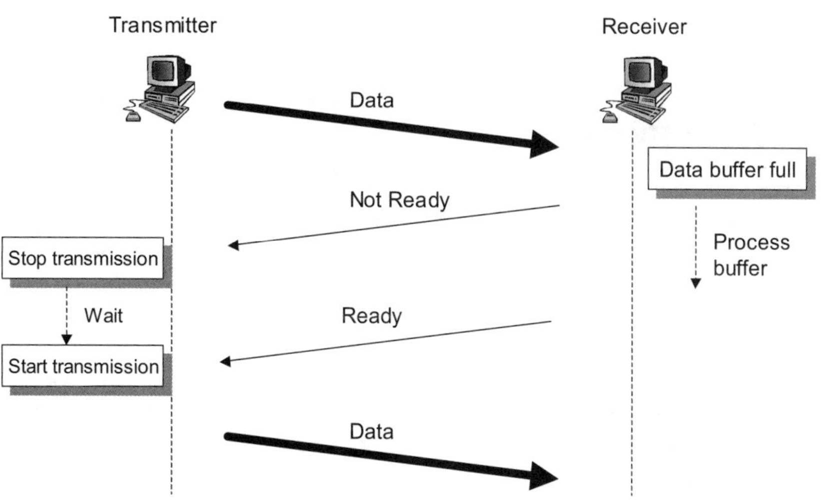

Figure 12.4 Flow control

Figure 12.5 shows the transmission of data segments with a window size of three. Initially the transmitter sends data segments with a send sequence number (S) of 1–3. It then waits for the receiver to send an acknowledgement, which it does by informing the transmitter that it expects to receive a data segment with a value of 4, next (R=4). If no acknowledgement was received from the receiver, the transmitter would resend the data segments 1 to 3. Note that the sequence numbers can either relate to the packet number (such as 1, 2, 3, …) or to the byte number of the data being transmitted (this is the case in TCP communications). The reason that there is a different send (S) and receive (R) number is that both nodes may be transmitting and receiving data, thus they must both keep track of the data segments that are being sent and received.

Often the start sequence number does not start at zero or one, as previous connections could be confused with new connections, thus a time-based initial value is used to define the start sequence number. Both the transmitter and the receiver agree on the start sequence number when the connection is negotiated.

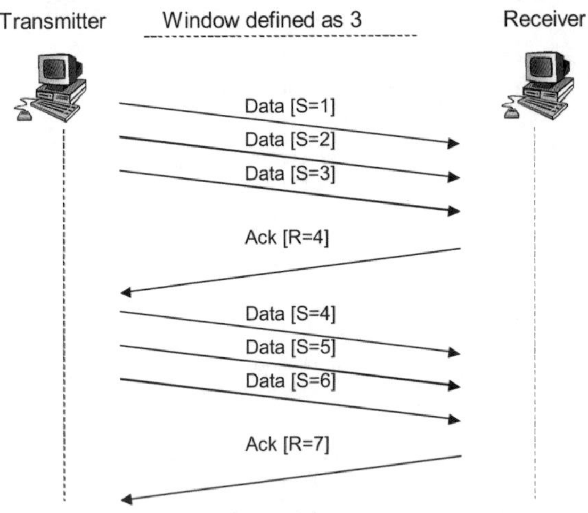

Figure 12.5 Windowing with a window of 3

12.3 TCP/IP model

No networking technology fits into the OSI model, as many of the existing networking standards were developed before the model was developed. Also the OSI model was meant to be an abstract method of viewing a network from its physical connection, through its hardware/software interface, right up to the application program. The key element that allows computers over the world to intercommunicate, no matter their operating system, their hardware, their network connection, or their application program is the networking protocol. At one time networking protocols were tied to specific systems, such as DECNET (for DEC-based network), DLC (for IBM-based networks), NetBEUI (for Microsoft networks) and SPX/IPX (for Novell NetWare networks). While most of these networking protocols are still used for local area networks, the most common protocol for worldwide communications is TCP/IP.

TCP/IP does not quite fit into the OSI model, as illustrated in Figure 12.6. The OSI model uses seven layers where the TCP/IP model uses four layers, which are:

OSI model	**Internet model**
Application *Presentation* *Session*	*Application*
Transport	*Transport (TCP)*
Network	*Internet (IP, ARP, ICMP, RARP)*
Data link *Physical*	*Network Interface*

TCP/IP supports most existing networking technologies, including Ethernet, ATM, FDDI, ISDN, and so on.

Internet applications:

- File transfer (FTP, NFS).
- E-mail (SMTP).
- Remote login (TELNET).
- Network management (SNMP).
- Domain naming (DNS).

- **Network access layer.** Specifies the procedures for transmitting data across the network, including how to access the physical medium, such as Ethernet and FDDI.
- **Internet layer.** Responsible for data addressing, transmission, and packet fragmentation and reassembly (IP protocol).
- **Transport layer.** Manages all aspects of data routing and delivery including session initiation, error control and sequence checking (TCP/UDP protocols). This includes part of the session layer of the OSI model.
- **Application layer.** Responsible for everything else. Applications must be responsible for all the presentation and part of the session layer.

TCP port values:

Used to identify the application (such as 21 for FTP). The ranges are:

- 0–255. Public applications.
- 255–1023. Assigned to companies for commercial products.
- Above 1023. Unregulated, and can be used by application programmers, or dynamically assigned by an application.

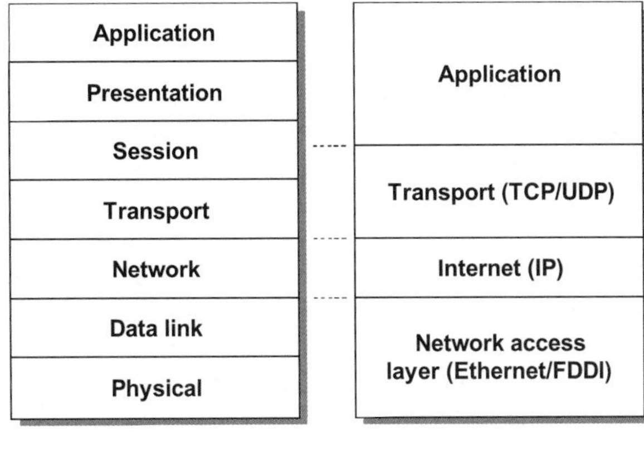

Figure 12.6 OSI and TCP/IP model

12.4 Transmission control protocol

In the OSI model, TCP fits into the transport layer and IP fits into the network layer. TCP thus sits above IP, which means that the IP header is added onto the higher-level information (such as transport, session, presentation and application). The main function of TCP is to provide a robust and reliable transport protocol. It is characterized as a reliable, connection-oriented, acknowledged and data stream-oriented server service. IP, itself, does not support the connection of two nodes, whereas TCP does. With TCP, a connection is initially established and is then maintained for the length of the transmission.

The main aspects of TCP are:

Window size. Defines the number of data segments that can be sent before an acknowledgement is required. The destination sends back an acknowledgement number for the data packet it expects to receive **NEXT**. Thus, if data segments 1, 2, 3 and 4 have been received the recipient sends back an acknowledgement value of 5.

Window size negotiation. This occurs when the connection is first made. The two hosts define the window in either direction (known as sliding window).

- **Data transfer.** Data is transmitted between two applications by packaging the data within TCP segments. This data is buffered and forwarded whenever necessary. A push function can be used when the data is required to be sent immediately.
- **Reliability.** TCP uses sequence numbers and positive acknowledgements (ACK) to keep track of transmitted segments. Thus, it can recover from data that is damaged, lost, duplicated, or delivered out of order, such as:

  - **Time-outs.** The transmitter waits for a given time (the timeout interval), and if it does not receive an ACK, the data is retransmitted.
  - **Sequence numbers.** The sequence numbers are used at the receiver to correctly order the packets and to delete duplicates.
  - **Error detection and recovery.** Each packet has a checksum, which is checked by the receiver. If it is incorrect the receiver discards it, and can use the acknowledgements to indicate the retransmission of the packets.

- **Flow control.** TCP returns a window with every ACK. This window indicates a range of acceptable sequence numbers beyond the last segment successfully received. It also indicates the number of bytes that the sender can transmit before receiving further acknowledgements.
- **Multiplexing.** To support multiple connections to a single host, TCP provides a set of ports within each host. This, along with the IP addresses of the source and destination, makes a socket, and a pair of sockets uniquely identifies each connection. Ports are normally associated with various services and allow server programs to listen for defined port numbers.
- **Connections.** A connection is defined by the sockets, sequence numbers and window sizes. Each host must maintain this information for the length of the connection. When the connection is closed, all associated resources are freed. As TCP connections can be made with unreliable hosts and over unreliable communication channels, TCP uses a handshake mechanism with clock-based sequence numbers to avoid inaccurate connection initialization.
- **Precedence and security.** TCP allows for different security and precedence levels.

TCP information contains simple acknowledgement messages and a set of sequential numbers. It also supports multiple simultaneous connections using destination and source port numbers, and manages them for both transmission and reception. As with IP, it supports data fragmentation and reassembly, and data multiplexing/ demultiplexing.

The set-up and operation of TCP is as follows:

1. When a host wishes to make a connection, TCP sends out a request message to the destination machine that contains unique numbers called

UDP

UDP has no sequence numbers, and thus does not use windowing or acknowledgements. Thus the application layer must provide reliability. UDP is designed for applications which do not send data segment sequences, and do not require to make a virtual connection with the other side.

Applications:

- **DNS.** Supports domain name mapping to IP addresses.
- **NFS.** Supports a distributed file system.
- **SNMP.** Supports network management for network devices.
- **TFTP** (Trivial FTP). A simplified version of FTP (typically used to update computers/routers with firmware updates).

a socket number, and a port number. The port number has a value which is associated with the application (for example a TELNET connection has the port number 23 and an FTP connection has the port number 21). The message is then passed to the IP layer, which assembles a datagram for transmission to the destination.

2. When the destination host receives the connection request, it returns a message containing its own unique socket number and a port number. The socket number and port number thus identify the virtual connection between the two hosts.
3. After the connection has been made the data can flow between the two hosts (called a data stream).

Table 12.1 Typical TCP port numbers

Port	*Process name*	*Notes*
20	FTP-DATA	File Transfer Protocol – data
21	FTP	File Transfer Protocol – control
23	TELNET	Telnet
25	SMTP	Simple Mail Transfer Protocol
49	LOGIN	Login Protocol
53	DOMAIN	Domain Name Server
79	FINGER	Finger
161	SNMP	SNMP

After TCP receives the stream of data, it assembles the data into packets, called TCP segments. After the segment has been constructed, TCP adds a header (called the protocol data unit) to the front of the segment. This header contains information such as a checksum, the port number, the destination and source socket numbers, the socket number of both machines and segment sequence numbers. The TCP layer then sends the packaged segment down to the IP layer, which encapsulates it and sends it over the network as a datagram.

12.4.1 Ports and sockets

As previously mentioned, TCP adds a port number and socket number for each host. The port number identifies the required service, whereas the socket number is a unique number for that connection. Thus, a node can have several TELNET connections with the same port number but each connection will have a different socket number. A port number can be any value but there is a standard convention that most systems adopt. Table 12.1 defines some of the most common values. Standard applications normally use port values from 0 to 255, while unspecified applications can use values above 255.

12.4.2 TCP header format

The sender's TCP layer communicates with the receiver's TCP layer using the TCP protocol data unit. It defines parameters such as the source port, destination port, and so on, and is illustrated in Figure 12.7.

The fields are:

- **Source and destination port number** – which are 16-bit values that identify the local port number (source number and destination port number or destination port).
- **Sequence number** – which identifies the current sequence number of the data segment. This allows the receiver to keep track of the data segments received. Any segments that are missing can be easily identified. The sequence number is the first

data byte of the DATA segment (except when SYN is present). If SYN is present the sequence number is the initial sequence number (ISN) and the first data octet is ISN + 1.

- **Acknowledgement number** – when the ACK bit is set, it contains the value of the next sequence number the sender of the packet is expecting to receive. This is always set after the connection is made.

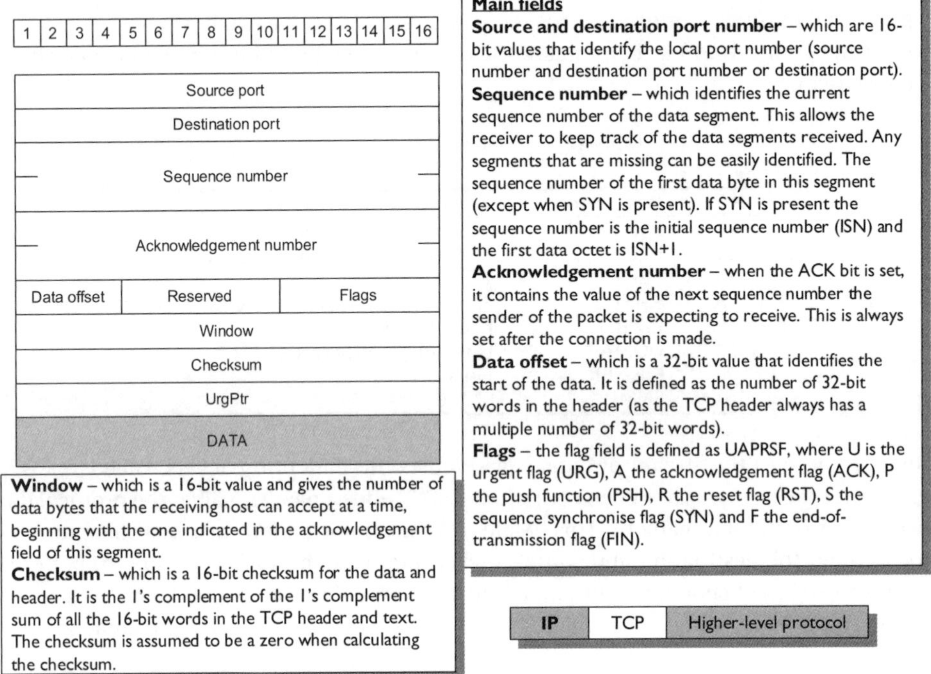

Figure 12.7 TCP header format

- **Data offset** – which is a 32-bit value that identifies the start of the data. It is defined as the number of 32-bit words in the header (as the TCP header always has a multiple number of 32-bit words).
- **Flags** – the flag field is defined as `UAPRSF`, where `U` is the urgent flag (URG), `A` the acknowledgement flag (ACK), `P` the push function (PSH), `R` the reset flag (RST), `S` the sequence synchronize flag (SYN) and `F` the end-of-transmission flag (FIN).
- **Window** – which is a 16-bit value and gives the number of data bytes that the receiving host can accept at a time, beginning with the one indicated in the acknowledgement field of this segment.
- **Checksum** – which is a 16-bit checksum for the data and header. It is the 1's complement of the 1's complement sum of all the 16-bit

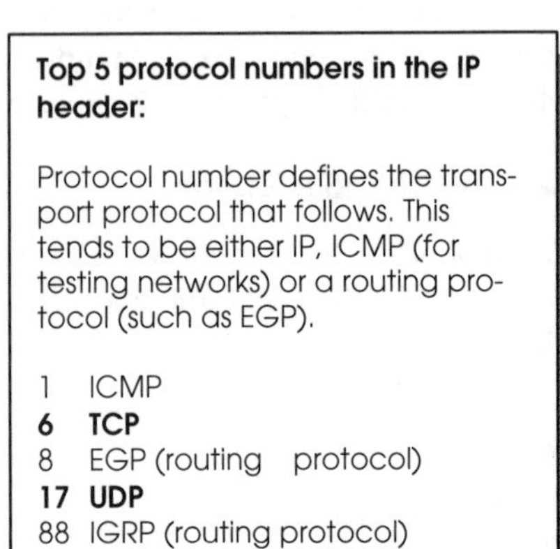

words in the TCP header and data. The checksum is assumed to be a zero when calculating the checksum.

- **UrgPtr** – which is the urgent pointer and is used to identify an important area of data (most systems do not support this facility). It is only used when the URG bit is set. This field communicates the current value of the urgent pointer as a positive offset from the sequence number in this segment.
- **Padding** (variable) – the TCP header padding is used to ensure that the TCP header ends and data begins on a 32-bit boundary. The padding is composed of zeros.
- **Options** – possibly added to segment header.

In TCP, a packet is termed as the complete TCP unit; that is, the header and the data. A segment is a logical unit of data, which is transferred between two TCP hosts. Thus a packet is made up of a header and a segment.

12.5 UDP

Top-down testing of a network

1. **Test application layer.** Use TELNET or application layer protocol to test the connection.
2. **PING.** If Step 1 fails, test if the node is responding to TCP/IP communications.
3. **TRACEROUTE.** If Step 2 fails, test the route to the node, to determine where the problem occurs.

TCP allows for a reliable connection-based transfer of data. The User Datagram Protocol (UDP) is an unreliable connection-less approach, where datagrams are sent into the network without any acknowledgements or connections (and thus relies on high-level protocols to provide for these). It is defined in RFC768 and uses IP as its underlying protocol. Its main advantage over TCP is that it has a minimal protocol mechanism, but does not guarantee delivery of any of the data. Figure 12.8 shows its format, which shows that the Protocol field in the IP header is set to 17 to identify UDP.

The fields are:

- **Source port.** This is an optional field and is set to a zero if not used. It identifies the local port number which should be used when the destination host requires to contact the originator.
- **Destination.** Port to connect to on the destination.
- **Length.** Number of bytes in the datagram, including the UDP header and the data.
- **Checksum.** The 16-bit 1's complement of the 1's complement sum of the IP header, the UDP header, the data (which, if necessary, is padded with zero bytes at the end, to make an even number of bytes).

UDP is used when hosts do not require to make a connection with the other side, and where reliability is built into a high-layer protocol. It is also used when there is no segmentation of data (as there are no segment values). Some applications are solely TCP or solely UDP, whereas the rest can use either. For example:

- **TCP applications.** FTP, TELNET, SMTP, FINGER, DNS and LOGIN.
- **UDP applications.** RIP, TFTP, NFS and SNMP.
- **TCP or UDP applications.** HTTP, POP-3 and ECHO.

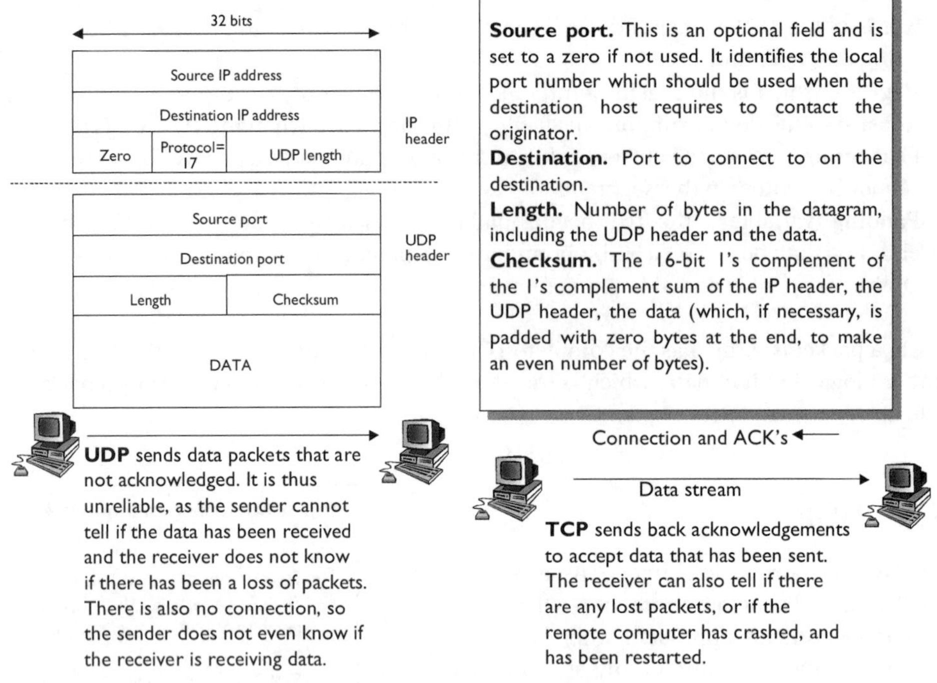

Figure 12.8 UDP header format

12.6 TCP specification

TCP is made reliable with the following:

- **Sequence numbers.** Each TCP packet is sent with a sequence number (which identifies byte numbers). Theoretically, each data byte is assigned a sequence number. The sequence number of the first data byte in the segment is transmitted with that segment and is called the segment sequence number (SSN).
- **Acknowledgements.** Packets contain an acknowledgement number, which is the sequence number of the next expected transmitted data byte in the reverse direction. On sending, a host stores the transmitted data in a storage buffer, and starts a timer. If the packet is acknowledged then this data is deleted, else, if no acknowledgement is received before the timer runs out, the packet is retransmitted.
- **Window.** With this, a host sends a window value which specifies the number of bytes, starting with the acknowledgement number, that the host can receive.

12.6.1 Connection establishment, clearing and data transmission

The main interfaces in TCP are shown in Figure 12.9. The calls from the application program to TCP include:

- OPEN and CLOSE. To open and close a connection.
- SEND and RECEIVE. To send and receive.
- STATUS. To receive status information.

The OPEN call initiates a connection with a local port and foreign socket arguments. A Transmission Control Block (TCB) stores the information on the connection. After a successful connection, TCP adds a local connection name by which the application program refers to the connection in subsequent calls.

The OPEN call supports two different types of call, as illustrated in Figure 12.11. These are:

- **Passive OPEN.** TCP waits for a connection from a foreign host, such as from an active OPEN. In this case, the foreign socket is defined by a zero. This is typically used by servers, such as TELNET and FTP servers. The connection can either be from a fully specified or an unspecified socket.
- **Active OPEN.** TCP actively connects to a foreign host, typically a server (which is opened with a passive OPEN) or with a peer-to-peer connection (with two active OPEN calls, at the same time, on each computer).

A connect is established with the transmission of TCP packets with the SYN control flag set and uses a three-way handshake (see Section 12.7). A connection is cleared by the exchange of packets with the FIN control flag set. Data flows in a stream using the SEND call to send data and RECEIVE to receive data.

The PUSH flag is used to send data in the SEND immediately to the recipient. This is required as a sending TCP is allowed to collect data from the sending application program and sends the data in segments when convenient. Thus, the PUSH flag forces it to be sent. When the receiving TCP sees the PUSH flag, it does not wait for any more data from the sending TCP before passing the data to the receiving process.

Question. *Okay. I understand that both the MAC address and the IP address need to be specified for a node to receive data, but how does a node know the MAC address of the remote destination?*

1. A host looks up its local ARP cache (which is in its own RAM, and not stored to the permanent storage) to see if it knows the MAC address for a known IP address.
2. If it does not find the MAC address, it transmits an ARP request to the whole of the network (ARP requests do not travel over routers). The host who matches the transmitted IP address then responds with an ARP reply with its own MAC address in the source address field in the data frame. This is received by the originator of the request, which updates its local ARP cache, and then transmits with the required MAC address.

Question. *Oh, yes. I think I see it now, but what if the destination is on another network, possibly in another country, how does it determine the address of the destination?*

1. The host knows the IP address of the gateway for the network (normally a router). It then uses the MAC address of the gateway, but with the destination IP address of the host that the data is destined for. The gateway senses that the data frame is addressed to itself, and forwards it to the next gateway, and so on.
2. If the node does not know the MAC address of the gateway it will send out an ARP request to the network with the IP address of the gateway.

Question: *What's the difference between a data segment and a data packet?*

The transport layer uses data segments, whereas the network layer uses data packets. Data segments allow two or more applications to share the same transport connection. These segments are then split into data packets which have a given maximum size (typically for IP packets this is 64 KB) and each are tagged with a source and destination network address. Different applications can send data segments on a first-come, first-served basis.

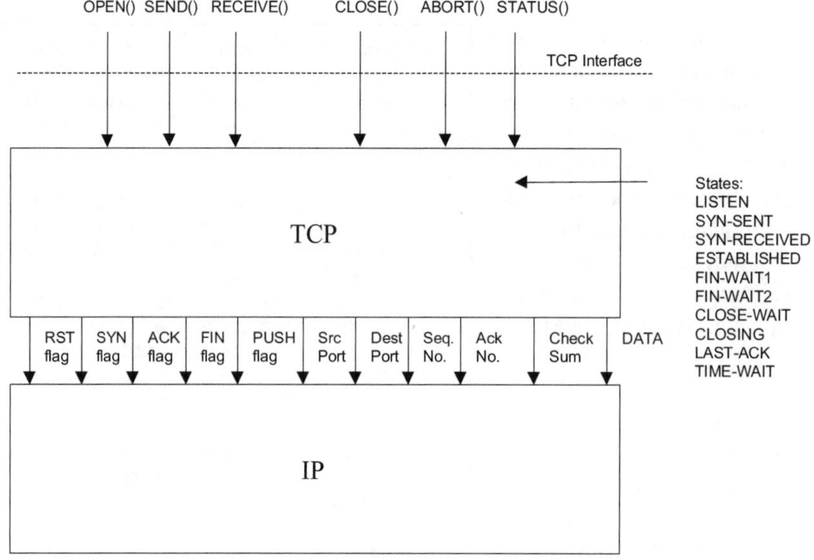

Figure 12.9 TCP interface

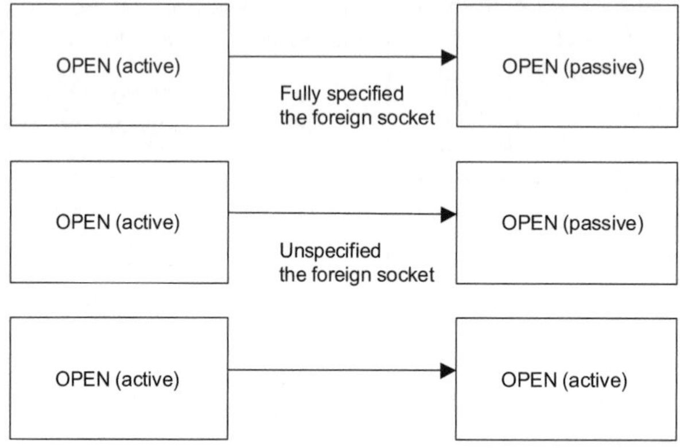

Figure 12.10 TCP connections

12.7 Connection states

Figure 12.11 outlines the states which the connection goes into, and the events which cause them. The events from applications programs are: OPEN, SEND, RECEIVE, CLOSE, ABORT, and STATUS, and the events from the incoming TCP packets include the SYN, ACK, RST and FIN flags. The definition of each of the connection states are:

- **LISTEN.** This is the state in which TCP is waiting for a remote connection on a given port.
- **SYN-SENT.** This is the state where TCP is waiting for a matching connection request after it has sent a connection request.

- **SYN-RECEIVED.** This is the state where TCP is waiting for a confirming connection request acknowledgement after having both received and sent a connection request.
- **ESTABLISHED.** This is the state that represents an open connection. Any data received can be delivered to the application program. This is the normal state for data to be transmitted.
- **FIN-WAIT-1.** This is the state in which TCP is waiting for a connection termination request, or an acknowledgement of a connection termination, from the remote TCP.
- **FIN-WAIT-2.** This is the state in which TCP is waiting for a connection termination request from the remote TCP.
- **CLOSE-WAIT.** This is the state where TCP is waiting for a connection termination request from the local application.
- **CLOSING.** This is the state where TCP is waiting for a connection termination request acknowledgement from the remote TCP.
- **LAST-ACK.** This is the state where TCP is waiting for an acknowledgement of the connection termination request previously sent to the remote TCP.
- **TIME-WAIT.** This is the state in which TCP is waiting for enough time to pass to be sure the remote TCP received the acknowledgement of its connection termination request.
- **CLOSED.** This is the notational state, which occurs after the connection has been closed.

Top 10 TCP ports

Port	Service
21	FTP
23	TELNET
25	SMTP (E-mail)
37	Time
53	DNS (Naming)
69	TFTP
79	FINGER
110	POP-3
161	SNMP
520	RIP

The following shows a sample session (using the `netstat` command). The local address is defined with the node address followed by the port number (for example for the first entry, artemis is the local address and the local port is 1023). Ports that are known (such as login, shell and imap) are given names, while non-assigned ports are just defined with a port number. It can be seen that the local host has three current logins with the hosts aphrodite and leto. These connect to the remote ports of 1018, 1023 and 1019. The send and receive windows do not vary on each of the connections, and are set at 8760. An important field is Send-Q, for which a nonzero value indicates that the network for that particular host is severely congested, as it defines the number of unacknowledged segments.

```
Local Address        Remote Address       Swind Send-Q Rwind  Recv-Q  State
-------------------- -------------------- ----- ------ -----  ------ -------
artemis.1023         poseidon.shell        8760      0  8760       0 FIN_WAIT_2
artemis.1022         poseidon.1022         8760      0  8760       0 ESTABLISHED
artemis.1021         poseidon.shell        8760      0  8760       0 FIN_WAIT_2
artemis.1020         poseidon.1021         8760      0  8760       0 ESTABLISHED
artemis.43939        hades.701             8760      0  8760       0 CLOSE_WAIT
artemis.login        aphrodite.1018        8760      0  8760       0 ESTABLISHED
artemis.login        leto.1023             8760      0  8760       0 ESTABLISHED
artemis.login        aphrodite.1019        8760      0  8760       0 ESTABLISHED
artemis.50925        poseidon.imap         8760      0  8760       0 CLOSE_WAIT
```

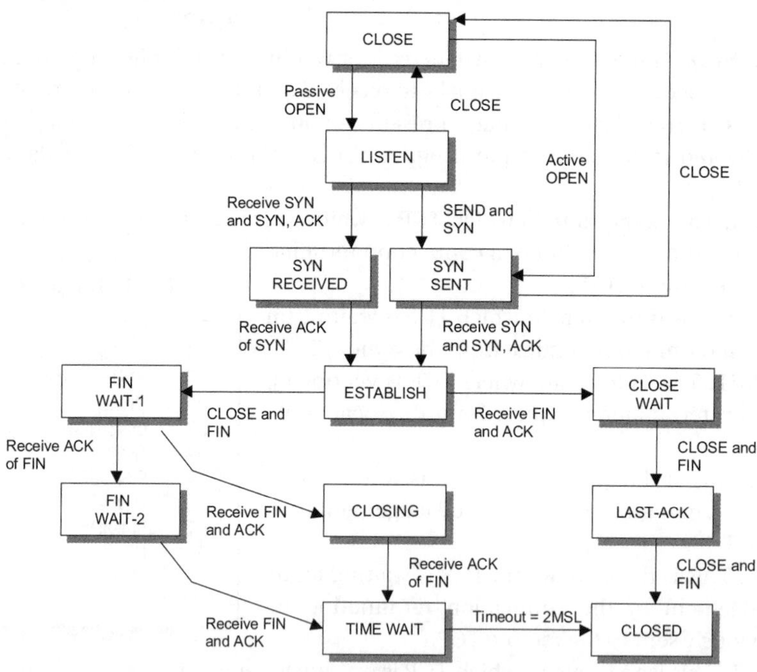

Figure 12.11 TCP connection states

12.7.1 Sequence numbers

TCP packets contain a 32-bit sequence number (0 to 4 294 967 295), which relates to every byte sent. It uses a cumulative acknowledgement scheme, where an acknowledgement with a value of VAL, validates all bytes up to, but not including, byte VAL. Each byte at which the packet starts is numbered consecutively, after the first byte.

When sending data, TCP should receive acknowledgements for the transmitted data. The required TCB parameters will be:

SND.UNA	Oldest unacknowledged sequence number.
SND.NXT	Next sequence number to send.
SEG.ACK	Acknowledgement from the receiving TCP (next sequence number expected by the receiving TCP).
SEG.SEQ	First sequence number of a segment.
SEG.LEN	Number of bytes in the TCP packet.
SEG.SEQ + SEG.LEN–1	Last sequence number of a segment.

On receiving data, the following TCB parameters are required:

RCV.NXT	Next sequence number expected on an incoming segment, and is the left or lower edge of the receive window.
RCV.NXT + RCV.WND–1	Last sequence number expected on an incoming segment, and is the right or upper edge of the receive window.
SEG.SEQ	First sequence number occupied by the incoming segment.
SEG.SEQ + SEG.LEN–1	Last sequence number occupied by the incoming segment.

12.7.2 ISN selection

The initial sequence number (ISN) is selected so that previous sockets are not confused with new sockets. Typically, this can happen when a host application crashes and then quickly re-establishes the connection before the other side can time-out the connection. To avoid this a 32-bit initial sequence number (ISN) generator is created when the connection is made, which is a number generated by a 32-bit clock, and is incremented approximately every 4 μs (giving an ISN cycle of 4.55 hours). Thus, within 4.55 hours, each ISN will be unique.

As each connection has a send and receive sequence number, these are an initial send sequence number (ISS) and an initial receive sequence number (IRS). When establishing a connection, the two TCPs synchronize their initial sequence numbers. This is done by exchanging connection establishing packets, with the SYN bit set and with the initial sequence numbers (these packets are typically called SYNs). Thus four packets must be initially exchanged:

- A sends to B. SYN with A_{SEQ}.
- B sends to A. ACK of the sequence number (A_{SEQ}).] Can be merged into a single state.
- B sends to A. SYN with B_{SEQ}.
- A sends to B. ACK of the sequence number (B_{SEQ}).

Note that the two intermediate steps can be combined into a single message, which is sometimes known as a three-way handshake. This handshake is necessary as the sequence numbers are not tied to a global clock, only to local clocks, and has many advantages, including the fact that old packets will be discarded as they occurred in a previous time.

To make sure that a sequence number is not duplicated, a host must wait for a maximum segment lifetime (MSL) before starting to retransmit packets (segments) after start-up or when recovering from a crash. An example MSL is 2 minutes. However, if it is recovering, and it has a memory of the previous sequence numbers, it may not need to wait for the MSL, as it can use sequence numbers which are much greater than the previously used sequence numbers.

12.8 Opening and closing a connection

Figure 12.12 shows a basic three-way handshake. The steps are:

1. The initial state on the initiator is CLOSED and, on the recipient, it is LISTEN (the recipient is waiting for a connection).
2. The initiator goes into the SYN-SENT state and sends a packet with the SYN bit set and then indicates that the starting sequence number will be 999 (the current sequence number, thus the next number sent will be 1000). When this is received the recipient goes into the SYN-RECEIVED state.
3. The recipient sends back a TCP packet with the SYN and ACK bits set (which identifies that it is a SYN packet and also that it is acknowledging the previous SYN packet). In this case, the recipient tells the originator that it will start transmitting at a sequence number of 100. The acknowledgement number is 1000, which is the sequence number that the recipient expects to receive next. When this is received, the originator goes into the ESTABLISHED state.

4. The originator sends back a TCP packet with the SYN and ACK bits set and the acknowledgement number is 101, which is the sequence number it expects to see next.
5. The originator transmits data with the sequence number of 1000.

Originator				**Recipient**
1. CLOSED				LISTEN
2. SYN-SENT	→	<SEQ=999><CTL=SYN>		SYN-RECEIVED
3. ESTABLISHED		<SEQ=100><ACK=1000><CTL=SYN,ACK>	←	SYN-RECEIVED
4. ESTABLISHED	→	<SEQ=1000><ACK=101> <CTL=ACK>		ESTABLISHED
5. ESTABLISHED	→	<SEQ=1000><ACK=101> <CTL=ACK><DATA>		ESTABLISHED

Figure 12.12 TCP connection

Note that the acknowledgement number acknowledges every sequence number up to but not including the acknowledgement number.

Figure 12.13 shows how the three-way handshake prevents old duplicate connection initiations from causing confusion. In state 3, a duplicate SYN has been received, which is from a previous connection. The recipient sends back an acknowledgement for this (4), but when this is received by the originator, the originator sends back a RST (reset) packet. This causes the recipient to go back into a LISTEN state. It will then receive the SYN packet sent in 2, and after acknowledging it, a connection is made.

TCP connections are half-open if one of the TCPs has closed or aborted, and the other end is still connected. Half-open connections can also occur if the two connections have become desynchronized because of a system crash. This connection is automatically reset if data is sent in either direction. This is because the sequence numbers will be incorrect, otherwise the connection will time-out.

A connection is normally closed with the CLOSE call. A host who has closed cannot continue to send, but can continue to RECEIVE until it is told to close by the other side. Figure 12.14 shows a typical sequence for closing a connection. Normally the application program sends a CLOSE call for the given connection. Next, a TCP packet is sent with the FIN bit set, the originator enters into the FIN-WAIT-1 state. When the other TCP has acknowledged the FIN and sent a FIN of its own, the first TCP can ACK this FIN.

Originator				**Recipient**
1. CLOSED				LISTEN
2. SYN-SENT	→	<SEQ=999><CTL=SYN>		
3. (duplicate)	→	<SEQ=900><CTL=SYN>		
4. SYN-SENT		<SEQ=100><ACK=901> <CTL=SYN,ACK>	←	SYN-RECEIVED
5. SYN-SENT	→	<SEQ=901><CTL=RST>		LISTEN
		(packet 2 received) →		
7. SYN-SENT		<SEQ=1 00><ACK=1000><CTL=SYN,ACK>	←	SYN-RECEIVED
8. ESTABLISHED	→	<SEQ=1 000><ACK=101><CTL=ACK><DATA>		ESTABLISHED

Figure 12.13 TCP connection with duplicate connections

Originator			Recipient
1. ESTABLISHED			ESTABLISHED
(*CLOSE call*)			
2. FIN-WAIT-1	→	<SEQ=1000><ACK=99> <CTL=SFIN,ACK>	CLOSE-WAIT
3. FIN-WAIT-2		<SEQ=99><ACK=1001> <CTL=ACK> ←	CLOSE-WAIT
4. TIME-WAIT		<SEQ=99><ACK=101><CTL=FIN,ACK> ←	LAST-ACK
5. TIME-WAIT	→	<SEQ=1001><ACK=102><CTL=ACK>	CLOSED

Figure 12.14 TCP close connection

12.9 TCP user commands

The commands in this section characterize the interface between TCP and the application program. Their actual implementation depends on the operating system. Section 12.10 discusses practical WinSock implementations.

12.9.1 OPEN

The OPEN call initiates an active or a passive TCP connection. The basic parameters passed and returned from the call are given next. Parameters in brackets are optional.

Parameters passed: local port, foreign socket, active/ passive [, timeout] [, precedence] [options]

Parameters returned: local connection name

These parameters are defined as:

- Local port. The local port to be used.
- Foreign socket. The definition of the foreign socket.
- Active/passive. A passive flag causes TCP to LISTEN, else it will actively seek a connection.
- Timeout. If present, this parameter allows the caller to set up a timeout for all data submitted to TCP. If the data is not

Question. *If a computer has no permanent storage, how does it know its own IP address?*

Diskless hosts use the RARP protocol, which broadcasts a message to a RARP server. The RARP server looks-up the MAC address in the source address field in the data frame and sends back its IP address in a reply to the host.

Question. *How is it possible to simply connect a computer to an Ethernet network, and all the computers on the network are able to communicate with it, and how do they know when a computer has been disconnected?*

Computers use the ARP protocol, which allows nodes to determine the MAC address of computers on the network, from given IP addresses. Once they discover the destination MAC address, they update their ARP cache. After a given time, the entries in the table are updated (known as ageing the entry).

Question: *How does a node broadcast to the network?*

There are two types of broadcasts. The first is a flooded broadcast, which has ones in all parts of the IP address (255.255.255.255). The other it a directed broadcast, which has all ones in the host part of a IP address. For example, to broadcast to the 146.176.151.0 network, the broadcast address is 146.176.151. 255, as all ones in the host part of the address specifies a broadcast. Routers forward directed broadcasts, but not flooded addresses (as these are local).

transmitted successfully within the timeout period the connection is aborted.

- Security/compartment. Specifies the security of the connection.
- Local connection name. A unique connection name is returned which identifies the socket.

12.9.2 SEND

The SEND call causes the data in the output buffer to be sent to the indicated connection. Most implementations return immediately from the SEND call, even if the data has not been sent, although some implementation will not return until either there is a timeout or the data has been sent. The basic parameters passed and returned from the call are given next. Parameters in brackets are optional.

Parameters passed: local connection name, buffer address, byte count, PUSH flag, URGENT flag [, timeout]

These parameters are defined as:

- Local connection name. A unique connection name which identifies the socket.
- Buffer address. Address of data buffer.
- Byte count. Number of bytes in the buffer.
- PUSH flag. If this flag is set then the data will be transmitted immediately, else the TCP may wait until it has enough data.
- URGENT flag. Sets the urgent pointer.
- Timeout. Sets a new timeout for the connection.

12.9.3 RECEIVE

The RECEIVE call allocates a receiving buffer for the specified connection. Most implementations return immediately from the RECEIVE call, even if the data has not been received, although some implementation will not return until either there is a timeout or the data has been received. The basic parameters passed and returned from the call are given next.

Parameters passed: local connection name, buffer address, byte count
Parameters returned: byte count, URGENT flag, PUSH flag

These parameters are defined as:

- Local connection name. A unique connection name which identifies the socket.
- Buffer address. Address of the receive data buffer.
- Byte count. Number of bytes received in the buffer.
- PUSH flag. If this flag is set then the PUSH flag has been set on the received data.
- URGENT flag. If this flag is set then the URGENT flag has been set on the received data.

12.9.4 CLOSE

The CLOSE call closes the connections and releases associated resources. All pending SENDs will be transmitted, but after the CLOSE call has been implemented, no further SENDs can occur. RECEIVEs can occur until the other host has also closed the connection. The basic parameters passed and returned from the call are given next.

Parameters passed: local connection name

12.9.5 STATUS

The STATUS call determines the current status of a connection, typically listing the TCBs. The basic parameters passed and returned from the call are given next.

Parameters passed: local connection name
Parameters returned: status data

The returned information should include status information on the following:

- local socket, foreign socket, local connection name
- receive window, send window, connection state
- number of buffers awaiting acknowledgement, number of buffers pending receipt
- urgent state, precedence, security/compartment
- transmission timeout.

12.9.6 ABORT

The ABORT call causes all pending SENDs and RECEIVEs to be aborted. All TCBs are also removed and a RESET message sent to the other TCP. The basic parameters passed and returned from the call are given next.

Parameters passed: local connection name

12.10 Visual Basic communication program

Visual Basic contains a Winsock control, which can be used to provide TCP or UDP communications. When it is added to a form it is invisible to the user.

The complete code for this program and documentation are available at:
`http://www.palgrave.com/studyskills/masterseries/buchanan`

Client operation
To create a client the following properties are set:

RemoteHost Set the IP address or the name of the server
RemotePort Set the remote port on which the server is listening

After this the client uses the Connect method.

Server operation
LocalPort Set the local port on which the server is listening

Next the server is set into the listen mode with the Listen method.

When a connection is made a ConnectionRequest event is caused. If the connection is to be accepted the Accept method is used.

Communication

After the connection has been set-up the SendData method is used to send data and the GetData is used to read data. The client or server knows that data has arrived with the DataArrival method.

The code for the **client** form is:

```
Private Sub about_Click()
    frmAbout.Show
End Sub
Private Sub show_status()

    If (myTCPClient.State = sckClosed) Then
        status.Text = "CLOSED"
    ElseIf (myTCPClient.State = sckOpen) Then
        status.Text = "OPEN"
    ElseIf (myTCPClient.State = sckListen) Then
        status.Text = "LISTENING..."
    ElseIf (myTCPClient.State = sckConnecting) Then
        status.Text = "CONNECTING"
    ElseIf (myTCPClient.State = sckConnected) Then
        status.Text = "CONNECTED"
    ElseIf (myTCPClient.State = sckError) Then
        status.Text = "ERROR"
    Else
        status.Text = myTCPClient.State
    End If
End Sub

Private Sub cmdConnect_Click()
    If (myTCPClient.State <> sckClosed) Then myTCPClient.Close ' close existing
connection
    'Connect to the server
    myTCPClient.Connect
    server_address.Text = AddressIP.Text
    Call show_status
End Sub

Private Sub cmdDisConnect_Click()
    'Disconnect from the server
    myTCPClient.Close
    myTCPClient.RemoteHost = AddressIP.Text
    myTCPClient.RemotePort = AddressPort.Text
    Call show_status
End Sub

Private Sub Command1_Click()
    Call show_status
End Sub

Private Sub Form_Load()
    portnamec.AddItem ("Test")
    portnamec.AddItem ("Echo")
    portnamec.AddItem ("Daytime")
    portnamec.AddItem ("FTP")
    portnamec.AddItem ("SMTP")
    portnamec.AddItem ("Telnet")
    portnamec.AddItem ("Char. gen.")
```

Method used to make a connection.

Parameters used to set the remote host and the remote port.

```
    portnamec.AddItem ("Port 37")
    portnamec.AddItem ("WWW")
    portnamec.Text = "Test"
    AddressIP.AddItem "127.0.0.1"
    AddressPort.Text = "1001"
    localipaddress.Text = myTCPClient.LocalIP
    Call show_status
End Sub

Private Sub HelpClient_Click()
    If (myTCPClient.State <> sckClosed) Then myTCPClient.Close
    myTCPClient.RemoteHost = "www.dcs.napier.ac.uk"
    AddressIP.Text = "www.dcs.napier.ac.uk"
    AddressPort.Text = "13"
    portnamec.Text = "Daytime"
    myTCPClient.Connect
End Sub

Private Sub PortNameC_Click()
    'Choice of the port (name)
    If portnamec.Text = "Test" Then AddressPort.Text = "1001"
    If portnamec.Text = "Echo" Then AddressPort.Text = "7"
    If portnamec.Text = "Daytime" Then AddressPort.Text = "13"
    If portnamec.Text = "FTP" Then AddressPort.Text = "21"
    If portnamec.Text = "Telnet" Then AddressPort.Text = "23"
    If portnamec.Text = "SMTP" Then AddressPort.Text = "25"
    If portnamec.Text = "Char. gen." Then AddressPort.Text = "19"
    If portnamec.Text = "Port 37" Then AddressPort.Text = "37"
    If portnamec.Text = "WWW" Then AddressPort.Text = "80"
End Sub

Private Sub myTCPClient_DataArrival(ByVal bytesTotal As Long)
    'Display incoming data
    Dim str1 As String, str2 As String, str As String  'declare old, new, to-
tal data
    str1 = ShowText.Text    'old data
    myTCPClient.GetData str2    'incoming data (new data)
    str = str1 + str2   'total data to display
    ShowText.Text = str 'display to ShowText
End Sub

Private Sub myTCPClient_Close()
    If (myTCPClient.State = sckClosed) Or (myTCPClient.State = sckClosing) Then
        Call show_status
    Else
        myTCPServer.Close
    End If

End Sub

Private Sub AddressIP_Click()
     If (myTCPClient.State <> sckClosed) Then myTCPClient.Close ' close exist-
ing connection
    'Choose IP Address
    myTCPClient.RemoteHost = AddressIP.Text
End Sub

Private Sub AddressIP_Change()
     If (myTCPClient.State <> sckClosed) Then myTCPClient.Close ' close exist-
ing connection
    'Enter IP or DNS address
    myTCPClient.RemoteHost = AddressIP.Text
End Sub
```

Method used to close the current connection.

```
Private Sub AddressPort_Change()
     If (myTCPClient.State <> sckClosed) Then myTCPClient.Close ' close exist-
ing connection
    'Change port number directly in the AddressPort box (manually)
    myTCPClient.RemotePort = AddressPort.Text
End Sub

Private Sub CloseC_Click()
    'Return to main menu
    End

End Sub

Private Sub SendTextData_KeyPress(KeyAscii As Integer)
    'When you press the ENTER key the contain of the top box is sent
    If KeyAscii = 13 Then
    myTCPClient.SendData SendTextData.Text + vbCrLf
    show_text_sent = show_text_sent + SendTextData.Text + vbCrLf
    SendTextData.Text = ""
    End If
End Sub
```

and the **server** code is:

```
Private Sub About_Click()
    frmAbout.Show
End Sub

Private Sub exit_Click()
    End
End Sub

Private Sub Form_Load()
    ' Set the local port to 1001 and listen for a connection
    listenport.Text = "1001"
    localipaddress.Text = myTCPServer.LocalIP ' Show local IP address
    Call show_status
End Sub
Private Sub show_status()

    If (myTCPServer.State = sckClosed) Then
        status.Text = "CLOSED"
    ElseIf (myTCPServer.State = sckOpen) Then
        status.Text = "OPEN"
    ElseIf (myTCPServer.State = sckListening) Then
        status.Text = "LISTENING..."
    ElseIf (myTCPServer.State = sckConnecting) Then
        status.Text = "CONNECTING"
    ElseIf (myTCPServer.State = sckConnected) Then
        status.Text = "CONNECTED"
    ElseIf (myTCPServer.State = sckError) Then
        status.Text = "ERROR"
    Else
        status.Text = myTCPServer.State
    End If
End Sub

Private Sub listenport_Change()
    If myTCPServer.State <> sckClosed Then myTCPServer.Close
    myTCPServer.LocalPort = listenport.Text
    myTCPServer.Listen
    Call show_status
End Sub
```

Method used to determine the state of the connection.

Set local port, and set the server into listen mode.

```
Private Sub myTCPServer_Close()
    If myTCPServer.State <> sckClosed Then myTCPServer.Close
    myTCPServer.LocalPort = listenport.Text
    myTCPServer.Listen
    ipaddress.Text = ""
    iphost.Text = ""
    remoteport.Text = ""
    Call show_status
End Sub

Private Sub myTCPServer_ConnectionRequest(ByVal requestID As Long)
    ' Check state of socket, if it is not closed then close it.
    If myTCPServer.State <> sckClosed Then myTCPServer.Close
    ' Accept the request with the requestID parameter.
    myTCPServer.Accept requestID
    ipaddress.Text = myTCPServer.RemoteHostIP
    If (myTCPServer.Protocol = 0) Then
        iphost.Text = "TCP"
    Else
          iphost.Text = "UDP"
    End If
    remoteport.Text = myTCPServer.remoteport
    Check1.Value = 1 ' show that remote has connected
    Call show_status
End Sub

Private Sub myTCPServer_DataArrival(ByVal bytesTotal As Long)
    ' Read incoming data into the str variable,
    ' then display it to ShowText
    Dim str As String
    myTCPServer.GetData str
    ShowText.Text = ShowText.Text + str
    Call show_status
End Sub

Private Sub SendTextData_KeyPress(KeyAscii As Integer)
    Call show_status
    If (KeyAscii = 13) Then
        myTCPServer.SendData SendTextData.Text + vbCrLf
        show_text_sent = show_text_sent + SendTextData.Text + vbCrLf
        SendTextData.Text = ""
    End If
End Sub
```

Event caused when the client connects to the server.

Event caused when data arrives from the client.

Method used to get the data which has just arrived.

Method used to send data to the client.

Screen shots from a development system are given in Figure 12.15. In this case a remote computer is set to listen for a connection. The client then connects into it by connecting to the server's IP address. The server will then show the connection. After this the user on the client machine and the user on the server can communicate using the text windows. In this case they connect using port 1001.

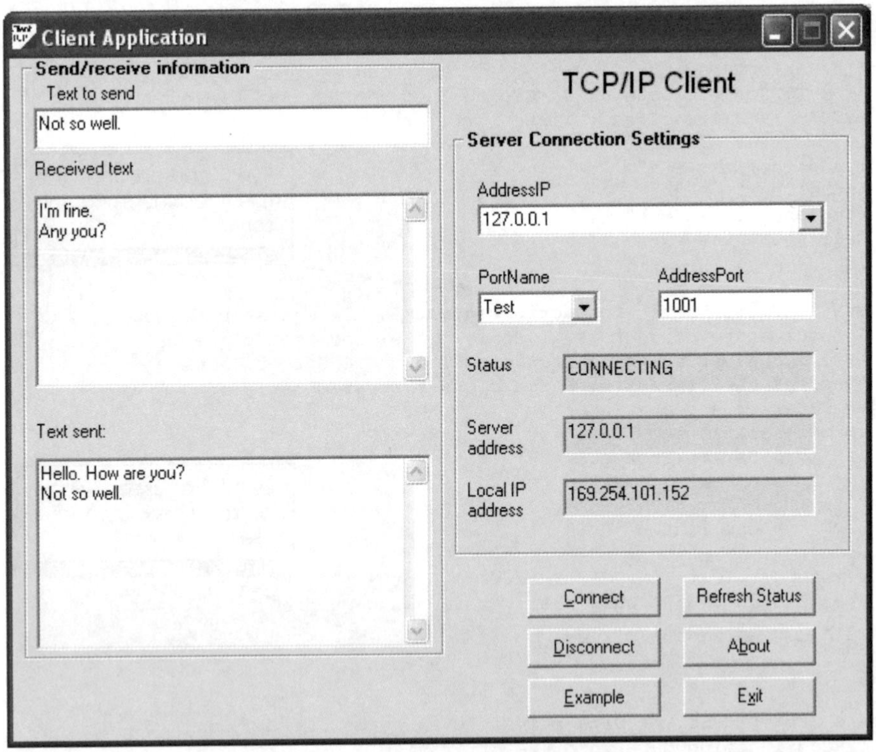

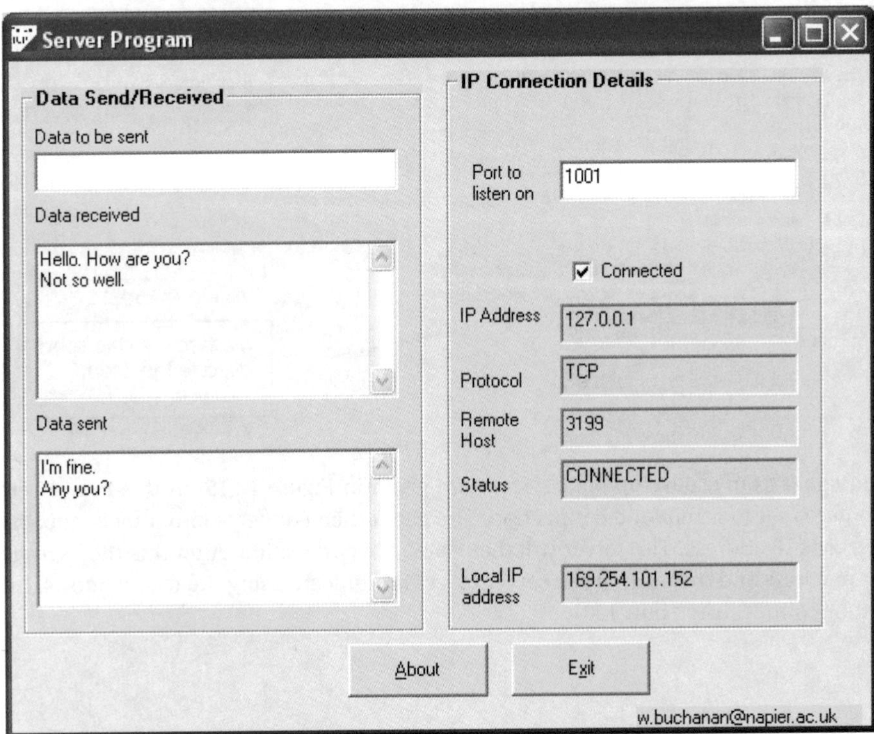

Figure 12.15 Client and server programs

12.11 TCP/IP services reference

Port	*Service*	*Comment*	*Port*	*Service*	*Comment*
1	TCPmux		7	echo	
9	discard	Null	11	systat	Users
13	daytime		15	netstat	
17	qotd	Quote	18	msp	Message send protocol
19	chargen	ttytst source	21	ftp	
23	telnet		25	smtp	Mail
37	time	Timserver	39	rlp	Resource location
42	nameserver	IEN 116	43	whois	Nickname
53	domain	DNS	57	mtp	Deprecated
67	bootps	BOOTP server	67	bootps	
68	bootpc	BOOTP client	69	tftp	
70	gopher	Internet Gopher	77	rje	Netrjs
79	finger		80	www	WWW HTTP
87	link	Ttylink	88	kerberos	Kerberos v5
95	supdup		101	hostnames	
102	iso-tsap	ISODE	105	csnet-ns	CSO name server
107	rtelnet	Remote Telnet	109	pop2	POP version 2
110	pop3	POP version 3	111	sunrpc	
113	auth	Rap ID	115	sftp	
117	uucp-path		119	nntp	USENET
123	ntp	Network Timel	137	netbios-ns	NETBIOS Name Service
138	netbios-dgm	NETBIOS	139	netbios-ssn	NETBIOS session
143	imap2		161	snmp	SNMP
162	snmp-trap	SNMP trap	163	cmip-man	ISO management over IP
178	nextstep	NeXTStep	179	bgp	BGP

12.12 Exercises

12.12.1 Which of the following is not part of a TCP header (select one or more):
(a) Host IP address (b) Time-to-live field
(c) Host port number (d) Acknowledgement number

12.12.2 Which port does a TELNET server listen to:
(a) 21 (b) 23 (c) 25 (d) 80

12.12.3 Which of the following best describes the function of the transport layer:
(a) Segments and reassembles segments into a data stream
(b) Establishes, maintains and terminates sessions between applications
(c) Routes data packets around interconnected networks
(d) Formats data in a form which can be transmitted over the network

12.12.4 Which of the following best describes the function of the session layer:
(a) Segments and reassembles segments into a data stream
(b) Establishes, maintains and terminates sessions between applications
(c) Routes data packets around interconnected networks
(d) Formats data in a form which can be transmitted over the network

Additional material and tutorial questions are available at:
`http://www.palgrave.com/studyskills/masterseries/buchanan`

13 Encryption

13.1 Introduction

The increase in electronic mail has also increased the need for secure data transmission. An electronic mail message can be easily intercepted as it transverses the world's communication networks. Thus there is a great need to encrypt the data contained in it. Traditional mail messages tend to be secure as they are normally taken by a courier or postal service and transported in a secure environment from source to destination. Over the coming years more individuals and companies will be using electronic mail systems and these must be totally secure.

Data encryption involves the science of cryptographics (note that the word *crytopgraphy* is derived from the Greek words which means hidden, or secret, writing). The basic object of cryptography is to provide a mechanism for two people to communicate without any other person being able to read the message.

Encryption is mainly applied to text transmission as binary data can be easily scrambled so it becomes almost impossible to unscramble. This is because text-based information contains certain key pointers:

- Most lines of text have the words 'the', 'and', 'of' and 'to'.
- Every sentence has a full stop.
- Words are separated by a space (the space character is the most probable character in a text document).
- The characters 'e', 'a' and 'i' are more probable than 'q', 'z' and 'x'.

Thus to decode a message an algorithm is applied and the decrypted text is then tested to determine whether it contains standard English (or the required language).

> **DEAR NET-ED**
>
> **Question:** *Some people talk about gateways, and I've got a gateway option in my settings for my network connection. So what's the difference between a gateway and a router?*
>
> A gateway is an old-fashioned way of defining the entry and exit point of a network. Most of the time a gateway is a router. You need to define the IP address of the gateway (the router) before you can communicate with external networks.
>
> **Question:** *So isn't a gateway a better definition for it?*
>
> Well I suppose it is, but it's a router, really. In the past computers were sometimes set up to run a routing protocol and had two or more network cards. These systems acted as gateways.

13.2 Encryption and the OSI model

It is possible to encrypt data at any level of the OSI model, but typically it is encrypted when it is passed from the application program. This must occur at the presentation layer of the model, as illustrated in Figure 13.1. Thus, an external party will be able to determine the data at the session, transport, network and data link layer, but not the originally transmitted application data. Thus encryption is useful in hiding data from external parties, but cannot be used (with standard protocols) to hide:

- The session between the two parties. This will give information on the type of session used (such as FTP, TELNET or HTTP).
- The transport layer information. This will give information on the data packets, such as, with TCP, port and socket numbers, and acknowledgements.
- The network address of the source and the destination (all IP packets can be examined and the source and destination address can be viewed).
- The source and destination MAC address. The actually physical addresses of both the source and the destination can be easily examined.

Most encryption techniques use a standard method to encrypt the message. This method is normally well known and the software which can be used to encrypt or decrypt the data is widely available. The thing that makes the encryption process different is an electronic key, which is added into the encryption process. This encryption key could be private so that both the sender and receiver could use the same key to encrypt and decrypt the data. Unfortunately this would mean that each conversation with a user would require a different key. Another disadvantage is that a user would have to pass the private key through a secret channel. There is no guarantee that this channel is actually secure, and there is no way of knowing that an external party has a secret key. Typically public keys are changed at regular intervals, but if the external party knows how these change, they can also change their own keys. These problems are overcome with public-key encryption.

Question: *So, apart from a World War, what relatively uninsured event could trigger a world-wide panic for over a week and end up costing over $15 billion of damage?*

A simple worm, which poked its head above the surface on the fourth day of May 2000. It was the day that will go down in history as the day that the world said 'I Love You'. Unfortunately it was not a message which would bring world peace, nor was it a sign of affection. Never before had such a global threat grown so quickly and attacked so many systems. So why was it able to spread so quickly and cause so much damage? The reasons are three-fold:

- **Internet transparency.** The Internet is of course, as it should be, a vast complex infrastructure that needs to have many different paths from one computer to another.
- **The openness and interconnection of global e-mail system.** Electronic mail is obviously an easy target as it is one of the most useful applications of the Internet. Thus it is a portal that allows external threats into an organization, but its usefulness typically outweighs its potential threats.
- **Microsoft's scripting tools.** This was caused by Microsoft's openness in allowing users to script system events and write simple programs which integrate into their office tools (normally known as Macros) and also perform powerful operating system commands, such as deleting files, and sending information over the Internet. Unfortunately, while they are extremely useful for some users, few users actually use the full power of their facilities, and would prefer that they did not exist, as they are a potential source of damage.

Most encryption is now public-key encryption (as illustrated in Figure 13.1). This involves each user having two encryption keys. One is a public key which is given to anyone that requires to send the user some encrypted data. This key is used to encrypt any data that is sent to the user. The other key is a private key which is used to decrypt the received encrypted data. No one knows the private key (apart from the user who is receiving data encrypted with their public key).

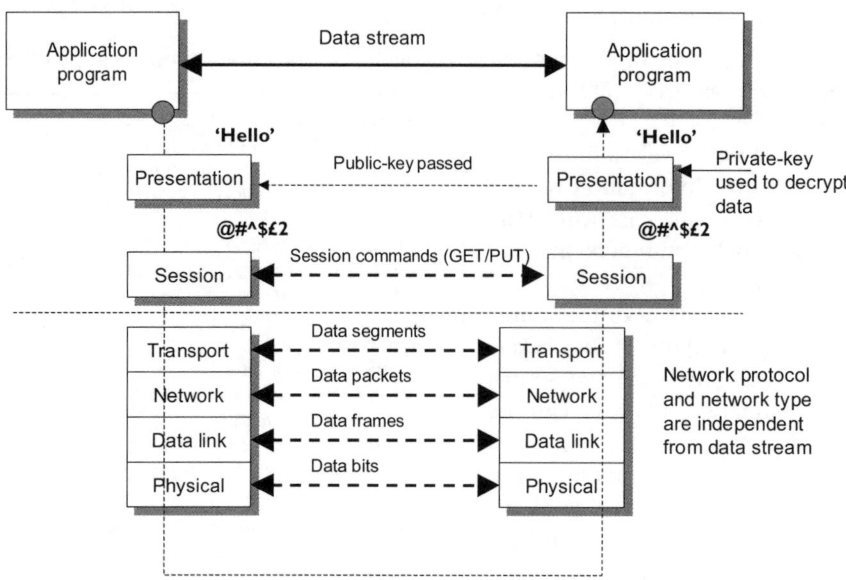

Figure 13.1 Encryption and the OSI model

13.3 Cryptography

The main object of cryptography is to provide a mechanism for two (or more) people to communicate without anyone else being able to read the message. Along with this it can provide other services, such as:

- Giving a reassuring integrity check – this makes sure the message has not been tampered with by non-legitimate sources.
- Providing authentication – this verifies the sender identity.

Initially plaintext is encrypted into ciphertext, it is then decrypted back into plaintext, as illustrated in Figure 13.2. Cryptographic systems tend to use both an algorithm and a secret value, called the key. The requirement for the key is that it is difficult to keep devising new algorithms and also to tell the receiving party that the data is being encrypted with the new algorithm. Thus, using keys, there are no problems with everyone having the encryption/decryption system, because without the key it is very difficult to decrypt the message.

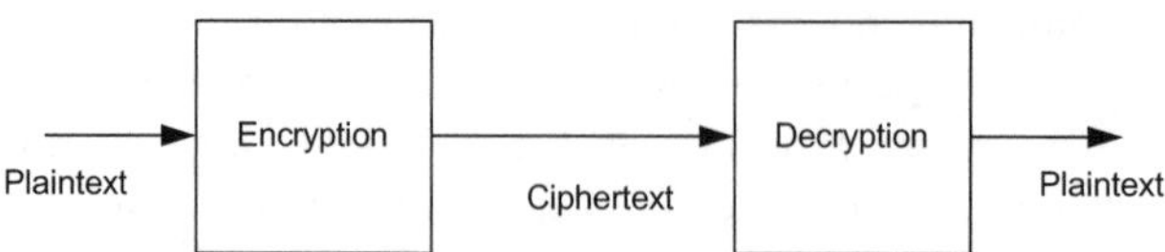

Figure 13.2 Encryption/decryption process

13.3.1 Public key versus private key

The encryption process can either use a public key or a secret key. With a secret key the key is only known to the two communicating parties. This key can be fixed or can be passed from the two parties over a secure communications link (perhaps over the postal network or a leased line). The two most popular private-key techniques are DES (Data Encryption Standard) and IDEA (International Data Encryption Algorithm).

In public-key encryption, each user has both a public and a private key. The two users can communicate because they know each other's public keys. Normally in a public-key system, each user uses a public enciphering transformation which is widely known and a private deciphering transform which is known only to that user. The private transformation is described by a private key, and the public transformation by a public key derived from the private key by a one-way transformation. The RSA (after its inventors Rivest, Shamir and Adleman) technique is one of the most popular public-key techniques and is based on the difficulty of factoring large numbers.

STOP PRESS:
Cntrl-Alt-Del defeats Trojan Horses

Trojan horse viruses pretend to be valid programs and can either present a common user interface or pretend to be useful programs. One Trojan horse virus, which is available over the WWW, is said to contain over 100 active viruses. Someone running this program will quickly be infected with these viruses.

The Happy99 virus typically attaches itself to e-mails and when the user runs the file it shows a lovely display of on-screen fireworks. Unfortunately it also replaces the existing TCP/IP stack with its own version, and copies itself to the most used e-mail addresses in a users address book (which is obviously embarrassing, as they tend to be friends or business colleagues).

One method of determining a user's login ID and password is to create a program which displays the user login screen. When the user enters their password it can be sent to the hacker. Windows NT/2000 overcomes this by having a login screen which can only be displayed when the Ctrl-Alt-Del keystrokes are used. It is extremely difficult to overrule this, as many programs use these keystrokes to reboot the computer.

13.3.2 Computational difficulty

Every code is crackable and the measure of the security of a code is the amount of time it takes persons not addressed in the code to break that code. Normally to break the code a computer tries all the possible keys until it finds a match. Thus a 1-bit code would only have 2 keys, a 2-bit code would have 4 keys, and so on. Table 13.1 shows the number of keys as a function of the number of bits in the key. For example it can be seen that a 64-bit code has 18,400,000,000,000,000,000 different keys. If one key is tested every 10 μs then it would take 1.84×10^{14} seconds (5.11×10^{10} hours or 2.13×10^{8} days or 5,834,602 years). So, for example, if it takes 1 million years for a person to crack the code then it can be considered safe. Unfortunately the performance of computer systems increases by the year. For example if a computer takes 1 million years to crack a code, then assuming an increase in computing power of a factor of 2 per year, then it would only take 500,000 years the next year. Table 13.2 shows that after almost 20 years it would take only 1 year to decrypt the same message.

The increasing power of computers is one factor in reducing the processing time; another is the increasing usage of parallel processing. Data decryption is well suited to parallel processing as each processor or computer can be assigned a number of keys to check the encrypted message. Each of them can then work independently of the other (this differs from many applications in parallel processing which suffer from interprocess(or) communication). Table 13.3 gives typical times, assuming a doubling of processing power each year, for processor arrays of 1, 2, 4 ... 4096 elements. It can be seen that with an array of 4096 processing elements it takes only 7 years before the code is decrypted within 2 years. Thus an organization which is serious about deciphering messages will have the resources to invest in large arrays of processors or networked computers. It is likely that many governments have computer systems with thousands or tens of thousands of processors operating in parallel. A prime use of these systems will be in decrypting messages.

Table 13.1 Number of keys related to the number of bits in the key

Code size	*Number of keys*	*Code size*	*Number of keys*	*Code size*	*Number of keys*
1	2	12	4 096	52	4.5×10^{15}
2	4	16	65 536	56	7.21×10^{16}
3	8	20	1 048 576	60	1.15×10^{18}
4	16	24	16 777 216	64	1.84×10^{19}
5	32	28	2.68×10^{8}	68	2.95×10^{20}
6	64	32	4.29×10^{9}	72	4.72×10^{21}
7	128	36	6.87×10^{10}	76	7.56×10^{22}
8	256	40	1.1×10^{12}	80	1.21×10^{24}
9	512	44	1.76×10^{13}	84	1.93×10^{25}
10	1 024	48	2.81×10^{14}	88	3.09×10^{26}

Table 13.2 Time to decrypt a message assuming an increase in computing power

Year	*Time to decrypt (years)*	*Year*	*Time to decrypt (years)*
0	1 million	10	977
1	500 000	11	489
2	250 000	12	245
3	125 000	13	123
4	62 500	14	62
5	31 250	15	31
6	15 625	16	16
7	7 813	17	8
8	3 907	18	4
9	1 954	19	2

Table 13.3 Time to decrypt a message with increasing power and parallel processing

Processors	*Year 0*	*Year 1*	*Year 2*	*Year 3*	*Year 4*	*Year 5*	*Year 6*	*Year 7*
1	1 000 000	500 000	250 000	125 000	62 500	31 250	15 625	7 813
2	500 000	250 000	125 000	62 500	31 250	15 625	7 813	3 907
4	250 000	125 000	62 500	31 250	15 625	7 813	3 907	1 954
8	125 000	62 500	31 250	15 625	7 813	3 907	1 954	977
16	62 500	31 250	15 625	7 813	3 907	1 954	977	489
32	31 250	15 625	7 813	3 907	1 954	977	489	245
64	15 625	7 813	3 907	1 954	977	489	245	123
128	7 813	3 907	1 954	977	489	245	123	62
256	3 906	1 953	977	489	245	123	62	31
512	1 953	977	489	245	123	62	31	16
1 024	977	489	245	123	62	31	16	8
2 048	488	244	122	61	31	16	8	4
4 096	244	122	61	31	16	8	4	2

13.4 Government pressure

Many institutions and individuals read data which is not intended for them; they include:

- Government departments. Traditionally governments around the world have reserved the right to tap into any communications which they think may be against the national interest.
- Spies who tap into communications for industrial or governmental information.
- Individuals who like to read other people's messages.
- Individuals who 'hack' into systems and read secure information.
- Criminals who intercept information in order to use it for crime, such as intercepting PIN numbers on bankcards.

Governments around the world tend to be against the use of encryption as it reduces their chances to tap into information and determine messages. It is also the case that governments do not want other countries to use encryption because it also reduces their chances of reading their secret communications (especially military manoeuvres). In order to reduce this threat they must do either of the following:

- Prevent the use of encryption.
- Break the encryption code.
- Learn everyone's cryptographic keys.

Many implementations of data encryption are in hardware, but increasingly it is implemented in software (especially public-key methods). This makes it easier for governments to control their access. For example the US government has proposed to beat encryption by trying to learn everyone's cryptographic key with the Clipper chip. The US government keeps a record of all the serial numbers and encryption keys for each Clipper chip manufactured.

13.5 Cracking the code

A cryptosystem converts plaintext into ciphertext using a key. There are several methods that a hacker can use to crack a code, including:

- **Known plaintext attack.** Where the hacker knows part of the ciphertext and the corresponding plaintext. The known ciphertext and plaintext can then be used to decrypt the rest of the ciphertext.
- **Chosen-ciphertext.** Where the hacker sends a message to the target, this is then encrypted with the target's private key and the hacker then analyses the encrypted message. For example, a hacker may send e-mail to the encryption file server and the hacker spies on the delivered message.
- **Exhaustive search.** Where the hacker uses brute force to decrypt the ciphertext and tries every possible key.
- **Active attack.** Where the hacker inserts or modifies messages.
- **Man-in-the-middle.** Where the hacker is hidden between two parties and impersonates each of them to the other.

- **The replay system.** Where the hacker takes a legitimate message and sends it into the network at some future time.
- **Cut and paste.** Where the hacker mixes parts of two different encrypted messages and, sometimes, is able to create a new message. This message is likely to make no sense, but may trick the receiver into doing something that helps the hacker.
- **Time resetting.** Some encryption schemes use the time of the computer to create the key. Resetting this time or determining the time that the message was created can give some useful information to the hacker.
- **Time attack.** This involves determining the amount of time that a user takes to decrypt the message; from this the key can be found.

13.6 Letter probabilities

The English language has a great deal of redundancy in it, thus common occurrences in text can be coded with short bit sequences. The probability of each letter also varies. For example the letter '*e*' occurs many more times than the letter '*z*'. The program on the WWW site gives a simple C program which determines the probability of letters within a text file. This program can be used to determine typical letter probabilities. Sample run 13.1 shows a sample run using some sample text. It can be seen that the highest probability is with the letter '*e*', which occurs, on average, 94.3 times every 1000 letters. Table 13.4 lists the letters in order of their probability. Notice that the letters which are worth the least in the popular board game Scrabble (such as, '*e*', '*t*', '*a*', and so on) are the most probable and the letters with the highest scores (such as '*x*', '*z*' and '*q*') are the least probable.

Scrabble™ letter values (placing in Table 13.4):

A	1 (3)	E	1 (1)
I	1 (4)	L	1 (9)
N	1 (6)	O	1 (5)
R	1 (8)	S	1 (7)
T	1 (2)	U	1 (14)
D	2 (11)	G	2 (15)
B	3 (19)	C	3 (12)
M	3 (13)	P	3 (17)
F	4 (16)	H	4 (10)
V	4 (21)	W	4 (18)
Y	4 (20)	K	5 (22)
J	8 (26)	X	8 (23)
Q	10 (24)	Z	10 (25)

Sample run 13.1

```
Char. Occur. Prob.      Char. Occur. Prob.
  a    1963   0.0672     b      284   0.0097
  c     914   0.0313     d      920   0.0315
  e    2752   0.0943     f      471   0.0161
  g     473   0.0162     h      934   0.0320
  i    1680   0.0576     j       13   0.0004
  k      96   0.0033     l      968   0.0332
  m     724   0.0248     n     1541   0.0528
  o    1599   0.0548     p      443   0.0152
  q      49   0.0017     r     1410   0.0483
  s    1521   0.0521     t     2079   0.0712
  u     552   0.0189     v      264   0.0090
  w     383   0.0131     x       57   0.0020
  y     278   0.0095     z       44   0.0015
  .     292   0.0100     SP    4474   0.1533
  ,     189   0.0065
```

13.6.1 Frequency analysis

Frequency analysis involves measuring the occurrences of the letters in the ciphertext. This can give many clues as the English language contains certain key features for deciphering, such as:

- Determine the probabilities of ciphertext letters. The least probable should be 'j', 'k', 'x' and 'z'. These have an accumulated occurrence of less than 1 per cent. One of the letters, an 'e', should have an occurrence of more than 10 per cent. Next the ciphertext letter probabilities should be measured against standard English language letter probabilities. If the two do not tie-up, it is likely that the text was written in another language.
- If the single letters do not yield the code, then two-letter occurrences of the same letter should be examined. The most common ones are: ss, ee, tt, ff, ll, mm and oo. If the ciphertext contains repeated letters, it may relate to one of these sequences.
- If there are spaces between the words, the two-letter words can be examined. The most popular two-letter words are: an, as, at, am, be, by, do, of, to, in, it, is, so, we, he, or, on, if, me, up, go, no and us (see Section 13.13).
- If possible, the list of letter probabilities should be related to the type of message that is being sent. For example, military communications tend to omit pronouns and articles (excluding words like he, a and I).
- Try and identify whole phrases, such as 'Hello who are you'. This can be used as a crowbar to get the rest of the code.
- If the ciphertext corresponds to correct letter probabilities, but the deciphered text is still unreadable, it may be that the code is a transpositional cipher, where the letters have had their positions changed. For example, every two cipher characters have been swapped around.

Table 13.4 Letters and their occurrence in a sample text file

Character	*Occurrences*	*Probability*	*Character*	*Occurrences*	*Probability*
SPACE	4474	0.1533	g	473	0.0162
e	2752	0.0943	f	471	0.0161
t	2079	0.0712	p	443	0.0152
a	1963	0.0672	w	383	0.0131
i	1680	0.0576	.	292	0.0100
o	1599	0.0548	b	284	0.0097
n	1541	0.0528	y	278	0.0095
s	1521	0.0521	v	264	0.0090
r	1410	0.0483	,	189	0.0065
l	968	0.0332	k	96	0.0033
h	934	0.0320	x	57	0.0020
d	920	0.0315	q	49	0.0017
c	914	0.0313	z	44	0.0015
m	724	0.0248	j	13	0.0004
u	552	0.0189			

13.7 Basic encryption principles

Encryption codes have been used for many centuries. They have tended to be used in military situations where secret messages have to be sent between troops without the risk of them being read by the enemy.

13.7.1 Alphabet shifting (Caesar code)

A simple encryption code is to replace the letters with a shifted equivalent alphabet. For example moving the letters two places to the right gives:

```
abcdefghijklmnopqrstuvwxyz
YZABCDEFGHIJKLMNOPQRSTUVWX
```

Thus a message:

```
the boy stood on the burning deck
```

would become:

```
RFC ZMW QRMMB ML RFC ZSPLGLE BCAI
```

This code has the problem of being reasonably easy to decode, as there are only 26 different code combinations. The first documented use of this type of code was by Julius Caesar who used a 3-letter shift.

13.7.2 Vigenère code

A Caesar-type code shifts the alphabet by a number of places (as given in Table 13.5). An improved code was developed by Vigenère, but as a shifted alphabet is not very secure. In this code, a different row is used for each encryption. The way that the user moves between the rows must be agreed before encryption. This can be achieved with a code word, which defines the sequence of the rows. For example the codeword GREEN could be used which defined that the rows used were: Row 6 (G), Row 17 (R), Row 4 (E), Row 4 (E), Row 13 (N), Row 6 (G), Row 17 (R), and so on.
Thus the message:

Keyword	`GREENGREENGREEN`
Plaintext	`hellohowareyou`
Ciphertext	`NVPPBNFAEEKPSY`

The great advantage of this type of code is that the same plaintext character will be encrypted with different values, depending on the position of the keyword. For example, if the keyword is GREEN, 'e' can be encrypted as 'K' (for G), 'V' (for R), 'I' (for E) and 'R' (for N). The greater the size of the code word, the more the rows that will be included in the encryption process. It is not possible to decipher the code by a frequency analysis, as letters will change their coding depending on the current position of the keyword. It is also safe from analysis of common two- and three-letter occurrences. For example 'ee' could be encrypted with 'KV' (for GR), 'VI' (for RE), 'II' (for EE), 'IR' (for EN) and 'RK' (for NG). A longer keyword would generate more combinations.

Table 13.5 Character-shifted alphabets

Plain	a	b	c	d	e	f	g	h	i	j	k	l	m	n	o	p	q	r	s	t	u	v	w	x	y	z
1	B	C	D	E	F	G	H	I	J	K	L	M	N	O	P	Q	R	S	T	U	V	W	X	Y	Z	A
2	C	D	E	F	G	H	I	J	K	L	M	N	O	P	Q	R	S	T	U	V	W	X	Y	Z	A	B
3	D	E	F	G	H	I	J	K	L	M	N	O	P	Q	R	S	T	U	V	W	X	Y	Z	A	B	C
4	E	F	G	H	I	J	K	L	M	N	O	P	Q	R	S	T	U	V	W	X	Y	Z	A	B	C	D
5	F	G	H	I	J	K	L	M	N	O	P	Q	R	S	T	U	V	W	X	Y	Z	A	B	C	D	E
6	G	H	I	J	K	L	M	N	O	P	Q	R	S	T	U	V	W	X	Y	Z	A	B	C	D	E	F
7	H	I	J	K	L	M	N	O	P	Q	R	S	T	U	V	W	X	Y	Z	A	B	C	D	E	F	G
8	I	J	K	L	M	N	O	P	Q	R	S	T	U	V	W	X	Y	Z	A	B	C	D	E	F	G	H
9	J	K	L	M	N	O	P	Q	R	S	T	U	V	W	X	Y	Z	A	B	C	D	E	F	G	H	I
10	K	L	M	N	O	P	Q	R	S	T	U	V	W	X	Y	Z	A	B	C	D	E	F	G	H	I	J
11	L	M	N	O	P	Q	R	S	T	U	V	W	X	Y	Z	A	B	C	D	E	F	G	H	I	J	K
12	M	N	O	P	Q	R	S	T	U	V	W	X	Y	Z	A	B	C	D	E	F	G	H	I	J	K	L
13	N	O	P	Q	R	S	T	U	V	W	X	Y	Z	A	B	C	D	E	F	G	H	I	J	K	L	M
14	O	P	Q	R	S	T	U	V	W	X	Y	Z	A	B	C	D	E	F	G	H	I	J	K	L	M	N
15	P	Q	R	S	T	U	V	W	X	Y	Z	A	B	C	D	E	F	G	H	I	J	K	L	M	N	O
16	Q	R	S	T	U	V	W	X	Y	Z	A	B	C	D	E	F	G	H	I	J	K	L	M	N	O	P
17	R	S	T	U	V	W	X	Y	Z	A	B	C	D	E	F	G	H	I	J	K	L	M	N	O	P	Q
18	S	T	U	V	W	X	Y	Z	A	B	C	D	E	F	G	H	I	J	K	L	M	N	O	P	Q	R
19	T	U	V	W	X	Y	Z	A	B	C	D	E	F	G	H	I	J	K	L	M	N	O	P	Q	R	S
20	U	V	W	X	Y	Z	A	B	C	D	E	F	G	H	I	J	K	L	M	N	O	P	Q	R	S	T
21	V	W	X	Y	Z	A	B	C	D	E	F	G	H	I	J	K	L	M	N	O	P	Q	R	S	T	U
22	W	X	Y	Z	A	B	C	D	E	F	G	H	I	J	K	L	M	N	O	P	Q	R	S	T	U	V
23	X	Y	Z	A	B	C	D	E	F	G	H	I	J	K	L	M	N	O	P	Q	R	S	T	U	V	W
24	Y	Z	A	B	C	D	E	F	G	H	I	J	K	L	M	N	O	P	Q	R	S	T	U	V	W	X
25	Z	A	B	C	D	E	F	G	H	I	J	K	L	M	N	O	P	Q	R	S	T	U	V	W	X	Y

The Vigenère code is *polyalphabetic*, as it uses a number of cipher alphabets.

13.7.3 Homophonic substitution code

A homophonic substitution code overcomes the problems of frequency analysis of code, as it assigns a number of codes to a character which relates to the probability of the characters. For example the character 'e' might have 10 codes assigned to it, but 'z' would only have one. An example code is given in Table 13.6.

Each of the codes is assigned at random to each of the letters, with the number of codes assigned related to the probability of their occurrence. Thus, using the code table in Table 13.6, the code mapping would be:

```
Plaintext    h  e  l  l  o  e  v  e  r  y  o  n  e
Ciphertext:  19 25 42 81 16 26 22 28 04 55 30 00 32
```

In this case there are four occurrences of the letter 'e', and each one has a different code. As the number of codes depends on the number of occurrences of the letter, each code will roughly have the same probability, thus it is not possible to determine the code mapping from the probabilities of codes. Unfortunately the code isn't perfect as the English language still contains certain relationships which can be traced. For example the letter 'q' normally is represented by a single code, and three codes represent a 'u'. Thus, if the ciphertext contains a code followed by one of three codes, then it is likely that the plaintext is a 'q' and a 'u'.

Table 13.6 Example homophonic substitution

a	b	c	d	e	f	g	h	i	j	k	l	m	n	o	p	q	r	s	t	u	v	w	x	y	z
07	11	17	10	25	08	44	19	02	18	41	42	40	00	16	01	15	04	06	05	13	22	45	12	55	47
31	64	33	27	26	09	83	20	03			81	52	43	30	62		24	34	23	14		46		93	
50		49	51	28			21	29			86		80	61			39	56	35	36					
63			76	32			54	53			95		88	65			58	57	37						
66				48			70	68					89	91			71	59	38						
77				67			87	73						94			00	90	60						
84				69										96					74						
				72															78						
				75															92						
				79																					
				82																					
				85																					

A homophonic cipher is a monoalphabetic code, as it only uses one translation for the code mappings (even though several codes can be used for a single plaintext letter). This alphabet remains constant, whereas a polyalphabet can change its mapping depending on a variable keyword.

13.7.4 Code mappings

Code mappings can have no underlying mathematical relationship and simply use a codebook to represent the characters. This is known as a *monoalphabetic* code, as only one cipher alphabet is used. An example could be:

```
Input:        abcdefghijklmnopqrstuvwxyz
Encrypted:    MGQOAFZBCDIEHXJKLNTQRWSUVY
```

Program 13.1 shows a C program which uses this code mapping to encrypt entered text and Sample run 13.2 shows a sample run.

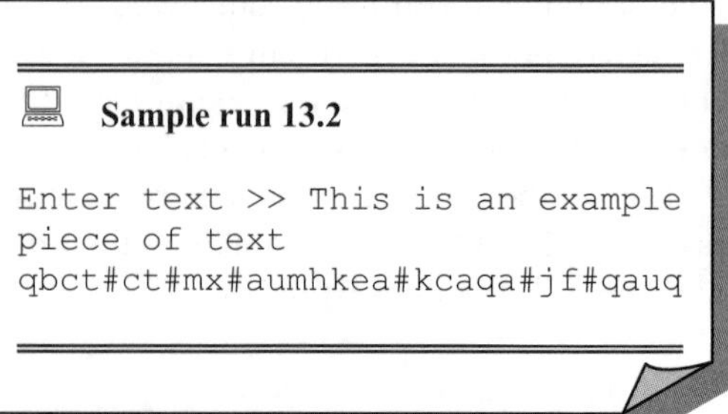

Sample run 13.2
Enter text >> This is an example
piece of text
qbct#ct#mx#aumhkea#kcaqa#jf#qauq

The number of different character maps can be determined as follows:

- Take the letter 'A' then this can be mapped to 26 different letters.
- If 'A' is mapped to a certain letter then 'B' can only map to 25 letters.
- If 'B' is mapped to a certain letter then 'C' can be mapped to 24 letters.
- Continue until the alphabet is exhausted.

Thus, in general, the number of combinations will be:

$$26 \times 25 \times 24 \times 23 \ldots 4 \times 3 \times 2 \times 1$$

Thus the code has 26! different character mappings (approximately 4.03×10^{26}). It suffers from the fact that the probabilities of the mapped characters will be similar to those in normal text. Thus if there is a large amount of text then the character having the highest probability will be either an 'e' or a 't'. The character with the lowest probability will tend to be a 'z' or a 'q' (which is also likely be followed by the character map for a 'u').

Program 13.1

```
#include <stdio.h>
#include <ctype.h>
int   main(void)
{
int   key,ch,i=0,inch;
char  text[BUFSIZ];
char input[26]="abcdefghijklmnopqrstuvwxyz";
char output[26]="mgqoafzbcdiehxjklntqrwsuvy";
   printf("Enter text >>");
   gets(text);
   ch=text[0];
   do
   {
      if (ch!=' ')    inch=output[(tolower(ch)-'a')];
      else inch='#';
      putchar(inch);
      i++;
      ch=text[i];
   } while (ch!=NULL);
   return(0);
}
```

A code mapping encryption scheme is easy to implement but unfortunately, once it has been 'cracked', it is easy to decrypt the encrypted data. Normally this type of code is implemented with an extra parameter which changes its mapping, such as changing the code mapping over time depending on the time of day and/or date. Only parties which are allowed to decrypt the message know the mappings of the code to time and/or date. For example, each day of the week could have a different code mapping.

13.7.5 Applying a key

To make it easy to decrypt, a key is normally applied to the text. This makes it easy to decrypt the message if the key is known, but difficult to decrypt the message if the key is not known. An example of a key operation is to take each of the characters in a text message and then exclusive-OR (XOR) the character with a key value. For example the ASCII character 'A' has the bit pattern:

100 0001

and if the key had a value of 5 then 'A' exclusive-OR'ed with 5 would give:

'A'	100 0001
Key (5)	000 0101
Ex-OR	100 0100

The bit pattern 100 0100 would be encrypted as character 'D'. Program 13.3 is a C program which can be used to display the alphabet of encrypted characters for a given key. In this program the ^ operator represents exclusive-OR. Sample run 13.4 shows a sample run with a key of 5. The exclusive-OR operator has the advantage that when applied twice it results in the original value (it thus changes a value, but does not lose any information when it operates on it).

Program 13.2

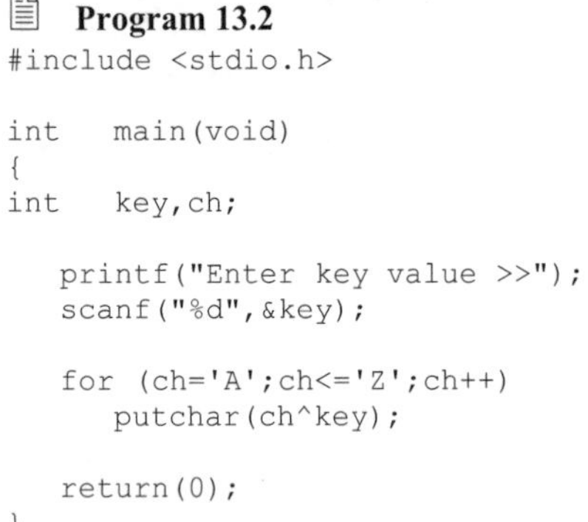

```
#include <stdio.h>

int   main(void)
{
int   key,ch;

   printf("Enter key value >>");
   scanf("%d",&key);

   for (ch='A';ch<='Z';ch++)
      putchar(ch^key);

   return(0);
}
```

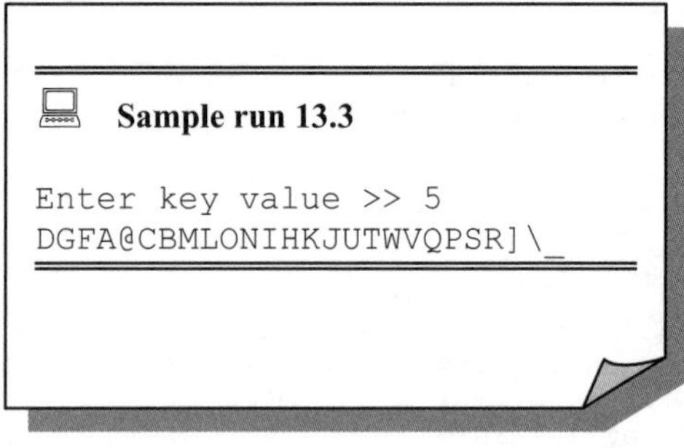

Sample run 13.3

```
Enter key value >> 5
DGFA@CBMLONIHKJUTWVQPSR]\_
```

Program 13.3 is an encryption program which reads some text from the keyboard, then encrypts it with a given key and saves the encrypted text to a file. Program 13.4 can then be used to read the encrypted file for a given key; only the correct key will give the correct results.

Sample run 13.4

```
Enter output filename >> out.dat
Enter text to be saved to file>> The
boy stood on the burning deck
Enter key value >> 3
```

Program 13.3

```
/* Encryt.c */
#include <stdio.h>

int   main(void)
{
FILE *f;
char  fname[BUFSIZ],str[BUFSIZ];
int   key,ch,i=0;

   printf("Enter output file name >>");
   gets(fname);

   if ((f=fopen(fname,"w"))==NULL)
   {
      puts("Cannot open input file");
      return(1);
   }
   printf("Enter text to be save to file>>");
   gets(str);

   printf("Enter key value >>");
   scanf("%d",&key);

   ch=str[0];
   do
   {
      ch=ch^key; /* Exclusive-OR character with itself */
      putc(ch,f);
```

```
      i++;
      ch=str[i];
   } while (ch!=NULL); /* test if end of string */
   fclose(f);
   return(0);
}
```

File listing 13.1 gives a file listing for the saved encrypted text. One obvious problem with this coding is that the SPACE character is visible in the coding. As the SPACE character is 010 0000, the key can be determined by simply XORing 010 0000 with the '#' character, thus:

SPACE	010 0000
'#'	010 0011
Key	000 0011

Thus the key is 000 0011 (decimal 3).

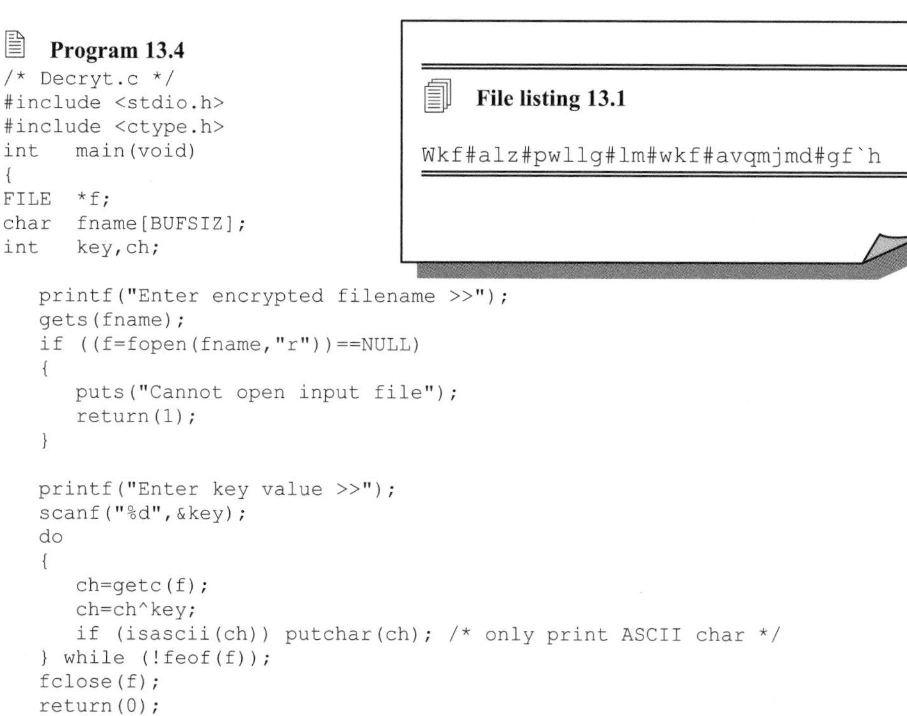

Program 13.4

```
/* Decryt.c */
#include <stdio.h>
#include <ctype.h>
int   main(void)
{
FILE  *f;
char  fname[BUFSIZ];
int   key,ch;

   printf("Enter encrypted filename >>");
   gets(fname);
   if ((f=fopen(fname,"r"))==NULL)
   {
      puts("Cannot open input file");
      return(1);
   }

   printf("Enter key value >>");
   scanf("%d",&key);
   do
   {
      ch=getc(f);
      ch=ch^key;
      if (isascii(ch)) putchar(ch); /* only print ASCII char */
   } while (!feof(f));
   fclose(f);
   return(0);
}
```

File listing 13.1

```
Wkf#alz#pwllg#lm#wkf#avqmjmd#gf`h
```

Program 13.5 uses the exclusive-OR operator and reads from an input file and outputs to an output file. The format of the run (assuming that the source code file is called `key.c`) is:
`key` *infile.dat outfile.enc*

where *infile.dat* is the name of the input file (text or binary) and *outfile.enc* is the name of the output file.

The great advantage of this program is that the same program is used for encryption and for decryption. Thus:

`key` *outfile.enc newfile.dat*

converts the encrypted file back into the original file.

Program 13.5

```
#include <stdio.h>

int main(int argc, char *argv[])
{
FILE *in,*out;
char fname[BUFSIZ],key,ch,fout[BUFSIZ],fext[BUFSIZ],*str;

   printf("Enter key >>");
   scanf("%c",&key);

   if ((in=fopen(argv[1],"rb"))==NULL)
   {
      printf("Cannot open");
      return(1);
   }

   out=fopen(argv[2],"wb");

   do
   {
      fread(&ch,1,1,in); /* read a byte from the file */
      ch=((ch & 0xff) ^ (key & 0xff)) & 0xff;
      if (!feof(in)) fwrite(&ch,1,1,out); /* write a byte */

   } while (!feof(in));

   fclose(in); fclose(out);
}
```

13.7.6 Applying a bit shift

A typical method used to encrypt text is to shift the bits within each character. For example ASCII characters only use the lower 7 bits of an 8-bit character. Thus, shifting the bit positions one place to the left will encrypt the data to a different character. For a left shift a 0 or a 1 can be shifted into the least significant bit; for a right shift the least significant bit can be shifted into the position of the most significant bit. When shifting more than one position a rotate left or rotate right can be used. Note that most of the characters produced by shifting may not be printable, thus a text editor (or viewer) cannot be used to view them. For example, in C the characters would be processed with:

```
ch=ch << 1;
```

which shifts the bits of `ch` one place to the left, and decrypted by:

```
ch=ch >> 1;
```

which shifts the bits of `ch` one place to the right.

Program 13.6 gives an example of a program that reads in a text file (or any file), and reads it one byte at a time. For each byte the program rotates the bits two places to the left (with `rot_left`) and saves the byte.

Program 13.6

```
#include <stdio.h>
unsigned char rot_left(unsigned char ch);
unsigned char rot_right(unsigned char ch);

int main(int argc, char *argv[])
{
unsigned char ch;
int i;
FILE *in,*out;
char fname[BUFSIZ],fout[BUFSIZ],fext[BUFSIZ],*str;
   if ((in=fopen(argv[1],"rb"))==NULL)
   {
      printf("Cannot open");
      return(1);
   }
   out=fopen(argv[2],"wb");
   do
   {
      fread(&ch,1,1,in);   /* read a byte from the file */
      ch=rot_left(ch);     /* perform two left rotates */
      ch=rot_left(ch);
      if (!feof(in)) fwrite(&ch,1,1,out); /* write a byte */
   } while (!feof(in));
   fclose(in); fclose(out);
}
// rotate bits to the left
unsigned char rot_left(unsigned char ch)
{
unsigned char bit8;

   bit8=(ch & 0x80) & 0x80;
   ch=ch << 1;
   ch = ch | ((bit8>>7) & 0x01);
   return(ch);
}
/* rotate bits to the right */
unsigned char rot_right(unsigned char ch)
{
unsigned char bit1;
   bit1=(ch & 1) & 0x01;
   ch=ch >> 1;
   ch = ch | ((bit1<<7) & 0x80);
   return(ch);
}
```

For example the text:

```
Hello. This is some sample text.

Fred.
```

becomes:

```
!•±±½¸□Q¡¥Í□¥Í□Í½µ•□Í…µÁ±•□Ñ•áÑ¸4(4(□É•'¸
```

This can then be decrypted by changing the left rotates (`rot_left`) to right rotates (`rot_right`).

13.8 Message hash

A message hash is a simple technique which basically mixes up the bits within the message, using exclusive-OR operations, bit-shifts or character substitutions.

- **Base-64 encoding.** This is used in electronic mail, and is typically used to change a binary file into a standard 7-bit ASCII form. It takes 6-bit characters and converts them to a printable character, as given on the WWW site.
- **MD5.** This is used in several encryption and authentication methods. An example conversion is from:

```
Hello, how are you?
Are you feeling well?

Fred.
```

to:

```
518bb66a80cf187a20e1b07cd6cef585
```

13.9 Private key

For more material on private-key encryption please visit our web site at
`http://www.palgrave.com/studyskills/masterseries/buchanan`

13.10 Public key

Public-key algorithms use a secret element and a public element to their code. One of the main algorithms is RSA. Compared with DES it is relatively slow but it has the advantage that users can choose their own key whenever they need one. The most commonly used public-key cryptosystems are covered in the next sections.

Private-key systems are not feasible for large-scale networks, such as the Internet or electronic commerce, as this would involve organizations creating hundreds or thousands of different private keys. Each conversation with an organization or even an individual within a company would require a separate key. Thus, public-key methods are much better suited to the Internet and, therefore, Intranets.

Figure 13.3 shows that a public-key system has two keys, a private key and a public key. The private key is secret to the user and is used to decrypt messages that have been encrypted with the user's public key. The public key is made available to anyone who wants to send an encrypted message to the person. Someone sending a message to the user will use the user's public key to encrypt the message and it can only be decrypted using the user's private key (as the private and public keys are linked in a certain way). Once the message has been encrypted not even the sender can decrypt it.

Typical public-key methods are:

- **RSA.** RSA stands for Rivest, Shamir and Adelman, and is the most commonly used public-key cryptosystem. It is patented only in the USA and is secure for key length of over 728 bits. The algorithm relies on the fact that it is difficult to factorize large numbers. Unfortunately, it is particularly vulnerable to chosen plaintext attacks and a new timing attack (spying on keystroke time) was announced on the 7 December 1995. This attack would be able to break many existing implementations of RSA.
- **Elliptic curve.** Elliptic curve is a new kind of public-key cryptosystem. It suffers from speed problems, but this has been overcome with modern high-speed computers.
- **DSS.** DSS (digital signature standard) is related to the DSA (digital signature algorithm). This standard has been selected by the NIST and the NSA, and is part of the Capstone project. It uses 512-bit or 1024-bit key size. The design presents some lack in key-exchange capability and is slow for signature-verification.
- **Diffie–Hellman.** Diffie–Hellman is commonly used for key exchange. The security of this cipher relies on both the key length and the discrete algorithm problem. This problem is similar to the factorizing of large numbers. Unfortunately, the code can be cracked and the prime number generator must be carefully chosen.
- **LUC.** Peter Smith developed LUC which is a public-key cipher that uses Lucas functions instead of exponentiation. Four other algorithms have also been developed, these are: LUCDIF (a key-negotiation method); LUCELG PK (equivalent to EL Gamel encryption); LUCELG DS (equivalent to EL Gamel data signature system) and LUCDSA (equivalent to the DSS).

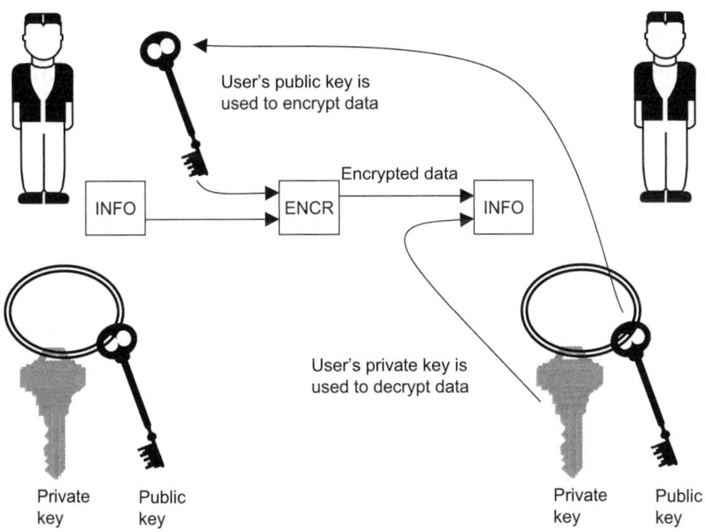

Figure 13.3 Overview of public-key systems

For more material on public-key encryption and PGP please visit our web site at `http://www.palgrave.com/studyskills/masterseries/buchanan`

13.11 Authentication

It is obviously important to encrypt a transmitted message, but how can it be proved that the user who originally encrypted the message sent the message. This is achieved with message authentication. The two users who are communicating are sometimes known as the principals. It should be assumed that an intruder (hacker) could intercept and listen to messages at any part of the communication, whether it is the initial communication between the two parties and their encryption keys or when the encrypted messages are sent. The intruder could thus playback any communications between the parties and pretend to be the other.

For more material on authentication please visit our web site
`http://www.palgrave.com/studyskills/masterseries/buchanan`

13.11.1 Digital signatures

Digital signatures provide a way of validating an electronic document, in the same way as a hand written signature does on a document. It must provide:

- Authentication of the sender. This is important as the recipient can verify the sender of the message.
- Authentication of the contents of the message. This is important, as the recipient knows that a third party has not modified the original contents of the message. Normally, this is also time-stamped.
- Authentication that the contents have not been changed by the recipient. This is important in legal cases where the recipient can prove that the message was as the original.

13.12 Internet security

As more information is stored on the Internet, and the amount of secure information, such as credit transfers and database transfers, increases, the need for a secure transmission mechanism also increases. The Internet has outgrown its founding protocol, HTTP. There thus has to be increased security in:

- Data encryption of WWW pages. This provides for secret information to be encrypted with a secret key.
- Message integrity. This provides a method of validating that the transmitted message is valid and has not been changed, either in transmission or in storage.
- Server authentication. This provides a method in which a server is authenticated to a client, to stop hackers pretending that they are the accessed server.
- Client authentication. This provides a method in which the client is authenticated to the server, to stop hackers from accessing a restricted server.

The main methods used are Secure Socket Layer (SSL) which was developed by Netscape, and Secure-HTTP (S-HTTP) which was developed by Enterprise Integration Technologies. Both are now being considered as international standards.

Two main problems are:

- Protection of transmitted information. For example, a person could access a book club over the Internet and then send information on the book and also credit-card information. The Book Club is likely to be a reputable company but criminals who can simply monitor the connection between the user and the Book Club could infiltrate the credit-card information.
- Protection of the client's computer. The Internet has little inherent security for the programs which can be downloaded from it. Thus, with no security, programs could be run or files can be download which could damage the local computer.

13.13 Occurrences of English letters, digrams, trigrams and words

Letters (%)		*Digrams (%)*		*Trigrams (%)*		*Words (%)*	
E	13.05	TH	3.16	THE	4.72	THE	6.42
T	9.02	IN	1.54	ING	1.42	OF	4.02
O	8.21	ER	1.33	AND	1.13	AND	3.15
A	7.81	RE	1.30	ION	1.00	TO	2.36
N	7.28	AN	1.08	ENT	0.98	A	2.09
I	6.77	HE	1.08	FOR	0.76	IN	1.77
R	6.64	AR	1.02	TIO	0.75	THAT	1.25
S	6.46	EN	1.02	ERE	0.69	IS	1.03
H	5.85	TI	1.02	HER	0.68	I	0.94
D	4.11	TE	0.98	ATE	0.66	IT	0.93
L	3.60	AT	0.88	VER	0.63	FOR	0.77
C	2.93	ON	0.84	TER	0.62	AS	0.76
F	2.88	HA	0.84	THA	0.62	WITH	0.76
U	2.77	OU	0.72	ATI	0.59	WAS	0.72
M	2.62	IT	0.71	HAT	0.55	HIS	0.71
P	2.15	ES	0.69	ERS	0.54	HE	0.71
Y	1.51	ST	0.68	HIS	0.52	BE	0.63
W	1.49	OR	0.68	RES	0.50	NOT	0.61
G	1.39	NT	0.67	ILL	0.47	BY	0.57
B	1.28	HI	0.66	ARE	0.46	BUT	0.56
V	1.00	EA	0.64	CON	0.45	HAVE	0.55
K	0.42	VE	0.64	NCE	0.43	YOU	0.55
X	0.30	CO	0.59	ALL	0.44	WHICH	0.53
J	0.23	DE	0.55	EVE	0.44	ARE	0.50
Q	0.14	RA	0.55	ITH	0.44	ON	0.47
Z	0.09	RO	0.55	TED	0.44	OR	0.45

13.14 Exercises

13.14.1 How many keys are used in the public-key system:
(a) 1 (b) 3 (c) 2 (d) 4

13.14.2 How many keys are used in the private-key system:
(a) 1 (b) 3 (c) 2 (d) 4

For more exercises and additional material please visit our web site at
`http://www.palgrave.com/studyskills/masterseries/buchanan`

14 Security

14.1 Introduction

An organization may experience two disadvantages in having a connection to the WWW and the Internet:

- The possible usage of the Internet for non-useful applications (by employees).
- The possible connection of non-friendly users from the global connection into the organization's local network.

For these reasons many organizations have shied away from connection to the global network and have set up intranets. These are in-house, tailor-made internets for use within the organization and provide limited access (if any) to outside services and also limit the external traffic into the intranet (if any). An intranet might have access to the Internet but there will be no access from the Internet to the organization's Intranet.

Organizations which have a requirement for sharing and distributing electronic information normally have three choices:

Ring-fenced firewall

Many organizations with several interconnected sites use a single firewall for all incoming and outgoing Internet traffic, as the network administrator can properly configure the firewall for the required security level, and also monitor any incoming and outgoing network traffic.

Note: Gateways into and out of a network, these days, are typically routers. At one time they were basically computers that connected to the internal and external network that filtered the traffic.

- Use a propriety groupware package, such as Lotus Notes.
- Set up an intranet.
- Set up a connection to the Internet.

Groupware packages normally replicate data locally on a computer whereas intranets centralize their information on central servers which are then accessed by a single browser package. The stored data is normally open and can be viewed by any compatible WWW browser. Intranet browsers have the great advantage over groupware packages in that they are available for a variety of clients, such as PCs, UNIX workstations, Macs, and so on. A client browser also provides a single GUI interface which offers easy integration with other applications, such as electronic mail, images, audio, video, animation, and so on.

The main elements of an intranet are:

- Intranet server hardware and software.
- TCP/IP stack software on the clients and server.
- WWW browsers.
- A firewall.

Typically the intranet server consists of a PC running the Linux (PC-based UNIX-like) operating system. The TCP/IP stack is software installed on each computer and allows communications between a client and a server using TCP/IP.

A firewall is the routing computer which isolates the intranet from the outside world. Another method is to use an intermediate system which isolates the intranet from the external Internet. These intermediate systems include:

- A proxy. This connects to a number of clients; it acts on behalf of clients and sends requests from the clients to a server. It thus acts as a client when it communicates with a server, but as a server when communicating with a client. A proxy is typically used for security purposes where the client and server are separated by a firewall. The proxy connects to the client side of the firewall and the server to the other side of the firewall. Thus the server must authenticate itself to the firewall before a connection can be made with the proxy. Only after this has been authenticated will the proxy pass requests through the firewall. A proxy can also be used to convert between different versions of the protocols that use TCP/IP, such as HTTP.
- A gateway.
- A tunnel.

> **Virus signatures and footprints**
>
> All viruses have a signature, or create a footprint when they are executed. Virus decoders must determine the operation of the virus in order for an anti-virus program not to make a mistake in thinking that a valid piece of program is virus code. Thus there is very little guesswork with a virus-seeking program, and most viruses must be carefully analysed before an anti-virus program can be updated to eradicate it.

Each intermediate system is connected by TCP and acts as a relay for the request to be sent out and returned to the client. Figure 14.1 shows the set-up of the proxies and gateways.

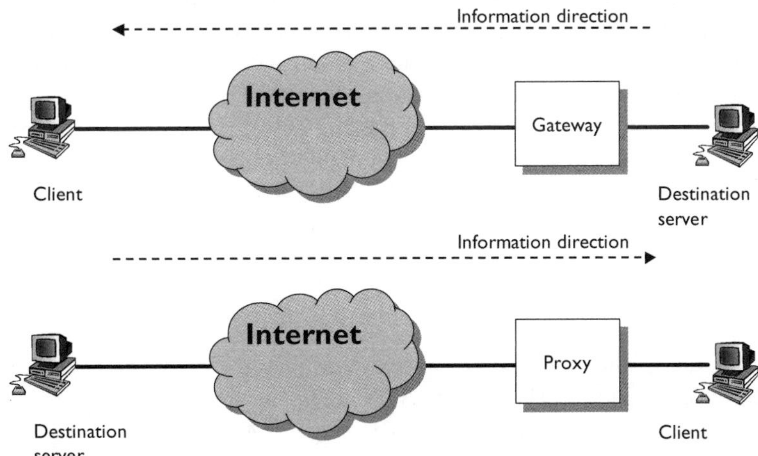

Figure 14.1 Usage of proxies and gateways

14.2 Firewalls

A firewall (or security gateway) protects a network against intrusion from outside sources. They tend to differ in their approach, but can be characterized either as firewalls which block traffic or firewalls which permit traffic. They can be split into three main types:

- **Network-level firewalls** (packet filters). This type of firewall examines the parameters of the TCP/IP packet to determine if it should be dropped or not. This can be done by examining the destination address, the source address, the destination port, the source port, and so on. The firewall must thus contain a list of barred IP addresses or allowable IP addresses. Typically a system manager will determine IP addresses of sites which are barred and add them to the table. Certain port numbers will also be barred, typically TELNET and FTP ports are barred and SMTP is allowed, as this allows mail to be routed into and out of the network, but no remote connections.
- **Application-level firewalls.** This type of firewall uses an intermediate system (a proxy server) to isolate the local computers from the external network. The local computer communicates with the proxy server, which in turn communicates with the external network, the external computer then communicates with the proxy which in turn communicates with the local computers. The external network never actually communicates directly with the local computers. The proxy server can then be set-up to be limited to certain types of data transfer, such as allowing HTTP (for WWW access), SMTP (for electronic mail), outgoing FTP, but blocking incoming FTP.
- **Circuit-level firewalls.** A circuit-level firewall is similar to an application-level firewall but it does not bother about the transferred protocol.

14.2.1 Network-level firewalls

The network-level firewall (or packet filter) is the simplest form of firewall and is also known as a screen router. It basically keeps a record of allowable source and destination IP addresses, and deletes all packets which do not have them. This technique is known as address filtering. The packet filter keeps a separate source and destination table for both directions, that is, into and out of the intranet. This type of method is useful for companies which have geographically spread sites, as the packet filter allows incoming traffic from other friendly sites, but blocks other non-friendly traffic. This is illustrated by Figure 14.2.

Unfortunately, this method suffers from the fact that IP addresses can be easily forged. For example, a hacker might determine the list of good source addresses and then add one of them to any packets which are addressed to the intranet. This type of attack is known as address spoofing and is the most common method of attacking a network.

14.2.2 Application-level firewall

The application-level firewall uses a proxy server to act as an intermediate system between the external network and the local computer. Normally the proxy only supports a given number of protocols, such as HTTP (for WWW access) or FTP. It is thus possible to block certain types of protocols, typically outgoing FTP (Figure 14.3).

The proxy server thus isolates the local computer from the external network. The local computer communicates with the proxy server, which in turn communicates with the external network, the external computer then communicates with the proxy, which in turn, communicates with the local computer. The external network never actually communicates directly with the local computer. The left-hand window of Figure 14.4 shows a WWW browser set up to communicate with a proxy server to get its access. In the advanced options (right-hand side of Figure 14.4) different proxy servers can be specified. In this case, for HTTP (WWW access), FTP, Gopher, Secure and Socks (Windows Sockets). It can also be seen that a proxy server can be bypassed by specifying a number of IP addresses (or DNS).

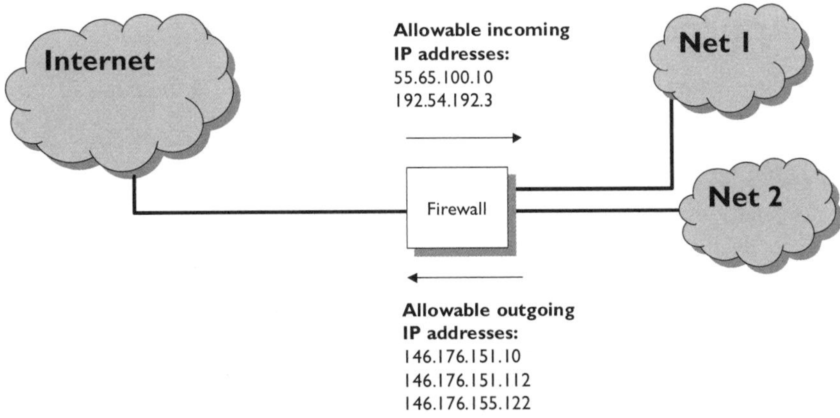

Figure 14.2 Packet filter firewalls

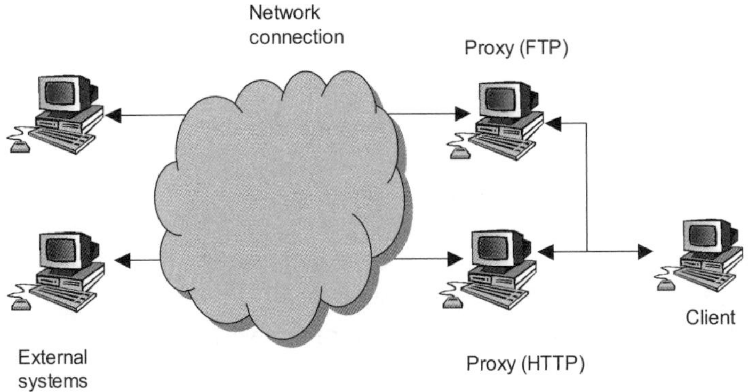

Figure 14.3 Application-level firewall

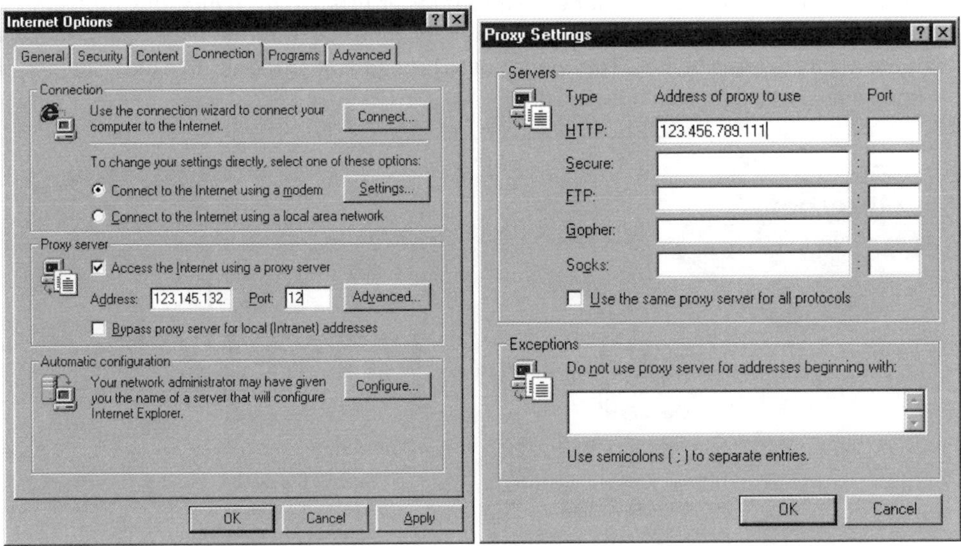

Figure 14.4 Internet options showing proxy server selection and Proxy settings

14.3 Application-level gateways

Application-level gateways provide an extra layer of security when connecting an intranet to the Internet. They have three main components:

- A gateway node.
- Two firewalls which connect on either side of the gateway and only transmit packets which are destined for or to the gateway.

Figure 14.5 shows the operation of an application-level gateway. In this case, Firewall A discards anything that is not addressed to the gateway node, and discards anything that is not sent by the gateway node. Firewall B similarly discards anything from the local network that is not addressed to the gateway node, and discards anything that is not sent by the gateway node.

Thus, to transfer files from the local network into the global network, the user must do the following:

- Log onto the gateway node.
- Transfer the file onto the gateway.
- Transfer the file from the gateway onto the global network.

To copy a file from the network, an external user must:

- Log onto the gateway node.
- Transfer from the global network onto the gateway.
- Transfer the file from the gateway onto the local network.

A common strategy in organizations is to allow only electronic mail to pass from the Internet to the local network. This specifically disallows file transfer and remote login. Unfortunately, electronic mail can be used to transfer files. To overcome this problem the firewall can be designed specifically to disallow very large electronic mail messages, so it will limit the ability to transfer files. This tends not to be a good method as large files can be split up into small parts, then sent individually.

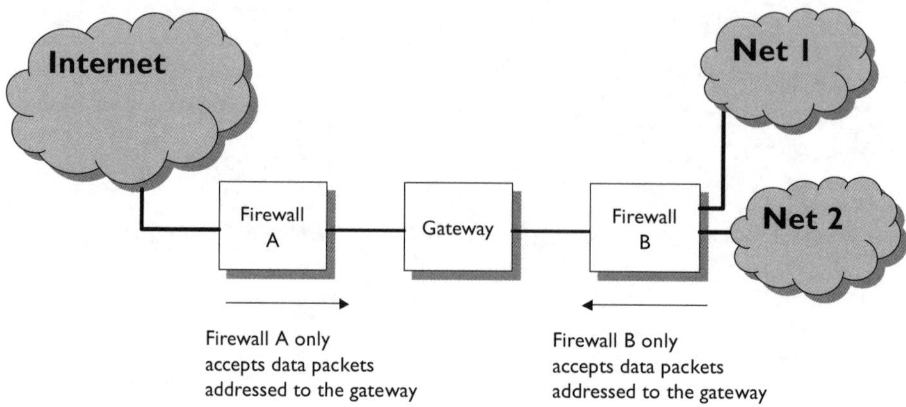

Figure 14.5 Application-level gateway

14.4 Ring-fenced firewalls

Many large organizations have several sites which are spread over a geographically large area. This causes a major problem for security, as the different sites would have to be administered separately. Any small breaches on a single site could cause the whole organizational network to become threatened. One solution is to centralize the gateway into and out of the organization network. An example is given in Figure 14.6 where the three sites each have a firewall which protects security breaches between each of the sites. These then connect to a common router, which then connects to a strong firewall. At the gateway to each of the sites and at the gateway to the entire organization network, there is an audit-monitoring computer, which will log all the incoming and outgoing traffic over time. This could monitor incoming and outgoing IP addresses, domain names, transport protocols, and so on. Any security breaches can be easily detected by examining these logs. The audit monitor could also be used against staff if it shows that employees have been acting incorrectly, such as copying files from the organizational network to an external network, or accessing inappropriate WWW sites.

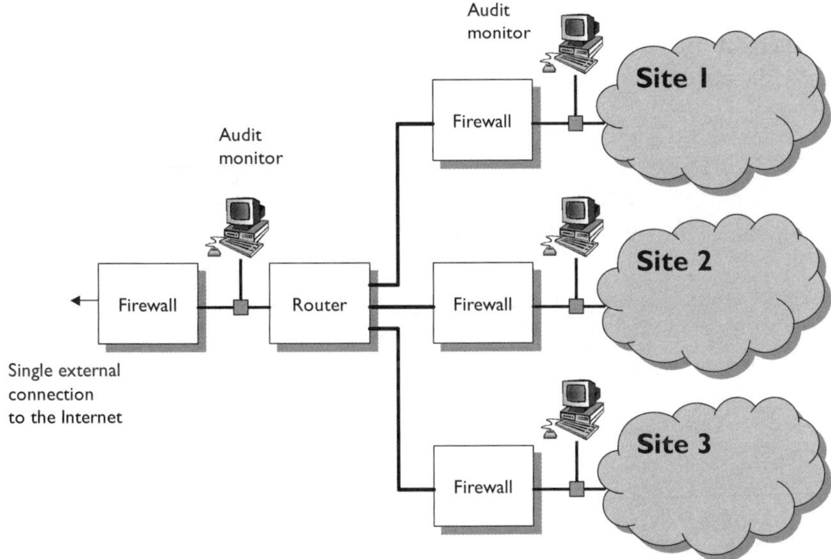

Figure 14.6 Ring-fenced firewall

14.5 Encrypted tunnels

Packet filters and application-level gateways suffer from insecurity, which can allow non-friendly users into the local network. Packet filters can be tricked with fake IP addresses and application-level gateways can be hacked into by determining the password of certain users of the gateway then transferring the files from the network to the firewall, onto the gateway, onto the next firewall and out. The best form of protection for this type of attack is to allow only a limited number of people to transfer files onto the gateway.

The best method of protection is to encrypt the data leaving the network then to decrypt it on the remote site. Only friendly sites will have the required encryption key to receive and send data. This has the extra advantage that the information cannot be easily tapped into. Only the routers which connect to the Internet need to encrypt and decrypt, as illustrated in Figure 14.7.

Typically, remote users connect to a corporation intranet by connecting over a modem which is connected to the corporation intranet, and using a standard Internet connection protocol, such as Point-to-Point Protocol (PPP). This can be expensive in both phone calls or in providing enough modems for all connected users. These costs can be drastically reduced if the user connects to an ISP, as they provide local rate charges. For this a new protocol, called Point-to-Point Tunnelling Protocol (PPTP) has been developed to allow remote users connections to intranets from a remote connection (such as from a modem or ISDN). It operates as follows:

- The data sent to the ISP, using PPTP, is encrypted before it is sent into the Internet.
- The ISP sends the encrypted data (wrapped in an IP packet) to the intranet.
- Data is passed through the firewall, which has the software and hardware to process PPTP packets.
- Next, the user logs in using Password Authentication Protocol (PAP) or Challenge Handshake Authentication (CHAP).
- Finally, the intranet server reads the IP packet and decrypts the data.

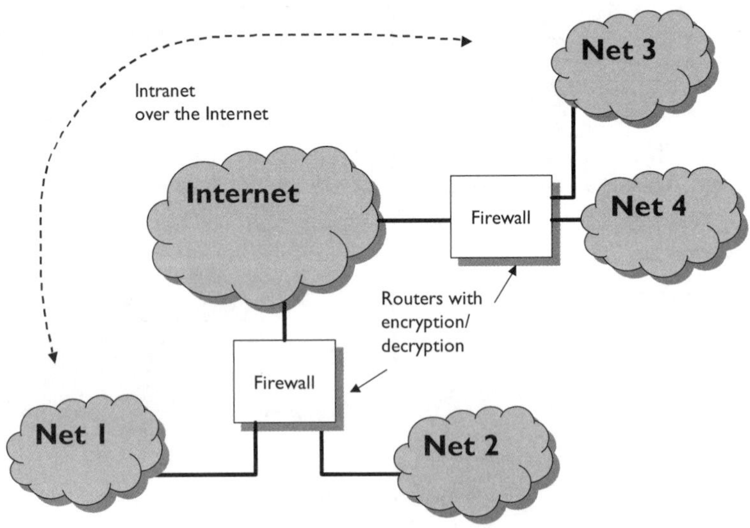

Figure 14.7 Encryption tunnels

14.6 Filtering routers

Filtering routers run software which allows many different parameters of the incoming and outgoing packets to be examined, as illustrated in Figure 14.8, such as:

- **Source IP address.** The router will have a table of acceptable source IP addresses. This will limit the access to the external network as only authorized users will be granted IP addresses. This unfortunately is prone to IP spoofing, where a local user can steal an authorized IP address. Typically, it is done by determining the IP address of a computer and waiting until there is no-one using that computer, then using the unused IP address. Several users have been accused of accessing unauthorized material because other users have used their IP address. A login system which monitors IP addresses and the files that they are accessing over the Internet cannot be used as evidence against the user, as it is easy to steal IP addresses.
- **Destination IP address.** The router will have a table of acceptable outgoing destination IP addresses, addresses which are not in the table are blocked. Typically, this will be used to limit the range of destination addresses to the connected organizational intranet, or to block certain addresses (such as pornography sites).
- **Protocol.** The router holds a table of acceptable protocols, such as TCP and/or UDP.

Integration generations

1st 1 bit per module
2nd 1 register per module
3rd Register-on-a-chip
4th Processor-on-a-chip
5th System-on-a-chip

- **Source port.** The router will have a table of acceptable TCP ports. For example, electronic mail (SMTP) on port 25 could be acceptable, but remote login on port 543 will be blocked.
- **Destination port.** The router will have a table of acceptable TCP ports. For example, FTP on port 21 could be acceptable, but TELNET connections on port 23 will be blocked.
- **Rules.** Other rules can be added to the system which define a mixture of the above. For example, a range of IP addresses can be allowed to transfer on a certain port, but another range can be blocked for this transfer.

Filter routers are either tightly bound when they are installed and then relaxed, or are relaxed and then bound. The type depends on the type of organization. For example, a financial institution will have a very strict router which will allow very little traffic, apart from the authorized traffic. The router can be opened up when the systems have been proved to be secure (they can also be closed quickly when problems occur).

An open organization, such as an education institution will typically have an open system, where users are allowed to access any location on any port, and external users are allowed any access to the internal network. This can then be closed slowly when internal or external users breach the security or access unauthorized information. For example, if a student is accessing a pornographic site consistently then the IP address for that site could be blocked (this method is basically closing the door after the horse has bolted).

To most users the filtering router is an excellent method of limited traffic access, but to the determined hacker it can be easily breached, as the hacker can fake both IP addresses and also port addresses. It is extremely easy for a hacker to write their own TCP/IP driver software to address whichever IP address, and port numbers that they want.

'A standalone computer is about promising as a standalone phone.'

- AT&T Vice President.

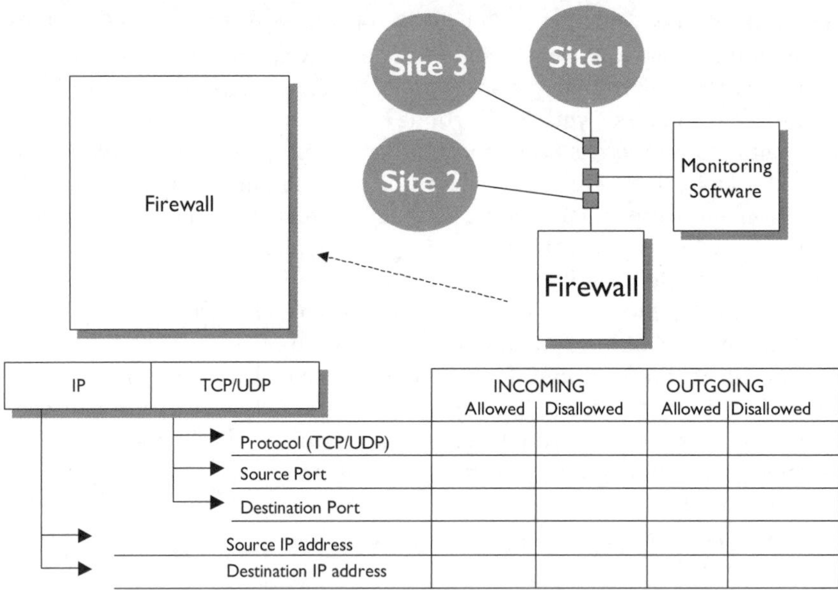

Figure 14.8 Filtering router

14.7 Security

Security involves protecting the system hardware and software from both internal attack and from external attack (hackers). An internal attack normally involves uneducated users causing damage, such as deleting important files, crashing systems. Another attack can come from internal fraud, where employees may intentionally attack a system for their own gain, or through some dislike for something within the organization. There are many cases of users who have grudges against other users, causing damage to systems, by misconfiguring systems. This effect can be minimized if the system manager properly protects the system. Typical actions are to limit the files that certain users can access and also the actions they can perform on the system.

Most system managers have seen the following:

- Users sending a file of the wrong format to the system printer (such as sending a binary file). Another typical one is where there is a problem on a networked printer (such as lack of paper), but the user keeps re-sending the same print job.
- Users deleting the contents of sub-directories, or moving files from one place to another (typically, these days, with the dragging of a mouse cursor). Regular backups can reduce this problem.
- Users deleting important system files (in a PC, these are normally AUTOEXEC.BAT and CONFIG.SYS). This can be overcome by the system administrator protecting important system files, such as making them read-only or hidden.
- Users telling other people their user passwords or not changing a password from the initial default one. This can be overcome by the system administrator forcing the user to change their password at given time periods.

Security takes many forms, such as:

Top financial losses due to security breaches

1. Theft of equipment.
2. Financial fraud.
3. Viruses.
4. Insider net abuse.
5. Sabotage.
6. Unauthorized insider access.
7. Laptop theft.
8. Denial of service.
9. Active wiretapping.
10. Telecoms eavesdropping.

2000, CSI/FBI Computer Crime and Security Survey.

- **Data protection.** This is typically where sensitive or commercially important information is kept. It might include information databases, design files or source code files. One method of reducing this risk is to encrypt important files with a password, and another is to encrypt data with a secret electronic key (files are encrypted with a commonly known public key, and decrypted with a secret key, which is only known by user who has the rights to access the files).
- **Software protection.** This involves protecting all the software packages from damage or from being misconfigured. A misconfigured software package can cause as much damage as a physical attack on a system, because it can take a long time to find the problem.
- **Physical system protection.** This involves protecting systems from intruders who might physically attack the systems. Normally, important systems are locked in rooms and then within locked rack-mounted cabinets.
- **Transmission protection.** This involves a hacker tampering with a transmission connection. It might involve tapping into a network connection or total disconnection. Tapping can be avoided by many methods, including using optical fibres which are almost impossible to tap into (as it would typically involve sawing through a cable with hundreds of fibre cables, which would each have to be connected back as they were connected initially). Underground cables can avoid total disconnection, or its damage can be reduced by having redundant paths (such as different connections to the Internet).
- **Using an audit log file.** Many secure operating systems, such as Windows NT/2000, have an audit file, which is a text file that the system maintains and updates daily. This is a text file that can record all of the actions of a specific user, and is regularly updated. It can include the dates and times that a user logs into the system, the files that were accessed, the programs that were run, the networked resources that were used, and so on. By examining this file the system administrator can detect malicious attacks on the system, whether it is by internal or external users.

14.7.1 Hacking methods

The best form of protection is to disallow hackers into the network in the first place. Organizational networks are hacked for a number of reasons and in a number of ways. The most common methods are:

- **IP spoofing attacks.** This is where the hacker steals an authorized IP address, as illustrated in Figure 14.9. Typically, it is done by determining the IP address of a computer and waiting until there is no-one using that computer, then using the unused IP address. Several users have been accused of accessing unauthorized material because other users have used their IP address. A login system which monitors IP addresses and the files that they are accessing over the Internet cannot be used as evidence against the user, as it is easy to steal IP addresses.

- **Packet-sniffing.** This is where the hacker listens to TCP/IP packets which come out of the network and steals the information in them. Typical information includes user logins, e-mail messages, credit card number, and so on. This method is typically used to steal an IP address, before an IP spoofing attack. Figure 14.10 shows an example where a hacker listens to a conversation between a server and a client. Most TELNET and FTP programs actually transmit the user name and password as text values; these can be easily viewed by a hacker, as illustrated in Figure 14.11.

> **Fragility of the computer industry**
>
> The fragility of the computer industry was shown in 1993 when a fire at the Sumitomo Chemical Company plant in Japan caused the price of memory to rocket, as the plant supplied over 60% of the world's supply of cresol, which was used in memory chip casings.

- **Passwords attacks.** This is a common weak-point in any system, and hackers will generally either find a user with an easy password (especially users which have the same password as their login name) or will use a special program which cycles through a range of passwords. This type of attack is normally easy to detect. The worst nightmare of this type of attack is when a hacker determines the system administrator password (or a user who has system privileges). This allows the hacker to change system set-ups, delete files, and even change user passwords.
- **Sequence number prediction attacks.** Initially, in a TCP/IP connection, the two computers exchange a start-up packet which contains sequence numbers (Section 12.7.1). These sequence numbers are based on the computer's system clock and then run in a predictable manner, which can be determined by the hacker.
- **Session hi-jacking attacks.** In this method, the hacker taps into a connection between two computers, typically between a client and a server. The hacker then simulates the connection by using its IP address.

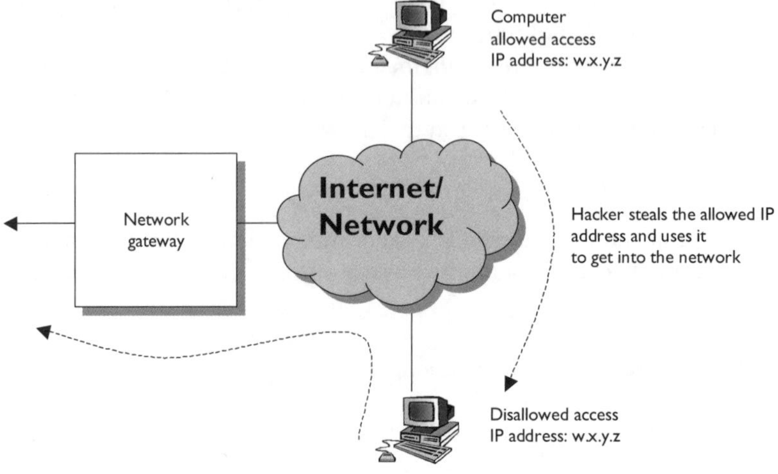

Figure 14.9 IP spoofing

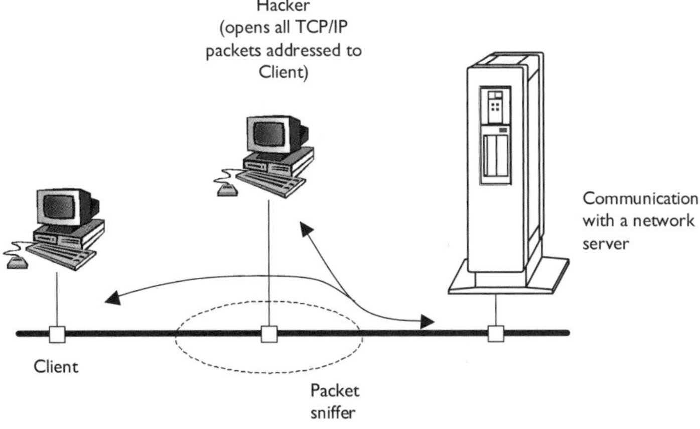

Figure 14.10 Packet sniffing

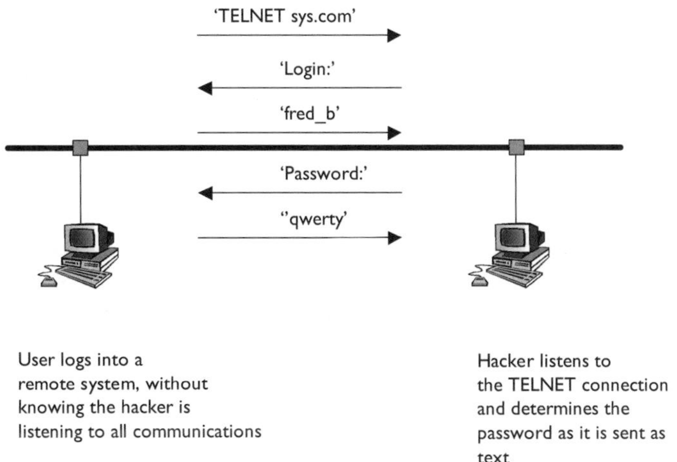

Figure 14.11 Packet sniffing on a TELNET connection

- **Shared library attacks.** Many systems have an area of shared library files. These are called by applications when they are required (for input/output, networking, graphics, and so on). A hacker may replace standard libraries for ones that have been tampered with, which allows the hacker to access system files and to change file privileges. Figure 14.12 illustrates how a hacker might tamper with dynamic libraries (which are called as a program runs), or with static libraries (which are used when compiling a program). This would allow the hacker to possibly do damage to the local computer, send all communications to a remote computer, or even view everything that is viewed on the user screen. The hacker could also introduce viruses and cause unpredictable damage to the computer (such as remotely rebooting it, or crashing it at given times).
- **Technological vulnerability attack.** This normally involves attacking some part of the system (typically the operating system) which allows a hacker to access the system. A typical one is for the user to gain access to a system and then run a program which re-

boots the system or slows it down by running a processor intensive program. This can be overcome in operating systems such as Microsoft Windows and UNIX by granting re-boot rights only to the system administrator.

- **Trust-access attacks.** This allows a hacker to add their system to the list of systems which are allowed to log into the system without a user password. In UNIX this file is the *.rhosts* (trusted hosts) which is contained in the user's home directory. A major problem is when the trusted hosts file is contained in the root directory, as this allows a user to log in as the system administrator.
- **Social engineering attacks.** This type of attack is aimed at users who have little understanding of their computer system. A typical attack is where the hacker sends an e-mail message to a user, asking for their password. Many unknowing users are tricked by this attack. A few examples are illustrated in Figure 14.13. From the initial user login, the hacker can then access the system and further invade the system. In one research study it was found that when telephoned by an unknown person and asked what their password was, 90% of users immediately gave it, without asking any questions.

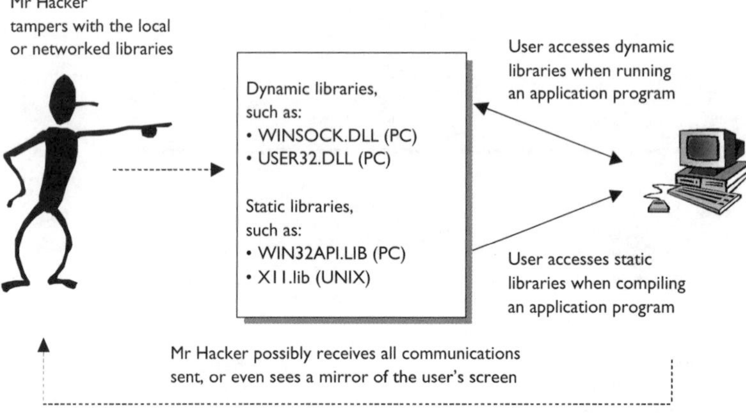

Figure 14.12 Shared library attack

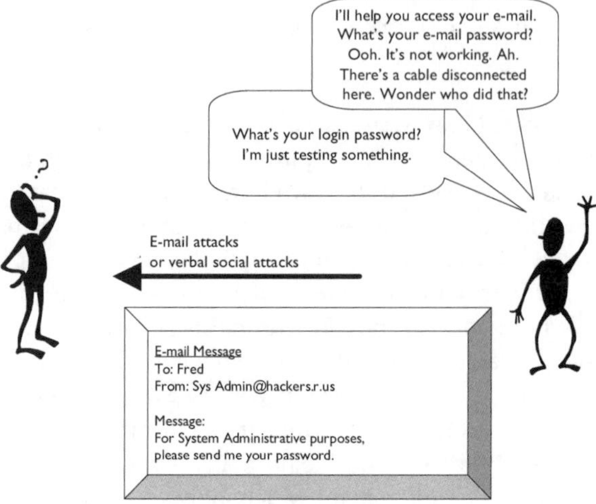

Figure 14.13 Social engineering attack

14.7.2 Security policies

A well-protected system depends mainly on the system manager. It is up to the manager to define security policies which define how users can operate the system. A good set of policies would be:

- **Restrictions on users who can use a given account.** The system administrator needs to define the users who can login on a certain account.
- **Password requirements and prohibitions.** This defines the parameters of the password, such as minimum password size, time between password changes, and so on.
- **Internet access/restrictions.** This limits whether or not a user is allowed access to the Internet.
- **User account deletion.** The system administrator automatically deletes user accounts which are either not in use or users have been moved to another system.
- **Application program rules.** This defines the programs which a user is allowed to run (typically games can be barred for some users).
- **Monitoring consent.** Users should be informed about how the system monitors their activities. It is important, for example, to tell users that their Internet accesses are being monitored. This gives users no excuse when they are found to be accessing restricted sites.

14.7.3 Passwords

Passwords are normally an important part of any secure network. They can be easily hacked with the use of a program which continually tries different passwords within a given range (normally called directory-based attacks). These can be easily overcome by only allowing a user three bad logins before the system locks the user out for a defined time. Novell NetWare and Windows NT/2000 both use this method, but UNIX does not. The system manager, though, can determine if an attack has occurred with the BADLOG file. This file stores a list of all the bad logins for a user and the location of the user.

Passwords are a basic system for providing security on a network, and they are only as secure as the user makes them. Good rules for passwords are:

- Use slightly unusual names, such as *vinegarwine, dancertop* or *helpcuddle.* Do not use names of a wife, husband, child or pet. Many users, especially ones who know the user, can easily guess the user's password.
- Use numbers after the name, such as *vinedrink55* and *applefox32.* This makes the password difficult to crack as users are normally only allowed a few chances to login correctly before they are logged out (and a bad login event written to a bad login file).
- Have several passwords which are changed at regular intervals. This is especially important for system managers. Every so often, these passwords should be changed to new ones.
- Make the password at least six characters long. This stops 'hackers' from watching the movement of the user's fingers when they login, or from running a program which tries every permutation of characters. Every character added multiplies the number of combinations by a great factor (for example, if just the characters from 'a' to 'z' and '0' to '9' are taken then every character added increases the number of combinations by a factor of 36).

- Change some letters for numbers, or special characters. Typically, 'o' becomes a 0 (zero), 'i' becomes 1 (one), 's' becomes 5 (five), spaces become '$', 'b' becomes '6', and so on. So a password of 'silly password' might become '5illy$pa55w0rd' (the user makes a rule for 's' and 'o'). The user must obviously remember the rule that has been used for changing the letters to other characters. This method overcomes the technique of hackers and hacker programs, where combinations of words from a dictionary are hashed to try and make the hashed password.

The two main protocols used are:

- **Password Authentication Protocol** (PAP). This provides for a list of encrypted passwords.
- **Challenge Handshake Authentication Protocol** (CHAP). This is a challenge-response system which requires a list of unencrypted passwords. When a user logs into the system a random key is generated and sent to the user for encrypting the password. The user then uses this key to encrypt the password, and the encrypted password is sent back to the system. If it matches its copy of the encrypted password then it lets the user login. The CHAP system then continues to challenge the user for encrypted data. If the user gets these wrong then the system disconnects the login.

14.7.4 Hardware security

Passwords are a simple method of securing a system. A better method is to use a hardware-restricted system which either bars users from a specific area or even restricts users from login into a system. Typical methods are:

- **Smart cards.** With this method a user can only gain access to the system after they have inserted their personal smart card into the computer and then entered their PIN code.
- **Biometrics.** This is a better method than a smart card where a physical feature of the user is scanned. The scanned parameter requires to be unchanging, such as fingerprints or retina images.

14.7.5 Hacker problems

Once a hacker has entered into a system, there are many methods which can be used to further penetrate into the system, such as:

- **Modifying search paths.** All systems set up a search path which the system looks into to find the required executable. For example, in a UNIX system, a typical search path is `/bin`, `/usr/bin`, and so on. A hacker can change the search paths for a user and then replace standard programs with ones that have been modified. For example, the hacker could replace the e-mail program for one that sends e-mails directly to the hacker or any directory listings could be sent to the hacker's screen.
- **Modifying shared libraries.** As discussed previously.
- **Running processor intensive tasks** which slows the system down; this task will be run in the background and will generally not be seen by the user. The hacker can then further attack the system by adding the processor intensive task to the system start-up file (such as the `rc` file on a UNIX system).
- **Running network intensive tasks** which will slow the network down, and typically slow down all the connected computers. As with the processor intensive task, the networking intensive task can be added to the system start-up file.

- **Infecting the system with a virus or worm.**

Most PCs now have virus scanners which test the memory and files for viruses. This makes viruses easy to detect. A more sinister virus is spread over the Internet, such as the Internet worm which was released in November 1988.

14.7.6 Internet problems

The Internet can cause a great deal of problems as it can allow open access for external users. Typical attacks include:

- **E-mail bombing.** This is where an external user(s) continually send an identical e-mail message to a particular address. E-mail spamming is a variant of this, where the same message is sent to many users, at a single time. This is made worse if the recipient actually responds back to the e-mail spamming message using all the recipients on the address list, as this will also flood the network with unwanted e-mail messages. E-mail bombing without the permission of the user is illegal in many countries and there should always be a message on the e-mail message which identifies the method that can be used to delete a user's name from an e-mail bombing database.
- **E-mail spoofing.** This is where external users setup incorrect e-mail addresses, and then send e-mails to other users. This could either be to cloak the identity of the person, or to try and pretend to be another known person. On a personal level, when pretending to be another person, this can be particularly disturbing, as many users think that the e-mail address in the From: field is always from that person. The cloaking is typically used with e-mail bombing, where a false user name is used to send e-mail bombs.
- **Denial of service** (DOS) attacks. These are severe attaches where external users continually try and access a server, typically a WWW server, an email server or network routers, and try and slow it down to the point that no-one else can get access to it. Unlike many other attacks there is very little that can be done about it, apart from tracing the source, and trying to block the transmissions.

A week of DOS attacks

1. **Yahoo.** 7 Feb 2000. The site was hit by a DOS attack which made it unavailable for up to three hours.
2. **Buy.com, eBay, CNN** and **Amazon.** 8 Feb 2000. eBay reached a 9% available for a few hours; only 5% of users could access the CNN site; Amazon's site was attacked for 30 minutes, where it took up to 5 minutes to access a page.
3. **ZDNet.com** and **Excite.** 9 Feb 2000. The ZDNet site was down for two hours; the Excite site availability dropped to less than 50% for over two hours.

14.8 Viruses

Before the advent of LANs and the Internet, the most common mechanism for spreading a virus was through floppy disks and CD-ROM disks. Anti-virus programs can easily keep up to date with the latest viruses, and modify their databases. This is a relatively slow method of spreading a virus and will take many months, if not years, to spread a virus over a large geographical area. Figure 14.14 illustrates the spread of viruses.

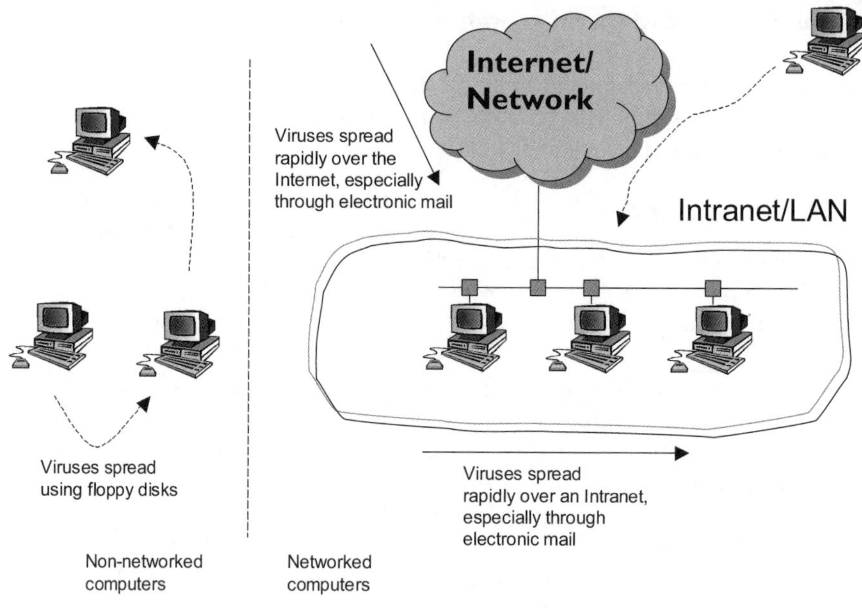
Internet/
Network
Viruses spread
rapidly over the
Internet, especially
through electronic mail
Intranet/LAN
Viruses spread
using floppy disks
Viruses spread
rapidly over an Intranet,
especially through
electronic mail
Non-networked
computers
Networked
computers

Figure 14.14 Spread of viruses

LANs and the Internet have changed all this. A virus can now be transmitted over a LAN in a fraction of a second, and around the world in less than a second. Thus a virus can be created and transmitted around the world before an anti-virus program can even detect that it is available.

A worm is a program which runs on a computer and creates two threads. A thread in a program is a unit of code that can get a time slice from the operating system to run concurrently with other code units. Each process consists of one or more execution threads that identify the code path flow as it is run on the operating system. This enhances the running of an application by improving throughput and responsiveness. With a worm, the first thread searches for a network connection and when it finds a connection it copies itself, over the network, to that computer. Next, the worm makes a copy of itself, and runs it on the system. Thus, a single copy will become two, then four, eight, and so on. This continues until the system, and the other connected systems, will be shutdown. The only way to stop the worm is to shutdown all the affected computers at the same time and then restart them. Figure 14.15 illustrates a worm virus.

14.8.1 Boot sector viruses

The boot sector resides on the first sector of a partition on a hard disk, or the first sector on a floppy disk. On starting, the PC reads from the active partition on the hard disk (identified by C:) or tries to read from the boot sector of the floppy disk. Boot sector viruses replace the boot sector with new code and moves, or deletes the original code.

Non-bootable floppy disks have executable code in their boot sector, which displays the message 'Not bootable disk' when the computer is booted from it. Thus any floppy disk, whether it is bootable or non-bootable, can contain a virus, and can thus infect the PC.

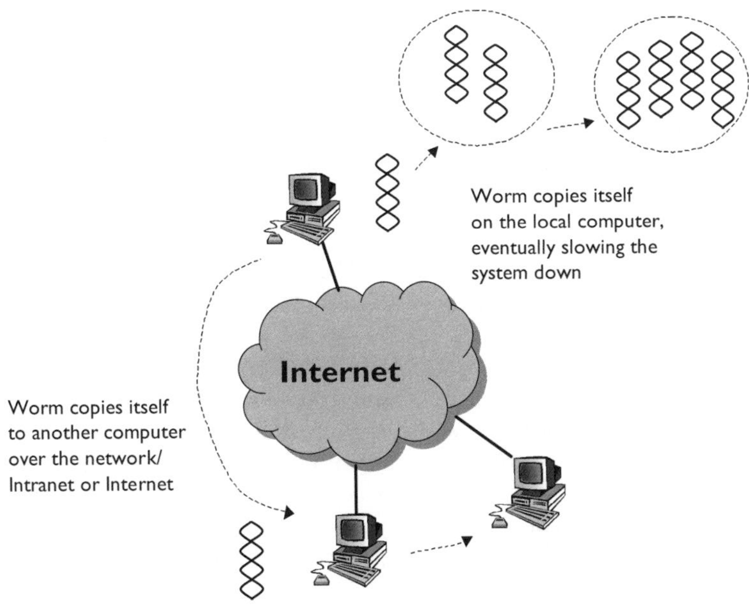
Worm copies itself
on the local computer,
eventually slowing the
system down
Internet
Worm copies itself
to another computer
over the network/
Intranet or Internet

Figure 14.15 Worm viruses

14.8.2 Partition viruses

When starting PCs, the system automatically reads the partition sector and executes the code it finds there. The partition sector (or Master Boot Record) is the first sector on a hard disk and it contains system start-up information, such as:

- Number of sectors in each partition.
- The start of the DOS partition starts.
- Small programs.

> Why was IBM named 'Big Blue'?
>
> Because its products were typically painted blue.

Viruses, which attach themselves to the partition sector, modify the code associated with the partition section. The system must be booted from a clean boot virus to eradicate this type of virus. Partition viruses only attack hard disks, as floppy disks do not have partition sectors. A partition is created with the FDISK program. Hard disks cannot be accessed unless they have a valid partition.

14.8.3 File viruses

File viruses append or insert themselves into/onto executable files, such as .COM and .EXE programs. An indirect-action file virus installs itself into memory when the infected file is run, and infects other files when they are subsequently accessed.

14.8.4 Overwriting viruses

Overwriting viruses overwrite all, or part, of the original program. They are easy to detect as missing files are easily detected.

14.8.5 Macro viruses

One of the most common viruses is the macro virus, which attacks macro or scripting facilities which are available in word processors (such as Microsoft Word), spreadsheets (such as Microsoft Excel), and remote transfer programs. An example virus is the WM/CAP virus which modifies macros within Microsoft Word Version 6.0. When a macro is executed it can cause considerable damage, such as deleting files, corrupting files, and so on.

The greatest increase in macro viruses is the number of viruses which use Microsoft Visual Basic for Applications (VBA) as this integrates with Microsoft Office (although recent releases have guarded against macro viruses). A macro virus in Word 6.0 is spread by:

- The file is either transmitted over e-mail, over a LAN or from floppy disk.
- The infected file is opened and the `normal.dot` main template file is modified so that it contains the modified macros. Any files that are opened or created will now have the modified macros. The WM/CAP macro virus does not do much damage and simply overwrites existing macros.
- VBA is made to be event-driven, so operations, such as File Open or File Close, can have an attached macro. This makes it easy for virus programmers to write new macros.

Newer viruses are typically spread through e-mail clients, where the virus is run as a script, or is run as an e-mail attachment, which then infects other computers by sending itself to addresses in the user's e-mail address book.

Figure 14.16 shows an example of a macro created by Visual Basic programming. The developed macro (`Macro1()`) simply loads a file called AUTHOR.doc, selects all the text, converts the text to bold, and then saves the file as AUTHOR.rtf. It can be seen that this macro is associated with `normal.dot`.

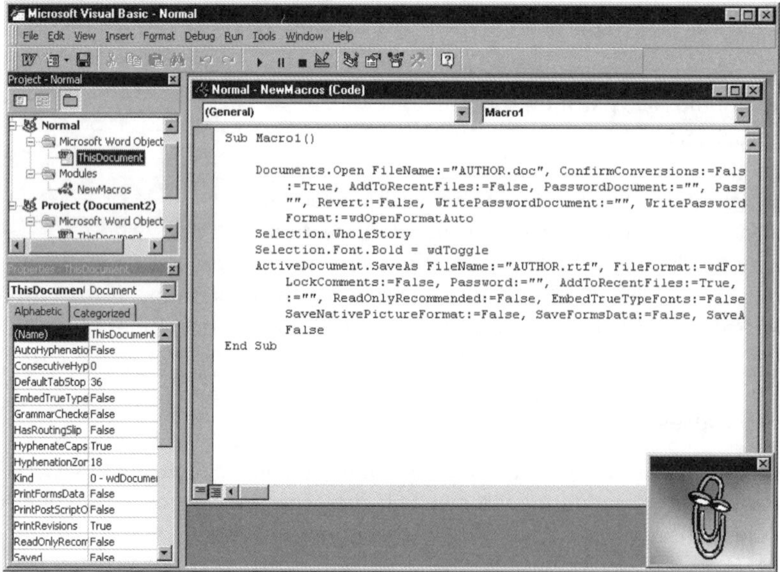

Figure 14.16 Sample macro using VB programming

These types of viruses typically exploit weaknesses in the security on the system. Fortunately, in most cases, these gaps can be plugged with software patches when they are found.

Newer viruses, such as the Code Red worm have caused great panic, but it is typically their modified form that causes the most damage, as the original virus can be patched with new software, but a new version can spread quickly as virus programmers modify the virus code.

14.9 Exercises

The following questions are multiple choice. Please select from a–d.

14.9.1 Which of the following best describes an intranet:
(a) A company-specific network using company-designed tools
(b) A local internet which is isolated from the Internet
(c) A totally incompatible system to the Internet
(d) A faster version of the Internet

14.9.2 The main function of a firewall is:
(a) To disallow unwanted users into the network and allow wanted traffic
(b) To allow users access to the Internet
(c) To allow faster transfer of data between the intranet and the Internet
(d) To convert one type of network to connect to another type

14.9.3 Which of the following best describes a proxy:
(a) It connects to a number of clients and acts on behalf of other clients and sends requests from the clients to a server
(b) A server that acts as if it is the destination server
(c) It passes messages to the client or server without modifying them
(d) It stores responses

14.9.4 Which TCP/IP application would be blocked if port 23 was blocked:
(a) TELNET (b) FTP
(c) WWW (HTTP) (d) Electronic Mail (SMTP)

14.9.5 Which TCP/IP application would be blocked if port 80 was blocked:
(a) TELNET (b) FTP
(c) WWW (HTTP) (d) Electronic Mail (SMTP)

14.9.6 Which is the best method of securing transmitted/received data:
(a) Firewalls (b) Encryption
(c) Proxy servers (d) Leased lines

14.9.7 Assuming an alphabet of 26 letters ('a' to 'z') and a password of 4 letters, how many password permutations are possible:
(a) 26 (b) 104 (26×4)
(c) 456,976 ($26 \times 26 \times 26 \times 26$) (d) 358,800 ($26 \times 25 \times 24 \times 23$)

Additional material and tutorial questions are available at:
`http://www.palgrave.com/studyskills/masterseries/buchanan`

15 Intelligence, agents and the future

15.1 Introduction

It is amazing how computers have changed over the past few years. Just a few years ago, computing basically involved computer systems and the programs which ran on them. Now computing includes multimedia, networking, software engineering, the Internet, digital media, computer hardware, interfacing, WWW development, security, operating systems, and so on. Thus predicting the future is all the more difficult as the subject area continues to expand and evolve. John von Neumann wrote in 1949:

> *'It would appear that we have reached the limits of what it is possible to achieve with computer technology, although one should be careful with such statements, as they tend to sound pretty silly in 5 years.'*

So, it's really easy to predict the future, but not so easy to get it right. Before we cover some of the techniques of the future, it is important to look back at some of the predictions that were made in the past. Each of these sounded sensible at the time, but have turned-out to be disastrously wrong. The best ones are:

> *'Computers in the future may weigh no more than 1.5 tons.'* –Popular Mechanics
> *'But what ... is it good for?'* – Engineer at the Advanced Computing Systems Division of IBM, 1968, commenting on the microchip
> *'This 'telephone' has too many shortcomings to be seriously considered as a means of communication. The device is inherently of no value to us'* – Western Union internal memo, 1876

Most people can see when a technological revolution is occurring and can predict its growth. It is currently happening with electronic commerce, the integration of video and audio over TCP/IP networks, the Internet, and so on. But some people just totally miss it, as with:

> *'I have traveled the length and breadth of this country and talked with the best people, and I can assure you that data processing is a fad that won't last out the year.'* Editor, Prentice Hall, 1957

While the growth and the increasing power of the PC have allowed computers to be accepted into the home, many great people, and large organizations totally missed the growth of the PC. Ken Olsen, at DEC, is a classic example. Before the birth of the PC, he had built a multi-billion dollar company on the back of the minicomputer and was starting to eat into IBM's lucrative mainframe market. When the PC arrived he completely missed the tremendous opportunity that it brought with:

> *'There is no reason anyone would want a computer in their home'*, Ken Olson, president, chairman and founder of Digital Equipment Corp., 1977

and, from the leaders of one of the great microcomputer companies of the past:

> *'I don't think it's that significant.'* Tandy president John Roach, on the IBM PC

15.2 Computers and intelligence

In 1950, Alan Turing declared that one day computers would have the same intelligence as humans, and proved it with a special test. For this, he asked human testers to ask a human and a computer random questions. If the computer gave the correct answer, the testers could not differentiate between the human and the computer.

At present, computers and humans have advantages over each other, but as computers become faster and contain more memory, they can replace humans in many situations. In Arthur C.Clarke's *2001: A Space Odyssey*, the spacecraft's on-board computer, HAL, played the captain at chess. The computer won and then took over the ship. Thus, if a computer could beat the best human intellect at a game which provides one of the greatest human challenges then computers are certainly capable of taking on the most complex of problems. This become a reality when, on 10th February 1996, Deep Blue, a computer developed by IBM, beat Gary Kasparov at chess in a match in the USA. It was a triumph of Artificial Intelligence (AI) over human intelligence. Gary actually went on to beat Deep Blue by four games to two, but the damage had already been done. It would only be a matter of time before a computer would beat the chess champion, as, on average, computers increase their processing capacity by 50% each year, as well improving their operation and the amount of information they can store. Thus, in a rematch in May 1997, Deeper Blue, the big brother of Deep Blue, beat Gary by 3½ to 2½. The best computer had finally beaten the best human brain. In reality, it was unfair challenge. Computers have a massive number of openings programmed into it, and can search through an almost infinite amount of situations. Kasparov knew the only way to beat the computer was to get it away from its opening encyclopedia as quickly as possible, he thus made moves which would be perceived as bad when playing against another human. An annoying feature of playing against a computer is that it never makes mistakes, as humans do. Computers also process data faster than the human brain and can search billions of different options to find the best.

Claude Shannon, in 1949, listed the levels in which computers could operate, each with a higher level of intellectual operation. Figure 15.1 outlines these. Figure 15.2 then outlines some of the main characteristics between computers and humans. It can be seen that humans have two great advantages over computers. These are:

> An excellent comment from Chris Mason at Microsoft is:
>
> 'Since human beings themselves are not fully debugged yet, there will be always be bugs in the code no matter what you do.'

- **Learning**. Humans adapt to changing situations, and generally quickly learn tasks. Unfortunately, once these tasks have been learnt, they often lead to boredom if they are repeated repetitively.
- **Strategy**. Humans are excellent at taking complex tasks and splitting them into smaller, less complex, tasks. Then, knowing the outcome, they can implement these in the required way, but can make changes depending on conditions.
- **Enterprise**. Computers, as they are programmed at the present, are an excellent business tool. They generally allow better decision making, but, at present, they cannot initiate new events.
- **Creativity**. As with enterprise, humans are generally more creative than computers. This will change over the coming years as computers are programmed with the aid of psychologists, musicians and artists, and will contain elements which are pleasing to the human senses.

Level	Current status
8. **Machines capable of logical deduction**	As yet, there are few practical applications in this area.
7. **Machines capable of orchestrating a melody.**	As yet computers cannot properly create music, which is pleasing to the human ear.
6. **Machines for making strategic decisions in simplifying military operations.**	Computers are beginning to make strategic decisions, but these are still checked by humans.
5. **Machines capable of translating from one language to another.**	Computers now act as translator for one language to another.
4. Machines for performing symbolic (non-numeric) mathematical operations.	Computers generally operate on data which is non-numeric, such as database applications or image processing.
3. Machines which will handle the routing of telephone calls based on individual circumstances rather than fixed patterns.	Switching exchanges have been available for some time, which route calls depending on the called number.
2. Machines for designing relay and switching circuits.	Digital logic design software packages have also been available for some time.
1. Machines for designing filters, equalizers, and so on.	CAD computers have been available for some time to design electrical and electronic circuits. These tend to be based on mathematical calculations.

Figure 15.1 Levels of intelligence

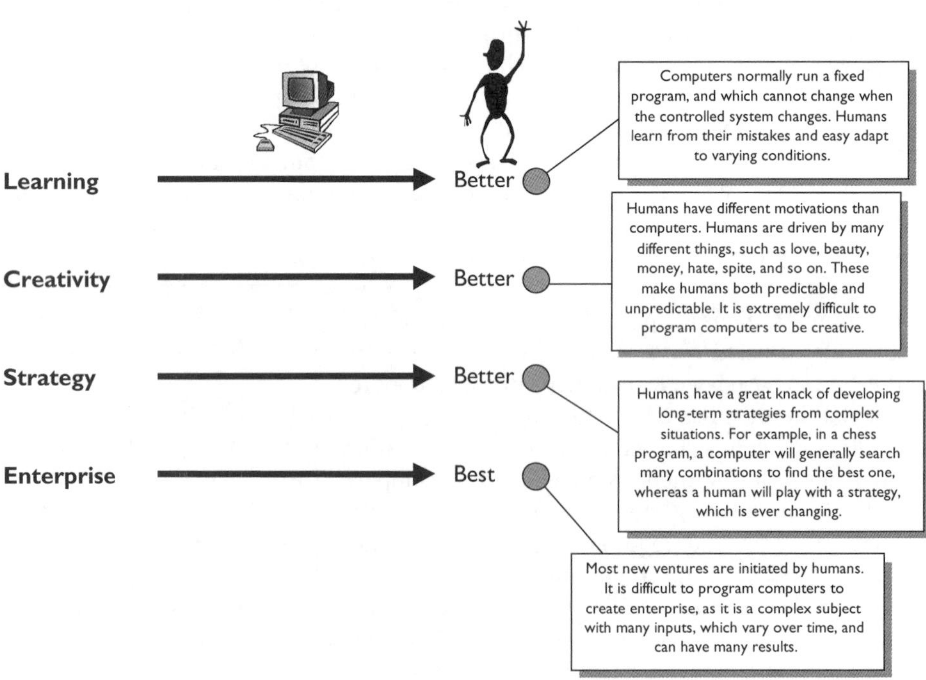

Figure 15.2 Computers v. humans

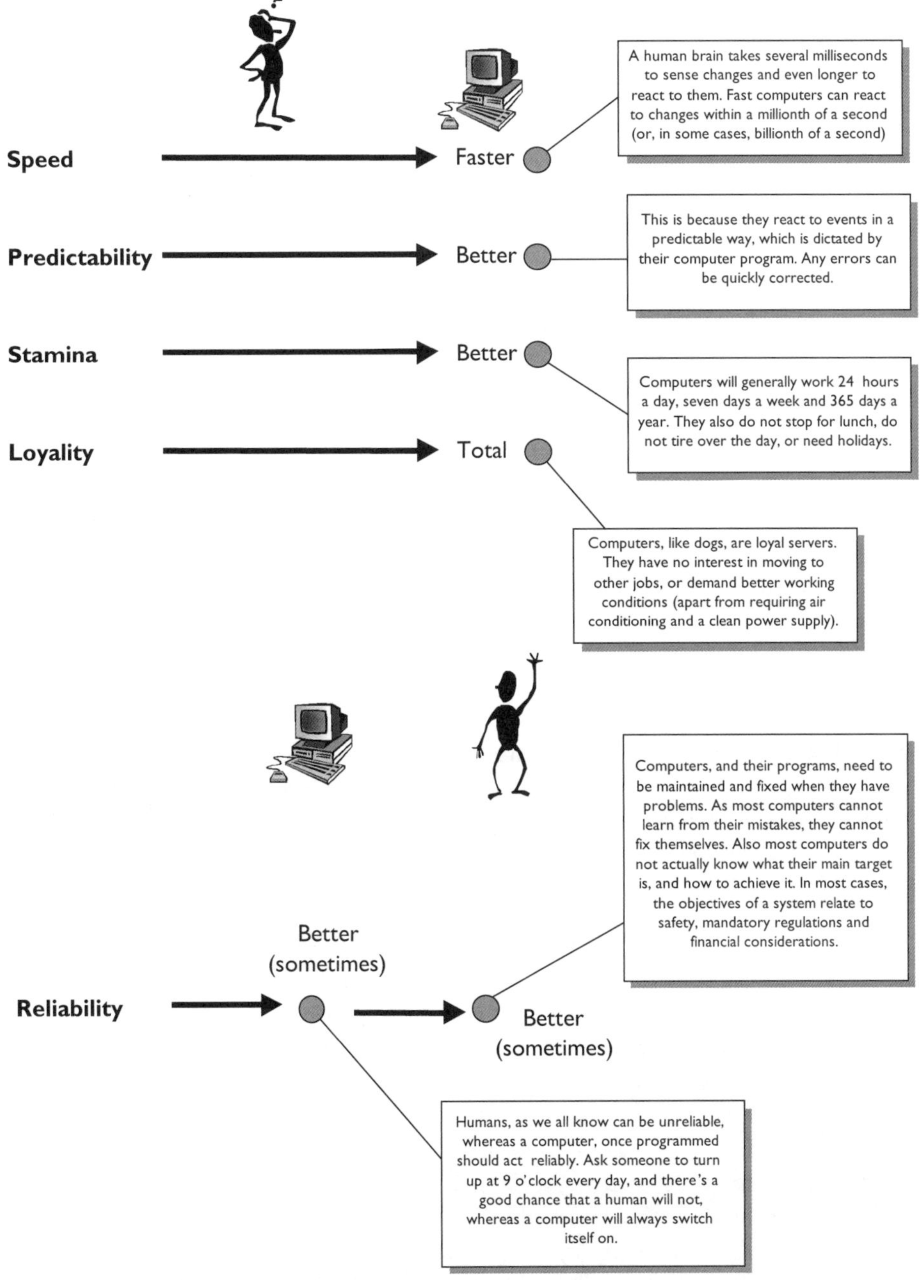

Speed
Faster
A human brain takes several milliseconds to sense changes and even longer to react to them. Fast computers can react to changes within a millionth of a second (or, in some cases, billionth of a second)
Predictability
Better
This is because they react to events in a predictable way, which is dictated by their computer program. Any errors can be quickly corrected.
Stamina
Better
Computers will generally work 24 hours a day, seven days a week and 365 days a year. They also do not stop for lunch, do not tire over the day, or need holidays.
Loyality
Total
Computers, like dogs, are loyal servers. They have no interest in moving to other jobs, or demand better working conditions (apart from requiring air conditioning and a clean power supply).
Computers, and their programs, need to be maintained and fixed when they have problems. As most computers cannot learn from their mistakes, they cannot fix themselves. Also most computers do not actually know what their main target is, and how to achieve it. In most cases, the objectives of a system relate to safety, mandatory regulations and financial considerations.
Better (sometimes)
Reliability
Better (sometimes)
Humans, as we all know can be unreliable, whereas a computer, once programmed should act reliably. Ask someone to turn up at 9 o'clock every day, and there's a good chance that a human will not, whereas a computer will always switch itself on.

Figure 15.2 continued

The key to improved strategy, increased enterprise and increased creativity is: LEARNING. If computers could learn, especially from their mistakes, they could outperform humans in most tasks. The key to learning is the neural network computer, which involves a computer thinking in the same way as a human does. Neural networks are based on the study of neural processing in the brain. Each of the processing elements with a neural network is similar to the neurons in a human brain, and hence, they are referred to as neuronmines, or artificial neurons, often known simply as neurons, as illustrated in Figure 15.3.

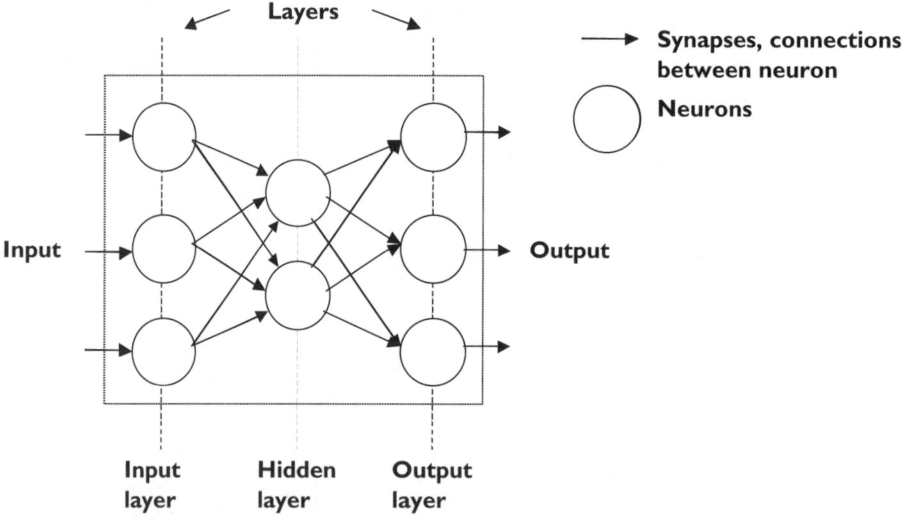

Figure 15.3 Neural network

At present, computers are very good at processing and transmitting data in a reliable and fast way. In terms of their architecture, they bare very little resemblance to the human brain, which is made up of 100,0000 million neurons (nerve cells) and is linked by over 100,000 billion synapses (neuron contacts). There is an almost unlimited amount of combinations of links possible in the brain (as illustrated in Figure 15.4).

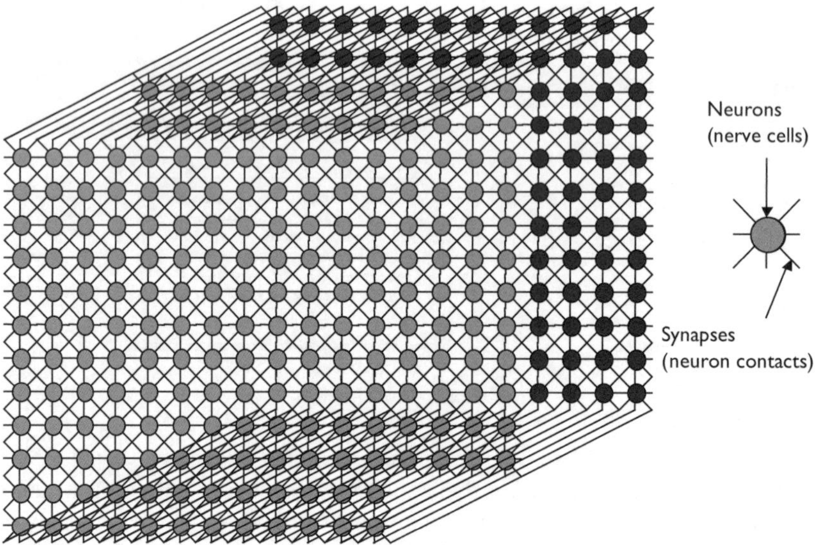

Figure 15.4 Neural network structure

15.3 Components of intelligence

There are seven main components of human intelligence, which, if computers are to match humans, they must implement:

- **Spatial**. This is basically the ability to differentiate between two- and three-dimensional objects. Computers, even running power image processing software, often have difficulty in differentiating between a two-dimensional object and a three-dimensional object. Humans find this easy, and are only tricked by optical illusions, where a two-dimensional object is actually a three-dimensional object, and so on. The objects on the right-hand side are a mixture of two-dimensional and three-dimensional objects. Humans can quickly determine from the simple sketches that the top two objects are three-dimensional objects, which have been drawn as a two-dimensional object, and the lower one is either a two-dimensional object, or that it is a three-dimensional object that has been drawn from above. A computer would not be able to make these observations, as it would not understand how these sketches relate to real-life objects, and that they were actually three-dimensional objects.
- **Perception**. This is the skill of identifying simple shapes from complex ones. For example, humans can quickly look at a picture and determine the repeated sequences, shapes, and so on. For example, look at the picture on the right-hand side, and determine how many triangles that it contains. It is relatively easy for a human to determine this, as they have great perception skills. This is because the human brain can easily find simple shapes from complex ones. Imagine writing a computer program which would determine all of the triangles in an object, then modifying it so it finds other shapes, such as squares, hexagons, and so on. *How many triangles are there in the picture?*

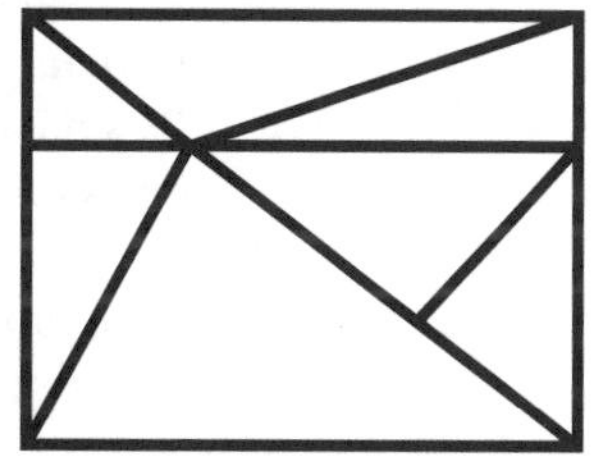

- **Memory**. This is the skill of memorizing and recalling objects which do not have any logical connection. Humans have an amazing capacity for recalling previous objects, typically by linking objects, from one to the next. Computers can implement this with a linked-list approach, but it becomes almost impossible to manage when the number of objects becomes large. For example look at the picture on the right-hand side for 30 seconds. Then, cover it up, wait 1 minute, and then try and name the objects that

were in it. Most humans will remember the picture by simplifying it, such as:
The person would try and visualize the picture by creating an imaginary story of the picture, such as:

- *A black horse jumps over a frog and then is eaten by a furious lion.*
- *A magician comes along on and turns the lion into a rabbit, which he pulls out of his hat.*
- *A shark suddenly jumps out and starts to bite the magician on the head.*
- *'Time for bed', announces the tortoise, and magician falls asleep.*

Imagine trying to get a computer to recognize these objects. The memory required on the computer would be massive, as it would not really be able to simplify the picture the way that a human would. Imagine how difficult it would be to get a computer to identify which object had been taken away, especially if they were in the wrong order, and they have been changed in some way (see picture on the right). Humans can also remember other things, apart from the types of objectives that they are, such as:

- *Was the magician male or female? (How do you tell a computer how to differentiate between the face of a woman and a man's face?).*
- *What did the magician have in his hands? (How do you tell a computer what hands are, and how they hold onto things?)*
- *Was the magician happy or sad? (How do you differentiate between happy and sad?)*

- **Numerical.** Most humans can manipulate numbers in various ways. Humans are by no way as fast as computers, but humans can often simply complex calculations, by approximating, or by eliminating terms which have little effect on the final answer. For example: *What is the approximate area for a room that is 6.9 metres and 9.1 metres?* [Many humans would approximate this to 7 times 9, and say that it is approximately 63 metres squared, whereas a calculator would say 62.79 metres squared]
- **Verbal.** This is the comprehension of language. Many computers now have the processing capability to speak in a near-human form. It is also now possible for even computers to understand accents, but it will be a long time before computers automatically learn verbal language without requiring the user to train them.
- **Lexical.** This is a manipulation of vocabulary. Why is it that Winnie the Pooh is more interesting to read than a soccer match report? It's all down to lexical skill. Currently virtually most of the creative writing in the world has been created by humans, as humans understand how sentences can be made from a collection of words, and in a form which is interesting for someone to read. Computers are very good at spotting spelling mistakes, and even at finding grammatical errors, but they are not so good at actually writing the material in the first place. When was the last time that you read something that was originated by a computer? Have a look at the text in the box on the

right-hand side of this paragraph. One of the sentences is active and interesting, while the other is passive and dull. Writing that is passive becomes boring to read, and most readers lose interest in reading it. *Write two pieces of text: one with an active style and the other with a passive style.*

> *(ACTIVE and INTERESTING)*
> The boy stood on the mountain top and smelt the clean, refreshing air.
>
> *(PASSIVE AND DULL)*
> On the mountain at the top, the boy stood and the air he smelt was clear and refreshing.

- **Reasoning**. This is induction and deduction. Humans can often deduce things when they are not given a complete set of information. For example, what is happening in the picture on the right-hand side? Most humans would reason that the two women had just attended a graduation ceremony, whereas a computer would have little perception about what the picture contained. If someone was asked a few questions, most people would reply with fairly positive answers, as they could reason things from this picture. *Are they male or female?* Female. *Did they pass?* Yes, they have parchments. *Are they pleased?* Yes, they are smiling. *Are they friends?* Yes, they seem to be. *Have they graduated with a degree?* Yes, I think so. They have mortarboards on. *Was it a PhD?* I don't really know, but I would say that it was just a degree, as they don't look old enough to complete a PhD. Anyway they look as if they are in a class together.

  Try getting a computer program to answer these questions, and you would require a whole team of expert psychologists, computer scientists, software engineers, image processing engineers, and so on.

15.4 Agents

The future is likely to see an increase in the use of agents. These are programs which automate user tasks, and are the next natural step in the development of distributed systems. Their great advantage is that they are designed to run over distributed computing systems, whereas traditional utility programs typically run on a peer-to-peer type connection. Figure 15.5 shows some of the applications of agents. They are particularly useful when working remotely from a server (especially when there is no current network connection), and for processing data that can be presented in a convenient form. For example, an agent could monitor the prices of stocks and shares, and then automatically buy and sell shares when a certain level is reached, or when the market behaves in a certain way. Another agent might seek the best price of an airline flight. This could involve the agent contacting server databases for airline prices and making requests for further details. The agent could then make a decision on which of the airline flights would be the best, for a given set of attributes (such as cost of flight, timing of flight, seat positions, airport locations, and so on).

At present, most agents are fixed in their programming, and cannot really change their operation without human input (mainly because many humans do not quite trust computer programs which change their operation and learn from their mistakes). Once artificial intelligence techniques become more reliable, agents will acquire the ability to learn their task, and, especially, learn from their mistakes. For example, a stock market agent could monitor how the market changed over time, and to identify trends. They could also monitor stock market announcements, and determine the elements which trigger stock market movements (such as changes relating to interest rates, inflation rates, and taxes). The agent would thus learn the best time to buy and sell (just as a human would learn to look for trends).

DEAR NET-ED

Question: *I'm very worried. I think that someone has installed an agent on my computer. How can I tell this has happened?*

Agents must communicate. First check to see if your TCP/IP stack has been replaced with a virus TCP/IP stack. This is typically done with a virus-checking program. If this gives the all clear, then you need to examine the TCP ports that your computer is using when it connects to the Internet. A port scanning program or NETSTAT will show all the current port numbers, and their source and destination addresses (the source will obviously just be the local computer). Use this to identify any ports which you are currently not using. Once identified, examine the processes which are currently running, and try and delete them to find out the process which is communicating with the port. The agent will either setup a LISTEN state on a port, and wait for a connection, or make an active connection with a remote server.

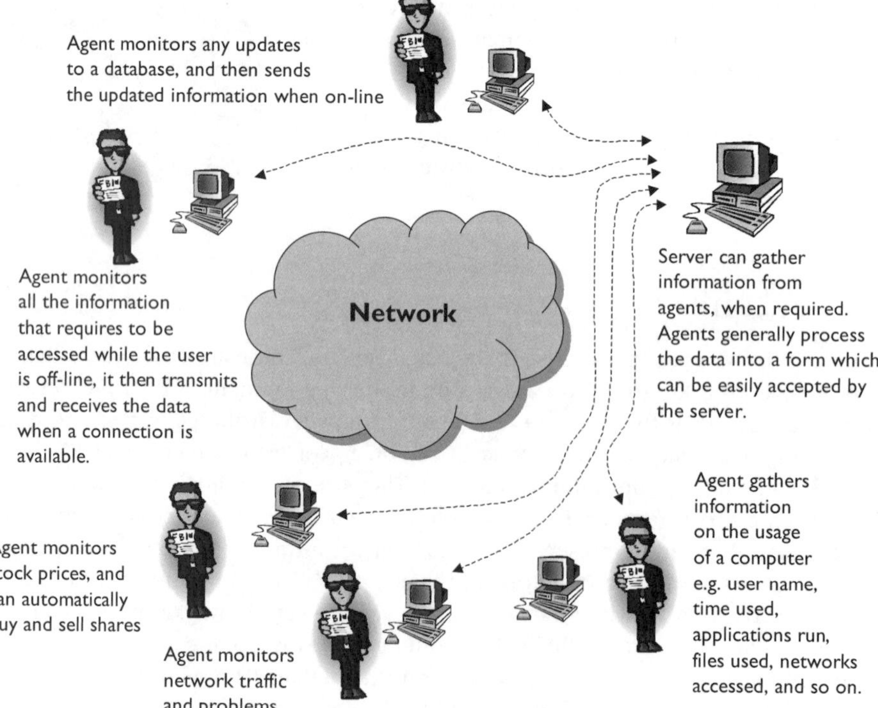
Agent monitors any updates to a database, and then sends the updated information when on-line
Agent monitors all the information that requires to be accessed while the user is off-line, it then transmits and receives the data when a connection is available.
Network
Server can gather information from agents, when required. Agents generally process the data into a form which can be easily accepted by the server.
Agent gathers information on the usage of a computer e.g. user name, time used, applications run, files used, networks accessed, and so on.
Agent monitors stock prices, and can automatically buy and sell shares
Agent monitors network traffic and problems

Figure 15.5 Agent applications

Great gains will come from *intelligent* agents, which use complex artificial intelligence (AI) methods to learn their tasks. Actually defining a task is not easy, as it typically requires a complete outline of the main objectives of the task (which are often difficult to define), and the weighting that each of these should be given. For example an agent could control a small area of industrial plant. The agent would have to be told that safety was the most critical area, and should overrule everything else. After safety was accounted for, the agent must then try to run the plant within statutory requirements (emissions, fuel consumptions, and so on). Once these have been met then the plant should run as optimally as possible, and produce a profit. All these requirements are difficult to define, and often humans do not understand the overall requirements of a system.

A typical usage of agents, in the future, will be for security purposes. One of the most prevalent attacks on a network is when a person logs into a valid user account that is not theirs. This can be difficult to overcome as the non-authorized user uses both the correct login name and correct password, which is then authenticated by the system. Biometrics could obviously be used to overcome this, such as using fingerprinting, or retina images, but these are normally too expensive to implement. It is also difficult to bar remote connections which do not have any biometric security. An improved method is to build up a profile of the user; the agent can then check the current usage against a standard profile for the user. With this, the local agent makes a request for a specific user profile to the server when the user logs in. The server then sends the user profile to the agent. This profile might include information on which application programs that the user would normally run, the types of files the user normally accesses, the type of networked resources the user uses, the times the user normally logs in, and so on, and even specific information that clearly identifies the user, such as the speed at which the user normally types, the amount of usage of the mouse, and so on. The agent can then check the current usage against the user's normal usage. Any differences in behaviour can be reported to the server, which can then be checked by the system administrator. In an extreme case the agent could use data mining, where information on the user is found from sources around the Internet. For example the agent could find out that the user normally shops at a certain high street store, and their normally monthly phone bill.

For security, the agent thus reduces the loading on the server, as the agent monitors the fine detail of the user's behaviour. The agent is also responsible for updating the profile of the user, and will thus resend the updated profile when the user has completed their tasks. This has minimized the communications with the server, as the agent only requires to send/receive data at log-in, when a problem occurs, or with an updated user profile, as user profiles are dynamic, and

DEAR NET-ED

Question: *I don't really see the difference between a user program and an agent. Aren't they the same?*

Agents are more like background processes that an operating system would run, such as for a print server, or a login program. A user program tends to be only run when required. The user should not be able to stop the execution of the agent. An agent, though, is not an operating system process, but, as it possibly accesses a high level of system, it requires a high level of privileged access that normal user programs would not be able to get (such as killing processes or examining audit logs).

Agents also tend to be relatively small in size and have a very fixed goal, rather than being general purpose. They also respond quickly to predetermined events, but their operation is not necessarily scripted. A key feature of all agents is that they do not exist on their own, and require to communicate with other agents or a server. User programs tend to exist on their own, if required.

change over time (but they tend to change slowly, thus sharp changes normally indicate a breach of security).

The requirement for agents increases for many reasons, such as:

- Increased requirement for management information for system administrators.
- Increased requirement for reliability for networked applications.
- Increased requirement for a certain quality of service from the network.
- Increased usage of many different types of computer systems, operating systems, networked operating systems, network technologies, and networking protocols.

Mobile agents are a further enhancement on agent technology. These can move around the network, and can actually migrate themselves so that they communicate with the server, on the server. This can have advantages in certain applications, as it reduces the command overhead of handshaking with the server over the network.

Traditional client-server architectures are typically wasteful in their usage of bandwidth. Agent mobility overcomes this by minimizing bandwidth consumption, as they:

- Support adaptive network load balancing.
- Solve problems caused by intermittent or unreliable network connections.

The main area that agents will bring benefits is where autonomy and mobility are required, such as in network management applications. The aim of mobile agent research is to adopt mobile agent architecture and to provide the framework on which to build a variety of network management tasks, as well as investigating the advantages of mobile agent architecture over client/server architecture. Most software development systems use object-oriented methods, and a mobile agent can be viewed as the next step in the evolution of the object-oriented design, where an agent object is also given a location.

DEAR NET-ED

Question: *As a bit of fun, I'm think of writing an agent which will send me some basic information on the programs that a user is running. How should I go about this?*

DON'T DO IT. Often things on the Internet can start as a bit of fun, but can end up with someone facing legal charges. There is a legal responsibility on the system manager to operate the network in a legal way. If anyone is caught misusing the network, they risk serious charges. There are many cases of users being blamed for anything that goes wrong with a network, such as computers crashing or the network going down, even although the changes they had made to a computer or a network could not have affected it in any way. What would happen if the agent caused the computer to crash and the user lost an important document? What would the financial and humanistic cost be?

Another serious problem is releasing an agent into the wild by mistake. This has happened with many macro viruses which spread from document to document, over networks, or by e-mail.

15.4.1 Agents

Agents are commonly used in other technological areas, such as:

- **Artificial intelligence**. For improving collaborative on-line social environments.
- **Distributed systems**. Enhancements to the client-server architecture.
- **Electronic gophers**. These can monitor the stock market and purchase shares, locate and purchase cheap flights, notify a network administrator of a network fault (and even execute fault rectifying procedures), or monitor a website.

Accurate definitions for agents are:

'An agent is anything that can be viewed as perceiving its environment through sensors and acting upon that environment through effectors.'

'Autonomous agents are computational systems that inhabit some complex dynamic environment, sense and act autonomously in this environment, and by doing so realize a set of goals or tasks for which they are designed.'

'Intelligent agents are software entities that carry out some set of operations on behalf of a user or another program with some degree of independence or autonomy and in so doing, employ some knowledge or representation of the user's goals or desires.'

These definitions, whilst informative, result from specific examples of agents, but are not truly representative as a global definition. The best definition is provided by Franklin and Graesser who have classified agents with the characteristics given in Figure 15.6.

In order to be useful, an agent must respond quickly to changes in the environment, as the information would arrive too late to be acted on. Also, the great benefit of agents is that they act autonomously and do not need to communicate with other agents or with the server for their operation. Thus all agents are autonomous, and should run continuously. Every agent satisfies the first four properties (reactive, autonomous, goal-oriented and temporally continuous), and the others are added as they are required for the application.

Many software packages already use agents, such as Office Assistants in Microsoft Office, which match the properties of agents (that is, reactive, autonomous, goal-oriented and temporally continuous). For example, a spell-checking agent continuously monitors the typing of a user and makes corrections on the fly. Spell and grammar checking agents are complex, and rely on AI for their functionality, as they display some characteristics of intelligence (in fact, in relation to grammar, they are often better than humans). However, these agents do not possess mobility, and are, at present, unable to operate in a distributed environment.

Weak agents

Wooldridge suggests that weak agents are autonomous (where they have control over their own actions and states) and have social interaction (agents interact with each other or humans via an agent-communication language). Agents of this type also react and respond to their environment through sensing and perceiving the changes in the physical world, and also display active knowledge of their goal through their actions.

Strong agents

Strong agents are defined by a similar set of properties to that of weak agents, and are constructed using a cognitive approach which bases the design of the agent on how a human may solve the problem, using knowledge, belief and intention.

There are potential benefits of producing an agent in such a manner (that is to reflect human behaviour) in that the agent may become more attuned to a particular environment or would be able to use its knowledge and intention to provide a 'reasoned' output to a particular set of inputs. There are also pitfalls in using this notion in that the more environment-specific the agent becomes, the more difficult it

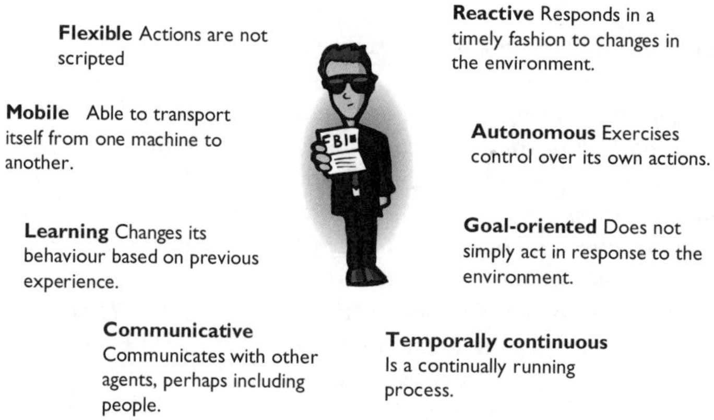

Flexible Actions are not scripted

Reactive Responds in a timely fashion to changes in the environment.

Mobile Able to transport itself from one machine to another.

Autonomous Exercises control over its own actions.

Learning Changes its behaviour based on previous experience.

Goal-oriented Does not simply act in response to the environment.

Communicative Communicates with other agents, perhaps including people.

Temporally continuous Is a continually running process.

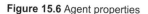

Figure 15.6 Agent properties

In a distributed system, mobility is a key property when considering the implementation of mobile agent architectures against traditional client-server architectures. In a client-server application, the client and the server programs normally exist on different systems, and communicate over the network. When the client requires data or access to resources from the server, the client sends a request to the server. The server then responds with a response to the client. This handshaking operation has a communications overhead, and will use some of the bandwidth of the interconnection. The main difference in mobile agent architecture is the place at which the communication takes place; as, in mobile agent architecture, the client does not talk to the server over the network. It does it at the server. It is the agent which moves itself over the network, than that the data passed between the agent and the server.

Mobile agents offer several advantages over traditional client-server models, such as:

1. Possibly reduce bandwidth requirements, as the handshaking between the client and the server does not occur over the interconnected network. Normally this response is a query or a transaction from the client to the server; this eliminates repetitive request/response handshakes.
2. They allow decisions about the location of code (client against server) to be made at the end of the development cycle when more is known about how the application will perform. This reduces the design risk.
3. They solve the problems created by intermittent or unreliable network connections. Agents can be easily created to work *off-line* and communicate their results when the application is back *on-line*.

Mobile agents have great advantages in network management applications, and solve several problems:

Interface agents

Maes defines interface agents as 'computer programs that employ Artificial Intelligence techniques to provide active assistance to a user with computer-based tasks.'

Maes research utilized existing applications and connected them to a learning interface agent, which gradually built a knowledge base of what the human operator may do in certain situations. It is desirable that an agent should exhibit a learning potential to improve its decision-making methods.

1. **Network bandwidth.** Client-server transactions use some of the available bandwidth, which could be reduced when the agent migrates itself onto the server (or, if it is off-line, when a connection can be made). The agent can also compile the required information from the collected data, and bring this information to the server, rather than the server communicating back and forth with the client.
2. **Protocol communications.** In developing traditional client-server applications, at an early stage the programmer must clearly define the roles, and the intent, of a client and server. As the client and server communicate using a well-structured protocol, there is little scope for modifications or enhancements. By contrast, mobile agent architecture allows more flexibility, as the agent can be allowed to visit several nodes on the network in succession, carrying out some task. The only requirement is that the node must accept the mobile agent and provide it with an operation environment. The communication occurs at a high level, normally with message passing (such as GET and PUT), is clearly defined and the programmer only requires to concentrate on the tasks of the agent (and not the communications mechanism).
3. **Intermittent connections.** Agent technology helps with unreliable network connections. With traditional methods a good reliable connection must be present for the complete time of a conversation. An agent can be dispatched to a node so that it can collect some data, process it, and send the information back to the server when connection becomes active. A good example of this is with a notebook computer which creates a dial-up connection with the server, where the server would send an agent to perform a remote monitoring task, and the results communicated to the server when the notebook next connects back onto the network.
4. **Load balancing.** Large computations can be split up into a number of smaller parallel tasks which can be executed by agents on different hosts. Agents perform the lower-level tasks, such as collecting data and processing it into a form that the server requires. The server is thus not burdened with major processing and is involved with the high-level management of the information.
5. **Real-time notification.** This is where an agent on a remote site can notify a server when events occur on the remote node.
6. **Heterogeneous networks.** Many networks contain a mixture of different operating systems, and computer types. Agents cope with this as they can reside within any type of system, and hide the computer type and operating system from the server.

Mobile agents

Mobile agents are software processes capable of moving around networks such as the Internet, interacting with other hosts, gathering information on behalf of their owner and returning with any information that was requested by the owner. Mobility is another way that agents can be classified, that is static or mobile.

Mobile agents have to stop execution in order to move around a network, and only continue executing when they arrive at a host that is capable of restarting and running the code. The suspension of execution is a serious disadvantage of mobile agents. A static agent on the other hand has the ability to execute other tasks while it is communicating with other static agents. Its execution never has to stop.

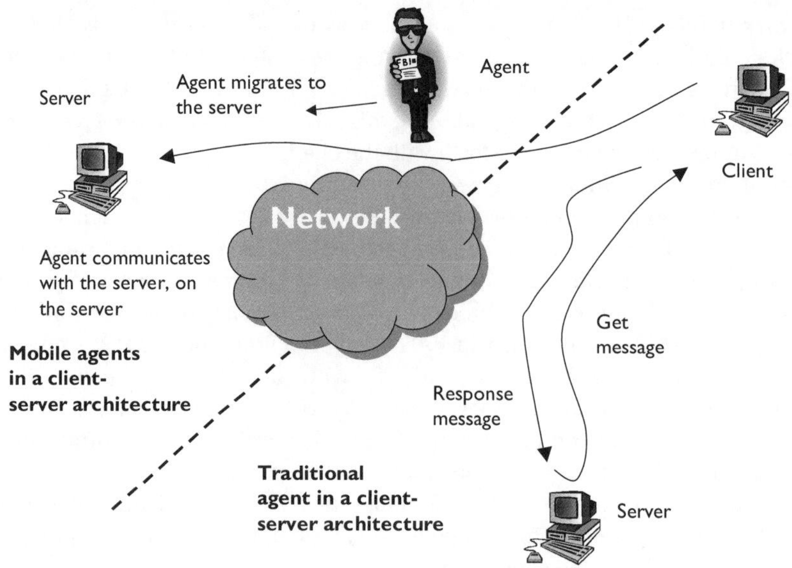

Figure 15.7 Mobile agents

Agent characteristics

Agent characteristics can be further grouped into a number of characteristics:

- **Tactile**. Mobility and persistence.
- **Social**. Communication and collaboration with other agents and/or server.
- **Cognitive**. Adaptation, learning and goal orientation.

> **Co-operative agents**
> A co-operative agent can communicate with, and react to, its environment. An agent's view of its environment would be very narrow due to its limited sensors. Co-operation exists when the actions of an agent achieves not only the agent's own goals, but also the goals of agents other than itself.

With current technology, agents can be easily made tactile and social. Mobility of code and computation towards the location of the data and the resources is not new to the WWW, as this is how Java and applets operate, as these allow portable components to be distributed over a network. This mobile code is dynamically loaded and executed by standalone programs. For an applet this is a WWW browser. Unlike the applet, however:

- An agent travels with its state of execution.
- An agent's characteristic of autonomy allows the agent to decide where it can go and what it will do.
- Agents can receive requests from external sources, follow a predetermined itinerary or make decisions such as to travel across the network to a particular host, all independent of any external influences.

Security, though, is a concern in any network. As more applications use connections over a network, the potential of attack also increases, especially with mobile code. Security is a problem with mobile agents, as agent architecture allows agents to move wherever they like over the network and which resources they can have access to. This can allow viruses to spread through a network, where virus agents pretend to be valid agents, and virus servers communicate with valid agents. A security mechanism must thus be developed to handle both trusted code, which is safe, and untrusted code, which is not safe.

> **Reactive agents**
> These are a special type of agent, which do not possess internal symbolic models of their environment. Instead, they react to a stimulus or input that is governed by some state or event in its environment. This environmental event triggers a reaction or response from the agent.

Every WWW browser implements security policies to keep applets from compromising system security. The following restrictions apply:

- An applet cannot read from or write to files on the executing host.
- An applet cannot make network connections except to the host it came from.
- An applet cannot read certain system properties.
- An applet cannot start any program on the executing host.
- An applet cannot load libraries or define native methods.

Such security measures are very necessary, but inhibiting. When considering mobile agent architecture we have to address some of these concerns whilst hopefully allowing greater flexibility to enable a mobile agent to carry out its work. Java provides a highly customizable security model, which allows us to go some way in achieving this aim. Thus, just as the applet requires a WWW browser in which to execute, so an agent needs a safe environment in which to be hosted. Figure 15.8 illustrates how an agent virus could inhabit a network, either as a virus agent which operates as a valid agent and either sends incorrect information to the server, or sends information to a remote server (the virus maker's server), or even causing damage to the host by deleting or moving files or running network or process intensive tasks. A server virus can also exist which receives valid agent information from valid agents. This information can then be used by the virus maker to view network activity, file usage, file information, and so on. The virus server can also get the valid agents to perform certain tasks (such as viewing or editing files).

To overcome these problems, as a minimum, an agent operating within its host must have:

- A unique identity.
- A means of identifying itself to other agents who are also operating within the host.
- A means of determining what messages other agents accept and send.

The host that is accepting an agent must:

- Allow multiple agents to co-exist and execute simultaneously.
- Allow agents to communicate with each other and with the host.
- Provide a transport mechanism to transfer agents to another host and to accept agents from other hosts.
- Offer a way of 'freezing' an agent's state of execution prior to transfer and conversely

'thawing' it so as to allow its execution to continue after transfer.
- Inhibit agents from directly interfering with each other.

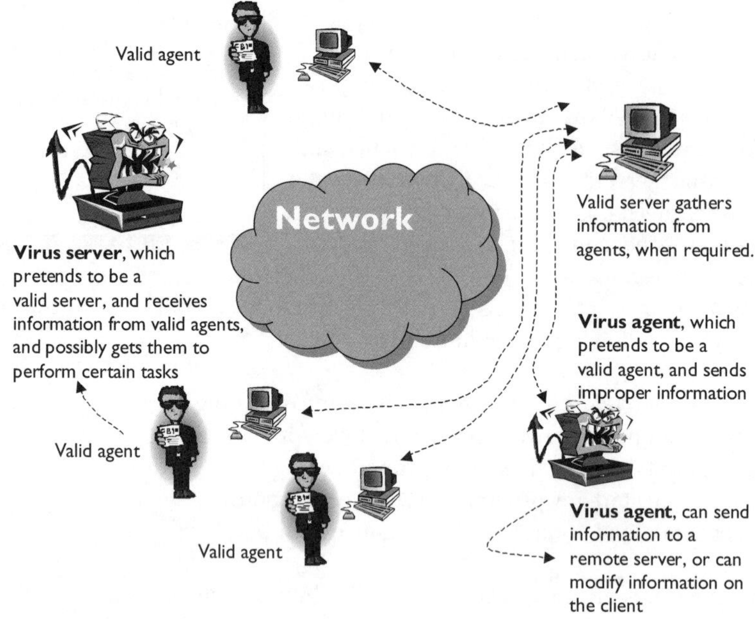

Valid agent
Network
Valid server gathers information from agents, when required.
Virus server, which pretends to be a valid server, and receives information from valid agents, and possibly gets them to perform certain tasks
Virus agent, which pretends to be a valid agent, and sends improper information
Valid agent
Valid agent
Virus agent, can send information to a remote server, or can modify information on the client

Figure 15.8 Virus agents

As well as giving the agent mobility, the agent must also be given a workplace (a context), where it gets access to only the resources and data that it requires. The context is a stationary object residing on the host computer, and:

- Maintains and runs agents in a uniform execution environment, in a way which secures the host against malicious agent attacks.
- Prevents an untrusted agent from having access to sensitive data or resources, whilst ensuring that a trusted agent has correct rights access to the resources that it requires.

It is relatively easy to create a security model to protect hosts against malicious agents, it is not so easy to protect agents against malicious hosts. If no protection is given against malicious hosts; a host could implant its own tasks into the agent or modify the agent's state. This could lead to the theft of the agent's resources, as a host could upload an agent's class file and state of execution, and then have access to such sensitive information. Thus, the agent's context must have some mechanism where rules can be set stating which privileges an agent has within its context. These privileges are likely to be based on knowledge of the agent's origin.

Agents interact with each other and applications through message passing. Message handling must be able to support both synchronous messages and asynchronous messages. The three types of messages are:

- **Now-type message**. These are synchronous and block the execution until the receiver has completed the handling of the message.

- **Future-type message**. These are asynchronous and do not block the current execution. The sending agent can then either wait for a reply from the recipient or continue processing its task and get a reply later.
- **Multicast**. These are messages which are simultaneously sent to all agents within a context. Only those agents who have subscribed to the message will receive it.

15.4.2 Why Java for mobile agents?

Mobile agents can use one of two fundamental development technologies: *mobile code* or *remote objects.* Java is well suited to these environments as it supports both of these through Object Serialization Remote Method Invocation (RMI).

Java has become the development language of choice for building distributed application components. It offers:

- Modular, dynamic, class-orientated compilation units.
- Portability and mobility of compiled code (class files).
- On-demand loading of functionality.
- Built-in support for low-level network programming.
- Fine grained and configurable security control.

The main sections of code required for a Java agent are:

- **Sockets**. In Java, the `java.net` package provides classes for communications and working with networked resources. The socket interface provides access to standard network protocols used for communications between nodes on a network. TCP/IP communications provides for the usage of a socket where applications transmit though a data stream, that may or may not be on the same host. Java supports a simplified object-oriented interface to sockets making their use considerably easier. Reading from and writing to a socket across a network is as easy as reading and writing any standard I/O stream.
- **Threads**. Multitasking involves running several processes at a time. Multitasking programs split into a number of parts (threads) and each of these is run on the multitasking system (multithreading). A program which is running more than one thread at a time is known as a multithreaded program. These threads allow for smoother operation. A server application that could only handle a request from one client would be of limited use. Threads provide a means to allow an application to perform multiple tasks simultaneously. Java makes creating, controlling, and co-coordinating threads relatively simple.
- **RMI**. RMI supports the information interchange between the server and client. It uses a distributed object application, where Java objects may be accessed and their methods called remotely to take advantage of a distributed environment and thus spread a workload over a number of network nodes. It also provides a means in which agents may communicate with each another.
- **Object serialization**. This is a process which enables the reading and writing of objects, and has many uses, such as RMI and object persistence. In developing agent applications it is serialization that can provide *mobility.* An object (an agent) may be serialized (converted to a bit stream), and moved (passed over the socket) to another host where it continues its execution. Thus, the agent is no longer bound to the host, but has the whole network as a resource. Through this process an agent object may be serialized, that is

converted to a stream of bytes, then written to any opened standard output stream (a file, memory, or a socket). Reading from and writing to a socket across a network is as easy as reading and writing any standard I/O stream. Prior to its imminent serialization the agent must be informed so allowing it to write to the heap all information necessary for its reconstruction. The agent complete with its state may then be reconstructed from the stream of bytes at its new location by reversing the process. In adopting this serialization technique, we also encompass persistence, both mobility and persistence being properties in the first of the characteristics required in a mobile agent architecture.

Java thus supports sockets, threads, RMI and object serialization, and is thus the ideal development environment for mobile agents, and any distributed application.

One important area is security. Agent architecture ultimately allows agents to move around a network, where the boundaries of hosts become blurred and access to local resources is available, security becomes a major concern. It could be easy to write agents which could corrupt the data on the systems connected to a network. Java offers a fine-grained and highly configurable security control that provides acceptable levels of security to protect hosts from malicious agents. A more difficult question, which is not so straightforward to address, is that of malicious hosts. As hosts upload an agent's class files and state of execution, it could potentially have access to sensitive information. Agent architecture must then include an environment in which agents can operate (known as a context). Rules can be adopted on what privileges an agent may be granted within this context based on knowledge of its origin. These rules are of considerable interest, and are currently being investigated as part of this research.

The original security model provided by Java (the *sandbox* model) allowed a very restricted environment in which to run untrusted code obtained from the open network. In this, local code is trusted to have full access to vital system resources, whereas downloaded code (an applet or agent) is not trusted and can only access limited resources provided inside the sandbox. A security manager is responsible for this. Security has changed over the versions of Java with:

- **Signed applet**. JDK 1.1 introduced this, where a digitally signed applet is treated like local code, with full access to resources, only if the public key used to verify the signature is trusted. Unsigned applets are still run in the sandbox.
- **Security policy**. JDK 1.2 introduced this in an attempt to integrate all aspects of security into a consistent approach. All code, regardless of whether it is local or remote, can now be subject to a security *policy*. This policy defines the set of *permissions* available for code from various signers or locations and can be configured by a user or a system administrator. Each permission specifies a permitted access to a particular resource, such as read and write access to a specified file or directory or connect access to a given host and port. The runtime system organizes code into individual *domains*, each of which encloses a set of classes whose instances are granted the same set of permissions. This fine-grained level of security will provide a highly customizable security mechanism necessary in a mobile agent architecture.

15.4.3 Agents and security

Computer network security mainly involves preventing intrusion of an unauthorized person onto a computer network. The number of users who connect to networks increases, thus the task of preventing unauthorized access also increases. Intrusion includes any action that attempts to compromise the integrity, confidentiality or availability of a computer system resource (for example, unauthorized distribution of sensitive material over the Internet).

The most commonly used security-enhancement method is a simple user name and a password, which is a simple and robust system, but suffers from many problems. The main drawbacks are:

- Once the password barrier has been breached, there are few means of preventing the system being modified or destroyed.
- Once the security system has been setup (proactively), it is often difficult to anticipate every possible case of abnormal behaviour.

One solution to these problems is to create and maintain historical user profiles of normal usage and compare them with current usage, and monitor the differences. These can be used as most users do not vary the way that they use the system. A historical user profile is built up over a defined time, and includes a mixture of:

- System wide level. For example, the type and mix of jobs being run.
- User level. This relates to specific user profiles, such as applications program types, process durations, user working times, typing speed, types of files accessed, and so on.

It can then be the task of the agent to gather this information, and report back its results to the server.

15.4.4 Monitoring software quality

The quality of many products has increased over the years, especially due to the application of quality assurance practices. In the car industry surveys are completed each year which monitors how reliable a make of car has been. This has had a great effect on car sales. The software industry still produces unreliable software, and it is not uncommon for a computer to crash several times a day. This is typically because it is impossible to test a software program in every possible combination. Thus a solution is to run agents on computers which monitor the operation of a specific software program. Any time that a program crashed the agent could gather details on it and the current environment. This information could then be sent back to the software producers, for them to investigate the crash, and hopefully find a method to make the software more reliable.

Another possible extension of this is for the software industry to be monitored in the same way as the car industry. For this the agent would send information on crashes to an independent organization, who would then compile details on the reliability of various software packages, and publish their results each year. This would have a great effect on software producers, and would give them a great motivation on improving software quality, and not as many do, increase the number of user facilities (Figure 15.9).

15.4.5 Mobile agents and network management

Distributed network management is an important task as networks have grown in their importance and the number of users who depend on them. Network managers face a difficult task in collating information. Agents may be one answer that could help in getting this information.

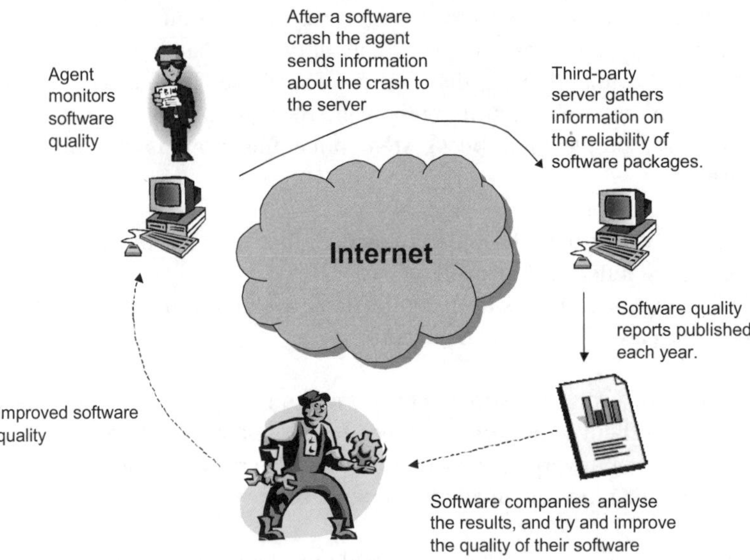
Agent
monitors
software
quality
After a software
crash the agent
sends information
about the crash to
the server
Third-party
server gathers
information on
the reliability of
software packages.
Internet
Software quality
reports published
each year.
Improved software
quality
Software companies analyse
the results, and try and improve
the quality of their software

Figure 15.9 Agent monitoring software quality

Typically networks and information on those networks are managed in a centralized manner, with a client-server-based architecture. With this, a server advertises a set of *services* which provide access to *resources* (such as databases). The executable code that implements these services is hosted locally by the server. The server, itself, executes the service, and thus has the *processor* capability. If the client needs to access a resource which is hosted by the server, it will simply use one or more of the services provided by the server. The client needs some limited 'intelligence' to decide which of the services it should use. The server then holds, in one central location, all of the facilities required: the services, the resources and the processing capability.

With mobile agents, the roles of client and server are less defined, as the agent can migrate to the server directly, taking with it the code that implements the service; thus the resources and services need no longer reside at the same host. This leads to a potentially more flexible and distributed system where computation migrates toward resources. Applications which could have advantages with migrating computation and mobile agents toward resources include:

- **Data backup management**. As networks grow in size and complexity, managing a consistent backup procedure becomes increasingly difficult. Agents could be allowed to roam around the network and check or confirm the backup status for every disk locally.
- **Software deployment**. Normally software deployment on a static network is relatively simple (that is, users do not physically move). Where users are mobile (perhaps use laptops which connect to a network) and only occasionally connect to the network, tracking software upgrades becomes difficult. Agents could be used to inform a user, when they connect to the network, of any recent software upgrades. This makes the task of tracking and informing all network users simpler.
- **Software acceptance trials.** In a trails network, an agent could be used to monitor how often a certain application gets accessed. The data could then be relayed to another

agent responsible for collecting and collating this data. These results could then be communicated to the network manager on a daily, weekly or monthly basis and could form the basis for software acceptance trials.

- **Accessing databases**. Typically data may be spread over a number of databases. An agent may be given an itinerary in which it is instructed to visit a number of database servers to collect information. The agent could then perform computationally intense retrieval tasks. This will not have any problems with network delay (latency) as the data is accessed locally.
- **Network usage**. Where network usage is heavy at certain key times, agents could be used to visit nodes locally and gather information relevant to network use. The agents could return to a common point of origin at a more appropriate time so relieving the network of extra traffic.
- **Intranet web site monitor**. Increasingly organizations use local web sites on their intranets as a means of sharing and distributing information. A monitoring agent could be used which could monitor specific documents for updates. When such an update occurs the agent could inform interested parties.

15.4.6 User agents

The future could see an increase in personal agents, which perform specific task for the user. As Figure 15.10 illustrates, an agent could be programmed by an agent programming station, where generic agents are given tasks by the user, such as searching the best airline ticket, or determining if there are any problems on a route for a journey. It may even be possible to create hi-fi agents who determine the tastes of the person who is listening. This type of approach should make computer programs less complex, as the agent only has a small task to achieve. The trend recently has been towards large, and multifunction programs which typically are unreliable.

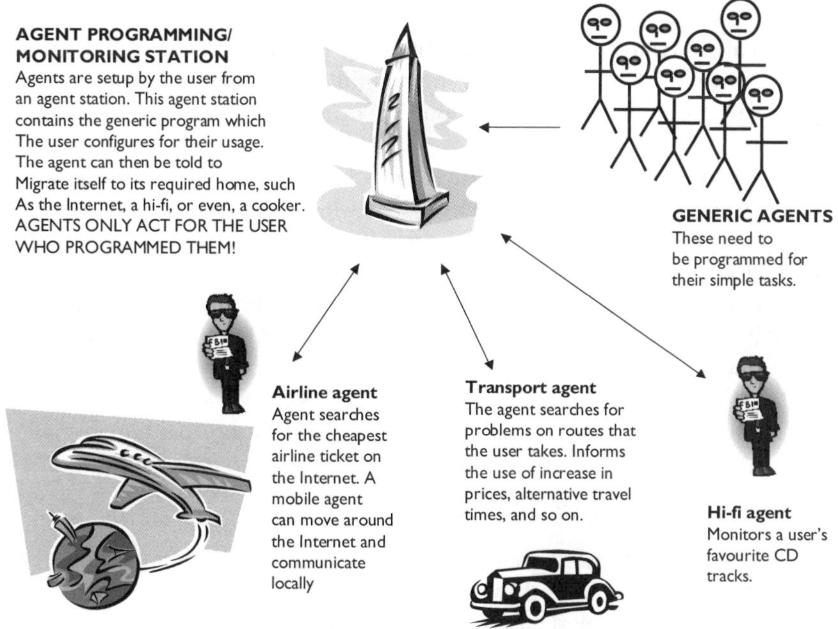

AGENT PROGRAMMING/
MONITORING STATION
Agents are setup by the user from
an agent station. This agent station
contains the generic program which
The user configures for their usage.
The agent can then be told to
Migrate itself to its required home, such
As the Internet, a hi-fi, or even, a cooker.
AGENTS ONLY ACT FOR THE USER
WHO PROGRAMMED THEM!
GENERIC AGENTS
These need to
be programmed for
their simple tasks.
Airline agent
Agent searches
for the cheapest
airline ticket on
the Internet. A
mobile agent
can move around
the Internet and
communicate
locally
Transport agent
The agent searches for
problems on routes that
the user takes. Informs
the use of increase in
prices, alternative travel
times, and so on.
Hi-fi agent
Monitors a user's
favourite CD
tracks.

Figure 15.10 Agent monitoring software quality

15.5 The future

So what areas will be the great growth areas of the future? Here are a few:

- **Electronic commerce**. Many organizations realize that many products, in the future, especially electronic-based one, will be bought over the Internet, using electronic commerce. A key growth to this will be the acceptance of secure standards for the transfer of credit card details. This can only be achieved properly with secure encryption techniques. Another growth area will be in downloading electronic material, such as application software, movies and music files, over the Internet. This will change the way that consumers buy their products, moving from buying hard goods, such as CDs and video cassettes, to purchasing licenses for using electronic material.
- **Audio and video over IP**. The great success of the Internet has been the general acceptance of the TCP/IP protocol. The IP part performs the routing of data around the Internet, while the TCP part allows application programs to communicate, over a network. The IP protocol can be used by other applications, apart from computer connections. One of the great growth areas will be to use the IP protocol to route telephone calls. This will allow users to communicate, worldwide, for the cost of a local rate call (or even, a free call, in some areas of the world).
- **Hand-held computers**. Computers are becoming smaller by the day, and it is now possible to fit a computer onto a single integrated circuit. The major problem has always been the size of the keyboard, but as miniature keyboards have become more robust, and easier to use, they are becoming accepted, especially to store database information. It is also now possible, with camera miniaturization, to integrate video cameras into small hand-held computers. A great increase with their usage is likely to occur with the increasing integration with the Internet, especially with remote communications using wireless connections. New versions of the protocol for these devices will allow for integration of audio and video.
- **Integration of electronic devices into the Internet**. With the growth, and acceptance, of IP routing, there will be an increase in the amount of different devices which connect via IP. Typical devices will be mobile phones, central heating systems, hi-fi equipment, and so on.
- **Public-key encryption and security**. Unfortunately, TCP/IP is a very open protocol. Any user that connects to any part of the network on which data travels, can read any of the TCP/IP data, and can thus read any messages that are sent or received. The best way to stop other users from reading messages that are not intended for them is to encrypt the data. Public-key methods are the best for this, as they allow users to easily publicize their public key, which is used to encrypt the data. The only key which can decrypt the message is the private key, which is not publicized.
- **DVD video**. VHS video has always been rather limited in its content. It has extremely poor sound quality, and does not offer any additional features that are normally available with standard TV transmission. DVD video supports many enhancements to the standard VHS video standard, including:

    - **Enhanced sound quality,** which uses a 5.1 audio channel (four surround sound speakers and an effects speaker).
    - **Enhanced digital picture quality and extra scenes.**
    - **Extra film text information, such as subtitles in different languages.**

- **MP3 audio**. MP-3 allows for many more music tracks to be stored on a given media, for example, a standard music CD can store at least 10 times the number of tracks, if they are stored in MP-3 format. This will also allow music tracks to be downloaded from the Internet, or a computer, onto an MP-3 music player with electronic memory.
- **Distributed processing/storage over the Internet**. As the storage capacity and the speed of the Internet increases, there will be a move to distributed data around the data. Each source can be a mirror of each of the other sources, and synchronize themselves for any updates to any one of the distributed databases. This has the advantage that if one of the sources becomes unavailable, other sources can be used as a backup.
- **Digital TV**. Conventional TV signals waste the available transmission bandwidth. In a digital form, hundreds of digital TV channels can be sent instead of a single analogue TV channel. Over the coming years, analogue transmission will be phased-out, in favour of digital transmission. Digital transmission offers enhanced picture and audio quality, as well as extra information, such as subtitles, interactive controls, and so on.
- **Self-configuring hardware**. Currently computers are typically difficult to setup and install. In the future it is likely that more software will be embedded into system, as embedded systems are typically easier to use, and setup. There is no reason why the operating system and application software could not be integrated into the computer. This would solve many of the problems that users have when setting up their computer. Increasingly it is also easier to add and delete devices from the computer. The key to this is to get rid of legacy devices and interface systems, such as the ISA bus in the PC, and move towards hub-based architectures, such as USB.
- **Database-driven WWW**. In the future more WWW pages will be generated using database data. For example a WWW page would present the current time in your time zone, and greet you with a 'Good Morning', a 'Good Afternoon' or a 'Good Evening'. It could also know the language that you most like to read, or the background colour that you prefer.

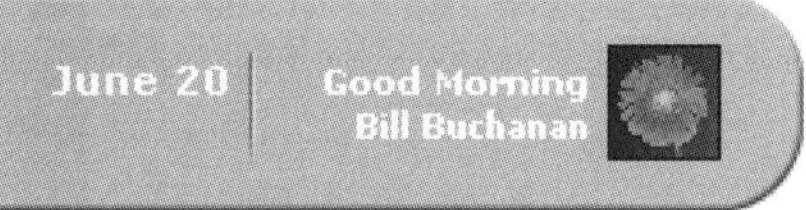

- **Data mining**. There is a great deal of information around the Internet on many subjects and also on users. Data mining allows databases to interrogate other databases to create a better viewpoint on a specific subject, or user. For example there will be a database somewhere in the world that will actually know the language that you speak. Other databases could interrogate this, in order to present you with a form in the correct language.

15.6 Exercises

15.6.1 Which of the following program is termed an agent program:

(a) Word Processor (b) Spreadsheet
(c) Grammar Check, as you type (d) Database

15.6.2 Which of the following is **not** a property of agents:

(a) Passive (b) Flexible
(c) Autonomous (d) Learning

Additional tutorial questions are available at:

`http://www.palgrave.com/studyskills/masterseries/buchanan`

16 Databases and data storage

16.1 Introduction

Databases store information in an easy-to-access format. They have an increasing role in virtually every area of computing. Many WWW pages are now generated from a database, where content is added to the database, and the WWW page reads it to generate the WWW page. This allows for more dynamic content within WWW pages. For example a database could contain a list of recommended WWW links, which were updated every hour. There may be many pages which use these links. Thus a good approach is to design so that the links are generated from the database, which is updated hourly.

We have a great deal of information on us already in databases. For example now it is possible to receive approval for a loan request in a matter of seconds. This is because there are databases around the Internet which contain much of your financial details, such as the number of times you have been late with your payments, your monthly salary, your current loan commitments, and so on. The loan application program thus goes and gathers the information on you and quickly generates a score which relates to your ability to pay back the loan. This type of approach is known as data mining where programs gather data on the user from several different sources. In the future, with data mining, it should be possible to determine many other things about a user, apart from their financial details. For example if a user purchases movie tickets on-line then a data-mining agent might determine the type of movie that the person preferred, and use this information for advertising new movie releases. This may lead to an increasing amount of personalization on WWW pages. For example if a person accessed amazon.com then, if the WWW browser knew the user, they would be greeted with a page which displayed the books that were recommended for that user, based on their interests. At one time the user would have to enter these preferences, but in the future they may be generated automatically. A typical technique, these days, is to store user details on a database, such as their credit card number, bank details, and so on, so that when the user purchases something on-line, these details are automatically entered. This makes shopping on-line easier.

Databases can be organized in a flat format where everything is added as a record in the complete database. For example a college could have a single database that contained staff details (**Lecturer**), then another database which contained all the modules on the courses (**Modules**), and another which had a database which contained the modules on a course (**Programme**). It would be inefficient to create a database for each of these, as the Programme database could use the modules defined in the Modules database. A relational database has the advantage that tables with records can be setup, and then the relationship between them can be defined. Figure 16.1 shows an example of a relational database with tables for Lecturer, Modules and Programme. The window below the main database window shows the relationship between the tables (this will be defined in more detail in the following sections).

The basic elements of a relational database are:

- **Record**. Databases are made up with a number of records which are a collection of data. For example the personal record for an individual could be that they are 42 years old (age), 2.2 metres tall (height), 57 kg heavy (weight) and that they're male (sex). This would constitute a personal record for an individual. A record can also be known as a row in a database.

- **Table.** In relational databases the table is one of the most fundamental elements of the database, and defines a particular category within the database (such as employees or sales stock). Figure 16.2 illustrates a Lecturer Table which is made up of a number of records (in rows), and a number of fields (in columns).
- **Field.** These are specific items of elements within a table. For example, in a table of personal details the fields could be age, height, weight and sex. An instance of these would constitute a record. Fields are represented in a database by a column within a table, as illustrated in Figure 16.2.
- **Item.** An item is the basic element that holds information in a database.

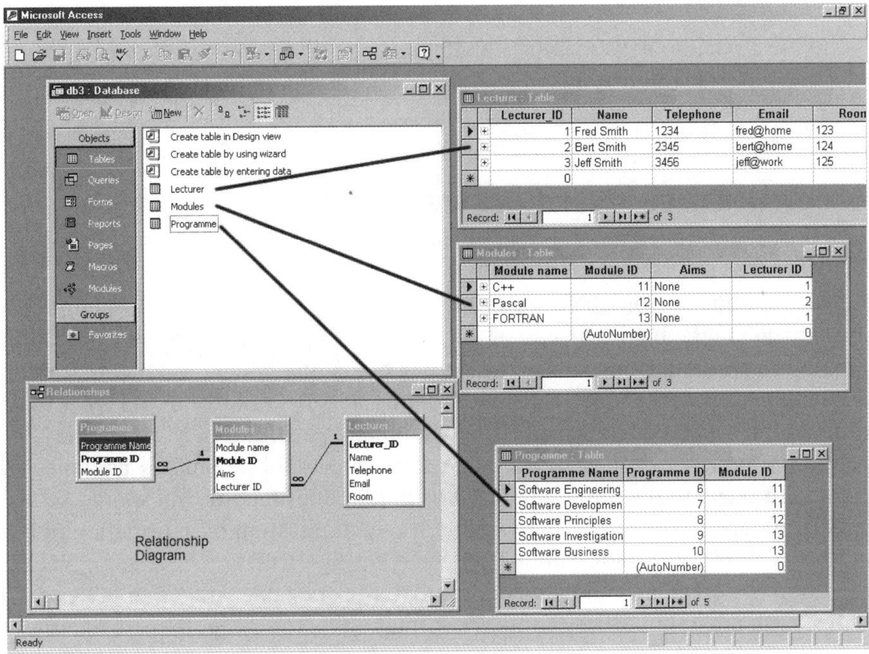

Figure 16.1 Example database

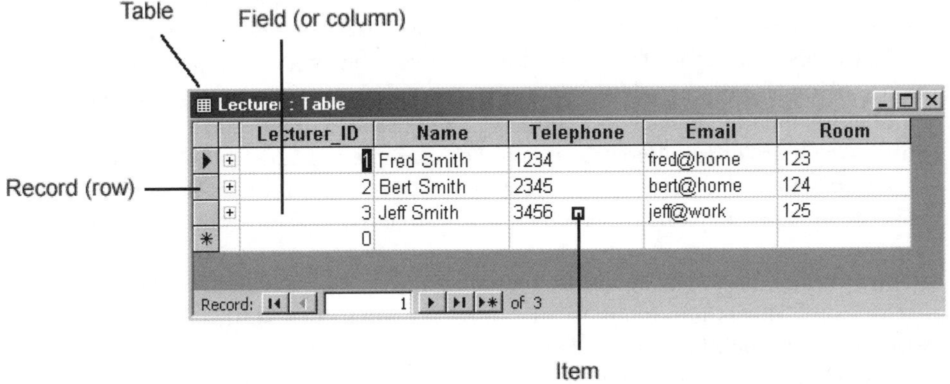

Figure 16.2 Database definitions

Relational databases bring information from different tables and use queries, forms and reports to present the information. These can be defined as follows:

- **Query**. This is a question about the data stored in multiple tables, or a request to perform an action on the data. This can provide the source of data for a form or report. Typically an SQL request is made to the database. Structured query language (SQL) is a language used in querying, updating, and managing relational databases.
- **Form**. This allows for taking actions or for entering, displaying, and editing data in fields.
- **Report**. This produces formatted information for displaying the results of database queries. Examples might be to produce monthly sales figures, or a weekly stock control report.

In order to use a relational database, each table must contain a primary key which uniquely identifies each record stored in the table. For example in Figure 16.2 the Lecturer_ID code is defined as the primary key for the Lecturers table.

16.2 Database creation steps

The steps in designing a database should include:

- **Define the aims**. To be able to produce a well-designed database it is important to properly define the main purpose of the database. If possible gather as much information on the required subject areas which will define the tables, and the information to be stored in each of the tables (the fields). If possible determine the data types of the information to be stored in the fields (such as numeric, text, currency, and so on).
- **Determine tables**. In this step the main subjects should be defined as tables. These should not relate to the information that is required for reports, but should be a structured approach to the data. There should be no duplication of information in a table, and between tables. A table should thus be a flat-file structure. When one piece of information is stored, it should only be stored in the one table, and other tables can refer to this. Each table should only contain information on the things that are required to be stored in that table. For example personal data on an individual would be stored in one table, and their scores for their sporting activities would be stored in another table. This would allow the sports scores to be easily deleted without affecting the personal details.
- **Determine fields**. After each of the tables have been determined, the next task is to define the fields in the table. For example a customer table might have fields for company name (name), company address (address), company city (city), company telephone number (telephone), and so on. If possible store the data in the smallest logical part as this makes it easier to differentiate data. For example the address field could be split into: number of street (street_no), street name (street_name), street area (street_area). This would allow someone to search for just a street name, and ignore the street number.
- **Define primary keys**. This involves identifying the field or fields with unique values in each record. This is important as they provide connections between separate tables, which uniquely identifies each individual record in the table.
- **Define relationships between tables**. Once the tables and primary keys have been defined, it is then necessary to define how the tables are inter-related, in order to build the data in a meaningful way.

- **Enter data and create database objects.** This involves actually entering the data in the records, and creating the objects which might be required (such as queries, forms, reports, and so on).

Of course at every stage the design should be refined, so that errors can be minimized. If possible prototypes of part of the database should be created in order to determine if the database achieves the required aims.

16.3 Relationships

After building tables, relationships allow the data to build back into a meaningful form. In the previous example, there were three tables: Lecturer, Module and Programme. Each module has a module leader which is defined in the Lecturer database, and each Programme has modules which are defined in the Module database. Thus there is a relationship between the Module table and the Lecturer table, and one between the Programme table and the Module table. A relationship works by matching data in key fields. Two things are common:

- Fields normally have the **same name** in both tables.
- Fields are typically a **primary key** from one table, which provides a unique identifier for each record, and a **foreign key** in the other table. For example, in the Module database the Module ID is the primary key as this is the place that stores the module ID data, while the Module ID field in the Programme table will be the foreign key, as it links to the primary key, which is in the Module table.

There are three main types of relationships between tables:

- **One-to-many relationship.** This is the most common type of relationship, and relates to when there is one matching record in one table, which can link to another table with many matching records. For example Table A can have many matching records with Table B, but there is only one matching from a record in Table B to Table A. For example there is a one-to-many relationship from the Module database to the Lecturer database, as each module can link to many possible lecturers, but there will only be one actual link from a lecturer to a module. A one-to-many relationship is created if only one of the related fields is a primary key.
- **Many-to-many relationship.** In this case, a record in Table A can have many matching records in Table B, and a record in Table B can have many matching records in Table A. A many-to-many relationship uses a third table (called a junction table) whose primary key consists of two fields, which are the foreign keys from both Tables A and B. Thus a many-to-many relationship is constructed with two one-to-many relationships with a third table.
- **One-to-one relationship.** This is the least common case, and relates to when a record in Table A can only have one matching record in Table B, and each record in Table B can only have one matching record in Table A. A one-to-one relationship is created if both of the related fields are primary keys.

16.4 SQL query

SQL queries allow the database to be interrogated with an SQL statement. Typical SQL queries are:

- `SELECT`. Select fields from a table or several tables.
- `WHERE`. Criteria for selection that determine the rows to be retrieved.
- `FROM`. Tables from which the field is defined.
- `GROUP BY`. Groups records.
- `HAVING`. Used by `GROUP BY` to define how the groups are grouped.
- `ORDER BY`. Criteria for ordering.

16.4.1 SELECT

A typical SQL query is to select information from several tables. For example to select all the fields from the Modules table:

```
SELECT *
FROM [Module marks]
```

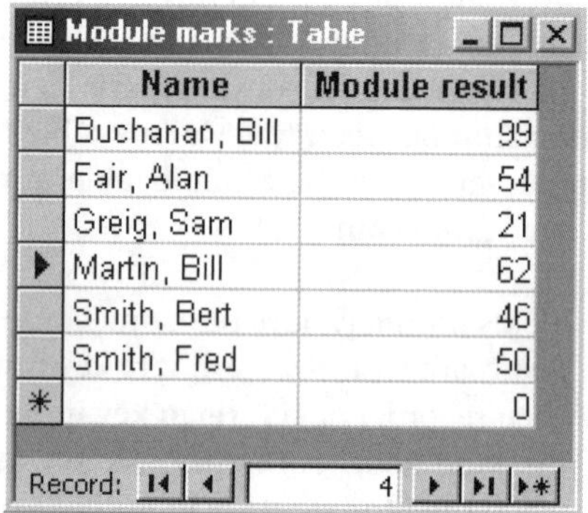

Module marks : Table

	Name	Module result
	Buchanan, Bill	99
	Fair, Alan	54
	Greig, Sam	21
▶	Martin, Bill	62
	Smith, Bert	46
	Smith, Fred	50
*		0

Record: 4

The * represents the wildcard, where all the fields are read, and the square brackets are used if there is a space between words in a field (or table). To retrieve one field the following could be used:

```
SELECT [Module results] FROM Modules
```

16.4.2 WHERE clause

The `WHERE` clause is used to locate records which match a certain criteria, and is added to the end of a `SELECT` query. For example, to find all the modules with a mark of over 50 (from the Mark field of the Module marks table):

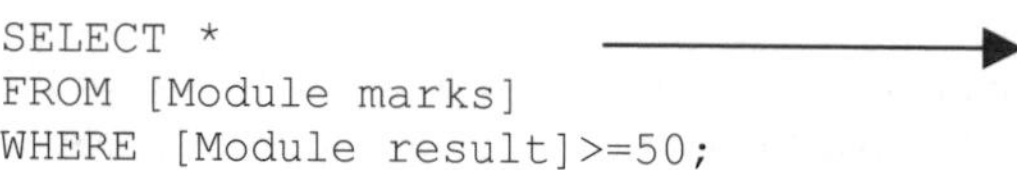

```
SELECT *
FROM [Module marks]
WHERE [Module result]>=50;
```

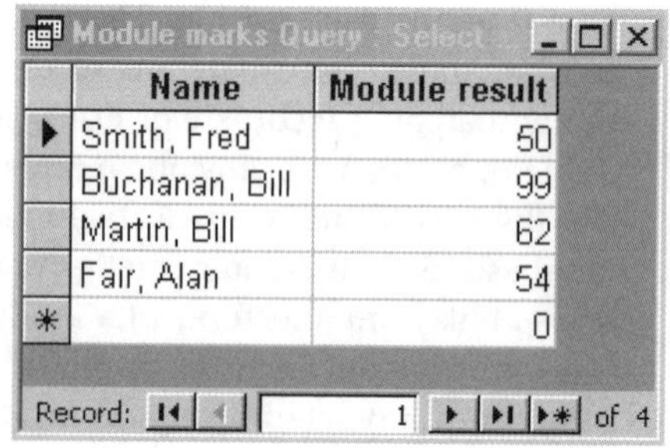

Module marks Query : Select ...

	Name	Module result
▶	Smith, Fred	50
	Buchanan, Bill	99
	Martin, Bill	62
	Fair, Alan	54
*		0

Record: 1 of 4

The operators that can be used with `WHERE` are < (less than), > (greater than), <= (less than or equal to), >= (greater than or equal to), = (equal to), <> (not equal to), or Like. The Like operator can be used to match string patterns. Typical examples are:

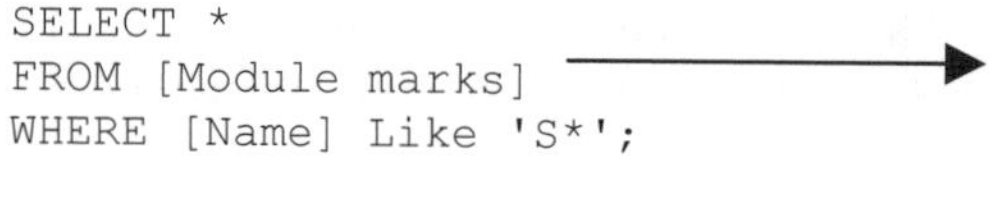

```
SELECT *
FROM [Module marks]
WHERE [Name] Like 'S*';
```

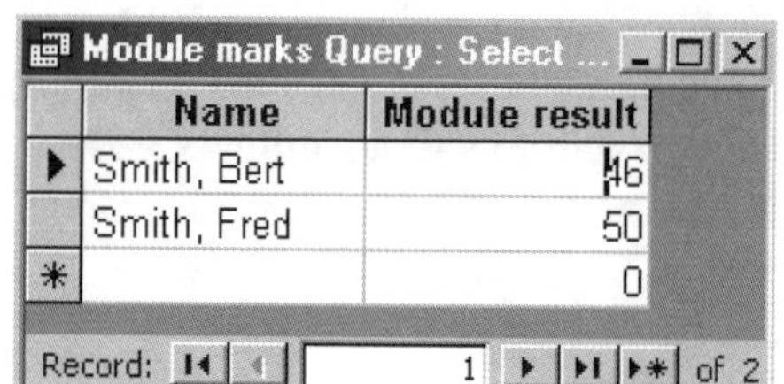

Module marks Query : Select ...

	Name	Module result
▶	Smith, Bert	46
	Smith, Fred	50
*		0

Record: 1 of 2

Which will list all the names in the Name field which start with the letter 'S', and followed by any other character sequence. The '?' character is used to signify any single character. A range of characters is signified by a hyphen, and enclosed within square brackets. For example:

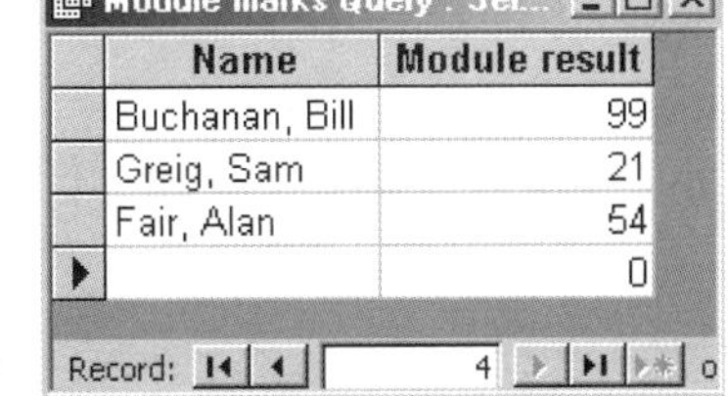


```
SELECT *
FROM [Module marks]
WHERE (([Module marks].Name) Like '[A-G]*');
```

Which will find all the names beginning with characters from 'A' to 'G' in the Names field.

16.4.3 ORDER BY clause

The `ORDER BY` clause is used to arrange the results of a query. The typical format is:

```
SELECT * FROM TableName ORDER BY field ASC
SELECT * FROM TableName ORDER BY field DESC
```

Where `ASC` is to order in ascending order, and `DESC` is for descending order. So, for example, if we wanted to order the marks from the database in descending order of name (where Name is a field of Module marks), then:

```
SELECT * FROM  [Module marks] ORDER BY Name DESC
```

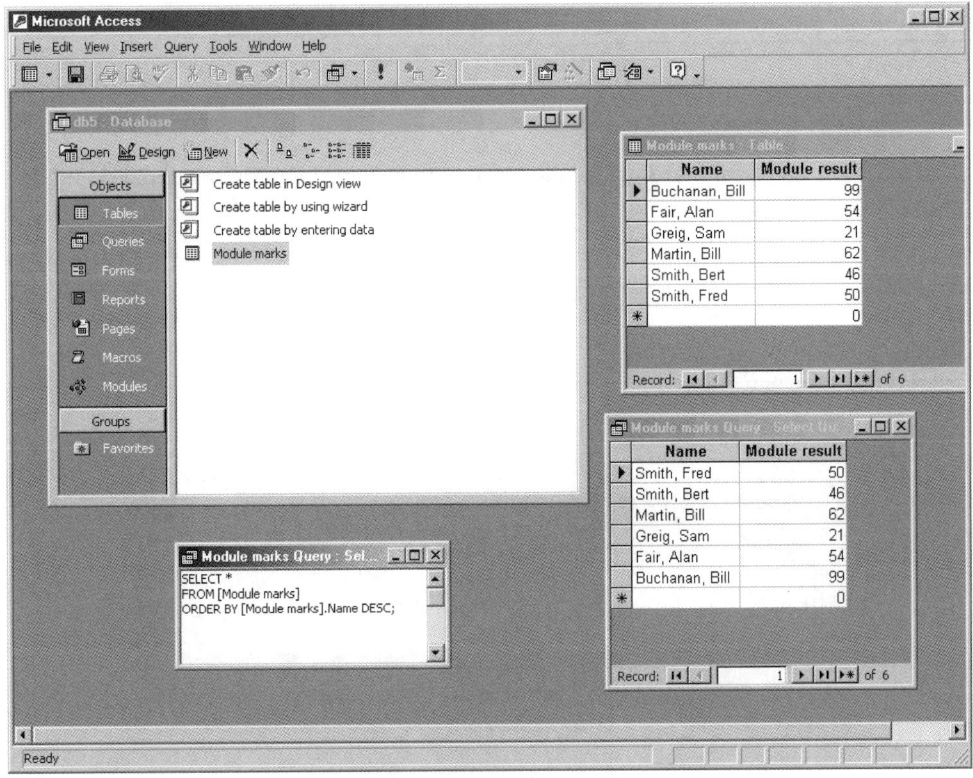

Figure 16.3 Example query

Figure 16.3 shows an example of a query in Microsoft Access. The table for the marks table [Module marks] is shown in the top left-hand window, and the query is shown in the bottom left-hand window. In this case the query is:

```
SELECT *
FROM [Module marks]
ORDER BY [name] DESC;
```

The result of the query is shown in the bottom right-hand window. It can be seen that it has put Smith, Fred at the top of the list, followed by Smith, Bert.

16.4.4 INNER JOIN

`INNER JOIN` is used to merge multiple tables together so that the merged tables can be searched. The standard format is:

`SELECT * FROM` *Table1* `INNER JOIN` *Table2* `ON` *Table1.field = Table2.field*

Where the `ON` part specifies the fields from each table that should be compared to determine which records will be selected. For example, if we add a new table named Details to the previous example, and then add the following records:

Name	Matriculation Number
Buchanan, Bill	1
Martin, Bill	2

Then to merge the search for the Module marks and Details database, we could do the following:

```
SELECT *
FROM [Module marks] INNER JOIN Details ON [Module marks].Name=Details.
Name;
```

The result is shown in Figure 16.4.

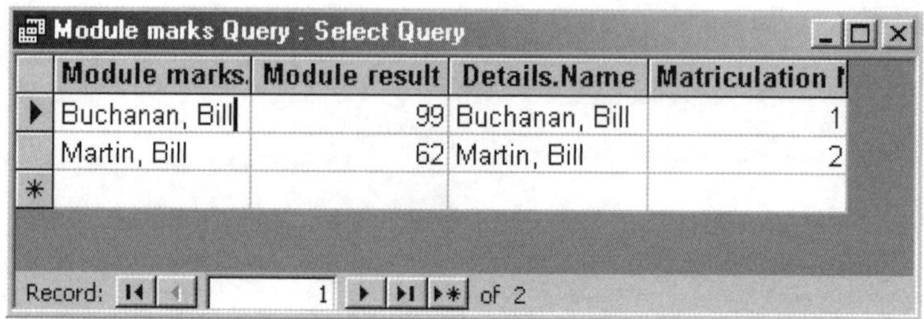

Figure 16.4 Example query

16.5 Data Protection

The increasing usage of databases causes a great deal of worry for individuals. For example what if someone typed in your postcode and house number instead of someone else who was on a credit black list. What could you do once the data was on the database, since this data could be sent around the world in seconds? Fortunately there are laws on what can be done with databases, such as those from the European Data Protection and Telecoms Protection Directives, which states:

- That the data is processed fairly and lawfully.
- That the data is collected for specific, explicit and legitimate purposes.
- That the data is adequate, relevant and not excessive in relation to the processes for which they are collected and/or processed.
- That the data is accurate and, where necessary, kept up to date.
- That the data is kept in a form which permits identification of data subjects for no longer than is necessary.
- That appropriate technical and organizational measures are taken by the data controller to protect personal data against accidental or unlawful destruction or loss, etc.
- That where the data controller chooses a data processor to process personal data for him, he must take appropriate measures to ensure that the data processor complies with the obligations of data controller.
- That the transfer of personal data to a country outside the EEA (the 15 member states of the EU plus Iceland, Norway and Liechtenstein) may take place only if the country in question ensures an adequate level of protection or there are appropriate contractual arrangements in place or the data subjects have given consent.

And individuals have the following rights:

- The right to information concerning the personal data held about them by a data controller.
- The alteration of personal data held by controllers where such personal data is incorrect.

Also special conditions are made for personal data on the racial or ethnic origin, political options, religious or philosophical beliefs, trade union membership, and information concerning the health or sex life of those still alive. For these areas individuals must give explicit permission for the data to be used for other purposes. Thus a company who wants to view the medical records of an individual would have to get the permission of the individual before they could do this.

Of course at one time this was easy to control, as requests for data were made via the postal service. These days data can be transferred from one place to another within a fraction of a second, and transferred around the world in seconds. Thus it is important that electronic data is kept in a secure form, which cannot be tampered with, especially personal data. As much as possible databases with personal data should be protected by passwords, firewalls, and all the other secure methods that were discussed in a previous chapter. When the data is transmitted over the Internet, it must be encrypted, as TCP/IP allows any listener to view the data. Any breaches in security can leave the organization responsible, and they could receive a heavy fine.

Any organization which does business in the EU must adhere to the following:

- Provide clear and concise notice for the purpose for which the data is being collected, and any third parties which may share the data.
- Offer the opportunity to choose whether and how personal information is used or disclosed to third parties.
- Enforce mechanisms that allow, at a minimum, independent complaint procedures.

The seven rules of providing safe data can be summarized as:

- **Notice**. This should be given about the reasons for the data collected.
- **Choice**. This gives individuals the choice as to whether they want their data collected, or not.
- **Onward transfer**. This gives individuals the choice as to whether they want the data to be forwarded to third parties, or not.
- **Access**. This gives individuals the right to access any data which the organization has on them.
- **Security**. The data must be kept securely.
- **Data integrity**. The data must be correct and up to date.
- **Enforcement**. There must be enforcement procedures for complaints.

16.6 Personalization and data mining

An increasing concept is personalization, where the WWW pages are designed especially for the user. The information to generate these is contained in databases. This personalization can either be:

- **Implicit personalization**. With this the pages are designed using users personal preferences. A good example of this is My Yahoo and MSN which allow users to design the WWW page for their preferences, such as the news articles that they would like on the page, the stocks that they would like to view, and so on.
- **Explicit personalization**. With this the pages are designed using data from the user's behaviours, and occur automatically without the user have any direct influence on the choices. A good example of this is Amazon's book recommendation service which offers customers books based on the books that they have purchased in the past.

This personalization has many advantages. A good example is Amazon's One Click service which allows the user's credit card details to be held in a secure manner, and used every time that the user wants to purchase a book. Users could also benefit from being offered products that another user with a similar profile has bought.

Computer generations

1st	Valves (ENIAC)
2nd	Transistors (PDP-1)
3rd	Integrated circuits/time-sharing (IBM System/360)
4th	Large-scale integration (ZX81)
5th	Systems-on-a-chip (Pentium).

For organizations, there is also an increased amount of targeted marketing, where complimentary services can be offered, such as a company which gives a holiday book, might also provide travel insurance to the user. Also marketing can be targeted at specific users, rather than, at present, with blanket marketing. Most users now ignore the advertising banners which appear at the top of many WWW pages. This database approach also leads to savings in WWW development, as template pages are produced, and the content for these are generated from the database. With a non-database driven system, the pages must be coded for every different type of page. Changes in products can also be quickly updated, as it only requires a single change to the database, rather than over many pages.

Examples of personalization include:

- **Customized user interface**. This could be with fonts, colours, layout, and structure.
- **Stimuli**. This could be related to the way that the content is delivered, such as differing ways of delivering content using images, video or audio.
- **Personalized content**. This allows users to select the types of content they wish to receive (such as My Yahoo), such as providing content on news, sports, events, and so on.
- **Personalized services**. This would allow registered users more access to services than a guest user.
- **Remembering details**. This allows the details of the user to be stored. Many sites now remember the name of the person who is accessing the site. These details are typically stored as a text file, called a cookie, on the user's computer. When the user goes back to the site, the cookie is loaded back, and the details of the site can be remembered. Secure information, such as credit card details will be stored on a secure database.
- **Match services or products**. Services can be exactly matched to the user's preferences.

Database Management Systems (DBMS):

MySQL. A common database program which is used on many sites. It is suitable for small to medium sized databases, and is free of charge. It is also excellent to learn how to use databases.
PostgreSQL. A popular DBMS, and is available free of charge. It is more advanced that MySQL, and supports virtually all of the SQL features. Unfortunately it is only available for UNIX and Linux systems.
Oracle. A high-powered database system, which is used on many of the high-end WWW servers, especially in on-line shopping sites. It is reliable, highly scaleable, and has a great deal of tools to manage the databases. Oracle is available for both Windows and UNIX.
Microsoft SQL. This is a powerful DBMS which is comparable to the power of Oracle. It uses many advanced features, such as OnLine Analytical Processing (OLAP), and data mining. Unfortunately it is only available on Windows systems.
Microsoft Access. This is a popular database program which is used in small to medium sized database applications.

Which one should I choose?
Well it all depends what you've got, and what your application is. If you have a small database, and you've already got Microsoft Access, then it makes a good start in database development. If you want your database on the WWW, then you can't go much wrong with MySQL, and using PHP to access it. Both are free, and are available on many types of servers. On large-scale systems, you can't go wrong with Oracle. It's a robust, and highly scaleable system that is used by many of the leading WWW sites. They used to say: 'No-one ever got fired choosing IBM'. Nowadays, it could be said that 'No-one ever got fired choosing Oracle'. The main thing, though, is that often, once you've picked your database type, it will remain your main system, as it's often difficult to change your DBMS over to another type. So pick wisely!

- **Pre-emptive customer service**. With this organizations can predict the requirements of the user, such as providing a graduation gown service in the month of June in the year that they graduate from college.
- **Product suggestions**. This is based on products that the user has bought in the past, or ones that similar users have purchased.
- **Cater for individual needs**. This caters for special needs that only apply for a few customers.

A good example of personalization is on the Dell.com WWW site (see Figure 16.5). With this the user enters the system service tag (or express service code) of their computer and the WWW site generates pages which relate specifically to the product. This allows Dell to provide details of software downloads, hardware updates, and so on, specifically for the computer. This overcomes one of the most annoying features when trying to find the correct documentation and software downloads for a specific product. It also allows Dell to quickly target specific products for bug fixes, and product updates.

The Dell database also keeps track of the complete history of a product, as the service tag is a unique code. This is shown as a text code, and also as a bar code, from which the servicing department can easily update and retrieve data on the system. The database knows the specification of the computer, and when it was shipped from Dell. It will also track the product and stores details of its operating system, its specification, and so on. These provide important information for the Dell Support team, and make it easier for them to make the correct decisions in providing help. Database systems are even used to track a product that is being fixed, because the user can contact Dell, and they are able to track the actual location of the system, and its current status.

An example of a Dell cookie is (stored as user@dell.txt):

```
SITESERVER
ID=e4f7cb198cb4880753345da5a68f6d37
dell.com/
642859008
31887777
2953433472
29419968
*
```

16.6.1 Cookies or remote storage of details

The personalization can be achieved in number of ways, e.g., simple cookies, which are stored on the user's computer. Cookies are simple text files (typically stored as TXT files in the WINDOWS\COOKIES folder on Microsoft Windows), and will contain relevant details on the user, and any of their preferences. As these are text files, they cannot do any damage to the local computer. Sometimes users delete these cookies, and all the previous information is lost, and they must then re-register for the system to be able to store their details. Other systems store details of the user on the server, and this allows the user to move around the Internet and still get access to their logged data. A good example of this is MSN Messenger which allows the user to login with a passport, and their contacts and other data is downloaded from the server. This allows users to read their e-mail or contact friends from any location on the

Internet. As the user's details and preferences (such as where they live, and their favourite links) are stored on a server, they can't be deleted when they erase the cookies on the own computer. Unfortunately the logon process can be quite time consuming, as the program must contact the server, which is likely to be processing many other logins. Problems can also occur when the server goes down, as users will not be able to login. These types of servers are targets for DOS (denial-of-service) attacks, and can be made to slow down their processing, if they have to respond to too many logins, at a time.

With cookies the data stored can involve:

- **User profile**. This would typically store details of the user, such as their name, date of birth, and so on. This could also store the user's login name and password (obviously this would not be shown in the cookie in a text form, and will be encoded in some way, so that the user's login and password details cannot be viewed from their cookies.
- **Session details**. This would store the date and time that the user last accessed the site, and the time they have spent there.
- **Customer identification**. This might contain a unique customer identification, which can be used to match-up with the organization's database entry.
- **Advertising profiles**. This typically defines the adverts that have already been displayed. For example many sites show an initial 'flash' screen which is useful initially to present a good image for the organization, but should not be displayed again, the user has already seen it. If the user has viewed it, then the cookie stores this information, so that it will not be displayed again (obviously if they were to delete the cookie, it would appear again).

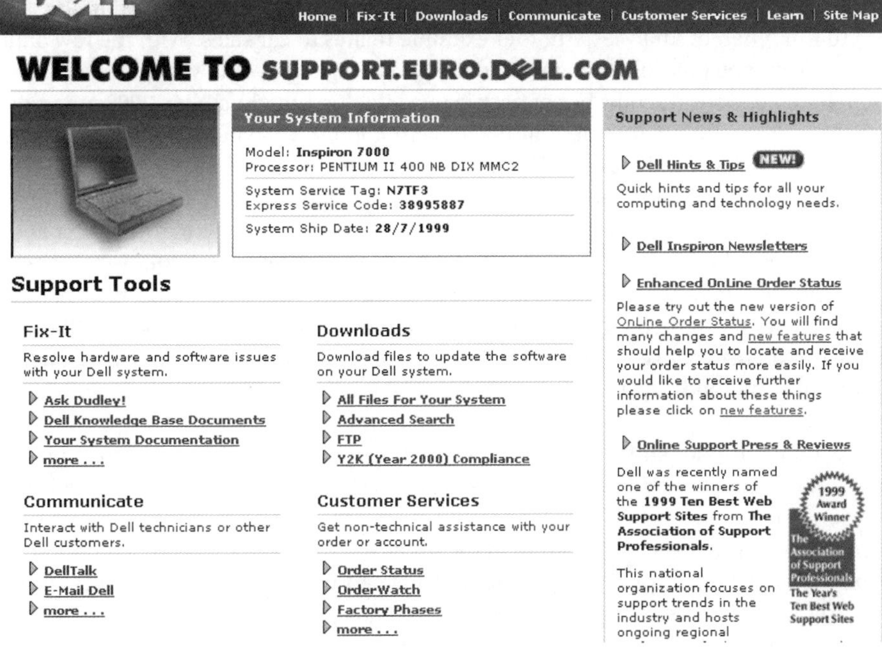

Figure 16.5 Dell.com personalized site

As cookies are just simple text files they cannot pass information on a user's computer, other than the information contained within the cookie. Also the cookie generated by a WWW site cannot be used by another WWW, because they can only be used by the WWW site that created it. Thus cookies cannot be used to track users around the Internet. The greatest drawback with cookies is that users typically do not get the opportunity as to whether they want the cookie stored to their local disk, or not.

An example of the usage of centralized market information is DoubleClick, who specialize in generating banner advertisements which are aimed at specific users. With this companies who subscribe to DoubleClick, have a cookie request from DoubleClick on their page. If the user has an existing one it is read for the user's details (otherwise a new one is generated). As DoubleClick has many organizations subscribing to it, they can search for the types of sites that the user has most frequently accessed. The user will then receive a targeted banner advertisement which is most relevant to them. Over time the advertising will become more focused as DoubleClick learn more about the user. Note all the cookies will be sent and received by DoubleClick, and not by the organization that subscribed to them.

16.6.2 Data warehousing

Data warehousing is a method which stores vast quantities of raw data, such as that generated from logs files. This data can then be prepared and reformatted for data mining process, which will try and create meaningful information from the raw data. This is similar to traditional paper-based storage, but it is obviously easier to store large amounts of electronic data in a small physical space. For example exam papers could be marked to get the final exam mark. The raw data for this would be the actual exam papers. This data could be analysed for the average number of words per question, or the average mark for each question, or the number of pages used, and so on. With the raw data, it is possible to analyse the data in many different ways, and find new insights on it. Without the raw data it is often difficult to run different analyses. Another example relates to car sales. With the raw data on car sales, it would be possible to determine the percentage of people within a certain street that bought red cars, or the number of people in a city that bought a blue, 2000cc car, or the number of people with a surname that began with a letter 'C', who bought a Ford van. All this data in warehouses will make marketing more refined in the future.

There is obviously a very fine line between personalization and personal intrusion, and the collection of data must comply with current laws. Unfortunately many data collection programs confuse the user by displaying great deals of text, for which the user is asked to read, and then agree to. Most users now, typically, just click the accept button without even bothering to read the agreement statement. For example, when was the last time that someone actually read the license agreement for a software program that they had just bought?

Data mining methods include:

- **Anonymous profile data.** This is generated whenever a user contacts a site, and might contain the network address (IP address), domain name, ISP provider, WWW browser version, and so on.
- **Cookies.** This provides information on the user.
- **Monitoring newsgroups and chat rooms.** This can used to determine information on the user. For example if the user subscribes to many job related newsgroups, then there is a good chance that the user is actively looking for another job.
- **Self-divulgence of information for a purchase.** This is data that is completed when purchasing a product.

- **Self-divulgence of information for free merchandise**. This typically related to on-line prize draws, where the user completes a form, in order to win a prize or receive a free gift.
- **Self-divulgence of information to access a web site**. This is where the user subscribes to a WWW site, and fills-in a form.

A registration form is an excellent method for an organization to get user data, and is an opportunity for the organization to ask questions about the user, which they could use for marketing purposes. For example, how many times have you been asked if you were male or female when you registered for a WWW site? It should not matter to the registration if you were male or female. So why do they ask? For marketing and data mining purposes. This form of data mining is **explicit**, where the user actually knows that the data is being stored. Many users do not like this form of data mining, as they feel that it is obtrusive. Newer forms of data mining are implicit, where users do not know that they are being monitored for their usage patterns. These include cookies, but WWW sites can also monitor how the user moves through a site, and the pages that they are most likely to spend time with. For example if the user on a bank site spends more time looking at the corporate page, then they may possibly be interested either in buying stocks in the company, or they are looking for a job with them.

Future technologies may include **spyware**. With these WWW pages code contains graphics files which are invisible to the user (as they may only contain a few pixels), but are resident on a data mining server. When the page is loaded the data mining server is contacted, and the details of the access can be logged. This will give details of where the user is located, their network address, their browser details, and so on. This could also be applied to e-mails, which contain graphics which are contained on data mining services. The server can then log the accesses to the graphics, and thus log when the e-mail was read, and from which location.

16.7 ASP interface to a Microsoft Access database

ASP code allows a WWW browser to gain access to a database, and add and delete records through standard SQL statements.

For more material on ASP interfaces to databases please visit our website at:
`http://www.palgrave.com/studyskills/masterseries/buchanan`

The first part of the code reads the IP address of the user, and then asks for their e-mail address. After they submit their details through a submit button, the `xt_mail.asp` file is called.

```
<% ip = Request.ServerVariables("REMOTE_ADDR") %>
<p>Enter your email address in the database (<%=ip%>) </p>
<form method="post" action="xt_email.asp">
<input type="text" name="EmailAddr">
<input type="hidden" name="IpAddr" value="<%=ip%>">
<input type="hidden" name="Day" value="<%=now%>">
<input type="submit" value="Submit" name="submit2">
<input type="reset" value="Reset" name="reset">
</form>
```

The `xt_mail.asp` file is given next. It opens the database with a full pathname, and then adds the e-mail address, IP address, and the current day.

```
<%
' File name is xt_mail.asp
'Create a connection to our database using a fileless dsn
Response.Buffer = true
dim cnn,rst
set cnn = Server.CreateObject("ADODB.Connection")
set rst = Server.CreateObject("ADODB.RecordSet")
cnn.Open "driver={Microsoft Access Driver
(*.mdb)};;DBQ=C:\Inetpub\wwwroot\staff\bill\email.mdb;"
sqltext = "SELECT * FROM email"
rst.Open sqltext,cnn,3,3

'Server Side form validation to keep our database clean
dim email,ip,day
addr = Request.Form("EmailAddr")
ip = Request.Form("IpAddr")
day = Request.Form("Day")

if addr = "" then
error = "You have not entered an email address."
Response.Write error
Response.End
end if

'If we pass through validation then store the information in the db
rst.AddNew
rst("EmailAddr") = addr
rst("IpAddr") = ip
rst("Date") = day
rst.update
'Lets redirect the user back to where they came from
Response.Redirect "user_details"
%>
```

Finally the database can be read back with the following:

```
<%
Dim szDSN, szSQL, rstData, intFields
' -- Specify the database to connect to via ODBC
' -- Use an existing data source name
'szDSN = "DSN=email"
' -- OR
' -- You can also use a DSN-less connection by providing the driver and data-
base
szDSN = "Driver=Microsoft Access Driver
(*.mdb);DBQ=C:\Inetpub\wwwroot\staff\bill\email.mdb"

' -- Create an ADO Recordset object
Set rstData = Server.CreateObject("ADODB.Recordset")

' -- Supply a SQL statement to query by
szSQL = "SELECT * FROM email"

' -- Execute the query on the data source
rstData.Open szSQL, szDSN

' -- Draw a table
Response.Write "<P><TABLE BORDER=1>" & vbCrLf
Response.Write "<TR>" & vbCrLf
```

```
' -- Make a table column for each field in the query
For intFields = 0 to rstData.Fields.Count - 1
Response.Write "<TD BGCOLOR=""#CCCCCC""><B>" & rstData.Fields(intFields).Name &
"</B></TD>" & vbCrLf
Next

Response.Write "</TR>" & vbCrLf

' -- Loop through the recordset and make a new row for each record
Do While Not rstData.EOF
Response.Write "<TR>" & vbCrLf
' -- Display the value for each field in the query
For intFields = 0 to rstData.Fields.Count - 1
Response.Write "<TD>" & rstData.Fields(intFields).Value & "</TD>" & vbCrLf
Next

Response.Write "</TR>" & vbCrLf
' -- Go to the next record
rstData.MoveNext
Loop
Response.Write "</TABLE>" & vbCrLf
' -- Clean up
Set rstData = Nothing

%>
```

16.8 SQL reference

The following gives a basic outline of the main SQL statements:

CREATE TABLE

CREATE TABLE is used to create a new table in the database. The name of the table is defined after the CREATE TABLE part, followed by the fields in the table, separated by commas. For example to create a table named mytab in the database, with fields from matriculation (8 digits), name (up to 255 characters) and fees (a floating-point value with 2 decimal places):

```
CREATE TABLE mytab
(
   matriculation INT(8),
   name CHAR(255),
   fees FLOAT(9,2)
)
```

INSERT

The INSERT statement allows records to be added to a table. It uses the INTO clause to define the table that the records are to be added to, and the VALUES cause to define their values. An example is:

```
INSERT INTO mytab (matriculation, fees) VALUES (12345678, 1200.10)
```

UPDATE

The UPDATE statement modifies data in the database. The name of the table is defined after UPDATE, followed by the SET clause which indicates the field to be updated, and the WHERE cause which defines the data to be modified. An example is:

```
UPDATE mytab SET fees = 2200.00 WHERE matriculation = 12345678
```

SELECT

The SELECT statement allows data to be retrieved from the data. The names of the fields which the data is required from are specified, the FROM clause defines the table that the data is taken from, and the WHERE clause specifies where the data to be taken from. It returns data in a table format (which is often called a result set). An example is: `SELECT matriculation,name FROM mytab WHERE fees>100.00`
DELETE
The DELETE statement removes data from a database. It uses the FROM clause to define the table and the WHERE clause to define the conditions for the data to be deleted. An example is: `DELETE FROM mytab WHERE fees<100.00`

16.9 PHP interface to a MySQL database

PHP code allows a WWW browser to gain access to a database.

For more material on PHP interfaces to databases please visit our website at:
http://www.palgrave.com/studyskills/masterseries/buchanan

The first part creates a table in an existing datatabase:

```
<?php
/* Data of SQL-server */
$server=    "db.myserver.co.uk";    /* Address of server                  */
$user=      "myuser";               /* FTP-username                       */
$password=  "mypassword";           /* FTP-Password                       */
$database=  "dbname";               /* name of database                   */
$table=     "datatest";             /* Name of table, you can select that */

/* Accessing the server and creating the table                            */
MYSQL_CONNECT($server, $user, $password) or die (
        "<H3>Server unreachable</H3>");
MYSQL_SELECT_DB($database) or die ( "<H3>database not existent</H3>");
$result=MYSQL_QUERY( "CREATE TABLE $table (
name varchar(25),email varchar(25))");

print "Result is $result";
/* Terminate SQL connection*/
MYSQL_CLOSE();
?>
```

To add a record:

```
<?
/* Data of SQL-server */
$server= "db.myserver.co.uk"; /* Address of server */
$user= "myuser";              /* FTP-username */
$password= "mypassword";      /* FTP-Password */
$database= "dbname";          /* name of database */
$table= "datatest";           /* Name of table, you can select that */
```

```
/* Accessing SQL-server */
MYSQL_CONNECT($server, $user, $password) or die (
    "<H3>Server unreachable</H3>");
MYSQL_SELECT_DB($database) or die ( "<H3>Database non existent</H3>");

MYSQL_QUERY( "INSERT INTO $table VALUES('Fred','fred@home.com')");
MYSQL_QUERY( "INSERT INTO $table VALUES('Bert','bert@myplace.com')");

/* Display number of entries */
$query="SELECT * FROM $table";
$result = MYSQL_QUERY($query);

/* How many of these users are there? */
$number = MYSQL_NUMROWS($result);

if ($number==0):
   echo "database empty";
elseif ($number > 0):
   echo "$number rows in database";
endif;
mysql_close();
?>
```

To read data from the database:

```
<?php
$server= "db.myserver.co.uk";       /* Address of server                     */
$user= "myuser";                    /* FTP-username                          */
$password= "mypassword";            /* FTP-Password                          */
$database= "dbname";                /* name of database                      */
$table= "datatest";                 /* Name of table, you can select that    */
/* Accessing SQL-Server and querying table                                   */
MYSQL_CONNECT($server, $user, $password) or die (
      "<H3>Server unreachable</H3>");
MYSQL_SELECT_DB($database) or die ( "<H3>Database non existent</H3>");
$result=MYSQL_QUERY( "SELECT * FROM $table order by name");

/* Output data into a HTMl table */
echo "<table border=\"1\" align=center width=50%";
echo "<tr>";
echo "<div color=\"#ffff00\">";
while ($field=mysql_fetch_field($result)) {
   echo "<th>$field->name</A></th>";
}
echo "</font></tr>";
while($row = mysql_fetch_row($result)) {
   echo "<tr>";
   for($i=0; $i < mysql_num_fields($result); $i++) {
      echo "<td align=center>$row[$i]</td>";
   }
   echo "</tr>\n";
}
echo "</table><BR><BR>";

/* Close SQL-connection */
MYSQL_CLOSE();
?>
```

and to delete a table:

```
<?php
/* Accessing the server and deleting the table */
MYSQL_CONNECT($server, $user, $password) or die (
```

```
      "<H3>Server unreachable</H3>");
MYSQL_SELECT_DB($database) or die ( "<H3>database not existent</H3>");
$result=MYSQL_QUERY( "DROP TABLE $table");
print "Result is ";
print $result;
/* Terminate SQL connection*/
MYSQL_CLOSE();
?>
```

Tutorial questions and additional material are available at:
http://www.palgrave.com/studyskills/masterseries/buchanan

17 Programming

17.1 Introduction

Some programs provide a framework for a user to manipulate data without the user having to produce their own program. Examples of this include word processors, spreadsheet programs, and so on, where the user writes macro, or script, programs which integrate within the package. With Microsoft products these can be written in Visual Basic. For example, in Microsoft Excel, a macro to select the whole of column A, and then make it bold, and finally to copy and paste it to the D column is achieved with:

```
Sub Macro2()
  Columns("A:A").Select
  Selection.Font.Bold = True
  Selection.Copy
  Columns("D:D").Select
  ActiveSheet.Paste
End Sub
```

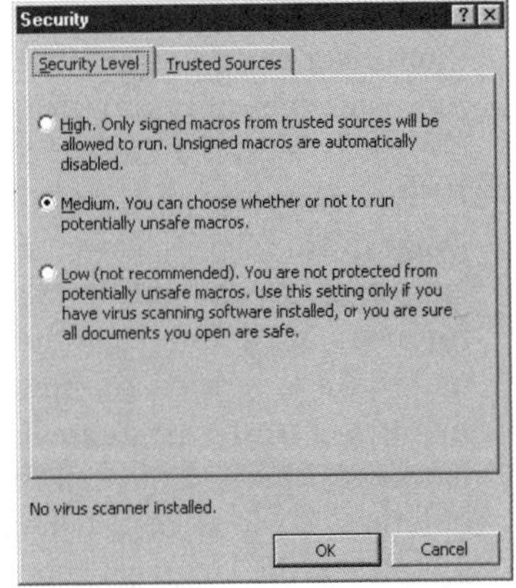

The user can easily call this macro up from a menu, or they can define a hotkey to activate it. In most cases the macro can be written automatically by following the user's actions (such as Tools→Macro→Record New Macro). These can be easily edited and tested, when they are written in Visual Basic, as this comes with an integrated editor and test environment. The Visual Basic scripts can be easily made to react to certain events, such as startup, file saving, and shutdown events.

The technique of generating macros has been popular with users, as it does not require a great deal of programming experience, or for quickly providing a foundation for code development. Unfortunately it has also proved an excellent opportunity for some people to write macro viruses. These are as easy to write for the virus programmer, as they are for the normal user. A typical technique for the virus programmer is to respond to one of the events which occur within a document, and perform some action. Thus, for example, the document could generate an event to copy itself somewhere, when the user opens the document. Normally this is to copy itself into another file (and thus self-replicate itself). A typical action is to copy the macro to the default template, thus all the new documents will have the virus macro. Macro viruses, and script viruses, in general, are one of the greatest causes of viruses, and allow an easy way for viruses to spread quickly, without initial detection. The global Internet has now allowed a fast channel for their spread.

In many cases though users require to customize their programs, and produce a program which will run on its own. This can be done by a programmer writing a program from scratch, or it could be to customize an existing program. Popular programming languages include C++, Visual Basic, Java and Delphi. A programmer can select a software language which is either scripted, interpreted, compiled or assembled. Table 17.1 outlines the main attributes of the different language classifications, which are:

- **Scripted languages**. These are languages which run within a specific environment and they cannot be run without it. Examples include Excel macros and remote access scripts. These scripted languages are often specific to the application package, and cannot be transferred to other similar packages.
- **Interpreted languages**. These are languages that are interpreted by an interpreter when they are run, and the interpreter performs the required operations. The language requires the interpreter to be present when they are run. Examples of interpreted languages are Java (in some cases), HTML and BASIC. Scripted and interpreted languages are the slowest of all the languages, as the interpreter or environment must interpret the language and make a decision on how to implement it on the system. Interpreted languages can also have problems with different versions of the language, as updates to the language can be interpreted by only certain versions of the interpreter. There are many different interpreted languages used on the WWW, including HTML, JavaScript, VBScript, ASP and PHP. These languages are either interpreted by the WWW browser (in the case of HTML, JavaScript and VBScript), or by the WWW server (in the case of ASP and PHP). With interpreted languages it is the interpreter that must be operating system and/or system dependent, and not the program. Thus HTML will work on every WWW browser, but a WWW browser type will only work properly on a certain type of operating system/system type. For example a different WWW browser program is required for an Apple Mac, as one required for a Microsoft Windows-based PC.
- **Compiled languages**. These are languages that are fed through a compiler which changes the high-level program into machine code (object code). The compiler catches all of the language syntax errors (syntax errors), and will typically highlight problems that could occur when running the program (run-time errors). The compiler will not produce an executable

The 586

After the 80486, most people expected to see the 80586, but it never happened. The reason for this was that Intel had tried to make the 386 one of their trademarks. Unfortunately, the US courts believed that the 386 number was so prevalent that it was almost a generic name (which led to the introduction of the term Intel386 for an Intel 386 processor). Instead of 586, they used the Pentium, so that they could trademark the name. This allowed Intel to invest their own money into developing the Pentium brand. Few users actually understand the technical specifications of the processors, and will typically buy a computer using the following judgements:

1. Brand name of the computer, such as IBM, Dell or Compaq.
2. Computer type is chosen depending on the brand name of the processor, such as Intel or AMD, and its clock speed.
3. Memory and hard disk capacities.
4. Software packages pre-installed.
5. Support and delivery times.

Dear Compression Agent. *Ah. You say that 24-bit colour uses 8 bits for Red, Green and Blue. So what does 32-bit colour use? Is it ten and two-thirds of a bit for each colour, or have they discovered a new primary colour?*

No. They haven't found a new primary colour. The extra 8 bits define an alpha channel, thus every single bit can have its colour set in RGB and also a transparency value from 0 to 255 (0 to 100%). Transparency allows the background colour to show thorough, depending on the setting of the transparency. Graphics files, such as PNG support this, along with layers which defines the objects that are above other objects.

program unless all the syntax errors are fixed. Typical compiled languages are C, Pascal and FORTRAN.

- **Assembled languages**. These are languages which use assembly macro commands for equivalent machine code commands. Assembled languages are generally the fastest of all the languages, as they are often optimized to the processor.

Compiled and assembled languages have the advantage over the other types of languages in that they create a single executable program, whereas interpreted and scripted languages require an interpreter or an application environment to run (such as a WWW browser for HTML). Interpreted languages tend to produce smaller programs, as much of the extra code is built into the interpreter (for example, there is no need to add code for interfacing to the keyboard or display, as the interpreter already has this code, for the specific operating system and system specification).

Figure 17.1 shows the sequence of events that occur to generate an executable program from a source code file (the filenames used in this example relate to a PC-based system). With this an editor creates and modifies the source code file; a compiler then converts this into a form which the microprocessor can understand, that is, its own machine code. The file produced by the compiler is named an object code file. This file cannot be executed as it does not have all the required information to run the program. The final stage of the process is linking, which involves adding extra machine code into the program so that it can use devices such as a keyboard, a monitor, and so on. A linker links the object code file with other object code files and with libraries to produce an executable program. These libraries contain other object code modules that are compiled source code.

The complication and linking stages generate either warnings or errors. If they generate errors then the source code must be modified to eliminate them and the process of compilation/linking begins again. A warning in the compile/link stage does not stop the compiler or linker from producing an output, but errors will. All errors in the compilation or linking stage must be eliminated, whereas it is only advisable to eliminate warnings.

The type of programming language is typically defined as either a high-level language or a low-level language. A high-level language uses an almost English-like syntax, so that it is easy to read and write the program. Typical statements are: if; for; while; and so on.

```
if (x> 3) then y=10;
```

which says that: 'if x is greater than 3 then y is equal to 10'. In a high-level language mathematical operations are also defined in a way which is similar to the format which is typically used for mathematical notation, such as:

```
x = 2 * y + 7 * z;
```

A low-level language uses statements which are similar to the machine code of the microprocessor. These are often difficult to remember, and understand, thus it normally takes a great deal of skill to write programs using a low-level language.

It's hot!

The Pentium processor initially ran with a voltage supply of 5 V at 60 MHz and 66 MHz. Unfortunately, the larger the clock frequency, the larger the power dissipation, and the larger processor supply voltage, the larger the power dissipation. It ran so hot that it required a fan to sit on top of the processor. Initially, the processor did not have thermal shutdown, and a failing fan would cause the processor to melt. New processor and memory designs use 3.3 V rather than 5 V, which reduces the power dissipation by over 56 per cent (as power dissipation varies with the square of the voltage).

Two creative developments from the 1960s which were created by individuals have stayed with us: UNIX and C. Two startling failures were developed by committee include:

- **ALGOL-68** (1968). It was an attempt to produce a language which was defined by a committee (International Federation for Information Processing – IFIP). It suffered from being too complex, and its main legacy has been Pascal, which was based on it, but much more tightly structured.
- **PL/I** (Programming Language, One - 1964). This was developed by IBM, and was meant to integrate the features of FORTRAN, COBOL and ALGOL. While it had excellent features, it was complex, and only IBM really supported it. Also FORTRAN and COBOL were, at the time, gaining a strong foothold on the market, in different market segments, so many programmers asked: why change?

Other programming languages which have not really been adopted, possibly because they were too specialized, include:

- **LISP** (List Processing). A language-oriented language which was oriented towards processing symbols rather than evaluating algebraic expressions.
- **Forth**. A specialist language for industrial control applications.
- **Occam**. A programming language for parallel processing applications, especially for INMOS Transputers (a great UK innovation, that also failed to be adopted).
- **Prolog**. A logic programming language.

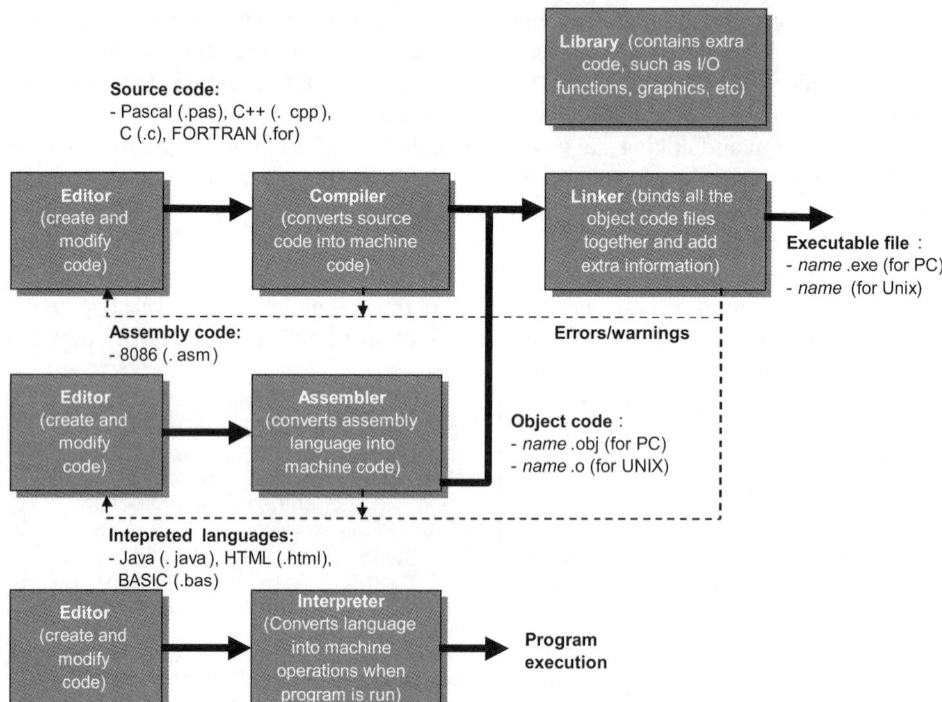

Figure 17.1 Compilation, assembly and interpretation

Table 17.1 Comparison of different types of software languages

	Interpreted languages	*Compiled languages*	*Assembled languages*
Examples	Java, BASIC and HTML.	C, C++, Visual Basic, Delphi, FORTRAN, Pascal and COBOL.	8088, 80386, 68000 and 6502.
Speed	**Slowest.** This is because the code must be read by the interpreter, and implemented with the required instructions, as the program is run.	**Medium.** Compiler normally tries to optimize the speed of the program.	**Fastest.** Developed code is exactly engineered for the application and the machine.
Portability	**Excellent**. Can be easily interpreted on another system or on any type of operating system.	**Medium**. Must be recompiled on other system. Problems can happen though on different operating systems, as many programs use different calls for system-dependent system calls, such as calls for windows, or operating system operations. For example a C program typically requires to be modified if it is run on a different system.	**Poor.** Microprocessors produced by different manufacturers tend to use different machine codes (mainly because of historical reasons), thus they tend to be incompatible with each other).
Syntax errors	**Poor**. Interpreter must run the program before errors can be found. It is often difficult to test the whole program for every time of run condition.	**Good**. The compiler should catch most syntax errors.	**Excellent**. The assembler should catch all syntax errors.

Table 17.1 Continued

	Interpreted languages	*Compiled languages*	*Assembled languages*
Run-time errors	**Poor**. Interpreter must run the program before errors can be found. It is often difficult to test the whole program.	**Excellent**. Most errors should be highlighted before the program is run.	**Poor**. Assembly language allows greater control of the system, but can lead to errors because even simple tasks require a great deal of coding, and understanding of the hardware.
Speed of development	**Normally fast.** The programs can be edited with most types of editors, and then easily updated.	**Medium.**	**Slow**. Often one line of a high-level language can be equivalent to many lines of assembly language. The amount of development on assembly language is normally kept to a minimum, and often a high-level to low-level convertor is used to initially generate large amounts of assembly language, which can then be customized for the required functionality.
Producing complex programs	**Medium**. This typically depends on the power of the language.	**Excellent**. Supports most user functions.	**Poor**. A single high-level statement typically requires many assembly language commands, thus it can be extremely difficult to write large and complex programs in assembly language.
Ease of upgrade	**Excellent**. Text files can be easily upgraded. Unfortunately the interpreter may require to be upgraded for changes in the language's specification.	**Medium**. Binary executables, and other binary files typically require to be upgraded.	**Poor**. Binary executables, and other binary files typically require to be upgraded. These may affect other programs.

17.2 Integrated development environment

At one time programs needed to use a separate editor to create their source code, a separate compiler program to compile the program and a separate linker to bind the compiled code with code from a library, to produce the executable program. Most development systems are now totally integrated, as illustrated in Figure 17.2, where the editor, compiler and linker are all part of the same integrated environment. An important tool is a debugger, which is used for two purposes:

- **To locate and fix errors.** A debugger can be set-up to break the program at given points (known as breakpoints), and then the developer can test any of the variables within the program. This helps to locate errors in the program. The developer can also execute the program one line at a time (known as step-through).
- **To perform a code walk-through.** Even if a program is successfully running, it is important to perform a code walk-through. This involves stepping through the program one line at a time, and watching the route that the code takes, and how the variables change. This is important as there may be something occurring in the program which is unwanted, such as taking more time to conduct an operation, than is necessary.

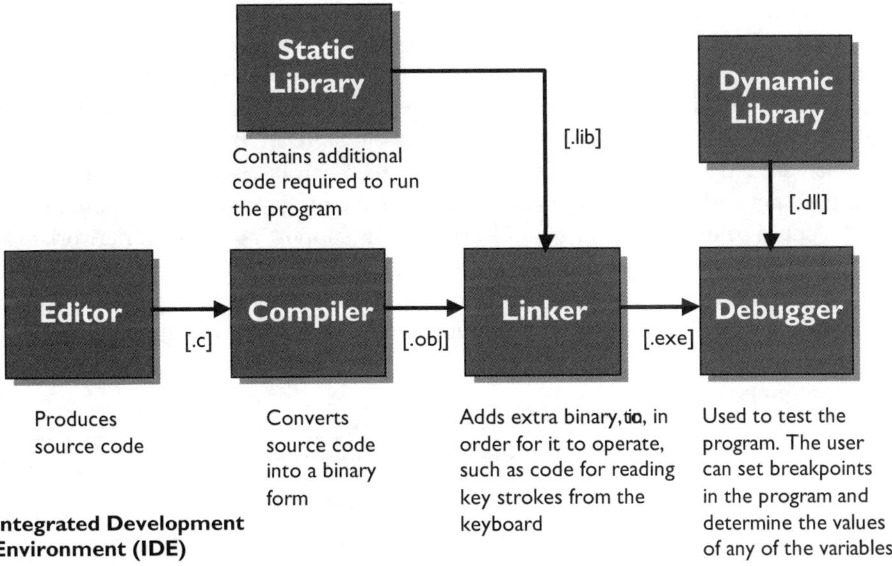

Figure 17.2 Integrated development environment

17.3 Procedural or modular programming

Modules are identifiable pieces of code with a defined interface. They are called from any part of a program and allow large programs to be split into more manageable tasks, each of which can be independently tested.

A module can be thought of as a 'black box' with a set of inputs and outputs. It has a sole purpose, and processes its inputs in a way dictated by its goal and provides some output. In most cases the actual operation of the 'black box' should be invisible to the rest of the program. This can be likened to an educational programme, where the course is broken down into a series of modules, which the student must undertake. For each module there is an initial specification (the input to the module, along with the students enrolled on the module), and the output are graduated students, with their results. As much as possible these modules should be taken independently from the other modules on the programme, as the teaching and operation of one module should not really have much affect on other modules. The amount that they are inter-related is known as cross-coupling. For example a student on a Computing course may be taking a Java module. The cross-coupling between this module, and the Legal Aspects of Computing module is likely to be zero, as the teaching of one does not affect the other. Some modules will have a strong coupling, such as the Object-Oriented Design Methods (OODM) and the Java module. With this the Java module will typically depend, in some way on the OODM module. If it was totally dependent on the way that it was taught and operated, then it would be 100% dependent. In most cases lecturers will try and reduce the amount of coupling, so that the module can run without affecting other modules.

> 'The use of COBOL cripples the mind; its teaching should, therefore, be regarded as a criminal offense.'
>
> - Dijkstra

A modular program consists of a number of 'black boxes' which, in most cases, work independently of all others, each of which uses variables declared within themselves (local variables) and any parameters sent to it. Figure 17.3 illustrates a function represented by an ideal 'black box' with inputs and outputs, and Figure 17.4 shows a main function calling several subfunctions (or modules). New techniques in software development use components, which are large general-purpose modules, which can be used in a number of ways. For example a networking component could be used in a program. If the component is well designed it could be used in a number of ways, such as supporting different network protocols, or different network types. These have led to the concept of component factories, where large software components are generated, which are general enough so that they can be reused for many different types of applications. These components could be stored around the Internet, and downloaded when a programmer needs to integrate them with their own program.

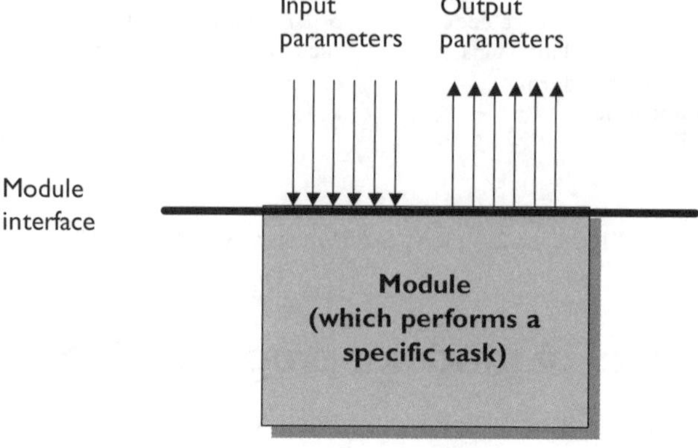

Figure 17.3 An ideal 'black-box' representation of a module

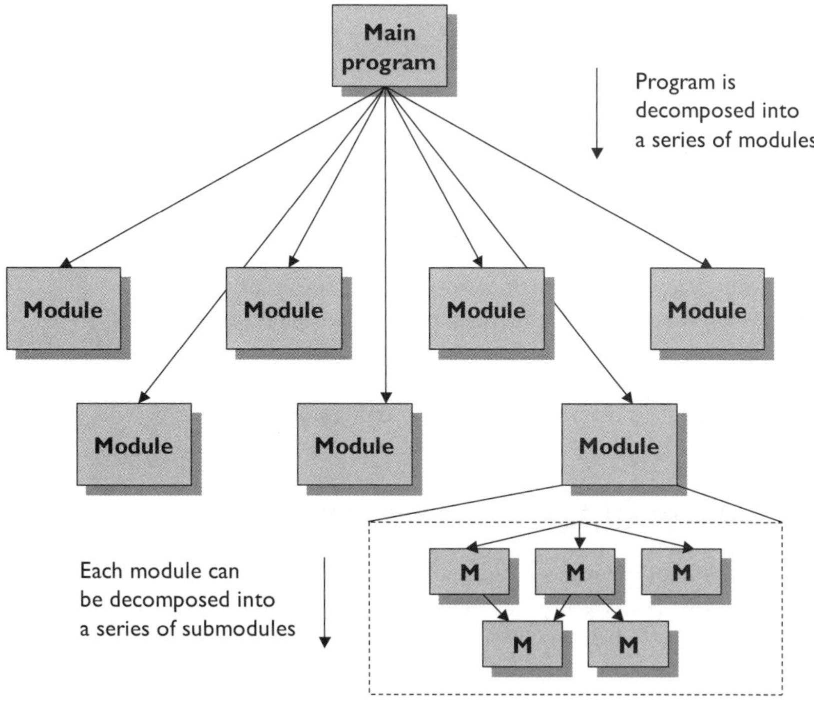

Figure 17.4 Hierarchical decomposition of a program

17.4 Event-driven programming

Traditional methods of programming involve writing a program which flows from one part to the next in a linear manner. The programs are designed using a top-down structured design, where the task is split into a number of subtasks (or submodules) and these are then called when they are required. This means that it is relatively difficult to interrupt the operation of a certain part of a program to do another activity, such as updating the graphics display. It is also an inefficient way of programming, as the program could be waiting for some other to occur, such as waiting for the user to press a key on the keyboard, because the computer could be doing something else while it is waiting.

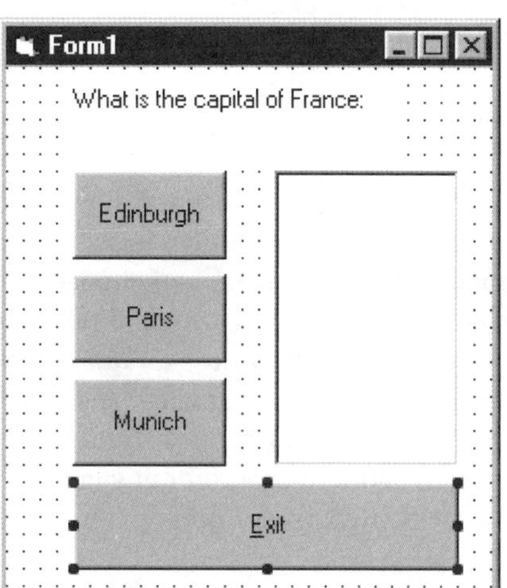

An event-driven program differs from this method, and is written to respond to events, such as:

- When the user clicks the mouse.
- When the user presses a key on the keyboard.
- When a character is received from a modem.

- When the printer becomes busy.

Event-driven programs are typically more responsive to the user, as they can be made to respond to many different types of events. For example, the following are events that can occur when the user has selected a command button:

- MouseOver event. Responding to the mouse cursor moving over the button.
- KeyPress. Responding to a key being press when the mouse cursor is over the button.
- KeyUp event. Responding to a key being released.
- KeyDown event. Responding to a key being pressed.
- DblClick event. Responding to a double-click of a mouse button.
- DragDrop event. Dragging another object on top of the button.
- MouseDown event. Responds to a mouse button down.
- MouseUp event. Responds to a mouse button up.
- LostFocus event. Responds to another object being selected.

17.5 Object-oriented programming

We live in a world full of objects; so object-oriented programming is a natural technique in developing programs. For example we have an object called a cup, and each cup has a number of parameters, such as its colour, its shape, its size, and so on. It is efficient for us to identify it as a cup, as we know that cups should be able to hold liquid, and we will place our cup beside all the other cups that we have. If we were a cup designer then we could list all the possible parameters of a cup, and for each design we could set the parameters. Some of the parameters might not actually be used, but for a general-purpose design we would specific every parameter that a cup might have. So let's design a cup. For a simple case we'll limit the choices for five main parameters:

Parameter	**Cup 1**	**Cup 2**	**Cup3**
Shape (Standard/Square/Mug)	Standard	Square	Mug
Colour (Red/Blue/Green)	Blue	Red	Green
Size (Small/Medium/Large)	Small	Large	Small
Transparency (0 to 100%)	100%	50%	25%
Handle type (Small/Large)	Small	Small	Large

Thus we have three choices of shape (square, standard or mug), three choices of colour (red, blue or green), three choices in size (small, medium or large) and two choices of handle type (small or large). Also we can choose a level of transparency of the cup from 0 to 100% (in integer steps. In object-oriented programs the collection of parameters is known as a class. Thus we could have a class for our cup which encapsulates all the design parameters for our cup. The instance of our class, such as Cup 1, Cup 2 and Cup 3, is known as an object. We can create many objects from our class.

Many modern programming languages, such as Delphi, C++ and Java, now typically use object-oriented programming. It involves:

- **Classes**. Defines a collection of parameters that can be used to define an object. For example, a class for a car may have the following parameters:
    - Car type.

- Colour.
- Engine size.

- **Objects.** Objects are created from classes. For example, as illustrated in Figure 17.5, two car objects could be created, as:

    - Car 1 (Object 1). Car type = "Toyota", Colour = "Blue", Engine size= "1600".
    - Car 2 (Object 2). Car type = "Ford", Colour = "Red", Engine size = "1000"

Object-oriented programming is an excellent programming technique as it involves creating a program around the data, and not, as in modular programming, around the modules. This allows for a much better definition of the problem.

Object-oriented design focuses on the data that is used in program, and not on the modules that are used. Objects are operated on by methods. These will be introduced in a following section.

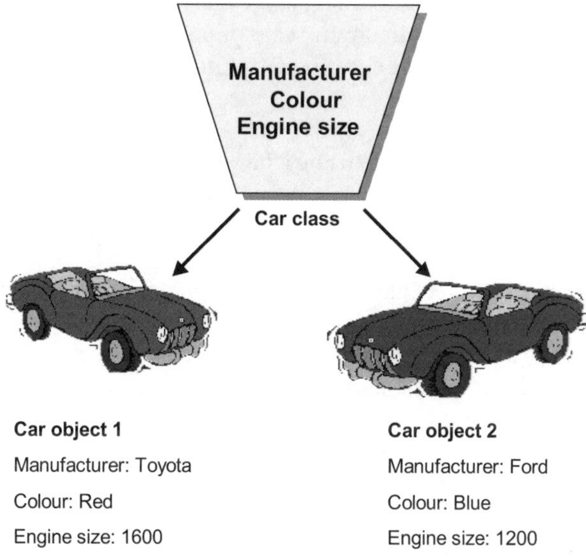

Figure 17.5 Car class and object

17.6 Interpreted languages

Interpreted languages have several advantages over other types of languages, such as:

- They are extremely portable, compared with compiled and assembled languages, because only the interpreter is required to interface to the hardware and the operating system. Thus, in the case of HTML, only the browser has to be compatible with the system.
- They are small in size, compared to compiled languages.
- They can be easily updated, with a change of the interpreter. An example of an interpreted language is HTML which is interpreted by a WWW browser. Users can easily

upgrade their system by downloading a new WWW browser, which may enhance one or more features. Unfortunately the developer of the code must decide on which version of the interpreter they will support.

- They can be easily upgraded and distributed, as all that is required is to distribute a text file. There are typically no binary files, such as library files, to be transported with them.
- Since the program files are text files, they are easily edited. Thus even a BASIC text editor can edit the program. Unfortunately, because they are available in a text form, they can be easily copied and changed. Sometimes, though, as in the case of ASP and PHP, a WWW server processes the code and converts it into another format (such as HTML), so that the requestor is not able to see the original code.

WWW-based languages such as HTML, and languages which integrate into HMTL, such as ASP, PHP, CGI, JavaScript and VBScript will be discussed in the next chapter.

17.6.1 Java

Java is a totally object-oriented programming language, and has been designed for Internet applications, but can be used for virtually any kind of programming. It has now become the most popular programming language, beating C++ into second place. It can be used as either:

- A **stand-alone** program which is run using a Java interpreter.
- An **applet** which is interpreted by a WWW browser, or can be integrated into a WWW page with JSP (Java Server Page).

The increased power of computers allowed the development of the Java programming language. It was first released in 1995 and was quickly adopted as it fitted well with Internet-based programming. It was followed by several other versions, such as Java 1.4, which gave faster interpretation of Java applets and included many new features. Java is a general-purpose, concurrent, class-based, object-oriented language and has been designed to be relatively simple to build complex applications. Java is developed from C and C++, but some parts of C++ (mainly the most difficult parts, such as pointers and parameter passing) have been dropped and others added.

Java has the great advantage over conventional software languages in that it produces code which is computer hardware independent. This is because the WWW browser interprets the compiled code (called bytecodes). Unfortunately, this leads to slower execution, but, as much of the time in a graphical user interface program is spent updating the graphics display, then the overhead is, as far as the user is concerned, not a great one. Most existing Web browsers are enabled for Java applets (such as Internet Explorer 3.0 and Netscape 2.0 and later versions). Figure 17.6 shows how Java applets are created. First the source code is produced with an editor; next a Java compiler compiles the Java source code into bytecode. An HTML page is then constructed which has the reference to the applet. After this a Java-enabled browser or applet viewer can then be used to run the applet.

The main advantages of Java, over other languages, include:

- **Networking support.** Direct support for the Internet and networking, especially for the transmission of compression image, audio and video formats.
- **Compatibility**. Allows programs to run on any type of system, no matter their operating system or their system type.

- **Threads**. Multitasking involves running several processes at a time. Java allows programs to be split into a number of parts (threads) and each of these is run on the multitasking system (multithreading).
- **RMI** (Remote Method Invocation). This supports the information interchange between the server and client. It uses a distributed object application, where Java objects may be accessed and their methods called remotely to take advantage of a distributed environment and thus spread a workload over a number of network nodes.
- **Object serialization**. This is a process which enables the reading and writing of objects, and has many uses, such as RMI and object persistence. In developing agent applications it is serialization that can provides *mobility*. An object may be serialized (converted to a bit stream), and moved (passed over the socket) to another host where it continues its execution.

The Java Development Kit (JDK) is available, free, from Sun Microsystems. This can be used to compile Java applets and standalone programs. There are versions for Microsoft Windows, Apple Mac and UNIX-based systems with many sample applets.

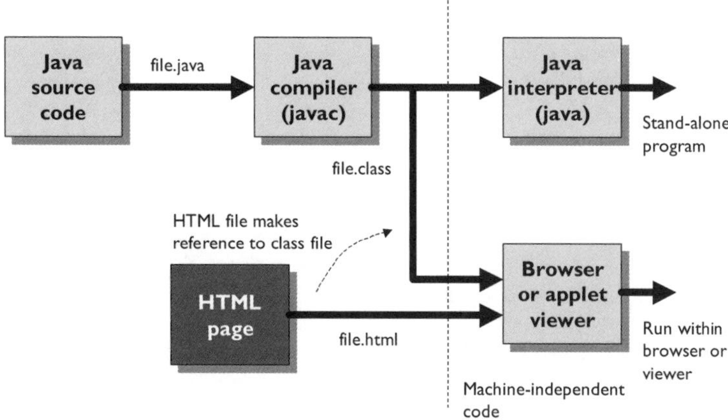

Figure 17.6 Constructing Java applets and standalone programs

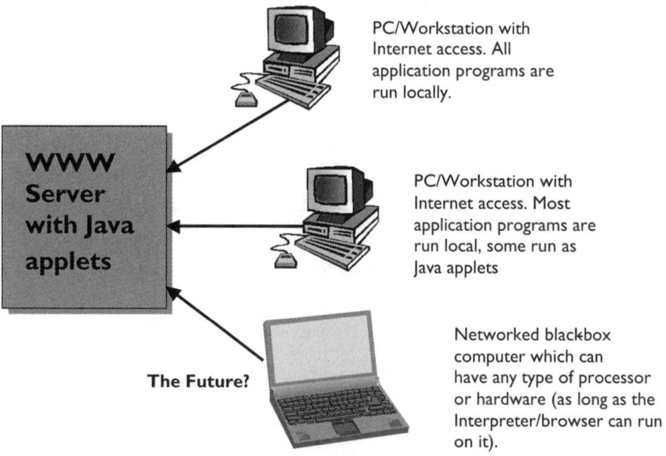

Figure 17.7 Internet accessing

An example Java applet is given next.

Java applet

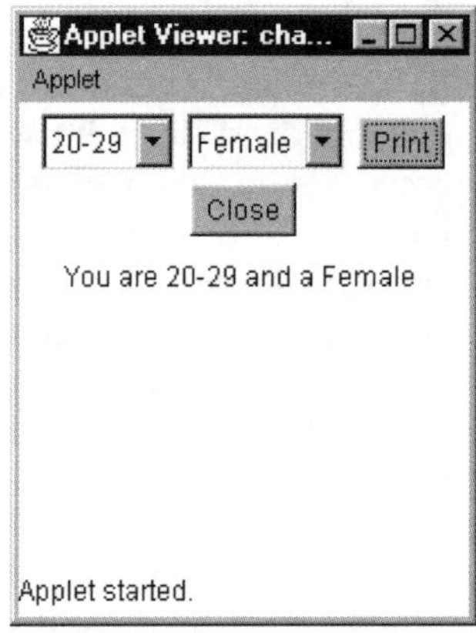


```
import java.applet.*;
import java.awt.*;
import java.awt.event.*;

public class chap9_15 extends Applet
  implements ItemListener, ActionListener
{
Choice age = new Choice();
Choice gender = new Choice();
Button print= new Button("Print");
Button close= new Button("Close");
String gendertype=null, agetype=null;

String Msg, Options[];
  public void init()
  {
      age.addItem("10-19");
      age.addItem("20-29");
      age.addItem("30-39");
      age.addItem("40-49");
      age.addItem("Other");
      add(age);

      gender.addItem("Male");
      gender.addItem("Female");
      add(gender);
      add(print);
      add(close);

      age.addItemListener(this);
      gender.addItemListener(this);
      print.addActionListener(this);
      close.addActionListener(this);
  }
 public void itemStateChanged(ItemEvent evt)
 {
  int i;
  Object obj;

     obj=evt.getItem();

  if (obj.equals("10-19")) agetype="10-19";
  else if (obj.equals("20-29"))
     agetype="20-29";
  else if (obj.equals("30-39"))
    agetype="30-39";
  else if (obj.equals("40-49"))
    agetype="40-49";
  else if (obj.equals("Other"))
    agetype="Other";
  else if (obj.equals("Male"))
    gendertype="Male";
  else if (obj.equals("Female"))
    gendertype="Female";
  }
public void actionPerformed(ActionEvent evt)
{
String str;

  str=evt.getActionCommand();
```

```
    if (str.equals("Print"))  repaint();
    else if (str.equals("Close")) System.exit(0);
 }
public void paint(Graphics g)
{
 if ((agetype!=null) && (gendertype!=null))
   Msg="Your are " + agetype + " and a " + gender-
type;
 else Msg="Please select age and gender";

 if (Msg!=null) g.drawString(Msg,20,80);
 }
}
```

JSP, which is a language which integrates the Java programming language with WWW pages, will be discussed in the next chapter.

17.6.2 BASIC

At the beginning of the 1960s the main programming languages were COBOL and FORTRAN. These languages were not well suited to introducing students to programming languages. Thus, in 1964, John Kemeny and Thomas Kurtz at Dartmouth College developed the BASIC (Beginners All-purpose Symbolic Instruction Code) programming language. It was a great success, although it was never used in many 'serious' applications, until Microsoft adopted it as the basis of their Visual BASIC, which provided an excellent opportunity to develop Microsoft Windows programs. The greatest weakness of many early versions of BASIC was that it was an interpreted language, thus users could actually view the source code, and easily copy it. Newer versions of BASIC included a compiler, and linker, which allowed the BASIC code to be compiled to an executable file.

The golden years for BASIC were when the first microcomputers appeared, and BASIC become a standard programming language on many microcomputer systems. Many of the classic microcomputers, such as the Sinclair ZX Spectrum, used BASIC to develop programs. Unfortunately, at the time, there were no real standards for the language itself, and many compiler developers added their own parts to the language, which made standardization difficult. Thus a BASIC program written on one computer may not run on another computer. Pascal came along and challenged BASIC for a while, but it was the C programming language which then provided the ultimate challenge to BASIC. It was small enough to run on a microcomputer, and was also available on large computers. Along with this it was quickly standardized, so that programs written on one type of computer would have a good chance to run on another type.

17.7 Compiled languages

Compiled languages are a good compromise between assembled and interpreted languages. The main advantages are:

- They are relatively fast, compared with interpreted languages.
- They are relatively easy to develop, compared with assembled languages.
- They are fairly reliable for run-time errors, compared with interpreted and assembled languages.

The main compiled languages are: Visual Basic, C/C++, Pascal and Delphi.

17.7.1 Visual BASIC

Visual BASIC is one of the best programming languages, and is probably the easiest programming language to actually get something to work, and operating in a Microsoft Windows environment. It uses BASIC programming language for its BASIC language syntax, but adds many new features. It is especially suited to Microsoft Windows programs and integrates well with other Microsoft application programs (such as Word and Excel). Visual BASIC has even been added to many of the Microsoft Office products, where users can develop macro programs in Visual BASIC. In general it is:

- **Object-oriented**. Where the program is designed around a number of ready-made and user-defined objects. Typical objects include buttons, windows and sockets (which are communication ports over a network).
- **Event-driven**. Where the execution of the program is not predefined and its execution is triggered by events, such as a mouse click, a keyboard press, and so on.
- **Designed from the user interface outwards**. The program is typically designed by first developing the user interface and then code is designed to respond to events within the interface.

Figure 17.8 shows an example Visual BASIC desktop, which contains a menu form, controls, main form, project windows and properties window.

An example Visual BASIC program is given next. The module name identifies the name of the object, and the event. For example `Command1_Click()` identifies the command button object named `Command1` which is called on the `Click` event. An additional file is used in Visual BASIC which defines the layout, and types of objects used. This is separate to the Visual BASIC code.

```
Private Sub Command1_Click()
Dim a, b, c As Double
Dim aval, bval, cval As String
    aval = Text1.Text
    bval = Text2.Text
    cval = Text3.Text
    a = CDbl(aval)
    b = CDbl(bval)
    c = CDbl(cval)
    If (Not (IsNumeric(aval)) Or _
        Not (IsNumeric(bval)) Or Not (IsNumeric(cval))) Then
        Text4.Text = ""
        Text5.Text = ""
        Text6.Text = "INVALID"
    ElseIf ((b * b) > (4 * a * c)) Then
        Text4.Text = CStr((-b + Sqr(b * b - 4 * a * c)) / (2 * a))
        Text5.Text = CStr((-b - Sqr(b * b - 4 * a * c)) / (2 * a))
        Text6.Text = "Real"
    ElseIf (b * b < 4 * a * c) Then
        Text4.Text = CStr(-b / (2 * a))
        Text5.Text = "j" + CStr(Sqr(4 * a * c - b * b) / (2 * a))
        Text6.Text = "Complex"
    Else
```

```
        Text4.Text = CStr(-b / (2 * a))
        Text5.Text = ""
        Text6.Text = "Singlar"
    End If
End Sub
```

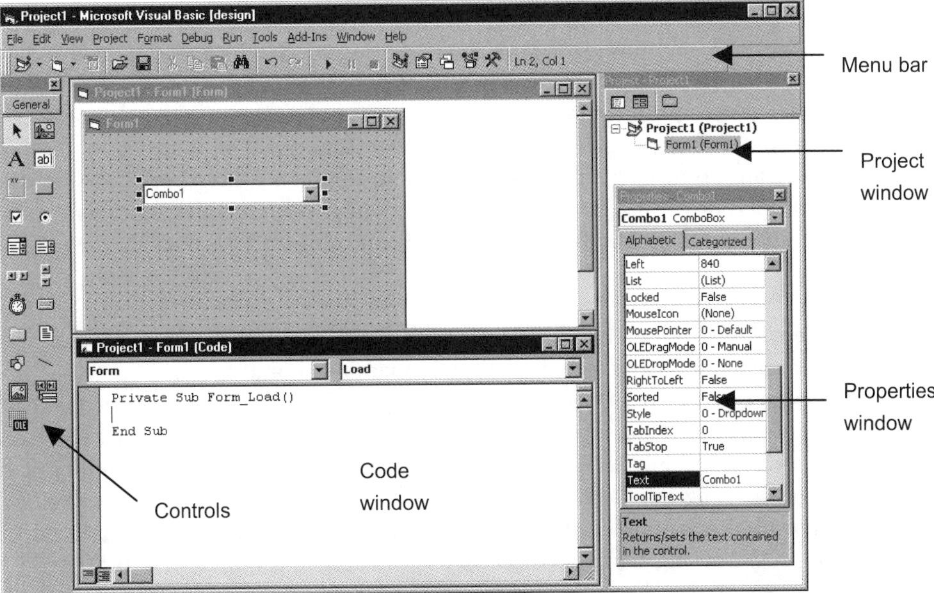

Figure 17.8 Visual BASIC desktop

Figure 17.9 shows two sample runs.

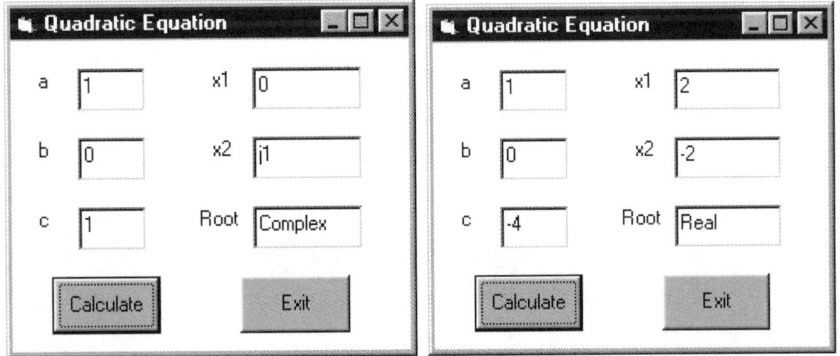

Figure 17.9 Sample runs

17.7.2 Pascal

Pascal was, at one time, one of the most widely used PC-based programming languages, but its popularity has waned against the strength of C++ and Java. It is an excellent programming language and is typically used to teach good software development techniques. Its popularity is almost solely due to Borland, who developed the excellent Turbo Pascal integrated development environment (IDE), and then enhanced it further, for Microsoft Windows programming, with Borland Delphi.

17.7.3 Delphi

Visual BASIC has the advantage over the other languages in that it is relatively easy to use and to program, but it suffers when the user needs to achieve complex programming. The greatest weakness of Visual BASIC is that variables do not need to be declared before they are used. Thus variables can be created, but misspelled, which could cause errors in the program. This also causes problems when the programmer performs an operation which is possibly not allowed, or intended. The BASIC compiler does not have a strong method of checking the programs, thus languages such as C++ and Delphi are often preferred for writing large, and complex programs. Figure 17.10 shows a sample Borland Delphi screen.

Delphi uses standard Pascal and can also used object-oriented Pascal (OOP). In general it is:

- **Event-driven**. Where the execution of a program is not predefined and its execution is triggered by events, such as a mouse click, a keyboard press, and so on.
- **Designed from the user interface outwards**. The program is typically designed by first developing the user interface and then coded to respond to events within the interface.
- **Component-based**. Delphi uses standard components which the programming can easily add to the program. These components are typically general-purpose modules which can be used in a number of ways, and in a number of environments. For example a network programming module could be used to transmit either UDP or TCP data packets.

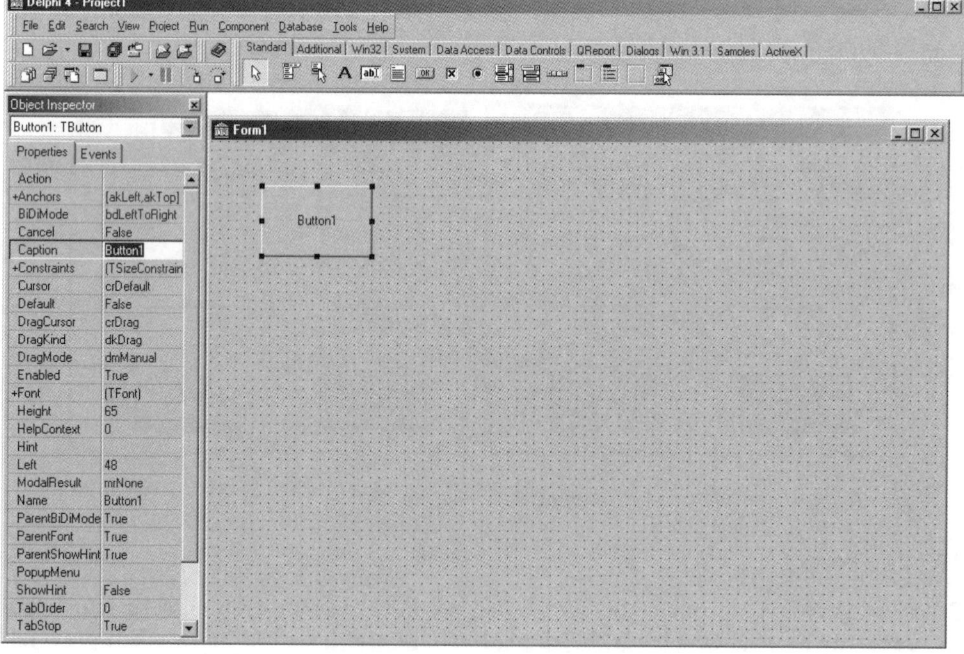

Figure 17.10 Delphi user interface

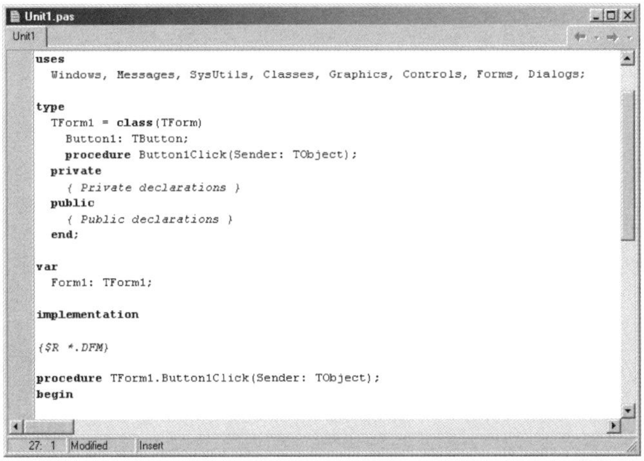

```
Unit1.pas
Unit1
uses
  Windows, Messages, SysUtils, Classes, Graphics, Controls, Forms, Dialogs;

type
  TForm1 = class(TForm)
    Button1: TButton;
    procedure Button1Click(Sender: TObject);
  private
    { Private declarations }
  public
    { Public declarations }
  end;

var
  Form1: TForm1;

implementation

{$R *.DFM}

procedure TForm1.Button1Click(Sender: TObject);
begin
27: 1   Modified   Insert
```

Figure 17.10 Continued

Delphi uses a number of terms to describe design procedures, these are:

- **Components**. The Delphi interface contains a window with component objects which are pasted onto a form. These components can be simple text, menus, spreadsheet grids, radio buttons, and so on. Each component has a set of properties that defines its operation, such as its colour, its font size and type, whether it can be resized, and so on. Some components, such as command buttons, menus, and so on, normally have code attached to them, but simple controls, such as text and a graphics image can simply exist on a form with no associated code. Example components are: TRadioButton (Windows radio button), TButton (push button control) and TListBox (Windows list box).
- **Forms**. A form is the anchor for all parts of a Delphi program. Initially it is a blank window and the user pastes controls onto it to create the required user interface. Code is then associated with events on the form, such as responding to a button press or a slider control, although some control elements do not have associated code. A program can have one or more forms, each of which displays and handles data in different ways. When adding components to the form, editing properties, or coding in the form unit, it is the form that is being edited. The following gives an example of some Delphi code, and Figure 17.11 shows a sample run:

```
procedure TForm1.Button1Click(Sender: TObject);
var         outstr,outstr1,outstr2:string;
            a,b,c,x1,x2:real;
            code:integer;
begin
     val(edit1.text,a,code);
     val(edit2.text,b,code);
     val(edit3.text,c,code);
     if (b*b>4*a*c) then
     begin
        edit6.text:='REAL';
        x1:=(-b+sqrt(b*b-4*a*c))/(2*a);
```

```
         x2:=(-b-sqrt(b*b-4*a*c))/(2*a);
         str(x1:6:2,outstr);
         edit4.text:=outstr;
         str(x2:6:2,outstr);
         edit5.text:=outstr;
      end
      else if (b*b=4*a*c) then
      begin
         edit6.text:='SINGULAR';
         x1:=-b/(2*a);
         str(x1:6:3,outstr);
         edit4.text:=outstr;
         edit5.text:='';
      end
      else
      begin
         edit6.text:='COMPLEX';
         x1:=-b/(2*a);
         x2:=sqrt(4*a*c-b*b)/(2*a);
         str(x1:6:2,outstr1);
         str(x2:6:2,outstr2);
         outstr:=outstr1+'+j'+outstr2;
         edit4.text:=outstr;
         outstr:=outstr1+'-j'+outstr2;
         edit5.text:=outstr;
      end;
end;
```

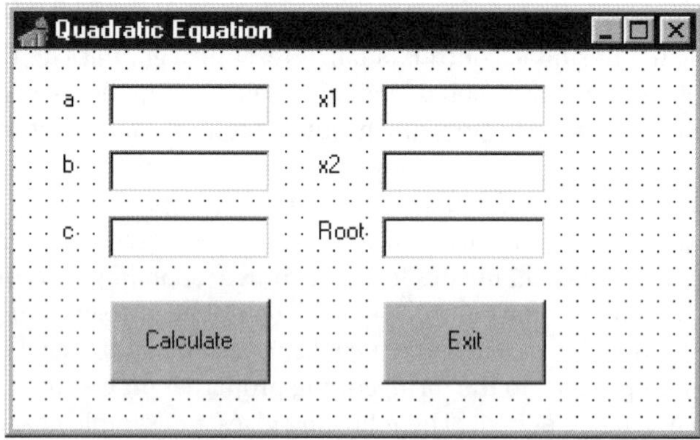

Figure 17.11 Sample run

17.7.4 C

Up to 1974, most programming languages had been produced either as a teaching language, such as Pascal or BASIC, or had been developed in the early days of computing, such as FORTRAN and COBOL. Both FORTRAN and COBOL had a large hold on the main-frame market, but the emerging microcomputers required much smaller programming languages, that could interface to many different types of hardware. Another factor which called for a new programming language was the increasing influence of operating systems. None of the existing programming languages properly interfaced to the operating system, thus Brian Kernighan and Dennis Ritchie developed the C programming language. Its main advantage was that it was supported in the UNIX operating system. C has since led a charmed existence by software developers for many proven (and unproven) reasons, and quickly took off in a way that Pascal had failed to do. Its main advantages were that: it could be both a high- and a low-level language, it produced small and efficient code, and that it was portable on different systems. Another major advantage was that it was a standardized software language, with ANSI C, that was supported on most operating systems. For this, a program written on one computer system would have a good chance to compile on another system, as long as both compilers conformed to a given standard (typically ANSI C). Pascal always struggled because many compiler developers used non-standard additions to the BASIC language, and thus Pascal programs were difficult to port from one system to another. FORTRAN never really had this problem, as it only had a few standards, mainly FORTRAN 57 and FORTRAN 77. C moved from the UNIX operating system to the PCs, as they became more advanced. It normally requires a relatively large amount of storage space (for all of its standardized libraries), whereas BASIC requires very little storage space.

The following program gives an example of a C program. As can be seen, it is an extremely terse language, which is difficult for non-C programmers to read.

```
/* prog.c          */
#include <stdio.h>

#define     MAX      150
#define     TRUE     1
#define     FALSE    0

void     get_values(int *n,float array[]);
void     print_values(int n,float array_in[]);
void     sort(int n,float input[]);
void     order(float *val1,float *val2);

int      main(void)
{
float    array[MAX];
int      nvalues;

   get_values(&nvalues,array);
   sort(nvalues,array);
   print_values(nvalues,array);
   return(0);
}

void     get_values(int *n,float array[])
/* *n stores the number of value in the array */
{
int      i,rtn,okay;

   do
   {
      printf("Enter number of values to be processed >>");
      rtn=scanf("%d",n);
      if ((rtn!=1) || (*n<0) || (*n>MAX))
      {
         printf("Max elements is %d, re-enter\n",MAX);
         okay=FALSE;
      }
      else  okay=TRUE;
   } while (!okay);

   for (i=0;i<*n;i++)
   {
```

```
      printf("Enter value >>");
      scanf("%f",&array[i]);
   }
}
void     print_values(int n,float array_in[])
{
int      i;
   printf("Ordered values\n");
   for (i=0;i<n;i++)
      printf("%8.3f ",array_in[i]);
}

void     sort(int n,float input[])
/* order array input to give smallest to largest */
{
int      i,j;
   for (i=0;i<n-1;i++)
      for (j=n-1;i<j;j--)
         order(&input[i],&input[j]);
}
void     order(float *val1,float *val2)
/* val1 is the smallest    */
{
float temp;
   if (*val1 > *val2)
   {
      temp = *val1;
      *val1 = *val2;
      *val2 = temp;
   }
}
```

Test run 17. 1 shows a sample run with 10 entered values.

Test run 17.1

```
Enter number of values be entered >> 10
Enter value >> 3
Enter value >> -2
Enter value >> 4
Enter value >> 10
Enter value >> 3
Enter value >> 2
Enter value >> 1
Enter value >> 0
Enter value >> 19
Enter value >> 14
Ordered values
  -2.000    0.000    1.000    2.000    3.000    3.000    4.000
10.000   14.000   19.000
```

17.7.5 C++

C is an excellent software development language for many general-purpose applications. Its approach is that data and associated functions are distinct, where data is declared and the functions are then implemented. Object-oriented programming languages allow the encapsulation of a set of data types and associated functions (called methods) into objects.

C++ is one of the most popular object-oriented languages (alongside Java) and was developed by Bjane Stoustrup at AT&T Bell Laboratories. Its great strength, and also one of its weaknesses, is that it was based on the popular C programming language. Its usage is now widespread and many current applications have been written using C++, whether they be for microcomputers, minicomputers and mainframe computers. The main drawback of C++ is that programmers could still use the C programming language, which, because of its looseness and simplicity, allowed the programmer to produce programs that would compile, but could crash because of a run-time error which was due to badly designed software. Typically errors were running off the end of an array, bad parameter passing into modules, or using memory that was not reserved for other purposes. Object-oriented programming languages are much tighter in their syntax, and the things that are allowed to be done. Thus, the compiler will typically catch more errors, whether they are run-time or syntax errors, before the program is run. Java has since overcome the problems of C++, as it is totally object-oriented, and much tighter in the rules of software coding.

Figure 17.12 shows a Microsoft Visual C++ development environment. C++ has many enhancements over C. These include:

- **I/O stream support**. This facility allows data to be directed to an input and/or an output stream.
- **Objects**. An object incorporates data definitions and the declaration and definitions of functions which operate on that data.
- **Classes**. These are used to implement objects and can be initialized and discarded with constructors and destructors, respectively.
- **Data hiding**. This allows certain data to be hidden from parts of a program which are not allowed access to it.
- **Overloading**. This allows more than one definition and implementation of a function.
- **Virtual functions**. These allow any one of a number of multiple defined functions to be called at run-time.
- **Template classes**. These allow the same class to be used by different data.

```
#include <iostream.h>

class circuit
{
private:
   float r1,r2;
public:
   void  get_res(void);
   float series(void);
   float parallel(void);
};

int   main(void)
{
   circuit  c1;
   float    res;

   c1.get_res();

   res=c1.series();
   cout << "Series resistance is " << res << " ohms\n";

   res=c1.parallel();
   cout << "Parallel resistance is " << res << " ohms\n";
   return(0);
}

void  circuit::get_res(void)
```

```
{
   cout << "Enter r1 >> ";
   cin >> r1;
   cout << "Enter r2 >> ";
   cin >> r2;
}

float circuit::parallel(void)
{
   return((r1*r2)/(r1+r2));
}

float circuit::series(void)
{
   return(r1+r2);
}
```

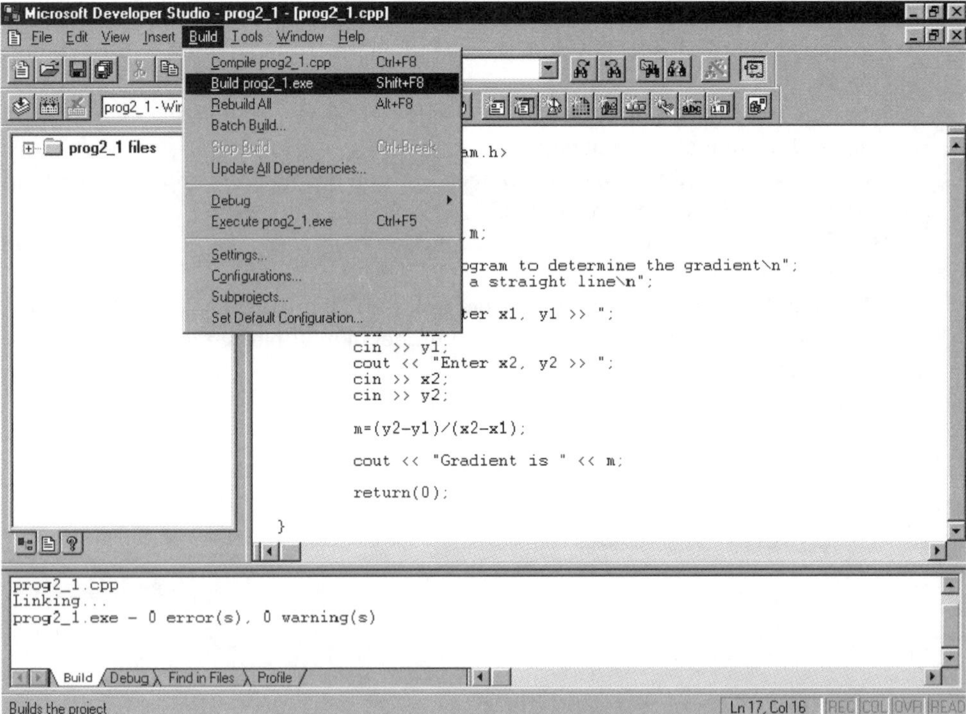

Figure 17.12 Microsoft Visual C++

Test run 17. 2

```
Enter r1 >> 1000
Enter r2 >> 1000
Series resistance is 2000 ohms
Parallel resistance is 500 ohms
```

17.7.6 FORTRAN

FORTRAN was developed by IBM in 1957, and caused a great revolution, since up to that point, computer programs were written in machine code. It grew to become one of the most popular computer languages in the world, but with the advent of new general-purpose languages, its popularity has waned. Where COBOL was used in data processing and business applications, FORTRAN was used primarily used in engineering and science. It is an extremely portable language and is mainly used on workstations and mini/main-frame computers. FORTRAN is not used in many PC-based applications mainly because it is poor in input/output, it also lacks some of the facilities to handle characters. It is also a relatively easy language to learn but it is very prone to errors. A standard for FORTRAN was developed by ANSI in 1977, and is known as FORTRAN-77. You may find it strange but there are still many FORTRAN programs around, which are still working quietly giving very few problems.

The program given next contains two subroutines called from a main program and test run 17. 3 shows a sample run.

```
      program calc_resistance
C     Program to calculate the parallel resistor of three resistors
      real R1,R2,R3,Requ
      print *,'Program to determine equivalent parallel resistance'
      print *,'of three resistors'
      print *,'Enter R1, R2 and R3 >>'
      read *,R1,R2,R3
      Requ=1/(1/R1+1/R2+1/R3)
      print 100,R1,R2,R3
 100  format(' R1 =',f8.2,' R2',f8.2,' R3=',f8.2,' ohm')
      print 200,Requ
 200  format(' Equivalent parallel resistance is',f8.2,' ohm')
      end
```

Test run 17.3 shows a run with values of 250, 500 and 1000 Ω.

Test run 17.3

```
Program to determine equivalent parallel resistance
of three resistors
Enter R1, R2 and R3 >>1000 500 250
R1 = 1000.00 R2  500.00 R3=  250.00 ohm
Equivalent parallel resistance is  142.86 ohm
```

When FORTRAN was first developed, the system used punch cards, thus the layout of the program follows the layout of a punch card, and is:

Field	Column(s)
Statement label	1 through 5
Continuation indicator	6
Statement	7 through 72

A comment can be indicated with the letter C or an asterisk (*) in column 1, and the compiler ignores this line. The statement field uses column 7 to 72. If a line is longer than this a character is inserted in the continuation column.

1	2	3	4	5	6	7	8	9	10	11	12	13	14	15	16	17	18
C						T	h	i	s		a		p	r	o	g	
	1	0	0			A	=	5									
	2	0	0			B	=	1	0	0							
						E	N	D									

17.7.7 Major problems with BASIC and FORTRAN

BASIC and FORTRAN are similar in their syntax, as BASIC was developed at a time that FORTRAN was the leading programming language. Most programming languages do not allow users to create variables without them first being declared by their data type. For example C declares variables as follows:

```
int      value1, value2;     /* two integers                    */
float    x, y;               /* two real values                 */
char     str1[10], ch;       /* a character string and a character    */
```

FORTRAN, Visual BASIC and BASIC allow variables to be used without them first being declared. It is possible to declare the variables, but it is not statutory. It is thus difficult for the compiler to tell the data type of the variable, and thus reserve enough space in memory for it. In FORTRAN data types are automatically assigned with relation to the first letter of the variable name. For example:

- Variable names which start with an I, J, K, L, M or N are integers (for example `Ival`, `Ndata1` and `Msubt` are all integer values, unless they are declared otherwise).
- Variables which start with an H are character strings.
- Variables which start with an R, S, T, U, V, W, X and Y are floating-point values.

In BASIC values have implied data types, which are defined in the way they are used. For example if the user does the following:

```
Dim  val as integer
Dim  x, y as double

   z= x * y
```

Then z would automatically be declared to be a double data type.

17.8 Assembled languages

Assembled languages, such as 8086, 6502, Z80 and 68000 are derived directly from the machine code of the processor. They are thus highly optimized as the programmer can directly control the operation to the program, rather than the compiler making the decisions. They have many major problems, and are hardly ever used to create large programs. An example 8086 assembly language programs is given next.

```
code          SEGMENT
              ASSUME cs:code

BASEADDRESS        EQU      01F0H            ; change this as required
PORTA              EQU      BASEADDRESS
PORTB              EQU      BASEADDRESS+1
CNTRLREG           EQU      BASEADDRESS+3
;  program to output to Port B counts in binary until from 00000000
;  to 11111111 with approximately 1 second delay between changes
start:
        mov dx,CNTRLREG        ; set up PPI with
        mov al,90h             ; Port B as Output
```

```
         out dx,al
         mov ax,00h
loop1:
         mov dx,PORTB
         out dx,al              ; output to Port B

         call delay
         inc ax
         cmp ax,100h
         jnz loop1              ; repeat until all 1s

         mov ah,4cH             ; program exit
         int 21h                ;

         ; ROUTINE TO GIVE 1 SECOND DELAY USING THE PC TIMER
DELAY:      push ax
         push bx
         mov ax,18              ; 18.2 clock ticks per second;
         ; Address of system timer on the PC is 0000:046C (low word)
         ; and 0000:046E (high word)
         mov bx,0
         mov es,bx
         ; Add the number of required ticks of the clock (ie 18)
         add ax,es:[46CH]
         mov bx,es:[46EH]

loop2:      ; Compare current timer count with AX and BX
         ;  if they are equal 1 second has passed
         cmp bx,es:[46EH]
         ja loop2
         jb over
         cmp ax,es:[46CH]
         jg loop2

over:       pop bx
         pop ax
         ret

code     ENDS
      END    start
```

Typically, these days, in-line assembly language is used alongside another programming language. For example, in C:

```
for (ival=0;ival<100;ival++)
{
   cout << "Outputting a value to the port"
   /* Assembly Language statements */
   _asm
   {
   mov dx, 01f0h
   mov al, ival
   out dx, ival
   }
   /********************************/
}
```

As a rule, as little as possible should be done in assembly language, as it is very easy to perform an incorrect operation. These days the major usage of assembly language is to write device drivers. In most cases, it is the operating system which communicates with the hardware, as illustrated in Figure 17.13.

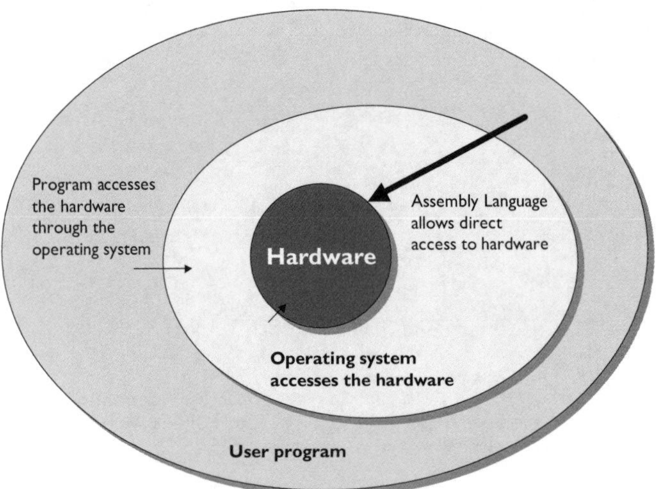

Figure 17.13 Accessing the hardware

17.9 Language comparison

The following table summarizes some of the feature of each programming language

	C	*C++*	*Pascal*	*Delphi*	*Visual BASIC*	*HTML*	*Java*	*COBOL*	*BASIC*	*FORTRAN*
Support for Windows programming	–	✓✓ 1	–	✓✓✓	✓✓✓	✗	✓ 2	✗	✗	✗
Easy to produce usable programs	✓	✓	✓✓	✓✓	✓✓✓	✗ 3	✓	✓	✓✓✓	✓
Available source code (4)	✓✓✓	✓✓✓	✓✓	✓	✓✓✓	✓✓✓	✓✓	✓	✓	✓
Support for Internet	–	✓✓	–	✓✓	✓✓	✓	✓✓✓	✗	✗	✗
Catches run-time errors (5)	– 6	✓✓	✓	✓✓	– 7	✓✓	✓✓✓ 8	✓	✗ 7	✗ 7

Availability of development tools	✓✓✓	✓✓✓	✓	– 9	✓ 9	✓✓✓	✓✓	✓	✓	✓
Support for object-oriented methods	×	✓✓	–	✓✓	✓✓	×	✓✓✓	×	×	×
Language power	✓✓	✓✓	✓✓	✓✓	– 10	×	✓✓✓ 11	–	–	–
Portability for different systems	✓✓	✓✓	✓	× 12	× 12	✓✓✓	✓✓✓	✓	✓	✓
Event-driven	×	✓ 13	×	✓✓✓	✓✓✓	✓ 14	×	×	×	×
Representation of problem/data	✓	✓✓	✓	✓✓	–	×	✓✓✓	×	×	×
Integration with other applications	–	✓✓	–	✓✓	✓✓✓	–	✓	×	×	×

The rating system is as follows:

✓✓✓ Excellent ✓✓ Good ✓ Fair
– Pass × Fail

Top five languages:

1. Java, which has won more of the sections than any other language.
2. C++, which consistently does well in virtually every measure.
3. Delphi which is another good all-rounder, but it fails in its acceptability because it is not widely supported by different vendors, and because it isn't portable between different systems.
4. Visual BASIC does extremely well in some sections, especially in its ease of use, its integration with other applications, and its support for event-driven programming, but its usage of the BASIC programming language is its biggest weakness.
5. C performs well in many situations and is extremely portable.

Notes:

(1) With Windows programming environments, such as Borland C++ and Visual C++.
(2) Java provides a generic approach to Windows programming.
(3) HTML does not support flow controls or repetition, thus without JavaScript it is difficult to have any user interaction.
(4) The available of example source code can have a great effect on the choice of a programming language. The Internet and development packages are full of source code for C, C++, Visual Basic and Java.
(5) A major problem with many languages is that the compiler does not catch possible run-time errors. A typical problem is when the program uses arrays, but the program accesses an array element which is outside the range of the array. This cases data to be read or written from an area of memory which is not assigned to the array, causing the program to act unreliably.
(6) C allows the programmer a great deal of freedom, and does not perform many checks that are necessary to get rid of run-time errors.
(7) Visual BASIC is particularly bad at detecting run-time errors, especially because the programmer does not need to declare variables. A common error is when a programmer uses two variables which have similar names, but are assumed to be the same variable. BASIC and FORTRAN are also similar in this respect. With FORTRAN, variables which begin with an I, J, K, M and N are assumed to be integers, while most other beginning letters are assumed to be floating-point variables.
(8) Java has a very strict syntax, and a strict set of rules for designing objects and classes. It is thus good at detecting run-time problems. It also allows for arrays to be resized, whenever required.
(9) Delphi and Visual BASIC are only supported by a single vendor. Visual BASIC, though, is likely to be well supported in the future by Microsoft.
(10) Visual BASIC uses the BASIC programming language for its BASIC language syntax which has little support for advanced programming language features, such as string manipulations, structures, and so on.
(11) New versions of Java allow for complex operations of data structures and object manipulation.
(12) Visual BASIC and Delphi are only available for PC systems, thus they cannot be ported between different systems.
(13) Microsoft Windows versions of C++ development systems allow for event-driven programming in C++, but it is not a standard part of the programming language.
(14) HTML can have limited event-driven facilities with Java Script.

17.10 Cross compiler

Often developers write programs which must be converted so that they can run on another system, possibly with a different processor and/or a different architecture. This requires a cross compiler, which either converts a high-level language to the machine code for the destination computer, or converts a machine code program on one computer to another one that runs on the destination computer. Typical reasons are:

- **Porting programs to other computers**. This can involve recompiling a program for another processor. The cross-compiler must thus know how to convert one type of machine code into another type.
- **Developing programs on a convenient computer**, and using a cross compiler to create the final executable version. This is typically used with game consoles where a programmer can use a PC to develop the code for games console (such as the Sony PlayStation) and then use a cross compiler to convert the code into a form that could run of the required system. Other example include cross compiling for an embedded system.
- **Developing for a prototype system**. Often the hardware is not initially available for software to be developed for a system. Thus often the software will be written for it on another system, and then compiled for the system using a cross compiler.
- **Using a less expensive development system**. Often when developing software for expensive systems it is easier to develop it on a cheaper system (such as a PC) and then port it over to the real system when the software is ready to be tested.
- **Programming microchips**. Typically it is much easier to write programs on a PC and then download the cross-compiled code to the device, rather than directly writing the code for it.
- **Availability of development tools**. Sometimes specific development systems are not available for the required system, thus it is often necessary to use a computer with the required development tools, and then cross compile for the final system.

Figure 17.14 illustrates examples of cross compilation. It should be noted that cross compilation can lead to many problems. This is because the system emulator and the cross compiler are never perfect and it is often difficult to fully test a program.

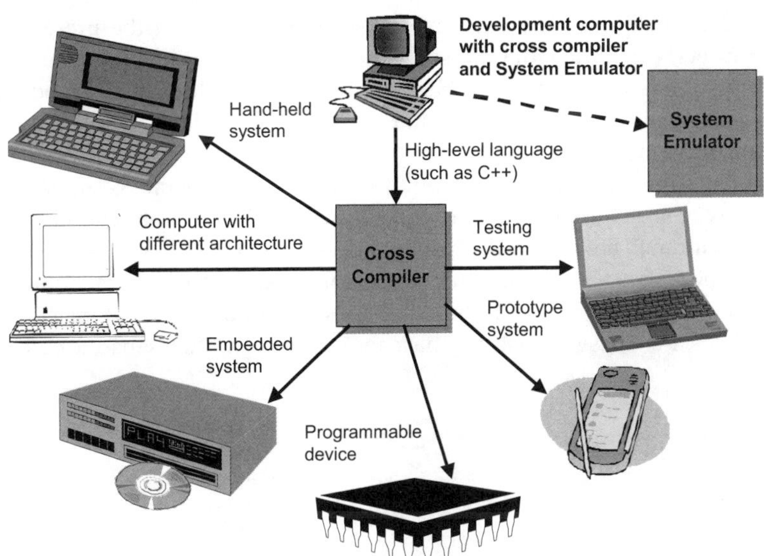

Figure 17.14 Examples of cross compilers

17.11 Three layers of programming

Just like in networking and the Internet, with its OSI model, most applications have three logical layers:

- **Data layer**. This manages the data used by the application. An application that stores its data in data files is said to implement the data layer itself. Many applications use a database to manage the storage of data. In these cases, the database itself is considered to be the data layer of the application.
- **Business logic layer**. This layer builds on the data layer, and contains the various rules and operations that the application performs on its data. For example, when an order is placed through an e-commerce Web site, the data layer stores the order details while the business logic layer performs all the required calculations, validates credit card numbers and ensures all the relevant information is present.
- **Presentation layer**. This layer builds on the business logic layer and presents and manages the display which enables the user to interact with the system. Graphical user interfaces (GUI) and web pages are typical examples of a presentation layer.

Applications can be categorized by the number of *tiers* they have. A tier is a grouping of the three layers into a single component of the application. Although there are only three sections (data, business logic, and presentation) there are actually four categories for an application.

- **Single-tiered applications**. All three sections combined into a single component, which is usually an executable program. Many PC applications fall into this category such as word processors and spreadsheets, and some simple web based applications.
- **Two-tiered applications**. The data layer is separated out from the presentation and business layers, while the latter are still combined. Although it is possible to separate the presentation layer and leave the business logic and data layers combined, this is not usual as most applications, which separate the presentation layer, will also separate the remaining two as well.
- **Three-tiered applications**. Separate the three layers into separate components. These applications typically use distributed middleware to allow disjoint components of the system to communicate and work together.
- **N-tiered applications.** Similar to three-tiered applications, but more distributed. An N-tiered application has many distributed objects spread across many machines, again using middleware. These objects may have their own individual, separate data layers.

Tutorial questions are available at:
`http://www.palgrave.com/studyskills/masterseries/buchanan`

18 WWW and WWW programming

18.1 Introduction

The World-Wide Web (WWW) and the Internet have more jargon words and associated acronyms than anything else in modern life. Words, such as

gopher, ftp, telnet, TCP/IP stack, intranets, Web servers, clients, browsers, hypertext, URLs, Internet access providers, dial-up connections, UseNet servers, firewalls

have all become common in the business vocabulary.

The WWW was initially conceived in 1989 by CERN, the European particle physics research laboratory in Geneva, Switzerland. Its main objective was:

to use the hypermedia concept to support the interlinking of various types of information through the design and development of a series of concepts, communications protocols, and systems

One of its main characteristics is that stored information tends to be distributed over a geographically wide area. The result of the project has been the worldwide acceptance of the protocols and specifications used. A major part of its success was due to the full support of the National Center for Supercomputing Applications (NCSA), which developed a family of user interface programs known collectively as Mosaic.

The WWW, or Web, is basically an infrastructure of information. This information is stored on the WWW on Web servers and it uses the Internet to transmit data around the world. These servers run special programs that allow information to be transmitted to remote computers which are running a Web browser, as illustrated in Figure 18.1. The Internet is a common connection in which computers can communicate using a common addressing mechanism (IP) with a TCP/IP connection.

The information is stored on Web servers and is accessed by means of pages. These pages can contain text and other multimedia applications such as graphic images, digitized sound files and video animation. There are several standard media files (with typical file extensions):

- **GIF/JPEG files for compressed images** (GIF or JPG)
- **QuickTime movies for video** (QT or MOV)
- **Audio** (AU, SND or WAV)
- **MPEG files for compressed video** (MPG)
- **MS video** (AVI)
- **Postscript files** (PS or EPS)
- **Compressed files** (ZIP, Z or GZ)
- **Java/JavaScript** (JAV or JS)

Each page contains text known as hypertext, which has specially reserved keywords to represent the format and the display functions. A standard language known as HTML (Hypertext Markup Language) has been developed for this purpose. Hypertext pages, when interpreted by a browser program, display an easy-to-use interface containing formatted text, icons, pictorial hot spots, underscored words, and so on. Each page can also contain links to other related pages.

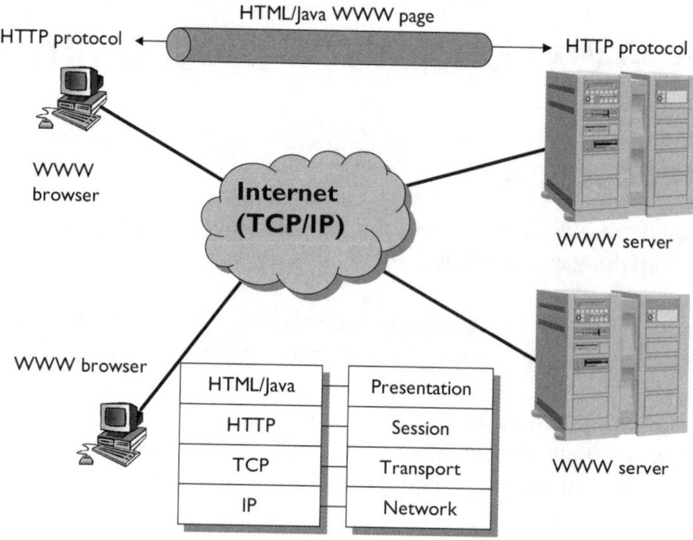

Figure 18.1 Web servers and browsers

The topology and power of the Web now allows for distributed information, where information does not have to be stored locally. To find information on the Web the user can use powerful search engines to search for related links. Figure 18.2 shows an example of Web connections. The user initially accesses a page on a German Web server, this then contains a link to a Japanese server. This server contains links to UK and USA servers. This type of arrangement leads to the topology that resembles a spider's web, where information is linked from one place to another.

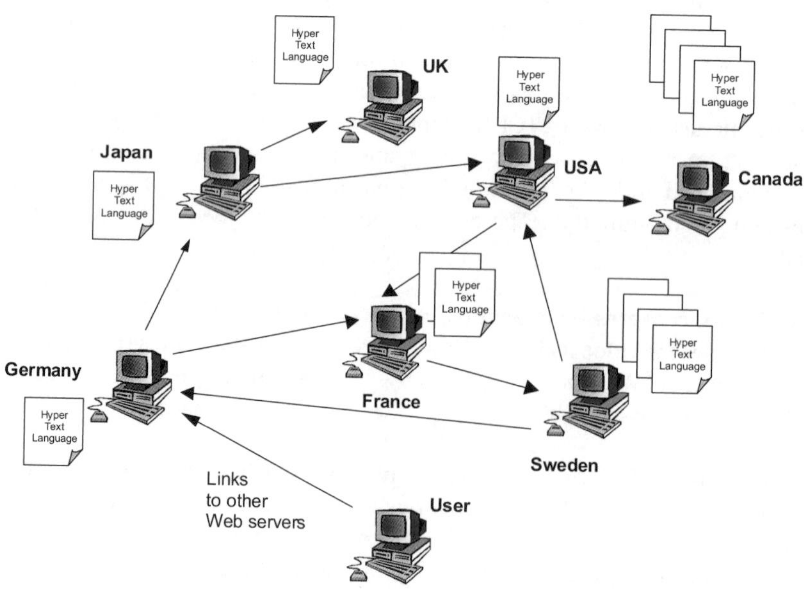

Figure 18.2 Example Web connections

18.2 Advantages and disadvantages of the WWW

The WWW and the Internet tend to produce a polarization of views. Thus, before analysing the WWW for its technical specification, a few words must be said on some of the subjective advantages and disadvantages of the WWW and the Internet. It should be noted that some of these disadvantages could be seen as advantages to some people, and vice versa. For example, freedom of information will be seen as an advantage to a freedom-of-speech group but often a disadvantage to security organizations. Table 18.1 outlines some of the advantages and disadvantages.

Table 18.1 Advantages and disadvantages of the Internet and the WWW

	Advantages	*Disadvantages*
Global information flow	Less control of information by the media, governments and large organizations.	Lack of control on criminal material, such as certain types of pornography and terrorist activity.
Global transmission	Communication between people and organizations in different countries which should create the Global Village.	Data can easily get lost or state secrets can be easily transmitted around the world.
Internet connections	Many different types of connections are possible, such as dial-up facilities (perhaps over a modem or with ISDN) or through frame relays. The user only has to pay for the service and the local connection.	Data once on the Internet is relatively easy to tap into and possibly easy to change.
Global information	Creation of an ever-increasing global information database.	Data is relatively easy to tap into and possibly easy to change.
Multimedia integration	Tailor-made applications with good presentation tools.	Lack of editorial control leads to inferior material, which is hacked together.
Increasing WWW usage	Helps to improve its chances of acceptance into the home.	Increased traffic swamps the global information network and slows down commercial traffic.
WWW links	Easy to set up and leads users from one place to the next in a logical manner.	WWW links often fossilize where the link information is out of date or doesn't even exist.
Education	Increased usage of remote teaching with full multimedia education.	Increase in surface learning and lack of deep research. It may lead to an increase in time wasting (too much surfing and too little learning).

18.3 Client/server architecture

The WWW is structured with clients and servers, where a client accesses services from the server. These servers can either be local or available through a global network connection. A local connection normally requires the connection over a local area network but a global connection normally requires connection to an Internet service provider. These providers are often known as Internet service providers (ISPs), sometimes as Internet connectivity providers (ICP). They provide the mechanism to access the Internet and have the required hardware and software to connect from the user to the Internet. This access is typically provided through one of the following:

- Connection to a client computer through a dial-up modem connection (typically at 28.8 kbps or 56 kbps).
- Connection to a client computer through a dial-up ISDN connection (typically at 64 kbps or 128 kbps).
- Connection of a client computer to a server computer which connects to the Internet through a frame relay router (typically 56 kbps or 256 kbps), or broadband communication, with ADSL.
- Connection of a client computer to a local area network which connects to the Internet through a T1, 1.544 Mbps router.

These connections are illustrated in Figure 18.3. A router automatically routes all traffic to and from the Internet whereas the dial-up facility of a modem or ISDN link requires a connection to be made over a circuit-switched line (that is, through the public telephone network). Home users and small businesses typically use modem connections (although ISDN connections are becoming more common). Large corporations which require global Internet services tend to use frame routers. Note that an IAP may be a commercial organization (such as CompuServe or America On-line) or a support organization (such as giving direct connection to government departments or educational institutions). A commercial IAP organization is likely to provide added services, such as electronic mail, search engines, and so on.

An Internet presence provider (IPP) allows organizations to maintain a presence on the Internet without actually having to invest in the Internet hardware. The IPPs typically maintain WWW pages for a given charge (they may also provide sales and support information).

18.4 Web browsers

Web browsers interpret special hypertext pages which consist of the hypertext markup language (HTML) and JavaScript. They then display it in the given format. There are currently four main Web browsers:

- **Netscape Navigator** – Navigator is one of the most widely used WWW browsers and is available in many different versions on many systems. It runs on PCs (running Microsoft Windows), UNIX workstations and Macintosh computers, and has become the standard WWW browser and has many add-ons and enhancements. The basic package also has many compatible software plug-ins which are developed by third-party suppliers. These add extra functionality such as video players and sound support.

- **NSCA Mosaic** – Mosaic was originally the most popular Web browser when the Internet first started. It has now lost its dominance to Microsoft Internet Explorer and Netscape Navigator. NSCA Mosaic was developed by the National Center for Supercomputing Applications (NCSA) at the University of Illinois.
- **Lynx** – Lynx is typically used on UNIX-based computers with a modem dial-up connection. It is fast to download pages but does not support many of the features supported by Netscape Navigator or Mosaic.
- **Microsoft Internet Explorer** – Explorer now comes as a standard part of Microsoft Windows and as this has become the most popular computer operating system then so has this browser.

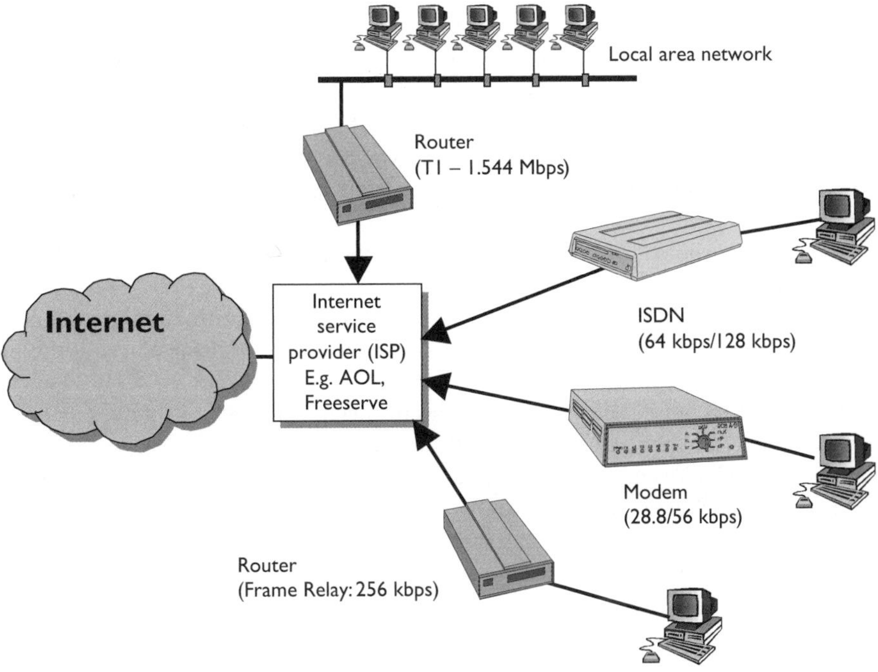

Figure 18.3 Example connections to the Internet

18.5 Universal resource locators (URLs)

Universal resource locators (URLs) are used to locate a file on the WWW. They provide a pointer to any object on a server connected over the Internet. This link could give FTP access, hypertext references, and so on. URLs contain:

- The protocol of the file (the scheme).
- The server name (domain).
- The pathname of the file.
- The filename.

URL standard format is:

<scheme>:<scheme-specific-part>

and can be broken up into four parts. These are:

```
aaaa://bbb.bbb.bbb/ccc/ccc/ccc?ddd
```

where

`aaaa:` is the access method and specifies the mechanism to be used by the browser to communicate with the resource. The most popular mechanisms are:

- `http:`. HyperText Transfer Protocol. This is the most commonly used mechanism and is typically used to retrieve an HTML file, a graphic file, a sound file, an animation sequence file, a file to be executed by the server, or a word processor file.
- `https:`. HyperText Transfer Protocol. It is a variation on the standard access method and can be used to provide some level of transmission security.
- `file:`. Local file access. This causes the browser to load the specified file from the local disk.
- `ftp:`. File Transport Protocol. This method allows files to be downloaded using an FTP connection.
- `mailto:`. E-mail form. This method allows access to a destination e-mail address. Normally the browser automatically generates an input form for entering the e-mail message.
- `news:`. USENET news. This method defines the access method for a news group.
- `nntp:`. Local Network News Transport Protocol.
- `telnet:`. TELNET. The arguments following the access code are the login arguments to the telnet session as `user[:password]@host`.

`//bbb.bbb.bbb` is the Internet node and specifies the node on the Internet where the file is located. If a node is not given then the browser defaults to the computer which is running the browser. A colon may follow the node address and the port number (most browsers default to port 80, which is also the port that most servers use to reply to the browser).

`/ccc/ccc/ccc` is the file path (including subdirectories and the filename). Typically systems restrict the access to a system by allocating the root directory as a subdirectory of the main file system.

`?ddd` is the argument which depends upon the access method, and the file accessed. For example, with an HTML document a '#' identifies the fragment name internal to an HTML document which is identified by the A element with the `NAME` attribute.

An example URL is:

```
http://www.toytown.anycor.co/fred/index.html
```

where `http` is the file protocol (Hypertext Translation Protocol), `www.toytown.anycor.co` is the server name, `/fred` is the path of the file and the file is named `index.html`.

18.5.1 Files

A file URL scheme allows files to be assessed. It takes the form:

file://*<host>*/*<path>*

where *<host>* is the fully qualified domain name of the system to be accessed, *<path>* is the full path name, and takes the form of a directory path, such as *<directory>*/ *<directory>*/ .../ *<name>*.

For a file:

```
C:\DOCS\NOTES\NETWORKS\NET_CHAP13.DOC
```

would be accessed as from `dummy.com` with:

```
file://dummy.com/C|DOCS/NOTES/NETWORKS/NET_CHAP13.DOC
```

Note, that if the host is defined as `localhost` or is an empty string then the host is assumed to be the local host. The general format is:

```
fileurl  = "file://" [ host | "localhost" ] "/" fpath
```

18.5.2 Electronic mail address

The `mailto` scheme defines a link to an Internet e-mail address. An example is:

```
mailto: fred.bloggs@toytown.ac.uk
```

When this URL is selected then an e-mail message will be sent to the e-mail address `fred.bloggs@toytown.ac.uk`. Normally, some form of text editor is called and the user can enter the required e-mail message. Upon successful completion of the text message it is sent to the addressee.

18.5.3 File Transfer Protocol (FTP)

The `ftp` URL scheme defines that the files and directories specified are accessed using the FTP protocol. In its simplest form it is defined as:

ftp://*<hostname>*/*<directory-name>*/*<filename>*

The FTP protocol normally requests a user to log into the system. For example, many public domain FTP servers use the login of:

```
anonymous
```

and the password can be anything (but it is normally either the user's full name or their Internet e-mail address). Another typical operation is changing directory from a starting directory or the destination file directory. To accommodate this, a more general form is:

ftp://*<user>*:*<password>*@*<hostname>*:*<port>*/*<cd1>*/*<cd2>*/ .../*<cdn>*/*<filename>*

where the user is defined by *<user>* and the password by *<password>*. The host name, *<hostname>*, is defined after the @ symbol and change directory commands are defined by the *cd* commands. The node name may take the form `//user [:password]@host`. Without a user name, the user `anonymous` is used.

For example the reference to the standard related to HTML Version 2 can be downloaded using the URL:

```
ftp://ds.internic.net/rfc/rfc1866.txt
```

and draft Internet documents from:

```
ftp://ftp.isi.edu/internet-drafts/
```

The general format is:

```
ftpurl     = "ftp://" login [ "/" fpath [ ";type=" ftptype ]]
fpath      = fsegment *[ "/" fsegment ]
fsegment   = *[ uchar | "?" | ":" | "@" | "&" | "=" ]
ftptype    = "A" | "I" | "D" | "a" | "i" | "d"
```

18.5.4 Hypertext Transfer Protocol (HTTP)

HTTP is the protocol which is used to retrieve information connected with hypermedia links. The client and server initially perform a negotiation procedure before the HTTP transfer takes place. This negotiation involves the client sending a list of formats it can support and the server replying with data in the required format.

Users generally move from a link on one server to another server. Each time the user moves from one server to another, the client sends an HTTP request to the server. Thus the client does not permanently connect to the server, and the server views each transfer as independent from all previous accesses. This is known as a stateless protocol.

An HTTP URL takes the form:

`http://`*<host>*`:`*<port>*`/`*<path>*`?`*<searchpart>*

Note that, if the *<port>* is omitted, port 80 is automatically used (HTTP service), *<path>* is an HTTP selector and *<searchpart>* is a query string.

The general format is:

```
httpurl      = "http://" hostport [ "/" hpath [ "?" search ]]
hpath        = hsegment *[ "/" hsegment ]
hsegment     = *[ uchar | ";" | ":" | "@" | "&" | "=" ]
search       = *[ uchar | ";" | ":" | "@" | "&" | "=" ]
```

18.5.5 News

UseNet or NewsGroup servers are part of the increasing use of general discussion news groups which share text-based news items. The news URL scheme defines a link to either a news group or individual articles with a group of UseNet news.

A news URL takes one of two forms:

`news:`*<newsgroup-name>* `news:`*<message-id>*

where *<newsgroup-name>* is a period-delimited hierarchical name, such as 'news.inter', and *<message-id>* takes the full form of the message-ID, such as:

<message-ID>`@`*<full_domain_name>*

The general form is:

```
newsurl        = "news:" grouppart
grouppart      = "*" | group | article
group          = alpha *[ alpha | digit | "-" | "." | "+" | "_" ]
article        = 1*[ uchar | ";" | "/" | "?" | ":" | "&" | "=" ] "@" host
```

18.6 Web browser design

The Web browser is a carefully engineered software package which allows the user to efficiently find information on the WWW. Most are similar in their approach, but differ in their presentation. Figure 18.4 shows the tool bar for Microsoft Internet Explorer. This has been designed to allow the user to move smoothly through the WWW.

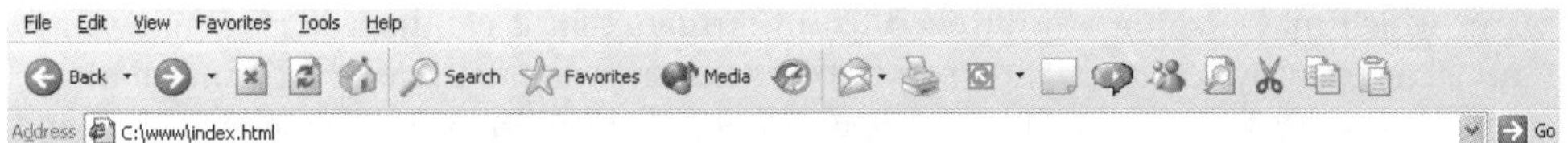

Figure 18.4 Microsoft Explorer tool bar

The Back and Forward options allow the user to traverse backwards and forwards through links. This allows the user to trace back to a previous link and possibly follow it.

The Stop option is used by the user to interrupt the current transfer. It is typically used when the user does not want to load the complete page. This often occurs when the browser is loading a graphics image.

The Web browser tries to reduce data transfer by holding recently accessed pages in a memory cache. This cache is typically held on a local disk. The Refresh forces the browser to reload the page from the remote location.

Often a user wishes to restart a search and can use the Home option to return to it. The home page of the user is set up by one of the options.

The Search option is used to connect to a page which has access to the search programs Microsoft Explorer typically connects to. An example screen from Microsoft search facility is given in Figure 18.6. It can be seen that this links to the most commonly used search engines, such as Yahoo, Lycos, Magallan and eXcite.

Often a user has a list of favourite Web pages. This can be automatically called from the Favorites option. A new favourite can be added with the Add To Favorites ... option. These favourites can either be selected from the Favourites menu option (such as Internet Start) or from within folders (such as Channels and Links). The favourites are organized using the Organize Favorites... option.

18.7 HTTP

The foundation protocol of the WWW is the Hypertext Transfer Protocol (HTTP) which can be used in any client/server application involving hypertext. It is used on the WWW for transmitting information using hypertext jumps and can support the transfer of plaintext, hypertext, audio, images, or any Internet-compatible information. The most recently defined standard is HTTP 1.1, which has been defined by the IETF standard.

HTTP is a stateless protocol where each transaction is independent of any previous transactions. Thus when the transaction is finished the TCP/IP connection is disconnected, as illustrated in Figure 18.5. The advantage of being stateless is that it allows the rapid access of WWW pages over several widely distributed servers. It uses the TCP protocol to establish a connection between a client and a server for each transaction then terminates the connection once the transaction completes.

HTTP also supports many different formats of data. Initially a client issues a request to a server which may include a prioritized list of formats that it can handle. This allows new formats to be easily added and also prevents the transmission of unnecessary information.

A client's WWW browser (the user agent) initially establishes a direct connection with the destination server which contains the required WWW page. To make this connection the client initiates a TCP connection between the client and the server. After this is established the client then issues an HTTP request, such as the specific command (the method), the URL, and possibly extra information such as request parameters or client information. When the server receives the request, it attempts to perform the requested action. It then returns an HTTP response, which includes status information, a success/error code, and extra information. After the client receives this, the TCP connection is closed.

18.7.1 Caches, tunnels and user agents

In a computer system, a cache is an area of memory that stores information likely to be accessed in a fast access memory area. For example, a cache controller takes a guess on which information the process is likely to access next. When the processor wishes to access the disk then, if it has guessed right, the cache controller will load from the electronic memory rather than loading it from the disk. A WWW cache stores cacheable responses so that there is a reduction in network traffic and an improvement in access times. Figure 18.6 shows an example use of a cache. Initially (1) the client sends out a request for a page, along with the date that it was last accessed. If the page has not changed then the server sends back a message saying that it has not been changed. The client will then use the page that is stored in the local cache.

Often Internet service providers use a network cache which stores pages that users have recently accessed. If a request is made for a page which has already been accessed, and is stored in the cache, the network cache can be used to provide the page to the requester. In the future, network caches could be used to considerably speed up WWW page download. Popular pages would be regularly downloaded to the cache, and sent to the clients when required. An important factor is keeping the cache regularly updated. For this HTTP requests must still be sent with the date and time that the page was last updated. If there is a change, the new updated page should be sent (and obviously also stored in the cache).

Some WWW browsers can also be setup so that they do not re-access a previously loaded page, if it is re-requested within a given time. This can be annoying for the user, especially if the page is updating itself within a short interval (such as with a WWW camera). A Reload button is typically used to force the WWW browser to re-request the page.

Tunnels are intermediary devices which act as a blind relay between two connections. When the tunnel becomes active, it is not seen to be part of the HTTP communications. When the connection is closed by both sides, the tunnel ceases to exit. A user agent, in HTTP, is a client which initiates requests to a server. Typically this is a WWW browser or a WWW spider (an automated WWW trawling program).

18.7.2 HTTP messages

HTTP messages are either requests from clients to servers or responses from servers to clients (Figure 18.7). The message is either a simple request, a simple response, full request or a full response. HTTP Version 0.9 defines the simple request/ response messages whereas HTTP Version 1.1 defines full requests/responses.

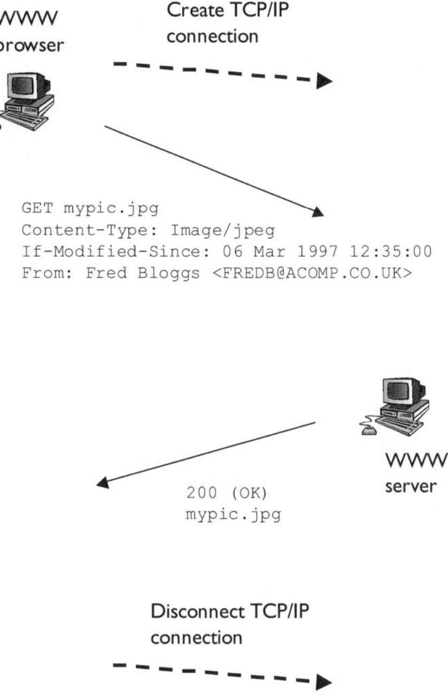

Figure 18.5 Example HTTP transaction

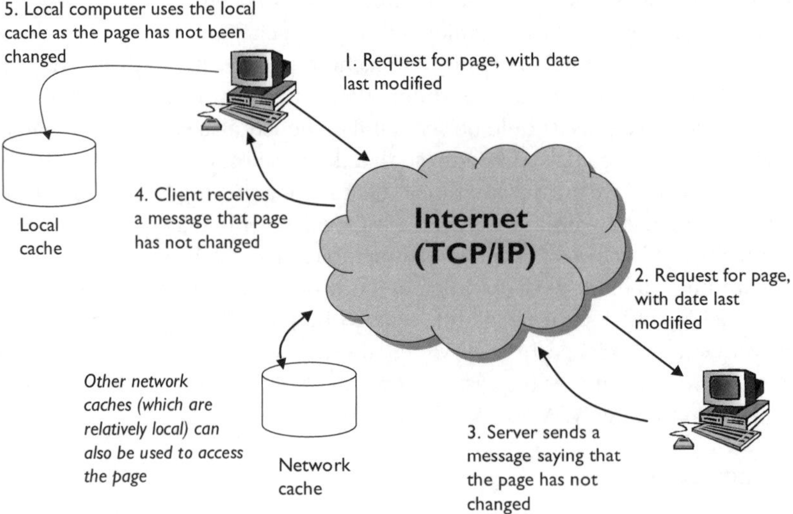

5. Local computer uses the local cache as the page has not been changed
1. Request for page, with date last modified
4. Client receives a message that page has not changed
Local cache
Internet (TCP/IP)
2. Request for page, with date last modified
Other network caches (which are relatively local) can also be used to access the page
Network cache
3. Server sends a message saying that the page has not changed

Figure 18.6 Using caches

HTTP is a stateless protocol where each transaction is independent of any previous transactions. The advantage of being stateless is that it allows the rapid access of WWW pages over several widely distributed servers. It uses the TCP protocol to establish a connection between a client and a server for each transaction then terminates the connection once the transaction completes.
HTTP also supports many different formats of data. Initially a client issues a request to a server which may include a prioritized list of formats that it can handle. This allows new formats to be easily added and also prevents the transmission of unnecessary information.

A client's WWW browser (the user agent) initially establishes a direct connection with the destination server which contains the required WWW page.
To make this connection the client initiates a TCP connection between the client and the server. After this is established the client then issues an HTTP request, such as the specific command (the method), the URL, and possibly extra information such as request parameters or client information.
When the server receives the request, it attempts to perform the requested action.
It then returns an HTTP response, which includes status information, a success/error code, and extra information itself.
After the client receives this, the TCP connection is closed.

Figure 18.7 HTTP operation Simple requests/responses

The simple request is a `GET` command with the requested URL such as:

```
GET  /info/dept/courses.html
```

The simple response is a block containing the information identified in the URL (called the entity body).

For more material on HTTP please visit our web site at:
http://www.palgrave.com/studyskills/masterseries/buchanan

18.8 WWW programming

This section discusses some of the methods which are used to program over the WWW. The WWW was initially conceived in 1989 by CERN, the European particle physics research laboratory in Geneva, Switzerland. Its main objective was to allow various different types of information, such as text, graphics and video, to be integrated together in an easy-to-use manner. It also supports the interlinking of information. The standard language developed is HTML (HyperText Markup Language), which is a text-based language which has certain formatting tags. These tags are identified between a less than (<) and a greater than (>) symbol. Most have an opening and closing version; for example, to highlight bold text the bold opening tag (<B>) is used and the closing tag is </B>. When a greater than or a less than symbol is required then a special character sequence can be used. It is fine for low quality and medium quality documents, but it is difficult to produce any high quality printed material. It is likely that new versions of HTML will support enhanced presentation. Table 18.1 defines some of the tags that are used in HTML. An example HTML is given next, and Figure 18.8 shows how it is interpreted by a WWW browser.

```
<HTML><HEAD><TITLE> Fred Bloggs</TITLE></HEAD>
<BODY TEXT="#000000" BGCOLOR="#FFFFFF">
<H1>Fred Bloggs Home Page</H1>
I'm Fred Bloggs. Below is a table of links.
<P>
<TABLE BORDER=10 WIDTH=90% LENGTH=50%>
<TR>
   <TD><B>General</B></TD>
   <TD><A HREF="res.html">Research</TD>
   <TD><A HREF="cv.html">CV</TD>
   <TD><A HREF="paper.html">Papers Published</TD>
   <TD></TD>
</TR>
<TR>
   <TD ROWSPAN=2><B>HTML/Java Tutorials</B></TD>
   <TD><A HREF="intro.html">Tutorial 1</TD>
   <TD COLSPAN=2><A HREF="inter.html">Tutorial 2</TD>
</TR>
<TR>
   <TD><A HREF="java1.html">Tutorial 1</TD>
   <TD><A HREF="java2.html">Tutorial 2</TD>
   <TD><A HREF="java3.html">Tutorial 3</TD>
</TR></TABLE>
</BODY></HTML>
```

Normally WWW designers do not write HTML code, as they can use a WWW page designer, such as Microsoft FrontPage or Macromedia Dreamweaver. Figure 18.9 shows a split between the design view and code view in Dreamweaver and Figure 18.10 shows a screen from FrontPage showing integrated HTML code. In most cases, the designer simply uses the graphical user interface to design the WWW page, and the design package produces the HTML code. If required the designer can edit any part of the HTML code, manually, thus an understanding of HTML is important.

Table 18.1 Example HTML tags

Open tag	*Closing tag*	*Description*
`<HTML>`	`</HTML>`	Start and end of HTML
`<HEAD>`	`</HEAD>`	Defines the HTML header
`<BODY>`	`</BODY>`	Defines the main body of the HTML
`<TITLE>`	`</TITLE>`	Defines the title of the WWW page
`<I>`	`</I>`	Italic text
`<B>`	`</B>`	Bold text
`<U>`	`</U>`	Underlined text
`<BLINK>`	`</BLINK>`	Make text blink
`<EM>`	`</EM>`	Emphasize text
`<FONT SIZE=+1>`	`</FONT>`	Increase font size by one increment
`<FONT SIZE=-1>`	`</FONT>`	Reduce font size by one increment
`<CENTER>`	`</CENTER>`	Centre text
`<H1>`	`</H1>`	Section header, level 1
`<H2>`	`</H2>`	Section header, level 2
`<H3>`	`</H3>`	Section header, level 3
`<P>`		Create a new paragraph
` `		Create a line break
`<!-->`	`-->`	Comments
`<SUPER>`	`</SUPER>`	Superscript
`<SUB>`	`</SUB>`	Subscript

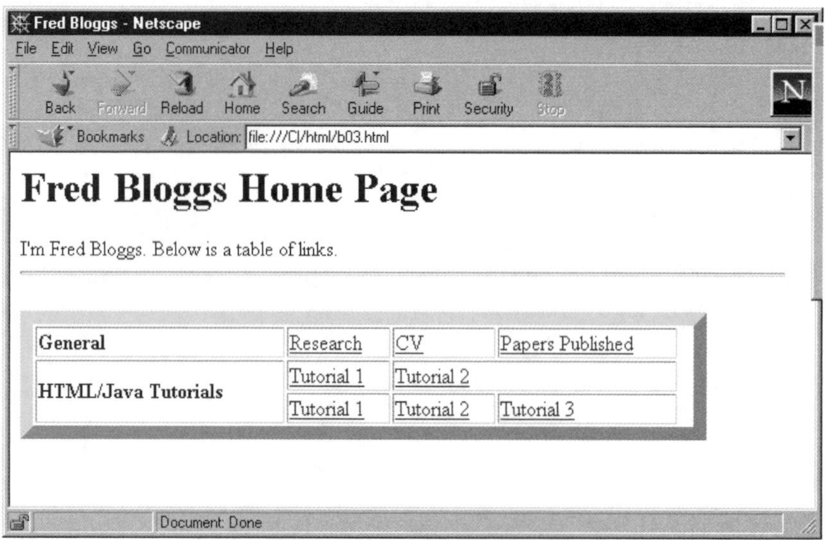

Figure 18.8 Example HTML page

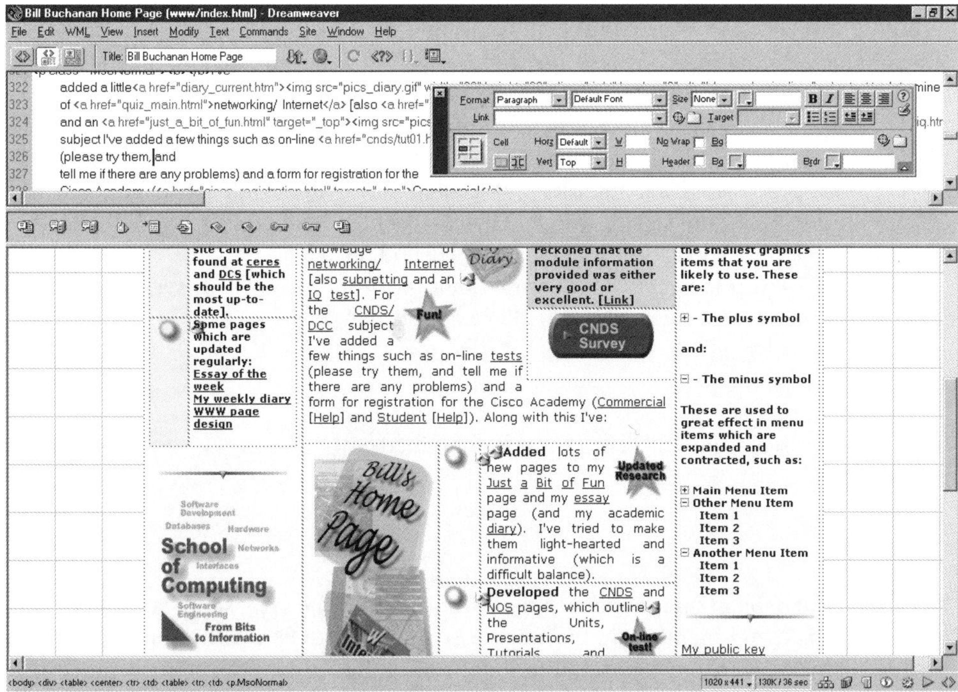

Figure 18.9 Macromedia Dreamweaver showing a split screen for the Code View and Design View

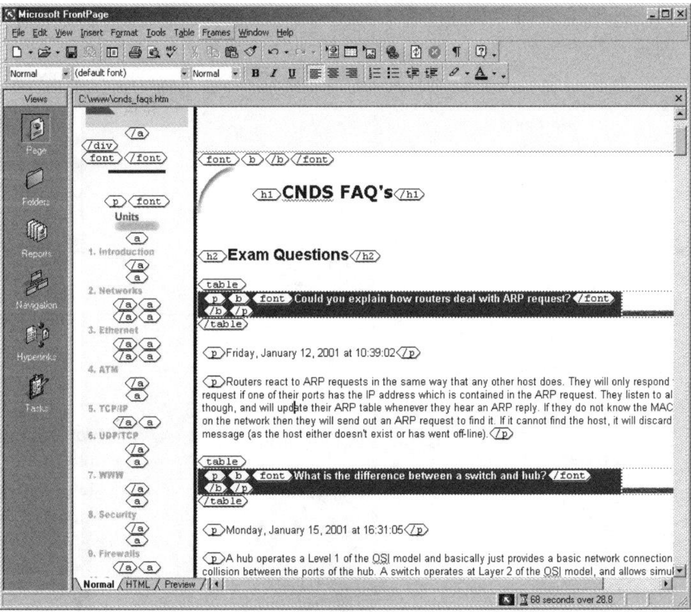

Figure 18.10 Microsoft FrontPage showing HTML tags

18.8.1 Languages which integrate with HTML

HTML is the standard language which is used to present WWW pages, and is interpreted by the WWW browser. Unfortunately HTML is a rather limited language, and can only really present static information. It is also not good at getting user interaction, languages have been added to HTML to enhance it. Typically this is to process user information, or to respond to user events (such as mouse clicks, or text input). The place where the processing of the additional script defines whether it is a server-side include or a client-side include. If the WWW browser processes the script, then it is a client-side include, otherwise it a server-side include, as illustrated in Figure 18.11. Typical client-side includes are VBScript and JavaScript, and typical server-side includes are PHP and ASP.

A server-side include is better for compatibility with the WWW browser, as it converts the additional script into standard HTML. For example in ASP:

```
<%=time()%>
```

would be processed as an ASP script (as it is contained with <% and %>), and converted to the HTML code:

```
<P>Thur, 5 Oct 2001</P>
```

Thus it does not depend on browser version. Unfortunately the extra script is dependent on the server, and any problems with this may cause the script to fail. With client-side include the code is processed by the browser, thus it depends if the browser can actually process the script. Fortunately most browsers are now fairly compatible with the client-side includes, but you can never be too sure how different browser versions are going to present the page.

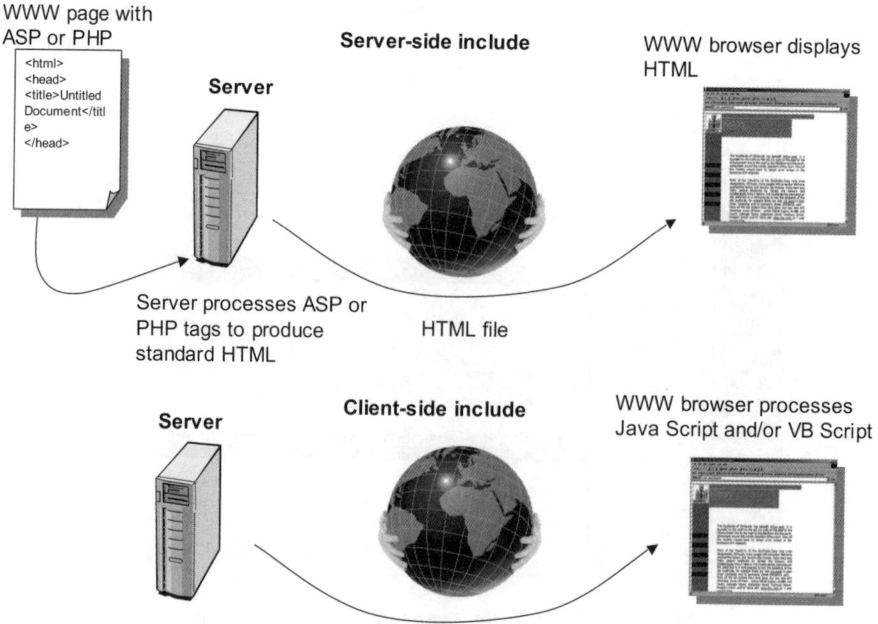

Figure 18.11 Difference between server-side include and client-side include

JSP also uses the <% and %> tags, but the files are named with a JSP extension. These files were initially developed by Sun Microsystems and are typically processed by a UNIX-based server. The basic language used is Java.

Typical JavaScript events:

onAbort()	onBlur()
onChange()	onClick()
onDblClick()	onDragDrop()
onError()	onFocus()
onKeyDown()	onKeyPress()
onKeyUp()	onLoad()
onMouseDown()	onMouseMove()
onMouseOut()	onMouseOver()
onMouseUp()	onMove()
onReset()	onResize()
onSelect()	onSubmit()
onUnload()	

18.8.2 VBScript

HTML is fine for basic formatting, but it is not so good at getting user interaction, thus VBScript is a simplified form of Visual BASIC (which is the most popular programming language in the world) and is used to provide some basic functions, such as time() to display the current time. VBScript integrates into HTML, and can hide itself from WWW browsers by embedding it in-between the <SCRIPT LANGUAGE= "VBSCRIPT"> and the </SCRIPT> tags.

```
<SCRIPT LANGUAGE="VBSCRIPT">
sub myheader_onClick
   myheader.Style.Color = "BLACK"
end sub
</SCRIPT>
```

18.8.3 JavaScript

JavaScript integrates into the HTML page within the <SCRIPT LANGUAGE= "JAVASCRIPT"> and the </SCRIPT> tags. It has a similar syntax to Java, but is not as strict on the syntax of the code. For example to print the current time (HH:MM) with JavaScript:

```
<p>Current time is
<script language="javascript">
var dat=new Date();
   document.write(dat.getHours() + ":" + dat.getMinutes());
</script>
```

Outputting to browser. The document.write() applies the write() method to the document object, and outputs a processed string to the browser screen. JavaScript has much of the power of a programming language and supports arrays, such as:

```
<script language="javascript">
var dat=new Date(),
mon=["Jan","Feb", "Mar", "Apr", "May", "June", "July", "Aug", "Sept", "Oct",
"Nov", "Dec"];
  document.write("Month is ");
  document.write(dat.getMonth());
  document.write(" and the name of the month is ");
  document.write(mon[dat.getMonth()]);
</script>
```

Decisions. As with most programming languages, JavaScript supports decisions with the if() and switch() statements, such as the following which determines if it is morning or afternoon, and greets the user either with a "Good Morning!", or a "Good Afternoon!":

```
<FONT COLOR="GREEN">
<script language="javascript">
var dat=new Date();;
   hr=dat.getHours();
   if (hr<12)
   {
      document.write("Good Morning!");
   }
   else
   {
      document.write("Good Afternoon!");
   }
</script>
</FONT>
```

Repetitive loops. JavaScript supports for() and while() loops. For example the following loops for values of `fsize` from 1 to 5, which are used to define the font size.

```
<script language="javascript">
var fsize;
for (fsize=1;fsize<=5;fsize++)
{
   document.write("<br> <FONT SIZE = ");
   document.write(fsize + ">");
   document.write("Hello</FONT>");
}
</SCRIPT>
```

Typical JavaScript method

Methods are applied to objects. An example JavaScript object is **String**. Typical methods include:

big()	make text large
blink()	make text blink
charAt()	find a character in a string
fontcolor()	set font color
fontsize()	set font size
italics()	set italic
link()	make a link
small()	make font small
sub()	make font subscript
toLowerCase()	convert to lowercase
toUpperCase()	convert to uppercase

User functions. Even user functions can be incorporated into the page. For example, a function call to a square function is as follows:

```
<script language="javascript">
function sqr(val)
{
   return val * val
}
var value=sqr(3);
   document.write("Three squared is " +
   value);
</SCRIPT>
```

Methods. In object-oriented design, methods are applied to objects. Typical objects in JavaScript are Math (which contains mathematical properties and methods), history (which contains a lists of the visited URLs), button (which contains the object for buttons) and document (which is the container for the information on the current page). An example JavaScript object is Math. For example, the following determines the square of a value:

```
The square root of 15 is
<script language="javascript">
   document.write(Math.sqrt(15.0));
</SCRIPT>
```

Another example is to determine the cosine of a value, by applying the cos() method to the Math object:

```
<P>The cosine of 1.5 radians is
<script>
document.write(Math.cos(1.5))
</script>
```

The string object has many useful methods, such as toLowerCase(), which converts a string to lowercase, and toUpperCase(), which converts a string to uppercase, as used in the following example:

```
TYPEwrITer in lowercase is
<SCRIPT>
document.write(("TYPEwrITer").toLowerCase())
document.write("and in uppercase it is");
document.write(("TYPEwrITer").toUpperCase())
</SCRIPT>
```

Using events. JavaScript has many useful functions, such as one to open windows of a certain size and with certain conditions, and also to respond to events, such as the onMouseDown() event when the user clicks on a graphic. The following opens a window (with the window.open() function) of width of 310 pixels and height of 200 pixels, when the user clicks on the referred graphic (message.gif). The onMouseDown() is an event which occurs when the user clicks on the graphic.

```
<script language="javascript">
function openWindow(theURL,winName,features) {
   window.open(theURL,winName,features);
}
</script>
<img border="0" src="message.gif" width="159" height="25"
   onMouseDown="openWindow('message.html','', 'toolbar=yes,
   menubar=yes, scrollbars=yes, resizable=yes, width=310, height=200')"
   align="left">
```

18.8.4 ASP

ASP is similar to VBScript, but rather than the browser processing the script, the WWW server actually does it before it sends the page to the WWW browser. ASP is a Microsoft technology and will typically only run on a Microsoft server (such as with an Microsoft IIS server). ASP pages are named with an asp file extension (such as default.asp), to differentiate them from normal HTML pages. An example is:

<B>Current time is <%=Time()%> </B>

which will display the current time. When this is sent to the WWW browser it will have the Time() function expanded into HTML code, such as:

```
<B>Current time is 10:35pm</B>
```

for which the WWW browser will display as:

```
Current time is 10:35pm
```

18.8.5 JSP

JSP (Java Server Page) allows Java code to be integrated into a WWW page. Like ASP, it uses the <% and %> tags to define Java code and uses the server to process the additional code into HTML. An extract from a JSP page is shown next. The highlighted areas show the JavaScript parts. It can be seen that, in this case, the JavaScript part hides an if() decision. The server process the Java parts and decides which parts on the HTML code it sends to the client.

```
<html><body>
<%
  String user = (String)session.getAttribute("user");
  if ((user == null)
      || (user.equals(""))){
%>
    <p> no user in session</p>
<%
  }
  else{
    session.invalidate();
%>
    <p>User <b><%= user %></b>
      logged out!</p>
<%
  }
%>
    <a href="login.jsp">login</a>
</body></html>
```

In this case, if `user` is an empty string then the following code will be sent to the client:

```
<html><body>
     <p> no user in session</p>
    <a href="login.jsp">login</a>
</body></html>
```

else the following will be sent:

```
<html><body>
    session.invalidate();
    <p>User <b><%= user %></b> logged
out!</p>
    <a href="login.jsp">login</a>
</body></html>
```

As with ASP and PHP, JSP allows an organization to keep its additional code private, so that all that the client sees is pure HTML (possibly also with JavaScript and/or VBScript).

CGI security settings

Normally files on a WWW server are protected so that external users cannot execute them. CGI scripts are different, as they must be executed by the WWW page. Thus the file security settings for CGI scripts are set so that anyone can execute them. In UNIX the settings are:

Owner = read, write, execute.
Group = read, execute.
All = read, execute.

The read attribute is set so that everyone can read the file, as the WWW browser must be able to read the file.

In UNIX the file attributes are typically defined rwxrwxrwx, where the owner's permissions are defined in the first three letters, their group's permission in the next three letters, and everyone else in the last three. Thus rwxr-xr-- means that the owner of the file can read, write and execute, his/her group can read and execute, and everyone else can only read the file. Thus in UNIX the CGI files must be rwxr-xr-x (this is sometimes defined in hexadecimal as 755).

18.8.6 PHP

ASP is a Microsoft technology for server-side includes in HTML pages, whereas PHP is a UNIX equivalent, and typically runs on an Apache WWW server. It is one of the oldest scripting languages for WWW pages, but is one of the most useful, as it interfaces with many different types of relational databases, such as Oracle, Sybas, MySQL and ODBC.

In PHP the additional code is added between the <? and ?> tags. For example the following prints a "Hello World" message to the browser:

```
<?php
print("Hello World");
?>
```

Variable are identified with a proceeding $ sign, such as:

```
<?php
$value=100;
print("Value is $value");
?>
```

Loops can use a while() statement, such as:

```
<?php
$value=0; //our variable
while($value<=10){
 print(" $value = ".($value*$value));
 print("<br />\n");
 $value=$value+1;
}
?>
```

A powerful usage of PHP is in string manipulation. The following example shows how PHP initializes an array of strings:

```
<?php
$colors = array('red','blue','green','yellow');
foreach ( $colors as $color )
{
   echo "Do you like $color?\n";
}
?>
```

The real power of PHP is the way that it supports e-mail, forms and access to databases, in a secure way. CGI was used in the past for this, but it is a complex language that does not integrate into the HTML page. An example of a form in HTML is as follows:

When form submitted, do the required action.

```
<form action="formmail.php3" method="POST">
<input type="hidden" name="recipient" value="fred@noemail.com">
<input type="hidden" name="subject" value="Reply Form">
<input type="text" name="input">
<input type="submit" value="Send">
</Form>
```

Button to press on the form. When pressed the action is invocated.

In this form the user can fill in one of the fields (the type is a 'text' field). When the user completes this field, and presses return, or presses the submit button, the action on the form is invocated. In this case the action is to call the PHP file named formmail.php3. The parameters from the form, in this case these are named recipient, subject, and input are then send to the script file (this action is know as posting the parameters). Note that the parameters recipient and subject are hidden to the user, but are passed to the script file. The contents of formmail.php3 then contain code which e-mail's the message to the recipient, such as:

```
<?php
$fmt_Response=implode("", file("response.htt"));
$fmt_Mail=implode("", file("mail.htt"));
while(list($Key, $Val)= each($HTTP_POST_VARS)) {
   $fmt_Response=str_replace("{$Key}", $Val, $fmt_Response);
   $fmt_Mail=str_replace("{$Key}", $Val, $fmt_Mail);
}
mail($HTTP_POST_VARS["recipient"], $HTTP_POST_VARS["subject"], $fmt_Mail);
echo $fmt_Response;
?>
```

Some SQL commands

ABORT, ALTER GROUP,
ALTER USER, BEGIN,
CLOSE, CLUSTER,
COMMIT, COPY,
CREATE DATABASE, CREATE GROUP,
CREATE OPERATOR, CREATE TABLE
CREATE USER, CREATE VIEW
DELETE, DROP DATABASE,
DROP TABLE, END,
INSERT, LOAD, LOCK, MOVE
SELECT, SELECT INTO
SET, SHOW, UPDATE

The file response.htt contains a basic message for the user when they have submitted the form, and the mail.htt contains the message which will be added to the e-mail that is sent.

Along with direct e-mail support, PHP supports many different types of databases, which can be accessed directly from the WWW page. To create a table (in this case the table is named datatest) within a database. The variable $server is the name of the SQL server (such as mysql-server.co.uk); $user is the login name for the user; $password is the password which is associated with the user; and $database is the name of the database. Initially these variables are used with the MYSQL_CONNECT() command to connect to the server, once connected, the database can be accessed with MYSQL_SELECT_DB() command. Next the SQL query: CREATE TABLE is used to create the table within the database. In this case it will create two fields within this table: name and e-mail, each with 25 characters. Finally the SQL_CLOSE() command closes the database.

```
<?php
/* Start of PHP3 Script */
/* Data of SQL-server */
$server= "$$$$";          /* Address of server */
$user= "$$$";             /* FTP-username */
$password= "$$$";         /* FTP-Password */
$database= "$$$";         /* name of database */
$table= "datatest";       /* Name of table, you can select that */

/* Accessing the server and creating the table */
MYSQL_CONNECT($server, $user, $password) or die ( "<H3>Server unreach-
able</H3>");
MYSQL_SELECT_DB($database) or die ( "<H3>database not existent</H3>");
$result=MYSQL_QUERY( "CREATE TABLE $table (name varchar(25),email var-
char(25))");

/* Terminate SQL connection*/
MYSQL_CLOSE();
?>
```

Data can then be written to the database with the INSERT SQL query (as highlighted):

```
<?php
$server= "$$$$"; /* Address of database server */
$user= "$$$$"; /* FTP-username */
$password= "$$$$"; /* FTP-Password */
$database= "$$$$"; /* name of database */
$table= "datatest";

/* Accessing SQL-server */
MYSQL_CONNECT($server, $user, $password) or die ( "<H3>Server unreach-
able</H3>");
MYSQL_SELECT_DB($database) or die ( "<H3>Database non existent</H3>");

MYSQL_QUERY( "INSERT INTO $table VALUES('Fred','fred@home.com')");
MYSQL_QUERY( "INSERT INTO $table VALUES('Bert','bert@myplace.com')");

/* Display number of entries */
$query="SELECT * FROM $table";
$result = MYSQL_QUERY($query);

/* How many of these users are there? */
$number = MYSQL_NUMROWS($result);

if ($number==0):
   echo "database empty";
elseif ($number > 0):
   echo "$number rows in database";
endif;
mysql_close();
?>
```

The data can then be read back with the SELECT query (as highlighted below):

```
<?php
$server= "$$$$"; /* Address of database server */
$user= "$$$$"; /* FTP-username */
$password= "$$$$"; /* FTP-Password */
$database= "$$$$"; /* name of database */
$table= "datatest"; /* Name of table, you can select that */
/* Accessing SQL-Server and querying table */
MYSQL_CONNECT($server, $user, $password) or die ( "<H3>Server unreach-
able</H3>");
MYSQL_SELECT_DB($database) or die ( "<H3>Database non existent</H3>");
$result=MYSQL_QUERY( "SELECT * FROM $table order by name");

/* Output data into a HTML table */
echo "<table border=\"1\" align=center width=50%";
echo "<tr>";
echo "<div color=\"#ffff00\">";
while ($field=mysql_fetch_field($result)) {
echo "<th>$field->name</A></th>";
}
echo "</font></tr>";
while($row = mysql_fetch_row($result)) {
   echo "<tr>";
   for($i=0; $i < mysql_num_fields($result); $i++) {
      echo "<td align=center>$row[$i]</td>";
   }
   echo "</tr>\n";
}
echo "</table><BR><BR>";
```

```
/* Close SQL-connection */
MYSQL_CLOSE();
?>
```

And finally, if the table needs to be deleted, the DROP TABLE query can be used (as highlighted below):

```
<?php
/* Accessing the server and deleting the table */
MYSQL_CONNECT($server, $user, $password) or die ( "<H3>Server unreachable</H3>");
MYSQL_SELECT_DB($database) or die ( "<H3>database not existent</H3>");
$result=MYSQL_QUERY( "DROP TABLE $table");
print "Result is ";
print $result;
/* Terminate SQL connection*/
MYSQL_CLOSE();
?>
```

As more content becomes database-driven, and more sites use electronic commerce, there will be a great increase in the usage of databases over the WWW, especially in accessing them from WWW pages. Just imagine if you computerized your own home, and you had a database setup which monitored all the conditions in your home, and saved them to a database. If this was interfaced to a WWW browser you could recall all your data. An excellent usage of database integration with a WWW browser is where users register their details on a database, and are sent e-mails at regular intervals to keep them informed of any products that they may be interested in.

Security in PHP

PHP can be used to prevent access to certain pages. For example the following PHP code and form read in the variables for login and password. When the user clicks on the submit button the login_page.php file is executed.

```
<form action="login_page.php"
method="post">
Login: <input type="text" name="login">
<BR>Password <input type="text"
name="password">
<input type="submit" value="Login">
</form>
```

The following shows an example of the login_page.php file, where the login and password variables are checked against 'fred' and 'bert', respectively. If they are the same the user is allowed to access the restricted page (in this case, cnds.html):

```
<?php
if ($login=="fred")
{
print "<H2>Login name is correct";
}
else
{
print "<H2>Login name is incorrect<BR>";
}
if ($password=="bert")
{
print "<H2>Password is correct<BR>";
}
else
{
print "<H2>Password is incorrect<BR>";
}
if ($name="fred" && $password=="bert")
{
print "<a href='cnds.html'><H2>Goto CNDS
page </a>";
}
else
{
print "<a
href='Javascript:history.back()'><H2>Login
again </a>";
```

18.8.7 CGI

A CGI program is one that is called from a WWW browser. These can be written in many languages, such as Visual BASIC, C++, Java and Perl. Visual BASIC, C++ and Java normally need to be compiled into an executable form to run on the server. Perl is different in that it is a scripted language, and does not have to be compiled before it is used. Normally Perl programs perform some sort of system function, such as getting information on the current WWW connection, or accessing data in a database. As they have a high level of priority, they must be kept in a secure way, so that external users cannot gain access to the server. This special place is a directory called the cgi-bin. Scripts placed in this place are allowed to gain access to the system. An example Perl program to show the IP address of the user is:

```
#!/usr/local/bin/perl
print "Content-type: text/html","\n\n";
print STDOUT "\n";
$remote_addr = $ENV{'REMOTE_ADDR'};
print STDOUT "<P>Your IP address is: ";
print STDOUT $remote_addr;
```

It operates by sending all of the required commands that a WWW server would normally add to the WWW page. For example "`Content-type: text/html","\n\n";`" is the string that is sent by the server before the main WWW page is sent, and defines that the page is an HTML page. In the case of Perl the STDOUT is normally sent to the monitor, but in a WWW page the output will be to the connection with the WWW browser. Also the first line of the Perl script defines where the operating system should find the Perl program (in this case it is /usr/local/bin/perl).

Perl, for all its power, is a very difficult language to use, and typically WWW developers use standard cgi scripts, which they can use for their purpose. Typical cgi scripts include page hit counters, form filling, and login user accesses to WWW pages. Perl's strongest feature is its string processing abilities.

Creating and reading cookies in PHP

A cookie is a saved text file which contains details on a session, which can be recalled the next time the user accesses a WWW page. In PHP a cookie is setup with:

```
<?php
setcookie("billscookie",
"Test",time()+3600);
/* format is name, value,
expiry time. In this case it will expire in 1
hour */
?>
```

and can be tested for its presence with:

```
<?php
if (isset($billscookie))
{
print "<P>A cookie exists on your computer";
} ?>
```

In this case, the cookie will have the form of:

```
billscookie
Test
localhost/
1024
142822656
*
```

18.8.8 XML

XML (eXtensible Markup Language) is a markup language which is similar to HTML. Its main application is to produce structured documents. It is much more powerful than HTML, as it is possible to define new tags. XML itself is derived from SGML (Standard Generalized Markup Language), which also defines sets of tags and the relationships among them.

Tags in XML are similar to HTML tags, and they consist of a tag name plus optional attributes, surrounded by angle brackets (< and >). Like HTML, the opening tag has < followed by the name of the tag, and the closing tag has the tag name preceded by a slash and then a >. For example we could define our own tags of <PARAGRAPH>, <BOLD> and <ITALICS>, and use them in the following document:

<PARAGRAPH>Some programs provide a <BOLD>framework</BOLD> for a user to manipulate data without the user having to produce their own program. Examples of this include word processors, spreadsheet programs, and so on, where the user writes <ITALIC>macro</ITALIC>, or script, programs which <BOLD>integrate</BOLD> within the package.</PARAGRAPH>

would be formatted (after we had properly defined our tags) as:

Some programs provide a **framework** for a user to manipulate data without the user having to produce their own program. Examples of this include word processors, spreadsheet programs, and so on, where the user writes *macro*, or script, programs which **integrate** within the package.

One difference between HTML and XML is that an empty tag (one that uses only a single tag, such as `<img>`, instead of an opening tag and a closing tag containing text or other material) must end with a slash just before the closing angle bracket. For example, an `<img>` tag in XML might look like this:

```
<img src="mygraphic.gif" />
```

XML, though, is much stricter and less forgiving about its syntax than HTML is; and files, which do not conform to the XML standard, are rejected by XML parsers.

Typical JavaScript methods

Methods are applied to object. An example JavaScript object is **Math**. Typical methods include:

Math.abs()	Absolute value.
Math.acos()	Inverse cosine.
Math.asin()	Inverse sine.
Math.atan()	Inverse tangent.
Math.ceil()	Returns the nearest integer, greater than the number.
Math.cos()	Returns the cosine.
Math.exp()	Return the exponential of a value.
Math.floor()	Returns the nearest integer, less than the number.
Math.min()	Returns the minimum of two values
Math.pow()	Returns the value of the first value raised to the power of the second value.
Math.random()	Returns a random number.
Math.round()	Rounds the value of the nearest integer.
Math.sin()	Returns the sine.
Math.sqrt()	Returns the square root.
Math.tan()	Returns the tangent.

Methods applied to the history object include:

history.back()	Go back to the last link
history.forward()	Go forward to the next link
history.go(-*n*)	Go back *n* links.

Methods applied to the document object include:

document.close()	Close a window
document.open()	Open a new win-

18.8.9 WML

There will be a great increase in the coming years in the usage of mobile computing devices. These devices will typically connect to the Internet through a radio link, and will possibly have a small display area. Thus, the existing WWW pages are not really relevant to this type of system, as they tend to be graphics-intensive, and are designed for a resolution of at least 640 by 480 pixels. Thus a new language has been developed to cope with this: Wireless Markup Language (WML). Basically

WML is a markup language which is based on XML and was developed for specifying content and user interface for devices which have low bandwidth connections, such as cellular phones and pagers.

WML is designed to work with small, wireless devices that have four characteristics:

- **Small display screens with low resolution**. Typically mobile phones can only support a few lines of text, with 8–12 characters on each line.
- **Limited capacity.** These devices typically have a limited amount of resources, such as a low-powered processor, limited amount of memory, limited power constraints, and limited storage space.
- **Limited user control**. Typically mobile phones have just a few special keys in which to navigate. It is unlikely that they would have a mouse or other pointing device.
- **Low bandwidth and high latency**. Mobile devices might only have a bandwidth of between 300 bps and 10 kbps network connections, with a delay of over five seconds.

The characteristics of WML are grouped into four major areas:

- It supports text and image support, and has a variety of formatting and layout commands.
- It is created from cards which are grouped into decks. WML decks are similar to HTML pages in that they are identified by an URL, and contain the main content for the page.
- It offers support for managing navigation between cards and decks, and includes commands for event handling. These are typically used to navigate.
- It allows parameters to be set for all the WML decks. Variables can be used in place of strings and are substituted at runtime.

All WML information is arranged as a collection of cards and desks. Cards normally specify one or more units of user interaction. This could be to present a menu, or to enter text in a field. The user then navigates through a number of WML cards, and makes choices before moving onto other cards. A deck is the smallest unit of WML that the server sends to the client. An example WML page is given next. With this the user will receive an ACCEPT option, which, if selected will take them onto the next card in the desk.

```
<?xml version="1.0"?>
<!DOCTYPE wml PUBLIC "-//WAPFORUM//DTD WML 1.1//EN"
"http://www.wapforum.org/DTD/wml_1.1.xml">
<wml>
        <card id="Card1">
                <do type="accept" label="Next">
                        <go href="#Card2"/>
                </do>
                <p> Select <b>Next</b> to go to the next card. </p>
        </card>
        <card id="Card2">
                <p> This is the second card </p>
        </card>
</wml>
```

18.8.10 Java and WWW pages

The Java programming language is the natural language for complex Internet and WWW based programming. These are standardized in the J2EE specification, and the main aspects of this are discussed on the following link.

For more material on Java and WWW pages please visit our website at:
`http://www.palgrave.com/studyskills/masterseries/buchanan`

18.8.11 CSS

Another particular problem with HTML is that it is not very good at precisely defining the format of text, especially between different types of browser. Thus the CSS standard has been defined. This involves including a CSS file in the HTML page, which contains definitions for the text styles used in the page. For example to define the first header (H1) style:

```
H1
{font: bold 16pt Verdana, Arial, Helvetica, sans-serif; background:
transparent; color: #000000}
```

which defines the header style (H1) is Verdana font, of 16 points, and black (#000000). Thus

```
<H1>Hello</H1>
```

will become:

Hello

18.9 Exercises

The following questions are multiple choice. Please select from a–d.

18.9.1 Where was the WWW first conceived:
(a) UCL (b) UMIST
(c) MIT (d) CERN

18.9.2 An MPEG file is what type of file:
(a) Image (b) Motion video
(c) Sound file (d) Generally compressed file

18.9.3 A GIF file is what type of file:
(a) Image (b) Motion video
(c) Sound file (d) Generally compressed file

18.9.4 A ZIP file is what type of file:
(a) Image (b) Motion video
(c) Sound file (d) Generally compressed file

Tutorial questions are available at:
`http://www.palgrave.com/studyskills/masterseries/buchanan`

19 Electronic mail

19.1 Introduction

Electronic mail (e-mail) is one use of the Internet which, according to most businesses, improves productivity. Traditional methods of sending mail within an office environment are inefficient, as it normally requires an individual requesting a secretary to type the letter. This must then be proof-read and sent through the internal mail system, which is relatively slow and can be open to security breaches.

A faster and more secure method of sending information is to use electronic mail, where messages are sent almost in an instant. For example, a memo with 100 words will be sent in a fraction of a second. It is also simple to send to specific groups, various individuals, company-wide, and so on. Other types of data can also be sent with the mail message such as images, sound, and so on. It may also be possible to determine if a user has read the mail. The main advantages are:

E-mail standards:

- **RFC821.** SMTP. Simple Mail Transfer Protocol. Defines the transfer of an e-mail message from one system to another.
- **RFC822.** Defines the format of an e-mail message, with heading to define the sender and the recipient.
- **RFC1521/1522.** MIME. Multipurpose Internet Mail Extensions. Defines a mechanism for supporting multiple attachments and for differing content types.
- **RFC1939.** POP-3. Post Office Protocol – Version 3. Creation of a standard and simple mechanism to access e-mail messages on a mail server. As it is simple it allows for many different types of programs to download e-mail messages.

- It is normally much cheaper than using the telephone (although, as time equates to money for most companies, this relates any savings or costs to a user's typing speed).
- Many different types of data can be transmitted, such as images, documents, speech, and so on.
- It is much faster than the postal service.
- Users can filter incoming e-mail easier than incoming telephone calls.
- It normally cuts out the need for work to be typed, edited and printed by a secretary.
- It reduces the burden on the mailroom.
- It is normally more secure than traditional methods.
- It is relatively easy to send to groups of people (traditionally, either a circulation list was required or a copy to everyone in the group was required).
- It is usually possible to determine whether the recipient has actually read the message (the electronic mail system sends back an acknowledgement).

The main disadvantages are:

- It stops people using the telephone.
- It cannot be used as a legal document.
- Electronic mail messages can be sent impulsively and may be later regretted (sending by traditional methods normally allows for a rethink). In extreme cases messages can be sent to the wrong person (typically when replying to an e-mail message, where a message is sent to the mailing list rather than the originator).

- It may be difficult to send to some remote sites. Many organizations have either no electronic mail or merely an intranet. Large companies are particularly wary of Internet connections and limit the amount of external traffic.
- Not everyone reads their electronic mail on a regular basis (although this is changing as more organizations adopt e-mail as the standard communications medium).

The main standards that relate to the protocols of e-mail transmission and reception are:

- Simple Mail Transfer Protocol (SMTP) – which is used with the TCP/IP protocol suite. It has traditionally been limited to the text-based electronic messages.
- Multipurpose Internet Mail Extension (MIME) – which allows the transmission and reception of mail that contains various types of data, such as speech, images and motion video. It is a newer standard than SMTP and uses much of its basic protocol.
- S/MIME (Secure MIME). RSA Data Security created S/MIME which supports encrypted e-mail transfers and digitally signed electronic mail.

19.2 Shared-file approach versus client/server approach

An e-mail system can use either a shared-file approach or a client/server approach. In a shared-file system the source mail client sends the mail message to the local post office. This post office then transfers control to a message transfer agent which then stores the message for a short time before sending it to the destination post office. The destination mail client periodically checks its own post office to determine if it has mail. This arrangement is often known as store and forward, and the process is illustrated in Figure 19.1. Most PC-based e-mail systems use this type of mechanism.

A client/server approach involves the source client setting up a real-time remote connection with the local post office, which then sets up a real-time connection with the destination, which in turn sets up a remote connection with the destination client. The message will thus arrive at the destination when all the connections are complete.

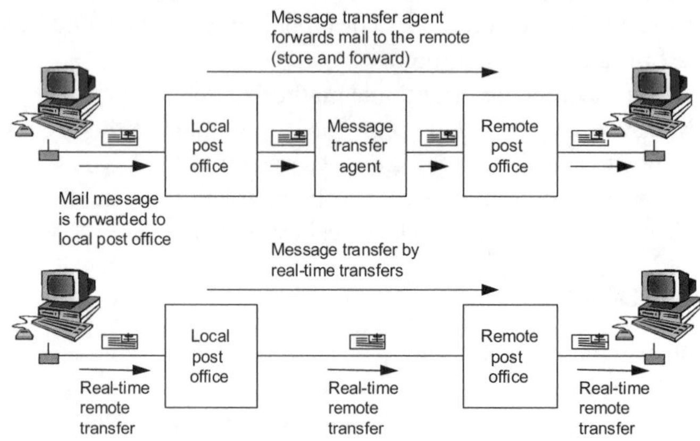

Figure 19.1 Shared-file versus client/server

19.3 Using an e-mail client

E-mail clients, such as Microsoft Outline, enables the user to create, send, read and file e-mails. Microsoft Outlook contains a series of folders in which e-mails are stored. When an e-mail is written, it is placed in the **Outbox** where it will remain until connection to the Internet, such as via an ISP. Likewise, when an e-mail is sent to your e-mail address, it is sent to the e-mail server, where it will stay in the **Inbox** of the server for your account. When you connect, the e-mails waiting for you will transfer to your computer and will be placed in the **Inbox** folder of the local computer. Typically the e-mail message is then deleted from the server, as it is already stored on the local computer. Figures 19.2 and 19.3 illustrates this principle.

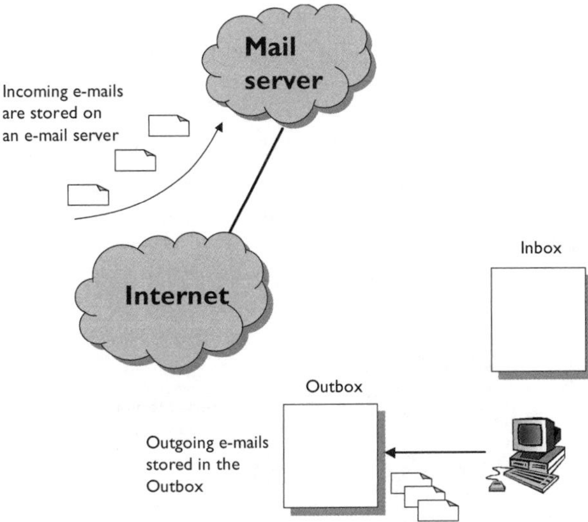

Figure 19.2 Before connecting to the Internet

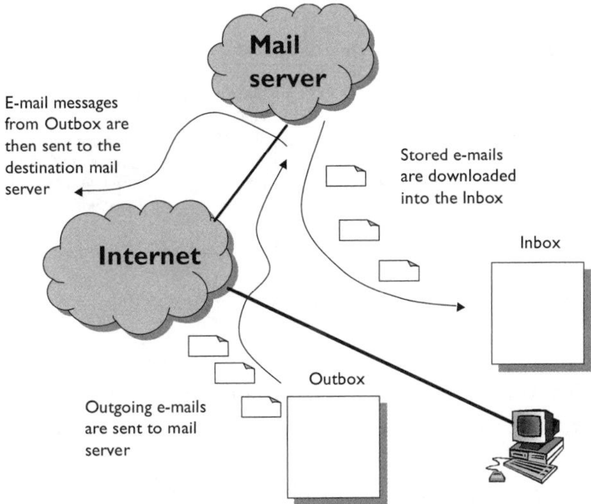

Figure 19.3 After connecting to the Internet

19.4 Electronic mail overview

Figure 19.4 shows a typical e-mail architecture. It contains four main elements:

1. Post offices – where outgoing messages are temporally buffered (stored) before transmission and where incoming messages are stored. The post office runs the server software capable of routing messages (a message transfer agent) and maintaining the post office database.
2. Message transfer agents – for forwarding messages between post offices and to the destination clients. This software can either reside on the local post office or on a physically separate server.
3. Gateways – which provide part of the message transfer agent functionality. They translate between different e-mail systems, different e-mail addressing schemes and messaging protocols.
4. E-mail clients – normally the computer which connects to the post office. It contains three parts:

   - E-mail Application Program Interface (API), such as MAPI, VIM, MHS and CMC.
   - Messaging protocol. The main messaging protocols are SMTP or X.400. SMTP is defined in RFC 822 and RFC 821, whereas X.400 is an OSI-defined e-mail message delivery standard.
   - Network transport protocol, such as Ethernet, FDDI, and so on.

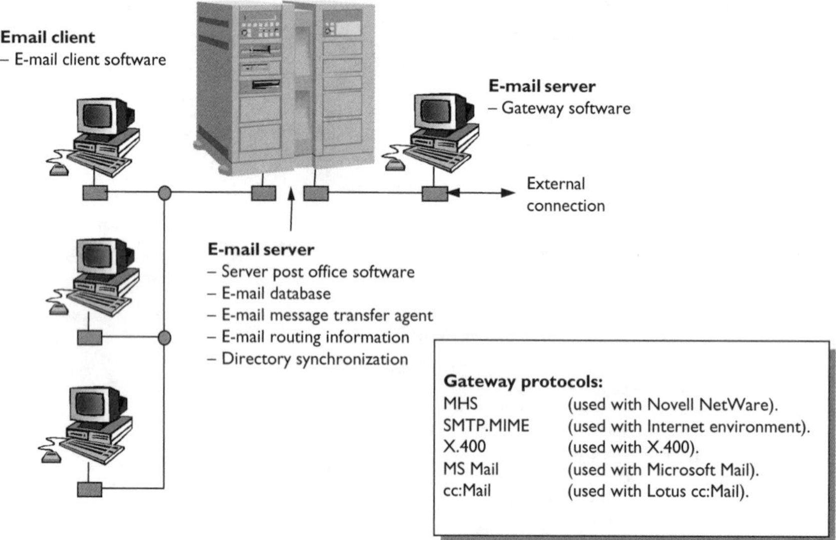

Figure 19.4 E-mail architecture

The main APIs are:

- MAPI (messaging API) – Microsoft part of Windows Operation Services Architecture.
- VIM (vendor-independent messaging) – Lotus, Apple, Novell and Borland derived e-mail API.
- MHS (message handling service) – Novell network interface which is often used as an e-mail gateway protocol.

* CMC (common mail call) – E-mail API associated with the X.400 native messaging protocol.

Gateways translate the e-mail message from one system to another, such as from Lotus cc:Mail to Microsoft Mail. Typical gateway protocols are:

* MHS (used with Novell NetWare)
* X.400 (used with X.400)
* cc:Mail (used with Lotus cc:Mail)
* SMTP.MIME (used with Internet environment)
* MS Mail (used with Microsoft Mail)

The Internet e-mail address is in the form of a name (such as `f.bloggs`), followed by an '`@`' and then the domain name (such as `anytown.ac.uk`). For example:

```
f.bloggs@anytown.ac.uk
```

19.5 SMTP

The IAB has defined the protocol SMTP in RFC821. As SMTP is a transmission and reception protocol it does not actually define the format or contents of the transmitted message except that the data has 7-bit ASCII characters and that extra log information is added to the start of the delivered message to indicate the path the message took. The protocol itself is only concerned in reading the address header of the message.

For more material on memory please visit our website at:
`http://www.palgrave.com/studyskills/masterseries/buchanan`

19.6 MIME

SMTP suffers from several drawbacks, such as:

* It can only transmit ASCII characters and thus cannot transmit executable files or other binary objects.
* It does not allow the attachment of files, such as images and audio.
* It can only transmit 7-bit ASCII characters thus it does not support an extended ASCII character set.

A new standard, Multipurpose Internet Mail Extension (MIME), has been defined for this purpose, which is compatible with existing RFC 822 implementations. It is defined in the specifications RFC 1521 and 1522. Its enhancements include the following:

* Five new message header fields in the RFC 822 header, which provide extra information about the body of the message.
* Use of various content formats to support multimedia electronic mail.
* Defined transfer encodings for transforming attached files.

The five new header fields defined in MIME are:

- MIME-version – a message that conforms to RFC 1521 or 1522 is MIME-version 1.0.
- Content-type – this field defines the type of data attached.
- Content-transfer-encoding – this field indicates the type of transformation necessary to represent the body in a format which can be transmitted as a message.
- Content-id – this field is used to uniquely identify MIME multiple attachments in the e-mail message.
- Content-description – this field is a plain-text description of the object with the body. It can be used by the user to determine the data type.

The rest of the material on MIME is available at:
`http://www.palgrave.com/studyskills/masterseries/buchanan`

19.7 Post Office Protocol (POP)

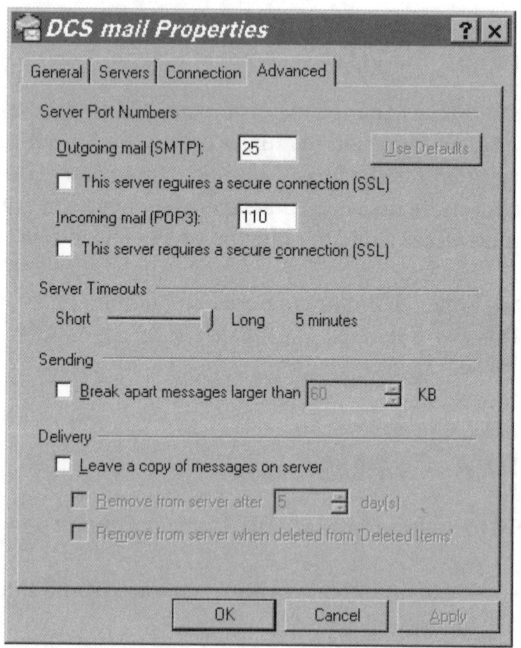

The Post Office Protocol was first defined in RFC918, but has since been replaced with POP-3, which is defined in RFC1939. The objective of POP is to create a standard method for users to access a mail server. E-mail messages are uploaded onto a mail server using SMTP, and then downloaded using POP. With POP the server listens for a connection, and when this occurs the server sends a greeting message, and waits for commands. The standard port reserved for POP transactions is 110. Like SMTP, it consists of case-insensitive commands with one or more arguments, followed by the Carriage Return (CR) and Line Feed (LF) characters, typically represented by CRLF. These keywords are either three or four characters long.

For more material on POP-3 and tutorial questions, please visit our website at:
`http://www.palgrave.com/studyskills/masterseries/buchanan`

20 Multimedia

20.1 Introduction

Human history has developed through the storage and distribution of information. Initially this involved writing and distributing material in a printed form such as with books, newspapers, leaflets and posters. One of the first changes to this type of distribution came when Ted Nelson, in 1960, published 'As We May Think', which was basically a description of a global document system, based on the **hypertext** principle. This paper inspired many people including Tim Bernes-Lee at CERN who, in the 1980s, actually developed the first prototype of the WWW. A major change has thus occurred over the last century where computers were used to distribute, store and present information.

Up until the end of the 1970s, computers systems could only really support text-based information, and were large, and difficult-to-use systems. The great change in computer systems came in 1981, when IBM released the PC. This was followed, in 1984, by the Apple Macintosh and in 1985 by the Commodore Amiga. The Macintosh and Amiga were based around GUIs and their applications used **WIMPs** (Windows, Icons, Menus and Pointers). These concepts allowed for proper multimedia. The PC would eventually catch up with the usage of Microsoft Windows, a GUI for the PC. Slowly the PC has supported multimedia, with the addition of graphical cards, audio cards and high-speed CD-ROM drives.

Before the integration of multimedia on computers, the media tended to be delivered in a non-computer-based way, such as through video, or audiotape delivery, or even over TV systems (such as used by the Open University). These systems did not provide much interaction between the trainer and the user. The new integrated multimedia systems supported the integration of audio, video, graphics and text. Initially the production of this material was difficult as there were very few development packages available, but over the 1990s, several companies, especially Macromedia and Adobe, produced development packages, which successfully integrated all the media into a single form.

Multimedia is the integration of many different media types into a single integrated unit. This normally involves converting the original media source, such as images, audio, video, text, and so on, into a digital form, so that it can be integrated into a digital package. This can then be delivered as a single entity. Figure 20.1 illustrates this. The text, video, sound and images are typically produced in a raw format. For example video is normally available in either an NSTC, PAL or SECAM format. This can then be digitized into a digital form. This will give RGB and pixel data, arranged in frames. Next the video can be compressed into a standard format, such as MPEG or AVI. Sound can be converted into MP-3, and images are typically converted into JPEG, GIF or PNG. The output from the media integration package depends on how the media will be delivered. The main forms are:

- **Stand-alone package**. This is where the media can be run without requiring any additional software viewer. Typically, it is compiled for the specific computer and operating system that it will run on.
- **Media player integration**. This involves converting the media into a form which can be played in a media player. Typical media players include Macromedia Shockwave Player (which plays DCR files), Macromedia Flash Player (which plays SWF files). The forms can also be integrated into a WWW browser (using the required browser plug-in).

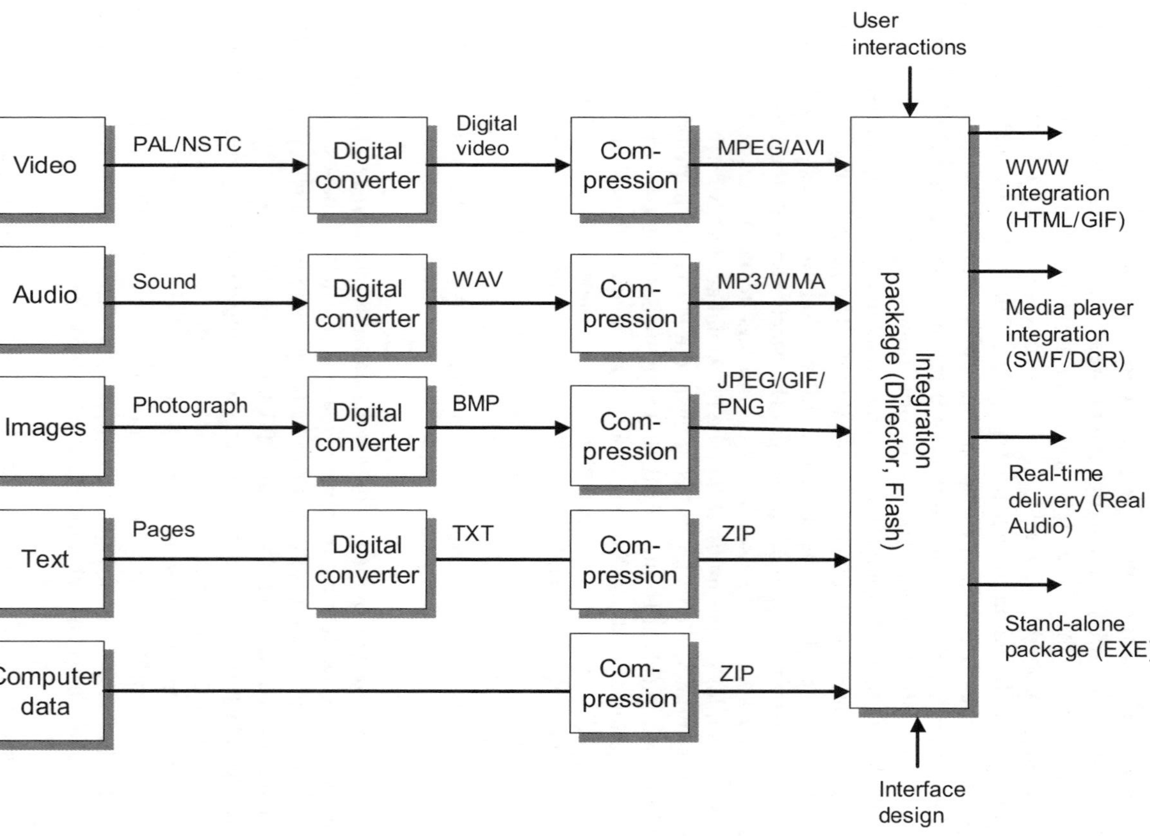

Figure 20.1 Media integration

- **WWW integration**. This involves converting the media into a form which can be viewed by a WWW browser. For this the media is converted into a number of HTML pages, which contain media content, such as AVI, MPEG, GIF, JPG and PNG files. Note that additional plug-ins are required for the delivery of AVI and MPEG movies. A typical player is Quicktime, which is available from Apple Computers.
- **Real-time delivery**. This involves delivering the media, in real time over a network connection. Sometimes this can involve the synchronization of images or video with sound. Typical real-time formats include the Real Audio (RA) format, and Windows Media Audio (WMA).

20.1.1 Applications areas

The use of multimedia systems has increased over the past decade and the main developments are: education, tourism, retail and entertainment, corporate markets, will increase over the next few years. With education there can be no replacement for the teacher, but multimedia has enhanced education with:

- Increased availability to information, especially over the Internet.
- Access to material produced by the best professionals. This can be backed-up by the teacher.
- Access to video conferencing and chat facilities which allows for remote conversations.
- Delivery of material in many different forms, such as video, audio, graphical and text. Multimedia allows for much richer content than traditional systems, and also provides faster linking of additional material.

A great increase of multimedia will come in the next few years, as more courses are delivered, and taken, on-line. This will provide for the delivery of educational material over the Internet, and will allow instant access to tutors. It will also support exams to be taken online, and instantly marked. Students will thus be able to pace their own training to the speed at which they learn best, rather than having to conform to college/university timetables.

Multimedia in tourism

In the past tourists relied on brochures, videotapes and books. Multimedia enhances this by providing a much richer form of presentation. Currently it is possible to view places around the world and sample them before travelling. For example, it is possible to get a 3D-view of the Coliseum in Rome, and to view in real time with web cameras. Tourists can also access information via kiosks in city streets, to get information, e.g. live shows to area maps. It is also possible to arrange bookings for travel and accommodation over the Internet.

Multimedia in retail

With retail, multimedia has allowed goods to be sampled remotely. This is especially useful if the media is already in a digital format. Areas, which have been successfully developed include the selling of books over the Internet (with Amazon.com), and the sale of music CDs (with Cdpoint.com). These have allowed users to view and review the content before they buy them. Also as they do not need a shop to view the goods, and as there is no sale person involved, the supplier can ship the material at a much reduce cost. Over the next few years multimedia and WWW integration will allow for many more goods to be purchased over the Internet. For example it is now possible to view a new car over the Internet, and then change its colour, and view how it would look. It is even possible, to drive a simulator of the car, and get a feel of how it would drive, without ever visiting a showroom. In the past consumers would have had to visit shops or use mail order catalogues to sample material.

Corporate use

In the corporate market the use of electronic mail has considerably increased commercial activities. Electronic mail now supports full multimedia with text, images, video and audio. There is also an increased amount of training conducted using multimedia. This saves time in travel, and in training costs. Video conferencing has allowed for remote meetings, but this still is not as widely used as the telephone.

Entertainment

The largest increase in the use of multimedia will come in the entertainment market. This will be in many forms. In TV, there is now a great amount of digital information sent along with the main content. This has even been expanded to support user interaction (especially in sports matches). Once TV is fully integrated with the Internet there will be scope for linking extra information from many sources. For cinema it is now possible to review films, and sample them before you book tickets, which can also be done on-line. Radio stations are also going on-line, and their content is being transmitted over the Internet. This allows radio stations to provide extra content, such as providing information on the songs, with their lyrics. Multimedia has improved many traditional forms of entertainment, such as:

- **Encyclopaedias**. These are now fully interactive with video and sound.
- **DVDs**. Analogue videos are being replaced with DVDs for movies, as DVD supports improved graphics quality and also enhanced sound, such as surround sound and a special effects channel. They also allow for users to view different scenes and angles, and support the integration of text and graphical data, alongside the video data.
- **Console games**. These have become more sophisticated, and it is even possible to play interactive games, over the Internet, with music and video.

For an educational multimedia system, what questions would you ask when you were designing it?

What type of people are they?
What will the course be taken?
What are the time schedules involved for learning?
What are they learning?
What level of IT knowledge do they have?
How motivated are they to learn?
What new skills will be required?
Are they adult learners?
What types of systems will they have access to?

20.1.2 Conclusions

A key to the future will be the integration of multimedia with all forms for current delivery. This will include its integration into traditional systems, such as TV, radio and telephone. The future is likely to involve the integration of many different content sources into a single system, which is likely to be delivered over a single transmission source: the Internet. The WWW is now a global database of knowledge, and search engines make it easy to locate information, in a way that was never possible before. Unlike libraries, which tended to support printed material, this material is now available in many different forms, and can be easily integrated to produce a single entity.

20.2 Multimedia development

Multimedia isn't really a very good term for the creation, production and delivery of media content. Unfortunately it has become a standard part of the IT vocabulary. Also many people still view it to be a single activity, but it actually involves many different skills from content design and media design, to software engineering and content delivery skills. For example many find it difficult to differentiate the creation of the content from its development as an integrated system. Many also cannot differentiate this development from the delivery of the material. Each of these stages is a definitive part of the process, and requires different skills at each stage. The stages might be:

- **Content creation**. At the creation phase there are normally expert users, who know how the system should operate, and who it is aimed at. For example, a French language teacher will know how to present a structured course in the teaching of French, for a certain level of knowledge. They may not know how the material would operate in a multimedia environment, but they can produce material in a form that could be used in this.
- **Content integration**. This is where IT skills are important, and normally involves integrating the content into a single package. As much as possible the developer must have communications with the content creators, and the delivery specialists.
- **Delivery**. This is an important stage as it involves delivering the content to the user's computer. Typically these days the delivery is over the Internet, or over a network, thus bandwidth is a major consideration. It is important that delivery issues are taken into account, before the decisions are taken on the design and development of the package.
- **Maintenance**. The material, once produced, must be kept up to date, and bugs fixed, and new material generated.

Just like software development, there is no defined way to develop multimedia. Each developed system will have its own aims; its own target audience; its own method of delivery, and its own special problems. The factors that typically affect the develop cycle include:

- **Aims of the content**. Different subject areas have differing requirements for the way that the content needs to be delivered. For example, a PhD student might require just a basic text-based document with simple line drawings for their research, but pre-school children would need a more graphically rich user interface, where text was replaced by pictures. The navigation would also be simpler.
- **Source content**. The source content can be available in a number of different formats, and it may have to be generated before the system was developed, or it may have to be produced after the system has been designed. Another major factor is the protection of the content against it being copied by others.
- **User system requirements**. This can have a great effect on the type of multimedia used, because it is no good at all to develop a totally graphical-based, animated system for a mobile computing device which has limited processing and memory capabilities. The operating system can also have a great effect on how the content is presented. It is extremely difficult to aim the requirements at every user, but market research will show the typical systems that the target user uses.
- **Compatibility**. This can be a major factor, for many reasons. If possible the amount of development for different types of delivery should be minimized. Thus it is a great ad-

vantage to a developer if they can develop the same material for both CD-ROM delivery and for Internet delivery.

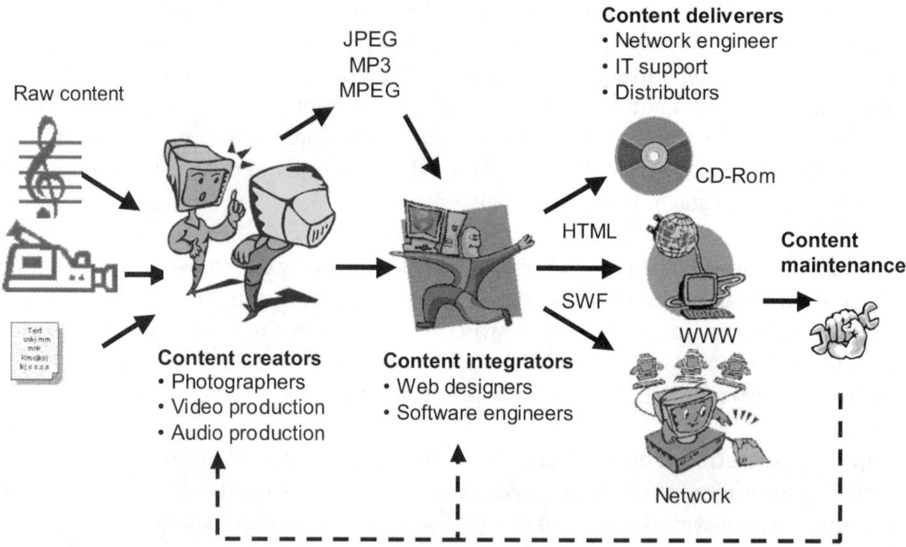

Figure 20.2 Content stages

- **Delivery**. This is a major factor, and the delivery type should be defined by both the user, and the type of material. A multimedia system which has a great deal of video content will typically not cope well with a modem connection to the Internet. Thus CD-ROM would probably give better delivery. Also it is difficult to deliver executable programs over the Internet (and, in some case, they should not be trusted), and CD-ROM distribution makes this easier.
- **Maintainability**. This is an important factor for the long-term development of a multimedia product. It is unlikely that the product will ever be completely finished, as new material is often added to it, or bugs fixed. Thus, maintainability is an important factor. It does little good to develop a system, which is extremely difficult to add to, or to change in any way. A good example of this is in the Adobe PDF format. In this a package known as Abode Acrobat can be used to convert from many types of documents, such as Word documents, to the PDF format. Acrobat can then be used to add navigation, movies, sound, menus, and so on. Unfortunately it is difficult to update the original material without starting from the beginning again (although there is a basic touch-up tool to make small changes). Thus it is often better to choose a system which can easily update the material and reproduce the product. It is thus an advantage to make the media elements as small as possible, as a change in these will not have a great effect on the rest of the material.
- **Resusability**. This is important, especially when parts of the multimedia system can be used in other systems. If possible content should be developed in a generic way, so that it can be easily modified so that it can be used again in another system. For example, a developer could develop a range of buttons, with associated interactions. If possible the developer should design them so that the could be easily used in another system. This might involve creating a way of changing the colour of the button, or the text, or the way that events occur on the buttons.

20.3 Content design and delivery

The stages of content development involve different types of people, with different skills. As much as possible the creators of the content should be kept up to date in the development of the project, as many software project fail as the software designers have not received continual feedback from the actual people who have initiated the idea for the project, or how they use the product.

A good approach in the development of the multimedia is to setup two design teams. These should be small enough to be efficient (as often the larger the committee, the slower that the work will proceed). These would be:

- **Instructional design team**. The objectives of this team are to analyse, to design, to build and to evaluate the product. Typically this team would be made up of content creators, such as graphics designers, and the idea generators. This is the main design team, and will feed ideas to the software design team. Representatives from the software design team should be part of this team, and should give the instructional team technical support for their ideas. This team will initially ask the software design team to produce prototypes which will be presented to the instructional design team, so that the instructional team can generate a design.
- **Software design team**. The objectives of this team are to prototype, to generate new ideas, to construct and code, and to test and evaluate the product. This team will be led by the instructional design team, and must report back to this team, as technical requirements should never overrule the aims of the product (unless the instructional team were to approve these). After the generation of initial prototypes, the instructional team will give outline designs for the product. These would be turned into a formal design specification by the software design team, which would be presented back to the instructional team, for their acceptance, or not. Once accepted the software design team can start to properly code and integrate the media. After this is complete they can feed differing versions to the instructional team, who would give feedback on their developments. Finally the product would enter the test and evaluate phase.

Any failure in the project is likely to be shared by the two teams, rather than resting on an individual. A good approach is to formalize meetings of the two teams. For example let's imagine that we have a language tool for primary school children. Initially the teams would be defined, and distributed to everyone. For example the instruction team could be:

Ms J. Goodie, French Teacher (Instructional Group Leader).
Mr M. Plode, Teacher, Design Department.
Mr R.Headingly, School Head.
Ms A. Bigwig, Legal Department, Local Authority.
Ms I.S. Techno, Multimedia Developer (Software Group Leader).
Ms A.N. Pupil, Senior Year Pupil.

This team should involve the main content creators (the teachers), and representatives of users of the system (the pupil). It also includes the School Head, who is likely to be able to make discussions on finance and resources. The representative from the Legal Department will help with copyright issues. Also the technical person (Ms Techno) is there to represent the Software Design team. Initially they would meet and define the main designs for the project, these would be fed to the software team, so that they can work on prototypes and the main design specifications. The software design team could be made up of:

Ms I.S. Techno, Multimedia Developer (Software Group Leader).
Ms J. Goodie, French Teacher (Instructional Group Leader).
Mr C. Plus, Software Developer.
Mr E.Ternet, IT Support.

This team includes someone from the instructional team, and will meet to discuss the ideas and the requirements from that team. The number of meetings of the teams depends on the project, but, in this case we could define:

- Formal instructional team meets every two weeks, to discuss documents and things like design details and content creation. An informal agenda is created for each meeting, and each meeting focuses on a specific aim.
- Software design team meets every two weeks, to discuss technical development. An informal agenda is created for each meeting, and each meeting focuses on a specific aim.
- Representatives from both teams meet every four weeks to discuss the progress. This meeting should have a formal agenda with documents and presentations tabled before the meeting, which are open to discussion. This meeting is fully minuted, and actions are put on people. Any major changes in the project are discussed at this meeting.

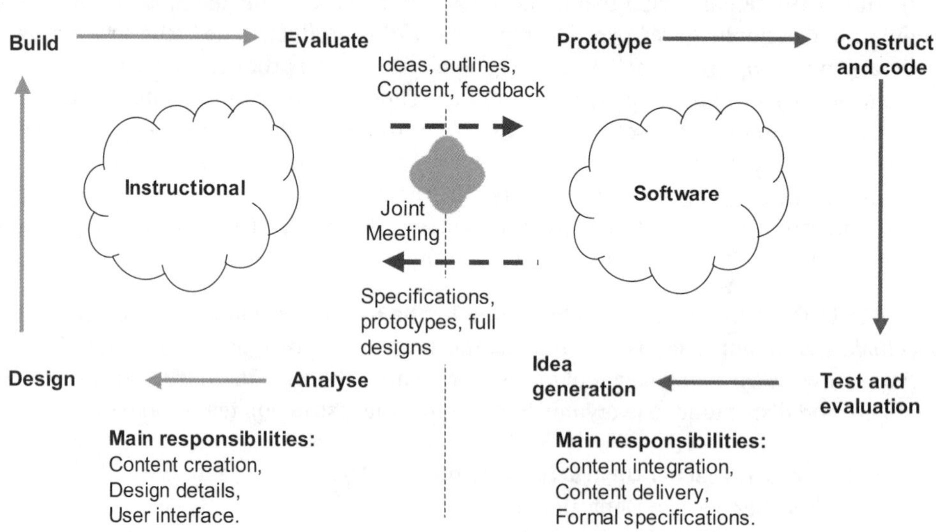

Figure 20.3 Content development teams

20.4 Multimedia package integration

In most cases the copyright of the original material should be preserved as much as possible. There does seem to be a focusing of integrating multimedia material with the WWW. Figure 20.4 shows an example of a possible flow of content in developing multimedia. If a WWW page is required the developer can simply use a WWW design package, such as Macromedia Dreamweaver or Microsoft FrontPage. The content, though, may have to be generated by another package such as Adobe Photoshop or Macromedia Flash. In many cases the content must be protected against copying of the original source, thus packages such as Macromedia Flash and Macromedia Director can be used to protect this. These packages also support enhanced user interaction, and excellent animation facilities. As the diagram shows the designer uses Flash and/or Director to produce SWF or DCR files, respectively. These can then either be integrated in a WWW page, or produced as a standalone package, using Director. Flash is an excellent package in that it allows media to be broken into small parts, which can then be integrated in the whole system. Flash content is often known as a Flash movie. The actual design files for Flash and Director are stored with FLA and DIR extensions, respectively. These files are typically not distributed, and should be kept in a secure way, as they contain much of the original source content.

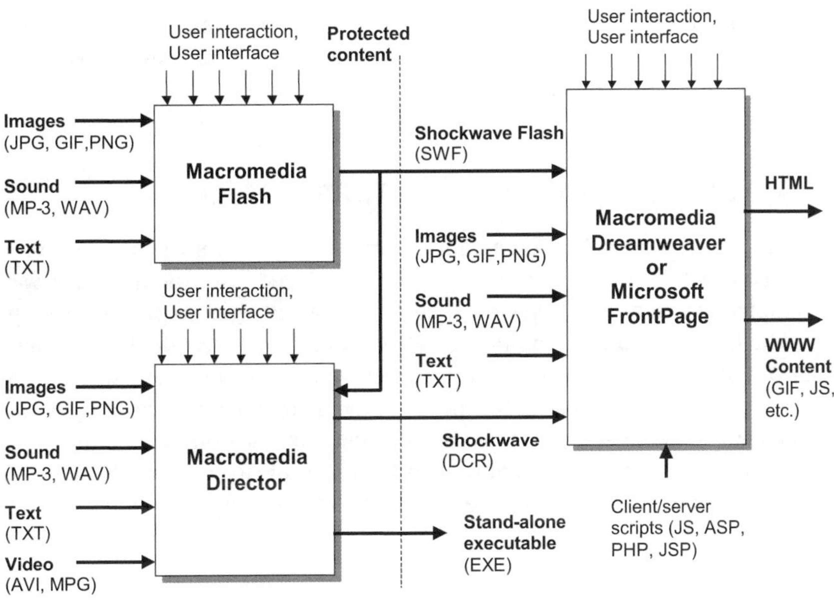

Figure 20.4 Typical media development

Macromedia Flash has many advantages, including:

- **Scaleable graphics**. Flash produces graphics which can be expanded or contracted without losing the definition of the graphics content. It does this by making the content vector based, rather than in a bitmapped format. Vector graphics are much more scaleable than bitmaps.
- **Streamed content**. Flash allows the content to be delivered in required stages. For example it is possible to transmit the parts of the content which the user needs to see first, and then load the rest in the background.
- **Timeline-based.** Each Flash movie is created along a timeline. This allows events within the animation to be synchronized. This is especially important when audio needs to be synchronized with video/images. This timeline-based system allows different movies to run at different speeds.

- **Optimized for the WWW**. Flash content is highly optimized for producing excellent graphics with the minimum amount of bandwidth required. This is because much of the graphics capabilities is available in the player, which plugs into the browser.
- **Scripted actions**. Flash content can contain actions on the elements of the content, such as mouse over events on graphics, or mouse down events on buttons.

Apart from Flash and Shockwave, the other main document format for protecting content is Acrobat PDF (Portable Document Format). With this, documents are converted into a form which can be protected against copying (such as from a copy-and-paste action), or protected against printing. As the document cannot be printed, it has better protection than a document in a paper form, as the document can be scanned, and then converted to text with an OCR (Optical Character Recognition) package. Many packages can now produce PDF documents, especially Adobe packages, and many have a plug-in to support it. The documents can either be displayed within the PDF Reader, or can be viewed within a browser with the required PDF Reader plug-in. PDF also has the advantage that it supports scaleable graphics, where the graphics (or text) can be zoomed-into without loosing any of the definition of the graphic (or text).

20.5 Audio components for multimedia

Speech and audio are normally in an analogue format. In order for them to be stored, analysed or transmitted by a computer they must be digitized also, the analogue waveform must be sampled at a fixed rate. Typically speech quality audio is sampled at 8,000 times per second and high quality audio is sampled at 44,100 samples per second. Each of these samples is converted into a digital form, with a given number of bits to define an analogue intensity. The greater the number of bits the more accurate the digitized sample. CD audio uses 16 bits per sample; telephone uses 8 bits per sample. The output from the digitization process gives results in a raw file format such as WAV, this file format can be inefficient in its storage, e.g. CD quality requires 10MB for every minute of stereo. Compact disks use the following parameters:

Sample rate:	44.1 kHz
Channels:	2 (stereo)
Bits per sample, per channel:	16
Levels per sample:	65,536
Total data rate (Mb/s):	1.4112

20.5.1 Compressed audio

A more efficient method of storing or transmitting audio is to use an audio compression algorithm such as:

MP3 This format was developed by the Motion Picture Experts Group (MPEG). Almost all MPEG files are recorded in MPEG 1 or MPEG 3. This format is well known for its excellent compression and good sound quality. The quality of the conversion is normally defined by the converted bit rate. A rate of 128 kbps gives almost CD-like sound quality.

WAV This was developed by Microsoft for the PC. It has become a standard on the Microsoft Windows operating systems. Many of the sounds produced by the Microsoft operating system are generated from WAV files. In general WAV files support either 8-bit or 16-bit samples with either a stereo or mono format. It also supports a wide range of sampling rates.

AU This format was developed by Sun Microsystems, and is comparable to the WAV format. It is mainly used with NeXT and SUN UNIX systems, and uses a format called the Sun u-law, which is an international compression standard. Like WAV files, it supports many sampling rates, of which the 8 kHz sampling rate is most common.

AIFF This format is Audio Interchange File Format, and was developed by Apple. It is mainly used for Macintosh and cross-platform applications. AIFF can files can support 8-bit or 16-bit using mono or stereo sound. It is also capable of many different sampling rates.

A logical extension to the delivery of audio content is to use the Internet, and deliver the audio when required. This technology is named **streaming** audio. With this, a server sends out compressed audio data in a continuous steam, and the receive stores the incoming samples and plays them when required. If the rate of playing the audio is faster than the rate that it is being received, then the player will play the audio without any interruptions. Typically, an audio player will try and store (buffer) as many audio samples as possible before it starts, so that they can be used if the received rate becomes too slow. Thus the concept of only ever listening to a radio station at the same time as everyone else will disappear in the future. With streaming technology it is possible for each user to listen to the audio (and video) when they require.

Typical formats for streaming audio over the Internet are WMA (Windows Media Audio) and:

RA The Real Audio file format by Real Networks is used for streaming audio in real time over the Internet and is a popular audio format for streaming audio. This format is optimized for compression over low data bandwidth such as a standard 56 k modem.

The two main applications, which are used to receive streaming audio, are Windows media player and RealNetworks Realplayer.

20.5.2 MIDI files

The MIDI (musical instrument digital interface) format is a standard interface between electronic instruments and music synthesizers. Software designed to compose and edit music usually provides input and output in the MIDI format. The MIDI format has several advantages over full digital sound files, in that it is much more compact, and can be easily edited. It allows for musical tracks to be easily combined. MIDI files can also be played in a Web browser. The main disadvantage of MIDI files is that some servers do not recognize them.

For more material on multimedia and tutorial questions, please visit our website at:
`http://www.palgrave.com/studyskills/masterseries/buchanan`

Index

WITHDRAWN FROM HAVERING COLLEGES
SIXTH FORM LIBRARY